Images, Iconoclasm,
and the Carolingians

THE MIDDLE AGES SERIES

Ruth Mazo Karras, Series Editor
Edward Peters, Founding Editor

A complete list of books in the series is available from
the publisher.

f this volume was supported by a grant from the Institute for Scholarship in the Liberal
rsity of Notre Dame.

f Pennsylvania Press
a, Pennsylvania 19104-4112

the United States of America on acid-free paper

8   7   6   5   4   3   2   I

oging-in-Publication record is available from the Library of Congress

978-0-8122-4141-9

Images, Ico
and the Care

Thomas F. X. Noble

The publication o
Arts of the Univ

Copyright © 20

All rights reser
this book may

Published by
University o
Philadelph

Printed in

10   9

A Cata

ISBN

PENN

University of Pennsylvania Press

Philadelphia

For Linda
    for everything

CONTENTS

Introduction

Thou shalt not make unto thee any graven image, or any likeness of anything that is in the heaven above or that is in the earth beneath, or that is in the water under the earth.
    —Exodus 20.4

In the history of European art it is difficult to name any one fact more momentous than the admission of the graven image by the Christian Church.
    —Ernst Kitzinger, "The Cult of Images"

GOD'S WORDS TO Moses, with Kitzinger's gloss, take us to the heart of a long, sometimes bitter, and always fascinating chapter in the histories of art, of Christianity, and of Western culture. This book focuses on one important but neglected and misunderstood segment of those histories. Between 790 and 840, in differing circumstances and with differing aims and intentions, Carolingian writers produced hundreds of pages of intelligent, interesting, and not infrequently polemical writing about Christian art. This book studies and interprets those texts. In about 790, Theodulf of Orléans, with the aid of several of his contemporaries, and on the express command of Charlemagne, began to write the *Opus Caroli*. This was a treatise of several hundred pages that ostensibly formed a response to the decisions of the Second Council of Nicaea of 787, a great assembly that had put a temporary end to Byzantine iconoclasm. Just after 840 Jonas of Orléans—that he and Theodulf were bishops of the same see is purely coincidental—put the finishing touches to his *De cultu imaginum*. Jonas's treatise, originally begun at the request of Louis the Pious in 827 and completed on the order of Charles the Bald, responded to the iconoclasm of Bishop Claudius of Turin and to much else besides.

Writings about Christian art, or about what visual arts Christians might have and how they might use them, began with the apologists in the second century.[1] Yet not until the eighth century did the Byzantine world sustain a serious discussion of the appropriateness of Christian figural art. The so-called "iconoclastic controversy"—as always the victors got to name the battle after the losers—has been called "one of the greatest political and cultural crises of Byzantium."[2] More than this, it was "undoubtedly one of the major conflicts in the history of the Christian Church. . . . All levels of life were affected by the conflict, all strata of society were involved in the struggle. The fight was violent, bitter and desperate."[3] Not surprisingly, then, a major authority can say that the iconoclastic controversy was "arguably the major manifestation of change and continuity in early medieval Byzantium."[4]

Byzantine iconoclasm ran two courses. The first lasted from 726 to 787 and the second from 815 to 842. As noted just above, Theodulf wrote the *Opus Caroli* to respond to the council that put an end to the first phase of iconoclasm. Did a Western controversy exist? If so, was it a great crisis? Did it shake the (Western) Christian Church to its foundations? Does it reveal significant forces of change?

Usually the answers to these questions are all in the negative. The Western image discussions are seen as a *Nebenerscheinung*, as a "side show," to the Byzantine main event. It is usually argued that the Carolingians in the 790s simply did not understand the basic issues involved in the Byzantine dispute. In the harshest telling, the Carolingians are alleged to have lacked Greek books and learning, as well as an understanding of the philosophical and theological traditions of the Greek Church. In the mildest telling, the Carolingians had poor translations of the *acta* of II Nicaea, perhaps indeed a mere extract from those voluminous documents. Carolingian writings were, in any case, without discernible influence on the continuing course of Byzantine iconoclasm and, say what one will about the Nicene *acta*, the subsequent writings of ninth-century Byzantine image theologians were either unknown or unremarked in the West. Although thirty years ago Peter Brown said that the iconoclastic controversy was "in the grips of a crisis of overinterpretation," no one could then or would now say the same about the West.[5] To this day there exists neither a comprehensive description or explanation of the Western response to Byzantine iconoclasm or a thorough account of Carolingian reflections on images.[6] This book constitutes a first such attempt.

There was, in fact, a Carolingian controversy about visual art but its ties to Byzantine iconoclasm are tenuous and complex. Thus there is an opportunity to ask what the Carolingian discussion actually is linked to. I do not deny that Theodulf took it as his first task to respond to the second Nicene council. But I do assert that his response is rooted deeply in central concerns of the Carolingian court in the years between about 780 and 800. Goaded by II Nicaea the Carolingians expressed themselves in distinctive ways about problems that were important to them and that were fundamentally different from many, but not all, of the problems that exercised the Byzantines. Viewed in this way, the *Opus Caroli* becomes less an incompetent or uncomprehending response to Byzantium than a cunning, albeit unfinished and unpolished, statement of basic Frankish concerns.

When the Franks returned to the subject of images in the 820s, they were prompted to do so by the Byzantines and, as in the 790s, traced a distinctive path. Emperor Michael II, a mild iconophobe, wrote to Louis the Pious to enlist his aid and support and to explain his own actions in the East. Louis assembled his theologians. At Paris in 825 they produced a large dossier of materials that seem to respond only partially to the letter of Michael II and to correspond only in oblique ways with the issues that had attracted the attention of Theodulf and Charlemagne's other key advisers. Once again, however, the context for the treatises written at Paris in 825 is to be sought amid major preoccupations of Louis the Pious and his key associates in the first fifteen or so years of the reign of Charlemagne's heir.

At just about the time when Louis's theologians were gathering in Paris the Frankish world encountered a home-grown altercation. Claudius of Turin, the Septimanian, probably Visigothic, bishop, theologian, and arch controversialist, went on a rampage of image destruction and iconophobic propaganda. Louis directed Jonas of Orléans, who had presided at the Paris deliberations, to respond to Claudius. He did so by beginning his *De cultu imaginum* but under slightly mysterious circumstances laid it aside, unfinished. Other writers, however, took up pens—one almost said cudgels—against Claudius: Theodemir, the abbot of Psalmody and Dungal, the chief schoolman in Pavia, most prominently. Agobard of Lyon, meanwhile, weighed in on his own with a treatise that expressed reservations about Christian art much graver than those articulated by the Paris theologians, Theodimir, or Dungal, but less reckless than those of Claudius. Still other writers—Hrabanus Maurus, Einhard, and Walahfrid Strabo, to mention the three most prominent ones—wrote on art too but did so in terms more approving than those expressed by Agobard and Claudius, yet quite different on key points from those of Jonas and Dungal. The context for this Carolingian logomachy is the turbulent world of the 830s when the Franks fought civil wars, endured foreign attacks, and attenuated the buoyant optimism that had characterized the reign of Charlemagne and the early years of Louis the Pious.

Standard works on Carolingian art history rarely discuss the treatises and documents just mentioned. To a degree this neglect is justifiable because many of these Carolingian texts about Christian art seem to have very little to do with art per se. As I shall repeatedly argue, controversies that were sparked by some problem having to do with art turned into major statements of or else quarrels about contemporary issues that did not have Christian art as their primary subject matter. Perhaps this is not so odd. Throughout history, heated debates about artistic representation, and the actual destruction of public and private works of art, have been by-products of other kinds of social, political, or religious movements.[7] One thinks immediately of Protestant iconoclasm in the sixteenth and seventeenth centuries; of the political iconoclasm of the French Revolution; of the ideological iconoclasm of both Fascist and Communist states and their successors; or of contemporary American disputes over flag burning and public subsidies for artistic work that some people deem blasphemous or obscene. The iconoclastic moment in these movements almost always provides the careful observer with a sharp view of the stresses and tears in the social fabric of a given place or time. In short, I shall ask the reader to look with me at certain problems in Carolingian history in ways that would seem perfectly normal to historians of other times and places. That is the broad view. In the narrow view, Carolingian historians may discover new things here as I invite them to reflect with me on neglected texts and problems. And I hope to persuade art historians to think in new ways about the subjects of their investigations.

Thus far the large issues to which this book is addressed. The next few pages provide a chapter-by-chapter orientation to how the book actually proceeds. Chapters 4 to 7 form the heart of the book. The first three chapters are not merely introductory, however. By looking in detail at the period from the fourth century to the eighth, these chapters establish the language, issues, and ideas which the Carolingians answered, modified, neglected. The chapters are long, but each addresses a basic and coherent bundle of problems within specific cultural and chronological contexts.

The first chapter turns to the ancient and late antique Mediterranean homeland both of Byzantine and Frankish art and of Christianity. I treat several issues in summary, synoptic fashion. What kinds of discussions about art took place in the Mediterranean world before the outbreak of Byzantine iconoclasm? What exactly are sacred icons, and what place do they occupy within the larger context of figural art generally, of support for or opposition to such art, and of religious practices in the East and in the West? What kinds of discussions of art took place in the West before the outbreak of iconoclasm and what cultic practices, if any, can be associated with works of art in the West? Without here anticipating the discussion that will follow, for the purposes of this study I acknowledge that any image could be an icon, but posit that sacred icons are not images of a particular style, size, or location but instead images that did, or that were expected to do, something. They were images to which cult was paid. These are huge subjects with elaborate, complex, and contentious bibliographies. Our aim here will merely be to pick out certain key themes so as better to understand some basic Carolingian positions. In sum, Chapter 1 asks what language, texts, and precedents were available to be accepted, rejected, or modified in the eighth century.

Chapter 2 opens with an inspection of a few battle sites in the *guerre des savants* over Byzantine iconoclasm. Everyone agrees that the Byzantine iconophilia following the first phase of Byzantine iconoclasm occasioned the *Opus Caroli,* so it is imperative to explore what else Theodulf and company *could* have responded to. This chapter extends the discussion begun in Chapter 1 of how East and West were alike and different in daily cult practice as well as in theological speculation. Another important objective of this chapter is to remind readers more familiar with the West than the East that recent scholarship has decidedly reduced the magnitude of the Byzantine controversy, the above quotations from Ladner and Florovsky notwithstanding. Byzantine iconoclasm was uneven, episodic, and never as devastating in human or material terms as formerly believed. Proceeding to the Carolingian world with this new understanding of Byzantium in mind will help us to see that we are not dealing with the bizarre and inexplicable asymmetry of a civilizational shock at one end of the Mediterranean that produced only a ripple at the other end. Finally, another important objective of this chapter will be a slimming of the intellectual, primarily theological, aspects of eighth-century iconoclasm, East and West. For too long scholars, mostly Byzantinists and most prominently the Russians among them, have gotten away with both proleptic and cataleptic readings of the eighth century that permit virtually all understandings of sacred icons to have been present then. If one assumes that the soaring theological flights of ninth-century writers such as the Patriarch Nicephorus and Abbot Theodore of Studion were already present in the early and middle decades of the eighth century, or that the lofty early eighth-century theology of John of Damascus was pervasive at the time of II Nicaea, then it is easy to portray Theodulf's theology as an ugly, flightless bird. We shall try to interpret the history a little closer to the order in which it actually happened.

Chapter 3 provides a discussion of the Western background to the *Opus Caroli*. The Anglo-Saxon Bede (673–735), whose writings were well known to the Carolingians, expressed himself on art several times in a variety of contexts. We shall find traces of his influence. The popes, moreover, with whom the

Franks entered into a solemn alliance in the 750s, were deeply distressed by Byzantine iconoclasm and explicitly objected to it on numerous occasions. From Gregory II (716–31) to Hadrian I (772–95) popes wrote frequently about the image crisis and held a series of councils that addressed images—among other things. Beginning in the 730s the Franks and the popes entered into increasingly intense relations with one another. There is some evidence that the Franks began taking notice of Byzantine iconoclasm in the 750s but the surviving sources convey little sense that images represented right away an important or interesting problem for the Franks. One task of Chapter 3, therefore, is to explain the differing perspectives of the popes and of the Franks on Byzantine religious policy in general, and on religious art in particular, in the central decades of the eighth century. Problems of rulership and church government were critical to those perspectives, but so too were cult practices associated with art. How was art actually used in the Frankish world, in Rome, and in Byzantium? In what ways did the Franko-papal alliance condition the partners' reactions to art, to Byzantine iconoclasm, and to one another? By the end of Chapter 3 the textual, political, and devotional scene will have been set with sufficient precision and clarity to make possible an understanding of Theodulf's work in his place and time.

Chapter 4 offers my reading of the *Opus Caroli* within the specific context of the Carolingian court during the most decisive, creative, productive years of the reign of Charlemagne. The chapter begins with a discussion of the making of the *Opus Caroli* that depends heavily on the magisterial work of Ann Freeman but that adds to her findings some perspectives and interpretations that arise from the wider view being taken in this book. The chapter continues with a lengthy summation of the contexts of the *Opus Caroli*, a treatise that has never been translated into a modern language and that has been more discussed than read, more often characterized than carefully studied. Next the reader encounters a delineation of the major arguments and themes that run through the *Opus*.

After Chapter 4's account of the major arguments in the *Opus*, Chapter 5 turns to the wider Frankish context by measuring themes in the *Opus Caroli* against annals, capitularies, diplomas, law codes, letters, poems, and works of Carolingian art and architecture. By reading the *Opus Caroli* against both the immediate Frankish context and a full understanding of the non-Frankish contexts, it will become possible, for the first time, to explain the central concerns of Theodulf's writings. Was he really out of step with Byzantine art talk in general? Did the *Opus* really accord badly with what was said and done at Nicaea? Does the *Opus* evince contention between the Carolingians and the very papacy they had pledged to love and defend? What religious value did the Carolingians assign to the visual arts? Does the *Opus* shed light on important contemporary issues? Do those issues help us to understand the *Opus*?

Chapter 6 opens with a discussion of the renewed outbreak of iconoclasm in Byzantium, explores some of the intellectual dimensions of and changes in Second Iconoclasm, and goes on to describe how and in what form "Second Iconoclasm"—as it is often called—came to the attention of the Franks in 824. The chapter continues with a presentation of what the Franks did in 824–25 by interpreting the lengthy dossier of materials produced in connection with the 825 Paris Colloquy—for it was not a council, as is usually maintained. The chapter examines the central themes in that dossier on their own terms and then compares those themes to contemporary Byzantine ideas and practices and to previous Frankish positions.

Chapter 7 then passes in review the major participants in the ninth-century image quarrel in the Frankish world and tells how they became involved. Their writings are summarized and their major arguments highlighted. The chapter moves to its conclusion by interpreting those themes in light of some of the major preoccupations evident in the sources for the reign of Louis the Pious. As with the *Opus* in Charlemagne's time, now the Paris dossier and the remnants of the Carolingian logomachy are read against other historical and artistic sources from the reign of Louis the Pious. This chapter attempts, finally, to show that an understanding of the Frankish world during Second Iconoclasm depends on disentangling the Franks' thoughts and actions from what was going on around them.

The way I read the central texts relevant to each phase of the Carolingian image discussion permits me to situate them within a series of broader discourses that were prominent in the Carolingian world. By "discourse" I mean no more than the shared information, attitudes, and modes of expression among the Carolingian elite. I have in mind something like Brian Stock's "Textual Communities," that is, groups of people united by common understandings of, and perhaps actions mobilized by, textual materials that were not necessarily known directly by all members of the group.[8] That such a discourse existed remains to be demonstrated. I do not wish to imply that I am claiming to have identified the *mentalité* of the Carolingian world. The discourse of which I speak was horizontal, not vertical, although I believe, and will try to show, that it was very wide. Also, as Stock demonstrates, people whose understandings were formed by common texts and experiences do not necessarily agree with each other all the time. But they do understand each other. We will discern sharp disagreements grounded in shared knowledge and understanding. If we listen carefully to fifty years' worth of Carolingian discourses about art, we can hear them talking about many of the things that were most important to them in the dramatic half-century bracketed by Charlemagne's greatest exploits and the civil wars and treaties that carved up his empire.

Three discourses recur in the art texts around which this study is organized. The first, labeled "tradition," concerns the attempt by the Carolingians to situate themselves in historical and ideological time. At one time or another the Carolingians thought of themselves as heirs of the Hebrews, of the apostles, and of the Romans. Because Theodulf and his contemporaries thought it important to deny that the Byzantines might have the same inheritances, the *Opus Caroli* is stridently anti-Byzantine. While the traditional discourse is the most powerful one in the *Opus Caroli*, it becomes a soft voice in the Paris chorus and is sometimes inaudible in the battle of treatises inaugurated by Claudius.

A second discourse gets the label "order." When we listen to this one we can hear the Carolingians talking about how to order a state or a church, asking questions about authority and legitimacy. What makes a good ruler? A good bishop? How is the business of government rightly conducted? Theodulf was, at least to some degree, concerned to refute the decisions of a council whose legitimacy the Carolingians doubted. He was also concerned to show how and why Charlemagne was the right kind of ruler while Byzantine emperors could not be, and why Carolingian bishops were proper churchmen whereas Tarasius, the patriarch of Constantinople, was not. Order was a major theme for Theodulf, second only to tradition, but it became the major theme at Paris in 825. Relations with Byzantium and with the papacy were discussed at length, along with the legitimacy of conciliar action and problems of consensus and dissent. Order diminishes slightly as an issue in the writings of the ninth-century authors provoked by Claudius. It is a commonplace in the scholarship on the Carolingians that they promoted "reform." Among other things, reform aims to remedy disorder. The Carolingian image texts identify and discuss disordered thought and practice. Other sources do the same thing.

The third discourse I call "worship." I array under this heading most of what the sources actually say about art. This discourse is rich with ironies. At Byzantium the *cult* of images was in dispute. Presumably this cult is what Theodulf attacked. Yet, as we shall see, there was, in reality, no cult of images in the West. Although Theodulf has some interesting and important things to say about worship, some fascinating things to say about Christian art, and a number of reflections on aesthetics, the ostensibly fundamental topics of his *Opus Caroli*—those touching the cult of images—are actually less prominent than the tradition and order discourses to which he contributed. In the Paris dossier, worship plays an exiguous role. The emperor and his theologians were attracted much more to the matter of who got to make decisions than they were to the particular decisions that were made. Order becomes central here. In the ninth-century logomachy worship, faith, belief, and the religious education of ordinary people are the basic concerns. For the first time, the cult of images receives serious and focused consideration in its own right. Tradition and order were the discourses of the optimistic in the late eighth century. Worship was the discourse of the cautious, perhaps of the pessimistic, in the middle of the ninth century.

During the great Carolingian century, from the elevation of Pippin to the Treaty of Verdun (751–843), the Carolingian elite continually asked, Who are we? What are we to do? How are we to do it? The art texts that undergird this study permit us to listen to some members of the Carolingian elite proposing answers to those questions. By comparing the art texts with laws, letters, poems, and other sources produced by and for the elite, we can judge the power and magnitude of the key discourses of the Carolingian world during that world's most dynamic and creative decades.

CHAPTER ONE

Art, Icons, and Their Critics and Defenders Before the Age of Iconoclasm

Someone asked Abba Sopatrus, "Give me a commandment, abba, and I will keep it." He said to him, "Do not allow a woman to come into your cell and do not read apocryphal literature. Do not get involved in discussions about the image. Although this is not heresy, there is too much ignorance and liking for dispute between the two parties in this matter. It is impossible for a creature to understand the truth of it."[1]

THIS CHAPTER LOOKS at the long period between the time when Christianity gained legal status in the Roman Empire and the eve of Byzantine iconoclasm: roughly, the years 300 to 700. Our focus will be on what writers in this period said about figural art. On the one hand, we will look at the points that various writers made for or against the possession and the use of the visual arts. On the other hand, we will look closely for moments—there were only a few—when writers actually seemed to engage one another. This chapter will lay the groundwork for an understanding of the furious arguments over religious art that broke out in the eighth century.

Art Talk in Late Antiquity

In order for defenders or critics of Christian art to have something to talk about, a distinctively Christian art had to arise and spread in the Mediterranean world.

The existence of the superb art works that are the glory of churches and museums the world over must not tempt us to think that such art was inevitable. Indeed, several forces militated against the emergence of Christian figural art. Moreover, words and concepts had to be discovered and disseminated and had to enter into common discourse, for discussions of art to take place. Each chapter of this book will have a section devoted to "art talk," a modest phrase intended to provide opportunities to gather together and to reflect upon those words and concepts. In this chapter, we will begin collecting those words and concepts so that they can be used routinely and clearly later on. In this first section, we will proceed chronologically from about 300 to 700, noting writers who accepted or rejected religious art, their terminology, and their arguments.

Classical, Biblical, and Early Christian Antecedents

Although the Greeks and the Romans produced much art of high quality and great beauty, their societies always had critics of visual representation. Among the Greeks, for example, Heraclitus criticized the stuff out of which images, presumably statues in particular, were made. Xenophanes ridiculed the idea that beings such as gods could somehow be depicted or portrayed in figures that looked alarmingly like ordinary mortals.[2] Here already we meet themes that will recur in later Christian discussions. Greek critics addressed the ontology of images, their basic mode of being, the substances of which they are made. Statues, after all, rot and rust; insects invade them; mice nest in them; birds foul them. Such dross matter is wholly unsuited to the depiction of sublime, perhaps ineffable, realities. In addition, many Greeks thinkers valued the intellect over the senses. That is, what could be perceived by the power of contemplation was superior to anything that entered consciousness by means of sensory experience. Put in slightly different terms, enlightened Greeks esteemed the spiritual more highly than the material, the abstract more than the particular, the mental more than the visual, and the universal more than the finite.

Some Romans feared that beauty was softening, that beautiful things would strip Roman men of their martial and manly values. Moreover, Romans feared, or some influential Romans affected to fear, outside ideas and always assumed that art would import the very notions they wished to repel.[3]

By the later decades of the second century, when most Christians rejected the Gnostic and Marcionite temptation to jettison the Hebrew Scriptures, the new faith had inherited the apparently strict prohibition of imagery expressed explicitly in Exodus 20.4 and implicitly elsewhere. The Old Testament prohibitions could be understood in several ways. To the extent that they focused on the matter of which images were made, they were similar to Greek and Roman reservations. But some new themes entered the discussion too. Some said that the faith of Israel depended on words, not on images. These observations opened a long debate over the relative value of seeing and of hearing, of looking and of reading. Others said that in making images, artists were usurping the creative act that belongs to God alone.[4]

In view of these strains of hostility to art, and in the absence of impressive physical evidence, scholars long maintained that early Christianity was aniconic.[5] In fact, a history of Christian images can be traced from about A.D. 200.[6] Moreover, it is now clear from the frescoes in the synagogues at Dura Europos, Ain ed-Duk, and Beth Alpha, as well as from the Via Torlonia in Rome, and also from artistic motifs taken over by Christian book painters from Jewish books, that Christianity's Jewish environment was not without visual representations.[7] Sparse and scattered literary testimonies reveal that early Christians were possibly iconophobic but certainly not iconoclastic. Christians were like Jews in worrying more about idolatry than about figural art per se. Origen (*Contra Celsum* 3.15) said that in instructing the young, one should teach them to hate idols and images. In a world where temples and images were among the most familiar and important features of the cultural landscape, it is easy to see why early Christian writers would have been concerned to condemn idolatry.[8] Justin Martyr too was concerned about the anthropomorphism of statues and about their being "soulless" (ἀψυχία) and "dead" (νεϰρά).[9] Although statues provoked criticism, there is no solid evidence for discussions of painting. And it is important to emphasize that the earliest Christian comments on images occurred in the writings of apologists who were often engaged in trying to persuade influential pagan notables that Christian worship was admirable because it was spiritual, that is aniconic. Apologists were not really talking about art per se.[10]

Early Reservations About Figural Art

In about 306 a church council at Elvira, in Spain, in a canon that was never again cited by a church council as far as I have been able to determine, said, "there ought not to be pictures in churches; for what is worshiped and adored ought not to be painted on walls."[11] In the early fourth century Eusebius of Caesarea (ca. 260–ca. 340) said that he knew of people who claimed to possess images of both Christ and the apostles made while they were alive.[12] An apocryphal life of the evangelist John either written or reworked in the third century tells of an image of him that he had actually seen and rejected as inappropriate.[13] But Eusebius was no passive observer of artistic representation even if his stories, like the Elviran canon, tell us coincidentally that such representations had appeared and that some people believed them to have been around for a long time.

Early in the fourth century Eusebius, a member of the imperial entourage, was asked by Constantia, a sister of Constantine, to send her an image of Christ. Eusebius refused to comply. He said he did not know which image of Christ he had been asked to provide: "the true and unalterable one which bears His essential characteristics, or the one which He took up for our sake when He assumed the form of a servant." He added that "dead colors and inanimate delineations" could not capture the "glistening, flashing radiance of such glory," and he reminded Constantia that even Christ's own disciples had been unable to stand His sight at the time of the Transfiguration. Eusebius added that the law forbade such likenesses, said that images were "banished and excluded from churches all over the world," and railed at pagans who worshiped images of their gods and philosophers.[14] This seems clear enough. Spiritual realities can be neither seen nor represented by humans, and, anyway, dead matter cannot be used to represent living reality. He is making the point that no image can be equivalent with what it seeks to portray. Eusebius's position was not completely iconophobic. In his *Life of Constantine* he mentioned, with no expressed or implied criticism, some statues that the first Christian emperor had put up in Constantinople: One was of a Good Shepherd and one depicted Daniel in the lions' den.[15] Eusebius was evidently prepared to accept images that were merely symbols that pointed to realities beyond themselves. Christ could not be depicted but some of God's mysteries could be revealed by artistic renderings.

Eusebius's observations yield some pertinent facts about emerging Christian attitudes toward art. First, at least some art is permitted. Permissible art may be symbolic, or it may stand as a memorial. In discussing a statue of the woman with a hemorrhage (Mark 5.25–34), Eusebius calls it a "wonderful memorial of the benefit the Savior conferred upon her."[16] Second, while not exactly approving of pictures of Christ, Peter, and Paul allegedly painted in their lifetimes, Eusebius attributes such pictures to the "ancients habitually following their own Gentile custom."[17] The point seems to be that some people make images innocently enough while others ought to know better. Perhaps, too, he is talking about the artist's intentions.

The Constantinian world evoked other criticisms of the new Christian art and its uses. Lactantius (ca. 250–ca. 325), whom Constantine appointed as tutor to his son Crispus, asked why anyone would worship images of the dead when they could turn their eyes to heaven. Images only commemorate those who have died and, as such, they are superfluous. As material things, moreover, they lack all sense and understanding.[18] Arnobius of Sicca (fl. late third century), Lactantius's teacher, asked with grim humor whether, if there were no images, the gods would not know they were being worshiped. As the work of artisans, and as creations from vile matter, images cannot bear any relationship to what they purport to represent. Thus there is absolutely no reason to have them.[19]

In these years around the Constantinian peace of the church, when Christian art was both emerging and drawing criticism from the imperial court right on down, there slowly arose a myth of Christian aniconism. David Freedberg is certainly correct to emphasize that from late antiquity to the Reformation and beyond there has been a persistent "myth of aniconism." The point of this myth is to claim for its adherents moral and spiritual superiority over those who possess or use images. People who worship a God who is separate from matter may well refuse to represent their God by means of matter and may also disdain those who do so. Persons who embrace the myth impute their position to all moments of the history of their people and faith and, accordingly, criticize those who are iconic, so to speak, as idolatrous and superstitious.[20]

Conditions may have been unpromising for the emergence of Christian figural art, yet the fourth and fifth centuries witnessed a veritable explosion of art in many forms: sculpture, painting, mosaic, glass- and metalwork. Roman evidence that clusters around A.D. 200 shows that, in catacombs, Christians had begun to use several abstract symbolic representations such as the Good Shepherd and various stylized biblical scenes.[21] Near one synagogue at Dura Europos was a Christian building with a picture of Adam and Eve before a font and also a Good Shepherd. Most Christian art that survives from before 300 is funerary and private; Christianity was, after all, illegal. After 300, however, Christian artists began regularly to represent subjects from Scripture including Christ Himself, even though it took more than a century for a basic repertoire of representational schemes to be worked out. After Christianity became licit, it attracted rich patrons accustomed to elegantly decorated spaces, and built or took over large buildings that provided space and scope for artistic talent; wall paintings, mosaics, and statues appeared everywhere. Fourth- and fifth-century discussions of art took place in an ever more richly ornamented environment, which had not been true in the pre-Constantinian period.[22]

Many explanations have been offered for why this happened. Some, sailing in the wake of Adolf von Harnack, suggest that popular superstitions combined with the persistence of pagan practices in an unholy accommodation of the sacred to the profane.[23] A long-standing interpretation holds that Christians appropriated to their own use themes and motifs of imperial art, although this explanation is better at describing what happened than it is at explaining why.[24] A recent view suggests that Christians embraced art as a means of "providing spiritual readings of the Old Testament and, hence, for rendering spiritual exegesis accessible. . . . Pictures could render the Jewish story intact and, at the same time, reveal its hidden significance." Put simply, Christians rendered Old Testament words in pictures of their own making.[25] Surely, the depiction of at least some Old Testament subjects is connected with emerging modes of typological exegesis: the Old Testament foreshadowed the New. This interpretation of pictures as exegetical tools would certainly explain some Old Testament representations, but not the full repertoire of New Testament scenes, nor depictions of saints. The cult of the cross and the cult of relics have been identified as possible sources.[26] In the case of the cross and of relics, however, it is easier to discern a contribution to practices associated with art, veneration most prominently, than to the emergence of the art itself. Late antique funeral portraits, such as those known from Egypt, may have been influential in the specific development of sacred icons, but their connection with Christian art in general is harder to fathom.[27] Likewise, the tremendous popularity of the column-sitting Stylites may have given a spur to reproductions of their pictures, and thus to icons, but it seems that traditions of Christian art were well under way before the first pillar was climbed.[28] An effort to appropriate both the representation and the potency of the healer, the wise man, and the magician could have played a role.[29] Munificence by members of the upper classes who were accustomed to a richly decorated environment may have been a factor.[30] Imperial rhetoric, speaking in terms of "magnificence" and "abundance," may explain some decorated environments.[31] Similarly, the fact that Christians appropriated many genres of classical literature may provide a clue as to why they eventually decided to appropriate as well the "language" of art.[32] No single explanation will ever cover all the evidence or persuade all the scholars. It suffices to say that across the fourth century diverse Christian arts arose and proliferated rapidly. That art adopted much from its pagan environment in terms of style, motif, and technique of production.[33]

The Elaboration of Arguments for and Against Art

During the fourth century the basic Christian defenses of images began to take shape against the background of artistic production on the one hand and ambivalence or hostility on the other. The fourth and fifth centuries would also witness more coherent arguments against art than the ones we have encountered so far. Among the defenses of art, one that grew in prominence in each succeeding generation maintained that worship was transmitted from an image to the person whom that image represented. This argument is associated with St. Basil (329–79). In a homily on the Holy Spirit, Basil was trying to explain how the Son and the Father could be two in person without being two gods. To make his point he used the analogy of the imperial images. If a person looks at an image of the emperor he will say, "That is the emperor," but there do not thereby appear two emperors since "the honor shown to the image is transferred to its model."[34] At roughly the same time a similar argument was presented by Athanasius (ca. 296–373) in his *Third Discourse Against the Arians*.[35]

A second line of defense emphasized the capacity of images to evoke emotional responses that greatly enhanced piety. Gregory of Nyssa (ca. 335–ca. 395), speaking about the sacrifice of Isaac, said, "I have often seen this tragic event depicted in painting and could not walk by the sight of it without shedding tears."[36] Basil, again, spoke of the way images call deeds to memory "just like writing. For feats of war done bravely are sometimes expressed by orators and sometimes by painters, these adorning those deeds with words, those painting them on tablets, and each one incites not a few to courage. For whatever of history language communicates through hearing, silent pictures put those images before the eye for imitation."[37] At about the same time John Chrysostom (347–407) mentions a tendency in Antioch to make images of St. Meletius, a former bishop: "For you [the Antiochenes] were not only touched by his name but also by the figure (τυπόν) of his body. And what you did with respect to his name you did also with respect to his image (εἰκόνα). Indeed, on rings, seals, vials, on the walls of dwellings, and everywhere many put up that holy image that they might not only hear his holy name but also see the figure of his body and take some consolation for his double exile."[38] John's account differs from those of Gregory and Basil in speaking of a proliferation of images intended to bring "consolation." Right down to the thirteenth century many writers maintained that words did not have the same capacity to arouse the mind and the heart as pictures.[39]

Third, images were seen to be useful for instruction. Gregory of Nyssa, again, said that "painting, even if it is silent, is capable of speaking from the wall and being of the greatest benefit. . . . When scenes of martyrdom are painted on the walls of a church . . . this is of the greatest benefit and is like writing."[40] Gregory was the first to draw a parallel between verbal eloquence and the visual arts. The word *graphē* could mean painting or writing, and *historiai* could mean a picture or a story. Gregory compared pictures to "a book endowed with speech." Eventually this became a topos in Christian discourse about art.[41] As both Basil and Gregory said, the point of gazing at Christian art was to induce emulation. Emulation, imitation, mimesis was a central theme of Christian writings from the Gospels to saints' lives. Art and theology were beginning to share perspectives and even, to a degree, a descriptive vocabulary. It was quite natural, therefore, that Christian art would be swept into the general flow of Christian discourse.[42]

Several features of these early discussions of art require emphasis. First, each writer said something about art while actually talking about something else entirely. Second, these writers were neither addressing one another nor defending themselves and their positions from any known assailant. Third, their defenses of art are couched in purely instrumental terms; aesthetic considerations are entirely absent. They talk about the effects that art can have. There is no question here of a cult associated with art. It is also interesting that none of these writers felt called upon to rebut a charge of idolatry.

Late in the fourth century Epiphanius of Salamis (ca. 315–403) spoke out against images in a serious and comprehensive way.[43] Three fragments from his writings are found among the works of Patriarch Nicephorus (758–828), whom we shall meet again.[44] John of Damascus (ca. 660–ca. 750), the great defender of images, was aware of Epiphanius. Ever mindful of ecclesiastical traditions, John seems to have felt that Epiphanius was virtually alone in opposing images and could be easily ignored: "one swallow does not make a spring."[45] It was always easy for later writers to strike Eusebius from the dossier because his Arianism tainted all his writings. Epiphanius was a perfectly orthodox bishop, however, so his ideas could have been more troubling to supporters of religious art.

In his *Testament* Epiphanius says that whereas the Fathers (he means Old Testament figures) "abominated the idols of the gentiles . . . we make images of the saints as a memorial to them and worship these in their honor." He goes on to mention people who have painted pictures of Peter, John, and Paul on the walls of their houses and says, "let those who believe that by so doing they are honoring the apostles, learn that they are rather dishonoring them." Epiphanius was the first writer to attempt a systematic differentiation between idols (εἴδωλα) and images (εἰκόνες). By keeping the apostolic commandments, Epiphanius says, we create the finest images of the apostles. Epiphanius also rejects the idea that by looking at pictures of the apostles people are thereby reminded of them. He criticizes too the ignorance and presumption of painters and the lifeless matter of their pictures.[46] In a *Letter to the Emperor Theodosius* Epiphanius complained that no "Father" (here he refers to both Old and New Testament figures) ever painted an image of Christ and put it in a church or a house and that no one had ever made a picture of Abraham, Isaac, Jacob, Moses, or of prophets, patriarchs, or apostles. He adds that painters depict such people according to their own whims, and produce markedly different representations. He concluded by asking the emperor to remove painted curtains from churches, baptisteries, houses, and martyria; to whitewash wall paintings; and to remove mosaics where possible.[47] Finally, in a *Letter to John, Bishop of Aelia* (Aelia Capitolina is Jerusalem), Epiphanius explained that he had discovered in a village called Anautha a church with a door curtain on which there was an image that the locals believed to be of Christ or of one of the saints. Epiphanius pulled it down and insisted that it be used as a burial cloth for a poor man. Epiphanius concluded by assuring the bishop of Jerusalem that he had sent a replacement curtain.[48]

Another testimony survives only among the documents presented at the Second Council of Nicaea in 787: two letters on images allegedly written by St. Nilus of Sinai (d. ca. 430).[49] Learned consensus has regarded these letters as authentic ever since 1668, when Leo Allatius, their first editor, included them along with the nearly one thousand letters that make up Nilus's collected correspondence. Recently, however, it has been shown that whereas the Nicene fathers accused an iconophobic council of 754 of doctoring these letters in a way hostile to images, it was in fact someone connected with II Nicaea who turned Nilus's cautious, mildly hostile position in the opposite direction.[50]

In the first letter Nilus supposedly tells of a man who was saved by St. Plato and who knew just who had saved him because he had often seen Plato's image. The story is not completely implausible but fits less comfortably in an early fifth- than in a seventh- or eighth-century context. The second letter takes the form of a response to the Exarch Olympiodorus who was thinking of decorating a church with crosses, animals, and hunting scenes. In the interpolated version, Nilus allegedly told Olympiodorus to use a cross along with Old and New Testament scenes because the naturalistic images would be distracting. The genuine version of this letter probably insisted on a cross and bare walls because in a church dedicated to the martyrs the memory alone of those who had died should suffice to sustain the faithful. Nilus may have said that the inclusion of a cross alone would be the mark of a "firm and manly mind." In other words, while Nilus surely did not endorse the introduction of images into churches, he seems to acknowledge with some diffidence their frequent presence. Unlike Epiphanius, as far as we know, he did not remove any.

Later Byzantine writers report that near the end of the fifth century Philoxenus of Mabbug (ca. 440–523), bishop of Hierapolis in Syria, claimed that it was unlawful to endow angels with bodies because they were incorporeal. He also said that the only true image of Christ was worship in spirit and truth (John 4.23–24). Wrong too, in Philoxenus's view, were portrayals of the Holy Spirit as a dove. Philoxenus also "took down and obliterated images of angels in many places, while those representing Christ he secreted in inaccessible spots."[51] Philoxenus was mainly concerned to combat paganism, however, so his actions against images may need to be situated in that context more than within an evolving Christian discourse on art.[52] Philoxenus reminds us that the polemical stance of the pre-Constantinian period was still alive.

The flowering of Christian literature in the fourth and fifth centuries alerted Christian writers to the difficulties of talking about God. The intensity of those difficulties is reflected in the quotation from Abba Sopatrus (fourth century) with which this chapter begins. Sopatrus was not really talking about artistic representations. Rather, he was referring to the "Origenist" controversies that turned around the problem of anthropomorphism.

The Origenists complained that prayer was impeded to the degree that the mind could not free itself of crude images. Such images arose in the mind because of an inevitable human attachment to material reality. Thus, Origenists held for a spiritualized, allegorized interpretation of all biblical passages relating to man as created in the image and likeness of God, and to the Son as the image of the Father. Whereas Origenists were initially cool to images as tools of language, or even as a kind of language, they eventually became averse to images as instruments of a kind of visual perception which they regarded as crude and material.

The Arians too were strongly opposed to both language and art that moved dangerously close to denying the absolute transcendence of God. Semi-Arians, like Eusebius, had reservations about depicting Christ while others argued that Christ's humanity could indeed be depicted as a means of displaying the gulf that separated Him from His Father. Athanasius countered this view decisively. The Cappadocian Fathers (Basil, Gregory of Nyssa, and Gregory Nazianzus) worked out the basic language for talking about God. As we have seen, Basil and Gregory of Nyssa, in particular, found images both licit and helpful in promoting spiritual awareness and affective piety.[53]

Hostile commentators raised several points that we have already met as components of the ancient iconophobic tradition and that we will meet again in the age of iconoclasm. First of all, they reveal to us the extent to which images had spread and the wide array of holy people who were being depicted. Epiphanius also provides the first unambiguous testimony that images were somehow being worshiped. Neither Eusebius nor any of the early iconophiles had said this. The theme of the superiority of spirit to matter is sounded here.

Material things are not suitable channels for worship, in part because of the matter of which they are made and in part because of the fallibility of the humans who make them. Pictures are also indeterminate. A corporeal angel is confusing, for instance, and in Anautha people were unsure whose image was on the curtain. Painters cannot agree on how to depict the sainted heroes of Christianity. Symbolic representation—the dove, for instance—was obviously spreading and was seen to be dangerous. This is interesting in light of Eusebius's apparent willingness to tolerate symbolic representations—the Good Shepherd, in particular. Anthropomorphic representations were held to be crude and distracting and positively damaging to the ineffable reality of a purely spiritual being. Finally, just as the iconophiles spoke about practices, so too the iconophobes addressed ordinary conduct which disturbed them. They did not explicitly address the supporters of images and they do not appear to have been challenged at the time. Theirs were lonely voices. But no less lonely than those which favored sacred art.

The sixth century saw renewed statements in praise of images. The church historian Evagrius (ca. 536–600) tells of a fresco at Apamea depicting a miracle. The image "was set up in the ceiling of the church to make known these events by means of painting to those who were ignorant of them."[54] At around the same time the historian Agathias (ca. 531–ca. 580) said, concerning an image of the archangel Michael, "The mortal man who beholds the image directs his mind to a higher contemplation. His veneration is no longer distracted: engraving within himself the [archangel's] traits, he trembles as if he were in the latter's presence. The eyes encourage deep thoughts, and art is able by means of colors to ferry over [to its object] the prayer of the mind."[55] These fragments are revealing but other writers of the time spoke at greater length and more systematically.

One of them, Hypatius, who was archbishop of Ephesus from 531 to, perhaps, 538, addressed some *Miscellaneous Inquiries* to Bishop Julian of Atrymitium. Julian had become alarmed about image practices in his diocese and turned to his metropolitan for counsel. Julian was concerned that "those who set up in the sanctuaries what is revered and worshiped, in the form of paintings and carvings alike, are once again disturbing divine traditions." Julian apparently cited biblical prohibitions against such representations but added that he permitted the worship of paintings but not of statues. Hypatius goes through a careful examination of why the Scriptures say seemingly contradictory things about images and he agrees that sacred writings, implicitly both Scriptures and saints' lives, are superior. "We take no pleasure at all in sculpture or painting," Hypatius says, "but we permit simpler people, as they are less perfect, to learn by way of initiation about such things by [the sense of] sight which is more appropriate to their natural development, especially as we find that, often and in many respects, even old and new divine commandments lower themselves to the level of weaker people and their souls for the sake of their salvation." Hypatius then passes in review several Old and New Testament passages to show precisely how God used images to meet people with familiar terms of reference. He continues, "For these reasons we, too, allow even material adornment in the sanctuaries, not because we believe that God considers gold and silver and silken vestments and gem-studded vessels venerable and sacred but because we permit each order of the faithful to be guided and led up to the divine being in a manner appropriate to it [the order] because we think that some people are guided even by these [gold, silver, etc.] to the intelligible and immaterial light." After saying that God is distinct from his creation and worthy of spiritual worship alone, Hypatius concludes that "We do not, then, disturb the divine [commandments] with regard to the sanctuaries but we stretch out our hand in a more suitable way to those who are still rather imperfect, yet we do not leave them untaught as to the more perfect [knowledge] but we want them to know that the divine being is not at all identical or the same or similar to any of the existing things."[56]

In the early seventh century Bishop Leontius of Neapolis (ca. 590–650) in Cyprus delivered a series of sermons against the Jews, the fifth of which is addressed especially to images. Leontius's opening is rather conventional: He defends images because God commanded Moses to put cherubim on the ark; because He commanded Ezechiel to decorate the Temple; because Solomon put images in the Temple. Leontius challenges the Jews to reprehend God Himself for commanding these images to be made. A Jew would respond—much of the sermon is cast as a dialogue—that the images were made only for memory and not for worship. The Christian would answer that "we hardly regard these likenesses (χαρακτῆρες) and images (εἰκόνες) and forms (τύποι) of saints as if they were gods." Likenesses are honored for what they represent, not for what they are. For example, "when two pieces of wood are put together to make a cross, I venerate (προσκινῶ) the figure on account of Christ who was crucified on it; afterwards, if the pieces of wood were separated again, I would throw them into the fire. And so, when someone receives an order from the emperor and he salutes the seal, he does not honor (ἐτίμησεν) the clay, the paper, or the lead, but he extends his veneration (προσκύνησιν) and respect (σέβας) to the emperor." Leontius then talks of boys who, when their father goes away, see his staff, cloak, or chair and embrace them with tears and kisses. As the boys honor these things because of their father, so Christians honor objects because they

remind them of Christ. Christians put up images everywhere "so that in inces-
santly looking at them we might remember, and never forget, as you have forgotten, the Lord your God." "Just as you," he continues, "in adoring the book
of the law, do not adore the hide and ink which are in it but the words of God
which lie there, so indeed I, in honoring an image of Christ, do not adore the
wood and colors but, in holding this inanimate likeness of Christ, I hope to
hold Christ through it." Leontius asks why, if nothing made is to be adored,
Jacob kissed Joseph's cloak or reverenced his staff. If our images are really idols,
why do we worship in temples dedicated to the martyrs who destroyed idols? If
Christians honor wood as a god, why do they honor martyrs who destroyed
wooden simulacra? Jews are stubborn, blind, and impious. They refuse to see
that images put demons to flight. They will not acknowledge how many visita-
tions, imitations, and effusions of blood come from images. They do not see
how many wicked, impious men, idolaters, murderers, fornicators, and robbers
have come to the recognition of truth through images. Leontius concludes by
reminding the Jews that they keep many manufactured things for the glory and
memory of God: the staff of Moses, the tables of the law, the burning bush, the
manna-bearing urn, the altar, the plate with God's name, the ephod, the Tabernacle. Christians are no different and do not deserve the charge of idolatry.[57]

The seventh century saw several other anti-Jewish dialogues, possibly
spurred by Heraclius's anti-Jewish legislation.[58] Among these, that of Bishop
Stephen of Bostra was particularly important both because it was influential later
on and because he was the first Greek writer to attempt a careful explanation of
the difference between adoration and veneration. His text survives in a very
fragmentary state. It appears that Stephen used only the most conventional
arguments. He says, for example, that everything made in God's name is good
and that Christians never worship manufactured things for themselves but for
the persons they represent. Moreover, since creation, everything is manufactured, is made by human hands. If no respect is to be accorded to manufactured
things, why do Jews venerate the wooden altar, the urn with manna, the table
and lights inside and outside the Tabernacle? Images are one thing, idols another. Since God made Adam in His image, are men somehow idols?[59]

Although the arguments contained in the dialogues of Leontius and Stephen are conventional and, for the most part, familiar to us by now, there are
some puzzles implicit in their writings. Were there really dialogues on the specific subject of images between particular Christians—whether Leontius, Stephen, or anyone else—and actual Jews? Are the texts that survive mere literary
inventions? Why argue with Jews at all, let alone in connection with images?

Even though we know comparatively little about the Jews in the sixth and seventh centuries,[60] scholars have in recent years devoted considerable attention to a substantial corpus of anti-Jewish literature that arose in this period.[61] This is not the place for a detailed assessment of that literature, but one aspect of its appearance deserves mention because it helps to place the writings of Leontius and Stephen into sharper focus. Byzantium was subjected to severe military pressure and frequent defeat by Slavs, Persians, and then, most disastrously, Arabs. The Arabs of course represented not only a military threat of immense proportions but also a profound religious challenge. In ways that are still a little hard to fathom, one element of Byzantium's response to this ongoing crisis was a series of literary polemics against the defenseless and unthreatening Jews. For David Olster the polemics "used the Jew as a rhetorical device to personify the doubts of their own community with a recognizable, evil, and most important, eminently defeatable, opponent."[62] Muslims were, on the other hand, triumphant and they were iconophobic, albeit less militantly so than has usually been assumed.[63] The dialogues of Leontius and Stephen may not represent actual Jewish-Christian dialogue so much as an imaginary way of addressing the legitimacy of the rising prominence of images. Once again, in other words, the very texts that seem at first to reveal an intense discussion of the legitimacy of sacred art may actually bear little connection to any such discussions and may not even have much relevance to the topic of art.

Along the Greek world's frontier, in seventh-century Armenia, there was some discussion of images. Apparently Vrt'anes K'ert'ogh, an influential churchman, was combating Christian iconoclasts in Armenia. One of his writings on images, or an extract from one of them, has survived. Vrt'anes begins by rejecting the heretics' contention that no paintings or images (statues?) should be in churches. Their charge is idolatry and it is based on the Old Testament. The immediate response is to cite Old Testament passages where God commanded images to be made. Vrt'anes then mentions Paul and the altar of the unknown God at Athens (Acts 17.23) and says that church fathers mention and approve of images. He adds that the cross is venerated because Christ died on it and then says, "what is astonishing is that you accept the commandments and you persecute the Lord; you prostrate yourselves before the symbol [the cross] but you stone the king [presumably a corpus on a crucifix]; you honor the cross and you outrage the crucified. For this is how the Manichaeans and the Marcionites behave who consider the Lord, who really took a body, an apparition, and when they see images of him they grow angry, become furious, and insult them." Vrt'anes then mentions the story in Eusebius (*Hist.* 7.18) of the woman at Paneas whose hemorrhage was cured by a statue of Christ. He then talks of all the pictures of Mary, martyrs, and saints that exist in the churches of the Christians and says that all the marvels of Christ are depicted, just as in the Scriptures: "Everything which the Holy Scriptures relate is painted in the churches. Are not books written with pigment? The same things are painted with pigment. In churches indeed the ears hear the scriptures, but the images, one sees them with the eyes and one hears them with the ears, and one understands them with the heart, and one believes." Heretics say that images are vile because they are lifeless but when Christians prostrate themselves before a beautifully decorated Gospel book, they do not reverence the precious materials but the word of God. If paints are vile, then so too are the vitriol, gall, and gum which make the ink with which the Scriptures are written. But actually paint is made from milk, eggs, arsenic, and other things, some of which are food and others medicaments. Vrt'anes concludes that we can know the invisible world through visible things.[64] On the whole, Vrt'anes's position is quite moderate. His words do signal, however, that issues drawing attention within the emerging Byzantine Empire were also familiar outside its boundaries, carried along, one assumes, by Christian texts and personal encounters.

At about the same time, another prominent Armenian cleric, John Mayragometsi, heard of some agitation against images by three monks who had urged people to scratch images off church walls, and he summoned them to appear before him. When they did so he asked them why they opposed images and they said, simply, that the Bible neither commanded nor permitted them. John responded with biblical arguments of his own. He recounted the decorations on Moses' tent and the adornment of the Temple. This text says nothing about the veneration of images and does not reveal a high degree of theological speculation on either side of this issue.[65]

Many of the statements by these writers are by now familiar to us. But three new notes have entered the music. First, Agathias talks, rather cryptically, of images directing the viewer to a higher contemplation. Hypatius, rather more clearly, speaks of a viewer being guided up to the divine being. This sounds very much like a passage near the beginning of *The Celestial Hierarchy* by Dionysius the Pseudo-Areopagite, an early sixth-century text that drew deep drafts from the wells of Neoplatonic thought. Pseudo-Denys said, "We are led up, as far as possible, through visible images to the contemplation of the divine."[66] For some people, perhaps many people, an image became a highly charged point where anagogy met theophany. The spiritual energy of the viewer was channeled upward just as heavenly grace and intercession were channeled downward. A picture thus became capable not merely of representing but in fact of mediating to the observer the thing observed. This is what Karl Morrison has called a "calculated, stylized misunderstanding."[67] There can be no doubt that Neoplatonic thought eventually contributed to a breakdown of the barrier that separated the image from the person whom it represented. But, judging from Agathias and Hypatius, Pseudo-Dionysius was, in the sixth century, understood as providing a way of thinking about referential prayer and devotion. The idea that the image participated (μέθεξις) in, or shared in the being of the person it represented had not yet been articulated. This would happen only in the ninth century. Second, Leontius and, less explicitly, Vrt'anes refer to miracles associated with images. This topic will loom larger and larger in later discussions of images. For now, it is worth noting that two very different writers could pass over this subject with complete equanimity. Third, Hypatius in particular does not so much defend images in general and on principle as suggest that they may be of value to the simple. Images were always seen by their supporters as useful in teaching but here we learn who was to be taught by them—not the whole community but only its humbler members. The implication is that the better sort of people were able to rise above mere sensory perception.

Embedded in the *acta* of the fifth session of II Nicaea, but not otherwise preserved, are statements from two late seventh-century Byzantine churchmen who had interesting things to say in defense of images. Bishop John of Thessalonica is quoted, in the first place, as having said a few quite traditional things. He defended images because they exist only for remembering and honoring those depicted. The images themselves, indeed, are not honored, but instead the servants and friends of God who intercede for people. But then John adds, "We make images of God, that is of our Lord and Savior Jesus Christ, in so far as he was seen upon the earth and talked with men. We paint this not that it [the image] be understood as God by nature . . . we depict the humanity, not the incorporeal divinity." John concludes by developing the same argument with respect to angels. Of course they are incorporeal but they appeared many times to men as if corporeal and so that is how they are depicted.[68] At about the same time Deacon Constantine, the Chartophylax (archivist, we might say) of Hagia Sophia, defended images of Christ for exactly the same reason that John did: Christ had appeared as a man and an image of him manifested that reality.[69]

Far from the heart of Byzantium, Anastasius of Sinai reflected on images in the late seventh century in ways that harkened back to old philosophical debates about the relative excellence of seeing and hearing or reading that accorded with contemporary concerns about the authenticity of texts and that addressed very current concerns, in the world of Monothelitism and the sixth council of 680, about Christ's full humanity. He said, defending depictions of the crucifixion, that "the best rule of the wisest men is this: material refutations and representations are stronger and more believable and mightier by far than both spoken words and learned quotes. For the material representation cannot be glossed or forged, whereas the spoken expositions of books often suffer additions and omissions at the hands of evil-speaking men."[70] Not until the ninth century did iconophile writers express the full equivalence between pictures and words, but Anastasius was obviously on that path. In his own time, however, he was, perhaps, less concerned with art itself than with refuting the Theopaschites who believed that God had suffered on the cross. For Anastasius, depiction of the crucifixion was an exercise in apologetics: It demonstrated that it was only the human, the fully human, Jesus who suffered and died.[71]

The last pre-iconoclastic writings on images are in some respects the most important. In 692 the council "in Trullo" (often called the "Quinisext" or "Fifth-Sixth") added a lengthy set of disciplinary canons to the dogmatic decisions of the Fifth (533) and Sixth (680) Ecumenical Councils. Three times the council addressed itself to the use of art in cult. In canon 73 the council fathers forbade the image of the cross to be put on the floor, presumably in a mosaic.[72] This canon actually did no more than repeat an edict of Theodosius II of 427 that had been taken up in Justinian's code.[73] It means that sacred images were to be accorded respect and, thus, not to be trampled underfoot. Canon 100 says that there should be no pictures that "catch the eye and corrupt the mind and excite base pleasures."[74] This canon is rarely noticed by historians of the image. Its meaning is ambiguous in the extreme: It could relate to secular or sacred art. It may bear some connection to the kind of thinking that later occasioned the interpolations in the letter of St. Nilus of Sinai (see above p. 18) who was alleged to be concerned that art in churches might be distracting and not instructive. Churches were places of worship, not of entertainment, and no art was justifiable that did not enhance the piety of worshipers. Finally, in its most famous image canon, number 82, the Trullan Council decreed:

> In some depictions of the venerable images, the Forerunner is portrayed
> pointing with his finger to a lamb, and this has been accepted as a
> representation of grace, prefiguring for us through the law the true
> Lamb, Christ our God. Venerating, then, these ancient representations
> and foreshadowings as symbols and prefigurations of truths handed
> down by the church, nevertheless, we prefer grace and truth, which we
> have received as fulfillment of the law. Therefore, in order that what is
> perfect, even in paintings, may be portrayed before the eyes of all, we
> decree that henceforth the figure of the Lamb of God who takes away
> the sins of the world, Christ our God, should be set forth in images in
> human form, instead of the ancient lamb; for in this way we apprehend

the depth of the humility of the Word of God, and are led to the remembrance of his life in the flesh, his passion and his saving death, and the redemption which thereby came to the world.[75]

It is sometimes said that this canon forbade the depiction of Christ as a Lamb. It does not have to be read in this way. Taken together with the words of John of Thessalonica and Constantine Chartophylax, and viewed in the context of the continuing Christological battles that disturbed the Orthodox Church, this canon can be taken to mean that, in order to assert the doctrine of the incarnation, Christ can and should be depicted as a man. Stated differently, this Trullan canon can be interpreted as an affirmation that, the Word having been made flesh, there was no need to provide symbolic representation of the grace to come.[76] With respect to images themselves, we have, in tracing a path from Eusebius to the Trullan Hall, reversed course. Eusebius could not imagine making an image of Christ but was happy with abstract, symbolic representations. The Trullan fathers were a little dubious about symbols and content with specific figural renderings. In any case, the Trullan Council marked the first time, at least the first time since the obscure Elviran canon quoted above, that the church pronounced officially on sacred art. It cannot be emphasized too strongly that the verdict was decidedly affirmative.

In the age before iconoclasm, therefore, certain basic positions had been staked out by both the attackers and the defenders of images. The former said that God was a purely spiritual being who could not be depicted. Depictions, in any event, were made of vile matter which was unsuited to the divine essence and also encouraged the worship of material creation. Creation itself, moreover, was God's work alone. People should not, in creating images, presume to share in God's work. Images were idols, or so very much like them as to make no difference. Finally, God had revealed himself in words, not in pictures.

The defenders of images used didactic arguments: Art was good for the instruction of the ignorant. Art stimulated the emotions in ways that words did not. Art encouraged people to think deeper thoughts about higher things. Art reminded people of the scriptural and ecclesiastical heroes whose example remained a continuing presence and comfort. Art helped to focus and to refer the prayers of the believers. Art was made of vile matter, perhaps, but the matter was incidental to the purposes of art. Moreover, God had created all things and had pronounced them good. Matter could be abused, certainly, but it was not intrinsically bad. In some cases seeing was preferable to hearing or reading. Images worked miracles in many places. Surely this helped to establish their legitimacy. Finally, images of Christ helped to proclaim the doctrine of the incarnation.[77]

Ernst Kitzinger once said that there was no time between the fourth century and the ninth when there was no discussion of images.[78] That is true. But it is also true that the discussions were rare in comparison with, for example, the fierce debates surrounding the person and nature of Jesus Christ. The most common charge against art was idolatry and the most common defense was that, in certain circumstances, God himself had commanded images to be made. In a way, the image quarrels were really battles over biblical exegesis. This may help to explain the emergence of the didactic defense of images. If, for example, an image could be "read" to support an incarnationist reading of the New Testament, then such an image was itself an exegetical argument against those who interpreted the Scriptures differently.

Maybe "argument" is the wrong word. Few of the writers whom we have mentioned appear to have been answering any of the other writers. Jews and heretics may have prompted some defenses of images, or they may have prompted no more than literary inventions cast in dialogue form. Popular excesses seem to have occasioned some attacks. But it would be wrong to think of a centuries-long debate. There were instead, during these dynamically creative centuries in the history of Christianity, occasional and isolated voices. Kitzinger also remarked that before the age of iconoclasm there was no systematic attempt to establish a Christian theory of images.[79] It is worth adding that there was no systematic theory on either side of the issue. Nothing is less predictable than that a bitter image quarrel should have arisen in the eighth century.

The Rise and Function of Sacred Icons

Before I could write these words I took in hand a mouse and clicked on a series of icons. These icons, of course, are mere symbols designed to convey to me various realities and possibilities hidden deep in the electronics of my computer. In late antiquity, more and more people clicked on religious icons in order to activate the religious forces of their age.

Εἰκών simply means image, picture. The word can refer to any image at all. Historians often use it, however, to refer to specific types of religious images. Reserving the word "icon" for religious pictures alone is actually a Russian usage, and a fairly recent one.[80] Nevertheless, art historians usefully distinguish between narrative pictures, *historiai*, and icons, *eikones*, which tend to represent one or a few figures frontally and totally out of temporal, historical context.[81]

Such arguments are based partly on stylistic considerations and in view of the small number of surviving, pre-iconoclast examples—fewer than twenty—it is probably dangerous to attempt to differentiate too sharply among the works of art at our disposal. In Belting's words, the icon "was nothing but a late classical panel picture that inherited the divine image, the imperial image, and the portrait of the dead. Thus the icon adopted a multiplicity of formal devices, each coming from a different tradition and from different genres. It had not yet evolved a style or aesthetic of its own. It embraced the conflict between the desire for commemorating an individual's likeness and the wish for obtaining an imperishable ideal."[82] This is helpful, but the point can be extended by saying that a work of art may be regarded as iconic when it makes no reference to words at all. It does not illustrate a biblical text or saint's life, does not tell a story, is not expected to draw the observer's mind back to something that he or she has read or heard.[83] Furthermore, as Gary Vikan has observed, insofar as "icon" simply means "image," the term should not be restricted to an abstract religious portrait painted in egg tempera on a gold-covered wooden board. What defined an icon in Byzantium, and already in late antiquity, was its use and what people believed it to be. An icon is a devotional image that demands reverence and respect; it is holy in the sense that it shares in the sanctity of the figure whose likeness it bears. "A painting became an icon at the moment when it began to function as an icon."[84]

Art and Cult

In asking about the rise and function of icons, I prefer to turn away from what they look like and to inquire about how they were used and what they did (or were believed, or expected, to do). There are many problems in this approach too, not the least of which is that the literary sources and the surviving art works cannot as a rule be brought into direct connection with each other. For instance, there is no incontrovertible evidence for the place of manufacture, original place of display, and cult practices, if any, associated with the famous pre-iconoclastic icons preserved in the monastery of St. Catherine in Sinai.[85] At the same time, virtually all extant literary allusions to icons relate to paintings that have long since vanished.

On one point most authorities are agreed: An icon is a work of art before which certain specific cult acts were performed.[86] Marie-France Auzépy says that "it is because one renders devotion to it that an image becomes an icon, that is to say, a place of communication between a devotée and the person who is represented."[87] Hans Georg Thümmel adds that an icon emerges when a picture that was honored and that was seen as efficacious was distinguished from other such objects or from general church decoration.[88] The first unambiguous reference to such acts is provided by St. Augustine, who said, "I know there are many who adore pictures of the dead."[89] Epiphanius, as we saw, expressed some concerns about how images were being used, but his words are less explicit than Augustine's.

Hans Belting thinks that the first step from a memorial image to a cult of the image was the practice of lighting candles and laying garlands before portraits at the graves of the dead. Soon, the portraits could be replicated and thus the cult was no longer tied to the place where the person depicted was actually buried. In some instances a particular person or community became a sort of impresario of a cult.[90] The fifth-century writer Theodoret reports of St. Symeon Stylites that he "became so famous in the great [city of] Rome that in the porches of all the workshops they set up little images of him so as to obtain protection and security."[91] Not only portraits were portable. The *Life of Symeon* (c. 231) refers to *eulogia*, an iconically stamped earthen token. Symeon tells a father who brought his son for a cure to take the image anywhere and to look at it to see him and his power. Some two hundred of these tokens survive in various collections. The *eulogia* makes the presence and efficacy of the saint available anywhere. We see here icons that could ward off evil and icons that could effect cures. Gary Vikan sketches a typology of these potent icons in these terms: "While the *charsterion* icon would have been made in response to the exercise of miraculous power (and might, after the fact, act miraculously), and the *eulogia* icon would have been made to help precipitate a miracle, the *phylacterion* icon, by definition, would have been created to be the source of it."[92] If by the fifth century people adored images and expected cures and protection from them, then in at least some instances, specific works of Christian art had acquired functions quite beyond those of stimulating, elevating, commemorating, and teaching. Such works of art may usefully be called icons. As I shall use the word icon here and throughout this book, I mean to bracket pictures that were holy, that *did* things, leaving aside all other pictures which were, by definition, icons too. At the same time, I am not concerned with matters of style. In my analysis, it does not matter what a picture looked like. What counts is what it did, or what it was expected to do. My definition is artificial and cuts against the grain of several historical traditions and disciplinary understandings. What this definition has going for it is clarity and consistency. Moreover, when we come to the Carolingians, we will see that they had many images but no icons.

A brief consideration of ordinary objects and images, even of objects with images on them, will serve as a reminder that icons, panel paintings, *eulogiai*, the cult of the dead, and the apotropaic powers of some pictures can all themselves be located within a wider context. Too often the discussion of icons is confined to a consideration of either the famous, beautiful, and ostentatiously public arts of late antiquity's churches, or else to those paintings that are called "icons," mainly on stylistic grounds. But there was a whole realm of domestic art, or arts, that we should not lose sight of. Symbolic representations of knots, eyes, circles, serpents, keys, or octagons were thought to ward off evil. Christian inscriptions over doorways could do the same thing, as could lambs, doves, letters, words, "holy Names," and, especially, crosses. Houses also had lamps, bowls, pitchers, and dishes with explicitly Christian images, some symbolic and some clearly representational.[93] John Chrysostom provides a revealing account of the prevalence of the cross, increasingly the Christian symbol par excellence:

> What once horrified everyone, its figure is now sought by all, and is discovered everywhere, among princes and subjects, among men and women, among virgins and married, among slaves and free. Everyone now presses that sign on the nobler parts of their bodies. . . . The cross seems to be celebrated everywhere, in houses, in the forum, in deserted places, in roadways, in mountains, in valleys, in hills, in the sea, in ships, in islands, in beds, on clothing, on weapons, in rooms, at banquets, on gold and silver vessels, in pearls, in wall paintings, on the bodies of pack-animals, on the bodies of those afflicted by demons, in war and in peace, in the daytime and at night, among troops of dancers, in communities of the ascetic. Everyone seeks its marvelous gift, its inexpressible grace. . . . No one affects shame or blushes when he realizes that this is a symbol of a damnable death; indeed, everyone adorns himself even more with it.[94]

Christians all over the Mediterranean world were becoming accustomed to being surrounded by a profusion of pictures and images that sometimes served to refresh their memories and that were sometimes thought to protect or heal them. If most attention is usually accorded to icons, then those icons should not be set off in sovereign seclusion from potent images.

The Proliferation of Icons

A consensus so broad that it requires no elaboration holds that icons spread tremendously in the sixth and seventh centuries. Abundant testimonies, some of them already mentioned in the previous section, tell us of icons (or images) in churches, houses, monasteries, and shops. We even hear of a man who carried an image of Sts. Cosmas and Damian in a sack under his arm.[95] Surely he was not unique.

The sixth century saw a comprehensive refiguring of imperial ceremonial designed to achieve a "style of governing which integrated the imperial government with contemporary taste."[96] That taste was religious. And it was cultivated in a world that was being "liturgified," amid processes "whereby the old classical survivals lose ground to a uniformly religious approach to life . . . whereby the emperor gradually sheds the traditional Roman attributes to emerge fully as the *philochristos basileus.*"[97] As emperors were integrating their office and the rituals connected with it into the religious life of their people, they identified special roles for images and icons to play in that process.

In their attempts to restore popular confidence in the generations after Justinian, emperors increasingly made Mary the patron and protector of Constantinople.[98] As early as the reign of Theodosius II the emperor's wife Eudocia sent from Jerusalem to his sister Pulcheria an image of Mary allegedly painted by St. Luke.[99] Justinian was particularly devoted to Mary.[100] During the Avar siege of 626, icons of the Virgin were carried around Constantinople.[101] Icons of Christ were also carried around the city in 626 and accompanied imperial armies into battle against the Persians and later against the Arabs. Justinian II placed images of Christ on his coins, an act of Christomimesis designed to proclaim that he was the sole legitimate earthly representative of the heavenly king.[102] Constantinople, the empire, and the emperor had all come under the special protection of the Virgin and of Christ. By extension, then, everyone in the empire enjoyed the same patronage and protection. The religious revaluation of the imperial office and regime was an integrative force in early Byzantine society. One key tool and manifestation of that force was the icon.

In a world so deeply Christianized, at least at the official level, in a world where Jesus and Mary, not the genius of the emperor or the strength of the legions, protected the empire and its people, icons represent one element in the "replacement of the remaining vestiges of classical culture by a codification of knowledge based on religious truth."[103] If icons protected the empire and the emperor, and did so in very public displays of power, then surely icons could protect, heal, and comfort ordinary people too. God had revealed himself by means of many signs in the past: the burning bush, the tablets of the law, the Ark of the Covenant, the cross, the Scriptures, water, manna, incense, and candles. Knowledge, like grace, comes, along approved channels, through revelation, not through secular learning. The rise of "authentic" icons and of miracle stories connected with many icons serves to show just how approved the channels of revelation were that joined viewers to the objects of their gaze.

It is surely not coincidental that a particularly authentic kind of image, the *achieropoietos*, the "image not made by human hands," began to gain in recognition and popularity in the sixth and seventh centuries. Here was a kind of image—the Camuliana that arrived in Constantinople from Syria in 574, the Edessa image[104] that protected its city from the Persians in 544, or the cloth in Memphis with a portrait of Christ left when He had washed His face[105]—whose source and materials could not be called into question. How could God oppose icons if He Himself made them for His people? How could the materials in icons be base if they came straight from heaven? The so-called Lucan Mary fits into this context too. A portrait by one of the evangelists, by one of God's own spokesmen, could not be illegitimate. And if Luke painted Mary from life, then there could be no question of the whims of the painter leading him to make any sort of picture he wished. Likewise, the Gallic bishop Arculf, reporting on his seventh-century travels in the Holy Land, told Adomnan of a cloth woven by Mary and bearing images of Jesus and the apostles.[106] These pictures were powerful precisely because they were so powerfully "authentic."[107]

The sixth and seventh centuries not only saw the proliferation of stories about icons "not made by human hands" but also witnessed a mushrooming of accounts of acts of reverence performed before icons and or miracles performed by them. The most common forms of reverence were *proskynesis* and *aspamos*. The latter means, most simply, kissing but can also mean touching or embracing. The former can have a wide range of meanings. Writers used it interchangeably with other words (especially forms of τιμαῶ) but could use it in one sentence or paragraph to refer to the worship, honor, adoration, or reverence paid both to God and to an icon. And writers did this even as they were trying by the force of their arguments to differentiate crisply between the kinds of reverence due to God and to icons that were only memorials. Icons were reverenced by genuflecting or kneeling before them; by approaching them with candles and incense; or by ceremonially bathing them.[108] No doubt the most frequent form of reverence was the quiet prayer. The key point is that while some writers continued to ruminate on the Basilian idea of the relationship between the image and its prototype, the sixth and seventh centuries begin to show evidence of practices, and of reflections on those practices, that bound some images, icons, and their viewers in psychologically and spiritually complex ways.[109]

Icons were meant to provide protection and security. They warded off ills and healed those already afflicted. They effected the return of runaway slaves.

Icons stood sponsor to children at baptism and brought them blessings later. Demons were driven out by icons. Dreams were authenticated when the dreamer looked at an icon and recognized the very person(s) who had visited him in his sleep. Scrapings from an icon could heal a sick person, as could the water with which an icon was washed. Icons were suspended from the walls and gates of towns to drive away enemies and icons were carried into battle.

Such, at any rate, is what Leslie Brubaker calls the "canonical" interpretation of the dramatic increase in the prominence of icons after about the 550s. Her use of the word "canonical" refers directly to the evidence collected and interpreted by Kitzinger. But Brubaker carefully collates two generations of scholarship on Kitzinger's evidence and calls almost every piece of it into question.[110] She makes three fundamental points. First, while it is true that from the seventh—note, not mid-sixth—century stories about images become increasingly common in texts of various kinds, and especially in saint's lives or collections of their miracles, it is very rare for any miraculous power to be assigned to the images in the stories. She looks closely at *The Miracles of St. Artemios, The Miracles of Cosmas and Damian,* and *The Life of Symeon the Younger* to make this point. In other words, even if images are becoming more and more evident, they are not yet becoming more and more powerful. They are not necessarily, in this interpretation, becoming icons. Literary testimonies about images are not at all the same thing as evidence for an increasingly prominent cult of icons. Second, virtually every story about a miraculous seventh-century image is embedded in a text at a point that gives rise to some suspicions of later tampering. A good example dating from around 600 is *The Spiritual Meadow* of John Moschos upon which Kitzinger and others have drawn heavily. In his collection of 243 edifying tales (in a recent version) only four concern images at all.[111] Three image stories are quite possibly later interpolations. Third, although the late sixth-century Piacenza Pilgrim is the first writer after Augustine to use the term "adorare" (*et nos eam adoravimus*) unambiguously in connection with an image,[112] only in the time of Arculf and Stephen of Bostra—that is, late in the seventh century—did *proskynesis* begin to become routine.[113] By my count, Stephen uses "προσκυνῶ" in one form or another nine times in a text whose surviving version runs to a mere forty-eight lines.[114] Practices that, as we shall see in more detail in the next chapter, had become commonplace by the 730s, when John of Damascus was writing, were fairly recent and not the inheritance of many centuries of steady development.[115] By 700 there were countless images in all kinds of media in many different places. There were also icons in the sense in which I am using the term. It is important not to conflate the two, and it is difficult to say what proportion of images were icons.

Art Talk in the Latin West Before Iconoclasm

Positive or negative references to pictures or to cult practices associated with them were as rare in the Latin West as they were in the Greek East. Once again, it is difficult to trace direct connections between one author and another. The range of opinions that we have already met on the positive side appears in the West, albeit with some new twists. There is no writer so negative as, say, Epiphanius but many Western authors were quite reserved where figural art is concerned.

The Terms of Discussion

Paulinus of Nola (353/4–431) was among the first Western authors to express himself on images. He did so in a poem in which he says that the houses of Felix (of Nola) were adorned with pictures on sacred themes in the hope that they "would excite the interest of the rustics by their attractive appearance." In particular, it seems that the peasants around Nola were especially given to feasting and drinking and so, by means of pictures of "the feast of fasting," the hunger of peasants would be "beguiled" and they would turn to better practices. Some at least of these pictures were given *tituli*, explanatory inscriptions, that the more literate could read to the less to enhance their instruction.[116] Paulinus may strike us as naive, but there was by his time a fairly strong tradition holding that art could move its viewers.

John Cassian (360–435), in his tenth *Conference*, said that the gentiles (he means pagans) dressed in human forms the demons which they worshiped (*excolebant*). "Now they think they can adore the incomprehensible and ineffable majesty of the true God under the form of some sort of image (*imaginis*), believing themselves to have or to hold nothing at all if they shall not have put up some sort of image." He goes on to say that man was created in the image and likeness of God but that to make images of God is to fall into the heresy of anthropomorphism.[117] John does not speak of idolatry. He reserves his objection to anthropomorphism. As a disciple of Evagrius and therefore as an Origenist, John may well be talking more about the anthropomorphic controversies raging in Egypt, which he visited, than about images per se. And he appears to be concerned about recent pagan converts and their habit of bringing their old practices with them into their new church. Be that as it may, Cassian's *Conferences* were widely read in the West, especially in monastic circles, but they do not seem to have deterred the production of art works, including depictions of the deity. It may be that his words were read primarily in the context of ancient heresies.

The prolific Augustine had little to say about art, and he was mainly indifferent to it. For him, words were always superior to pictures. We noted above Augustine's disparaging remark about "adorers" of pictures of the dead. In one of his treatises on the Scriptures Augustine expressed concern about the tendency of artists to engage in anachronisms that distort the meaning of the Bible. For instance, he complained about the tendency of painters to portray Christ, Peter, and Paul together as if they had been contemporaries.[118] Augustine clearly had doubts about the ability of pictures to teach what was in the words of Scripture. The second book of Augustine's *On Christian Doctrine* spells out the saint's ideas about signs. Artistic representations can be signs; they can convey information about something other than themselves. But because pictures were inferior to words, and because it was necessary for a person to be well prepared in order to look at a picture and see what it signified, Augustine regarded paintings and sculptures as "superfluous creations."[119]

Augustine was a wordsmith. It is perhaps not surprising that he privileged the written and spoken word over visual forms of communication. In his *On the Trinity* (8.4–5) Augustine says, perhaps thinking about the anthropomorphist controversy, that no one can love God before he knows Him. "And what is it to know God, except to see Him mentally and to perceive him clearly." In saying this, Augustine moves beyond words to contemplation. He did not think it was possible for an image to resemble its subject because images were the products of human imagination and every believer or artist imagines God in his own way.[120] His qualms about representations are clearly expressed in another passage in *On the Trinity*:

> Who having read or heard read or heard what the apostle Paul wrote, or what was written about him, will not fashion in his mind a face for the apostle, and for everyone else who is mentioned in these texts. And since each member among the vast multitude of those to whom these texts are known will think of the lines and shape of their bodies differently, it is completely uncertain who thinks most closely and accurately. Our faith is not concerned with what physical face those men had, but with how they lived through the grace of God, and what they did, which things are witnessed in those writings.[121]

In one of his sermons, Augustine argues that Christ's ascension was necessary, and that it had to happen in the sight of the apostles, because otherwise they would have remained fixated on his human form and would have been unable to contemplate his invisible divinity.[122] By contemplation, therefore, Augustine means seeing the invisible, and he spoke eloquently on this kind of sight in his *Literal Commentary on Genesis*:

> What is seen actually, not as in an image, and not through the eyes of the body, is seen by that vision which surpasses all others. In so far as the Lord will help me, I will try to explain the types of vision and how they differ. Behold when this one precept is read—"You shall love your neighbor as yourself"—three kinds of vision arise: one through the eyes by which we see the letters themselves; another through the spirit by which the neighbor is contemplated even though he is absent; and a third through a perception of the mind whereby this very love is seen to be understood. Among these kinds of vision, the first is clear to everyone for in this way heaven and earth are seen and everything in them is perceived by our eyes. Nor is that other one, by which absent bodies are contemplated corporally, difficult to explain. Indeed, we can think about heaven and earth and all that we can see in them even when we are standing in the dark and seeing nothing with our bodily eyes and yet contemplating bodily images in our soul. These might be true images, in so far as we have seen those bodies and kept them in memory, or imaginary images in so far as our thinking has fashioned them. So it is one thing to think of Carthage, which we know, and another thing to think of Alexandria, which we do not know. The third kind of vision, by which love is seen to be understood, concerns those things which have no images or likenesses which are not what they themselves actually are. For a man, or a tree, or the sun and whatever other bodies there are in heaven or on earth are seen when present in their own forms and are contemplated when absent in images impressed on the mind. They generate two kinds of vision: one through the perception of the body and another through the spirit in which those images are contained. Is love, however, seen in one way when it is present in the manner in which it exists and in another way when it is absent in some sort of an image like itself? No. But in so far as it is possible to perceive with the mind this love is seen more clearly by one and less clearly by another. But if some bodily image is contemplated, then it is not love that is seen.[123]

Augustine's "visionary imagination" may be characterized as embracing "corporeal, pictographic, and conceptual" sight arrayed in a precise hierarchical order where the corporeal is the least excellent and the conceptual, the most.[124] Augustine extended this line of thought in his suggestively entitled work *On Faith in Things Unseen:*

> There are some who think the Christian religion ought to be ridiculed rather than upheld. The reason for this is that in it, not the thing which may be seen is set forth, but faith in things which are not seen is imposed upon men. For the sake of refuting those who, prudent in their own opinion, seem to be opposed to believing what they cannot see, we surely have not the power to present to the eyes of men the divine truths which we believe. Yet we do show the minds of men that even those things which are not seen ought to be believed. Now, as regards those whom folly has made so servile to the eyes of the body that they do not think they ought to believe anything which they do not perceive through those eyes, they ought, in the first place, to be reminded of how many things there are which cannot be seen with such eyes—things which they not only believe but also know.
>
> These things are innumerable in our mind itself, whose nature is invisible—to say nothing of other things, like the very faith by which we believe, or the thought process by which we know either that we believe something or that we do not believe it, although it might be entirely outside the realm of those eyes. What is there so bare, so clear, what so certain to the interior perceptions of our minds? How, therefore, must we not believe what we do not see with our bodily eyes, when we perceive beyond any doubt either that we believe or do not believe where we cannot employ the eyes of the body?[125]

Augustine's relative indifference to works of art rested on a firm principle: What the body's eyes could see in the world is vastly inferior to and ultimately less important than what the mind's eye could see. And the mind itself could be properly instructed only by words. As we shall see in Chapter 5, Augustine's ideas were profoundly influential in the Carolingian world.

In the fifth century, in the south of Gaul, Caesarius of Arles (ca. 470–542) expressed himself on art in a passage of his *Rule* for nuns. He says "Do not put up painted tablets, nor should there be any pictures on the walls or in the rooms, for in a monastery there should only be things that please the spiritual, not the human, eyes. There should be no pictures at all except on handkerchiefs and face-towels when the abbess has so ordered."[126] This was not so much a comment on art as it was a piece of sumptuary legislation for a cloistered community of religious women. But it is interesting to note that Caesarius seems to have felt that paintings would be distracting.

Isidore of Seville (560–636), in his wide-ranging *Etymologies*, had only a few things to say about images. On one occasion he demonstrates a concern about idolatry. He says there were once "certain brave men, the founders of cities, for whom, after they had died, the people who loved them put up likenesses (*simulacra*) that they might have some comfort from contemplation of the images (*imaginum*). But a little later, on the urging of demons, this error was found among the people: Those whose images they had honored solely for the honor of the name, their successors took to be gods and worshiped them." Isidore does not say anywhere that this "error" was to be found among Christians. He goes on to talk of demons, and also of likenesses, simulacra, images, and so on. Throughout, he emphasizes that God alone is to be worshiped.[127] Elsewhere he says that "an icon *(icon)* is an image *(imago)* which tries to express the figure of something else by means of something similar." On another occasion he says that a "painting *(pictura)* is an image *(imago)* expressing the appearance of something else which, while it is being viewed, brings it back to the memory. A painting, however, is called artificial, for it is a fashioned image, not the truth."[128] In his *Three Books of Opinions*, Isidore took a slightly different line. He says "Many imitate the life of the saints and they take up an image *(effigies)* of virtue from the way of life of another such that if any image *(imago quaelibet)* is being regarded intently then from it likeness *(similitudine)* a sort of painted image can be formed. Thus the one who lives in the likeness of the image becomes like the image."[129] Isidore, thus, recognizes the danger of idolatry but he, perhaps like John Cassian, assigns a higher degree of risk to pagans than to Christians. As for images themselves, Isidore is coolly analytical, as always. He explores words and their meanings. In doing so, he discovers that images are not real, they are not anything in themselves. As in Augustine's reckoning, images are signs. But like other ancient thinkers, Isidore thinks that images can refresh the memory. While he does not go as far as some writers in suggesting that images can teach, he is sympathetic to the idea that they can provoke emulation, can arouse virtue.

The writings of Gregory of Tours (d. 594) open before us the world of late antique and early Frankish Gaul. Gregory describes many churches, and his voluminous writings, plus those of his contemporaries and successors, at least mention numerous others. Many, perhaps most, of these churches were richly decorated. Gregory transmits an interesting anecdote concerning the wife of Bishop Namatianus of Clermont who sat with a book in her lap dictating to the painters who were decorating the walls of St. Stephen's basilica with "stories of ancient deeds."[130] There survives from the pen of Venantius Fortunatus a poem that describes a cycle of narrative paintings on the life of St. Martin that Gregory had installed in his rebuilt cathedral.[131] The church of La Daurade in Toulouse had a rich set of mosaics.[132] Literary testimonies reveal thousands of pictures.[133] Greogry's world must have been covered with pictures.

Gregory sponsored works of art, described or referred to many, and once spoke of people who had Christ's law in their hearts but who had pictures of his "meritorious deeds" in their homes and churches, the better to remember those deeds.[134] That is a commonplace. More interesting are two other elements of Gregory's art talk. Herbert Kessler argues persuasively that Gregory saw a role for art in missionary work in the still-pagan parts of Gaul.[135] If he is correct, then Gregory may have been yet another author who believed that art had the power to move its observers.

A Cult of Images?

Robert Markus discovers in Gregory's writings a cult of icons in sixth-century Gaul.[136] Gregory tells of a crucifix in Narbonne that was stolen by a Jew and that bled to reveal the theft.[137] He also speaks of a naked image of Christ that asked to be clothed.[138] To Markus's slim dossier may be added two cases he overlooked. In his *Life of St. Martin* Gregory relates that in Ravenna there was an image of Martin with an oil lamp burning beneath it. Oil from that lamp was capable of healing the sick.[139] In the church of St. Martin in Tours there was an inscription attributed to Paulinus of Perigueux. This inscription addressed a person who, prostrate, might be praying before an image of Martin in hopes of obtaining a cure.[140]

It is possible that the cult practices and actual icons associated with Eastern devotions reached and dispersed through Gaul. There were many easterners in Gaul, not least numerous Syrian communities.[141] And Symeon the Stylite, whose immense popularity is judged by some scholars to lie at the base of the rise of icons, was a Syrian. Yet the evidence for a cult of icons in Gaul is meager, and if we remember that Brubaker has dammed up Kitzinger's flood of sixth- and seventh-century icons in the eastern Mediterranean, then it may be that there was less influence available to the West than has been thought until now.

There is room for serious doubt about a widespread cult of icons in Gaul. Neither the crucifix that bled nor the image that asked to be clothed give evidence of the cult practices elsewhere associated with icons. The one case may be about anti-semitism and the other about prudery or asceticism or social compassion. In addition, the Narbonne image addressed itself to a priest with a Greek name, and did so exactly once. This may be no more than a pale reflection of current concerns in the East.[142] Moreover, these are not miraculous images in the sense of those in the East that were expected to, indeed that were believed to, provide miracles for various people on a regular basis. These images worked only once, with the possible exception of the ones in Ravenna and Tours, as far as we know. Gregory once mentions tokens from the Holy Land, surely the *eulogiai* discussed above, but he equates them with relics, saying, "Faith believes that everything the sacred body touches is holy."[143] Gregory takes works of art very much for granted, but with one possible exception (Tours), he does not once portray anyone prostrating himself before an image; and even then he merely cites an inscription written by someone else. Yet he does say that people laid down before tombs and the cross.[144] The lamp and image from Ravenna sound more like the Eastern cases that are so familiar. But Ravenna was, for all practical purposes, an Eastern city. It was the seat of the exarch, the Byzantine commander of northern and central Italy after about 580. It would be imprudent to generalize about the West from a single Ravennese case. The oil, moreover, not the picture, is assigned credit for Venantius's cure, although it does seem that the oil acquired its potency from the picture (icon?). In addition, Gregory, the successor to St. Martin, had every incentive to report anything marvelous or miraculous relating to the founder of his see. But these stories are the only ones that Gregory could, or did, associate with an image of Martin. The situation of the Stylites or, for that matter, the way John Chrysostom describes the practices associated with St. Meletius in Antioch could not have been more different. Finally, the inscription in Tours may well reveal acts of worship conducted before an image but it seems that the cult of Martin is more important here than the cult of images. The image is meant to remind the petitioner of who his patron is.

A complicating factor in the West of Gregory, Venantius, and others has been limned by Patricia Cox Miller, Giselle de Nie, and Joaquín Martinéz Pizarro. According to Miller, late antiquity was a time when almost everything was understood in terms of images. Images, however, could be understood, among other possible ways, as allegorical, oneiric, or visionary. People shared a world view based on analogies, an "insistently figural way of viewing the social, psychic, religious, and philosophical dimensions of life."[145] In de Nie's opinion, "imagistic associations are not limited by discursive principles such as contradiction and incongruity" such that "an image could present multileveled, dynamic truths in a way that abstract statements could not."[146] The point will be familiar to anyone who has read much in Gregory of Tours or Venantius Fortunatus.

They both had a stunning capacity to paint word-pictures that were obviously meant to evoke images—no matter how one wants to take that word—in the minds of their readers. There is more than a whiff here of Augutine's writing about the "mind's eye." But this is where Pizarro enters the discussion with the astute observation that Gregory used, first of all, textual strategies: "Rather than say that Gregory of Tours thought in images, I would prefer to say that he wrote in images."[147] What power those images might have possessed, whether they were mental or textual, and how one is to interpret that imagistic way of thinking, is hard to tell. But one can confidently say that people did not kiss, wash, place in shops, or carry into battle mental pictures or textual fragments.

Along with Augustine the most influential of all late antique commentators on art was Pope Gregory I (590–604). His comments came not in the form of a systematic treatise but exclusively in two letters he dispatched to Bishop Serenus of Marseilles in July of 599 and October of 600 when he learned that his episcopal colleague had been destroying works of art and scandalizing the population. Gregory was distressed to learn that Serenus "seeing certain people adoring (*adoratores*) images, broke them up and threw them out of the churches." Gregory praised Serenus for his zeal in preventing manufactured things (*manufacta*) from being adored but tells him that he should on no account destroy pictures because "pictures are used in churches so that those who do not know letters may at least read by seeing on the walls what they cannot read in books." Gregory concluded his first letter by reiterating that pictures should be put up for the instruction of those who lack letters and by reemphasizing that pictures are never to be adored.[148] More than a year later Gregory wrote again because he had heard that Serenus persisted in his iconoclasm, apparently believing that Gregory's first letter to him was a forgery. Gregory assures Serenus of the authenticity of his first letter and then, once again, insists that Serenus cease from breaking images. "Tell me brother," Gregory says, "when have you ever heard of any priest doing what you did?" Gregory says again that it is wrong to adore pictures but that in pictures one can see what is to be adored. Gregory reminds Serenus not to scandalize the "gentiles" who have "savage minds." Gregory goes on to remind Serenus that, as a pastor, his greatest concern should be the spiritual health of the flock that has been entrusted to his care. Pictures can be helpful to Serenus in carrying out his pastoral responsibilities, first by educating the uneducated and second by eliciting compunction.[149]

Much that Gregory says on art, as on so many subjects, is quite conventional. Pictures can teach. Pictures can stir the emotions and induce better behavior. Pictures are not to be adored. Recent scholarship has, however, brought some new perspectives to bear on Gregory's words. Kessler, again, sees in these letters more evidence for the value of art among pagan or only partially Christianized populations. I agree. Celia Chazelle, in a finely nuanced study of both Gregory and his predecessors, establishes that Gregory dealt more fully and explicitly than they with the idea that in order for an unlettered person to "read" a picture, that person had to be carefully prepared. Pictures could not truly be "live writing" for someone who did not know what the writing said. Should anyone want an example to illustrate the point, let him or her imagine an ordinary Christian standing before the triumphal arch of Santa Maria Maggiore in Rome or the processional frescoes of Sant'Apollinare Nuovo in Ravenna. Surely that viewer would have been baffled. Again, I agree. And I would add that a further proof for Chazelle's thesis is to be found precisely in Gregory's admonitions to Serenus to preach, teach, and set an example for his flock. This is classic Gregory. Preaching, teaching, and setting a good example are central to his greatly influential *Pastoral Rule*, and they are themes that come up again and again in Gregory's letters. Gregory is, therefore, just like many of the other late antique figures whom we have discussed. He turned to the subject of art only when prompted to do so by something else entirely. Even then, he integrated his comments on art neatly into his wider, his long and consistently held, views on the episcopal office.

It might be asked whether or not Serenus's hostility to people who "adored" pictures could be taken as added weight for Markus's idea about an image cult in Gaul. This view is not impossible. But I note that Serenus's case is absolutely isolated. That very isolation is intriguing, however. Serenus was scandalized by something. But what? Since it is in all probability wall paintings, or possibly mosaics, that Serenus was destroying, we are left wondering about the practices that evoked his ire. Were people kissing these images, or scraping bits of paint off them, or prostrating themselves before them, or venerating them with candles and incense? We do not know. And, even granted all the dangers inherent in arguments from silence, we neither hear of such practices elsewhere in the West nor are we informed of another churchman who behaved as Serenus did. Gregory himself asked Serenus if he had ever heard of anyone else doing what he had done. Likewise we do not know if Serenus was agitated by Gauls or by foreigners. Marseilles is a port city on the south coast of Gaul. Even if there was a widespread image cult there, it is likely that it had associations with that city's substantial Eastern population. Finally, as Gregory was concerned with "gentiles," that is with pagans, it may be that in this case we have evidence for the kind of people who evoked concern from John Cassian and Isidore of Seville. Newly or partially converted Christians may have had some difficulties in relinquishing all the vestiges of their former practices and in seeing the difference between Christian images and pagan idols.

These Western writers make most of the same points that their Eastern counterparts had already made. Idolatry was an absolute, unforgivable evil. But as God himself had on certain occasions commanded images to be made, they could indeed be fabricated or painted for the right reasons. Those reasons were to educate the uneducated, to reveal God's holy mysteries, to remember, and to inspire compunction. In places in the sixth-century West there was still a lingering concern with idolatry. John Cassian and Isidore of Seville give evidence of that, and so does Gregory of Tours in an interesting passage castigating the idolatry of the Franks before their conversion.[150] A desire to avoid any hint of luxury impelled Caesarius to forbid paintings to his nuns. The great Augustine regarded art as superfluous. Gregory of Tours seems to have taken it very much for granted. New in the West, at least compared to the East, was a heightened sense of the implications of preparation for visual literacy. A person could not "read," could not recall to memory, what he or she had not been carefully taught to recognize and understand. Likewise, art was seen to have possibilities for missionary work.

Conclusion

When we turn in the next chapter to the outbreak of Byzantine iconoclasm and in the one after that to the initial Western reactions to iconoclasm, we shall do so on the basis of a few basic points. First, a distinctively Christian figural art had arisen and spread rapidly and widely in the world of late antique Christianity. No part of the Christian world was demonstrably imageless, aniconic. Second, in both East and West, voices had been raised in defense of art and also against it. Defenders everywhere raised pretty much the same issues in their apology. Art could teach, remind, delight, and inspire. Attackers generally pointed to idolatry. Third, there simply was no coherent, centuries-long debate about sacred art. Instead, particular authors, drawing on a small, common stock of traditional ideas and texts, wrote in specific circumstances. Often those circumstances are unknown to us. Sometimes art got folded into theological debates such as those labeled "anthropomorphism" or those which turned on the fullness of Christ's humanity. Sometimes comments on art turned up in anti-Jewish polemics which are unlikely to have been occasioned by real disputes about pictures. Fourth, in the East there does seem to have been an incipient cult of icons. Even if one must admit that earlier scholars exaggerated the extent and intensity of the Eastern cult, one must still ask whether the icon, defined not as a picture evincing a certain style but as an object or locus of cult, was ever a significant feature of the spiritual landscape of people in the Latin West. In so far as iconoclasm was an attack on icons, we have reason to wonder whether the East and the West could readily have understood each other's concerns.

CHAPTER TWO

Byzantine Iconoclasm in the Eighth Century

The Greeks held in especially high honor a picture of the Mother of God
which they believed to have been painted by St. Luke, for this foolish, stupid
people imagined that the spirit of the divine Mother lived in the image;
which nonsensical opinion was speedily damned by Pope Innocent III. For
all I know such errors may be entertained by others of the faithful who pay
such inordinate heed to such images.[1]
　　—Ludovico Antonio Muratori

THE LEARNED AND garrulous Muratori (1672–1750) introduces, apart from his peculiar insertion of Innocent III (1198–1216), what might still pass for a textbook summary of the issues in eighth-century Byzantine iconoclasm. In the usual telling, Emperor Leo III (717–41) unexpectedly took a profound dislike to Byzantium's ubiquitous and miraculous religious images and sought to eliminate them. His son and successor, Constantine V (741–75), expressed his own opposition to religious images by developing sophisticated theological arguments against them, by destroying a great quantity of art, and by persecuting iconophiles, especially the monks among them. In the 780s, Irene, ruling as regent for her son Constantine VI (780–97), worked to restore images to their accustomed place of reverence and finally did so by means of an ecumenical council which she assembled, albeit only with great difficulty, in 787 in the historically evocative city of Nicaea. At that council the victorious iconodules declared officially that the veneration of images was an article of faith. Given that each side in the long dispute laid claim to authentic tradition, it has, in view of the iconophile triumph that was only temporarily interrupted by a renewed outbreak of iconoclasm between 815 and 842, been easy to assume that iconophilia represents the one consistent tradition of the Eastern Church. The iconoclasm of Leo III and his dynasty appears, on the contrary, to be a puzzling aberration.

This chapter surveys the origins, course, and nature of Byzantine iconoclasm. It also considers the strains of iconophilia that eventually triumphed at II Nicaea. The chapter, Janus-like, looks forward and backward. That is, it takes account of the kinds of art talk that I have already discussed for the pre-iconoclastic period and also looks for new arguments that arose in the eighth century and that were available to the Carolingians when they took note of the controversy, briefly in the 750s and 760s, and at great length in the 790s. In other words, what actually happened in the East and what impact did the East have on the West? I shall explore various phases of the eighth-century controversy—no one denies that there was a controversy; disagreement surrounds its intensity and significance—to say a little about what happened and why it happened. Finally, I shall attempt to discern, amid a notoriously fractious body of evidence, the actual arguments used on all sides.

Scholarship has in recent decades fundamentally altered our view of the so-called "iconoclastic controversy." The explanatory tumult has taken two forms. In the first place, the magnitude of the iconoclastic controversy itself has been dramatically reduced in proportions and the situation of iconoclasm within the total context of eighth-century Byzantium has been sharply relocated. At the beginning of this book I quoted three scholars on the meaning of iconoclasm. It is important to note that whereas George Florovsky and Gerhart Ladner saw iconoclasm in virtually apocalpytic terms, Averil Cameron, a leader in the modern rethinking of early Byzantine history, subtly shifts the focus. For her, iconoclasm reveals other changes. It was not itself the major change, nor even the major crisis. The seventh century was extraordinarily difficult for Byzantium.[2] Protracted but finally successful wars against Persia afforded not a well-earned respite on the Mesopotamian frontier but instead a new and more dangerous onslaught from the fervent adherents of the new faith of Islam. The Balkan frontier was menaced by Avars, Bulgars, and Slavs. The late antique economy was slowly vanishing and the eventual shape of its successor was only dimly visible. The administrative arrangements of Justinian were evolving into new forms. Orthodox Christianity was losing forever its control of lands that may have formed a "Byzantine Commonwealth," but whose Jacobite and Nestorian Christians had long looked at Constantinople with suspicion.[3] Inside the territories that remained to the empire politically and ecclesiastically, a wrenching process of redefinition was underway. Iconoclasm must, therefore, be seen as no more than one link in the massive chain that was dragging Byzantium from the late antique world into the fully developed mid-Byzantine period. Whereas earlier scholars saw iconoclasm as fundamentally disruptive, Gilbert Dagron now says that "the quarrel over images did not upset the empire. It accompanied its transformation." Iconoclasm was not a crisis but a period of stability and consolidation after a crisis.[4]

In the second place, scholars have always known that almost all the evidence for iconoclasm, and especially for its earliest phase, is late and hostile. Nevertheless, it was long felt that if the sources were employed with due caution they could be made to yield reliable information. It is increasingly apparent that sources written in the ninth century are valuable primarily for indicating the outlook prevailing in the decades when they were written. Many sources, even the *acta* of II Nicaea, are so riddled with interpolations, when they are not the product of sheer invention, that their use is hazardous in the extreme. In short, we can now be more confident that we know how later iconodules wanted the story of iconoclasm to be told than about what actually happened or how the iconoclasts might have presented their own positions. We must be skeptical of what the sources say about the iconoclasts and about the outbreak of iconoclasm.

Images of Orthodoxy

To enter the sacred spaces of Orthodoxy today, or for most of the last thousand years, is to set foot in a realm of color, light, and image that is almost indescribably dazzling. Dramatic mosaics fill majestic apses. Stirring mosaics and frescoes decorate triumphal arches and side walls. A veritable wall of pictures, the iconostasis, separates the sanctuary from the nave. When the eyes of the head and of the soul have adjusted to the surroundings, they see that the images are strikingly alike in design and perhaps even in execution. There is a comforting sameness to their look no matter where they are or when they were made.

But it was not always so. Before the age of iconoclasm the artistic programs of later centuries had not yet appeared. The iconostasis, for instance, did not achieve its customary form before the fourteenth century.[5] Many spaces that were richly decorated in later times were virtually aniconic at the dawn of the eighth century.[6] Surprisingly, perhaps, the most famous church of Byzantium, Hagia Sophia, was without large-scale pictures before the 860s. The iconoclastic council of Hiereia—about which I say much more below—observed that there was no prayer for the consecration of an icon.[7] The tenth-century *Book of Ceremonies* finds no place for icons. The liturgical prominence of icons is late.[8]

We saw in the previous chapter that there were certainly images in, for example, Armenia and Atrymitium. Literary and archaeological records prove the existence of images in such places as Hosios David, St. George, and St. Demetrius in Salonica; in the Church of the Dormition at Nicaea; and in Constantinople's churches of St. Mary at Blachernae and St. Eirene.[9] Thus we are left to wonder, how common were images in churches? How common were private and personal images like the one of Sts. Cosmas and Damian that a fellow carried around in a sack under his arm? Generalizing from scanty evidence or arguing from the silences of the sources is dangerous. But there must be serious questions about the extent to which ecclesiastical and public environments were decorated with the kinds of images that became so familiar in later times.[10]

While it is true that any picture was, is, potentially an icon, it is no less true that not all pictures became or became recognized as icons. Some of those who, between the fourth century and the seventh, raised their voices against pictorial representations may not have been objecting to icons per se as much as to any figural representation that seemed to violate the Exodus prohibition. And some of those who worried about superstitious practices—most of which were approved and even sometimes recommended in later centuries—had no qualms about representations as such. The evidence, in other words, makes it exceedingly difficult to form a clear impression of the antiquity, scale, intensity, or meaning of the iconophilia to which the iconophobes of the eighth century (and those of the ninth century to whom I shall turn in Chapter 6) took exception.

We must therefore embark on the present discussion with a clear understanding that objections to religious art were not new in the eighth century. I have shown that such objections had not been systematically formulated in earlier centuries. Precisely in the age of the quarrel over icons careful and intellectually cogent arguments against religious art were first set down in detail and with rigor. It was also during this same period that arguments in favor of religious art were articulated in ways that, for much of the Orthodox world, became normative. In fact, as we shall see, arguments on behalf of religious art, and in particular on behalf of icons, underwent some important developments across the eighth and ninth centuries. No one council or thinker arrived in a single moment of blinding insight at the doctrine of images that subsequently held sway in Orthodox Christianity.

And yet there are potent streams in current Orthodox image doctrine that take an atemporal, unhistorical view. The twelve-hundredth anniversary of the

Second Council of Nicaea generated a spate of reflections on that council and on images. Fr. Michael Azkoul is typical when he says that icons "in the proper sense" existed from the beginning. He argues that it is wrong for scholars to infer from a lack of positive evidence that later doctrines of the image were not both widespread and widely held from the beginning.[11] Archbishop Methodios says without hesitation that the icon *is* metaphysical; that it is holy. Icons bear gifts that belong to the supernatural world. An icon is fundamentally a theological statement. Because icons reveal the uncreated essence of the faith, the painter of icons must in the first place be gifted in spirituality.[12] If these views might seem to have been cast in this particular form by men of the cloth, compare them to the words of an able secular scholar, Daniel Sahas: "The icon is not a form of visual and aesthetic art as such; it is, primarily, an expression of the theological experience and faith of the Church, and a statement of it. This is how it has been treated *from the earliest days of the Church*" (emphasis mine).[13] Finally, let us hear the great theologian Leonid Ouspensky: "Since in its essence the icon, like the word, is a liturgical act, it never served religion but, like the word, has always been and is an integral part of religion, one of the instruments of the knowledge of God, one of the means of communication." And "The Church sees in its holy image not simply one of the aspects of Orthodox teaching, but the expression of Orthodoxy in its totality, the expression of Orthodoxy as such."[14] Like Azkoul, Methodios, and Sahas, Ouspensky believes that such views are part of the common stock of early Christian teaching. Yet their earliest authority is St. John of Damascus, who wrote in the 730s and 740s after the image quarrels were well under way. Moreover, John's teaching was, as I shall argue, deliberately set aside at Nicaea. Some of what current Orthodox writers say about images can be found in the writings of the ninth-century authors Patriarch Nicephorus of Constantinople and Abbot Theodore of Studion. But none of this had yet been said, embraced, argued, or refuted when images first were attacked. Robin Cormack treats the subject historically when he says that after iconoclasm "one could not claim to be Orthodox and criticise the icon." He adds that only after 843 was "the icon not just a tolerated object; it was the sign and symbol of Orthodoxy, a distinguishing feature of the full, agreed dogma of the eastern church."[15]

There is a fascinating story behind both the ahistorical interpretations so often applied to icons and the intriguing similarity among virtually all existing icons. In 839 Adolphe Napoléon Didron set out to discover why all Eastern religious images looked so much alike.[16] His quest for an answer took him to Mt. Athos, where he discovered painters working according to manual. He had stumbled upon the *Painter's Manual* of Dionysius of Fourna (1670–1745/6), written in the 1730s but seemingly based on very old materials. He tried in vain to acquire the book but did obtain a Greek transcription, from which he prepared a French translation. The work caused quite a stir. Scholars, romantics, and novelists—Didron dedicated his work to Victor Hugo—believed that they had unlocked the secret to Byzantine art. But the *Manual* was recent and there had been no lawlike formulation of the rules of Byzantine art in the actual Byzantine period. "The work gives the impression," says Belting, "of being a codification of a tradition no longer living and therefore endangered, written to prevent the tradition from being further distorted." That tradition, although recently invented, has been retrojected into the earliest periods of Byzantine and Christian history, much to the confusion of both. Some scholars, recognizing that the tradition found in the *Manual* cannot be traced back before the iconoclastic period, assign to the so-called "art statute" of II Nicaea[17] responsibility for fixing both the themes and the styles of Byzantine religious art.[18] They are seeking to explain central features of Byzantine art history: Why was there so little innovation? Why did certain iconographical modes emerge so early and definitively? But the art statute is in reality no statute at all.[19] The fathers at Nicaea were, on the negative side, refuting Hiereia and, on the positive side, affirming the traditions of the fathers. Hiereia had not made statements about artistic themes and styles that Nicaea could have refuted. Moreover, the 787 council meant basically to say that the authority of icons descended from the fathers and not from the whims of painters. One must, that is, look to a time later than the iconoclastic era, indeed later than the Middle Ages, for the stabilized iconography of those works of art that we call icons.

Recent theologians speak more of spiritual meaning than they do of style. Here again, the views which they associate with the earliest days of Christianity are comparatively recent and, what is more, Russian in provenance. In the late nineteenth century two processes related to images led to the elaboration of what passes today, as the above quotations show, for the normative view. The first unfolded between the time when Bishop Porphiri Uspensky acquired two icons from Mt. Athos in 1845 and 1850, and the 1890s when N. P. Kondakov began to study the Russian icon. Many in Russia had tired of the Europeanization of Russian culture that had been so marked a feature of official life since the late seventeenth century. Among many attempts to recover the authentic origins and characteristics of Russian culture, the icon was discovered and held up as a special and ancient Russian achievement. The second process involved the formulation by Russian Orthodox theologians of a series of Neoplatonic explanations of icons that derived much from the thought of John of Damascus while attributing that thought to the whole chronology of what was claimed as the sole authentic Christian tradition.[20]

To sum up, then. To understand what happened in Byzantium in the eighth century we must avoid anachronistic views of both Byzantine art and of the meanings that can be attributed to or derived from that art. For generations proleptic and kataleptic readings of the Christian tradition as it applies to art have obscured attempts to come to grips with basic issues. No one with eyes to see can deny the serene traditionalism of classical Byzantine religious iconography. But that tradition took its rise in the intellectual battles of the eighth century and expressed itself in the art of later times. Likewise, no one can deny the profundity of the Russian contribution to modern Orthodox image doctrines. But there were no Russians in the eighth century.

The Outbreak of the Controversy

Here is a common account of the outbreak and subsequent course of Byzantine iconoclasm: "He [Leo III] caused the destruction of a venerable image of Christ above the Bronze Gate of the imperial palace. A civil war ensued that lasted, from high to low, until 843: immense ruins; martyrs without number; the destruction of almost all icons; and finally the most profound discussion of the theology of aesthetics."[21] Recent research has called into question almost every aspect of this familiar formulation. Today, we cannot be certain just what Leo did. Likewise, we do not know exactly when he acted. Moreover, his motivations are almost beyond our reach. In turning to Leo III now, it will be well to add a forecast that, in subsequent sections, I shall have occasion to raise doubts about that civil war, those martyrdoms, and even the wholesale destruction of works of art.

Deciding what Leo III actually did depends entirely on what sources are called upon as witnesses to the possible events of the late 720s and early 730s; or perhaps, on the recipe of source-ingredients that the historian-chef prepares. Late sources, such as Nicephorus and Theophanes, have often been accorded high value because they seem to provide the most circumstantial accounts. Contemporary sources, such as the correspondence of Patriarch Germanus and the Roman *Liber Pontificalis*, are usually expected to add flavor and color to the main dishes because they do not provide a satisfying meal—support a narrative—by themselves.

The Sources

The oldest of the late sources, in other words the one closest in time to the events it recounts, is the *Short History* of Nicephorus, the future patriarch of Constantinople who wrote this "oeuvre de jeunesse" in the late 780s. According to Nicephorus, Leo heard of volcanic eruptions on the islands of Thera and Therasia and, taking these natural disasters to be signs of divine wrath, "he took up a position contrary to the true faith and planned the removal of holy icons. . . . He tried to expound his own doctrine to the people."[22] The newer of the late sources, the *Chronicle* of Theophanes, a product of the years around 815, repeats some of Nicephorus's information and adds other details. Under the year 722–23 the chronicler tells a remarkable tale. Theophanes says that a Jewish wizard went to Caliph Yezid (Izid) and told him that he could expect a reign of forty years "if he destroyed the holy icons that were venerated in Christian churches throughout his dominions. The senseless Izid was persuaded by him and decreed a general constitution against the holy images." "The Emperor Leo," Theophanes continues, "partook of the same error, a grievous and illicit one, and so became responsible for inflicting many evils upon us. He found a partner in this boorishness—a man called Beser. . . . Because of his physical strength and like-mindedness in error, he was honoured by the same Leo. . . . Another of his wicked coadjutors was the bishop of Nacoleia who was filled with every kind of impurity and lived in similar boorishness." Then, after a garbled account of developments in Italy that actually date from the 750s but that Theophanes assigns to 723–24, the chronicler picks up his discussion of Leo under the year 724–25. "This year," he says, "the impious emperor Leo started making pronouncements (ποιεῖσθαι λόγον) about the removal of the holy and venerable icons. When Gregory, the pope of Rome, had been informed of this, he withheld the taxes of Italy and of Rome and wrote Leo a doctrinal letter to the effect that an emperor ought not to make pronouncements concerning the faith nor to alter the ancient doctrines of the Church which had been defined by the holy fathers." Under the year 725–26 Theophanes reports the volcanic eruptions on Thera and Therasia and, like Nicephorus, adds that Leo "thinking that God's wrath was in his favour instead of being directed against him, . . . stirred up a more ruthless war on the holy and venerable icons." Again without going into specifics, Theophanes mentions Beser, Leo's ally in this "senseless-ness." Theophanes goes far beyond Nicephorus in adding that the "populace" of the imperial city, "much distressed by the newfangled doctrines," purposed to attack Leo. In that they were not successful, but they did kill some of the emperor's men "who had taken down the icon of the Lord that was above the great Bronze Gate." As a result, "many of them were punished in the cause of the true faith by mutilation, lashes, banishment, and fines, especially those who were prominent by birth and culture." Heaping further abuse on Leo, Theophanes adds that the impious emperor closed the schools that had been Constantinople's glory since the days of Constantine. Also under the year 726, and then again under the years 728 to 730 Theophanes records attempts by Leo to get the Patriarch of Constantinople Germanus to go along with his views. In an account brimming with confusion, Theophanes adds that Leo, because he had Germanus under his control, expelled him from his office. Meanwhile Pope Gregory "reproved him openly in his widely known letters" while John "Chrysorrhoas" (that is, John of Damascus, with whom I shall be much occupied) anathematized the emperor. Nothing daunted, Leo summoned a *silention* (a solemn gathering of key imperial advisers that usually had ceremonial or judicial significance) "against the holy and venerable icons" on January 7, 730. To this meeting Leo summoned Germanus to ask him if he would subscribe to the imperial view and, when he refused, Leo permitted him to retire to his ancestral home. Germanus died in exile in 733. On the twenty-second of January Anastasius, Germanus's *synkellos* (private secretary), was named patriarch. Gregory refused to recognize Anastasius, wrote letters condemning what had happened, and separated Rome and Italy from imperial authority. Leo was infuriated and "intensified the assault on the holy icons." Many clerics, monks, and pious laymen earned the crown of martyrdom. Leo reigned until June of 741 but Theophanes does not mention his image policies during the last eleven years of his life.[23]

To this basic outline, a little more may be added from late sources. The *Life of St. Stephen the Younger*, written in 809, says that the crowd which attacked the soldiers who destroyed the Christ icon at the Chalké Gate was led by women.[24] A tenth-century *Synaxarion* (an enumeration of feasts, often with readings) names the chief defender: Theodosia.[25] The *Synodicon Vetus*, a work of the late ninth century, repeats the tale of Beser's and Constantine of Nacoleia's contributions and says that Gregory organized a synod, anathematized the iconoclasts, and sent criticisms to Leo.[26] Clearly those elements of the story had become fixed in memory.

The evidence that is contemporary must somehow be fitted into this basic outline. The major source is the *Lives* of Gregory II (715–31) and Gregory III (731–41) in the *Liber Pontificalis*. Chapters 13 through 16 of the *Life of Gregory II* recount struggles in central Italy between, on the one side, locals and Lombards and, on the other side, imperial agents and papal officials who were preventing Constantinople's men from collecting taxes.[27] The emperor sent various delegates to Italy in an attempt to force the pope to comply and, in the midst of narrating all of this purely secular and political contention, the *Liber Pontificalis* says in chapter 17, "Orders having been dispatched, the emperor decreed that no image of any saint, martyr or angel should be kept in a church. He declared them all accursed." The emperor further told the pope that to retain his favor he would have to comply, otherwise he would be deposed. Gregory instead "despised the prince's irreligious order, and now he armed himself against the emperor as against an enemy, denouncing his heresy and writing to Christians everywhere to be on their guard."[28] This chapter continues with the secular, political rejection of imperial authority in terms that make it hard to perceive exactly what role the emperor's "order" or "decree" against icons may have played. It is clear that some in Italy sided with the pope and his men while others on the scene remained loyal to the emperor. Sometimes those who followed the pope are called people who "kept the faith" or something similar. The author of this text was not particularly interested in laying down a precise chronology, although most of what he says is organized in rough chronological sequence. The events discussed up to this point must all be assigned to the period between 725 and 727.

After discussing developments that can be dated to 728 and 729, the *Life* goes on to say "later the emperor's wickedness that made him persecute the pontiff became clear: to force his way on everyone living in Constantinople by both compulsion and persuasion to take down images, wherever they were, of the Saviour, his holy mother and all the saints, and, what is painful to mention, to burn them in the middle of the city. . . . Since many of that city's population were preventing this crime, some were beheaded and some paid the price by mutilation." A revision probably prepared in the 750s adds that all the painted churches were whitewashed. The *Life* also tells of Germanus's deposition and says that, in letters, Gregory refused to acknowledge the new patriarch, Anastasius, and complained to the emperor.[29] The other relevant biography in the *Liber Pontificalis*, the *Life of Gregory III* tells us that Gregory was bishop in the time of Leo and Constantine (V) while "there was raging the persecution they started for the removal and destruction of the sacred images of our Lord Jesus Christ, God's holy mother, the holy apostles and all the saints and confessors." Like his predecessor, the *Life* says, Gregory III sent letters to the east to warn the emperor about the evil of his ways. The letters never reached Constantinople because the envoy was too terrified to carry out his mission.[30] After a council in the spring or early summer of 731, which the *Life* mentions but does not describe, the same unfortunate envoy was again sent to the imperial city. This time he was detained in Sicily by imperial agents. In November of 731 Gregory held another council which pronounced anathema upon anyone who would henceforth dare to "remove, destroy, profane and blaspheme against this veneration of sacred images." Messengers bearing news of the council's action were sent to Constantinople but like the previous one they were held captive in Sicily. People from all over Italy also "sent writings of supplication to the princes for the setting up of images" but these too were seized by the emperor's henchmen. One last time, the *Life* says, Gregory wrote to the emperor and to Anastasius. No information is provided about the outcome of this attempt. The rest of the *Life of Gregory III*, some three-fourths of the whole, omits any further mention of the east, the emperor, or iconoclasm.

Theophanes and the *Liber Pontificalis* both say explicitly that Popes Gregory II and Gregory III wrote letters to the East in attempts to persuade the emperor and the patriarch to change their ways. Such letters would be invaluable sources, if they survived. The *acta* of II Nicaea do indeed have, standing right at their head, two letters purporting to be missives from Gregory II to Leo.[31] Scholarly verdicts on the authenticity of these letters have flip-flopped several times since the late nineteenth century. Today, it seems safest to admit that, even if there is in them some substratum of original material, the surviving versions of Gregory's letters are so badly contaminated by later alterations and interpolations that they simply cannot be used. Likewise, the alleged letter of Gregory II to Germanus must be treated as forged or deeply contaminated.[32]

The *acta* of Nicaea do contain some perfectly genuine letters of Germanus to three Bithynian bishops, John of Synada, Thomas of Claudiopolis, and that very Constantine of Nacoleia whom a number of the late sources associated with Leo III.[33] Metropolitan John of Synada wrote to Germanus, probably in 726 or 727, to seek advice on how to handle Bishop Constantine of Nacoleia who had been agitating against images. Germanus wrote back to John, first to say that he had already interviewed Constantine and, second, to offer some fairly traditional and largely perfunctory defenses of images. The patriarch assured John that Constantine had already agreed to accept the traditional teachings and to cease scandalizing people. Evidently, once he was away from the capital, Constantine resumed his opposition to images and this opposition prompted John's letter. Pursuant to John's letter, Germanus attempted to restore hierarchic discipline. He wrote to Constantine "for the heresy had begun with him." Germanus urged Constantine to present this letter to John and to submit to his metropolitan in all things. Germanus's letter also says that Constantine had insisted that he had not actually taken action against images but had merely pointed out scriptural passages that prohibited the worship of created things. Germanus threatened to relieve Constantine of his office if he did not mend his ways.

Germanus's third letter is to Bishop Thomas of Claudiopolis. It is clearly a little later than the letters to John and Constantine,[34] and it may reveal that opposition to images was growing in Bithynia. Germanus says that he had heard rumors about Thomas and that they surprised him because never before had Thomas raised questions about images. Germanus learned that Thomas was teaching that it was acceptable to prohibit and even destroy images. Germanus also says that on account of this new teaching cities and peoples were being thrown into confusion. Alas, Germanus does not name those cities or peoples, does not explain their confusion, does not name any additional iconophobe or iconoclast bishops, and does not provide any details about what may have been a growing movement.

The evidence from Germanus's letters is confirmed in two chapters that Germanus added, either before his deposition or during his years in exile, to the seventh-century treatise *On Heresies and Synods*.[35] In these Germanus says that a "certain bishop of Nacoleia, a little bitty town in Bithynia"—he does not even bother to name him—looked on his own into the Scriptures and found reasons to reject the teachings of the fathers. "He inflamed a war in the church," says the patriarch. What does that mean? Beyond these two chapters by Germanus, a third chapter was added to the treatise by an anonymous author who spoke about imperial and official fury and punishments, tortures, and exiles. This chapter is without doubt a later interpolation so its testimony is without value for Germanus's views or time.[36] As in his letters, Germanus's additions to *On Heresies and Synods* suggest that he was either discreet or ignorant. Constantine he virtually dismissed; Thomas surprised him; and yet there was a "war."

There is one other contemporary source, the three *Orations* (or *Apologies* or *Addresses*) of St. John of Damascus *Against Those Who Attack the Divine Images*.[37] Dating these texts is not easy.[38] The first appears to have been written in the late 720s, perhaps shortly after John got wind of what was going on in Constantinople. The second was clearly written after Germanus had been deposed; so, after January of 730. The first and second *Orations* may have been prepared about the same time, the second being presented as a clarification of the first. Dating the third *Oration* is especially difficult. It may have been written shortly after the other two to add more material and to clarify some lines of argument. But John may have written the third in the 740s when he was revising many of his earlier works. The first two *Orations* therefore take us to the early days of iconoclasm and the third may do so or may contain later reminiscences by an engaged party.

"I see the Church of God . . . battered as by the surging sea overwhelming
it with wave upon wave, tossed about and troubled by the grievous assault
of wicked spirits, and Christ's tunic, woven from top to bottom, rent, which
the children of the ungodly have arrogantly sought to divide, and his body cut
to pieces, which is the people of God and the tradition of the church," says
John.[39] He goes on to say that "compelled to speak by a fear that cannot be
borne, I have come forward . . . for the oracular pronouncements of a king (τῶν
βασιλικῶν . . . θεσπισμάτων) exercise terror over his subjects."[40] On other
occasions John speaks explicitly to or about Leo. "It is not for emperors to legislate
for the church."[41] John asks rhetorically, "Are you now going to write the Gospel
according to Leo?"[42] John makes no mention of persons who influenced or collab-
orated with the emperor. John speaks explicitly only of Germanus's troubles:
"And now the blessed Germanus, radiant in his life and his words, is flogged
and sent into exile, and many other bishops and fathers, whose names we do
not know."[43] John addresses himself to "the people of God"[44] but does not tell
us where or when those people were gathered. John was a monk at St. Saba
outside Jerusalem so his writings, like those of the popes, indicate that news of
Leo's actions spread quite widely, and fairly quickly if the first two *Orations* are
to be dated around 730. What, exactly, did John find objectionable—apart from
imperial interference in dogma? In one place John says that "For certain have
risen up, saying that it is not necessary to make images."[45] In another place,
John offers the intriguing remark that "But then they say 'make an image of
Christ and of his Mother who gave birth to God, and let that suffice.'"[46] John
chose to interpret the latter remark as an attack on the cult of saints.

What Happened?

Let us gather in the harvest from these small fields of evidence. Our aim is to
answer this question: What happened? In about 725 or 726 Emperor Leo III
began to agitate against icons. Scholars have debated for years whether or not
Leo issued a formal legislative decree against icons.[47] I do not believe that he
did. The sources say he "expounded his views," that he "spoke," and Theophanes can find no better word than *logos*, which is no word at all for a law.
Papal sources speak of "orders" and of "decrees" but do so in the midst of a
rather complicated account of imperial attempts to cope with open rebellion in
Italy. No later emperor ever rescinded a decree by Leo and no later church
council refers unambiguously to such a decree, anathematizes such a decree, or
demands the removal of such a decree. The *silention* of 730 was not a legislative

assembly. The *Life of Stephen the Younger* may imply that Constantine V later turned the *silention* into a legislative session but it was not that in Leo's time.[48] The meeting that deposed Germanus was a consultation among courtiers. Let there be no mistake about it: Leo III decided to oppose images. Gregory II, Gregory III, John of Damascus, Nicephorus, and Theophanes place the blame squarely on Leo.

Was Leo incited to take action? Did he stir up a movement? Germanus, displaying a discretion entirely appropriate to the man who held a high and sensitive office, shifted the blame to Constantine of Nacoleia. A century and a half later the *Synodicon Vetus* repeated the accusation against Constantine. Germanus's correspondence reveals surprise and disappointment that Thomas of Claudiopolis had gone over to the heretics, but that same correspondence demonstrates that the important metropolitan John of Synada maintained the traditional faith in icons.[49] In the capital, Germanus's replacement, the Patriarch Anastasius trimmed his sails to the imperial winds. Still, he took broadsides from iconophile writers for replacing the revered Germanus, not for any specific, named acts or teachings against images. Germanus was tolerated for, perhaps, four, five, six years, quietly deposed, and permitted, evidently, an honorable retirement. The weird stories about the Jewish wizard, Caliph Yezid, and the mysterious Beser are all late.[50] I shall have occasion to return to them. For now, let it be said only that they represent, first, an attempt to situate the image quarrels within the context of the old Christian-Jewish debates (elements of which came up in Chapter 1) and second, an effort to exculpate the ruling house at a time when a later member of that house was acting in defense of religious images. None of this suggests much of a movement.

What kinds of action did Leo take? Exactly one destroyed image is mentioned anywhere: The image of Christ over the Bronze Gate of the imperial palace. The destruction of that image by soldiers in 726 is usually seen as the inception of iconoclasm in action. But the vivid scene may well be the later literary representation of a polemical legend.[51] That is, it may never have happened, or it may have happened differently than later writers claimed. Theophanes' account of Leo's alleged destruction of this image is the familiar one, but it is not the first. The *Life of St. Stephen the Younger*, several years older than Theophanes' *Chronicle*, tells of the destruction of the image but places it in the time of Patriarch Anastasius, that is, after 730.[52] No source accords any prominence to this image in the eighth century,[53] and attempts by later writers to create a venerable past for the image are suffused with legend. Germanus, in his letter to Thomas, does mention an image on the front of the palace, but it is not the famous Christ image. Sometime between 720 and about 729 Leo himself had placed an image of apostles and prophets "in front of the imperial palace."[54] This statement is revealing. It shows that Leo was not always an iconophobe and that, perhaps, there were images that he was prepared to tolerate. Maybe he conformed with traditional practices for a while until they began to offend him. In an account that is almost hysterical, the *Liber Pontificalis* speaks of images being gathered up and burned in Constantinople. But this statement lacks corroboration, and it is hard to believe that the iconophiles would have overlooked such an opportunity to smear Leo. The point is quite simple: It is impossible to name with certainty a work of art destroyed by Leo or destroyed in his time. The originator of iconoclasm may have been no more than an ardent iconophobe.

Theophanes knows of persecutions but, apart from the *Liber Pontificalis*, contemporary sources do not. Germanus, in his letters and in the chapters he added to *On Heresies and Synods*, makes no mention of fellow sufferers. John of Damascus says he does not know how many people may have suffered. Stephen's biographer and Theophanes, writing long after the events they described, create vivid pictures of the mob in Constantinople and their mistreatment by the soldiers who supposedly took down the Chalké image. For the latter, the leaders are women, for the former, the intellectual elite of the city. But other sources do not pick up this story, and, given the colorful history of the Constantinopolitan populace, it is hard to imagine that significant incidents of popular insurrection escaped the notice of all but two writers. Surely the iconophiles would have had every reason to shout from the rooftops about the popular defense of images. No source names names, except for the shadowy Theodosia. We hear of exiles, but can only adduce Germanus as an example.

Byzantine iconoclasm got off to a decidedly slower and smaller start than the usual accounts would lead one to believe. All the action must be packed into the years between 725 and 730, and if there is anything at all to the connection later drawn between Leo's actions and the volcanic eruptions, then the action must be compressed into the years after 727 or 728. Following his *silention* of early 730, Leo took no other action against images as far as we know. He died in 741 and the empire was disturbed for a time by civil strife. Eventually, Leo's son Constantine V secured the throne. Although history would mark him down as the arch-iconoclast, he took no known actions against images before the late 740s, at the earliest. In Jerusalem, John of Damascus provides no hint of new iconoclastic campaigns in his third *Oration*, a text that perhaps dates from the 740s. In Rome the over ten-year pontificate of Zachary (741–52) is related in a detailed *vita* that contains not one word about an image controversy. The pope did enter into relations of some sort with Constantine V and received from the emperor the gift of two estates near Rome.[55] All of this stands as a sharp reminder that Byzantine iconoclasm or iconophobia was episodic, not continuous.

Byzantine Iconoclasm Under Constantine V

After a flurry of shrill denunciations of Leo III, the major Byzantine chroniclers, Nicephorus and Theophanes, carry their accounts forward for many years with no mention at all of any controversies relating to images. It has been remarked that only about 20 percent of these texts treats the image controversy.[56] True, the chroniclers reserve their sharpest focus and hottest prose for their passages dealing with iconoclasm, but this aim and heat cannot be allowed to obscure the fact that, in reality, recorded events arising from disputes over icons were few and far between. The reign of Constantine V (741–75) illustrates this fact clearly.[57]

The Council of Hiereia, 754

The sources for Constantine's reign exceed in quantity and quality those for the reign of his father, but they are no easier to interpret. In addition to the historians Nicephorus and Theophanes, three treatises[58] and a major saint's life[59] contain important information. What is more, some fragments of Constantine's own writings[60] survive as do the *horos* and the anathemas from a major church council held under the emperor's aegis in 754.[61] If the historian of Constantine's reign is grateful for a comparative abundance of material, she is nevertheless stymied in her attempts to stitch together a coherent narrative and to work out a detailed chronology.

The very start of Constantine's reign was troubled by an attempted coup d'état by Artabasdos, an old companion in arms of Leo III who had been rewarded for his loyalty and good work with high offices and even with the hand of one of the emperor's daughters. Nicephorus vaguely implies that Artabasdos restored images[62] while Theophanes says that the people accepted the would-be emperor precisely because "he was orthodox and a defender of the divine doctrine." Indeed, "he restored the holy icons throughout the city."[63] Earlier scholars, such as Ostrogorsky, were inclined to accept the historians' view of Artabasdos,[64] but it seems more likely that they transmitted legends, engaged in invention, or passed along "unsubstantiated iconophile hearsay."[65] Be that as it may, there is no secure evidence that Constantine V encountered or prompted a dispute over images at the outset of his reign.

In his account of the year 745–46 Theophanes reports an earthquake in Palestine, Jordan, and Syria as well as a plague that reached the Balkans from Sicily and Calabria. Oddly, he says that these disasters "restrained the fury" of Constantine against icons and the churches.[66] This is curious for two reasons. First, it would appear to be a reversal of the events of 726–27 when a volcanic eruption incited Leo's wrath against images. Second, it contradicts Nicephorus who says that the calamities of 746–47 provoked an attack on images.[67] Once again, it seems that, years later, people did not really know what had happened and that they patched together bits and pieces of various stories, some of which may have had authentic components. Speck, for example, thinks that after the earthquake and pestilence Constantine may actually have begun removing images from the areas in churches near the altar where they might have been a distraction from the eucharistic liturgy.[68] That is a clever guess, but it is no more than that.

Whether or not Constantine took any action in about 746, the first hints of anti-image activity come from the time just before the Council of Hiereia in 754. There is evidence. But its meaning is anything but clear. Perhaps it took Constantine ten or twelve years to develop his mature iconophobic, and even iconoclastic, point of view. Perhaps, in view of civil insurrections, natural disasters, opportunistic campaigns against the Muslims as the Umayyad Caliphate cracked apart between 748 and 750, a close watch on the always dangerous Balkan frontier, and major financial reforms, Constantine simply did not put images at the top of his working agenda. If this supposition is valid, then it highlights the degree to which iconoclasm was an element of and not the driving force behind developments at Byzantium in the eighth century. As we have neither Constantine's own views nor the views of anyone sympathetic to him, we are reduced to reasoned speculation.

The treatise *Against Constantine* says that after—immediately? merely at some time *after*?—he came to the throne the emperor sent out an edict to the provinces under his authority that holy images were to be destroyed.[69] The *Admonition of the Old Man* (Nouthesia) says that Constantine sent out "messengers of his cruelty."[70] The *Life of Stephen* says that Constantine gathered the people and made them swear not to worship images and goes on to say that messages were sent to all provinces to summon officials and bishops to a council.[71] Theophanes recites a discordant litany of charges. He says the emperor devised measures, convened a *silention*, propagandized the public, and prepared for "complete impiety."[72] Nicephorus says Constantine "terrified bishops with chains, prisons, threats, and innumerable other horrible treatments," but he does not name a single person thus terrorized, and no one else ever did either.[73] Returning to the *Admonition*, its most interesting section consists of a debate between the elderly George of Cyprus and an imperial agent named Cosmas conducted at a synod called by this Cosmas. The text may be read as implying that such disputations were common at about this time. Cosmas also refers to the edicts, commands, and words of the emperor.[74] These edicts may relate to the convening of the council, to the propaganda vaguely mentioned by Theophanes, or to actual iconoclasm. Stephen's biographer seems to say, with reference to this pre-Hiereia period, that images were destroyed and whitened over.[75] At II Nicaea, Patriarch Tarasius said that the Council of Hiereia found all the images destroyed.[76] This is a huge exaggeration but may refer accurately to some iconoclastic activity before 754.

If we apply a bit of imaginative puzzle solving to these statements, we can see that various later writers all had parts of the same story. That story goes something like this. Constantine, perhaps in 752 or 753, decided to call a church council to deal with the image question. He may have treated the populace of the capital to harangues on the subject. He may have sent trusted agents throughout his empire to whip up support. Some works of art may have been removed, or elevated so that they could not be touched or kissed, or whitewashed. Such actions definitely occurred in the 760s, and we cannot be confident that later writers did not retroject events from that decade into the previous one. If any individuals suffered personally, we hear nothing about it. Most likely Constantine put his bishops to work collecting the texts that were cited at Hiereia. At some point during these years, Constantine wrote his *Peuseis*, his *Inquiries*. In early February of 754 the emperor convened a council of 338 bishops.

I shall turn to the theological arguments offered at Hiereia in a later section of this chapter. For now it suffices to say that for the first time there arose a systematic, coherent presentation of the case for opposing figural religious art. The 338 bishops present at the council are many more than those who attended the Trullan Council and about the same number as those who would attend II Nicaea in 787. Leo III and Constantine V had had many years to appoint bishops favorable to their cause. The assembled bishops should not be seen as imperial lackeys but instead as men who had made their own the church's long-standing uneasiness about religious art. There is no evidence for violence or threats. The bishops sincerely saw themselves as standing within the church's great tradition, and they called their council the seventh to put it firmly within the line of the first six ecumenical councils. That their view did not prevail in later times owed more to changing historical circumstances than to any eccentricity of the arguments advanced in 754.

The council also took firm steps against religious art and its proponents. The records of Hiereia provide the first concrete and official evidence for an icon *policy* in the Byzantine Empire. The council named and anathematized exactly three iconophile leaders: Germanus, the patriarch deposed in 730; John of Damascus, author of three *Orations* in defense of images; and George of Cyprus, the key figure in the *Admonition*.[77] This is not a lengthy list of iconophile enemies of the iconophobes. Then the council also said "We decree unanimously . . . that every icon, made of any matter and of any kind of gaudiness of colours by painters, is objectionable, alien, and repugnant to the Church of the Christians."[78] This decree does not call explicitly for the destruction of icons. "He who from now on," says the council, "attempts to make an icon, or to venerate one, or to set one up in a church or in a private home, or to hide one, if bishop, presbyter, or deacon, let him be unfrocked; if monk or layman, let him be anathematized and subject to the royal laws, as an opponent of the commandments of God and an enemy of the doctrines of the Fathers."[79] This portion of the decree seems to grant a sort of amnesty to persons and actions of the past: "from now on." Nicephorus later said that they "set down a proclamation of the destruction of the holy icons," but that goes beyond what the text actually says.[80] Then, in an attempt to prevent the kind of vandalism that might have followed from excessive zeal in observing its dictates, the council forbade the alteration of sacred vessels, altar veils, or vestments without the expressed approval of the patriarch and the emperor. Moreover, the council forbade laymen to put their hands on churches.[81] This hardly looks like the grimly determined destruction of religious art and the merciless persecution of art's devotees that iconodule sources and modern writers usually portray. For several years after Hiereia the sources again fall silent, apart from a brief remark in the *vita* of Paul II (757–67) in the *Liber Pontificalis* to the effect that the pope badgered the emperor to restore the veneration of images.[82] We have absolutely no testimony about the implementation of Hiereia's decrees in the aftermath of the council.

Strife in the 760s

During the 760s Constantine V took several steps against individual monks and against the monastic order in general. Later iconodule writers interpreted these actions in connection with Constantine's anti-image policy and thus turned that policy into one attended by cruel persecutions. In fact, Constantine's harshness in the 760s was indeed directed against monasticism and also against people who had engaged in an attempted coup. But these phenomena appear to have been unconnected with each other, and neither had any demonstrable connection with the defense of images.

Monks had become immensely prominent in the Byzantine world since the seventh century. Byzantium acknowledged ninety new saints between the seventh century and 1453 and of these seventy-five were monks. Between 705 and 1204, forty-five of fifty-seven patriarchs were monks. In 700 as much as one-third of all land in the empire was in the hands of monasteries. Contrary to older views that monks tended to be lower class and uneducated, the interpretation prevailing today is that they came from all social classes and that their level of culture was impressive and improving. In a world that needed young men for the armies and talented men for the court, monasticism was seen by Constantine as a drain on the essential human resources of the state.[83] Constantine was not himself opposed to monasticism in principle. He was a great patron of the monastery of St. Anthusia and he named one of his daughters abbess of that house. In 775 Leo IV appointed several higoumens to bishoprics so prominent monks were still around then, and the huge number of monks active at II Nicaea proves that the order was not eradicated. Constantine's anti-monastic policy was focused, pragmatic, and institutional.[84]

That policy seems to have arisen in the years after Hiereia, if Nicephorus's none-too-precise account can be made to yield hard information. He says "the holy regiment of monks was lawlessly persecuted" and those who wished to "cling to their habit" or who "opposed the unholy doctrine of those men" were subjected to torture and outrage. Persons could escape such ill treatment only by putting off their monastic garb and accepting imperial service. Some of these monks were beaten with painted boards, with icons.[85]

The first named victim of this turmoil was Andrew Kalybites in 761. Theophanes says of Andrew only that "he had reproved his [Constantine's] impiety and called him a second Valens and a second Julian."[86] These charges could, of course, relate to the council of 754 or they could pertain to the harassment of monks in general. About Andrew himself absolutely nothing is known. Theophanes swept him up in his general condemnation of Constantine's actions in the 760s. In reality, however, there is no unimpeachable evidence for hostility to monks or to monasticism between 741 and 766.

The most famous victim of the alleged monastic persecution of the 760s is Stephen the Younger. His *vita*, written more than forty years later under deeply iconophile influence, is a crucial but problematic source. It says that Stephen and his family fled Constantinople in the time of Leo III and settled in the mountains of Bithynia. Evidently Bithynia was not an impossible place for iconophiles despite Constantine of Nacoleia and, perhaps, some of his episcopal colleagues. Stephen became a monk on Mt. Auxentius. The *vita* then mentions Constantine's destruction of images and the council of 754. Many monks—apparently they were able to travel quite freely—went to Stephen for advice. They asked him if there were any safe places, and he rattled off an impressive list that describes essentially the frontiers of the empire, places, in other words, where the imperial writ did not run. The emperor then sent an important nobleman to Mt. Auxentius to get Stephen to sign the synodal *acta*. Stephen refused and was placed under house arrest but freed a week later because war broke out with the "Scythians." The emperor's minions now tried a new tactic. They induced a monk named Sergius to circulate all sorts of damaging stories about Stephen. Interestingly, these stories had to do with sexual improprieties, not with defending or displaying images. The imperial agents did discover that noble women were abandoning their secular lives to follow Stephen, and this conduct seems to have puzzled the authorities. The *Synkellos* George was then dispatched to Stephen, and the saint tried to convert him. An exasperated emperor then brought Stephen to the capital, where he was kept under loose guard. His biographer says that he kept images in his confinement and that many people came to him seeking advice. Secular and episcopal authorities kept on trying to get Stephen to accept the *horos* of 754. After various changes in his place of confinement, Stephen was finally executed, or martyred, for his staunch opposition to Hiereia. Three hundred and forty two of Stephen's followers were rounded up, imprisoned, tortured, and mutilated.[87]

The *vita,* then, stresses Stephen's refusal to accept the decrees of 754 but Nicephorus and Theophanes tell a different story. They had every incentive to make Stephen an iconophile martyr. Nicephorus says that when Stephen was apprehended, "They brought against him a charge relating to religion" (perhaps to "loyalty") saying in the process that "he deceived many men by teaching them to despise the glory of this world, to disregard family and relatives, to avoid the imperial court, and to adopt the monastic life."[88] Theophanes says that Stephen was punished because "he admonished many people to enter the monastic life and had persuaded them to scorn imperial dignities and money."[89] The ninth-century *Life of Nicetas of Medikion* is instructive too. It says that Constantine hounded the monastic order, "punishing some by exile, killing some, flogging some and spilling their guts" (he mentions Stephen the Younger here). But in this whole overheated passage he says not one word about images.[90]

In 766 Constantine staged a public humiliation for the monks in Constantinople. He made monks parade into the hippodrome hand in hand with women while the crowd spat upon them.[91] In 771, Michael Lakhanodrakon, *strategos* of the Thrakesion theme, carried out a brutal purge of the monasteries in his jurisdiction. He seized monks and nuns, monasteries, religious paraphernalia, and books. All these he sold and transmitted the proceeds to the emperor. Some monks he flogged and others he degraded by setting their beards on fire.[92]

Clearly, Constantine set out quite systematically to attack the very symbols of the monastic order: their beards, their habits, their celibacy, their learning. He subjected them to public ridicule to demystify their persons and status. But he did all this for reasons related to the security of his state. Images played a minor role, if any role, in all of this.[93]

In the midst of their narrations of Stephen's travails both Nicephorus and Theophanes say that some officials ("men vested with authority") and soldiers were accused of venerating icons and were punished. All public officials were asked to pledge that they would not venerate icons. A few days after the abbots were paraded in the hippodrome, nineteen secular officials were executed. In 765 Constantine made the patriarch, also named Constantine, hold up a cross and swear that no one was venerating icons. The emperor also tried to get him to abandon his monastic state and adopt the status of a secular cleric. He even tried to get him to eat meat at the imperial table and to join in courtly entertainments.[94] The ruler seems both to have suspected the patriarch's loyalty and to have taken an opportunity to belittle monasticism once again. Shortly after these proceedings, Constantine was deposed from the patriarchate. Constantine had apparently been the target of opposition, and although that opposition may have involved the defense of images, it seems to have been, at its core, traditional military, courtly, and bureaucratic wrangling.[95]

Leaving aside the isolated cases of Andrew the Kalybite and Michael Lachanodrakon, it appears that critical events transpired between 765 and 767. Later writers connected these events with devotion to images and with monks, although they did not always explicitly say that monks were persecuted for their devotion to images. The reality is more complex. The years 765 and 766 were tremendously challenging for Constantine V. He won great military victories against Arabs and Slavs but suffered diplomatic reversals with the papacy and the Carolingians. He also faced problems with the church, an abandonment of the relative theological quiet since Hiereia, and a massive plot against his rule led by both civil and ecclesiastical elites. In putting Stephen to death, deposing and executing the patriarch, humiliating higoumens and both humiliating and executing civil "*archontes*," extracting an oath of allegiance to Hiereia, and, finally, in attacking some monks and seizing some monastic property, Constantine was attempting to put his house in order. Images played only a small role in this strife. Moreover, the attack on the monks was not so much an attack on monasticism itself as a precise campaign waged against those who were manifestly disloyal, who threatened the *basileia*. Viewed through the lens of later iconophile texts, appearances are very deceiving in these critical years.[96]

Except for a few scattered references to works of art that were removed or whitewashed, the last decade of Constantine's reign was without incidents related to iconoclasm. As we have seen, his reputation as the scourge of iconodules is vastly exaggerated. Once the monks are taken off the list of iconodules who suffered persecution, torture, or even death specifically because of their veneration of icons, the list of those who did actually suffer becomes very short indeed. Iconophile historians and hagiographers had every reason to name names. Such writers overlooked no opportunity to besmirch the reputations of Leo III and Constantine V, but they found few chances to connect their generalized besmirchings with particular victims. Stephen, it is true, refused to sign the acts of 754 but none of the sources blames his death on this refusal. Andrew the Kalybite may have been attacked for his devotion to images, but this is not clear. John, higoumen of Monagria, was thrown into the sea, but he may well have been a victim of Constantine's campaign against monks. It is remarkable that no monastic figures can be shown to have spoken up for images during the 760s, and the funeral oration of the iconophile Plato of Sakkudion shows that he was able to move about quite freely and that he held official positions around 775.[97] In the end, there was a period of intense anti-monastic activity between 765 and 767 and then again in 771–72 in the Thrakesion theme. None of this activity is obviously or necessarily connected with the veneration or prohibition of icons. The *vita* of Stephen the Younger is most instructive. Although its author sought to provide a long catalogue of woes, the careful reader can see that the court was concerned to win Stephen over and tried many stratagems to achieve that end. Stephen was handled with kid gloves.[98]

I found no concrete evidence for persecution in the time of Leo III, and now I argue that there is very little evidence for the harrying of iconophiles in the time of Constantine V. In Leo's reign I detected a period of iconophobic activity right around the year 730 with, possibly, some antecedents in the years between 725 and 730. During the reign of Constantine V, there was a time of intense iconophobia in the year or two preceding the council of 754 and then possibly in the mid-760s as the emperor sought to solidify his rule against monastic opposition and a coup attempt. In other words, iconoclasm is not the story of the eighth century in Byzantium. It is an occasional, albeit memorable, character in that story.

Iconoclasm and Art

What impact did iconoclasm have on art? For all of the 117 years between 725 and 842 only twenty to twenty-five works of art can be certainly identified as destroyed or covered over. We have already seen that it is by no means clear what, if anything, happened to the Chalké image in the time of Leo III. The fathers of II Nicaea said astonishingly little about ruined art works. One speaker mentioned a book with silver images that was thrown into a fire and another with pages *discussing* images that were cut out—although the latter book's covers with silver images of saints were undamaged. Another speaker said that in his city thirty books were burned—a suspiciously round number and vague testimony as to whether the books were burned to destroy their images or their texts. Yet another speaker said he had an Old Testament with a *scholium* on images that had been erased albeit not so completely that it could not still be read. Two other speakers complained of books from which pages had been cut containing, respectively, accounts of the Camuliana icon and the Abgar image. The patriarch himself offered in evidence a book from his own library that was missing all the pages on images.[99] Where books are concerned, then, it seems that the iconoclasts were more zealous about removing image texts than they were about snipping images themselves.

The best-known cases of destruction or removal are in buildings with which the emperors had important associations.[100] For instance, a cycle of New Testament images in St. Mary's church in Blachernai was replaced with foliage, and a set of depictions of the six councils in the Milion of the imperial palace was replaced with scenes of chariot races. Only in 768/69 did Patriarch Nicetas replace medallions of Christ and the saints with crosses in the secretum of the patriarchal palace.[101] Justinian II had put the image of Christ on his coins whereas Leo III, Constantine V, and Leo IV put small crosses on their coins. This was less an act of iconoclasm, however, than a return to earlier schemes of numismatic iconography.[102] Nicetas also scraped off some mosaics and frescoes in the patriarchal palace and painted over other images there and in the Abramaion. He may have removed some images from the gallery level of Hagia Sophia.[103] As de' Maffei has pointed out, much more art was painted over than destroyed, a point confirmed by the famous miniature in the early ninth-century Khludov Psalter depicting an iconoclast whitewashing an image.[104]

In the provinces, iconoclasm was very unevenly applied. In the Koimesis church in Nicaea the apse mosaic was chipped out and replaced with a cross. The same was done at Hosios David in Salonica. But the churches of St. Demetrius and St. George in Salonica were undisturbed.[105] Liturgical art was expressly spared by the council of 754, which also tried to prevent vandalism.[106] We noticed above that St. Stephen was able to direct people to many safe areas.

The fact that comparatively little art survives from the heartlands of the Byzantine Empire during the iconoclastic era must, therefore, be attributable to causes other than wanton destruction.[107] The court was officially iconophobic and the court was always a great patron of art. The official church, the church of the bishops, was perforce iconophobic. Many commissions must have been lost. This was also a time of desperate military challenges, frequent natural disasters, as well as major financial, legal, and administrative reforms. The state was spending money but seldom on artworks of any kind—palaces, churches, civic amenities. The fact that iconoclast emperors put up athletic and naturalistic scenes suggests that they were neither opposed to art as such nor aesthetic bumpkins.[108] They simply opposed images of Christ, and perhaps too of Mary and the saints. But, to conclude, there was no wholesale destruction of art in the eighth century, any more than there was a wanton persecution of iconophiles.

Empress Irene and II Nicaea

After a long reign whose many successes have been obscured by iconophile writers, Constantine V died in 775. He was succeeded by his son Leo IV, who reigned only until 780. From some remarks by Theophanes and a few other scattered bits of information, historians have concluded that Leo relaxed current prohibitions on the cult of Mary and reversed his father's sharp opposition to the monks. Why he took these steps is not clear. In any case, no source reports any concrete steps taken against images or their worshipers. Some monks were appointed to key offices, including bishoprics, and when the iconophobe patriarch Nicetas died in 780 Leo selected as his successor the Cypriot Paul who "tried to excuse himself on account of the reigning heresy," according to Theophanes. Whether Paul was actually an iconophile is difficult to say but Leo did make him swear an oath not to worship images.[109]

Irene from Regent to Basilissa

When Leo died he left behind a nine-year-old son, Constantine VI, and a remarkable widow, Irene. Because Irene summoned the Nicene council that put an end to eighth-century iconoclasm, she became a heroic, even legendary, figure among later iconophile writers. Thus it is important to understand her situation precisely and to observe very carefully what she actually did. For instance, Theophanes says that after Paul was consecrated as patriarch some court officials were dismissed when it was discovered that they had images in their possession, whereas the much later Cedrenus alters the story so that in his telling Irene had images under her pillows.[110] There is actually no solid evidence that Irene was particularly iconophile, either before or just after 780. It is, after all, hard to believe that Constantine V would have permitted his eldest son and presumptive heir to have married a known image worshiper. Scholars have not embraced the idea that Irene, as a woman, was more inclined to iconophilia than a man would have been. The old notion that because she was an Athenian Irene would have supported images derives from antiquated juxtapositions of "Hellenic" and "Asiatic" sensibilities that had a lot of currency a century ago but no value at all today.[111] The point is that, in the years just after 780, Irene decided to reverse official policy.

It is almost impossible to exaggerate the difficulty of Irene's position in 780. She was regent for her son but had no independent power base of her own. She had five brothers-in-law, sons of Constantine V by a later marriage than the first one which had produced Leo IV, who had claims on the throne at least as good as those of Irene's son Constantine VI. The army and civil administration had been carefully cultivated by Constantine V and owed Irene nothing. Military threats surrounded the empire with the forces of the caliph, whose annual income was probably sixteen to eighteen times greater than Byzantium's, representing the direst challenge. The Orthodox Church was separated from all other Christian communities and, particularly owing to official iconoclasm, had been divided from Chalcedonian Christians for a half century.[112]

Forty days after coming to power Irene faced a conspiracy led by various palace dignitaries who were acting on behalf of Nicephorus, the eldest of Irene's brothers-in-law. She managed to prevail over her opponents and began putting her own people into key positions of power. She also began to rule more or less in her own name as *basilissa* and, in this capacity, she attached herself to the most potent aspect of the memory of Constantine V: She initiated military campaigns. In the East these resulted in a useful truce in 782 whereas in the Balkans Irene's forces actually won major victories and recovered territories. In 781 Irene sent envoys to "Karoulos" to enquire about a marriage alliance. One may infer from this initiative that Irene was seeking to end her diplomatic isolation from other Christian powers while also attempting, in particular, to settle the matter of Italy. That is, it would appear that Irene was prepared to cede to Charles, and to his papal protégé, possession of northern and central Italy if the Franks and the papacy would, in turn, give Byzantium a free hand in the south.

Presumably the Lombard duchy of Benevento was to serve as a kind of buffer zone. In the midst of this frantic activity, Theophanes says, "The pious began to speak freely."[113] Almost certainly this means the monks who had been threatened and occasionally terrorized in recent years. During these years, basically 780 to 784, there was not a word about images.

In 784 the patriarch Paul fell ill, retired from office, and entered a monastery. On being asked why he had done this, Paul said he was deeply grieved that his church was separated from all other Christians. He insisted that there was need of an ecumenical synod to repair the damage which, in the circumstances, can only have meant the decisions of the Council of Hiereia in 754. Given Paul's reluctance to assume the patriarchal throne in 780 because of "the reigning heresy" much rings true in the report of his actions in 784.[114] On Paul's abdication, Theophanes reports, "The question of the holy icons began to be discussed and disputed by everyone."[115] Irene and Paul had appointed known iconophiles to bishoprics, monks had gotten a favorable ear from the regime, and there had been no hostile actions against either images or image worshipers in many years. Perhaps, therefore, residual iconophilia bubbled to the surface in this more favorable environment. Perhaps, too, Irene, sensing a movement from which she could profit, or maybe, even, which she could lead, encouraged the iconophiles.[116] Possibly, in the ingenious suggestion of Mark Whittow, Irene saw a restoration of iconophilia as the "necessary revolution" that would create or cement genuine support for her in a world where her position had been precarious.[117] Be that as it may, icons were back on the Byzantine agenda for the first time since Paul had promised not to worship them in 780 and since Patriarch Nicetas had covered up images in the patriarchal palace in the late 760s: another reminder of just how infrequently images were a topic of major contention in the "Age of Iconoclasm."

But when the circumstances of Paul's abdication are examined more closely some peculiarities emerge. Paul abdicated on August 31, 784. Theophanes gives us this date and says that when she learned of Paul's withdrawal Irene, along with her son, went to see him to ask why he had done this. He told her of his distress at leading a church separated from all others. On hearing this Irene sent for the "chief men of the Senate" so that they could hear Paul's words and his call for an ecumenical council.[118] What is peculiar is, first of all, that Irene had written to Pope Hadrian on August 29, 784 (the letter bears the date IV Kal. Sept. Indict. VII), lamenting the long-standing opposition to images and inviting the pope to an ecumenical council.[119] Second, Irene says in her letter that she had been talking about these very matters face to face with Bishop Constantine of Leontine in Sicily whom she was now sending to Hadrian. The letter also mentions the bishop of Naples in a way that might imply that he too had been involved in such discussions.[120] Ostrogorsky thought that Paul had been persuaded to abdicate.[121] That is possible, but it may also be the case that Theophanes has simply compressed events and recorded them slightly out of order. Perhaps Paul did want a council and he and Irene might have been talking about restoring images, holding a council, and identifying a new patriarch for some weeks or months before Paul vacated his throne.

At some point after Paul died Irene gathered "all the people" at the Magnaura Palace and told them that it was necessary to find someone "who is able to tend us like a shepherd and to fortify the Church with his words of instruction." The people were unanimous in calling for the chief imperial secretary, Tarasius. Irene said that she too wished for Tarasius to become patriarch but that he was "being disobedient." Thus, she put Tarasius before the throng and asked him to explain himself. He delivered a long speech in which he said, predictably, that he was unprepared and unworthy and, moreover, that he could not in good conscience accept the leadership of a church that was cut off from all other Christians of the world. Again and again he insisted on the need for ecclesial unity. Finally the people agreed that there was need for a council. Then, as if to remind them once more what was at stake, Tarasius said that Leo III had destroyed the icons and had upset an ancient custom of the church.[122] On December 25, 784, nearly four full months after Paul's abdication, Tarasius was consecrated.

Once again this narrative is deceptive. Is it significant that Irene's bit of theater at the Magnaura was not staged until after Paul died? Why was a good teacher and pastor only to be found among the lay dignitaries of the palace? Given that Tarasius was "being disobedient," how long had he been discussing the patriarchal office with Irene? Why was he reluctant? The version of Tarasius's speech contained in the synodal *acta* of II Nicaea differs from Theophanes' account in one interesting respect: It says that "some few" people in the crowd at the Magnaura disagreed with the idea of holding a council.[123] Perhaps Tarasius had a healthy fear of such people or perhaps he and Irene were working to overcome opposition. Tarasius was a layman and had to be rushed through the clerical grades before being consecrated patriarch. Even so, it took a long time to enthrone him. The opposition may have been stiffer than the iconophile sources imply.

Tarasius wrote to Pope Hadrian to announce his election and to profess his orthodoxy. This letter is not extant but there survive, from October of 785, Hadrian's responses to both Irene and Constantine VI and to Tarasius.[124] From these letters we learn that Hadrian was told that both the rulers and the patriarch were planning for a council. "If," said the pope, "it is impossible to restore the holy and venerable images without a council," then let one be held that will, in the presence of the pope's legates, anathematize the pseudo-council of 754. For his legates the pope chose the Roman archpriest Peter (basically the head of the ecclesiastical personnel of the Roman Church) and another Peter, the abbot of the Greek monastic community of St. Saba.[125] It may be significant that Hadrian did not send high-ranking secular clerics, for instance, one or two of the suburbicarian bishops. It may also be important that Hadrian sent a Greek speaking envoy.[126] One also wonders if it is coincidental that the vicar of Peter sent two men named Peter to represent him.

Hadrian's letters are intriguing in several respects. Given that Irene wrote to him in late August of 784, why did he wait more than a year to respond? Why was he cool to the idea of a council?[127] His basic arguments may provide the answer to this question. Hadrian said insistently that his predecessors since Gregory II had been entreating Constantinople's rulers to put aside the heresy of iconoclasm. In short, the council of 754 was completely illegitimate, no legitimate ecclesiastical forum had pronounced on images, and so there was need only to return to the true faith. The pope's letters are full of Petrine references. They repeatedly assert and emphasize the authority of the bishop of Rome as Peter's successor. Hadrian wants the Greeks to acknowledge both his own authority and the ancient traditions which he and his predecessors have always faithfully kept.[128] Hadrian also raised other matters: Tarasius's having been elevated to the patriarchal office from the laity; the fact that the imperial *sacra* calls Tarasius "ecumenical"; the church provinces and revenues seized by Leo III; papal rights to ordain archbishops and bishops in southern Italy. Hadrian also says that only if the Eastern rulers hold tightly to Petrine teaching, as the great King Charles does, can they expect to have victories. Finally, he says that one thing his legates will do is make him "more certain" about the true orthodoxy of the path on which Constantinople has evidently embarked. Hadrian's words on images proper, to which I shall turn in detail in Chapter 3, are remarkably restrained. The Byzantine documents lay primary stress on the restoration of unity in the church while the papal letters emphasize papal authority. Images play an oddly secondary role here in the drama of which they are normally seen as the title characters. And the pope seems less than confident that he really knows what is going on in the East.

The East was learning how to walk on eggshells. A council was indeed summoned to meet on August 1, 786, and, perhaps just after hearing from the pope, letters were dispatched to the Eastern patriarchs inviting them to come or to send representatives. Irene's truce of 782 with the caliph was still in place and it may have been possible to get messages though. Unfortunately, the truce collapsed in 786 and the Eastern churches were represented only by two monks who were treated with great respect but whose official standing is not too clear.[129]

How many bishops had assembled in Constantinople by late July of 786 is not known, but shortly before the council could begin its work on August 1, Tarasius learned that many bishops and some laymen were still iconoclasts and that they were attempting to prevent the council from meeting.[130] The patriarch forbade meetings among such persons. The bishops had been called to meet in the palace but were told to assemble in the Church of the Holy Apostles by the rulers. No sooner had the meeting begun than local troops invaded the proceedings to break them up. The iconophobe bishops who did not want a council shouted, "We have won." Irene told the assembly to disband but some of the bishops and their military sympathizers stayed around long enough to read and affirm the decisions of Hiereia. Then everyone went home.

Irene's next moves were brilliant.[131] She sent Stauracius, her chief supporter in the imperial administration, to Thrace to persuade the troops there to help her rid the city of the disloyal troops. Then, amid rumors of an Arab attack in the East, she sent the rebel tagmatic troops out of the city, and when they had reached the first important staging post on the road to the Eastern frontier she cashiered them. With loyal troops in control and the disloyal ones dismissed, Irene had little to fear from the bishops. Accordingly, she called for a new council to meet at Nicaea in September of 787. Nicaea was close to Constantinople but just far enough away to create a sense of security. Nicaea was in the Opsikion theme whose commander was a loyal appointee of Irene's. The city itself had deep historical resonances with the first council held there in 325 and, certainly quite consciously, Irene, in choosing Nicaea, meant for everyone to draw parallels between her son and Constantine the Great and between herself and Helena, the sainted mother of the first Constantine. Still, the events of 786 stood as a disquieting reminder of the hurdles that lay in the path of any attempt to reverse some fifty or sixty years of official policy.

II Nicaea, 787

The basic story of the Second Council of Nicaea has been told many times and there is no reason to retell that story.[132] It suffices to highlight basic issues. The events of 784, along with the studied diplomatic ambiguities of Hadrian's letters, plus the tumultuous events of 786 will have combined to teach Tarasius and

Irene that they had to tread very carefully—as if not to break eggshells. The laymen and clerics who shouted at Tarasius in 784 and who disrupted the council of 786 were a group to be reckoned with. But how large was the group? No further lay opposition emerged. As for the tagmatic troops, it seems likely that they were more loyal to the memory of Constantine V and to his policies than they were to iconoclasm per se.[133] Where the bishops are concerned it is well to bear in mind the words of one of those who was reconciled in 787. After having been asked whether he and the other iconophobe bishops had been constrained to adopt their heresy, Hypatius of Nicaea said no but "we were born, educated, and grew up in this heresy of ours."[134] The key point, of course, is that except for an unknown number of putatively iconophile bishops appointed between 780 and 787, every bishop in the Byzantine Empire was, at least officially, an iconophobe. Some of these men were perhaps sincere in their beliefs. Others were, always had been, quite prepared to trim their sails to the prevailing winds. It is interesting that there was never a counter party in the church. We hear of no organized or numerous opponents in the years between 730 and 754, in the years around Hiereia, or in the period during and following II Nicaea. Although some people were willing to take a modest stand for iconoclasm in 784 and again in 786, there was no large party that was willing to sacrifice everything to defend the views of Leo III and Constantine V.[135] But, let me repeat, there was no discernible iconophile party in the church after 730.[136] It appears that images were less important between 730 and 787 than they became in later years among iconophile writers. The exception may be the papacy, but it seems fair to argue that images in themselves were less important to the popes than the large and complex matter of papal authority.

Among the iconophile writers who later demonized the iconoclasts, the monks were especially prominent. We have seen that monks did suffer from the regime of Constantine V but also that they probably did not suffer primarily because of their iconophilia. Still, the monks were angry in 787 and wanted a pound of iconoclast flesh.

Irene's position was tricky too. She was still ruling as regent for a boy who was growing older all the time, whose majority would come soon, and whose exact views on the great issues of the day were not publicly known. Irene may have embraced the iconophiles to create some distance between herself—and also her son?—and the legacy of Constantine V. But that was a calculated gamble, as the trouble caused by the troops in 786 showed all too well. Irene had to move cautiously and she dared not indulge in a thoroughgoing *damnatio memoriae* of her own and particularly her son's dynasty.

Under the baton of maestro Tarasius every discordant note was avoided.

His direction of the Second Council of Nicaea is one of the most astonishing feats in the history of Christianity and of Byzantium.

The council opened with some 252 bishops; later sessions had as many as 365. This suggests that between September 24 and October 13 Tarasius won a larger consensus. One hundred and thirty-one abbots and monks also attended, an unusually high number. Irene stayed away but was represented by Petronas, the count of the Opsikion theme and thus the local military commander, and by John, the military logothete, a trusted eunuch.[137] As soon as the council fathers had assembled in the Church of St. Sophia, the bishops of Sicily nominated Tarasius to open the synod (999C).[138] This provided him with the legitimate position he needed to manage affairs. The patriarch reminded the gathering of the aborted synod of 786 and of the mob that had been stirred up, he said, by "certain bishops whom it would be easy to identify but whose names I willingly pass over" (999D–E). He then stressed that the rulers had summoned the synod, and he concluded by inviting in the bishops who had been responsible for the previous year's troubles (1002A–C). Obviously, the vast majority of Eastern bishops had been admitted with no questions as to their orthodoxy. Only the troublemakers of 786, and possibly the surviving bishops of Hiereia,[139] were excluded from the opening rites. These amounted to ten only, and another seems to have arrived a bit later. Already Tarasius was displaying moderation.

After his opening discourse, Tarasius and the others invited the ten excluded bishops to enter. Before giving them any chance to speak, however, the council ordered the reading of the imperial *sacra*, or letter of convocation (1002D–1007C). I shall return often to this remarkable document. For the moment it is enough to see how both the assembled bishops and the dubious newly admitted were treated to a clear statement that the council had met with imperial authority. Irene and Constantine speak of how they were deeply distressed by the divisions in the church. They desire to achieve "unity and concord," to restore "harmony in the priesthood," to reestablish agreement with the decisions of the old councils, to "restore the ancient rules and orders." The rulers say that it was the former Patriarch Paul who advised them of the problems besetting the church, namely that Constantinople stood under the anathema of all other Christian communities because "they say that some synod or other" (σύνοδον τινα λέγουσι) had been held to subvert pictures and images. Paul had said that a council was necessary to undo the damage and Tarasius, for his part, would only accept the patriarchal office if such a synod were to be held. So a council has been called to bring the church together in the tradition of the fathers.

These words having been read out, three of the just admitted bishops, Basil of Ancyra, Theodore of Myra, and Theodosius of Amorion, were brought forward. Basil spoke first, saying that he had examined the issue before the council and now wished to approach the Catholic Church (1007D–1011B). Basil then read out a long and quite traditional profession of faith toward the end of which he embraced images of the incarnate Jesus, of Mary, angels, apostles, prophets, martyrs, and saints. He then delivered the anathemas against those who "slander Christians" (that is, iconoclasts), as well as against a series of rather elementary iconophobic stances, for instance that images are idols. The council responded to Basil with "Thanks be to God who has united what had been separated." Basil was thus readmitted to full communion and Theodore of Myra was brought forward. He too asked to be reunited to the church and then read out the same profession of faith that Basil had just spoken (1011C–D). When Theodore finished, Euthymius of Sardis said, "Blessed be God who has united him to the Catholic Church." Next Theodosius then came forward (1011D–1015B). He apologized for saying and teaching so much against images (he mentions no iconoclasm) and said that he had seen the error of his ways and now wished to be reunited with "all other Christians." In session five of the council we learn that Theodosius had been present at Hiereia (13: 173D). He then proceeded to read a *libellus* which he himself had prepared. He added six anathemas much like the ones his predecessors had spoken. The council then agreed that Theodosius was worthy of admission, and all three bishops were bidden to take their seats.

The council then turned to a touchier subject. Seven more bishops were hailed before the assembly, and Tarasius harangued them for their participation in the problems of 786 (1015E–1018A). The bishops then abjectly apologized for their conduct, saying that they were deceived by their teachers and the prevailing conditions of the church. Having seen the folly of their ways, they now wished readmittance to the church (1018A–1019B). The council pronounced them worthy of readmission, but then John, one of the Eastern legates, urged that the council scour the writings of the fathers to see exactly how the church should go about readmitting heretics. The conciliar records now go on for columns and columns in the standard edition in a diligent, almost fastidious, recitation of patristic and conciliar pronouncements on the reception of heretics (1019B–1050C). The clear impression is promoted that everything is to be done according to strict rules and in absolute conformity with ecclesiastical traditions. On several occasions, however, the monks spoke up with serious objections. They were concerned that readmitted heretics not be admitted to the priesthood; that persons who embraced heresy willingly not be easily readmitted; and that persons ordained by heretics not be permitted to exercise clerical ministry. Tarasius and the bishops skillfully overcame each monastic objection and, finally, the monks agreed that the proposed solutions were satisfactory. The seven bishops were then asked to read their recantations. Their full reception was, however, postponed to a later session of the council, probably to proclaim that their culpability was greater than that of the three bishops who were received immediately after their recantations.

As the second session of the council opened an imperial messenger arrived with Bishop Gregory of Neocaesarea who was also seeking reconciliation. Gregory was questioned very closely and then his case was postponed until a future session (1051D–1054D). The main business of the second session was the reading of Pope Hadrian's letters to Irene and Constantine (1055A–1076D) and to Tarasius (1078C–1084D). As we have already seen, Hadrian's letter to Irene was read in an expurgated version that served well to avoid controversy. Essentially the pope affirmed the authority of St. Peter, of the pope as Peter's vicar, and of the Roman Church. He expressed his pleasure at the change of heart on the part of Byzantium's rulers. And he laid out a good many biblical and patristic citations in defense of images. Throughout his letters the pope emphasizes the necessity of ecclesiastical unity under his leadership. One can easily imagine that the Byzantines would have preferred letters with a little less stress on the papacy but, at the same time, given their own strategy of emphasizing unity, the pope's words were welcome and tolerable. After the pope's letters had been read the synod offered many affirmations of their teachings (1086C–1111E). Here was another potent sign of unity.

The third session opened by admitting the bishops whose cases had been postponed in each of the first two sessions. The bishops who had already recanted were invited in along with Gregory of Neocaesarea, who was at one point in the proceedings labeled the chief of the heretics (1118A), and the head (ἔξαρχος) of the previous "unholy" synod (1118B). Gregory read his recantation and then was questioned closely on whether or not he had caused anyone to suffer on account of his devotion to images. Gregory denied that he had injured anyone, or had ordered anyone to be harmed (1115B–1119B). As no one came forward to contradict him—was everyone being discrete, were few people left from the 750s, or, as I suspect, were very few people ever actually harmed for their iconophilia?—it was decided that all the remaining bishops could be seated.[140] Abbot Sabas of Studion gave thanks for the newly restored unity of the church.

Bishop Constantine of Constantia in Cyprus, who was acting as master of ceremonies, then asked that Tarasius's letter to the Eastern clergy be read out (1119D–1127A). After the letter was read the pope's legates affirmed that Hadrian had received just such a letter, a matter of some importance since Tarasius's letter to Hadrian is not extant (barring later interpolations of the records, which cannot be ruled out). Tarasius kept to a very high level of generalization. He mentioned how Providence had brought him, even though a layman, to the patriarchal dignity; how he found a war of words raging in his realm; how he must adhere to custom and lay down a profession of faith. There follows a long and wholly traditional *professio fidei* which concludes with an interesting set of affirmations of the six ecumenical councils. He then presents his call for an ecumenical council and describes the complete support of the rulers for this plan. Tarasius asks for legates so that the unity of the church and faith can be restored, that the divided be united, that the wounded be healed. The synod then heard the letter of the Eastern patriarchs, who were unable to attend because of Muslim hostility, and the synodical letter of Patriarch Theodore of Jerusalem (1127C–1146C). These documents express great joy that a council will be held to repair the rift in the church and offer professions of faith. These take the form of a credal statement followed by an enumeration and affirmation of the six ecumenical councils, along with a condemnation of the pseudo-seventh council of 754. Interestingly, the documents affirm the traditions of the councils, the cult of the saints, and the cult of images, in that order. After the documents had been read the bishops confirmed their teachings.

The fourth session was taken up with the reading and approval of a whole series of biblical, patristic, and hagiographical texts pertaining to images. It concludes with a profession of faith by the assembled clergy (13: 128C–133A). The profession begins with a creedlike statement of faith, continues with a condemnation of the "Jewish Conventicle" that "barked" against images, and carries on with an affirmation of the cult of Mary and the saints, the cult of the cross, and then the cult of images. The session concludes with the subscriptions of all the bishops and higoumens present.

Session five works its way through a long list of ancient heresies and concludes by attaching iconoclasm to the long list of errors. A set of anathemas rebukes those who in any way reject images (157A–201E). Session six, the longest in the council, consists of a reading out and point-by-point refutation of the *horos* of Hiereia (204A–364D). In yet another nice specimen of management, Tarasius had Gregory of Neocaesarea, who had been present in 754, read out the *horos* piece by piece as the council proceeded to refute it. The session concludes by rescinding the anathemas pronounced in 754 against Patriarch Germanus, George of Cyprus, and John of Damascus. Session seven was devoted to a reading of the *horos* of II Nicaea along with a set of anathemas (364E–413A). Most of these are directed against those who attack images, but among them several deserve special notice. First, virtually the whole blame for Hiereia is placed on the heads of three long-dead bishops: Theodosius of Ephesus, Sisinnius Pastillas, and Basil Triccacabus (400A). Second, condemnation falls on the three patriarchs of the iconoclastic era: Anastasius, Constantine, and Nicetas (400A). Third, Bishops John of Nicomedia (otherwise deeply obscure) and Constantine of Nacoleia are called the heresiarchs (400B). The council then sent letters to Irene and Constantine (400D–408D) and to the clergy of Hagia Sophia and of Constantinople generally (408D–414A). These letters go out of their way to praise Irene's role in calling the council and to trumpet the council's adherence to the ancient and universal traditions of the church.

Scholars have long noticed that, compared to earlier ecumenical councils, II Nicaea's records contain rather little theology.[141] To that theology I shall turn shortly. For now it is important to see why administrative arrangements took up so much time in 787. Let us recall the tense situation between the summers of 784 and 786. Tarasius's handling of the council must be seen against that background.

Surely there were iconophiles among the bishops in 787 but the majority must still have been men appointed under the iconoclastic regime. Apparently they were not fanatical about images but they still had to be reconciled. The monks, in particular, were leery of their old foes. Thus, Tarasius followed several courses simultaneously to achieve his desired outcome: a church at one and at peace. A condemnation of iconoclasm, or an affirmation of iconophilia, I take to be a secondary objective—not an unimportant one but not *the* important one.[142]

First, Tarasius secured and broadcast as loudly as he could both imperial support and the support of Rome and the Eastern patriarchs. By this means he could be seen to be acting with the complete approval of the rulers, a point that will not have been lost on those who knew perfectly well that past rulers had been largely responsible for iconoclasm. He could also fulfill Paul's wishes, and his own, that the Orthodox Church no longer be separated from all other churches. This gave those who were still iconoclasts in 787 some cover to rejoin the church. They did not have to be seen as caving in to the patriarch alone or to a faction in the Orthodox Church itself. Second, document after document tediously recites the teachings of the six ecumenical councils while also citing biblical and patristic texts relevant to images. Here again the theme of unity was sounded. The wayward were being asked to join a tradition, to affirm a faith. A relatively tiny number of persons were singled out for public recantations. At least two of these had been present at Hiereia and seven others had been ringleaders in the disturbances of 786. No one else was subjected to any embarrassing scrutiny. Where iconoclasm itself was concerned—and I will come back just below to what II Nicaea said about Byzantium's iconoclast rulers—no one alive and present was blamed for it. Constantine of Nacoleia was turned into the heresiarch, and three eminently forgettable bishops were blamed for Hiereia. Three patriarchs, the last of them dead for more than seven years, were censured, and three iconophile heroes were rehabilitated. That is all. There was no hunt for heretics. There were no blanket condemnations. Tarasius practiced that *oikonomia* for which the Byzantine world is justly famed: the cautious, principled reconciliation of divergent points of view.[143] Tarasius had to find a way to remove iconoclasm without permanently alienating the iconoclasts. He succeeded.[144]

Let us look, much more briefly, at the way Tarasius dealt with the monks in 787.[145] Historically monks had not been accorded a prominent role in ecumenical councils. Tarasius involved as many as 132 monks in II Nicaea. He permitted them to attend all sessions, to speak on a regular basis, to question the bishops who were being reconciled to the church, and to bring forth image testimonies in sessions four and six. Tarasius and Irene may have seen in the monks a natural support group for their plans, and restoring images was one effective way of winning over a majority of the monastic clergy even though not all monks were iconodules. Yet Tarasius knew perfectly well that he could not operate a church without the bishops and he knew too that, particularly in light of the suffering of the monks in the 760s, there were bad feelings between the monks and the bishops. Thus, the patriarch did not let the monks press for extreme measures on such matters as readmitting heretics, but he let the monks have a visible role in the council which condemned the iconoclasm which had been a hallmark of the imperial and episcopal regime that had harried them mercilessly on at least some occasions. It is also tempting to speculate a little on the twenty-two canons that are appended to the acts of the council. It is not known exactly when or how the acts were prepared. Most of them derive in one way or another from earlier conciliar legislation (only numbers 2, 4, 8, 9, and 17 are new).[146] There had not been a significant council of the Byzantine Church in almost a century so the Nicene fathers may have perceived a need to introduce a few disciplinary measures. Still, many of these are decidedly interesting in that they touch on the faith, morals, and ecclesiastical conduct of the bishops. Possibly Tarasius and the monks agreed to address episcopal conduct in these canons instead of relentlessly attacking episcopal beliefs in the acts: *Oikonomia* again.

Finally, Tarasius, and perhaps Irene too, finessed the imperial involvement in iconoclasm.[147] The court did not want iconoclasm labeled an imperial heresy. Irene was in the delicate position of simultaneously embracing and distancing herself from the "Isaurian" legacy. She could not permit an outright condemnation of her predecessors. The constant stress on Irene's desire to put right the wrongs in the church might have rung a little hollow if Irene and Tarasius had at the same time castigated earlier imperial activities.

Looking at the conciliar records is instructive in regard to Tarasius's plan of action. Hadrian's letter, in the version that was read out, never names Leo III, Constantine V, or Leo IV. The pope speaks only of "your great-grandfather," "your grandfather," and "your father." Irene's letter to Hadrian refers diplomatically to "those who ruled before us." In the fifth session John, one of the Eastern legates, told a tale of one mysterious Tessarokontapechys, a Jewish wizard who promised the caliph Yezid a reign of thirty years if he would destroy images. Somehow this teaching reached Constantine of Nacoleia who, along with his supporters, destroyed images (197A–200B). Leo is not named. This story is suspiciously like the one that Theophanes tells under the year 722/3.[148] In the historian's telling, an unnamed Jewish wizard went to Yezid and promised him a forty-year reign if he would destroy images. A Christian named Beser, who had been a captive in Syria, communicated this teaching to Leo III, "who was responsible for inflicting many evils upon us." Leo had Constantine of Nacoleia as an ally. It seems clear that a common stock of stories served as a source for both the council fathers and Theophanes. But whereas the latter named Leo, both agreed in placing primary blame on a Jew, Muslims, and a wayward bishop.[149] As we shall see in our discussion of Nicaea's theology, the writings of John of Damascus are strangely neglected in 787. One reason could well be that John was savage in his criticisms of the rulers, and he also attacked the rights of any ruler to intervene in theological matters.[150] Making too much use of John would have been an affront to the whole dynasty and so he was gingerly kept on one side. Constantine V and Leo IV were explicitly named only in session six at points where the *horos* of Hiereia was being quoted (209D, 352E). There is one particularly revealing example of the way in which the rulers were silently excluded. As he was reading it out, Gregory of Neocaesarea quoted one portion of the *horos* as saying that God had raised up "our faithful kings, the ones equal to the apostles" to lead and teach and to abolish diabolical cunning. When Deacon Epiphanius read out the council's refutation of this section of the *horos* he said "because the members of that council were bishops . . ." (225D, 228C). One would not know, from these documents, that Constantine V had worked hard to prepare for the Council of Hiereia or that the council had taken into consideration some sophisticated theological speculation on the emperor's part. Here is how the council summed up its view of Irene's ancestors: "Their great deeds, the victories gained over enemies, the subjugation of barbarous nations, the solicitude they showed for their subjects, the wise measures they took, the constitutions they promulgated, their civic institutions, and the improvements effected by them in the cities . . . such is the title of the dead emperors to fame, that which secures to them the gratitude of all their subjects" (13: 355)."[151] This is neither the view nor the language of the three mid-century treatises or of the *Life of Stephen the Younger.*

Tarasius achieved a notable result.[152] Just as he had reconciled the bishops and appeased the monks, so he whitewashed the imperial role in iconoclasm. Iconoclasm owed its start to Jewish wizards, Muslim potentates, and one misguided bishop. Rulers were somehow infected with the contagion but it was not their fault. Hiereia was attributed to three bishops, not to the whole episcopate or to Constantine V. The whole point of II Nicaea, from one point of view, was to undo the damage wrought by the council of 754. That damage was carefully attributed to a small number of zealots whereas iconoclasm itself was blamed on loners from within or oddballs from without the empire. We have already seen that there may never have been any formal iconoclastic edict in 730 or at any other time. Be that as it may, Irene could not easily issue an edict abolishing iconoclasm without thereby attacking the actions and thus the memory of her predecessors. Tarasius found a way not so much to exculpate Leo III and Constantine V as to leave them out of the story.

Looking back, one can say that II Nicaea began by legitimizing its participants, then legitimized images with arguments drawn almost entirely from history and tradition, then delegitimized the council of 754, partly by adducing more "authentic" traditions and partly by impugning the texts or interpretations used in 754, and then issued a *horos* that is amazingly jejune as a statement of image theology. The reasons are to be found in the rather long discussion we have just been pursuing. The Second Council of Nicaea was about many things. All of those things were acutely important in the Byzantine world in the 780s. Only some of those things were themselves primarily about images.

Byzantium in the Eighth Century

Let us sum up this account of Byzantium in the first era of iconoclasm. Some criticism was lodged against images by Leo III in about 730. We do not really know what he did. Nothing else pertaining to images, at least that we know about, happened until about 752 when Constantine V began the agitation that led to the deeply iconophobe council of 754. In the 760s a few prominent works of art were removed from conspicuous public places. Some manuscripts were mutilated. When Paul was selected for the patriarchal office, he was asked to offer assurances that he would not worship icons. That is just about the whole history of iconoclasm as we can actually know it. It is a history with episodes but no plot.

Patriarch Germanus peacefully stepped aside. Bishops acceptable to the iconophobe rulers Leo III, Constantine V, and Leo IV were gradually put into office. We hear of no purges. We hear of no sharp opposition to the new bishops. In 754 the bishops gathered in synod and declared their opposition to image worship. We hear of no opposition to them, except from papal Rome. In the 780s the old Patriarch Paul, if the sources can be believed, had a crisis of conscience because he presided over a church divided from all other churches. Obviously the division was occasioned by iconoclasm, but it is noteworthy that the sources do not explicitly attach Paul's anguish to images. By 784 Irene and Tarasius were ready to reunify the church and to establish their own power base within the empire. To do this they decided to restore image worship. Perhaps they were sincere. Perhaps they were calculating. There was some opposition in 784 and again in 786, but it was adroitly overcome, and then Tarasius's superb management of the council in 787 allowed all parties a share in the newly won domestic tranquility and ecclesiastical harmony.

The clergy should not be seen as spineless in all of this. Nor should they be seen as the willing tools of a series of dominating rulers. Clergy and rulers had great respect for each other's roles in the smooth operation of the universal Christian commonwealth that since Constantine the Great depended on "one emperor, one empire, one faith." Hélène Ahrweiler reminds us pointedly that we must abandon caesaropapism, that "contemptible neologism."[153] It is useless as a historical interpretation of the complicated working relationship between Byzantium's secular and spiritual officials. The clergy of Byzantium were always prepared to support and to cooperate with the rulers whenever they could.[154] In the eighth century they almost always could. This tells us not that the clergy were stooges but that images were either not such a big issue—certainly not "orthodoxy as such"—or else not so unambiguously defined by the tradition as to make one and only one position palatable, honorable. It is only in the light of the final iconodule victory that, as we have noted already in this study, iconophobia was made to appear bad in itself and out of step with continuous Christian teaching.

Iconoclasm was important in eighth-century Byzantium mainly because two emperors laid some stress on it on at least a few occasions. But iconoclasm is not the story of eighth-century Byzantium. Wars in Anatolia and the Balkans were more important. Legal, administrative, and fiscal reforms were more important. The kinds of tensions that led to coup attempts in 741, in the mid-

760s, and probably again in 776 and 780, along with the currents that exposed themselves in the short but brutal attack on the monks in the 760s and again in one theme in the early 770s, were more explosive than any of the forces generated by iconoclasm. This is already one important gain in perspective for our ultimate task of explaining what happened in the West. We need not reckon with, at one end of the Mediterranean, a decades-long crisis of constant and searing intensity and, at the other end, practically nothing at all.

Art Talk in Eighth-Century Byzantium

Having surveyed what might be called the external history of Byzantine iconoclasm in the eighth century, it is time to look inside, to see what kinds of things were said about religious art, to turn again to the kinds of words and concepts we encountered in Chapter 1. The time of Leo III is critical in many respects but from Leo himself not a word survives. Our evidence for the early iconophobe position must be inferred from the letters of Germanus to the Bithynian bishops. As we saw earlier, popes wrote several letters but these do not survive, at least not in their original form. Nicephorus and Theophanes probably transmit some accurate information but it is hard to separate their embroidery from the plain cloth on which they put it. Germanus alone, therefore, permits some insight into how the iconophobes argued their case. Germanus also leaves us some clues as to what an iconophile argument might have looked like. But it is really John of Damascus who presents, for the first time, a detailed, cogent argument for the iconophile case. John's writings rarely permit inferences, however, about the exact positions that he might have been rebutting.

Germanus and the Papacy

Some of the inferences permitted by Germanus's letters seem absolutely secure. For instance, Germanus told John of Synada (100C) that Constantine of Nacoleia had become concerned after reading Exodus 20.4: "This is how he defended himself," said the patriarch. In his letter to Constantine himself, Germanus repeats the bishop of Nacoleia's insistence that no created thing be worshiped (105D), which is essentially the same point Germanus had made in his letter to John, saying there that Constantine had insisted that nothing "made by hands," "made by men" (100C) should be worshiped. In his long letter to Thomas of Claudiopolis Germanus undertakes a lengthy defense against a charge of idolatry

(109B–E, 112C–D, 117B–121D, 124C) that he believed to be grounded in a poor reading of the Scriptures, or brought forth "as if from the scriptures." Idolatry, then, understood as a contravention of the Mosaic Law, of the Exodus prohibition, was at the base of whatever iconophobia emerged in the 720s.

Other inferences drawn from Germanus's letters are a little harder to treat with confidence. Germanus's letter to John says that it is impossible to depict God, to make an image of the invisible Godhead (101A). It is possible that the iconophobes had argued thus. Again in the letter to John, Germanus appears to be refuting a charge that hearing and reading are superior to seeing, saying "because we are made of flesh and blood we are forced to know more certainly those things which through sight offer real assurance to the soul" (101E). In his letter to Thomas, Germanus cites Basil to the effect that pictures show to the eye what the ear hears. Seeing and hearing both incite to virtue and are equivalent (113B–116A). Possibly, then, the iconophobes had raised the issue, noted in Chapter 1, of the superiority of reading and/or hearing to seeing. But it may also be that Germanus uses the argument of the equivalence of these modes of perception, even suggesting the superiority of sight, as one element in his repertoire of defenses of images. That is, he may not have been answering a charge so much as advancing an argument of his own. In a brief passage in the letter to Thomas, Germanus says that it is not true that because there are images people do not have to attend regular church celebrations (123A). Perhaps some of those who had concerns about images raised this issue; if they did so, this is a new criticism of images.

If little new was said against images at the outbreak of iconoclasm, little new was advanced on behalf of images. Germanus presents five basic defenses. First, he says that no created thing is ever worshiped by Christians, that true worship (λατρεία) is reserved for God alone; that Christians never make images of the invisible Godhead; and that Christ has freed all his followers from idolatry (100C, E, 101A, 112C–D). Second, he argues that because Christ appeared as a man, he can be depicted acting in the various historical settings in which the Gospels place him. Likewise, Mary can be depicted "according to the flesh" as well as apostles, martyrs, prophets, and saints (101A–D, 116A). Third, Germanus insists that depictions of Christ or of the great figures of the Scriptures and the church inspire imitation and urge people to give glory to God (101D, 113B–116A, 117B). In other words, images do not exist for themselves. Fourth, the patriarch returns again to the argument that images are of long standing in the church and have never been condemned by ecclesiastical authority (109A, 116C–D, 124D–125A, 125A–E). Finally, Germanus pleads with his correspondents not to embrace the arguments of Jews and Muslims whose only aim is to destroy God's church (109B–E, 124D–125A).

There is absolutely nothing in Germanus's defense of images that we have not met already. New in the 720s was the involvement of the emperor. Scholars have labored prodigiously to explain Leo's actions on all kinds of grounds: He sought to gain control over the church which had most of the images; he sought to direct loyalty and even reverence to the imperial office and had to divert it from images; he was promoting a cult of victory and could not bear competitors; he was making concessions to the populations of his Eastern provinces.[155] I see no reason to suppose that any of these explanations has the whole truth or that any of them lacks wholly in truth. For my part, I am inclined to suppose that Leo was sincere in believing that images were idolatrous.[156] Let us remember that it is only in view of the ultimate victory of intense iconophilia that the whole history of Christian images, at least in the East, has been trimmed to fit one procrustean bed of interpretation. Yet, as we have seen, there were in antiquity many people who had reservations about Christian figural art and, in the eighth century, two of Orthodoxy's monotheistic contemporaries eschewed figural art. Leo's position does not seem odd at all. And his actions were probably a great deal more moderate than his later calumniators would have us believe. Moreover, if the years between the middle of the seventh century and the early decades of the eighth had seen an upsurge in acts of veneration connected with images and a rising belief in the miraculous power of images themselves, if in other words, these were relatively recent phenomena, and not ancient practices, then it may be possible to regard Leo, and Constantine of Nacoleia too, as conservatives, as upholders of tradition.

Perhaps in view of the Roman Council of 731, and obviously after 726, someone in Rome prepared a modest florilegium of iconophile texts. From later citations of some of the extracts contained in this florilegium, it can be shown to have had at least twenty-three chapters. To some of its testimony I shall turn in Chapter 3 in a discussion of art talk in the West. For present purposes it is enough to say that the texts collected in this florilegium are all familiar and that this specific collection does not appear to have had any influence in the East, albeit Eastern writers were aware of and sometimes themselves cited passages found in the Roman material.[157]

John of Damascus

Safe from Byzantium's reach in Palestine, John of Damascus took up his pens like swords in or shortly after 730. The date is provided by a reference in the opening section of John's first *Oration* which talks about truth being stronger than the might of kings, and about the need of good people to disobey evil laws of kings.[158] John addressed himself to the Christian people, but just which Christian community he had in mind we do not know. Evidently his first *Oration* was considered impenetrable by some and so John quickly prepared a second one. These first two texts are polemics of high intensity. Thus it is interesting to note that the third *Oration*, probably written during the 740s when John was revising a good many of his earlier works, reads like a "sober and technical theological treatise," to use the words of John's editor, Bonifatius Kotter.[159] It may be that John saw an opportunity to provide a systematic exposé of image thought and it may also be that the 740s were largely without significant image controversies so that John's last words on the subject could take on a serene air notably absent from his earlier communications. Another product of the 740s, John's *Exposition of the Faith*, treats images without the polemical tone of the first two *Orations*.[160] With his writings John changed forever the shape of the image discussion.

John made three fundamental contributions to a discussion that had been going on sporadically since the fourth century. First, he addressed himself in an extended, indeed almost in a systematic, way to the whole problem of images in the church. Second, as a sophisticated theologian and philosopher, John perceived flaws in the arguments for and against images and provided for the first time a profound reflection on Christian art. Third, John amassed a substantial body of evidence in support of his views.

John's first two *Orations* are rather like many of the writings we have noted already in this book. That is, they take up a wide array of topics in no particular order or sequence. It is hard to tell if John is responding to texts written by the opposition or simply taking up relevant subjects as they occurred to him. In the third *Oration*, however, John is greatly more systematic.

John points out that many terms regularly used by Christians—"Trinity," "consubstantial," "one nature of the Godhead," "three persons," "one person with two natures"—are not found in the Scriptures but have been interpreted by the fathers, and those are anathematized who refuse to accept them (3.11).[161] So too, John says, God himself commanded images to be made and these images have long been accepted (3.12). In other words, John rejects prohibitions based on what he views as a simplistic reading of Scripture. Then John asks, "What is an image?" Here is his definition: "An image is therefore a likeness and pattern and impression of something, showing in itself what is depicted; however, the image is certainly not like the archetype, that is, what is depicted, in every respect—for the image is one thing, and what it depicts is another—and certainly a difference is seen between them, since they are not identical" (3.16). After attempting to clarify the field of discussion, John asks why images are made. He answers, "All images reveal and make perceptible those things which are hidden." To illustrate his point John says that a person cannot have immediate knowledge of something that is invisible—the soul, for example—or of things that are far away in space or time. Images exist, then, to advance knowledge by revealing and making perceptible secret things. Images are helpful (3.17).

At this point John turns to an enumeration of all the possible kinds of images.[162] There are six (3.18–23). The first is the Son as a perfect image of the Father. This is a natural image and must precede all other kinds. The second is God's foreknowledge of things to come. Since God's plan is immutable, His designs for His creation are too. The third kind of image is man, made by God as an image of Himself. Man does not of course share in the divine essence but images God by imitation. The fourth kind of image is the "shadows and forms and types" of invisible and bodiless things which are mentioned in the Scriptures. The example John gives is angels. But his main point here is to say that we use "familiar, every-day media" to produce mental analogies that make it possible for us to contemplate higher, spiritual realities. A fifth kind of image prefigures what will happen. Here John means types in the exegetical sense. So the burning bush or the rod of Aaron which foreshadow the Theotokos, or the clouds and waters of the sea which point to baptismal grace. The sixth kind of image is made for remembrance of past events. John is obviously seeking to overwhelm those critics who have rejected one or another kind of image in an attempt to discredit all images. The matter is very complex, John shows.

John asks what may be depicted and how are images to be made (23.24–25). Predictably, John says that images may be made of "physical things that have shape, bodies which are circumscribed and have color." But images can also be made of beings that have no physical shape, of angels, for example. Bodily images of these can be fashioned, as Moses made images of the cherubim. Those who are worthy look upon such images and perceive "a bodiless and intellectual sight made manifest through physical means." John is really saying that images can be made of the projections of our thoughts and that an active congress between our thoughts and such images produces understanding of the deeper realities behind both the image and our thoughts about it.

John then insists that it was God Himself who first made images, beginning with his Son—the "natural image" (see the first kind above). John talks of Adam, Abraham, Jacob, Moses, Joshua, Isaiah, Daniel, and Paul, who saw in some way an image of God. God did not reveal in this way His divine nature but an "image and figure." All the persons who saw such images fell down and worshiped them, not as if they were God but in respect of God whose image they were. People today can do likewise, John says (3.26).[163]

This brings John to his last main topic: worship.[164] John differentiates between the absolute worship that is due to God alone and the relative worship that may be paid to created things. John's point is surely valid on theological grounds but, as Parry notes, the distinction between *latreia* and *proskynesis* "is a purely nominal distinction which cannot de distinguished in practice."[165] Lowden calls this kind of argument "weak" because it "requires every individual Christian to observe the subtle distinction between worship and veneration."[166] Auzépy, in her translation of the *Life of Stephen the Younger*, always translates *proskynesis*, in any form, as "prostration" so as to make clear that actual practices and not verbal abstractions are at issue.[167] Some later iconophobes were uneasy about this distinction and, as I shall show in later chapters, Western writers tended to be dubious about it.

For John, there are five kinds of absolute worship (3.28–32). First, the adoration given to God alone. Second, the awe and yearning we have for God because of His glory. Third, the thanksgiving we feel for all our blessings. Fourth is the hope we have that God will meet our needs. Fifth is repentance and confession. Of relative worship there are seven kinds (3.33–39). First is reverence for the holy places where God has rested. Second is the reverence for the places and things by means of which God has effected our salvation. Third is the reverence due to objects dedicated to God such as liturgical vessels. Fourth comes the images of future things seen by the prophets. Fifth stands our veneration for each other. The sixth concerns the veneration due to those who rule over us. Seventh is the respect paid by servants to their masters.

In few respects was John's thought original. Primarily he was comprehensive and organized where his predecessors, on both sides of the issue, had taken narrow views of limited aspects of the whole problem posed by images. Scattered through John's *Orations* are many comments on topics that we have already encountered. He says sight is our noblest sense (1.17). He complains about those who reject matter or who cannot abide the works of human hands (2.13–14, 19, 22). He insists that images can remind us of past deeds and help us to emulate them (2.10, 11). Christians simply are not idolaters and those who say that they are just do not know how to read the Scriptures (1.4, 5, 8, 24; 2.4, 7, 8). In all things the traditions of the church are to be maintained (1.2, 23, 26; 2.16, 20). Finally, John spoke angrily about the emperor's interference in dogmatic issues that were none of his concern in the first place, never mind that in his time Leo III was especially in error (1.1; 2.4, 12, 16; 3.41).

Writers had been saying for a long time that images of Christ could be painted because Christ had appeared as a man and His humanity was capable of description. This was an old argument by John's time. But John was a good enough theologian to know that Christ was not a "mere man." John realized that an image of Christ was more than a depiction of His humanity. Gerhart Ladner once said that the Christian concept of the image "was elaborated in the realm of the most fundamental dogmas about God and man."[168] Patrick Henry argued that the iconoclastic controversy was essentially about Christology.[169] Horst Bredekamp insisted that it was "inevitable" that the image controversy should emerge in the context of the Christological controversies.[170] What these writers fail to recognize is that it was none other than John of Damascus who made the argument over images into an argument about Christology in the first place.[171]

Prior to John's time people had often said that one could paint Christ's human nature. Yet Ladner observed, without quite sensing the implications of his observation, that John was the first to realize that the key issue was not nature but the more fundamental question of hypostasis.[172] John saw that the representation of the hypostasis of the second person of the Trinity was a very complicated issue.[173] It was not possible to represent the humanity alone because the humanity alone did not exist apart from the hypostasis of the Logos. It was also too simple to say that no one could depict the divine nature of Christ because no one had ever seen it. Once again, the key point was that the divine nature had no independent existence apart from the Logos. Thus, Christ had appeared as a man and had been seen. The being who had been seen could be depicted like any other being. But Jesus Christ was not like any other being. As one, discrete metaphysical being, one hypostasis, Christ had two natures, one human and one divine. But as these natures had no independent existence so neither could be depicted alone, or separately. Any depiction of Christ, therefore, revealed, in some mysterious way, the single Logos. To John this was not a sort of theological game, for any denial that Christ could be depicted threatened the reality of the incarnation and thus called into question the central mystery of the Christian faith and the whole divine economy of salvation. John had transposed an ancient discussion into a new key. He made the debate over images into a Christological controversy.

John's third contribution to the image controversy is to be found in the large collection of authoritative sources that he appended to his *Orations*. The surviving manuscripts do not make it easy to perceive the original form of the patristic (35), conciliar (2), and hagiographic (6) sources that John assembled.[174] John may have gone searching for just these references or he may have encountered them in the course of his long life and wide reading. One student of John's work asserts that John's oeuvre contains no fewer than 738 citations of 258 works by 48 authors.[175] John was a scholar of formidable erudition. Writers on images before John tended to cite a few biblical passages and sometimes one of the classical image texts, such as the well-known passages from Basil or Gregory of Nyssa. John, however, pulled together an unprecedented dossier of materials.

With characteristic acuity Averil Cameron has studied the way in which texts became weapons in the early Byzantine period.[176] As early as the fifth century polemical literature, often in dialogue form, began to proliferate. At the time of the Fifth Ecumenical Council (553) vast florilegia of proof-texts began being adduced. In 680 the Sixth Council, famously called by Adolf von Harnack a council of "antiquaries and paleographists,"[177] was concerned about falsified extracts and brought in whole books under lock and key. During the seventh century, as we have seen, there were Christian-Jewish arguments about images—witness Leontius of Neapolis and Stephen of Bostra. Before John of Damascus no one had so thoroughly surveyed the Christian past for the texts that bore on images, although there was the modest anthology put together in Rome between 726 and 731. Recently, Alexander Alexakis has demonstrated the preparation of a massive iconophile florilegium, probably in Rome, in about 770. This collection was then expanded in 774 or 775 and, probably in its shorter version, sent by Hadrian I to Tarasius along with his letter of 785. Thus, John's collection, plus the one of 770, perhaps as emended a few years later, served as the basis for the texts cited at Nicaea in 787.[178]

In all cases, attempts to pull together clinching testimonies was an exercise in appropriating tradition. We have seen that iconophiles usually said that images were of ancient usage and that no church council had ever prohibited them. By assembling a body of evidence from the traditions of the church, John buttressed this argument from tradition as never before. In doing this, John inserted images into the agenda of issues, previously mainly Christological, that had been debated by textual jousting matches in the previous two or three centuries. John also put opponents of images in a difficult position. Even if they were not satisfied by his refutation of the charge of idolatry, by his patient differentiation of the various kinds of images, and by his delineation of the types and objects of worship, then those opponents now had to tackle his scholarly dossier. They had to challenge either the authenticity or the relevance of his citations, or else they had to come up with authorities of their own. As noted above, the period down to the early 750s was, as far as can be discerned, quiet on the subject of images. That silence would lift.

Constantine V, Hiereia, and the Peuseis

During the reign of Constantine V we finally get substantial, coherent evidence for the iconophobe position. The *horos* of Hiereia was read out at Nicaea *in extenso* along with its biblical and patristic florilegium. This precious source permits us to hear the iconoclasts speaking in their own voices (I assume this; others might not). Similar in deriving from an iconoclast but dangerous as to their provenance are the *Peuseis* (*Inquiries*) of Constantine V.[179] The emperor apparently delivered as many as thirteen speeches on the topic of images between about 752 and 754 and then prepared two sets of questions which he submitted to the bishops for scrutiny and confirmation. The speeches do not survive and it is not clear that they are in any case identical in substance or argument to the *Peuseis*.[180] The latter survive only as fragments extracted by George Ostrogorsky from the *Antirrhetikoi* of Partriarch Nicephorus. The fragments are probably reasonably accurate; the technique of quoting the passage to be refuted having a long pedigree in Christian argumentation. Moreover, canon 9 of Nicaea (751D–E) required that copies of the iconophobes' books be put in the patriarchal library. Nicephorus would have had easy access to those books. But, then, he wrote his *Antirrhetikoi* between 818 and 820 when he was in exile and away from his library. Let us suppose that his memory was good or that he had notes. There remains the fact that in quoting only short extracts Nicephorus deprives us of any sense of the context, sequence, or elaboration of Constantine's arguments. Still, we are glad to have some of his *ipsissimi verbi*.[181] Finally, the *Nouthesia*, the treatise *Adversus Constantinum Caballinum*, and the treatise *Adversus Iconoclastas*,[182] although iconophile and polemical, supply some valuable information.

There exists a complex relationship between the *Peuseis* and the *horos*. Let us begin with the former. The first *Peusis* opens by confessing that the Catholic Church and all its members hold Jesus Christ to be one person in two natures, His divinity and humanity having been joined together without confusion (frag. 141). An image, Constantine says, must be one in being with what it represents (frag. 142, καὶ εἰ καλῶς ὁμοούσιον αὐτὴν εἶναι τοῦ εἰκονιζομενοῦ). So Constantine puts the question of how it would be possible to make an image of a being who has two natures, one spiritual and one material (frags. 144–46). No image is possible, the emperor says, because any attempt to make one necessarily involves "circumscribing" the divine nature and this is impossible (frags. 150–51).[183] Likewise, the artist cannot make an image of the flesh alone. If a painter makes an image of the flesh alone then he adds a fourth person to the Trinity—three divine persons and a human one (frag. 149). Thus it is impossible to describe in an image of one nature a person who exists in two natures. There is no image capable of achieving this (frags. 156–59).

The second *Peusis* explores whether or not the eucharist can be an image of the body—of the human nature—of Christ (there being no possibility of having an image of the divinity). Constantine referred to the bread and wine of the eucharist and said that Christ commanded His disciples and apostles to transmit these as a visible reminder of His love (frags. 164–65). Here is an image of Christ's body that comes from Christ Himself. This is the only proper and possible image for the bread and wine are the body and blood of Christ (frags. 166–67). Not all bread and wine figure Christ, of course, but only those consecrated by the priest. Thus what had been made by human hands becomes that which was not made by human hands (frag. 168).

Constantine may not have used Chalcedonian terminology quite correctly but his ideas are basically consonant with important strains in ecclesiastical tradition.[184] When the Council of Hiereia met to address the image question and to respond to Constantine's inquiries, the bishops basically added rigor and precision to the ideas of the emperor.[185] The council did not take up Constantine's idea that an image ought to be *homo-ousios* with what it represents.[186] Instead, the bishops developed Constantine's Christological reflections. Those who misunderstood Christ's humanity, they said, were the heirs of Arius and of the *Acephaloi*—the extreme Monophysites—while those who would separate the divine and human natures were descendants of Nestorius (241E–245E). Fundamentally they agreed with Constantine about the impossibility of making an image that did not either circumscribe the uncircumscribable divinity or else separate the humanity from the inseparable union of natures (252A–260A).[187] Constantine's idea about the eucharist as an image was retained but refined a bit (261E–264C).[188] Obvioulsy the bishops at Hiereia were not subservient. They responded thoughtfully to Constantine's "questions."

But the bishops did more than just respond to the emperor. "The first and recurrent motif of the *horos*," says Stephen Gero, "is the argument that Christian image worship is an artifice of the devil, and represents a resurgence of idolatry." The council betrays, he goes on, "a genuine hatred and fear of a poisonous remnant of paganism."[189] Lucifer, out of rage and jealousy, decided to alienate man from God by tempting him to worship creation instead of the creator (212E–213A).[190] Jesus may have saved humans from idolatry but the devil has cleverly reintroduced it (216D–221D). Paganism and idolatry were important issues for the iconophobes. But even more important to them was rejecting the idea that images were somehow equivalent to words.[191] They would not accept that images could convey true knowledge of theological realities. Byzantium's rulers therefore assembled bishops to scour the Scriptures for what they say about how false colors draw the mind down from pure spiritual worship to the base worship of material creation (229D–E). Worthless and dead matter simply cannot capture the glory of God or the virtue of the martyrs and saints. Texts alone can do this (277C–D).[192] One of the council's anathemas excoriates those who through "material colors" seek to understand the Word in His humanity (336E), and another anathema savages those who attempt to reproduce in themselves the virtues of the saints by looking at "inanimate and speechless icons made of material colors" when they could turn to books, to "animate icons" (345C–D). An interesting remark says that there is no prayer to consecrate an icon (268C). A picture is, and remains, common and worthless.

Much of this line of argumentation is familiar to us by now, but to place it in context, one must reach back over the age of Leo III to arguments more typical of the fourth and fifth centuries. It is true that Hiereia's biblical florilegium has the scriptural prohibitions of images, although it may be significant that Exodus 20.4 is missing, having been replaced by Deuteronomy 4.12 and 5.8. The biblical catena opens with John 4.24, and continues with 1.18, 5.37, and 20.29 (280E–284C). In other words, any straightforward application of the Mosaic prohibition has been avoided. Perhaps this owes something to John of Damascus's theology. It cannot be mere coincidence that John is accorded a particularly personal and brutal anathema (365D); he clearly was a thinker with whom the Hiereian bishops felt a need to reckon. But it may be that the references to John's Gospel reveal what is really going on here and show an advance in iconophobe thought. The repeated emphasis on worship "in spirit and in truth" coupled with complaints about dross matter suggest a deeply felt sense that worship, to be authentic, had to be fundamentally spiritual. Nothing in this created world is commensurate with the uncreated divinity, and nothing made by humans can elevate humans to an understanding of God. Notice how, in his eucharistic thought, Constantine talks of how what had been made turns into something unmade (ἐκ τοῦ χειροποιήτου πρὸς τὸ ἀχειροποίητον). Only in this unmade state can the eucharist figure the body of Christ. There is a Platonism here of a sort that had severe doubts about material reality and there is a theology here that is profoundly transcendent.[193] There is also a theology here that realizes the full implications of John of Damascus's Christological reflections on images.[194] Whereas John was drawn to say that in some mysterious fashion an image of Jesus' humanity could reveal His divinity, the bishops assembled at Hiereia were at great pains to show that this simply could not be the case. For the first time, in other words, image theologians are really grappling with each other's ideas.

In a second area Hiereia extended a bit beyond Constantine. The emperor was at some pains to argue that he had never separated himself from the church, and he appended a patristic florilegium to his *Peuseis* as a way of asserting his adherence to tradition.[195] At the council, bishops talked constantly about tradition. Again and again, the bishops trumpeted their faithful adherence to the six ecumenical councils (217A–B, 233B–237C). In an adroit move, the bishops cited the ways in which the six councils addressed the great Trinitarian and Christological issues of antiquity and of how they themselves agreed with the findings of those councils. This move assumes its full meaning when it is taken in conjunction with the council's perfectly Chalcedonian (237D–E) profession of faith and Christological argumentation about icons. The bishops were saying that, because a proper understanding of the second person of the Trinity, namely theirs, forbids icons, then all earlier ecumenical councils had also forbidden icons because they too had this proper understanding of the being of Christ. The fact that the council appended a patristic florilegium was another way of claiming solidarity with the church's great tradition, and at the same time of disputing John of Damascus's appropriation of that tradition on behalf of images (292D–324A). The Council of Hiereia was professedly conservative. High on its list of aims was an attempt to show that the iconophiles were innovators. And, to repeat, there are historical grounds for arguing that "traditional" iconophilia was *relatively* innovative in the century before Hiereia.

From the various iconophile writings that are contemporary with Constantine V, it is possible to form some sense of the current thinking of those who defended images. Some sense only: For as we have only Nicephorus's extracts from Constantine's *Peuseis,* so too we have from the iconophiles mainly their attempts to refute Constantine's propaganda campaign, the *Peuseis,* and the *horos.* Much of their thinking is quite clear but we do not have, as in John's case, a full and systematic exposition.

No less than their opponents, the iconophiles laid claim to the ancient and universal traditions of the church. The author of the treatise *Adversus Iconoclastas* cried out in anguish that images had been honored for 745 [*sic*] years and were only now being attacked.[196] As an interesting way of taking up the patristic duel, the author of *Adversus Constantinum Caballinum* says it is better to follow Basil, John Chrysostom, and Gregory Nazianzus than Pastillas, Triccaccabus, and that "foul pest" the patriarch Constantine.[197] Having had professions of faith hurled at them, the iconophiles flung them right back.[198] To the charge that Christ did not command images to be made, the iconophiles responded that images are of ancient usage and there are many things in the church which reach right back to the apostles even if one cannot find that Christ or an apostle commanded their observance.[199] There are two novel developments in iconophile argumentation. First, they began appealing to certain ancient images. Specifically, they referred to the Lucan portrait of Mary and to the Abgar image of Christ,[200] a tactic called by Robin Cormack "one of the more desperate suggestions of the iconophiles to support their case" and "an audacious strategy."[201] Second, in their recitations of the six councils, to which they professed complete allegiance, the iconophiles began citing the eighty-second Trullan canon, the one that commanded the representation of Christ as a man rather than as a symbol, for instance, a lamb.[202] This text, not surprisingly, was not cited at Hiereia and would be prominent at II Nicaea. On both sides, then, we can see that the battle over images was becoming a battle for the right to define the traditions of the church, to keep the church's memory, to validate its history—understood dually as the past itself and the right to record that past. Indeed, the last years of the eighth century and the first years of the ninth were rich in historical writings and reflections, almost entirely by iconophiles.[203] By making icons contemporary with Christ, by insisting that all six earlier ecumenical councils had affirmed icons, and by asserting that the unbroken tradition of the church validated icons, the iconophiles made icons an inseparable part of the *paradosis*. They took long steps toward creating, with respect to icons, that sense of immobility that has so long been attributed to Byzantine history.

Next, the iconophiles carried on with the old argument that matter had its uses and was not necessarily evil. After protesting that they do not worship manufactured things and that they do not adore walls, colors, or matter,[204] the iconophiles reformulate their exculpations more positively, as their predecessors had long done. That is, they say that many manufactured things are worthy of veneration: the cross, the Gospels (that is, books), liturgical vessels, the church, the altar.[205] Another reason for defending images is that they can help to lift people from the world of everyday reality to the higher realms beyond. Images can draw their viewers up "from sensible things to invisible ones."[206] The iconophiles and their opponents have two very different approaches to the world of material reality. If the iconophobes are Platonists, there is a sense in which the iconophiles are Aristotelians. It would be hazardous in the extreme to insist that either camp was consciously or explicitly following one of the Greek masters, but the general thrust of their thought is unmistakable.[207]

Finally, the defenders of images said that painters merely paint what writers put into books. "Every image that we *read* in church," says the author of *Adversus Constantinum Caballinum*, "*narrates*, like a speaking image,' and opens the feelings and the mind that we might emulate them" (my emphasis).[208] Images can indeed remind their viewers of the deeds and of the virtues of the saints.

Gazing at a scene of the crucifixion can inspire worship.[209] The iconophiles of mid-century, like John of Damascus before them, believed sight to be the noblest of senses.

As far as I can see, no iconophile thinker of this particular period took up Constantine's idea that an image should be one in being with what it represents. Likewise, the eucharistic teaching of both Constantine and Hiereia seems to have gone unremarked. The Christology of these writers is a little hard to grasp. They rejected the charge that they were guilty of circumscribing God's divinity or of separating His natures, but they did not advance a positive doctrine of their own. If they agreed or disagreed with John of Damascus's rather daring treatment of the Christiological implications of images, they did not say so.[210] The iconophiles did object to the idea that Hiereia was ecumenical, both because it had no patriarchal representation and because it departed from the ancient traditions of the six councils.[211] This argumentation was based on prevailing synodal theory and found easy acceptance at II Nicaea. It is easy to see why the bishops at Hiereia were so insistent on calling their synod ecumenical. The arguments about tradition, about matter, and about sight were old and had recently been reiterated by John of Damascus. They too found acceptance at Nicaea.

Yet just as John himself is, at least by name, almost absent from Nicaea's records, so too are the iconophile writings of mid-century. The reason, I would argue, is that the *Nouthesia* as well as the treatises *Adversus Constantinum Caballinum* and *Adversus Iconoclastas* were relentless in their repudiation of Constantine V. Indeed the *Adversus Constantinum* put about the story that the emperor got his nickname Copronymous ("Dung Named") because he had fouled his baptismal font.[212] The ideas these authors proffered were already available but they themselves would have been an irritant to Tarasius's elegant *oikonomia*.

The Arguments of II Nicaea

In addition to treating a number of extremely sensitive issues, such as rehabilitating iconophobe bishops and not tarnishing the reputations of Leo III and Constantine V, II Nicaea also had to address the topic of images. The assemblage did this primarily by negation. That is, rather than offering a systematic and comprehensive statement about images, as both John of Damascus and Hiereia had done, Nicaea's bishops took the cautious line of devoting most of their attention to a detailed refutation of the decisions of Hiereia. Even in advancing their refutation, however, the bishops confined themselves mainly to criticizing

Hiereia's interpretative techniques and that council's departure from tradition. In other words, Nicaea repeatedly said, "It is wrong to believe *that*," but almost never went on to say, "and so it is necessary to believe *this*." From Nicaea's negations it is possible to form a tolerably clear sense of what the iconophiles in 787 chose to present as the chief faults of the iconophobes but only a limited sense of what the iconophiles themselves actually believed about images.

In the midst of session one, as bishops Basil of Ancyra, Theodore of Myra, and Theodosius of Amorion were admitted to the council, each bishop had to follow his profession of faith with a set of anathemas (1010C–1011B). These anathemas are repeated, almost verbatim and in nearly the same order, at the end of sessions four and five, the sessions which reviewed the Bible and the church fathers as well as the writings of ancient heretics (128C–E, 201B–D). At the end of session seven, after the *horos* and signatures (397C–400A), and again in session eight (416A–C), the formal conclusion of the council held back in Constantinople at the Magnaura Palace, the anathemas are repeated once again. These condemnations reveal clearly the problem as Nicaea wished to frame it. Nicaea anathematized those who apply passages of Scripture against idols to images; those who call images idols; those who say the church ever admitted idols; those who say that Christians regard images as gods; those who ascribe deliverance from idolatry to anyone but Christ; those who add to or detract from the teachings of the apostles and fathers; and those who innovate. In one form or another, the anathemas also touch those who refuse to salute (usually some form of ἀσπάζομαι to salute, greet, embrace, kiss) the holy and venerable images. The anathemas in session eight also attack those who refuse to accept all written and unwritten traditions of the church as well as those who reject Gospel stories expressed by images.

What we meet here is the ancient charge of idolatry. This charge played a role in 754, to be sure, but took a place there alongside arguments about how images confused or separated the natures of Christ and about the priority of hearing (or reading) to seeing. The latter two subjects did indeed come up elsewhere in Nicaea's documents, as I will show. But 787's primary view of the failings of 754 amounted to its false accusation of idolatry. A second issue is plainly to be seen in the anathemas: innovation. Nicaea claimed that heresy infused the proceedings in 754 precisely because the bishops gathered there departed from tradition and, in so doing, innovated. Reduced to essentials, the argument from negation holds that images should be embraced, images are not idols, no one should depart from the traditions of the church. This hardly does justice to the sophisticated thinking of Constantine V and his bishops. Nicaea tends more to polemic than to apologetic.

How did Nicaea get to these negative conclusions? The bishops under Tarasius's direction proceeded in a rather interesting way. In the fourth session, Nicaea's bishops assembled the biblical and patristic testimonies used in 754. In the fifth session Nicaea dredged up virtually all imaginable heresies. And in the sixth session Nicaea cited and refuted the *horos* of Hiereia. In case after case, Nicaea's bishops demonstrated how a passage had been taken out of literary or historical context and, in isolation, had been taken as a general statement. Nicaea was especially harsh in attacking Hiereia's use of mere extracts (πιττάκια), and the Nicene fathers were careful to use whole books, mostly drawn from the patriarchal library and in a few cases presented by participants.[213] In some cases, when Hiereia had cited a particular passage from a work by a church father, Nicaea cited other passages from that father to show that the preponderance of that writer's testimony told for and not against images. In the case of a writer like Eusebius, the bishops in 787 agreed that he had spoken against images but then they dismissed him as an Arian heretic: wrong about one thing, wrong about everything. Finally, Nicaea adopted the strategem, especially in the case of Epiphanius of Salamis, of denying the authenticity of his allegedly iconophobe writings. All of this exegetical and hermeneutical labor is sophisticated and impressive. But it has the overall effect of negating what 754 said by challenging how 754 went about its work.[214] It does not have the effect of substituting positive doctrine for erroneous.

The council also expressed itself in affirmative terms. First and foremost, II Nicaea became the first church council to endorse images and the veneration paid to them. In its *horos* Nicaea says:

> We declare that, next to the sign of the precious and life-giving cross, venerable and holy icons—made of colours, pebbles, or any other material that is fit—may be set in the holy churches of God, on holy utensils and vestments, on walls and boards, in houses and in streets. These may be icons of our Lord and God the Saviour Jesus Christ, or of our pure Lady the holy Theotokos, or of honourable angels, or of any saint or holy man. For the more these are kept in view through their iconic representation, the more those who look at them are lifted up to remember and have an earnest desire for their prototypes. Also [we declare] that one may render to them the veneration of honour: not the true worship of our faith which is due only to the divine nature, but the same kind of veneration as is offered to the form of the precious and life-giving cross, to the holy gospels, and to the other holy dedicated items. Also [we declare] that one may honour these by bringing

to them incense and light, as was the pious custom of the early [Chris-
tians]; for "the honour of the icon is conveyed to the prototype." Thus,
he who venerates the icon venerates the hypostasis of the person depicted on it. (377D-E, trans. Sahas, p. 179)

The eighty-second Trullan canon had merely said that if there were to be images,
then they should be figural and not symbolic. Nicaea declares that images *may*
be put up and that they *may* be venerated. It is important to see that the council
did not require the presence of images and did not enforce worship (veneration)
of them.

Before analyzing in more detail this key section of the *horos*, let us note the
structure of the *horos* as a whole. The definition begins by saying that Christ
delivered his people from idolatry and then promised to be with them for all
time. Some people deviated from right thinking and from tradition and introduced heresy by failing to distinguish between the sacred and the profane.
Therefore Constantine and Irene called together a council so that by common
deliberations the ancient traditions of the faith might be reaffirmed. Central to
those traditions is the faith itself, to affirm which the council's definition cites
the Nicene Creed. The council then anathematized all those who, beginning
with Arius, spoke against the teachings of the six councils, each of which met to
affirm a particular teaching that had been attacked. The bishops then say that,
in sum, they preserve all the traditions of the church that exist in written or
unwritten form. Only at this point, about two-thirds of the way through the
horos, did the bishops speak the words quoted above. That set of remarks about
images is followed by yet another claim of adherence to tradition.

The importance of adhering to tradition is the absolutely central argument
of II Nicaea.[215] "There is," says Kenneth Parry, "a sense in which the entire
controversy over images could be said to center on the place of tradition in the
Byzantine church."[216] The imperial *sacra* read out in session one say that the
council has been called to decide in accord with the six councils, with the regulations of the fathers, and with the ancient rules of the church. Only through
tradition can there be unity in the church. John, the legate of the East, was
concerned that the council establish the admissibility of formerly iconoclast
bishops on immaculately traditional grounds so that the present council would
be in good order. Tarasius told Gregory of Neocaesarea that he would have been
much better off had he held fast to tradition and avoided profane innovation
(citing 2 Thess. 2.15 but changing κενοφωνίας into καινοθωνίας). When
Hadrian's letters were read they were followed by a series of affirmations to the
effect that the pope's statements were in accord with tradition. In writing to the

Eastern bishops, Tarasius cited Trullan canon eighty-two and in session four Elias, the archpriest of Blachernai, said that very canon changed him from a persecutor to a worshiper of images. The whole of session four was devoted to a scrutiny of the holy books of the Christian tradition. In session five Tarasius said that there were sufficient proofs from the holy fathers to establish that icons were of ancient lineage in the church. Again and again Nicaea asserted that the first six councils accepted icons and, therefore, there was no call to challenge them. The *horos* of the council appeals to tradition repeatedly. In the first place, then, II Nicaea was claiming for itself ecumenical validity because it was in conformity with the tradition of the church.

Obviously Nicaea was also asserting that one of the key traditions was cult images. Image testimonies are cited abundantly in session four, and in session five an attempt is made to show that, in the past, only heretics had attacked images. In session six the council says that the painting of images goes back to the apostles, as one can tell from looking at churches and from reading histories (220A). The six councils of the church preserved faithfully all the written and unwritten traditions, and one of these is the painting of images. Indeed, every council except the one of 754 accepted images so images must be alright and 754 must be wrong. Nowhere in all of this argumentation and testimony do the fathers of Nicaea attempt to justify images only on their own terms. Always it is a matter of tradition first.

But it is not exclusively a matter of tradition. That is, images are also valid for certain didactic reasons.[217] They help to call to mind the scenes of the Bible, the struggles of the martyrs, and the labors of the saints. Images strengthen belief. They awaken all the senses. They lift people up to the glory of God. They encourage ordinary people in their daily travails (for example, 1014C–D, 9D–E, 9E–12A, 17E–20D, 220E–221A, 225A, 232B, 288C–D, 300C, 301C, 304A, 348C–D, 360C; these statements are so common that it would be otiose to cite more examples). Images may be particularly helpful for instructing the unlettered (1014D, 9E). Images are a "form of writing" (1014E). They are the equivalent of the written word, a substitute for it, an extension of it (1014E, 20C–D, 220A, 232C, and so on).[218] "We learn the same things, that is, how to recall what has taken place" (221A). Images are thus traditional but also utilitarian, pragmatic. They can actually help to teach, to inculcate the very traditions of which they are a part.

As the *horos* says, images are holy in respect of what they represent, not in respect of what they are. Images are material, to be sure, but matter should not be condemned simply on the grounds of its sheer materiality. It is important to ascertain what matter is used for. Similarly painting is neither good nor bad

(241B–C). It is, once again, a matter of why the painter paints and what he paints. The council affirms saints, relics, and images—in that order. The council draws parallels between images and the cross, the Gospels, veils and vestments, and sacred vessels. Broadly speaking, one can say that iconophiles were open to many channels of divine grace. Some of these were material and some were human in the form of the monks admitted to the council and showered with sympathy for their recent sufferings. The iconophobes, on the other hand, sought to limit rather severely the channels along which divine grace could flow.[219] Essentially they stopped at the word of God and of approved writers, at the consecrated bodies of ordained priests and bishops, and at the eucharist. It is important to bear in mind, however, that images were, even at Nicaea, only one means of sanctification and not necessarily the most important one.[220] The council records, for instance, refer far more frequently to miracles performed by the saints themselves or by their relics than by their images.[221]

Just as Nicaea's bishops were anxious to establish that images were not worshiped as gods, so too the council was keen to show that pure worship, worship "in spirit and truth," was accorded only to God, never to an image, to Mary, or to the saints. Images received the relative worship of honor. Images are venerated, honored, approached, saluted, kissed, embraced only because of their prototypes and because they remind people of those prototypes and awaken zeal for them (56A–B, 68D–69A, 212C, 225A, 232C–D, 240A, and so on). In addition to repeated discussions in the council's sessions there is a long disquisition on worship in the council's letter to Irene and Constantine (404D–408D). Nicaea's treatment of the topic of worship appears to me to be the only place where the writings of John of Damascus were used in a serious way.[222] Even here, however, John was not cited by name. The point of all the words lavished upon worship is really to establish once and for all that images had always been accorded an appropriate measure of respect and Hiereia had perversely misunderstood this.

With this the basic teaching of II Nicaea stops. Let us review the basic points. Tradition permits, almost demands, images. Images are functionally equivalent to words. Texts and pictures can each recall to memory the narratives of the Bible, the heroism of the martyrs, the virtues of the saints, and the teachings of the fathers. Those teachings can both provide examples and lift up the viewer to the contemplation of the higher, more glorious realities of the heavenly realm. Images are owed a deep and reverent respect because of the stories or persons they represent. Acts of reverence undertaken before an image are referred to the prototype. In many respects these were old ideas. One can search the tradition from the fourth century to the early eighth and find, scattered all across the textual landscape, virtually every element of this teaching. What was new in the eighth century was the rigorous and comprehensive definition and affirmation of these ideas.

Yet some issues that arose in the eighth century did not reappear fully at Nicaea. The issue raised by Constantine V in his second *Peusis*, namely that the eucharist was the authorized icon of Christ's body, was rejected in one brief passage of the sixth session's refutation of Hiereia (264D–268A). It is interesting to note that this argument, although central to Constantine's second inquiry, was not actually affirmed by Hiereia. That Nicaea addressed it at all suggests, first, that the *Peuseis* may have been available at Nicaea and second that, here again, the Nicene bishops did not wish to address the former emperor directly. Thus they left this argument aside.

More important is the way Nicaea dealt with the Christological argumentation that was central to the thought of both Constantine and Hiereia. It will be recalled that in the 750s the iconophobes maintained that any image of Christ either confused or divided His divine and human natures. This line of thought marked a considerable advance on earlier iconophobe arguments to the effect that, because "no one has ever seen God," no one could make an image of Him. I argued above that Constantine and Hiereia did not introduce this Christological dimension but instead that they were responding to the ideas of John of Damascus. John was not content to say, with the tradition, that because Christ had appeared as a man His human nature could be depicted like the human nature of any man. For, as John says, Christ was not a "mere man." He was a single being with two natures. Any image of Christ was likely, in some fashion, to reveal—and perhaps too to recall to mind—both God and man. Moreover, since God had become human precisely to make it possible for humans to become more like God, the whole economy of salvation depended in some way on the depiction of Christ. To deny His "depictability" was in some way to attack the reality of His incarnation and thus to call into question the possibility of salvation. The iconoclasts seem to have understood this argument and to have tried hard to counter it.

Nicaea spoke on the matter of Christology many times but in a rather timorous way. Although de' Maffei thinks that the writings of John "ooze out continuously from between the folds of the Council of Nicaea,"[223] it seems to me that Nicaea actually blanketed John so as to make him invisible. He is named exactly once—at the point where his anathema was rescinded (357B–C). On this occasion John is praised as one who lifted up his voice in protest against those who attack Christ and Christ's people, but nothing is said about John's actual teaching. In all the patristic references—thirty-one authors in fifty-two texts plus twenty-three hagiographical sources—John is not mentioned once.²²⁴ The one place where John's teaching may have made a real contribution is in the sections dealing with the kinds of worship properly accorded to God and to other holy things. I have argued that Nicaea did not wish to bring up John for to have done so would have exposed his deep hostility to imperial interference in dogma. But I think there is another reason. Nicaea did not wish to raise the level of Christological speculation occasioned by images. In a real sense, the council of 787 held to the line that had been articulated by Germanus and by many before him. Because Christ had appeared as a man He could be depicted and such depictions were neither idolatrous nor blasphemous because they did not "circumscribe" Christ's divinity.²²⁵

Because John, Constantine, and Hiereia had raised the level of Christological debate, however, and because Nicaea chose to proceed more by negation and refutation that by positive argumentation, the bishops in 787 were led into some slightly ambiguous or even contradictory statements. The only explicitly Christological statement in the *horos* says, "he who venerates the icon venerates the hypostasis of the person depicted on it" (377E). If this statement is to be related to Christ, then it might appear to correspond with John's teaching. The picture of any saint or apostle would reveal only that person's hypostasis as a human, albeit the picture would, or would not, depending on one's general attitude to images, reveal the virtues of that person. But Christ was a unique hypostasis, a unique person, in which two distinct natures had been enhypostatized. Thus a picture that revealed *His* hypostasis might well be though to reveal His divinity. This goes beyond what Germanus had said and goes to the heart of what Hiereia had tried to prevent.

Reading this single line from the *horos* against earlier statements, however, makes it a little difficult to see exactly what the Nicene fathers intended. For instance, in rejecting what Hiereia had to say about the Nestorian implications of an image of Christ, Nicaea said that true Christians make an image "in so far as 'the Word became flesh'—that is a perfect man—'and dwelt among us.' God the Word circumscribed Himself when He came to us in the flesh. No one could possibly think of reproducing His divinity, however, because 'no one has ever seen God.' He is uncircumscribable, invisible, and incomprehensible, although circumscribable according to the humanity" (244A–B, trans. Sahas, p. 77). This passage refutes the charge of Nestorianism effectively but leaves open just a little the possibility that an image reveals the Word who became flesh in more than merely His human form. But as the text goes on that door is closed a bit but not shut tight. "For we know Christ to be of two natures, and in two natures, that is a divine and a human one, without division. The *one*, therefore, which is uncircumscribable and the *one* which can be circumscribed *are seen* in the *one* Christ [my emphasis]. The icon resembles the prototype, not with regard to the essence, but only with regard to the name and to the position of the members which can be characterized" (244B). Continuing, the passage says that a painter who depicts a man does not seek his soul in the depiction and that no one who looks at such an image sees a body separated from its soul. Hiereia is accused of "hair-splitting." This is certainly more than Germanus had been willing to say, but less than John had said.

A bit later in the sixth session, the Nicene fathers approached even closer to John. "If the divine nature was circumscribed together with the human nature by his being laid down and wrapped in swaddling clothes inside a manger, so is his uncircumscribable divinity in the depicted image of his human nature. So it is (N.B. *is*, not *was*: the reference is either to the eternal presence of the crucifixion or else to the particular presence of that event in an image) on the cross. If the divine nature was circumscribed with the human nature, so is his uncircumscribable divinity together with the depicted image of the human nature" (253D–E, trans. Sahas, pp. 86–87). This statement appears to push to door open a bit farther but then comes another qualification. "They accuse Christians of describing the incomprehensible and undescribable nature of Christ. . . . Christians . . . iconograph Him in so far as 'the Logos became flesh'" (256C). "No one of sound mind," they continue, "looks in any way to the image for the qualities of the prototype" (257D). From this point on the Nicene fathers turn to a demonstration that the image and its prototype differ in essence (260E–261D). By shifting the discussion to the ontology of images, by saying that the image is not one in being with its prototype and Christ is one in being with His father, the council narrowed once again the door's opening but they did not close it. That is, they did not finally, definitively say what the image represents, what it reveals. Nor did they say *how* an image reveals. Nor did they say what an image is.

Nicaea took as its task the refutation of Hiereia's Christological argument that an image of Christ either confused or split His natures. In this refutation Nicaea was quite confident. But at the same time, the council did not assume responsibility for defining the essence of the hypostasis depicted in an image of Christ. The council fathers went farther than Germanus and the tradition had gone, but less far than John had gone. Only in the ninth century, as I will argue in Chapter 6, did the question receive a fuller explication. That Nicaea left things on a slightly ambiguous plane is only to be expected. The council wished to reject recent novelties and to assert faithfulness to the ancient teachings of the church. Grand speculations about images would not have served either purpose.[226] This may be why Nicaea did not take up John's careful differentiation of the many kinds of images any more than Hiereia had done so. This set of ideas was not part of the tradition. There is also, finally, the profoundly pastoral dimension of II Nicaea that we have noted already in other contexts. The council of 787 wished only to say to the council of 754, "You departed from tradition. Let us agree to put things back as they always were." The Council of 787 did not wish to say, "Let us all agree to something new." That might have been very difficult to accomplish in the tense circumstances of the mid-780s. "One has the impression," says Schönborn, "that the fathers wished to avoid all disputed questions."[227] Or, in the elegant formulation of Aidan Nichols, Nicaea displayed "a certain intellectual chastity."[228]

Conclusion

This long and detailed discussion has attempted to identify the most crucial things that were done and said during Byzantium's eighth-century encounter with images. The following chapters will turn to the West on the basis of an understanding of what ideas were in the air.

Ideas about the place of icons have become fixed in Orthodox thinking, but have done so in ways that make it seem as though both iconodulia and its theological defenses are part of the most ancient traditions of the church. As we have seen, there was much about which it was possible to argue in the eighth century precisely because widespread iconodulia was rather recent and no *consensus patrum* had ever been formulated on this charged topic. Later iconophile writers depicted the iconophobes and the iconoclasts as persons who broke with the authentic traditions of the church. In fact, those who opposed the possession or veneration of icons viewed the devotions to which those objects were increasingly subject as innovations and as a form of idolatry. Worship, they said, was to be "in spirit and in truth," and could not be relayed to God or to the saints through material objects, and should never be directed to those objects themselves.

Iconophile writers defended images as consistent with the most ancient traditions of the church. Faced with the charge that neither the Scriptures nor the fathers spoke unambiguously about images, let along about icons (in the narrow sense in which I have been using that term), the iconophiles adverted to unwritten tradition, in a sense to arguments from silence. On both sides, there was a keen desire to lay claim to tradition. The image quarrel was fundamentally a battle for tradition, for a right reading of history. But that history looks different now than it did to the victors in 787: "The Second Council of Nicaea did not reestablish the cult of icons; it established it."[229]

One iconophile writer, John of Damascus, brought the full weight of his massive learning to bear on images. He developed further than anyone before him an intricate set of differentiations among forms of worship and among types of images. One might say that for John there existed a vast hierarchy of images that began with Jesus as an image of the Father and that extended downward to any icon. In this view, images were both evidence for and participants in the whole economy of divine salvation, which was itself rooted in the incarnation, the historical act that, in a way, legitimized images in the first place: Jesus was a man and could be depicted like any man. Yet John's ideas were too bold, too novel, too difficult to be fully embraced in the eighth century.

John's writing moved iconophobes to refine their treatment of the subject of idolatry and to address for themselves the ontology of images. For the iconophiles it was axiomatic that images were legitimate just because they were different from the person they represented. For iconophobes an image had to be like, not just look like, its subject. With the single exception of the eucharist, no "be like" image existed. Moreover, iconophiles were relatively open to material, visible channels of grace whereas iconophobes thought that matter was incapable of communicating invisible grace.

Issues that had for centuries appeared only occasionally and in isolated contexts were in the eighth century gathered together and aired quite fully. But in the end, at Nicaea, traditional positions were adopted. The boldest thinker, John of Damascus, was deftly shunted aside just as, interestingly enough, the most original iconophobe, Emperor Constantine V, was carefully sidestepped by the bishops at Nicaea. This is the intellectual background against which the West must be set.

The "iconoclastic controversy," supposedly running from the 720s to the 780s, was also about loud shouting, persecution, harassment of monks, and the destruction of art. Actually, there were only a few brief periods of active hostility to images: the years just around 730, the period, roughly, 752 to 754, and the years from 765 to 767. The last of these periods was actually so complicated in its actions and motivations that it is hazardous to say what proportion iconophobia or iconoclasm possessed within the totality of what took place. Iconoclasm, whatever caused it and whatever it meant, happened rarely and never seems to have absorbed the full energies of the Byzantine state.

It is difficult to find many victims of iconoclast persecution. Germanus was forced to resign, but he was hardly the only patriarch who failed to get along with a reigning emperor. It is impossible to name another victim in the time of

Leo III. Victims in the years just around Hiereia are hard to discover. There were plenty of victims in the mid-760s, and then in about 771, but it is rarely easy to say with confidence that those victims suffered because of their attachment to icons, no matter what later sources might have said or implied.

It is, finally, simply not the case that Byzantium's patrimony in religious art was destroyed. As it happens, the familiar and exuberant decorative schemes of Byzantine churches are the products of the post-iconoclastic era. Some of the reasons for this fact will attract our attention in later chapters. We must not suppose, however, that iconoclasts had available to them the innumerable repertoire of targets that it is all too easy to imagine. Some images survived right through the period, usually ones that were safely out of reach. But surely it is striking that those arch iconoclasts Leo III and Constantine V tolerated for so long so many offending pictures in the palaces and churches of Constantinople. The last few years of the 760s seem to have seen the destruction or covering-up of more art than the whole rest of the iconoclastic period taken together. There was destruction. But it was not systematic. People and art were not continuously in grave peril in eighth-century Byzantium.

Finally, the eighth-century texts discussed here regularly use the word *eikon*, which as I said in Chapter 1 can refer to any image, be it a fresco or mosaic or a portable panel painting. One surprising element in all the texts, however, is the relative absence of references to the kinds of pictures I discussed in Chapter 1, to icons proper. Nicaea did authorize the veneration of images. The bishops said that veneration usually took the form of *aspamos*, kissing, touching, hailing, embracing. But the range of practices that supposedly proliferated in the period between about 500 and 700 are conspicuous by their absence. The surviving sources afford limited access to the objections of the iconophobes. Scanty though it is, none of that evidence portrays anyone recoiling in horror before scenes of people bathing icons, scraping their surfaces to obtain healing powder, or hanging them outside their shops. On the other side, iconophiles were modest in their claims on behalf of icons. It is hard to find any explicit defense of the kinds of practices that Ernst Kitzinger took to be characteristic of icon practices in the sixth and seventh centuries. It may well be that, as I argued in Chapter 1, the icon was still relatively new and rare in the eighth century. Therefore, iconophobes objected to images of any sort and iconophiles did not treat icons as central to the tradition. Perhaps Nicaea's limited statements about cult practices associated with religious art add up to one more instance of the avoidance of novelty.

CHAPTER THREE

Art and Art Talk in the West in the First Age of Iconoclasm

Throughout the world, wherever Christianity is to be found, these holy images exist and are honored by all the faithful so that by a spiritual effect our mind may be elevated through the visible countenance to the invisible majesty of the divinity through the contemplation of the figured image according to the flesh which the son of God deigned to take on for our salvation.
—Pope Hadrian I, letter to Charlemagne, 792

BEFORE THE FRANKS became involved with the image controversy, the eighth century in the West was bracketed by two authors who talked about art in terms bearing substantial similarity to those with which we have become familiar in surveying late antiquity and early Byzantium. One of these is the Anglo-Saxon Bede and the other is Pope Hadrian I. For most of the eighth century, the evidence is sparse and unforthcoming; it is rarely easy to make sense of what people thought, said, and did during the period when Byzantium was addressing the problems and possibilities posed by images. The present chapter has a two fold aim: to tease out a history of Western art talk in the eighth century and to set the stage for the extensive Frankish discussions of the 790s.

We saw in Chapter 1 that, apart from some strange doings in Serenus's Marseilles and some ambiguous and, I insisted, atypical passages in Gregory of Tours, there was no real discussion of art, and certainly no arguments about it, before the eighth century. Bede was aware of the earliest stages of Byzantine iconophobia, and by the 790s the Franks were excoriating the "bogus council of the Greeks," that is, II Nicaea. So it stands to reason that the Western discussion was engendered by the Eastern one. That the Western discussion was not indigenous is already one important point to establish. More important, however, is establishing what people in the West knew, when they knew it, and how they responded in the decades before Theodulf wrote the *Opus Caroli*.

Put a little differently, this chapter, and the ones that follow, argue along vertical and horizontal planes. The vertical argument is basically chronological. It explores how the positions eventually adopted in the Frankish world were built up from preceding developments. The horizontal argument follows two parallel tracks. One investigates the extent to which what the Franks said was spurred by, consistent with, or opposed to what was being said in the East. The other explores how what the Franks said about art sheds light on what they said about other topics, and vice versa.

Art Talk in Bede's World

The first Western echoes of the quarrel over images sounded far from the Mediterranean, in Northumbria. They rang in the writings of Bede (673–735), a scholar of immense learning and wide connections. Bede commands attention not only because he is the first transalpine witness to the new controversy over images, but also because he provides some hints about what was being said in various places in the early stages of that controversy. He himself actually had a good deal to say about art and therefore provides at least one gauge of Western views on that general subject. Finally, his writings circulated widely and were highly influential.

Chapter 2 mentioned in passing the little that the *Liber Pontificalis* says about concrete issues in the early days of the image quarrel. It is important to have in mind what the *Liber Pontificalis* said because Bede is believed to have had a working copy of the *Liber Pontificalis* containing an as yet unfinished *Life* of Gregory II.[1] Between 729 and 731, and probably closer to the latter year,[2] Bede interrupted his allegorical exegesis of the Old Testament's description of Solomon's Temple to say this: "There are people who think we are prohibited by God's law from carving or painting, in a church or any other place, representations of either humans or animals or objects of whatever kind, on the grounds that He said in the Ten Commandments 'You shall not make.'"[3] This explicit reference to the Exodus prohibition does not appear in the *Liber Pontificalis* and that work speaks only of a prohibition of images of Jesus, Mary, the apostles, and the saints; it does not speak of animals or objects. There are two issues here, one relevant to these immediate circumstances and one important for the whole historical context of the early phase of the image controversy. The first point is where did Bede get his information? The *Liber Pontificalis* does say that Gregory II wrote to Christians everywhere.[4] Conceivably some such letter reached England. More likely, Bede learned what was going on in Rome and Constantinople from his trusty informant on Roman affairs, Nothelm.[5] A larger and more important point is that Bede's informant, whether Nothelm or someone else, told him only of the condemnation of images on the basis of Exodus 20.4. This was the gravamen of the charges that circulated among the Bithynian bishops and between them and the imperial court. Bede thus provides an interesting confirmation of the relatively modest intellectual focus of the controversy at its inception.

Bede had a discerning eye, a keen interest in material culture, and an ability to create beautiful word pictures.[6] Any reader of his *On the Temple* or *On the Tabernacle* could not possibly overlook the sheer delight Bede took in describing and then allegorizing gold, silver, bronze, cedar and olive wood, rich colors and thick textures in wool, linen, and animal skins. Bede always thought that only the finest things were worthy of symbolizing God, on the one hand, and of honoring Him, on the other. He evinces absolutely no trace of the tendency we detected in various late antique and also eighth-century Byzantine writers to speak of dross matter as intrinsically unsuited to holy purposes. Such matter could be abused, of course, but properly employed it was positively beneficial. He says explicitly that "[t]he making of objects or animals is not forbidden. Rather, what is entirely prohibited is making them for the purpose of idolatry."[7] He cites Exodus 20.3–5 as a clear statement about images of alien gods made by the gentiles for cult and worship.

Bede's attitude as to why cult art is permitted is worth quoting, even though it is not original. He says, again in *On the Temple*: "They (the iconophobes) would not say any such thing if they called to mind either the work of Solomon . . . or if they considered the works of Moses."[8] He goes on to say, "If it is permissible to raise up the brazen serpent on a tree that the Israelites may live by looking at it, why is it not permissible that the exaltation of the Lord our Saviour on the cross . . . be recalled to the minds of the faithful pictorially, or even His miracles and cures . . . since the sight of these things often tends to elicit great compunction in the beholders and also to make available to those who are illiterate a living narrative of the story of the Lord. For in Greek too a painting is called ζωγραφία, that is living writing."[9] Just a little further on, in describing the great purification basin in the Temple and its decorative details, he asks why, if sculptures ran along this basin to a length of ten cubits, we cannot "carve or paint"[10] stories of the saints and martyrs?

All of this was by then familiar and traditional. The Bible itself warrants the making of images and describes many of them. Images have the capacity to move people in commendable ways. And images can teach the illiterate what the literate learn in other ways. If there is anything at all new here, it is Bede's passing remark that images might be sculpted as well as painted. As far as I know, Bede never expresses the "referential" defense of images—the idea that an act of worship performed before an image is referred to the person represented. Nor does he ever offer a Christological defense of images. The referential defense had deep roots in antiquity but it had either not reached England or failed to take root there. Christological arguments, as I argued in Chapter 2, must primarily be attributed to John of Damascus who was in Bede's time utterly unknown in the West (and whose first two *Orations* were written near the very end of Bede's life). There had long circulated what I have called the relatively simple "incarnational" defense of images—Jesus was a man and could be painted like a man—but Bede does not mention this defense.

Bede actually did talk a good deal about art, and historians of art and architecture are delighted to have his descriptions and commentaries because much of the material evidence for the visual arts in Bede's world has vanished. I have mentioned already his luxurious accounts of the Temple and Tabernacle. Such descriptions are ubiquitous in Bede's exegetical works. Perhaps statements in his more obviously historical books can serve, *pars pro toto*, as examples of the kinds of things Bede is likely to have said.

In the first book of his *Ecclesiastical History* Bede recounts the arrival in England of Augustine and his companions, dispatched to the ends of the earth by Pope Gregory I. The intrepid missionaries landed on the isle of Thanet just off the coast of Kent, and when they informed King Æthelberht of their arrival, he ordered them to stay where they were. After a few days the king himself came to Thanet and ordered Augustine and his entourage to approach him. They complied "bearing as their standard a silver cross and an image of our Lord and Saviour painted on a panel. They chanted litanies and uttered prayers to the Lord for their own eternal salvation and the salvation of those for whom and to whom they had come." The account then continues without further mention of the cross or panel painting. One senses in this account a rather grand liturgical procession designed both to impress and to reassure. Æthelberht had insisted on meeting the missionaries in the open air for fear that, in an enclosed building, they might subject him to some magic.[11] The cross and panel painting will both have come from Rome. The cross itself will have been like the processional crosses that are met repeatedly in Roman sources. The painting is more interesting, but it is impossible to say anything about it: where it was made, what it looked like, where it had been before Augustine and company acquired it. Nevertheless, Bede does not say that it was some kind of palladium or that anyone was expected to venerate it. Indeed, he seems uninterested in its details.

Early in his *History of the Abbots* (of Wearmouth and Jarrow) Bede enumerates things that Benedict Biscop brought back from Rome. In fifth and last place he mentions: paintings of holy images which he brought back to adorn the church of blessed Peter the Apostle which he had built; and also an image of the blessed mother of God and ever virgin Mary and likewise of the twelve apostles which he attached plaque by plaque to an arched beam in the center of the nave stretching from wall to wall; and images of the Gospel story with which he decorated the south wall; and images of the visions of the apocalypse of blessed John with which he equally adorned the north wall so that everyone who did not know letters, no matter which way they looked, would always be able to contemplate on the lovable sight of Christ and of his saints, although in an image.[12] A little further on he relates that after his sixth visit to Rome Benedict brought back numerous books and, once again, images. These included "paintings of the Lord's story," with which he encircled the church of Mary in the monastery; paintings in the monastery of St. Paul illustrating the concord of the Old and New Testaments; Isaac carrying the wood with which he was to have been immolated, and a corresponding painting of the Lord carrying his cross; another pair of Moses holding up the brazen serpent and of the cross holding Jesus.[13]

What Bede actually says about discrete images in his own monastery accords well with his more theoretical statements. These images are beautiful and enhance worship. They help the unlettered to learn. In and of themselves, they represent straightforward representations of biblical scenes. For Bede, that is enough. He does not describe the images in detail, does not say what they looked like, who painted them, or where they came from in the first place (if not Rome). He never mentions them again. He certainly never speaks of any act of veneration connected with these images or of any miracles associated with them.

That Bede declines an explicit attribution to images of the power to do more than inspire and teach may just be significant in view of his treatment of a text which he knew well: Adomnan's *On the Holy Places*. Supposedly Adomnan had an opportunity to interrogate a shipwrecked pilgrim who had made a pilgrimage to the Holy Land and who was an eyewitness to the miraculous punishment of persons who had desecrated images of St. George and of Mary.[14]

Adomnan, for his part, transmits this story without comment. He wrote before iconoclasm and, as far as we can tell, expressed no views on art, sacred or otherwise. But Bede, near the end of his *Ecclesiastical History*, mentions Adomnan and his informer Arculf and then cites several passages from *On the Holy Places* describing some key sites in the life of Jesus.[15] The *Ecclesiastical History* was finished in 731, not long after Bede wrote the lines quoted above concerning Byzantine iconophobia. Arguments *e silentio* are always dangerous, but it is worth thinking about whether Bede might have mentioned the miraculous chastisement of those persons who damaged images if such occurrences seemed familiar, or even likely, to him.

Before leaving Bede, it is worth pointing out just how widely his works circulated and how influential he was. One has only to scan the pages of Laistner's *Hand-List of Bede Manuscripts* to see what a massive presence Bede was for later medieval people.[16] Generalizations apart, however, Bede's countrymen played a decisive role in the religious and intellectual life of continental Europe in the eighth century. Willibrord, the "Apostle of Frisia" who lived until 739, was a fellow Northumbrian. Boniface founded churches, monasteries, and schools all over what is now central Germany. Late in his life he was asking for works by Bede.[17] In the 760s, in circumstances that will be considered later in this chapter, Lull of Mainz, Boniface's successor, requested a copy of Bede's *On the Temple* from Wearmouth.[18] Alcuin, who was one of Charlemagne's key advisers, knew and admired Bede and was, in a sense, the great Northumbrian's intellectual grandson. Theodulf knew Bede. Indeed, he cited him in the *Opus Caroli* and drew inspiration from him in decorating his own chapel at Germigny.

To sum up: In Bede, and perhaps by extension in Bede's readers, we can perceive the initial dimensions of what the West knew about the East, and of what the West itself was thinking. On the first point, the West knew only—it seems—that some people understood the Exodus prohibition in extremely and unacceptably literal terms. On the second point, God was worthy of beautiful things; matter was created by God and therefore not quintessentially bad; art could inspire; and art could teach.

Textual Evidence from Rome, ca. 726 to ca. 760

Between the 720s and the mid-750s the political and institutional life of Rome experienced crucial changes as the popes liberated themselves from the Byzantine Empire and allied with the Franks. Several factors were of high significance in this process: Byzantine tax policies, namely efforts by the administration in Constantinople to raise money in Italy for use in defending Anatolia and the Balkans; continuing Lombard attempts to expand their holdings in central Italy and to join together the kingdom proper in the north with the Duchies of Spoleto and Benevento that lay astride and to the south of the lands in central Italy claimed by the popes; and the religious policies of the imperial government, particularly iconoclasm.[19] With the invasion of Lombardy by Pippin III in 755 and 756 the Franko-papal alliance commenced in practical terms, while the years between the late 750s and the late 760s witnessed a complicated triangular diplomacy among popes, Franks, and Byzantines. This section addresses what can be known about Rome's reactions to and continuing interest in Byzantine iconoclasm.

Normally, when investigating the papacy in the early Middle Ages, the historian must blend together the evidence of the papal correspondence with that of the *Liber Pontificalis*. For present purposes, however, the letters are useless. On the one hand, the letters of Gregory II allegedly read at II Nicaea are so corrupt that they cannot be put in the dock and interrogated. On the other hand, the surviving and authentic papal letters say almost nothing about images or any controversy concerning them until 766/67.[20] This fact may just be of some significance. If we compare the letters pertaining to the 760s, 770s, and 780s with those that survive from the period down to about the mid-750s, one thing is striking. In the later letters, no matter what the pope had on his mind at the time, he almost always managed to say something about Lombard depredations and then, after the fall of the Lombard kingdom, about his properties in Italy. The relatively few surviving letters from the period 726 to 750 address various concerns but never raise the issues of images, Byzantine heresy, or papal defense of the faith.[21] If these were central issues to the popes, in either personal or policy terms, it is odd that they never come up. I would not care to suggest that the popes were uninterested in or unaware of the image controversy in Byzantium, but I do think it worth asking whether, on the basis of the surviving correspondence, we should view the issue of images as ranking rather low on the priority list.

The *Liber Pontificalis* has more to say and is a work of semi-official character that emerged from the papal administration itself.[22] It presents a different picture than the letters but there are ways in which the two kinds of evidence agree with each other.

In chapter 17 of the *Life* of Gregory II, right in the middle of an extended discussion of intense political squabbling over the emperor's attempts to raise taxes in Italy and to impose his will there, we read: "In the mandates he later sent, the emperor had decreed that no church image of any saint, martyr or angel should be kept, as he declared them all accursed; if the pontiff would agree he would have the emperor's favour; if he prevented this being carried out as well he would be degraded from his office. So the pious man despised the prince's profane mandate, and now he armed himself against the emperor as against an enemy, denouncing his heresy and writing that Christians everywhere must guard against the impiety that had arisen."[23] The "mandates" do not survive. But it appears from this account that they involved more—"as well"— than just the issue of images. Indeed, Gregory had led a tax revolt and thwarted the will of a series of imperial officers.

Gregory II's *Life* continues, mainly narrating the ongoing strife in Italy, and then in chapter 23 says that the emperor was attempting to force his will on everyone in Constantinople to take down images "wherever they were"—in chapter 17 only images in churches are mentioned—to burn them in the center of the city, and to whitewash painted churches. Chapter 24 continues the thread by saying that many people opposed the emperor and that some were mutilated and others beheaded. The deposition of Germanus is also mentioned along with Gregory's refusal to countenance his successor, Anastasius, unless he returned to the Catholic faith. The *Life* then concludes, quite traditionally, with lists of Gregory's donations to Roman churches and his ordinations.[24] These accounts are decidedly stingy with details.

The *Life* of Gregory III (731–41) is not much different. From that text, from references in the poorly transmitted records of a Roman Synod of 769,[25] and from references to Gregory's work in the correspondence of Hadrian I (772–95),[26] we know that he held councils to condemn eastern image policy 731.[27] The second chapter of Gregory's *Life* reads as follows: "He was bishop in the time of the emperors Leo and Constantine, while there was raging the persecution they started for the removal and destruction of the sacred images. . . . On behalf of these, just as his predecessor of sacred memory had done, this holy man sent written warnings, with the authority of the apostolic see's teaching, for them to change their minds and quit their error."[28] We saw in Chapter 2 that Gregory's emissaries were unable to proceed to Constantinople. Gregory now called the largest synod to have met in Rome since the middle of the seventh century—seventy-nine bishops according to one source (Hadrian's letter), ninety-three according to another (*Liber Pontificalis*)—along with the priests and deacons of Rome and the local nobility. The *Liber Pontificalis* reports that this synod decreed, "If anyone thenceforth, despising the faithful use of those who held the ancient custom of the apostolic church, should remove, destroy, profane and blaspheme against this veneration of the sacred images . . .

let him be driven forth from the body and blood of our Lord Jesus Christ and from the unity and membership of the entire church."[29] The decrees of this council or a summary of its views were sent to Constantinople but once again the emperor's people prevented the documents from arriving. A little later, the *Life* says, people all over Italy rose up in defense of images and the pope wrote yet another letter to the emperor and to the patriarchal intruder, Anastasius. Gregory held another synod in 732, to which we will turn shortly, but with the report of the synods of 731 the *Life*'s treatment of Gregory's involvement with the image controversy breaks off. About three-quarters of the *Life* is silent on the subject. But the anathema just might be helpful as an explanation of why papal sources subsequently say so little about the image controversy. Perhaps Rome's view was that, once the iconophobes had been excommunicated, and given that they included in their number the emperor and the patriarch, the case was closed until the Byzantines decided to change course.

From later evidence we learn that Gregory's second council in 731 prepared a patristic florilegium in defense of images.[30] As we observed in Chapter 2, battle by florilegium was by the eighth century a well-tested method in the Eastern Christian world, and it had been used at the Roman Synod of 649. It is not surprising that Gregory put local scholars to work collecting relevant testimonies. Papal officials probably knew Greek and had access to key texts. Moreover, there was a large Greek religious community in Rome.[31] Gregory's response to the issues posed by images were a little precocious and suggest a higher degree of concern about images than his letters. That is, as we saw in Chapter 2, Emperor Leo III called no councils and, as far as we can tell, John of Damascus, acting in a private capacity, first assembled a dossier in favor of images in the East.[32] Hiereia then produced the first dossier against images. Gregory demanded that the iconophobes return to the true faith. Perhaps to clinch any arguments about what the faith was, which means what the tradition held, he had his florilegium prepared.

Unfortunately, only a few fragments of that florilegium are extant, and then only in later writings. The fragments that can be recovered give at least some idea of what kinds of arguments were used in Gregory's Rome. The bishops who assembled in 769 said that all their predecessors had defended the honor and respect due to images and that images were useful to the memory and elicited compunction.[33] From the wording of the passage and from its context, it seems certain that the florilegium prepared in connection with the council of 731 is meant here. With a little detective work, it is possible to reconstruct at least some of that florilegium.[34] Twelve *testimonia*, three biblical and nine patristic, can with considerable assurance be assigned to the council of 731. On a conservative reconstruction, the florilegium of 731 contained these references:

Biblical *testimonia*:
1. Exodus 25.1–22: Description of the adornment of the Temple.
   Hadrianum, 1. 12, p. 19.
2. 3 Kings 6.23, 32: Description of the cherubim on the Arc sculpted from olive wood and the cherubim carved into the doors of the Temple.
   Hadrianum, 1. 12, p. 19.
3. Numbers 21.8–9: Moses setting up the brazen serpent as a sign.
   Hadrianum, 1. 26, p. 27.

Patristic *testimonia*:
1. Pseudo-Athanasius, *Quaestiones ad Antiochum ducem*: Why, if statues and likenesses are not adored, images are. The answer is that images are not adored the way statues of the pagan gods are, or were.
   Hadrianum, 1. 34, pp. 31–32; Conc. Rom, p. 87; Böhringer, pp. 102–3.
2. Pseudo-Dionysius the Areopagite, *Epistula X ad Iohannem*: Visible things can lead one to invisible things.
   Hadrianum, 1. 36, p. 32.
3. Pseudo-Dionysius the Areopagite, *De coelesti hierarchia*: Images can elevate minds from the corporeal to the incorporeal.
   Hadrianum, 1. 36, pp. 32–33.
4. Cyril of Alexandria, *Thesaurus de sancta et consubstantiali Trinitate*: Looking at a carefully made image of the emperor leads to admiration for the emperor, not for the image; and the same is true in recognizing someone's signature.
   Hadrianum, 1. 37, p. 33.
5. Gregory Nazianzus, *Oratio 45 In Sanctum Pascha*: God commanded Moses to make everything just as things had been shown to him on the mountain. Again, theme of visible and invisible things.
   Hadrianum, 1. 47, p. 36.
6. Gennadius of Marseilles, *Liber sive diffinitio ecclesiasticorum dogmatum cap. 73*: On the appropriate honor due to relics.
   Hadrianum, 1. 59, p. 41; Conc. Rom., p. 87 (?).
7. *Preces clericorum et monachorum ad Iohannem constantinopolitanum*: Account of the conciliar condemnation of a heretic who removed

gold and silver images of doves and who said it was not necessary to call holy the Holy Spirit in the form of a dove.

Hadrianum, 1. 59, pp. 41–42.

8. Pseudo-John Chrysostom (Severianus of Gabala), *Sermo in quinta feria pascha*: Proper understanding of the honor to be paid to imperial images.

Hadrianum, 2. 13, p. 47.

9. Gregory I, *Epistola ad Serenum*: Unlettered read in pictures what the lettered read in books.

Hadrianum 2. 1, pp. 42–43.

It must be remembered that reconstructing the materials used in 731 from later records, especially from Hadrian's letters, is risky because Hadrian had occasion to cite only those texts which he needed in 785 and 793, and not a whole florilegium. Put differently, it is unlikely that we have more than a fraction of the texts contained in the 731 florilegium.

Looking cautiously at the evidence at our disposal permits a few insights into what was discussed in Rome in 731. The biblical passages adduced there all pertain to instances where God commanded images to be made. These are wholly traditional in this context and, as noted above, they accord with Bede's remark that people would not object to images if they only considered God's words to Moses. Bearing in mind that Bede seems to have heard something about an excessively rigid application of the Exodus prohibition at Byzantium and then cited the Bible itself as authorizing images, it is interesting to note that in Rome the same position was being adopted and, with the passage on Moses' brazen serpent, the very same passage was being cited. But we have seen that passage turn up in many contexts over the years, always with the same strategy: If someone cites Exodus 20.4 against images then cite back against him other passages where God commanded images to be made.

The patristic passages brought forward in 731 also raised traditional arguments. These may be grouped into several categories. In various ways the topic of imperial images comes up as a suitable analogy for thinking about Christian images. The old point is made that it was not the image of the emperor that was honored but the emperor whose image it was. Although we only know of Rome citing this point directly by means of the peculiar pseudo-Athanasian text and indirectly by an extract from Cyril, it was an old argument that could have been buttressed by many relevant passages. Gregory and Cyril, although in quite different ways, say that images can recall to mind biblical stories in the one instance and people in the other. A philosophical argument is advanced that images have the ability to elevate human thoughts from this world to the next. That is the point of the citation from an alleged letter of Dionysius the Areopagite to John the evangelist. Dionysius argued that images are merely visible versions of invisible things, that when the "invisible cohorts" are painted with colors, it is possible for our minds to grasp them. Put a little differently, material (visible) things permit us to pass over to immaterial (invisible) things. There must have been some discussion of the ontology of images. Fathers were cited to show that images themselves were not holy because of what they were made of and that they did not share in the being of the persons whom they represented. An Antiochene allegedly asked Athanasius why, if he did not adore statues and likenesses, he did adore images. Athanasius responds that the faithful do not adore images as if they were gods, as the pagans do, but rather for love of the person depicted. He then says that if there were once an image on some wood but that the image had been effaced, then the wood could be burned. Athanasius supposedly said that Jacob adored the staff of Joseph not for any quality of the staff but because of whose it was. All of these kinds of arguments could perhaps have been advanced with better texts but all of the arguments themselves are familiar to us by now. Moreover, the little we can know for certain about issues then current at Byzantium suggests that these kinds of arguments fit well into their historical and chronological context.

Two other aspects of the deliberations in Rome are a little different and require separate consideration. There is a slightly obscure passage from Gennadius of Marseilles which maintains that relics ought to be honored as if they were "*membra Christi*" as well as basilicas dedicated in the names of saints and places devoted to worship. Two other fragments that appear in Werminghoff's edition without attribution seem to me to be related to this one and the three may originally have formed part of a longer passage that made clearer sense. This fragment says that it must be carefully guarded against that, on account of icons, or perhaps because of discussion of them, a bad situation does not grow worse and someone prohibit the veneration of relics just as the "*membra Domini*" are venerated. The next fragment says "if we wish to have the company of the saints, then we really ought to venerate the relics not only of their bodies but also of their clothes, the basilicas dedicated in their names, and their images and their countenances, wheresoever painted, with the most frequent marks of respect." This strange set of extracts implies that there was discussion of images and relics, to be sure, but also of the locus of the holy; at least that is how I think one must take the statements about basilicas and places dedicated to worship. It is not otherwise known that this set of issues was discussed in Byzantium so perhaps these texts open up a view on an issue unattested in extant Eastern sources. Yet it is hard to see why people in Rome would have meandered off down this path without provocation.

The second issue that calls for a bit of independent discussion pertains to miraculous or what we might call "active" images. Pseudo-Athanasius says that a demon promised to stop tormenting some people if they would cease honoring an image of Jesus and Mary. This only shows that in Jerusalem, where the events allegedly took place, some people honored an image of Mary holding Jesus on her lap. The extract does not tell us the end of the story but does go on to say that if images did not have in them the power of God they would not ooze holy oil and would not bleed if pierced by a missile. This is, as far as I can see, the first instance of "active" images turning up in the West in an authoritative (papal, conciliar) context which extends beyond the ambiguous hints in Gregory of Tours and Venantius Fortunatus. We noted in Chapter 2 that miraculous images, despite what later iconodules said about them, were comparatively recent and not very numerous. Still, the topic may have had just enough currency around 731 that such images either had to be defended or else themselves served as a defense against iconophobia.

Two final points may be made about the evidence that derives from the Roman Council of 731. First, it was the Roman Council of 731, and not II Nicaea, that for the first time required the veneration of images under pain of anathema. This will be well to bear in mind as we consider later papal and Frankish positions in the image controversies. Second, the language in these fragments, on the very subject of what sort of cult was offered to images, is completely inconsistent. The words *adorare* and *venerare* are used interchangeably, and are mixed with *colere, diligere,* and others. This deserves emphasis because Augustine much earlier, John of Damascus a bit later in the eighth century, and Theodulf in the *Opus Caroli* all tried to maintain a sharp distinction between "adoration" and "veneration" but it seems that, at least in Rome, no such distinction was observed.

Turning back to the *Liber Pontificalis,* one has to wait until chapter 20 (of 29) of Zachary's *Life* (741–52) for even a hint of the image controversy. And it is only a hint. We read that he sent an "orthodox synodic letter" to the "church of Constantinople" and another to "the serene prince."[35] Normally patriarchs, at the time of their own installation, sent their peers synodic letters, a combination greeting, introduction, and profession of faith. Similar letters were usually sent to emperors as well, although this matter is a bit more complicated because in at least some cases emperors insisted on a prior right of approval before an elected candidate was consecrated and installed. In any case, Zachary wrote to the *church* of Constantinople, if the *Liber Pontificalis* is accurate, and not to

Anastasius. Moreover, he notified the emperor of his election—he was the last pope to do so. But the *Life* indulges in no rhetoric on this occasion: not a word about images; not a single charge of heresy; not one personal attack on the emperor or patriarch, although Zachary's failure to name the patriarch might be an implicit criticism. Once again, judging only from this *Life* one would have to conclude that images were not the primary issue on the pope's agenda.

The *Life* of Stephen II (752–57) has no reference at all to the image controversy. This is particularly striking in view of the fact that the Council of Hiereia met in 754. To be sure, Stephen faced acute Lombard pressure in Italy and he initiated complex diplomatic maneuvers, first with the Byzantines and then with the Franks, to try to alleviate the strains and to reclaim lost properties. Stephen figures prominently in the general history of Europe because in 754 he traveled to Francia, concluded a formal alliance with the Franks, and crowned Pippin as their king. These were important and pressing concerns but surely it is striking that the *Life* has not a word to spare about heretical Byzantines or about Hiereia.

The *Life* of Paul I (757–67) is unusually short. Early on it says, without comment, "He was bishop in the time of the emperors Constantine (V) and Leo (IV)." There is one other reference to Byzantium and also to images: "He strenuously defended the orthodox faith, which is why he frequently sent his envoys with apostolic letters to entreat and warn the emperors . . . to restore and establish in their erstwhile status of veneration the sacred images."[36] But there is no explicit mention of Hiereia or the alleged brutal persecutions of the 760s, either in this *Life* or in the one letter to Pippin that discusses, briefly, the pope's efforts on behalf of images.[37] As we will see below, Paul was concerned about Byzantium, but his concerns were primarily connected with the, to him, alarming prospect of a Franko-Byzantine entente that might have left him defenseless against the beaten but unbowed Lombards.

Visual Evidence in Texts from Rome

In addition to what the *Liber Pontificalis* says about the basic historical issues involved in the iconoclastic controversy, the papal lives also provide significant evidence about papal patronage of works of art and describe some works of art in varying degrees of detail. Quite often the art works themselves and the places where the popes put them reveal important aspects of the papacy's response to Byzantine iconoclasm. It is true that the Roman economy was improving across the eighth century and that, therefore, some artistic endeavors were possible then which would have exceeded the means of most seventh-century popes.

Still, the real economic boom of the century followed the elimination of the Lombard kingdom in 773–74 and manifests itself most visibly in the pontificates from Hadrian I's to Leo IV's (772–853).[38] The art talk of the popes of the first half of the eighth century came less in words than in deeds, and those deeds took the form of impressive and provocative works of art that may well have represented serious drains on limited material resources.

Gregory III held a synod on Palm Sunday (April 12), 732 to institute a new oratory in St. Peter's and then to provide decorations and liturgical arrangements for that oratory. The oratory was intended to honor the Savior, His holy mother, the holy apostles, and all the holy martyrs and confessors "resting in peace throughout the world." The feasts of the persons there commemorated were to be celebrated with vigils kept by the monks of the local monasteries and masses were to be celebrated on their *natalicia,* that is, the days of their deaths when they were "born" into a new life in heaven. Thus far the only striking thing about this oratory is the breadth of its dedication: to all saints everywhere. Perhaps the pope was claiming that he had taken charge of looking after all the saints just as, in his excommunications the previous November, he had set himself up as guardian of the faith everywhere.

Into this oratory, however, the pope introduced an image of Mary and he adorned the image with a crown, jeweled necklace and earrings, and a silver cover (or frame). This evidence alone might lead us to infer a deliberate, spectacular, and solemn denial of imperial iconoclasm, but there is more evidence which turns inference into certainty. The *Life,* in detailing the liturgical arrangements instituted by the pope to maintain cult in his new oratory, says that these were "inscribed on stone panels."[39] A substantial fragment of that inscription survives. Moreover, ninth-century manuscripts transmit the canons of the Palm Sunday council. When marble and parchment are juxtaposed it appears that, in a case almost unique in early medieval Rome, the records of a church council were inscribed and hung in public. It is fascinating to observe that the conciliar records are dated by indiction year only and not by the regnal years of Leo III.[40] In 731 Gregory III had condemned Leo and his image policy. In early 732 the pope erected and consecrated with ostentatious ceremony an opulently decorated a new oratory dedicated to the cults of the Savior, Mary, and the saints whose images Leo was prohibiting; introduced an image of Mary into that oratory; and proclaimed, publicly and visibly, that the emperor's authority was no longer valid in Rome. Taken together the synod and oratory represent the implementation in Rome of the conciliar decisions taken in 731.[41] In revenge, Leo sent a fleet to ravage the Adriatic coast and transferred valuable patrimonies and church provinces in southern Italy, Sicily, and Dalmatia out of the pope's control. Bullying and tax gouging by imperial officials plus iconoclasm had combined to effect a split in the age-old ties between Rome and Constantinople.[42] Gregory seems to have gone on an image-decorating campaign in Rome. Perhaps shortly before the installation of his new oratory, he got six twisted onyx columns from the Exarch of Ravenna, Eutychius. These he arranged near the *confessio* of St. Peter in conjunction with the six similar columns donated to the basilica by Constantine and later moved when Gregory I rearranged the presbyterium. On top of these columns he placed beams which he coated with silver on which there were "depicted in relief" the Savior and apostles on one side and Mary and holy virgins on the other. In the oratory dedicated to the Bethlehem crib at Santa Maria ad Praesepe (later Maggiore), he placed a "gold image of God's mother embracing our Lord and Saviour, with various jewels, weighing 5 lbs." He "silvered an ancient image of God's holy mother and covered it with fine silver weighing 50 lbs." The image in Santa Maria sounds like a small statue while the unknown one that was "silvered" may well have been a painting that was given a magnificent frame and cover not unlike, say, the one of Innocent III that still covers the Lateran icon of Christ kept in the chapel of St. Lawrence (the *Sancta Sanctorum*) at the top of the Scala Santa. The *Liber Pontificalis* says that he restored the church of San Crisogono and installed "paintings" there.[43] These are now to be found, in an advanced state of decay, in the church that is below the level of the current basilica.[44] At the very least there were pictures of popes and martyrs. This artwork, too, appears to have been a calculated affront to the emperor's policies.[45] He restored and "painted" Santa Maria in Aquiro. He rebuilt and painted the *accubita*—probably the accommodation for the poor—at St. Peter's. Finally, he repainted the apse and donated a gold image, perhaps another statue, to St. Andrew's at St. Peter's.[46]

Gregory III's work was continued by his successors. Zachary built a new triclinium—a banqueting and reception hall—at the Lateran and covered it with mosaics and paintings. He built a tower at the Lateran, placed in front of it a "figure" of the Savior, perhaps a statue, and decorated one room with an image of the world. There has been some reasoned speculation as to whether the image of the Savior was a deliberate provocation occasioned by Leo's alleged removal of the Chalké image in Constantinople. This is possible, but it should be remembered that there is controversy over whether Leo actually removed a Christ icon from the gate to the imperial palace or replaced such an icon with a cross. That controversy turns, in part, around the relatively late date for the sources that report the removal. Thus, it is difficult to know what Zachary knew. Suffice it to say that the image was provocative. For instance, if Zachary's image referred to the Lateran fastigium of Christ, then the pope may have been drawing an implicit comparison between a good emperor, Constantine, and a bad emperor, Leo III. It is necessary to leave on the margin the question of whether Zachary's provocation was a direct response to a specific act on Leo's part.[47] Zachary's image of the world has been plausibly interpreted as a claim to universality.[48] He also adorned St. Sylvester's and the portico with "sacred images." Zachary's attention to the institutional center, to the government offices, of the Lateran is significant as a gesture for these were the first examples for more than a century of new construction in the area of the Lateran. Placing images in these very public places—the new triclinium was probably used for the Roman Council of 745—can hardly have escaped the attention of anyone who was aware of recent history. Zachary also gave altar cloths to St. Peter's bearing images of the nativity.[49]

The *Life* of Stephen II provides only one example of a new image which he caused to be made and placed in a Roman church. He put an "*imago*" of Mary in Santa Maria Maggiore depicting Mary seated on a throne and holding Jesus on her knees. He adorned it with jewels and placed it between two older images of Mary in silver; these he gilded. This particular image, which appears to have been a "Maria Regina" type, must have been a painting with an elaborate frame. I will come back to the image of Mary as queen. But under Stephen II another kind of image appears for the first time and with it another aspect of Rome's involvement with images. In 752 Aistulf was threatening Rome. Stephen "held a procession and litany in the usual way with the holy image of our Lord and Saviour called the *acheropsita*." The text goes on to say that a vast procession proceeded to Santa Maria Maggiore and that the pope carried the image on his own shoulders. The four major Marian feasts—Purification, Annunciation, Assumption, Nativity—had been organized by Pope Sergius I (687–701).[50] This passage is the first witness to the procession that, each year, set out on the vigil of the Assumption for the forum region where, after a *statio* in the old *Curia Senatus,* by then the church and deaconry of Sant'Adriano, the procession proceeded through the suburra to Santa Maria for morning mass. The image "not made by hands" is mentioned here for the first time too. Almost certainly this is the famous Lateran icon of Christ referred to above.[51] Images "not made by human hands" had appeared from time to time in Eastern sources by 752 but this is their first, or possibly second, such mention in Rome.[52] Was the image seen as a palladium? The *Liber Pontificalis* does connect this procession with the image to Aistulf's depredations in the countryside. But this might be a coincidence. That is, the Lateran icon was carried in procession annually on August 14–15 which probably provides a date for Aistulf's attack but cannot be taken to indicate that the icon was paraded through Rome's streets only because the Lombard king was threatening the city. There is no other account like this one.

The *Life* of Paul I attributes a number of images to him. He translated the body of St. Petronilla, allegedly St. Peter's daughter, from a cemetery outside Rome to a beautifully refurbished chapel just outside St. Peter's on the south side. Into this chapel he placed "wondrously beautiful pictures." Also near St. Peter's he remodeled a small church dedicated to Mary, Santa Maria ad Grada, and "decorated it magnificently." In another chapel near St. Peter's dedicated to Mary he introduced mosaics and an effigy of Mary "standing upright, of gilded silver weighing 150 lbs." This is undoubtedly a statue. Later he turned his own house into a monastery, San Silvestro in Capite, and he introduced mosaics.[53] Leaving aside the work in his own house, Paul's work was mostly taking place in the region of St. Peter's, an area with profound religious, ecclesiological, and ideological significance. This was the prime destination of Roman pilgrims, and the general vicinity of the residential quarters for foreigners. Prominent Franks routinely visited St. Peter's and Pippin's officials placed there, over St. Peter's grave, copies of the Franko-Lombard peace treaties and records of the submission of many of Italy's cities to Rome and the pope. The chapel of Petronilla became basically a Carolingian private chapel in Rome. The placement of images in this region is in a way a counterpart to Zachary's work in the Lateran region.[54]

Some additional interpretations can be teased out of these often vague references in the *Liber Pontificalis*. First of all, words. The *Liber Pontificalis* does not use the word *icona* before the middle of the ninth century. Normally the *Liber Pontificalis* uses the words *imago, effigies,* or *pictura*.[55] Any one of these words might signify an icon but, as Belting emphasizes, an icon is a moveable and autonomous image which usually features a single figure or a small group of figures. It permits the viewer to enter into particularly intimate relations with it and its physical existence is dramatized when it is put into motion.[56] Apart from the *acheropsita* mentioned in the *Life* of Stephen II in connection with the Assumption procession of 752, we have no evidence of an image that was carried around from one place to another. Moreover, large mosaics and frescoes are not conducive to intimacy. Occasionally the *Liber Pontificalis* mentions what were probably statues; references are ambiguous and may well refer to the beautiful gilding and framing often applied to pictures. Not once is an image described in detail.[57] We are never once told what one of them looked like. When the popes rebuilt or embellished a church they are said to have "decorated" it or to have "adorned" it, perhaps "beautifully" or "wondrously." One easily perceives a joy and pride in display, not unlike that which Dominic Janes takes to be characteristic of late antique church decoration and its associated ways of seeing, feeling, and thinking.[58] One encounters here a papal rhetoric and aesthetic that adapts the imperial "munificence" and "abundance" of late antiquity.[59] Not once, finally, does an image *do* anything. Even the *acheropsita* failed to stem the Lombard flood—if that is what it was asked to do—and its solitary appearance marks the only case where something was, perhaps, expected of an image.

Visual Evidence from Rome: Physical Remains

This is not the place to attempt a history of papal artistic patronage in eighth-century Rome, much less to survey the art itself. My primary focus here will rest on the papacy's adoption of the "Maria Regina" image in the eighth century and on what that image says about Rome and the popes in the age of iconoclasm. I shall also investigate some other images of Mary from Rome and some of the paintings in the Theodotus Chapel in Santa Maria Antiqua in an effort to understand the uses to which images may have been put in eighth-century Rome. In other words, I am going to study political and devotional images.

Beginning with John VII (705–7), whose pontificate fell before the iconoclastic controversy but who had poor relations with Byzantium, the papacy promoted an explosion of Marian imagery in Rome. Some of those Marian images took a very specific form—the so-called "Maria Regina"—and almost every pope of the eighth century put up his own image in connection with a Maria Regina image. This proliferation of regal Marys in association with popes requires an explanation.

What, exactly, is a "Maria Regina" image?[60] This is an image of a crowned and enthroned Mary. In the porch of Santa Maria in Cosmedin there is an inscription whose image has disappeared. It reads: *Praeclara virgo caelistis superexaltata et gloriosa domina mea Dei genetrix mater.*[61] Hadrian I installed in Santa Maria Antiqua a Maria Regina with the inscription MARIA REGINA; hence the name for the image. In this image, Mary wears rich clothing, perhaps richer even than that of a *basilissa*, and copious jewels. The familiar image of Theodora from San Vitale in Ravenna provides an excellent sense of what this image looks like, as do, in another medium, the coins of Licinia Eudoxia from the fifth century. The pictures seem to have been taken over from imperial art not only in appearance but also in composition. That is, Mary is often flanked by angels who are like the soldiers that flank imperial portraits. Moreover, and this has not been emphasized by earlier scholars, the Maria Regina images are sometimes depicted holding in their left hands the *mappa* (or *mappula*),[62] an imperial attribute that was later transferred to the consuls. This was the little napkin that was dropped to start races or games.

During the eighth century Maria Regina images were placed in St. Peter's, Santa Maria in Trastevere, Santa Maria Antiqua, San Clemente, San Lorenzo fuori le Mura, and Santa Susanna.[63] It is usually argued that the Maria Regina is an especially Roman image.[64] Ursula Nilgen calls it the "madonna of the popes." The first possible example appears to come from the triumphal arch of Santa Maria Maggiore and can be confidently dated to the third or fourth decade of the fifth century. One depiction of Mary on the arch as a *femina clarissima* anticipates, in a very public place, some features of the later Maria Regina.[65] The first unquestionable Maria Regina was painted on the so-called palimpsest wall in Santa Maria Antiqua in the early decades of the sixth century. By 575 that wall had been painted over so its image was not available as a model to John VII. What is more, the Maria Regina was placed in this building before it became a church. It may have been secular officials who were responsible for it. The seventh century saw no further Maria Regina images in Rome. There is a pyx from Grado whose cover bears the image and an isolated example from Durrës (ancient Dyrrachium).[66] The program on Santa Maria Maggiore's triumphal arch actually emphasizes Christ, however, not Mary.[67] Moreover, Rome did not have a strong cult of the Virgin before the eighth century.[68] Pope Boniface IV (608–15) did secure the Pantheon in Rome from Emperor Phocas and rededicated it as the church of Mary and All the Martyrs—later Santa Maria ad Martyres.[69] Pope Sergius I (687–701) regularized in Rome the four main Marian liturgical feasts.[70] There is, therefore, something unusual about the choices made by John and his successors.

In the sixth and seventh centuries the cult of the Virgin and corresponding representations of Mary became more and more prominent in Byzantium. There may have been "imperial" images of Mary in Constantinople for a long time.[71] At about the same time that the Maria Regina image was painted in Santa Maria Antiqua, the poet Corippus, in a panegyric addressed to Justin II, spoke of "Virgo, creatoris genetrix sanctissima mundi, excelsi regina poli" (Most Holy Virgin, mother of the world's creator, queen of heaven on high).[72] The Virgin came to be seen as the protectress of the city and her intercession was the city's primary salvation.[73] In about 600 the emperor Maurice introduced the feast of the Assumption.[74] The role played by Mary's images and intercession at the time of the Avar siege of Constantinople in 626 appears to have been the decisive moment in Mary's emergence as the capital's chief patron.

Starting with John VII popes began placing their own images in Roman churches much more frequently than their predecessors had done.[75] John put his image in a mosaic in his new oratory in St. Peter's (a fragment of it remains in the Vatican gardens), in two further mosaics in Santa Maria Antiqua, and in a majestic Marian image on a panel painting now in Santa Maria in Trastevere—the "Madonna della Clemenza."[76] Zachary, Paul I, and Hadrian I placed their images in Santa Maria Antiqua as well.[77] John also put his image in his new Marian oratory just inside the right hand portal of Old St. Peter's. Both the location of these images and their composition are rich with meanings. The *Liber Pontificalis* says that John contemplated moving the papal administration to the imperial palace on the Palatine Hill.[78] Nothing came of this plan and, as noted above, Zachary began the long process of refurbishing and expanding the government complex at the Lateran. But John did twice put his own picture in Santa Maria Antiqua, a church that had been created in portions of what was once part of the entryway to the imperial palace. That church lies just off the Via Sacra in the Forum Romanum and opposite the former Curia Senatus. There was no more "Roman" place in Rome. That John and then several of his successors put their images there "cannot be without political significance" and surely "involved a certain claim of autonomy by the church of Rome."[79] An accident of history had made the Constantinian basilica, St. John Lateran, Rome's cathedral church. But St. Peter's was and is the great symbol of Christian Rome and of the papacy. John's image there too was potentially rich with meaning.

In his oratory in St. Peter's John placed an inscription reading "beatae Dei Genetricis Servvs" and on his octagonal ambo in Santa Maria Antiqua he put up inscriptions in both Latin and Greek reading, respectively, "Johannes Servu[s] S[an]c[t]ae M[a]riae" and "'Ιοάννου δούλου τῆς Θεοτοκόυ."[80] If the Madonna della Clemenza really is John's, then he is the pope kneeling at Mary's left knee. He really does appear as the "servant" of the Mother of God, or of Holy Mary. As Gerd Ladner put it, John appears as "der Knecht der Mutter Gottes." No pope had ever before had himself depicted in such a posture before any figure, heavenly or otherwise.[81] Other eighth-century popes associated themselves with Reginas in more traditional poses. Zachary appears in Santa Maria Antiqua, for example, on the complex eastern wall of the Theodotus chapel. This wall has a large crucifixion scene surrounded by symbols of the evangelists. Beneath that large set of pictures one finds a Maria Regina flanked by Peter and Paul—let us remember the emperor flanked by soldiers—the Eastern saints Quiricus and Julitta, martyrs to whom Theodotus dedicated this chapel, Theodotus himself donating his chapel, and Zachary.

Textual evidence repeats, mantralike, what Arnold Angenendt has called a "formula": Christ, Mary, Saints.[82] Images of Christ were comparatively rare in eighth-century Rome but images of Mary were put everywhere. These words and images speak the language of intercession. Santa Maria Antiqua was itself a deaconry, a food distribution center that dispensed the produce of the papal patrimonies.[83] Beginning with Gregory II popes protected the Romans from tax gouging, heterodoxy, and Lombards whenever possible. By claiming Mary for Rome and then by associating themselves with her in visible ways, the popes were very publicly using the media available to them to tell the Romans three things. First, Mary was made the patroness of Rome and, by extension, Constantinople was denied this claim upon her. Neither the Romans nor the popes answered to any earthly ruler, but only to the queen of heaven. Second, the pope was Rome's intermediary between Mary and God, the ultimate source of all favors and blessings. The prayers that were recited on each of the Marian feasts continually emphasize intercession.[84] These pictures were ideological, yes, but theological and even eschatological too. That is, if the Regina images proclaimed intercession in direct ways then other images which placed living popes in a scene with heavenly figures—Jesus, Mary, saints—were meant to remind the viewer that this very pope was going to await them in, to introduce them into, heaven.[85] Third, the emperor's prohibition of images was without force in Rome.

The Maria Regina images are large and public. They do not necessarily inspire feelings of intimacy and reverence but rather sentiments of awe and allegiance. They are not autonomous, and they do not permit a single "detachable" interpretation.[86] They are not windows into another world so much as commentaries on this world. As Clifford Geertz observes, important connections either exist or need to be created between the social realities of power and the symbolic forms of expression which that power may take. One should not draw a neat line between the symbols, or trappings of rule, and its reality, its substance.[87] The magnificent Marian images of early eighth-century Rome open for us vistas on emerging and changing power relationships and some of the ways that were found to articulate the new situation. Guglielmo Matthiae some years ago made the simple but important point that at Rome, given the Gregorian tradition of the didactic value of art, it was easy for relatively simple religious images to do multiple service. That is, they could decorate and please, but they could also teach. In teaching, they could communicate biblical narratives but they could also take part in the articulation of genuine political programs.[88] More recently Daniel Russo has argued, with particular reference to the Marian images under discussion here, that these images served to claim legitimacy for the rulers associated with them and to mark out the boundaries of the territories, both physical and symbolic, over which those rulers claimed authority.[89]

From political images of Mary, let us turn to devotional images. Santa Maria Antiqua has another image of Mary that is different than the Regina images we have been discussing. In a small niche to the right of the nave there is a small and beautiful Marian fresco at eye level. This image is intimate. The image stands alone and Mary is alone in it. The surfaces around the image are pockmarked in ways that suggest that petitions or thank-yous were once affixed there.[90] This might well be an icon in almost all senses of that term. But it cannot be dated securely to the eighth century, except on stylistic grounds.[91]

One aspect of that image is arresting, however. The style of the Mary depicted there is simple and elegant. She wears only a maphorion,[92] no robes, crowns, or jewels. If she is enthroned, we do not see this. This image of Mary has a great deal in common with the several surviving Roman icons of Mary that most scholars think date from the fifth to the sixth century even if they have been so dramatically altered over the centuries that we cannot confidently say how much like the originals the extant versions are.[93] These are the images of the Pantheon, of the Monasterium Tempuli, of Santa Maria Nova (Santa Francesca Romana), and of Santa Maria Maggiore (the Salus Populi Romani). To this small group may be added the enthroned but not regal Marys of the "Turtura" painting from the catacomb of Commodilla[94] and the fresco from the lower church of San Clemente. These Marian icons are very much like relics and in the Pantheon, for example, they may have functioned as substitutes for relics. They too speak the language of intercession.[95] They were sites of private and personal prayer and devotion and seem to lack the political and ecclesiological connotations associated with the Reginas. No source tells us if these images were kissed or if candles and incense were offered to them, but it is reasonable to suppose that these kinds of devotions were known in Rome.

The Theodotus chapel in Santa Maria Antiqua provides further hints about the meaning of Rome's images in the early days of Byzantine iconoclasm. This private chapel was installed in the northeast corner of the building by a wealthy layman while Zachary, who is depicted with a square nimbus indicating that he was alive, was still pope—before 752, that is.[96] Theodotus was the *dispensator*, chief administrator, of the deaconry. He was also the uncle of the future, blue-blood pope Hadrian I. According to the most recent, comprehensive, and persuasive interpretation of the cycle of paintings that cover all four walls of the chapel, Theodotus created his chapel as a memorial to his dead daughter and wife.[97] As intercessors he chose the Eastern saints Quiricus and Julitta. These were Cilician saints who suffered during Diocletian's persecution. Quiricus was the three-year-old martyred son of Julitta. Their *vita* was known in Rome by the early eighth century when the saints were inserted into the calendar.[98] It seems that Theodotus chose them as both emblems of and intercessors for his recently deceased wife and daughter.

The north wall was described above. Its large crucifixion scene may represent an overt statement that Rome was continuing to produce images, in spite of Byzantine prohibitions.[99] But on the south wall there is a particularly interesting scene. Here we find Theodotus himself kneeling and holding in his hands two votive lamps. He is shown in front of Julitta, a Christ child, and Quiricus. Theodotus's face is, however, turned back, as if toward the viewer, but actually toward the crucifixion scene on the opposite wall across the room. Theodotus is, in other words, appealing to Christ for the souls of his dead wife and son and drawing upon the intercession of the saints in the image. It is important to emphasize that Theodotus is not venerating the image of the saints. He and they are within the same picture frame. Theodotus is honoring the image of Christ with his lamps, probably in imitation of actual liturgical rites celebrated in Rome during the Easter vigil.[100]

The Theodotus chapel, therefore, is evidence for the intensity of the cult of the saints in Rome. Thus I cannot agree with Nordhagen's argument that Santa Maria Antiqua *as a whole* testifies to the intensity of the cult of images in Rome.[101] Its central scenes, within and without the Theodotus chapel, are related to the theology of intercession in quite traditional ways. The inclusion of Pope Zachary may be taken as an indication that the artwork in the chapel was acceptable to the Roman Church. The paintings in the chapel are beautiful and must have been exquisite when new. They will have been moving not least because they commemorated recent events and prominent people. But none of these images is autonomous, nor designed for intimacy. Indeed, the whole cycle of paintings around all four walls must be grasped in order to make sense of the discrete details of any one painting within the cycle. Here, perhaps more fully than anywhere else in early eighth-century Rome, at least to judge by what survives, we see the point and power of images. They adorned, they beautified, they taught, and they reminded. They made powerful political statements. They confirmed the formula: God, Mary, Saints. And they were licit.

The West in the Early Eighth Century

From the Western world of the early decades of the eighth century, apart from Anglo-Saxon England and Rome, discussed above, there survive only a few fragments of evidence which provide any insight into the place which images might have occupied or how people thought and talked about images. While it seems safe to suggest, on the basis of Elsmarie Knögel's inventory of 1,078 artifacts that are mentioned somewhere in a literary or documentary source from the period 500 to 750, that the Merovingian world was rich in visual delights, it must also be admitted that virtually nothing survives. For interpretations, we are reduced to educated guesswork.

Paul the Deacon, who spent time at Charlemagne's court and who wrote his *History of the Lombards* in the late eighth century, tells one story about an image that is interesting from three different points of view. The story: Duke Alahis was in a severe struggle with King Cunincpert (679–700) and just as their conflict was about to be resolved by battle, Alahis refused to take the field because saw among Cunincpert's soldiers an image of St. Michael on which, or like the one on which, he had sworn allegiance to the king.[102] The first point to be made is that this is the only story like this in Paul's rather long history. And he tells the tale without comment. He gives his reader no opportunity to decide if this situation was normal or highly unusual. The second point is that Paul does provide an unambiguous testimony about an image that was *used* for something other than visual adornment. An oath was evidently sworn on this image. This sounds more like the sort of thing that would appear in a Byzantine source. The third point is a little harder to work out. It is not possible to determine, from Paul's telling of the story, if Alahis saw the actual image on which he had sworn his oath or whether he saw in the ranks of his enemies an apparition of St. Michael that he recognized because of the image on which he had sworn his oath. If the former possibility is to be entertained, then we have here a unique case of the Lombards carrying an image of St. Michael into battle as a palladium. This, again, sounds Byzantine. If the latter possibility is to be considered, then we have here a unique case in the West of an image verifying, authenticating, a vision even though the story was told in the 780s about an event that allegedly occurred a century earlier. Such cases are known in Byzantine sources, and will crop up again in the West after 769, but are unattested in the West in the early eighth century.

Paul's countryman, Andreas Agnellus, adds a few insights. Beginning in about 831 he wrote his history of the bishops of Ravenna from the beginning of the see down to his own times.[103] It is not always easy to work out Agnellus's canon of inclusion and exclusion. I wish to draw attention to two aspects of his long, entertaining tale. First, to the undying gratitude of art and architectural historians, Agnellus talks at length and in detail about the artistic patronage of the archbishops of Ravenna and he lavishes attention on specific works of art. Agnellus tells two stories that might be signs of the adoration of images, that might point to icons. But there is not a word about Byzantine iconoclasm in his long and substantial treatment of Ravenna during the two periods of Byzantine iconoclasm. Agnellus's most recent student believes that as a staunch anti-Roman he was somewhat upset by the fact that the patriarchs of Ravenna regularly sided with the popes on the image questions and therefore decided to avoid the whole issue.[104]

The first of Agnellus's two stories can be dated to the period 726 to 744 because it relates to the episcopate of John V. A desert hermit pleaded with Christ every day "that He might show him the form of his incarnation." One night Christ appeared to him and told him to go to Classe to the basilica Petriana. "There," Christ said, "you will see me depicted on the walls as I was in the flesh in the world." The hermit went to went to Ravenna, accompanied by two lions, and on finding the image "fell down prone on the ground and, weeping, adored (*adoravit*) it." The lions then killed him and later all three were buried together.[105] The second story cannot be dated, but it does follow the story just recounted in Agnellus's work, so it may be later. Two men, one the godfather of the other, stood before an image (perhaps a mosaic or fresco) of Christ who appeared with His right hand extended. The image of Christ was flanked by images of Peter and Paul. The godson lent his godfather 300 solidi and asked Christ to stand as guarantor (*fideiussor*) for the loan while Peter and Paul were to function as witnesses (*testes*). After some time had passed and the loan had not been repaid, the loaner prayed before the image that Christ make good on His promise. The recipient of the loan, then in far-off Constantinople (and having fared well in his business dealings) had a dream, returned to Ravenna, and repaid his debt.[106] Both of these stories depend on older, Eastern prototypes. It is difficult to know how Agnellus came by them. Perhaps they were common knowledge in Ravenna. And in telling the stories, Agnellus is unlikely to have overstepped the boundaries of his fellow citizens' imaginations.[107] The archbishop of Ravenna who attended the Roman Synod of 769 said that "holy images ought to be venerated by all Christians with a great disposition of honor."[108] Nevertheless, Agnellus does not say that the image of Christ with His right arm extended routinely guaranteed debts—or did anything else, for that matter—and the image of Christ at Classe that was adored by a desert hermit does not, on Agnellus's telling, receive such devotion at any other time from anyone else. Sansterre says "one should not, certainly, exaggerate the importance of the two stories."[109]

The world of the Anglo-Saxon missionary Boniface provides a few more clues and hints. Boniface knew what an idol was. In his missionary endeavors in central Germany and in Saxony he repeatedly encountered what he called idols and idolatry.[110] He never tells us in detail just what he meant by these words.

At the least, his words are probably catchalls for the pagan religious practices of the peoples whom he encountered. The same is surely true for Boniface's slightly older contemporary Willibrord, who also encountered idols and idolatry in Frisia. Boniface had a sharp sense of how he might dazzle his pagan contemporaries. He once wrote to his friend Eadberga and asked her to send him a copy of St. Peter's *Epistles* written in gold letters so that he could "impress honor and reverence for the sacred scriptures visibly upon the carnally minded to whom I preach."[111] Note that it was scriptures written in gold, not an image of any kind, that Boniface requested. When Augustine came ashore in Kent he and his associates bore images. Boniface did not. Perhaps out in the missionary wilds of Germany he realized that any use of images was likely to be misunderstood.[112] Bede describes in loving detail the artistic embellishment of Wearmouth and Jarrow but in all the accounts of Boniface's church foundations there is no mention of pictures of any kind. Surely prudence rather than iconophobia was at work here. The absence of evidence from the realm of Boniface may serve as a reminder that there were important Christian communities where artwork was unimportant and perhaps nonexistent, at least for a while. Something else absent from the sources pertaining to Boniface is worthy of mention. Boniface worked as the special agent of the papacy. He had long, detailed, and harmonious dealings with Gregory II and III, and Zachary. Many of his letters to these popes survive as do some of their letters to him. Boniface visited Rome three times. Boniface was deeply concerned with the integrity of the faith and he rooted out heresy, quite apart from paganism, on several occasions. Yet from the Bonifatian sources it would be impossible to learn that an iconoclastic controversy existed.

Also from Boniface's world we have the *Hodoeporicon* of his kinsmen Willibald and Wynnebald written by Huneberc of Heidenheim, itself a monastery founded by Wynnebald.[113] Between 722 and 729 Willibald and Wynnebald undertook a long journey across Europe, down through Italy, across Byzantium, and then on to the Holy Land by way of Asia Minor. Sometime in, probably, the 760s, the brothers related their tale to Huneberc and she recorded it in considerable detail. This story too is most striking for what it does not say. The brothers visited the tombs of many great figures in Christian history and they called on certain living holy men, such as a pair of Stylites. In the Holy Land they visited virtually every place that had any connection with Christ's life. They expressed interest in certain relics: the true cross, one of the wine jugs from Cana, and even a church at Emesa that had once, allegedly, sheltered the head of John the Baptist. In this whole narration the brothers mention exactly one image. While they were in Constantinople, they decided to visit Nicaea where the great church council had been held and there they observed the portraits of the 318 bishops who had attended the council.[114] But let us back up a bit. The brothers were in Constantinople. In fact, they visited there from 727 to 729, just when iconoclasm was supposedly raging. What is more, they traveled back from Constantinople to Rome with papal and imperial envoys. And yet, they either told Huneberc nothing about iconoclasm or she somehow neglected to record what she heard. In any case, the brothers seem not to know anything about icons or iconoclasm. One does not learn from this text that there was any such thing as iconoclasm. One hears nothing of the destruction of images or of the punishment of image worshipers. One hears of no miraculous images. This may, again, be oblique evidence for the rather modest and episodic nature of Byzantine iconoclasm. Or it may be oblique evidence supporting the views of those scholars who invite us to question how widespread image veneration actually was in the pre- and early iconoclastic periods. Or it may be oblique evidence for the degree to which westerners just did not notice or think about the same things that easterners did.

Another traveler's account of sorts provides more negative evidence. In a ninth-century manuscript from Einsiedeln there is a pilgrim's itinerary for the city of Rome and a collection of transcriptions of monumental inscriptions that were still visible in the city.[115] The text of the itinerary can probably be dated to the eighth century, but there are many problems surrounding it. I only wish to draw attention to the fact that exactly once, in Route I which entered Rome at the Gate of St. Peter's and wound through the city to the baths of Trajan, does the compiler of the itinerary mention images. The ninth "stop" on this tour is Sancta Agatha—now Santa Agata in Suburra or Santa Agata dei Goti—and the itinerary says "*ibi imagines Pauli et Scae. Mariae.*"[116] This itinerary provides twelve routes through Rome. Dozens and dozens of churches and ancient monuments are named. From the testimony of the *Liber Pontificalis* we know that many of those churches had beautiful images both ancient and contemporary. Nothing is actually known about the images of Paul and Mary in Santa Agata. We will probably never know why the author of the Einsiedeln itinerary chose to mention them. But the fact that he mentions no others suggests that northern visitors to Rome were not especially interested in the city's artistic treasures either for aesthetic or for sacred reasons. People went to Rome to visit the tombs of saints and martyrs, not their images.

From the Frankish world in general in the early decades of the eighth century, there survives neither a portable image that might be called an icon nor any reference to such an image. There are no stories of oaths being sworn on images, of people being recognizable in dreams and visions because they looked like their images, or of images before which people prayed. In fact, very few images of any kind survive from the early eighth century. Some wonderful images were put into books at such places as Echternach, and they are important to art historians in their quest to understand what one scholar has recently called "cultural interplay" in the eighth century.[117] But I am unaware of any source which says that people prostrated themselves before such images, or kissed them, or approached them with candles and incense.

There may just possibly be a single exception. In the third year of Pippin's reign, probably 754 but, if his reign were dated from his papal coronation in 754, then 757, at a now unidentifiable place called Vosevio, a scribe named Gundohinus produced a Gospel book with images.[118] Compared with, say, the Trier Gospels produced at Echternach, the Gundohinus Gospels seem clumsy and amateurish. But they do have some intriguing features. The book contains a *Maiestas* image, a figure that was to have a bright future in Carolingain art. The *Maiestas* image of Christ is flanked by two angels labeled "cyrubin." Facing the *Maiestas* image are pseudo-Hieronymian texts on the Trinity. Given that the cherubim of the ark figured in pro- and anti-image arguments from the beginning and given that the image of Christ in majesty coupled with pseudo-Jerome's Trinitarian texts might be a solid affirmation of Christ's full humanity and divinity and a distant but vague echo of the deliberations at Hiereia, one could find a plausible context for this book in the years just around the council of 754. The Franks and popes had been in intensive contact in the years from 752 to 754 so they could have learned about recent events at Byzantium. If the book's date device can be read 757 instead of 754, then there is even more of an opening for the book to be a response to recent developments in Byzantium.[119] The book is almost certainly based on an earlier model, so it is possible that its maker(s) was/were, like iconophiles in the East, asserting that images had always been a part of the church's tradition. Still, in the absence of corroborating evidence it would be dangerous to insist on the Gundohinus Gospels as evidence for an early Frankish response to Byzantine iconoclasm.

The West beyond Rome, therefore, shows little interest in images as such, little awareness that there was any controversy about them, and not much evidence for ways in which images were used or perceived. Negative evidence, or arguments from silence, should always be treated with extreme caution. But in the present circumstances I think it has been worthwhile to detail the remarkable convergence of both the scanty records that do survive and the kinds of things that all sources ignore. Put differently, the Western evidence alone would neither signal that serious battles over religious art had been going on nor suggest that a controversy was about to break out in Frankish Europe.

Diplomacy and Images in the 760s

The entry for the year 767 in the *Royal Frankish Annals* reads, in part: "Then the lord King Pippin in the above mentioned estate [Gentilly] held a great synod between the Romans and the Greeks about the Holy Trinity, or (*vel*) about the images of the saints." The so-called "revised" version of the *Annals* is slightly different: "A dispute about the holy Trinity and (*et*) about the images of the saints having arisen between the eastern and western church[es], that is between the Romans and the Greeks, King Pippin, having gathered together an assembly in Gentilly, held a synod concerning this dispute."[120] Before attempting to understand just what is going on here, let us note some features of these two accounts. The annalist says only that Pippin, when he discovered some contention between Greeks and Romans, which can only mean the Byzantines and the popes, held a synod to explore the issue. What is more, Pippin was holding a general assembly, a normal annual event, when he decided to turn it into, or to add to it, a synod, an ecclesiastical meeting. The original account speaks only of a "great" (*magnum*) synod while the revised version says that there was an assembly which became a synod. Great could mean "large" or it could mean "important." Finally, the "dispute" in the former text concerned the Trinity or images while in the latter it was about both. The original annals were composed in the years right around 790; the revised annals date from the last years of Charlemagne's reign—more than twenty years later, that is. By the end of Charlemagne's reign there had been fierce contention over images and the procession of the Holy Spirit. Hindsight may have improved official memories of what happened at Gentilly.[121]

I must ask at least three questions: What actually happened? Why did the issue of images come up in the Frankish world in 767? What is the meaning of a dispute "*de Trinitate*"? Answers to the first and second of these questions seem to lie within the extremely complicated network of diplomatic initiatives that wove together the imperial, papal, and Frankish courts in the years following Pippin's Italian campaigns in the mid-750s. An answer to the third question may lie in that same diplomatic nexus, or it may lie a bit later in some creative manipulation of the historical record.

Rightly or wrongly, the judgment of history has always associated cunning, even devious, diplomacy with Byzantium. In the early 750s the empire attempted one last time to win the popes over to some kind of effort against the Lombard juggernaut of King Aistulf. The Byzantines may even have glimpsed the possibility that the pope's new friends, the Franks, could be won over to an alliance of some kind. After all, there will have been historical records available in Constantinople to remind the current regime that, in the sixth century, emperors had enlisted Frankish help in Italy. In any case, Pippin allied himself with the popes and then campaigned in Italy twice, in 755 and 756, to compel the Lombards to hand over to papal Rome various territories which the Lombards had recently seized from the empire.[122] Because the popes had been laying claim to those very lands for some decades, Pippin regarded the Lombard confiscations as having come at the papacy's expense. As Pippin was heading for Italy for his second campaign, a Byzantine legation called on the pope in Rome and then headed north to meet Pippin. The Greeks, joined by a papal emissary, sailed to Marseilles where they learned that Pippin had already crossed the Alps and entered Lombardy. The Byzantine envoys apparently felt that the pope was doing all he could to prevent them from meeting with Pippin. One of these envoys, George, traveled to Italy, met Pippin, and offered him many inducements to hand over to the emperor Ravenna and other cities of Italy. Pippin told George that he had already given the lands to St. Peter for the love of the saint and for the remission of his sins. George headed for Rome and then back to Constantinople via Naples, while the other member of the delegation, John, remained in the West; he was still in Francia in 757.[123]

The entry in the *Royal Frankish Annals* for 757 says that "Emperor Constantine sent King Pippin many gifts, including an organ."[124] These gifts, and those who brought them, arrived during a general assembly at Compiègne. Of this organ Michael McCormick says, "More than simply symbolising superior technology, a Byzantine organ was a strictly secular instrument used chiefly in ceremonies glorifying the emperor. Its ostentatious presentation to the usurper king at the assembly of his unruly magnates suggests that the Byzantines curried royal favour by supplying the means to magnify a nascent monarchy."[125] Byzantine relations with the papacy had been almost unrelievedly sour for some thirty years. Byzantium still had important interests in Italy and, because of serious threats in the Balkans and Anatolia, few resources to spare in advancing them. A Frankish alliance may well have struck the authorities in Constantinople as a possible means of stabilizing the situation in Italy and perhaps even of tipping the balance back in Byzantium's favor. The Franko-papal alliance was new, and, as I have just argued, there was no reason for Byzantine leaders to think that the Franks had any views on the potentially divisive subject of images.

Over the next decade there were fairly frequent diplomatic encounters between Byzantium and the Franks. In addition to the meeting at Compiègne in 757, there appear to have been contacts in 760, 763–64, and 766–67.[126] McCormick thinks that Byzantine attempts to win the Franks to their view of the Italian scene were alluring and Auzépy observes that, much to the consternation of Pope Paul I, Pippin rebuffed all attempts get him to return to Italy or to bring undue pressure to bear on the new Lombard king Desiderius.[127] It is true that Pippin had other priorities in the 760s. He campaigned every year from 760 to 763 in Aquitaine, and then returned there from 766 to 768. But his refusal to respond to Paul's requests for help may well have been a result of successful Byzantine diplomacy. Indeed, for usurpers like the Carolingians, the Byzantine stamp of approval must have been a welcome legitimation. Sometime in the 760s, perhaps around 766, Pippin seriously entertained the prospect of marrying his daughter Gisela to Leo IV, Constantine V's designated heir.[128] If the Franks knew or cared anything about Byzantine iconoclasm, then other advantages of a Byzantine alliance must have carried more weight. But the sources, which are admittedly scanty throughout this period, are silent about the topic of images until the year of, and the year before, the synod at Gentilly.

Thanks to Michael McCormick's brilliant analysis of two critical letters in the *Codex Carolinus*, numbers 36 and 37, it is now possible to form a much clearer picture of what happened at Gentilly and why.[129] Without entering into all of the details of his reconstruction of events, here are the essentials. Letters 36 and 37 were dated by their editor, Wilhelm Gundlach, to the years 764–66. In this he followed Philipp Jaffé. Other scholars sometimes expressed doubts about these dates but no one tried seriously to suggest alternatives. On the basis of Gundlach's chronology one had a significant Frankish-papal-Byzantine diplomatic initiative in the years 764–66 but then a gap in the evidence which made Gentilly fly in out of the blue in 767. That alone need not have aroused suspicion because there had been fairly intensive Franko-Byzantine encounters since 755. But McCormick persuasively reverses the order of the letters and then situates number 37 in late 766 and number 36 in, perhaps, March of 767. What is more, he dates Gentilly to February of 767. In other words, McCormick brackets Gentilly with two important letters that, together, provide important details about the first recorded instance of the Frankish court's having addressed the issue of images.

We now know that in 766 an embassy that probably had its origins in the Frankish court and that may have been connected with the proposed marriage alliance set out for Byzantium. Moreover, we know that papal envoys went along too. In addition, we are told that the popes had been pressing the Byzantines continually on the image question and, finally, we hear that Constantine V complained that his views were being misrepresented by the Roman authorities. This embassy then returned to Pippin's realm late in 766 and the king wrote to the pope to tell him about it. Letter number 37 is Paul's response. From it we learn that the pope granted permission for the members of the embassy to remain with Pippin through the winter and for the king, his bishops, and his magnates to debate about what response should be given to the information they had received. Presumably, this means what they had learned in Constantinople.

There followed a dispute "about the images of the saints" in a "great synod" that was an adjunct to a Frankish general assembly. After the assembly, as letter number 36 indicates, the pope expressed satisfaction at the outcome of the debates in Pippin's presence between his people and the emperor's, and he thanked Pippin for sending him detailed records. Of those debates themselves, letter 36 says only that they touched "the maintenance of the orthodox faith" and "the holy tradition of the fathers." While it would be dangerous to read too much into these few words, it does seem possible to suggest that, in 767, the fundamental issue at stake was whether the Greeks or the Romans adhered more faithfully to the ancient traditions of the church. The papal delegates may well have had in hand the patristic dossier prepared in 731 while the Greeks may have put the dossier of 754 on the table. Only the outcome permits us to cast a retrospective light on what followed the assembly of Gentilly.

McCormick believes that the debate was held before the Frankish elite because the issue of the marriage alliance was at the top of the agenda. To put this little differently, there would have been no reason to debate recondite matters of theology alone in a Frankish general assembly that was itself being held unusually early in the year owing to the pressing need to get on with a campaign in Aquitaine. But if the Franks and Byzantines had been dealing cordially with each other for a decade, and if they had gotten far enough along in their relations to discuss a marriage alliance, then it is very difficult to suppose that either of them put the divisive issue of images, or the traditions of the church, on the table. It simply must have been Paul I or his envoys who thrust this issue on the assembled parties. For a decade or more the popes had been worried about the possibility that a Frankish alignment with Byzantium might be damaging to their territorial interests in Italy. Finally, Rome raised religious issues and they trumped other considerations. The marriage alliance did not take place and, if the sources do not deceive us, there were no further contacts between Constantine V and the Franks.

If Byzantine recognition seemed attractive to the Franks, then in the end they must have realized that they really owed their crown in the first place to papal actions on their behalf. Since the time of Charles Martel the Carolingian family had been collaborating with religious officials such as Boniface to promote sound doctrine and effective ecclesiastical organization. If Boniface and his predecessor Willibrord opened up the channels of communication between

Rome and Francia, then those channels were tended in Pippin's time by such prominent men as Chrodegang of Metz and Fulrad of St. Denis. McCormick shows that some of the personnel on all sides who were involved in the complicated diplomacy of the 750s and 760s turn up again and again. They were old hands. They must have known just which issues would attract the most attention. The Franks who, sometime in the 760s, reissued the Salic Law with its so-called "Second Prologue" were indeed "strong in the faith" and "untainted by heresy." This theme of orthodoxy would be sounded again and again throughout the Carolingian period. It mattered. The popes knew that. But, still, what the Franks knew or cared about images *stricto sensu* is hard to determine.

That leaves the matter of the debate about the Trinity that supposedly took place at Gentilly. In the past most scholars have assumed that this argument represented the first appearance in the West of the *filioque* controversy, the problem of the procession of the Holy Spirit in the first place and of the wording of the text of the creed in the second place. This issue appears in the *Opus Caroli* and there was a lively controversy over it in 808 and 809 (to which we will come in Chapter 5). In the middle of the ninth century Ado of Vienne believed, perhaps reflecting a widespread belief, that the *filioque* had been at issue in 767.[130] But as McCormick points out, the *filioque* clause had not been adopted in Rome in the eighth century—it would not be officially adopted there until the early eleventh century—and it was never adopted in Byzantium. It is, therefore, pretty hard to imagine a papally sponsored debate with Byzantines over the *filioque* in 767.[131] I see two possibilities for explaining the somewhat anomalous report of the annals. First, and bearing in mind that Constantine V complained about misrepresentations of his views, it could be that some of the Christological reflections from Hiereia were laid before the Frankish assembly/synod in a way garbled enough to have left behind only an enigmatic trace when the annals were written down more than twenty years later and revised twenty or so years after that. If—*if*—the Trinitarian texts in the Gundohinus Gospels represent some sort of Frankish response to what was perceived to be dubious Byzantine Christology, then this view would be strengthened. Second, and bearing in mind that the *Royal Frankish Annals* were prepared in the first instance in close collaboration with Charlemagne's court around 790, then it could be that the business about a debate "*de sancta Trinitate*" in 767 is a later confection designed to add historical precedent to the theological concerns of a later time.[132] In sum, in the midst of a Frankish assembly that was dealing with important matters of diplomacy concerning the Byzantines, papal envoys raised the issue of images and possibly too the issue of the Trinity, or of the procession of the Holy Spirit, as a way of relaxing the bond between the Franks and the Byzantines that had itself been tightening for more than a decade. Territorial interests in Italy were important to the popes, and potentially complicated by a Franko-Byzantine alliance but religious issues were significant too.

The Roman Synod of 769

If images came up rather unexpectedly in 767 they did not have to wait long to be discussed again. Pippin died in 768 and was succeeded by his two sons, Charles and Carloman. The latter died in 771 but for some three years there was bad blood between the brothers and intrigues that reached to Bavaria, Lombardy, and Rome. In Rome itself, Paul I died in the early summer of 767, and for more than a year the city was the scene of bitter and bloody political strife.[133] When Pope Stephen III (768–72) finally got a secure grip on the papacy, he called a church council.[134] The majority of that council's time was devoted to investigating the recent troubles and to proposing some new regulations governing papal elections. But the council also addressed images. And an impressive delegation of Franks was present.

The *acta* of the council of 769 are transmitted only in poor texts. The *Life* of Stephen III in the *Liber Pontificalis* provides most of the basic details and then, as with the Roman Council of 731, one must turn to the *Hadrianum* to fill in a few blanks. There are things we just do not know, or know very imperfectly. Why were Franks invited? Were images always meant to be a part of the agenda of the council since the strife of 767–68 was the primary issue? Regardless of whether or not images were on the agenda from the beginning, how much, and exactly what, was said about them?

The *Liber Pontificalis* says that immediately after his election and consecration Stephen III sent Sergius, the *secundicerius* and *nomenclator*—an impressively high official—to Pippin and his sons. In the meantime, Pippin had died so Sergius presented letters to his sons urging them to send "some bishops who were knowledgeable (*gnaros*) in all the divine scriptures and deeply learned (*eruditos*) and widely experienced (*peritissimos*) in the rules of the holy canons."[135] The passage goes on to say that a council was to be held to address the actions of the papal usurper, Constantine. It does not say that images were to be discussed, or that the Franks were informed of any pending discussion of images, or that the Franks themselves insisted on discussing images. The passage then names the Frankish bishops who went to Rome and calls them "learned and proven men in divine scriptures and in the proper observance of the holy canons (*sanctorum canonum cerimoniis*)." Given that delicate matters such as the treatment of a man who had been elected pope in questionable circumstances and the institution of new rules for papal elections were handled in the council, and indeed constituted the work of the council which is best and most fully transmitted, then it may be possible to read these statements about the Frankish participants in a very specific way. That is, the emphasis is on their prudence and experience and on their knowledge of sound canonical procedure. Stephen, it seems, wanted to be sure that he got good advice but also that the Franks would understand the situation in Rome and see things the pope's way.

The council itself met in the Lateran basilica in four sessions spread over four days: April 12–15. By criteria of its size, the distinction of its participants, and the geographical range of its attendees, this was perhaps the most important Roman council of the eighth century.[136] The first two days dealt with Constantine's case and the third day proposed new rules for electing popes. Day four addressed images. The *Liber Pontificalis* says that "diverse testimonies of the holy fathers concerning the sacred images of the Lord God and Savior Jesus Christ and of Mary the holy, glorious, and ever-virgin mother of our Lord, and of the blessed apostles and all the saints and prophets and martyrs and confessors (N.B. the "formula") were laid before that council." The text goes on to say that all the popes and fathers agreed that images were to be venerated, that they served memory and evoked compunction, and that the recent council, that is Hiereia, was to be anathematized "for casting down sacred images."[137] Werminghoff, the editor of the conciliar records, believes that nothing really new was said about images because only a single day was devoted to the topic. Fundamentally, he thinks that the decrees of 731 were reiterated with just a few exceptions that are fairly easy to explain.[138] In short, it looks as though, from the papal point of view, images were not the critical issue in 769. This might seem odd if it was papal representatives who forced the issue of images onto the agenda at Gentilly. But it may be that all the pope wanted to do at that time was separate Byzantium and Francia and signal clearly to the Franks that the Byzantines were heretics. Thus, it seems likely that it was the Franks who laid images on the table for discussion in Rome.[139] There is additional evidence that points to this conclusion. Shortly before the Roman council Lull of Mainz wrote to Wearmouth and Jarrow to request a copy of Bede's *On the Temple*.[140] As Michael McCormick says, the timing of Lull's letter is unlikely to be coincidental.[141] One of the Frankish bishops at Rome, Erlolf of Langres, put into the record a letter of Gregory I to Secundinus in an already interpolated version.[142] It is significant that a Frankish bishop appeared in Rome with an image text in his bags and that the text in question was a doctored version of a letter of Gregory I. Perhaps indeed the doctoring was fairly recent, had taken place in Francia, and betokens a certain Frankish interest in the whole issue of images. Finally, Bishop George of Ostia, who had become the bishop of Amiens, was probably present in both Gentilly and Rome.[143]

Why would the Franks have wanted to see images on the Roman agenda? Perhaps because the synod of Gentilly where, as far as we know, the Franks encountered the image controversy for the first time in any kind of official setting was too small and local to settle a matter that, after all, had driven a wedge between the Frankish and Byzantine courts and was known, or was *by then* known, to have opened a gap between papal Rome and imperial Constantinople. Moreover, as I shall argue in more detail in later chapters, the Franks generally did not take so positive a view of images as Rome did and certainly had not worked out any theology of sacred art. Thus a large council, in Rome, under papal leadership, with Franks present, might have been reassuring to all parties. The Franks got an opportunity to learn in some detail about the issues involved in the iconoclastic dispute, and the pope was able to present the Roman case more fully than would have been possible at Gentilly.

What did the council say on the subject of images? First of all, it appears that the patristic passages adduced in 731 were brought forward and affirmed. Second, an anathema was hurled at the Council of Hiereia. Third, a few small bits of testimony were added from new sources: from a synodical letter of three Eastern patriarchs sent to Paul I; a modest remark from Ambrose of Milan put into the record by Sergius, the deacon of the patriarch of Ravenna; the interpolated latter of Gregory I mentioned above; and a text that, according to later manuscripts, Pope Stephen himself contributed. In full perspective, then, the council of 769 seems to have added little to the ongoing discussion of images.

The letter of the three Eastern patriarchs brings forth nothing new but does add to the Western discussion one point that had not been there before.[144] The author of the letter, after quoting the end of John's Gospel to the effect that Jesus did many things that were not written down anywhere and urging the pope to be steadfast in his defense of the faith, cites the story of Abgar of Edessa and his miraculous image of Christ. The logic of the passage would seem to be that if someone were to assert that the Bible did not mention images then, well, the Bible did not mention lots of things, as John himself said. Among those things, presumably, was the image that Jesus Himself sent to Abgar. I noted in Chapter 2 that precisely this kind of argumentation was advanced at Nicaea in 787. The Frankish bishops would have encountered it for the first time in 769. The passage from Ambrose tells of his being weak and sleepless owing to fasting and of his seeing a vision of Paul that he recognized to be Paul precisely because of an image that he had seen.[145] I do not know of another text like this from the

West at this time—unless Paul the Deacon's story about the angel Michael is relevant—but the basic point and theme here are familiar to us by now. The interpolated letter of Gregory insists that images are not cherished as if they were God but desired because they bring God's birth, passion, or glory back to mind.[146] Thus, the letter says, Gregory sent Secundinus two shields (*surtarias*) with images on them of Jesus, Mary, Peter, and Paul. Here again there is nothing new, apart from the dubious statement that Gregory sent someone actual images on shields and this can safely be left aside. There remains the contribution of Stephen himself, if that is what it is.[147] After talking about how the ark, tablets of the law, and golden urn (to preserve the manna) were the work of human hands and yet worthy of veneration, the text goes on to defend images which are also made by humans. Predictably, the text then defends things made of dross matter because it is not the matter in them which is venerated. The cross is cited as a good example but then so are bread, wine, and oil. Here Stephen's point is that perfectly ordinary things can be consecrated to holy purposes and thus become worthy of a respect they could never claim in their normal state. There are two points to be retained from the Roman synod. The synod said nothing new on matters of doctrine while introducing, or deepening the familiarity of, a dozen Frankish bishops to the issues involved in the image controversy.

There is one curious footnote to the discussion of images in 769. One of the minor figures in the political strife of 767–68 was a priest named Waldipert. When the authorities went looking for him they found him in the church of Sta. Maria ad Martyres, the former Pantheon. He was holding a picture of Mary.[148] Before jumping to the conclusion that this action on Waldipert's part signifies the use of images as palladia in Rome, there is another, more plausible interpretation to consider. Almost certainly Waldipert was not holding a portable image but rather standing near, perhaps touching, the Pantheon icon of Mary. He was claiming asylum and refuge,[149] which claims were summarily ignored. The point is that, apart from the story of the Abgar image, of the images that emitted blood or oil (reported above in connection with 731), and the "acheropsita," there is no other evidence at this early date for miraculous images in Rome.

By 769, then, the Franks and the popes had been brought into the Mediterranean discussion of images as talking partners. For the moment, it seems as though the Byzantines have receded from the scene as either potential allies for the Franks or as political, military, and theological sparring partners for the popes. The discussion of images, as far as it had gone, was pretty basic. No signs had yet appeared of a quarrel within the West itself. The episodic nature of the

Eastern quarrel which was detailed in Chapter 2 seems to have been replicated in the West. That is, some kinds of action touching on images seem to have been taken in the late 720s, in 731, 732, 767, and 769. In between there were, on Hadrian's later testimony, letters from the popes to the emperors, and the production of a good deal of artwork, some of which was certainly polemical in intent. But images were not a commanding issue and they had never attracted the best minds and most concerted energies of the popes or the Franks. That would change in the late 780s and early 790s.

Pope Hadrian I and the Defense of Images

As far as I can see, images attracted attention only once in the papal or Frankish worlds between the Roman Synod of 769 and Hadrian's initial preparation in 785 for the Second Council of Nicaea. In about 770, in Rome, an anonymous compiler produced a massive iconophile florilegium, and in 774 or 775 that compiler, or possibly someone else, revised that text substantially. Either or both of these texts may have been placed in the papal library and, as we saw in Chapter 2, there is a possibility that Hadrian sent one of them, probably the version from 770, to Constantinople along with his response to the invitation of Irene and Constantine to attend a church council dealing with images. The painstaking research of Alexakis has identified these collections of *testimonia* as the most likely source for the statements on images contained in Hadrian's letter to the Eastern rulers and also in his letter to Charlemagne of 793.[150] Those letters provide an excellent vantage point for assessing the authoritative papal view on images in the 780s and 790s. But the florilegia themselves make no known appearances in the papal sources for some ten or fifteen years after their preparation and they do not seem to have circulated in the Frankish realm. The popes and Franks dealt with each other intensively in this period, the Franks initiated new diplomatic contacts with Byzantium, and the popes watched warily as the Byzantines tried one or another political or military move in Italy.[151] Still, not a word was spoken about images.

In presenting Hadrian's views on images it is well to bear in mind that, on two separate occasions, he expressed those views in response to initiatives by other people. Irene and Constantine invited him to a council to consider images, and Charlemagne sent him a long document that attacked the work and conclusions of II Nicaea. For present purposes our discussion of Hadrian's views on images will be confined to what we can learn from his letter to Irene and Constantine and from the *Liber Pontificalis*. The latter source speaks generally about developments throughout Hadrian's pontificate and its information seems widely applicable to an investigation of the pope's views. The former source was written in 785, before Nicaea. Moreover, there is nothing in Irene and Constantine's invitation to Hadrian that called for a papal statement on images. It is reasonable to assume, therefore, that Hadrian said basically what he wanted to and what he felt needed saying. When, eight or so years later, he wrote the *Hadrianum,* he did so against the background of Nicaea's *acta* and in the immediate context of a massive Carolingian attack on Nicaea. The Hadrianum, arrayed in eighty-five chapters, is an exact response to eighty-five objections to Nicaea's image doctrines developed at the Frankish court. This letter, in other words, is less likely to represent Hadrian's considered views on images than the pope's rhetorical and polemical strategy in a very tense situation. Thus a detailed discussion of that letter will appear in Chapter 4 where the contours of that situation can be limned.

The great majority of early medieval papal letters are rescripts.[152] That is, apart from some rhetorical and often ideological introductory matter and spiritual closing matter that we may regard as Lateran boilerplate, the core of the letters constitute answers to questions that came to the pope from some outside source. Such letters cannot be read as general statements of papal policy. Centuries later canon lawyers often gathered up such statements and organized them systematically so as to create the appearance of policy, of precedent, of fixed law. But that was later. Hadrian's letter to Irene and Constantine was, to be sure, an answer to a letter he had received. But it does not have the distinguishing marks of a rescript. It can be read as a fundamental statement by Hadrian of his essential views. Hadrian's views on images are much in evidence in this letter, but he talks about other key topics too. It is important not only to see the full range of issues addressed by Hadrian but also to note the order in which he raised them.

Hadrian begins by expressing his delight at the steps which Byzantium's rulers were taking to restore images to their accustomed place of honor. He also expresses his sadness that the ancestors of the present rulers had fallen into heresy. Then he praises Constantine VI and Irene as a new Constantine and a new Helena, and does so while emphasizing that the first Constantine and his mother had honored Pope Sylvester. This serves as Hadrian's point of departure for a disquisition on St. Peter, the pope and his *principatus,* the absolute necessity of regarding the Roman Church as the "*caput omnium ecclesiarum,*" and the obligation for all Christians to respect the "power" and "authority" of the bishops of Rome.[153] Obviously Hadrian was upset by the long-standing heresy of iconoclasm. But his first tactic in addressing this heresy was to say that it resulted primarily from a failure in the East to pay due attention to the popes. It is precisely in this context that Hadrian incorporates his first image text. He cites the old story of Constantine's dream in which he saw Sts. Peter and Paul. In the story, the emperor summoned Pope Sylvester, who showed him a picture of Peter and Paul, whom Constantine immediately recognized. But then, the story goes on, Sylvester baptized Constantine, cured him of leprosy, and started him on his career as a dutiful son of the church. Hadrian does not tell this story as a proof-text for images but rather as evidence for the honor and respect that is to be accorded to Peter and Paul, and to Peter's vicar—he uses this very word. Then he goes on to say that under papal guidance the church has kept to the apostolic traditions for all these centuries until Leo and Constantine (V) lapsed into heresy. In precisely this place in the letter Hadrian cites his second image text, namely Gregory's letter to Serenus. He says that "the tribe of pagans, having seen the divine story painted, can be turned from the cult of idols and the statues of demons, just as our distinguished father and worthy preacher Gregory, bishop of this apostolic see, said: 'those who do not know letters, can at least read by looking at a wall what they cannot read in books.'" In other words, Hadrian here artfully turns the story of Constantine and Sylvester into a proof of the power of images to teach the uninitiated and to make them into good servants of the Roman Church.

Hadrian then turns to the subject of images, but at first in a very general way. That is, he lays out a series of specific defenses of images without elaboration. He tells how his predecessors going back to Gregory II and III had repeatedly attempted to restore images to their proper place of honor and respect. He says that Jesus can be painted "according to his incarnate human form." He says that wherever there is "Christianity" (*christianitas*) there are images and that they are honored by all the faithful. Everywhere images use a "visible countenance" (*visibilem vultum*) to make present "the invisible majesty of God" (*invisibilem divinitatis majestatem*). God, in heaven, is worshiped as a spirit, Hadrian says, citing John 10. We make images then, because Jesus appeared on earth and to gain some glimpse of the ultimate heavenly reality. But we do not deify those images "as some say." God made man, after all, in His own image and likeness. Moreover, God permitted Himself to be honored and glorified by all sorts of natural and manufactured things. Hadrian continues by arguing that, on the one hand, it is never the material out of which images are made that is worthy of honor, and that, on the other hand, God Himself commanded certain images or likenesses to be made. "Oh, what craziness of the whiners" it is to deny that images are not to be made or venerated. "If we believe that the Israelites were saved from looming calamity by the sight of the brazen serpent, do we doubt that we are saved by gazing at and venerating the likenesses of Christ our Lord and the saints?" He concludes this section by citing Isaiah 19 and Psalms 6, 19, 25, 26, 44, and 95 on the beauty of God's house and how that beauty honors God. This, Hadrian says, is exactly why we decorate our churches.

The heart of Hadrian's argument is built up on assertions concerning papal authority and its custody of the church's traditions. Some support for this way of interpreting Hadrian's letter comes from his own *vita* in the *Liber Pontificalis*. Of Hadrian's contribution to II Nicaea, the biographer says simply that Hadrian sent his envoys and a letter "to set up sacred images, as they are orthodoxly venerated in the holy, catholic and apostolic Roman Church by the warrant of the scriptures and the tradition of the approved fathers from olden times to the present."[154] Tradition had been at the core of all discussions of images from the fourth century. Since at least the preliminaries to the Council of Chalcedon (451), the popes had been asserting their special role as keepers and guardians of authentic tradition. What is new in Hadrian's letter is merely the pope's speaking so forcefully on behalf of tradition as it pertained to images. But it may well be that Hadrian was neither asserting nor claiming any more than his predecessors going back to Gregory II when a quarrel over images appeared on the papacy's horizon for the first time. As far as his actual defenses of images are concerned, they are wholly traditional. Images teach. Images disclose invisible realities. Christ was a man and could therefore be depicted. God himself commanded images to be made on many occasions. Beautiful decorations of God's house are a means of honoring God Himself not of setting up material, manufactured rivals to Him. As the Roman Synods of 731 and 769 had done, Hadrian says that images are to be venerated.

Hadrian then attached his patristic florilegium, as if to display the very traditions on which he has already built up his argument.[155] Hadrian's florilegium is rather modest, containing only about a dozen extracts, and while it buttresses and even expands upon each point made in the earlier sections of the letter, it does not follow the same order of thematic presentation. I cannot detect an obvious logic in the construction of the florilegium itself. Nevertheless, its basic points are easily grasped.

Hadrian shifts from his general reflections to his florilegium with an interesting device. He says that the eminent prophet David, in announcing the coming of the Savior and His incarnation, warned especially that His "face" (some form of *vultus* as Hadrian quotes the Psalms but sometimes a form of *facies* in the *Vulgate*) "according to the disposition of His humanity" should be sought. Then he cites three Psalms (26.8: "Your face, O Lord, shall I seek"; 44.13: "All the rich among the people shall entreat your countenance"; 4.7: "The light of your countenance, O Lord, is signed upon us"; in that order) and follows with a quotation from "blessed Augustine the most distinguished father and best teacher": "What is the image of God except the face of God in which the people of God is signed?" In fact, scholars have not been able to trace this passage in Augustine's works. But Hadrian's train of thought is not difficult to see. David predicted Christ's coming as a man with a human face and God's people had long been seeking the "face" of God. Jesus is an image of the Father, and humans are created in the image and likeness of God. Hadrian could not imagine a stronger justification of images.

Hadrian then cites Gregory of Nyssa twice. The first citation is the familiar one about Gregory's weeping every time he sees the image of the passion and the second established that acts of reverence before an image are passed to the prototype. Other authors usually turn to Basil to make this point but Hadrian cites Basil on the traditions of the church with respect to "honoring, adoring, and venerating" images and on the widespread custom of painting churches. He then draws another extract from Basil to establish the essential equivalence of painted or written stories. John Chrysostom is then quoted twice in connection with imperial images. The first quotation makes the point that any harm done to an imperial image actually redounds to the emperor and not to the image itself and the second quotation says that when imperial images enter a town crowds greet them not to honor the image but rather to honor the emperor. Cyril of Alexandria is then cited first to say that it is possible to paint the Word that became flesh and second to say that images help to make the invisible visible. Athanasius is then quoted to the effect that images can be made and remade; the materials of which they consist are not important. Ambrose of Milan and Epiphanius of Salamis are then cited to prove that when you have an image of the emperor you do not thereby have two emperors or that in making an image of Christ you do not split His humanity and divinity and thereby create two separate beings. Stephen of Bostra, in Hadrian's longest quotation, says that everything made in the name of God is good, that an image is one thing while a "*simulacrum*" is something else entirely, that the materials of which images are made are irrelevant to the respect paid to them, and that images serve to commemorate the persons represented on them. Hadrian concludes with a quotation from Jerome of Jerusalem which stresses that God commanded Moses to make images.

Hadrian's letter, therefore, falls into two parts. In the first and longer section he develops an argument based on papal authority and ecclesiastical tradition to say that the emperors of the East should never have affronted the sacred teachings of the Church and led the people of God into heresy. In this section of the letter, images are not to the fore. Any heresy could have been involved. The critical issue was authority. In the second section of the letter Hadrian quotes from the tradition to say what the authoritative position on images ought to be. Given the huge array of texts that could have been cited by 785, indeed no fewer than 133 in the iconophile florilegium that Alexakis believes to have been in the papal library, it is perhaps surprising that Hadrian was so selective in his range of citations. He uses a selection of passages from 731 and 769. Moreover, he often neglects to cite the passages one would have expected even on the points he does raise. The example of using Gregory of Nyssa instead of Basil on type and prototype is a good one.

I suggest that the rather spartan character of the second section of the letter is in a critical way related to the first section. That is, Hadrian began by saying that if people in the East had paid attention to the popes and had acknowledged that the popes are the guardians of authentic tradition, then none of these terrible problems would have emerged in the first place. But people did ignore both popes and the ancient teachings of the church and, as a result, plunged into heresy. The second section of the letter seems to me to contain Hadrian's sense of the terms of the heresy. He identified the old Christological attack on images in both its forms: There could be no image of God because "No one has ever seen God" and any image of Christ tended to split His divine and human natures. He identified the problem of materiality and the closely related issue of idolatry. In his letter to Tarasius, written at the same time as the one to the empress and her son, Hadrian said explicitly that he wanted a condemnation of "that *pseudosyllogus* which was held improperly without the papal see and illogically (*insyllogistice*)."[156] The fairly narrow range of Hadrian's patristic dossier may be read as a carefully articulated set of instructions on what positions or arguments were to be condemned at the new council that was going to be called. In sum, Hadrian wanted his authority to be recognized and he wanted what he took to be the most contagious germs of iconoclasm to be eliminated. If this way of interpreting Hadrian's letter is not off the mark, then its structure and relative brevity make another point reasonably clear. The pope was not going to be drawn into an argument over images. Hadrian's stand casts a retrospective light on the rather modest patristic florilegia presented in Rome in 731 and 769.[157] Granted that the sources provide us with a very imperfect sense of what was said and done in the two Roman councils, the fact remains that the limited set of patristic *testimonia* presented there resemble Hadrian's letter in a significant way. Iconoclasm was not refuted point by point. Iconoclasts were told to get back on the path of tradition. The relatively few patristic *testimonia* constitute less an argument for images than a set of pointed rejections of the theology of the iconoclasts. Always, then, the popes refuse to argue with heretics. That refusal by the popes to dignify their opponents by treating their views fully and in detail may explain the relative absence of explicit statements about iconoclasm after the anathemas of 731.

It may be worth mentioning the kinds of things Hadrian did not say. He mentioned no miraculous or "active images." True, he mentioned the image that permitted Constantine to recognize the men he had seen in his dream. But he did so in a context where the image itself is almost irrelevant to the story. Hadrian said nothing about images "not made by human hands." The only time that such a story turned up in a Roman source was when the Eastern patriarchs put the story of Abgar of Edessa on the table in the 760s. But their letter also and more importantly affirmed the allegiance of the whole East to the teachings of the six councils. Hadrian cites only church fathers, not hagiographical texts. He talks again and again about the decoration of churches but never mentions a portable image. He never mentions an image that was used as a palladium or as a phylactery. Like Gregory II and the council fathers in 769, Hadrian says that images are to be venerated. But he does not describe the forms that such veneration might take and he does not say which images are to be venerated. Just as scholars have detected a certain "chastity" in the work of II Nicaea, so too there is a palpable reserve in the views of the eighth-century popes.

This discussion of Hadrian may conclude with an assessment of what the *Liber Pontificalis* says about his images and his ideas. Hadrian was the first pope to profit from the Carolingian imposed *Pax Italiae*, achieved after Charlemagne's definitive defeat of the Lombards in 773–74. The most immediate consequence of this new situation in Italy was a peace and prosperity unmatched since late antiquity. Accordingly Hadrian presided over a building boom in Rome that continued into the ninth century and that was unrivaled until the Renaissance.[158] His *vita* is therefore filled with details on his building projects. If Gregory III, for instance, seems to have deliberately undertaken an image campaign as a response to Byzantine prohibitions, Hadrian's actions are a little more difficult to interpret. Hadrian's *vita* tends to stress the value of the images and decorations he introduced into Rome's churches. For instance, Hadrian donated to Roman churches at least 165 silk veils with images, and to all the title churches, deaconries, and monasteries, veils with crosses.[159] He "restored and decorated for the praise of God all God's churches both inside and outside this city of Rome."[160] He installed images either made from silver sheets or with silver coverings in many places in Rome. He placed "various representations" amounting to three hundred pounds of gold, in St. Peter's *confessio*. He put images of the Gospels—just what these were it is impossible to say—in St. Paul's and St. Lawrence's (outside the walls). He refashioned an image of Jesus, Mary, Peter, Paul, and Andrew at St. Peter's and he put representations of some kind on the doors of St. Paul's.[161] What we find here, in short, is a massive program of decoration. Given Hadrian's own testimony in his letter to Irene and Constantine, this is just what we ought to expect. The tradition had always permitted, indeed encouraged, the adornment of God's house. Now that he had the means to do so, Hadrian undertook that adornment on a grand scale. He acted on a more majestic level because he had the peace, stability, and financial resources to do so. Proud Roman that he was, Hadrian enhanced the beauty and appeal of his city. Tradition had triumphed, at least as far as that tradition was understood in Rome. Where art was concerned, that tradition went straight back to Gregory I. Where Rome itself was concerned, that tradition reached back a millennium.

Conclusion

From Bede to Hadrian, people in the West took a very consistent set of positions on the topic of images. Images can move their viewers. They can elicit compunction. They can elevate the mind from this world to the next. They can reveal, however imperfectly, invisible realities. They teach, especially the unlettered. The Bible itself authorizes images. There is an absolute difference between the matter of which images are made and the person(s) represented by the image. Honor paid to an image immediately passes to the person represented. Art makes the environment beautiful and if that environment happens to be a church, a place of worship, then the beauty offered there is a gift to God, an attempt to honor Him, a thanksgiving. Images can be venerated, according to papal sources. All of this, it will be recalled, is remarkably similar to the final decisions of the *horos* of Nicaea. In many respects, East and West were not very far apart in 787.

There are also persistent similarities in Western writers and church councils with respect to things said rarely or cautiously, and to things not said at all. It is just possible that there was some feeling that an image might confirm a vision but otherwise miraculous, or "active," images make almost no appearance. Images do not seem to have been used as palladia. Bede mentions panel paintings but otherwise only the *Liber Pontificalis* does so explicitly and then only on a few occasions. Active images, palladia, phylacteries, and portable panel paintings were probably less prevalent in the East than heretofore assumed, so East and West may not have seemed so different on the eve of II Nicaea.

In the West as in the East, images came up only occasionally and even then did not seem to dominate discussion. Modest flurries of activity can be identified in the late 720s and early 730s, in the 760s, and in the mid-780s. Apart from the obvious case of the Council of Hiereia, this replicates the chronology we saw in the East in Chapter 2.

The heavy burden of Chapter 4 will be to show how such limited raw materials were assembled into so huge a controversy in the 790s at the Frankish court.

CHAPTER FOUR

The Franks and Nicaea: *Opus Caroli Regis*

If he who scandalizes one of the least shall fall under the most dreaded
sentence, how much more terrible will be the judgment against the one who
either drives almost the whole church of Christ to adore images or binds
with anathema those who spurn the adoration of images. Both should be
avoided with great caution so, whether adhering to one party or the other,
one does not do more than good order demands.
— Theodulf of Orléans, *Opus Caroli Regis*

SHORTLY AFTER THE conclusion of the proceedings at Nicaea a poor Latin translation of the council's records reached Charlemagne. Although Rome must have been the provenance for the documents that came into Charlemagne's possession, it is not clear just how or why he received them. He sent the records, or a copy of them, to his trusted collaborator Alcuin, who was then in England, and he made another copy available, or later gave the original copy, to a new member of his court circle, Theodulf, later the bishop of Orléans. Alcuin wrote something in response to Nicaea's *acta* but his words do not survive. Theodulf produced a massive treatise, formerly known as the *Libri Carolini* but now more correctly entitled the *Opus Caroli Regis contra synodum*. The present chapter discusses the preparation of the *Opus* and summarizes its contents. Shortly after the *Opus* was concluded the Franks, lay elites and clergy alike, assembled at Frankfurt and, among many acts, condemned II Nicaea in an odd and ambiguous way. This chapter also places Theodulf's work into the framework created by Frankfurt.

The Franks had made some contribution to the eighth-century image controversy through the participation of twelve Frankish bishops in the Roman Synod of 769. But in the years after 769 there is no solid evidence for any further Frankish involvement with the dispute. As I have shown, the period from the mid-760s to the mid-780s witnessed little discussion of images in the East. In the 780s, Charlemagne embarked on a complicated diplomacy with the Byzantines that parallels in some ways the relations which his father had sustained with Constantinople in the years 756 to 767. Like his predecessor Paul I, Pope Hadrian was alarmed at the prospect of a Franko-Byzantine rapprochement and his concerns primarily focused on Italian territorial arrangements. Little in the international context, therefore, helps to explain the appearance of Nicaea's records in the West or the virulently negative reaction which they evoked.

One must turn to the Frankish context for insights into the Frankish reaction to Byzantium's repeal of iconoclasm. The years between about 785 and 795 were filled with military successes for the Franks. This was the time when the most significant of Charlemagne's court scholars gathered in the newly emerging capital at Aachen and began to produce their most mature and important works. The first of the beautiful court manuscripts were produced, some of the stunning achievements of Carolingian architecture were built, and major legal, administrative, institutional, and educational reforms were instituted. In this period the Frankish world encountered, in adoptionism, a significant home-grown heresy which elicited theological reflection of unprecedented fervor and rigor. In short, the arrival of the records of II Nicaea and the Frankish response to them took place in a time of intense, dynamic, and creative activity.

From Nicaea to Frankfurt, 787–94

The course of events between II Nicaea and the Council of Frankfurt is deceptively easy to tell. Hadrian's envoys returned in triumph from a council (II Nicaea) that restored ecclesiastical unity, affirmed the pope's magistracy in the church, and affirmed the pope's stance on images. The official records of Nicaea were placed in the papal library and a Latin translation was sent to Charlemagne. Nicaea's records were disconcerting to the Carolingian court. Despite having discussed images on essentially Roman terms at Gentilly in 767 and again at Rome in 769, the Franks had now come to a *via media* along which they insisted that both destroying and worshiping images were forbidden. Charlemagne set two of his most trusted theological advisers, the Anglo-Saxon Alcuin and the Goth Theodulf, to study the Nicene *acta*. The results of a preliminary Frankish assessment of Nicaea's perceived shortcomings, the *Capitulare adversus synodum,* was sent to Rome in 792. Meanwhile, at the court, Theodulf continued to work on his *Opus Caroli Regis contra Synodum*, a massive critique of Nicaea. In 793, or possibly 794, Pope Hadrian's lengthy and devastating rejection of the *Capitulare* reached Charlemagne. Nevertheless, Frankish plans continued apace for a major, indeed universal, church council. That council, the largest and most auspicious of Charlemagne's reign so far, met at Frankfurt and handled a lengthy agenda of ecclesiastical and secular business. On that agenda, conducted in the presence of papal legates, was a curious, ambiguous, limited condemnation of II Nicaea.

The Nicene Acta *Reach the Carolingian Court*

The immediate aftermath of Nicaea is the most straightforward aspect of the history of these years. But it is not without puzzles. Hadrian's envoys to Nicaea, Peter the Archpriest of the Roman Church and Peter the abbot of St.-Saba, returned in the autumn of 787 bearing the *acta* of the council and imperial letters. Hadrian had the *acta* translated into Latin and placed in the papal library "as a worthy, permanent memorial of the orthodox faith."[1] As the abbot of the Greek monastic community of St.-Saba, Peter was almost certainly bilingual. It may have been this skill that recommended him as one of the two papal legates to Nicaea alongside a very high ranking member of the papal administration. Nevertheless, the Latin translation was hastily and poorly done. It seems that someone with connections to the papal court, a modest knowledge of Greek, and glossaries on his desk prepared the Latin version.[2] Why a more skilled translator was not selected will never be known. Under Pope John VIII (872–82), Anastasius Bibliothecarius prepared a new Latin translation.[3] While this version survives intact, only fragments of the original, flawed Latin version are extant in the writings of some people who cited it. The imperial letters vanished without a trace.

Under somewhat mysterious circumstances that Latin version wound up in Charlemagne's hands, perhaps as early as 788 but possibly a little later. An entry under the year 792 in the Northumbrian *York Annals* says, "King Charles of the Franks sent the synodal book to Britain that had been sent to him from Constantinople."[4] We will return to the statement that Charles sent the book to Britain. For now, it is interesting to note that in England, where Charles's close associate Alcuin then was visiting, there was a belief that Charles had gotten his documents straight from the imperial court in the East. As Ann Freeman has shown, the Franks do indeed seem to have responded to the *acta* as if they were working with an official record. No source betrays the slightest hint that the Franks thought they were working with a translation.[5] Why it did not occur to someone at the Carolingian court that a Byzantine council would have conducted its business in Greek is impossible to say. In the middle of the ninth century Hincmar of Reims said that Charles got the *acta* from Rome.[6] This is almost certainly true, but Hincmar does not say why he believed this to be the case. It is quite possible that Hadrian himself forwarded the documents to Charlemagne. But it is not impossible that someone else in Rome sent them, someone who might have known that the Franks were, at the present time, unlikely to be pleased with the results of Nicaea's deliberations.

If Hadrian himself sent the documents, it is surprising that no cover letter survives and that no mention of the documents appears in the routine Franko-papal correspondence preserved in the *Codex Carolinus*. Perhaps Hadrian simply assumed that his endorsement of II Nicaea would have received Frankish concurrence. After all, the Franks had witnessed a debate on images at Gentilly in 767, and twelve Frankish bishops had participated in the Roman Synod of 769 where the then-reigning Byzantine iconophobia was condemned and the veneration of images was affirmed. Still, as the *Opus Caroli* and certain allied documents make clear, the Frankish view on images had shifted dramatically in twenty years. If Hadrian knew this, it might be possible to argue that he was not himself responsible for sending the Nicene records to Charles because he did not want to stir up a debate with his ally, friend, and protector.

But did Hadrian know this? And what did the Franks know about Byzantium's volte-face on images? Here is where the events after Nicaea get very murky. One can only offer reasoned speculations. These speculations turn around who knew what, and when they knew it. Charlemagne had entered upon a marriage alliance with the Byzantines in 781 when he affianced his daughter Rotrud to the young Constantine VI.[7] This engagement was broken off in 787 but for a few years there will have been reasonably frequent communications about it. What is more, a Byzantine courtier was sent to Francia to instruct the future princess.[8] In 786 Byzantine envoys found Charles in southern Italy where he was campaigning against the Beneventans and tried to get him to send Rotrud back with them. He refused to do so. In 788 the Byzantines attacked Frankish interests in southern Italy, allegedly because by this time Charles had definitively broken off the engagement.[9] This sequence of events suggests that there were fairly continuous Franko-Byzantine contacts between 786 and 788, the very years when Nicaea was being planned and actually took place.[10] An entry in the *Royal Frankish Annals* for 798 says that in that year Charles granted Sisinnius, the brother of Patriarch Tarasius, leave to go home. He had been captured in Italy "*iam dudum*," "a long time ago," in all probability amid the skirmishing in 788.[11] If Sisinnius were at the Carolingian court, where so eminent a hostage might well have been kept, for nearly a decade, he could have been a valuable source for what had been going on in Constantinople. Charles and Hadrian were in regular contact through the 780s and Charles himself visited Rome in 787. In 786 a papal legation crossed Francia on its way to England where it held a series of legatine councils. One key member of that legation was George of Ostia, the bishop of Amiens who had resided in Francia since 753 and who was, surely, one of the last living participants in the Roman Synod of 769. He could have been a valuable source of information.[12] Finally, scholars detect Alcuin's hand in the drafting of the legatine reports of 786.[13] If, as Donald Bullough has suggested, Alcuin became a full-time member of Charlemagne's court circle only after 786, and not from 782 as is usually assumed,[14] and since Alcuin did indeed meet with George of Ostia in England in 786, then he too might be seen as a valuable informant about Byzantine and papal affairs when he settled in Francia. Michael McCormick's prodigiously detailed demonstration of the frequency and intensity of trans-Mediterranean contacts in the early Middle Ages provides yet more potential context.[15] One can make an impressive case that all parties in the late 780s ought to have known each other's views and activities quite fully. And yet there was confusion about how the Franks got their copy of the Nicene *acta,* and serious differences had arisen between the papal and Frankish views on images without people in either Rome or Francia knowing or admitting that those differences existed.

The Preparation of the Opus Caroli

Exactly what happened when the *acta* reached the Frankish court is not clear either. In the preface to the *Opus Caroli* Theodulf refers to a council that "took place roughly three years ago."[16] Freeman believes that this remark dates the preface to 790 or 791.[17] So the thread of the story can be picked up in Francia in the dawning 790s. Some of the work of refuting Nicaea was already going on for Theodulf had begun drafting the *Opus Caroli* under unknown circumstances.[18] But the entry for 792 in the *York Annals* cited above says that Charlemagne sent the *acta* to England. Even if we suppose that this remark is true, it does not tell us when the documents were dispatched to England; we only know that the anonymous York annalist chose to record this information under the year 792. Why would Charlemagne have sent Nicaea's records to England? Because Alcuin, his most trusted adviser and intellectual jack-of-all-trades, was in England during the period 790–93.[19] The same passage in the *York Annals* does say that Alcuin submitted some sort of written response to the Nicene materials but, unfortunately, that document vanished and we do not know when he wrote it, when he sent it, if it arrived, or who read it.[20]

If Theodulf was already working in 790 or 791 and if at some point shortly thereafter the essential sources were sent to England, what was Theodulf working with before Alcuin's return in 793? It has been suggested that the Franks received from Rome only extracts of the Nicene *acta* in the first place.[21] Although, as I shall show in detail below, Theodulf seems to have misunderstood the context of some of the statements in the *acta*, his overall reactions are too detailed and thorough to support an argument that he *never* had more than extracts to work with. But recently, in light of the York annalist's statement, Freeman has suggested that Theodulf may have worked for a while with the full Nicene text, made extracts of his own before the full set of documents was sent to Alcuin in England, and then once again grappled with the complete text after Alcuin's return.[22] This is plausible. But it seems unlikely to me that the court's primary respondent to II Nicaea would have been forced to work from extracts and that the only full text was sent across the sea.

Little can therefore be said confidently about how the Frankish court reacted to Nicaea and the image question in 790–91. The identities and roles of the key personalities are no less intriguing that the events themselves. Alcuin's is a schoolhouse name. Theodulf's is not.[23] He was a Goth, perhaps from Saragossa, or maybe from Septimania, who was born around 760 and who suddenly appears in the Carolingian sources in around 790. In addition to writing the *Opus Caroli*, he was a superb biblical scholar, a gifted theologian, and the finest poet of the Carolingian age. It is not at all surprising that so talented a man came to Charlemagne's attention or that his talents were applied to the complicated matter of responding to Byzantium. The problem for scholars is that, as far as is known, Theodulf appeared out of nowhere and immediately assumed a leading role at the Carolingian court. It should not be forgotten that the shadowy presence of Alcuin hovers over the early months of the eighth century's last decade.

After the year 792 the web of evidence grows more dense, but no easier to interpret. In the summer of that year a provisional version of the Frankish court's answer to Nicaea was sent to Hadrian in Rome. The *Opus Caroli* was eventually assembled in four books totaling 120 chapters. The provisional work, which is organized differently, has eighty-five chapters in two series, one of sixty chapters and one of twenty-five. When the eighty-five-chapter Carolingian draft reached Rome, it evoked a howl of protest. Hadrian responded—hereafter the *Responsum*—to what he called the *Capitulare adversus synodum* in one of the longest papal letters of the early Middle Ages.[24] The *Capitulare* itself does not survive. Its contents can be partially reconstructed from the *Responsum*.[25] That is, the pope cites one chapter title after another and then rebuts the implicit or explicit criticism of Nicaea suggested by each title. Hadrian's letter begs an unanswerable question: Was the *Capitulare* a treatise or merely a list of objectionable Nicene passages that Theodulf—and others?—had identified and wished to call to the pope's attention? We will turn to the arrival of the *Responsum* in, probably, 793 just below. For now, I mention it only as evidence for the *Capitulare* of 792.

As they worked through the Nicene *acta* the Franks made what must have been a distressing discovery, and the way they reacted indicates that they wished to avoid provoking the pope. Standing near the head of the Nicene materials was Hadrian's letter of 785 to Constantine VI and Irene (JE 2448: the *Hadrianum*). This letter was read out during Nicaea's second session. Some statements pertaining to images that the Franks deemed most objectionable appeared precisely in this letter. The Franks had no desire to attack Hadrian personally so they adopted the subterfuge of looking hard for references to these passages elsewhere in the Nicene *acta*, usually in *actio IV*, and then assigned the offending remarks to that source. On a few occasions they simply made vague references without specifying an *actio*. Sometimes, when Hadrian had cited one text by an author the Franks referred to a subsequent Nicene citation of a completely different text by that same author. This took skill and is a first pointer to Theodulf's complete and intimate familiarity with the *acta*. In other words, Theodulf and his associates had no intention of attributing directly to Hadrian what they took to be dubious citations and questionable teachings.[26] Thus as the *Capitulare* was being drafted the Franks knew beyond a doubt that they and the pope disagreed on the subject of images and on the evidence that could be cited in defense of images. Given the information assembled above about the numerous contacts between and among Constantinople, Rome, and Francia in the 780s, it is difficult to understand how the Franks could have, for several years, badly miscalculated the substance and import of the pope's acceptance of II Nicaea. Or, in light of those contacts, and of Gentilly (767) and Rome (769), perhaps the Franks had not altered their own views on images until the early 790s. After all, many of the passages in the *Hadrianum* of 785 reiterated citations from the Roman Synods of 731 and 769. The Franks had attended the Synod of 769 and that synod's specifically reaffirmed the teaching of the Synod of 731. Once they saw the Nicene *acta*, however, they perceived a much more serious problem in Nicaea's comprehensive defense of image worship. The magnitude and vehemence of the *Responsum* may have been startling to the Franks, but they should have been ready for some disagreement.

Another development in 792 sheds light on the tension between Hadrian and the Franks. It should be noted, however, that none of the surviving narrative sources from the Frankish world contains a word about Theodulf, the *Capitulare*, or the *Opus Caroli*. From these sources, as indeed from Einhard's later biography of Charlemagne, one would not know that a discussion of images was underway. The most informative sources for the year 792 say that while the king was wintering (that is, the winter of 791–92) with his court at Regensburg, Felix, the bishop of Urgel in the Spanish March, was condemned for his allegedly dubious Christological reasoning. His error has long been labeled "adoptionism." Supposedly he maintained that Jesus was adopted as a son by God the Father at the moment of his baptism in the River Jordan by John the Baptist.[27] We will meet Felix and his co-heretic Elipandus of Toledo again shortly. For now it is important to note two facts: the Frankish sources make it appear that adoptionism was the really serious theological problem at this time, and Felix was sent to Rome with Angilbert, one of Charlemagne's most trusted counsellors. The *Responsum* says explicitly that Angilbert brought the *Capitulare* to Rome.[28] This permits a secure date of 792 for this preliminary stage of work on the response to Nicaea. There is no evidence for how long Angilbert stayed in Rome. Since Angilbert did have contact with the pope in the case of Felix, and since on that matter the Franks and the pope were in perfect accord, it is a fair hypothesis that Anglibert also discussed the *Capitulare* with Hadrian. There is no evidence to prove or disprove that he brought back Hadrian's response. What he learned, what impact if any he had on the pope, or what personal message the pope might have given him are all gone beyond recovery. What is more, careful prosopographical research reveals that Charlemagne had with him at Regensburg virtually all of his key Roman and Byzantine advisers, men with experience reaching back a decade or more.[29] This discovery adds to the mystery surrounding the dispatch of the *Capitulare* to Rome. Did this group of wily diplomats devise the textual legerdemain that was used to deflect criticism from Hadrian himself? If the tactful approach of the *Capitulare* was Theodulf's work, are we to suppose that no one bothered to tell the assembled "old hands" that a serious problem had arisen, or that they were so informed but recommended that the *Capitulare* be transmitted anyway?

The records of the Paris Colloquy of 825 provide a clue that sheds further light on events in 792 and that will help to move the narrative along to 793. The bishops who assembled at Paris under the aegis of Charlemagne's successor, Louis the Pious, were addressing the renewed outbreak of iconophobia in Byzantium. They say, referring to the first dispute, that at a meeting of some kind the material was read out for Charlemagne's approval.[30] Those records actually associate the public discussion with the *Capitulare* that Angilbert took to Rome. If that statement is strictly accurate then the public assessment "by himself [i.e., Charles] and his men" must have taken place at Regensburg in 792.

The Vatican manuscript of the *Opus* sheds additional light on this period while deepening the mysteries that surround it. Vaticanus Latinus 7207 is the actual working manuscript of the *Opus Caroli*. It is a unique document. Although this manuscript now lacks the preface, the opening of book one, and all of book four,[31] it still displays at least 3,400 corrections.[32] Some of these amount to no more than the alteration of a letter or two within a single word. Sometimes, however, whole passages, running to dozens of lines, were either crossed out, erased, or erased and replaced. In general terms we can say that the "editors" corrected Theodulf's Hispanisms, rephrased passages, added references, or softened (and/or shortened) the text's vicious criticisms. Freeman discerns at least four hands among the correctors. None can be identified. The overall impression conveyed by the Vatican manuscript is of a "team" effort at the court even if, as Freeman's meticulous researches have demonstrated, Theodulf was primarily responsible for the shape and argument of the *Opus*. Serious attention was lavished on this work. The Vatican manuscript reveals a major collaboration among Charlemagne's brain trust.

In the margins of the manuscript Freeman finds and deciphers at least eighty-one, and possibly eighty-three, notes in Tironian shorthand. In a further twenty-eight cases she detects evidence for the existence of a note that can no longer be read. As a result of a careless rebinding of the book in the nineteenth century a good many more notes were sliced off the edges of the pages. Some of them have left just a hint that they were once there.[33] These notes, virtually always one or two words such as *acute, bene, catholice, perfecte, sapienter*, or *totum bene*, record either the actual reactions of Charlemagne as the work was read in his presence or the collective reactions of his key courtiers. We may be sure, in other words, that both the work as a whole and dozens of its individual arguments had the king's expressed approval. Indeed, the work is ascribed to Charles himself—*The Work of Charles against the Synod*—a fact somewhat obscured by the former title, *The Caroline Books*.

But when did it get his approval? The easiest answer is to say "at Regensburg." There is no doubt that such an answer would be true. But it might not be complete. That is, when the *Capitulare* was sent to Rome it contained, as noted, eighty-five chapters in two series of sixty and twenty-five. The first sixty chapters of the *Capitulare* are not arranged exactly like the first sixty chapters of the *Opus,* but there is an overall similarity and both focus heavily, in these sections, on matters of biblical interpretation. The *Capitulare's* second series of chapters treat a wide range of issues in no systematic order. Eventually many of those issues found their way into books three and four of the *Opus.* Book four cannot be incorporated at this point into the present discussion because it is only known from the ninth-century Paris manuscript. That manuscript exhibits neither the corrections by Theodulf and others to the original text nor the Tironian notes. But book three has many corrections, albeit fewer than books one and two; indeed, book two, the shortest in the *Opus,* is the most massively corrected. Book three also has thirteen Tironian notes and Freeman has been able to identify four cases where there was once a note that is no longer legible. The point, quite simply, is that work continued all the while on the *Opus* and that such work probably extended well into 793 and possibly into 794.

Both the text of the *Opus* and the Vatican manuscript provide evidence for events in the course of 793. Concerning the text of the *Opus* two point may be made. First, the serious issue of adoptionism, which for obvious reasons had played absolutely no role at Nicaea, imposed itself on the *Opus* in several places. Such references may have been incorporated at Regensburg or may have been incorporated later as a result of the consultations on adoptionism that took place there. Such references might well have been inserted during the course of 793 or 794 as plans were underway for the Council of Frankfurt where the issue of adoptionism literally topped the agenda. Second, in just a few places in book four the influence of Alcuin has been detected.[34] It is not impossible that some contributions from Alcuin's letter from England found their way into books one and two which are largely devoted to criticizing Nicaea's biblical references. Alcuin was himself a formidable biblical scholar and his letter, or treatise, was based "on the authority of the divine scriptures." But the point that bears re-membering is that Alcuin did not return from England until sometime late in the first half of 793. Too, it is hard to believe that Charlemagne would not have wished to hear Alcuin's voice on a matter that had been discussed at his court and that had been written into a massive treatise that itself was the work of a great scholar and a troupe of collaborators. While we cannot say for certain just what was going on in 793, the text and the manuscripts of the *Opus* do point to continued revision.

The corrections in the Vatican manuscript tell other stories. Even though we cannot state conclusively what stage the *Opus* had reached when Angilbert departed for Rome in 792, it seems clear that the Vatican manuscript had not yet been begun. So one story told by the manuscript is that it was written between Angilbert's departure and late 793 or early 794. Another story told by the manuscript is best heard in Freeman's words:

> There is a curious demarcation in the Vatican manuscript where production standards suddenly and markedly decline. Up to LC [i.e., *Libri Carolini*, as it was then called] 3.13 the scriptorium used its finest parchment and supplied fine, large initials for each chapter, all of which were written in an elegant early Caroline minuscule; when discussion of the contents resulted in revisions, these were accomplished with great care. After LC 3.13 the character of the script deteriorates, becoming looser and coarser, most of the initials are small and mean, holes appear in the parchment, and whole pages are roughly crossed out, instead of being carefully erased and rewritten, as before. It appears that something has happened by which the enterprise has been blighted, but not halted.[35]

Freeman believes, and I think she must be right, that the arrival of the *Responsum* showed the Franks just how wide a chasm separated them from papal Rome. The *Opus* was brought to completion, or at any rate Vat. Lat. 7207 was completed hastily, without the usual polish. The work as such could not be sent to the pope, or disseminated generally, without advertising a sharp divide between the pope and Charles. Given the deferential tone of *Opus* 1.6, the most rigorously pro-papal in the whole treatise, alongside many other marks of respect paid to the popes and to papal traditions, the identification of such a divide was no doubt disconcerting but an advertisement of it was unthinkable. We will never know what a final, revised, and corrected version of the *Opus* might have looked like as a book, and we cannot be sure that all of its arguments would have stood exactly as we now read them.

The Vatican manuscript tells yet another story. In the course of its ongoing revision, several passages were rewritten to condemn adoptionism.[36] Letters from Elipandus of Toledo and his fellow Spanish bishops explaining their teachings to Charles and to the Frankish bishops arrived in Francia in 792 or 793.[37] These letters must have been a sober warning that Felix's condemnation at Regensburg in 792 was not going to put an end to a serious doctrinal quarrel that touched the very person of Jesus Christ. Accordingly, references to Christ's consubstantiality and coeternity with the Father, or to His being *"genitus"* not *"adoptivus"* were subtly introduced into the *Opus*. It is possible that Alcuin was summoned from England precisely to deal with the adoptionist issue for he certainly wrote a great deal on the subject in the next few years.[38] If this is true then this story connects textual and manuscript evidence while also revealing how Theodulf's book on images was sometimes influenced by other people and issues.

And there is a final story. Because it draws on evidence from book four it is as much a "text" as a "manuscript" story, but there is good reason to suppose that if we had the Vatican manuscript's version of book four we would be able to visualize the editorial ministrations that are the characters in this last tale. It seems that *Opus* 4.13, which criticized the claims of II Nicaea to universality, was originally meant to be the *Opus*'s last chapter.[39] But the end of the book as we now know it, 4.28, is a chapter that lays out a new theory regarding the universality of councils. The differences between these chapters will be discussed later but for now it is only important to say that, as plans for Frankfurt continued, the Franks were building a case for it to be a universal council and their deliberations on this matter found their way into the *Opus*. All of these stories help us to situate the *Opus* and the image controversy within the events of the year 793 as planning continued for Frankfurt.[40]

The Council of Frankfurt, 794

The whole situation surrounding the Council of Frankfurt (June 794) is also enigmatic. This is not the place for a full assessment of the problems surrounding and the accomplishments of that council.[41] I shall explore three issues. How did the council treat the subject of II Nicaea and of images? What does the council reveal about Charlemagne's relations with Pope Hadrian? What kind of a council was it?

Late in 793 papal envoys who were "presented with great gifts" met Charlemagne in southwestern Germany shortly before he went to St.-Killian's in Würzburg for Christmas.[42] Charlemagne then moved to Frankfurt where he spent the winter of 794, the Easter season (Easter was March 23), and the time down to the general assembly of the Franks appointed for Frankfurt on 1 June.[43] In the midst of that assembly Charles held a "great synod" including "the bishops from his whole kingdom," according to one source, or the "bishops of Gaul, Germany, and Italy," according to another. The synod was held in the presence of the papal legates Theophylact and Stephen.[44] It is likely that these were the same two legates who met with Charles late in the previous year. But it is possible that a new legation was sent by Hadrian.

The *Opus* was already very far advanced by late 793. The *Responsum* should probably be attributed to the papal embassy at the end of that year. Freeman reads the key passage on gifts to mean that the envoys brought the gifts to

Charlemagne to soften the blow.[45] I read the Latin the other way around and maintain that, on the contrary, the envoys got gifts from Charlemagne. Perhaps this was a peace offering on his part after he realized that his *Capitulare* had received a less than welcome reception in Rome. It is unlikely that papal legates were traipsing about Alemannia in the late autumn looking for Charlemagne who was visiting his huge canal project. Possibly they met him at St.-Killian's or, more likely, at Frankfurt early in 794. As the winter of 794 progressed, and as preparations for the assembly and council of Frankfurt continued apace, the Franks now knew for certain that Hadrian had rejected their condemnation of II Nicaea and their views on images. Von den Steinen believed that he could detect some modest alterations to the final text of the *Opus* designed to bring it a little more into line with the pope's views. Freeman is skeptical.[46] Whatever conversations passed between the Franks and the papal legates, the *Opus* was hastily concluded and silently filed away in the royal archives.

The prime annalistic source for the Council of Frankfurt says only that it was held to condemn, for the third time, the heresy of Felix. The text then moves on directly to the death and burial of Charlemagne's wife Fastrada. A later hand then interpolated into the entry for 794, at its end, "The pseudosynod of the Greeks, which they held for the adoration of images and which they falsely call the seventh, was rejected by the bishops."[47] The later revised version of the *Royal Frankish Annals* also mention Felix's condemnation, then adds, "The synod, too, which was assembled a few years ago in Constantinople under Irene and her son Constantine and called by them not only the seventh but even universal, was cast aside by everyone as completely and totally useless so that it would not be considered or called seventh or universal."[48] Neither of these sources mentions Theodulf, Alcuin, or the *Opus*.

The actual canons of Frankfurt are in perfect accord with the annalistic sources in one key respect: Felix's condemnation stands first. Then canon two addresses images and Nicaea but does so in an astonishing way. The canon reads: "The question of the recent synod of the Greeks, which was held in Constantinople for the adoration of images, was entered into the discussion; one finds written there that they who do not pay to the images of the saints the same service or adoration as to the divine Trinity are bound by anathema; our above mentioned most holy fathers, utterly rejecting such adoration and service, hate it and agree in condemning it."[49] The Latin is strange but the tactic adopted here is even stranger.

At Nicaea Bishop Constantine of Constantia in Cyprus had explicitly and carefully said that images were not to be paid the service or adoration paid to the holy Trinity.[50] Somehow his statement was garbled in the transmission, probably in the poor Latin version of the *acta* that Charlemagne received, and came out with him insisting that "I receive and embrace honorably the holy and most venerable images according to the service of adoration which I pay to the consubstantial and life-giving Trinity."⁵¹ This statement was severely criticized by Theodulf, but no more so, really, than dozens of others. In the *Responsum* Hadrian addressed this passage by saying that the Greeks had struggled with all their might to revert from heresy and that, for their actual views on images, one should turn to the definition of the synod as a whole.⁵² He did not directly address the charge itself. Perhaps the Franks reasoned that this one statement would be seen by the papal legates as so outlandish, and so indefensible, that they would concur in its condemnation. If they had looked at the faulty Latin version of the *acta* they would have been able to satisfy themselves that Constantine had, indeed, said this. A look at the Greek *acta* might have straightened them out, but no one seems to have used the Greek version through all these years. What the Franks got, then, was a very qualified condemnation of one statement allegedly uttered at Nicaea. But what of the amazingly ambiguous Latin of canon two? The last clause can be read, as I did above, to mean that one statement, and one statement only, was condemned. But the participles in that sentence are plural and could be either nominative or accusative, either the subjects or the objects of the two main verbs, or adjectives modifying the holy fathers, that is the bishops assembled at Frankfurt. The clause could be read as a rejection of Nicaea *tout court*.⁵³ It is hard to believe that papal legates would have accepted that. Is the ambiguity innocent?

Some clues to an answer to that question were mentioned above.⁵⁴ The *Royal Frankish Annals*, which stood close in time to the events they described, mentioned only the condemnation of Felix. Later, at a date that simply cannot be determined, someone interpolated a statement with two fundamental elements: Nicaea was a "pseudosynod" and Nicaea was falsely called the "seventh." We also saw that the revised annals, which certainly post-date Frankfurt by a good twenty years but often supply solid information for this earlier period, rejected any notion that Nicaea was the seventh ecumenical council of the church or a universal council. Two other annalistic sources that are nearly contemporary with Frankfurt also reveal some of these characteristics. The *Lorsch Annals* make no mention at all of Nicaea, images, or the Greeks, provide an unusually long, detailed description of Felix's condemnation, and call Frankfurt a "universal" council.⁵⁵ The *Maximinian Annals* do not call Frankfurt universal, but like the *Royal Frankish Annals*, they enumerate all the places that bishops came from, even adding Bavaria to the list. This source also uses the word "pseudosynod" for Nicaea and rejects numbering it as the seventh council.⁵⁶

Pulling these disparate sources together permits a few inferences about authoritative Frankish thinking. They themselves rejected Nicaea and refused to let it be called "seventh" or "universal." But they did not go so far as to put this rejection on the record at Frankfurt in the presence of papal legates. At least they did not do so if one gives a minimalist reading to the bizarre phrasing of the last part of canon two. Given that some of the best minds of the Frankish world had been addressing the image question and II Nicaea for some four to five years, and given that at least once and maybe twice the image issue was argued out in Charlemagne's presence, it seems a little odd that so much effort produced such modest results at Frankfurt and that the *Opus* was so quickly forgotten. But there was a need to avoid an outright break with Rome. By looking closely at how the Franks and the pope dodged the image question, and by comparing their treatment of that specific issue with some other issues that were then being discussed by the Carolingian and papal courts, we will be able to see more precisely how to understand where the image controversy fits in the larger framework of the history of this particular period.

Later sections of this chapter will treat Franko-papal relations in more detail. For now, I wish to focus on the years between about 790 and 794 and to look closely at the two issues that have come to our attention already, Nicaea and adoptionism, and then to add one more issue, namely the procession of the Holy Spirit. The ways in which these issues were treated in the four or five years under review illuminate each other, help to clarify the ways in which Charles and Hadrian dealt with the problem posed by Nicaea, and shed light on the work of the Council of Frankfurt itself.

Right away, one point needs reiteration and expansion. We saw already that in preparing the *Capitulare* Theodulf and his associates were extremely careful not to attribute to Hadrian himself any statement that they intended to attack. Obviously they did not wish to provoke or to impugn the orthodoxy of the pope whose assent they were seeking. Of course, they did not know, at least not in detail, what Hadrian's reaction would be until late in 793 or perhaps even early in 794. We have also seen that it is very difficult to discern actual changes in the text of the *Opus* that were occasioned by Hadrian's letter. But we can look at other sections of the *Opus*, some of which may have been finished in 792 when the *Capitulare* was completed but a few of which were definitely composed later in 792 or in 793.

Several times in the course of the *Opus* Theodulf either cited directly or alluded indirectly to the *Decretum Gelasianum*, a work composed somewhere in northern Italy in the early sixth century and long attributed to Pope Gelasius I (492–96).[57] This book was a list of works deemed authentic and authoritative, allegedly by the authority of the pope. By turning to it a number of times either to buttress the reliability of his own arguments or to attack the credibility of Byzantine testimonies, Theodulf implicitly hewed to the papal standard.[58] There is a certain irony here, however. *Opus* 1.6, the most rigorously pro-papal chapter in the book, did not appear in the *Capitulare* and seems not to have been Theodulf's work in the first instance.[59] Its inclusion in the final version of the *Opus* provides an excellent example of the nature and impact of the process of revision at the Carolingian court. Thedoulf, as an Iberian Goth, had a somewhat wary attitude toward actual papal power and intervention. Texts that arose in Spain in the earliest stage of the adoptionist controversy betray the same reservations about Rome.[60] He never mentions the pope in the preface to the *Opus*, focusing instead on the right and responsibility of the king to look out for the church and its faith. At the Carolingian court there was also an elevated sense of the king's prerogatives but, at the same time, a powerful feeling that authentic traditions came from Rome and had to be learned and implemented in all possible cases. In the sixth and seventh centuries, the Franks, although by no means hostile or indifferent to Rome, did not have this same sharp perception of the Rome-centeredness of the faith and church.[61] It seems to me that it was the Anglo-Saxon missionaries and scholars, who maintained close associations with the Carolingians going right back to Charlemagne's great-grandfather, Pippin II, who slowly but surely insinuated this Roman perspective into Frankish thinking.[62] Be that as it may, we can see that while the *Opus* was being composed Theodulf himself had a hearty respect for Roman traditions, if not necessarily for the authority of the reigning pope, while others at court had a profound devotion to papal authority.

This issue of how to deal with Rome only arises in the first place because of an age-old tendency in the scholarship on this period to see either the *Opus* or the second Frankfurt canon as majestic statements of Charlemagne's domination of the church and of the papacy. Some even speak of his having humiliated the pope by promulgating canon two in the presence of his legates.[63] These views are anachronistic. What is more, they are actually contradicted by the *Opus* itself and by the whole course of events surrounding Frankfurt. But it is important not to go too far in the opposite direction. That is, one cannot argue that as a loyal son of the church Charlemagne backed down when the pope informed him of this disagreement. Freeman thinks, for example, that Charlemagne was dissuaded from "publishing" the *Opus*.[64] I think it is hard to see just how the work might have been disseminated in the first place. It is very long, 461 quarto pages in Freeman's edition, 192 folios in the incomplete Vatican manuscript, and 244 folios in the Paris manuscript. Clearly, the book could not have been copied and distributed widely. Its weak manuscript tradition is about as strong as that of the unquestionably important and authoritative Council of Frankfurt.[65] And one is reminded of famous literary texts, say *Beowulf* or *La chanson de Roland,* which are weakly attested by surviving copies. The final version of the *Opus* has Charlemagne's name proudly and prominently on its first page in beautiful script: "INCIPIT OPUS INLUSTRISSIMI ET EXCEL-LENTISSIMI SEU SPECTABILIS VIRI CAROLI, NUTU DEI REGIS FRANCORUM, GALLIAS, GERMANIAM ATQUE ITALIAMQUE SIVE HARUM FINITIMAS PROVINTIAS DOMINO OPITULANTE RE-GENTIS, CONTRA SYNODUM, QUE IN PARTIBUS GRAETIAE PRO ADORANDIS IMAGINIBUS STOLIDE SIVE ARROGANTER GESTA EST."[66] This is the only treatise from Charlemagne's long reign that bears his name. He had no intention of humiliating the pope and he did not in some sense retire from the controversy. Charlemagne and Hadrian did not deal with each other that way, and early medieval popes did not yet have, and rarely even claimed, the right to impose their will in dogma. What the Franks wanted from Rome was less the orders of the current pope than the assurance that they were adhering faithfully to the living Roman tradition.[67]

The materials with which we have been dealing provide an interesting per-spective on the relations between the Franks and the popes with respect to dogmatic issues. On the subject of adoptionism, there was complete agreement on the basic point that Felix, Elipandus, and their followers were wrong. Coop-eration in dealing with this issue was easy. But the issue was not brought to Hadrian's attention in the first place by the Franks. Rather, Hadrian received notice in the mid-780s directly from Spain, and he wrote to the Spanish bishops, despite having very little accurate information, to reject what he had learned of their teaching on the subject of Christ's having been "*adoptivus,*" and he referred in a general way to the decrees of the Council of Ephesus that had condemned Nestorius.[68] It was the Franks who really took the lead in combatting adoption-ism. Felix was apprehended and interrogated at least three times. In the run-up to Frankfurt several major treatises were written against adoptionism. Alcuin composed several works of his own against the adoptionists, in addition to pre-paring Charlemagne's letter to the Spanish bishops and, perhaps, the letter of the Frankish bishops to Spain. Although there was Franko-papal concurrence, it looks as though the Franks themselves really took the lead in dealing with adoptionism. But there is another intriguing hint about Frankish relations with Rome. John Cavadini has brilliantly extracted the actual teachings of the adop-tionists from the doctrines ascribed to them by their antagonists. Hadrian, as noted, accused the adoptionists, more by implication than by detailed argument, of a species of Nestorianism. When the Franks, and Alcuin in particular, addressed adoptionism they treated it as, again, a kind of Nestorianism. It would be interesting to know if this was an independent intellectual result or an attempt to come into line with Roman, papal teaching. Either way, the basic level of cooperation remains intact.

We have seen that on images the Franks and the popes, on the broadest possible reading of the evidence, agreed to disagree. Neither finally imposed a view on the other. There is another case of the same kind from roughly the same period which yields a like conclusion. The first chapter of the *Capitulare* castigated the profession of faith which Tarasius pronounced at Nicaea because he said the "Holy Spirit proceeds from the Father *through* the Son" (emphasis added). Hadrian's reply, one of the longest in the *Responsum*, defends the Byzantine position on the authority of numerous patristic citations.[69] At some point the Franks had inserted into their recitation of the creed—the "Nicene" Creed was not yet recited at every celebration of Mass—the word *filioque* which produced this phrase: *ex Patre filioque procedit Spiritus Sanctus*. In this formulation the Holy Spirit proceeds not *through* the son but *from* the Father *and from* the Son. East and West both accepted the "double procession" of the Holy Spirit but articulated their understanding differently. Rome had not adopted the word *filioque* and did not do so until the eleventh century.[70] Theodulf, meanwhile, repeatedly attacked the Greeks for a faulty understanding of this essential doctrine.[71]

There the matter rested until in 809 a council was held in the Frankish world because some Frankish monks on the Mount of Olives near Jerusalem had been criticized by Greek monks for reciting a creed with *filioque* in it. The Frankish monks wrote to Pope Leo III, asked him to settle the matter, and told him that they had heard *filioque* recited in Charlemagne's chapel. Leo merely referred the case to the Franks. Charles, as was his custom, sought and received the views of several of his most reliable theological advisers. Several treatises were prepared defending the Frankish version of the creed and of the theology that undergirded it, and a deputation was sent to Rome to attempt to persuade Leo of the correctness of the Carolingian view.[72] Leo would not budge. In other words, and exactly as in the image controversy, the pope and the Franks agreed to disagree. Neither side imposed itself on the other. There were no charges of heresy. Cordial relations persisted.

These comparisons can be drawn out a little more so as to make them as clear and telling as possible. Let us think back to the letter written by Alcuin and drawn from "the authority of the divine scriptures." That might have been a very personal reaction by him to the Council of Nicaea. But given Alcuin's fame, connections, and involvement with the legatine decrees of 786, it might also have been a more or less official pronouncement on behalf of the church in England. There was also the *Capitulare*, a preliminary tract or the outline for one, vigorous discussions on one or more occasions in the Frankish court, and the *Opus* itself. If the materials pertinent to the image controversy are viewed in this way, then they compare favorably, in both quantity and circumstances of composition, to the sets of treatises produced before and after Frankfurt in connection with adoptionism and around 809 in connection with the *filioque* dispute.

The way Albert Werminghoff printed the Frankfurt materials in the MGH creates a sort of optical illusion. That is, one finds in his edition six collateral treatises or epistles and then the conciliar canons.[73] This appears to be a closed group of materials relevant to canon one and creates the impression that canon two, dealing with Nicaea, is fundamentally different, poorer, weaker somehow. Yet no manuscript of the Frankfurt canons transmits this body of material exactly as Werminghoff printed it, and only two manuscripts attach even one of the treatises, that of Paulinus of Aquileia, to the canons.[74] The materials produced in 809 are likewise never transmitted as a closed group and often do not appear in manuscripts containing the canons of the council of 809.[75] Viewed in this way, the Frankfurt materials do not appear to slight the image question or the *Opus*.

Charlemagne and his closest associates seem to have had one consistent method for dealing with doctrinal problems. Whenever a problem was discovered, it was brought to Charles's attention. He then summoned the people whom he believed to be most capable of dealing with the issue. He also notified Rome that a problem had arisen and spelled out his plans for dealing with it. Work then proceeded, often along several fronts simultaneously. Two clues in the Frankfurt materials reveal how final decisions were reached. First, canons one and two of Frankfurt were issued with the following dispositive language:

> Canon One: "sanctissimi patres . . . contradixerunt atque . . . statuerunt" ("the most holy fathers contradict and . . . declare").

> Canon Two: "sanctissimi patres nostri . . . contempserunt atque . . . condempnaverunt" ("our most holy fathers . . . despise and . . . condemn").[76]

Thereafter the dispositive language either shares responsibility between the king and the synodists or else attributes action to the king alone. Two examples will suffice:

Canon Four: "Statuit piissimus domnus noster rex" ("Our most pious lord king decreed").

Canon Six: "Statutum est a domno rege et sancta synodo" ("It was decided by the lord king and the holy synod").[77]

Long ago Hans Barion concluded that "dogmatic issues were being independently decided legally by the bishops."[78] Second, in the Frankfurt dossier there is a letter of Charles to the Spanish bishops, probably written by Alcuin.[79] Charles tells the bishops that they will find in this letter the orthodox faith as it has been taught by the apostolic teachers, kept by the church, and now laid out by his men. He urges them to adhere to it. He then tells them that he had assembled a council from all the areas under his control to discern "the holy unanimity of everyone." He especially emphasizes that he sent envoys to Rome three or four times to learn what apostolic tradition taught on the matter at hand. He concludes by saying that although the Spanish bishops have appealed to him, they must be urged to adhere to the "unanimity" that he has discovered. He says that he holds "with every effort of my mind, with all the eagerness of my heart" to the teachings of the papacy and of the ancient church. And he says that he holds "without doubt" to whatever they will find written in the books that stem from that august tradition.[80] This is exactly like Barion's judgment with respect to Frankfurt's canons: the church studies and decides and Charles adheres to and enforces the decision.

The last sections of the *Responsum* illustrate the diplomatic climate very well. After having devoted page after page of a long document to refuting the Frankish criticisms of II Nicaea, Hadrian played two intriguing gambits in closing. First he praised Charles, the "official" author of the *Capitulare,* for citing the letter of Gregory I to Serenus of Marseilles. That letter was cited in the *Capitulare* but in a truncated fashion that omitted Gregory's teaching about the didactic value of images. Undeterred by details, Hadrian praised Charles for holding to Gregory's teaching and suggested that this, and this alone, was Charles's real view and that the rest of the *Capitulare* reflected the views of others which Charles could safely abandon. Then Hadrian said that if the Byzantines did not soon return a favorable decision on the matter of his lost patrimonies, provinces, and revenues, he might yet declare them heretics. He held out to the Franks the hope that they might yet achieve from the pope a condemnation of the Byzantines, if not a rejection of II Nicaea.[81] We will see in more detail below that that prudent concession on Hadrian's part was extremely valuable to the Franks. For the present, it is enough to emphasize that, on the one hand, there was no rupture in Franko-papal relations because of the image question and, on the other hand, popes and Franks could work together effectively and praise each other to the high heavens, without agreeing on everything.

Finally, then, what was the Frankish view of Frankfurt? This is not an easy question to answer. The basic sources cannot necessarily be brought into relation to one another. The records of Frankfurt, as published by Werminghoff, are entitled *Capitulare Franconofurtense*. As the annalistic sources say, Charlemagne held at Frankfurt a general assembly in the midst of which there was a council. Normally an assembly issued capitularies, a basically legislative document divided into chapters—*capitula*, whence the name—and a council issued canons. The Frankfurt documents as we have them start with purely theological matters and then turn to a vast array of both secular and ecclesiastical business. These hybrid records are not unprecedented in the Carolingian age but Frankfurt's do seem unusually complex. For the present, let us say only that as the product of a general assembly Frankfurt's enactments would certainly appear to have the stamp of official approval.

We have seen that the *Opus* absolutely refused to consider Nicaea as universal and refused to enumerate it as the seventh ecumenical council of the church. We have also seen that later sources, in looking back on Nicaea, likewise refused to call it universal or seventh. Here we should add that no source calls Frankfurt the seventh council; indeed, the *Opus* continually refers to the *six* councils (Nicaea 325, Constantinople 381, Ephesus 431, Chalcedon 451, Constantinople 553, Constantinople 680) and insists on strict, faithful Frankish adherence to those councils. Even when we bear in mind that the first six ecumenical councils only gradually acquired what we might call "numbered" status, that within the church as a whole it took a long time for Nicaea II to receive its official number, and that many Christian traditions, especially in the East, rejected one or another of the seven councils, as the Roman Catholic and Orthodox world eventually enumerated them, it is striking that no "ecumenical" claim was made for Frankfurt.[82] Does this mean, therefore, that the council was not ecumenical; that it was "local"?[83]

It used to be argued confidently that the Franks refused to accept Nicaea's ecumenicity because they were not invited,[84] because "each and every part of the church" had not been consulted.[85] This view is true, but it is only a fraction of the truth. The ancient church had built up a conciliar theory that had both "vertical" and "horizontal" dimensions. The vertical ones involved authoritative, accepted teaching that reached back through the church fathers to the Bible. The horizontal ones meant representation and acceptance by the "pentarchy" of ancient patriarchates (Jerusalem, Alexandria, Antioch, Constantinople,

Rome) and the churches they represented.[86] In the *Opus* one finds abundant evidence that Theodulf was conversant with both of these points of view. He constantly refers to the Bible and the fathers, virtually always to argue that the Franks, and not the Byzantines, are true to the "vertical" tradition. In *Opus* 4.13, originally intended to be the grand, rhetorical conclusion to the work Theodulf spelled out why II Nicaea could not be compared to I Nicaea; they shared only the name of the place where they met. All of this is conventional. There is something new, however. Sieben detects a Frankish introduction of the principles of *scrutinium* and *ratio*. On this basis the Franks thought that every passage adduced had to be studied carefully, fully to see that it did indeed accord with the tradition. Theodulf cites three times each two biblical passages that bear on this theme: 1 Thessalonians 5.21, "But test all things; keep that which is good" (4.8, 4.10, 4.11), and 1 John 4.1, "Believe not every spirit, but try every spirit to see if they are of God" (2.17, 3.26, 4.11). Some representative passages demonstrate Theodulf's commitment to discrimination. In 2.17 he objects to the citation of a passage he does not know from Gregory of Nyssa and says it must be tested and then he cites St. Paul, insisting that he thus acts *rationaliter*. In 3.11 he says the Greeks should have "investigated" what each part of the church thought about images. In 3.25 he insists on the need to "discriminate" among signs. In 3.26 he puzzles over what dreams "prove" if their information has not been compared against scripture. In 4.5 he provides a detailed analysis of a letter of St. Symeon Stylites. A look at Freeman's index under such words as *indagatio* (Theodulf's preference, it seems), *investigatio*, or *ratio* will reveal quite clearly his ongoing concern for testing the truth of any proposition instead of merely accepting it because it seems to be old.[87]

But *Opus* 4.28, the last chapter in the work as it now stands, contains a bold new synodal theory. The chapter itself is brief and its key section may be quoted:

> If the bishops of two or three provinces come together, armed with the body of teaching found in the ancient canons, and establish some point of teaching or dogma which does not diverge from the doctrine of the ancient Fathers, then the point they establish is catholic and can indeed be called universal, for although it was not established by the bishops of the universal world, nevertheless it does not diverge from the universal faith and tradition. We know that this has frequently happened in many parts of the world, as circumstances have required, for many councils have been held through whose actions the holy Church is both defended and strengthened.[88]

On the basis of this statement, and indeed on the basis of the whole argument developed in the *Opus*, the Greeks had recently departed from the teachings of the ancient fathers and therefore what they did was neither catholic nor universal. The "vertical" argument in the *Opus* is left much as antiquity had bequeathed it. But the "horizontal" argument has been altered significantly. Now the pentarchs are left out of account. Either or both of two explanations may be relevant. Perhaps Theodulf had some "vertical" reservations about Hadrian and Tarasius (and as we will see about Nicaea's legate from the Eastern patriarchs) or maybe he realized that the Muslim conquests of the seventh century had permanently shattered the pentarchy. In the current circumstances he may have doubted whether the pope could function alone as a Western patriarch.[89] Having left pentarchy aside as the measure of "horizontal" legitimacy, the Franks turn to what might be called a "locally horizontal" theory that required a tight bond to the vertical theory. In other words, when the "bishops of two or three provinces" come together and teach what the Catholic Church has always taught, then whatever those bishops accomplish is well and truly "catholic" and "universal." We need to bear in mind that the annalistic sources stressed this very aspect of Frankfurt as did Charlemagne's letter to the bishops of Spain. A variety of people from different locations discussed images, adoptionism, and the *filioque*. In each instance, according to the emerging view of the 790s, the Frankish actions were universal. Thus, and once again, it is not so important, really, whether the *Opus* was in some sense "published." The views which it contained represented the most up-to-date thinking of the Frankish court.

Opus Caroli Regis: A Summary of Its Contents and Organization

In the years between Nicaea and Frankfurt the Carolingians had an opportunity to take stock of what had been done at Nicaea, to reflect on several serious dogmatic issues, to deal with the pope on very sensitive and controverted problems, to think about their place within the church, and to produce a remarkable book. That book is a stunning achievement in biblical exegesis, a penetrating theological assessment of a whole series of interrelated problems, and the first Western discussion of art and aesthetics since antiquity.

Preliminary Considerations

The *Opus* is a work of deep learning that responded in luxuriant detail to the *acta* of II Nicaea. It is also a polemic of white-hot intensity. The author and his associates missed no opportunity to register their scorn for virtually everything said and done at Nicaea. Here is a representative sample of the kinds sour notes with which Theodulf scored his rancorous composition: absurd, childish, delerious, demented, depraved, fatuous, imprudent, incautious, laughable, mindless, obtuse, perverse, pointless, rash, reprehensible, ridiculous, risible, silly, stupid, supercilious, and useless. To be sure, the *Opus* grapples, rigorously and tenaciously, page after page, with profound theological problems. But one must wonder about Theodulf's rhetoric of disputation. Why is his tone so bitter, so relentlessly denunciatory? Theodulf was acidulous in other writings.[90] Perhaps this was a personal quirk. As we will see in Chapter 7, Claudius of Turin and Agobard of Lyon, Goths like Theodulf, could also write with poisoned pens. It may be that a specialist in Visigothic Latin could determine whether or not brutal invective is a distinguishing characteristic. Nevertheless, one gets the impression that more is involved here than merely the refutation of one or more arguments with which the author disagrees. One can see why Walter Schmandt called this work a "political tract."[91] Among our tasks an important one will be to respect the integrity of Theodulf's theological concerns, to discern his way of dealing with them, and, above all, to understand the political dimensions that suffused his treatise.

Whatever kind of text Theodulf wrote, past scholarship forces me to ask if Theodulf actually understood the materials to which he was responding. We have already seen that Theodulf was compelled to work with a poor Latin translation of the Nicene *acta*. There is a chance that, for some period in the very early 790s, he had only extracts to study, probably his own. There are only a few passages in the *Opus* that lend support to the argument that Theodulf never had more than extracts.[92] These concern several cases where Theodulf seems not to understand that, at Nicaea, Deacon Epiphanius was forced to read out the *horos* of Hiereia so that the Nicene fathers could meet it with their objections. Theodulf seems sometimes to have attributed Hiereian statements directly to Nicaea. There are not too many such cases and because we do not have the bad Latin text from which he worked—however long he worked with it—I think it is dangerous to attribute to Theodulf misunderstandings that may have been prompted by his sources. Be that as it may, others have suggested that the whole flow of Theodulf's argument suggests that he did not understand the Byzantine arguments contained in the Nicene records and that his problems may be attributable either to a truncated version of the *acta*, to a persistent failure to understand the Greek distinction between *proskynesis* and *latreia*, both of which he or his source regularly read as *adoratio*, and to a generally lower level of theological sophistication in the West than prevailed in the East.[93] If Theodulf simply did not, or could not, understand what was said at Nicaea, then it follows that the polemical side of his work would still be of value to historians and that the *Opus*'s character as a *Staatsschrift* would claim primacy in any interpretative scheme. But if Theodulf really did understand what happened at Nicaea, then the political aspects of his work assume significance alongside the theological, and Theodulf's labors provide us with a privileged look into the world of Carolingian learning and culture in the 790s. A good deal is at stake here.

Recently two distinguished Byzantinists, Marie-France Auzépy and Hans Georg Thümmel, and a younger French scholar, Kristina Mitalaité, have dealt devastating blows to almost every aspect of the traditionally invidious comparisons between Theodulf and his Eastern contemporaries.[94] We have seen already in this study that in both Eastern and Western art talk there was considerable ambiguity concerning the use of *proskynesis* and *latreia*, *veneratio* and *adoratio*. At Nicaea too there was some ambiguity in the application of these terms and in the observation of careful distinctions between them. John of Damascus had worked out the differences in considerable detail but, as with so many of John's ideas, his contribution on this topic, at least his deep philosophical argumentation, was neglected at Nicaea. On the one hand, then, the East was a good deal less consistent on this important topic than has usually been assumed. On the other hand, and regardless of what stood on the pages of the translation that Theodulf was reading, several passages in the *Opus* show that Theodulf did understand the distinction. He simply felt that the Byzantines failed to observe it.[95] Theodulf also saw that many biblical passages adduced at Nicaea were irrelevant to the matter at hand.[96] We will discuss his exegetical interests and strategies just below, but for now we must insist that he knew exactly what was going on in the citation of Scripture. Next, Theodulf understood perfectly well what was at issue when, say, Basil of Ancyra and Theodosius of Amorion confessed a faith in images but failed to mention the remission of sins, the resurrection of the dead, and life everlasting (*Opus* 3.6). The Franks understood the difference between honoring a person and honoring an image, they had well established views on the limited circumstances under which matter could be said to be holy, and they felt that the Greeks had too often crossed the line.[97] Finally, because of the relatively intense diplomacy of the 750s and 760s, and because of the discussions at Gentilly in 767 and in Rome in 769, the Franks understood Isaurian theology very well and, apart from rejecting its iconoclasm, actually embraced a good deal of it. In both East and West, it was II Nicaea that was "a veritable revolution."[98] Again and again the *Opus* objected to the introduction of "novelties."[99] The adoration of images was certainly such a novelty and Theodulf understood this perfectly well. There is only a problem if one succumbs to the argumentation of II Nicaea to the effect that the adoration, or the veneration, of images was an ancient and well-nigh universal tradition in the church. As we have seen, such practices were actually quite recent in the East and, perhaps with the exception of Rome, were completely unknown in the West. Theodulf knew all of this.

Auzépy concludes that "[o]n the whole, the author of the *Libri Carolini* understood perfectly the sense of the argumentation of II Nicaea and even its contorted subtleties."[100] Thümmel agrees and adds that the eighth century had been a bad time for intellectual life in the East, that Nicaea itself was not a model of intellectual rigor or profundity, and that theologians like Theodulf may well have been superior to their contemporaries at the other end of the Mediterranean.[101] We may therefore proceed to a summation of Theodulf's work on the confident assumption that he knew what he was talking about. But I must also note that Theodulf was speaking as if he were Charles. His work is an "autobiographical fiction . . . a dramatic soliloquy in which 'Charles' constructs a narrative of himself." Indeed, the Frankish counterattack required Charles to reveal something of himself.[102]

The Structure of the Opus

Because the *Opus* is a long and complicated work of which only small fragments have ever appeared in translation, its structure, organization, and contents are not widely familiar. To be sure, many scholars have provided characterizations of the work or have drawn specific evidence from it in various kinds of historical discussions. It is not as if the work itself is unknown, but it does seem fair to say that its overall message has not been widely appreciated. Accordingly, as a prelude to an analysis of Theodulf's primary arguments, the reader may appreciate a fairly detailed summation.

In the *Preface* to book four Theodulf spins a set of metaphors about there having been four rivers of paradise, four Gospels, four virtues, and four kinds of wood in the Ark of the Covenant. From this it may be concluded that the plan for the work always called for four books. The work has 120 chapters so it seems that the original plan was for each book to have a preface and thirty chapters. In fact, for reasons that cannot be determined, each book has its preface, but the number of chapters varies: thirty in book one, thirty-one in books two and three, and twenty-eight in book four. The eighty-five sections of the *Capitulare* are strewn throughout the chapters of the *Opus*, which is in any case thirty-five chapters longer, leaving out of account its four prefaces. This means that the

Capitulare was not only a preliminary draft but also that its organization and contexts provide few clues about Theodulf's intentions for the eventual *Opus*. When studied carefully, the *Opus* reveals a tightly controlled and on the whole logical organization through books one and two. Book three is less tightly structured, although it is tolerably coherent down through chapter fourteen and, even after that, the rest of its material is consistent with what precedes even if not as neatly arranged. This situation accords well with Freeman's determination that the quality of work on the Vatican manuscript remains at a high level down to 3.13. Book four is much harder to understand. There is no obvious development or progression in it. Many of its topics had been dealt with previously. Often the chapters in book four seem only to expand on a problem already discussed. Freeman's analysis of the language in the *Opus* as a whole demonstrates persuasively that it is fundamentally Theodulf's work. Two hypotheses may be offered for the fact that the second half of book three and all of book four lack the tight and transparent organization of books one and two and the first half of book three. First, the earlier sections, and especially books one and two which deal most directly with biblical passages, may have been composed at an early stage while Theodulf had the full text at his disposal, or else resulted from his having run through the Nicene *acta* again carefully, before the *acta* were sent to England (if they actually were!), to note the biblical passages that he wanted to argue about. Second, when the full set of *acta* were once again available in 793, Theodulf began to work more closely with patristic passages, theological concerns having to do with images, and related problems that fill up books three and four. Or, as a corollary to this possibility, after Theodulf had marked out the more particularly theological passages for discussion and had begun drafting his responses to each issue, the *Responsum* arrived and rendered fruitless a final ordering of the last third of the *Opus*. In sum, while we can be certain that we are reading a book written by Theodulf, revised by other unidentifiable parties, perhaps contributed to by Alcuin, certainly argued over vigorously at least once or twice at the court, and approved by Charlemagne himself, we cannot be sure that we know just how the work would have looked had it been finished with the same artistic and intellectual precision with which it had been begun.

Detailed Summation

The *Preface* to book one sets the tone and introduces the major themes of the work as a whole.[103] God grants rule to those who will preserve unity and defend the faith. People who depart from received traditions, who abandon the fathers, who refuse to teach what they were taught, who introduce novelties are arrogant and ambitious. Some years ago the Greeks held a council in Bithynia "both negligently and of indiscriminate impudence" (p. 99) where "they abolished images put up for the adornment of churches and for the commemoration of things done by those in former times" (p. 99). Recently they have held a new council even worse than the former one because "Everywhere, whether in passages of divine scripture or in the commentaries of the holy fathers, whenever they found a mention of images they turned it into a judgment for adoration" (p. 100). "We, however," Theodulf says, "are content with the prophets, evangelists, and apostolic writings, and are imbued with the teachings of the orthodox fathers, who do not deviate in their teachings from that which is 'the way, the truth, and the life' (John 14.6). We accept the six holy and universal synods which were held by the holy and venerable fathers to deal with a variety of heretical attacks, and we reject all verbal novelties and stupid inventions, and not only do we not receive them but we truly hate such filth as that synod which was held in the region of Bithynia on account of the most imprudent tradition of adoring images. The text of its writings, lacking in eloquence and sense, has reached us" (p. 101). He concludes by saying that having gathered the concurrence of the bishops in the "kingdom granted to us by God" (Theodulf speaks in Charles's name) and having assembled the testimonies of the scriptures and fathers, we are compelled to object to this heresy coming from the East to the West. "Charles" compares himself to David in the need to put to flight the company of the wicked.

Book one opens by picking up one particular thread in the *Preface*, the one having to do with God's institution of rulers and of what a proper ruler should be. Chapters one to four[104] draw from the letter which Constantine and Irene sent to Hadrian in 785[105] and attacks the rulers on a series of related grounds. Chapter one is addressed to those rulers who say "through Him, God, who coreigns with us."[106] Theodulf takes this as a sign of unmitigated arrogance and says that the Greeks violate the principle of humility. They do not realize the chasm that separates God from us. David, he says, never dared to utter such a statement. He also provides a long discussion of time to "prove" that God and the Greeks are not, as it were, contemporaries and a grammar lesson on the various meanings and implications of "*con-*" (i.e., "with"). In chapter two Theodulf attacks a statement by the Greeks that "because we sought his glory He has chosen us." No, Theodulf says, their arrogance proves that they seek only their own glory. Moreover, he continues, if they are worshiping images and seeking to impose that worship on the whole church, then they are not worshiping God, not following Jesus, who said He was the "way, the truth, and the life," and therefore they are not seeking the glory of God. He provides a tidy discussion of what an image is and again some grammar lessons and reflections on the meaning of words. Chapter three tackles the way the Byzantines refer to their letters ("*divalia*") and to themselves ("*divos*"). Clearly Theodulf does not recognize here some perfectly traditional Roman chancery practice. He takes these expressions to mean that the Greeks have the temerity to equate themselves with God, or with the gods. Amid more grammar lessons, Theodulf says this is "reckless vanity" and "Roman ostentation more than apostolic tradition." Chapter four attacks a passage in the imperial letter of 785 where the rulers said, "We ask your paternity, and especially God asks." Predictably, Theodulf takes this to mean that the Greeks, in addition to being arrogant, simply do not know how to talk about God. God does not "ask," Theodulf says. So the *Opus* begins with a searing condemnation of Byzantium's rulers.

Having established to his satisfaction that the Byzantium's rulers are unfit to serve, Theodulf turns to four transitional chapters (1.5–8) that lead him on from a major theme in the preface to the central subject matter of book one: the interpretation of the Bible. Chapter five makes the simple point that Scripture must not be interpreted willfully, must not be subverted to the needs of the moment. There is a tradition of interpretation that must be strictly observed. Chapter six, which was not one of Theodulf's original ones, sets out the argument that on all difficult, disputed matters Rome must be consulted. Only those writings that have been approved by the popes or that are found in such books as Gelasius's *Decretum* are to be consulted. Peter preceded all the apostles, Theodulf says, so the bishop of Rome precedes all others now. Jerome, one of the greatest of the church fathers, did not hesitate to consult Pope Damasus and more recently Pippin eagerly sought Rome's advice on matters of worship, and after God handed Italy to "us" we have consulted Hadrian on the same problems. In all things the see of Peter must be followed, especially by us who have been given by God the rule of Gaul, Germany, Italy, and the Saxons. Chapter seven introduces the first biblical passage explicitly addressed by Theodulf but not so much to refute a particular line of interpretation as to establish *the* line of interpretation. Theodulf comments on Genesis 1.26ff., "For God created us in his own image, . . . " to say that this Scripture must not be understood in a literal sense as having to do with images when, in fact, it should be taken in a spiritual sense. Then Theodulf cites Ambrose's treatise, *On Faith*, to show that the noble interior of man, the soul, bears the image and likeness of God. He says that the soul bears in itself a certain image of the Trinity in that it is composed of understanding, will, and memory: "For just as the Son is generated from the Father, and out of the Father and the Son proceeds the Holy Spirit,[107] so the will is generated from understanding and memory proceeds from these two" (p. 139). Man is furthermore the image of God in his adherence to and display of godly virtues—love, justice, patience, mildness, generosity, mercy. Theodulf then cites Augustine on how the soul can be renewed and thereby take on a likeness to God while departing from sin and abandoning its former likeness to Adam. He continues with Augustine's observation that the likeness which the Son bears to the Father is different from the likeness that the human soul can bear to God. God, soul, and virtues are incorporeal, Theodulf insists, and the Greeks are wrong to equate them with manufactured things, that is with images. This provides Theodulf in chapter eight with an opportunity to discuss image, likeness, and equality. He believes that the Greeks think these to be essentially equivalent but they must be distinguished "because everything which is an image is a likeness but not everything that is a likeness is an image since an image never lacks likeness but a likeness often lacks an image and quite often both an image and a likeness are known to lack equality" (pp. 146–47). To explain this rather abstruse point Theodulf gives an example: "Every egg is similar to every other egg, in so far as it is an egg. But a partidge's egg, in so far as it is an egg, is similar to a hen's egg, but is nevertheless not its image because it is not expressed by it, and it is not its equal because it is smaller and comes from a different kind of animal" (pp. 147–48). In short, Theodulf says that the Bible must be read correctly, that the safest guide to correct reading is the Roman tradition, that passages quoted by the Greeks should be taken spiritually, as the fathers have done, and not literally, and that it is critical to understand what is meant by image in the first place. Having set forth the rules, he says, we can now turn to scriptural verses quoted by the Greeks. Two of his rules require emphasis. The spiritual meaning is always more important than the literal and the understanding that one attempts to derive from a text must be in agreement with what the fathers have already said.[108]

The next fourteen chapters (1.9–122) criticize specific Old Testament passages that the Nicene fathers quoted in defense of images.[109] We need not summarize each one here. It will be enough to give a few examples and to describe Theodulf's critical strategies. We can see Theodulf following along with the *acta* and therefore proceeding book by book through the Old Testament. So he comes to and rejects statements quoted at Nicaea that Abraham adored the people of the land (Genesis 23.7) and that Moses adored Jethro, the priest of Midian (Exodus 18.6–7). He also says that Jacob did not adore pharaoh (Genesis 47.7–10) and that Daniel did not adore Nebuchadnezzar (Daniel 2.46). He says that Jacob blessed pharoah but did not adore him (Genesis 47.10) and that

Nathan's adoration of David is not like the adoration of an image.[110] Theodulf's response to these citations shows one of his characteristic ways of working. First, he contends on the literal level but says that the Greeks got it wrong. That is, the "worship" of one person for another is a mark of respect or honor and has absolutely nothing to do with worship paid to things that lack movement, voice, or sense (p. 149). He then quotes 1 Peter 2.17, "love your brother," and quips that Peter did not say "submit yourself to an image." As for the stories of Jacob and Daniel, he says that he cannot find them in the Hebrew or in Jerome (i.e., the Vulgate) (pp. 151–52). Then he says that Jacob did not "adore" pharoah, he "blessed" him, a different thing altogether. And besides, he says, even if he had adored him he would have done so out of humility not to set a precedent for worshiping images (p. 152). Then, he goes on, the Greeks shift words in their treatment of the scriptures, they exchange *adorare* for *benedicere*, and they exchange *adorare* for *habere, salutari, osculare, venerare* (pp. 152–53). As for Nathan's worshiping David (3 Kings 1.23), he did this as a mark of respect for a man placed in power by God. He then cites, on the point, Paul (Romans 13.1) that all power comes from God and Titus (3.1) on the need for humble submission. In other words, he tells the Greeks that they cannot read the plain words before them and do not know how to read the Old Testament in light of the New.

He then mentions Jacob's pillow stone, and how he anointed it as a title (Genesis 28.11–18), Jacob's weeping over Joseph's coat (Genesis 37.32–34), his adoring the tip of Joseph's staff (Genesis 47.31),[111] and the story of Moses and the brazen serpent (Numbers 21.8–9).[112] Theodulf's criticisms of these passages take several forms. He says that Jacob's stone has three levels of meaning and that none of these authorize images. He says that the story of Joseph's coat prefigures the sacraments and that the brazen serpent prefigures the redeemer who can only be seen with the mind's eye ("*internis oculis*"). But he also attacks the Greeks for saying that Jacob put Joseph's coat over his eyes and kissed it and for saying that Jacob worshiped the tip of Joseph's staff instead of at the foot of his bed. Theodulf scores the Greeks for "mutilating" the Scriptures. Literal meanings are never enough, he believes, but no level of interpretation is possible if the text is quoted incorrectly. As for Joseph's coat, he says that even if the story were accurate the way the Greeks tell it, this would only point to a perfectly human reaction by a father who believed his beloved son to have been devoured by beasts. The story never has anything to do with images, much less with kissing or embracing them. Moses put up his brazen serpent to ward off snakebites, Thedoulf says, because the Hebrews were not strong enough to place their hope in "things not seen" (Romans 8.24). The brazen serpent itself was a matter of indifference; Hezekiah later destroyed it.

Three times (1.15, 19, 20) Theodulf addressed statements about the Ark of the Covenant and its cherubim. Theodulf repeats in each instance that these things were made on God's expressed orders and that they cannot be compared with images made by humans. He also says that the Ark and the cherubim were erected "as a most holy prefiguration of future mysteries" (p. 169). In chapter fifteen Theodulf deals at length with the typological significance of the cherubim and draws heavily on Augustine's *Questions on the Heptateuch* (pp. 169–75). But his fundamental point is well expressed in chapter nineteen: "We, who follow not the dead letter but the living spirit, who are not the carnal but the spiritual Israel, who having rejected things seen contemplate things not seen, rejoice in having accepted greater mysteries not only than images, which lack all mystery, but also greater and more distinguished signs of mysteries than those tablets or two cherubim" (pp. 193–94). Chapter twenty also contains Theodulf's first sustained attack on Patriarch Tarasius who would come in for repeated tongue lashings in the early sections of book three. This time, Tarasius is criticized because he was rushed so quickly from the lay to the clerical state without due education in theology and the priesthood that he did not know any better than to lead his people into the foolish worship of material things.

With chapter twenty-three Theodulf inaugurates a series of fifteen chapters, running down to 2.8, that deal with the psalms. This series is broken only for 1.30 which, among other things, explores the difference between seeing and hearing, and for the preface to book two. In all, Theodulf responds to seventeen specific psalm verses quoted at Nicaea.[113] We need not go through them all, but we may observe some of his techniques for interpreting them. In citing the psalm verses quoted in the *acta*, and in citing other verses which buttressed his quibbles or refutations, Theodulf used psalm versions from the Mozarabic antiphonary. This discovery has relevance to any understanding of the text of the *Opus* but was also a major element in Freeman's demonstration that Theodulf was in fact the author of the *Opus*.[114]

Theodulf deals with the psalms in much the same way that he dealt with the other Old Testament passages. For example, he again urges typological readings. When the Greeks cite Psalm 4.7 ("The light of your countenance is signed upon us"), Theodulf says, first, that the "light of God" is the Son of God through whom it is possible to have a glimpse of divinity. But then, he goes on, the light of the Lord signed upon us is "not to be sought in material images which lack, like other qualities, light, but in the banner of the cross because we have accepted baptism through the most holy flow of anointing impressed on our foreheads" (p. 211). In other words, he relates this passage to the sacraments and denies that it has anything to do with images. Similar is his treatment of Psalm 25.8 ("Lord, I have loved the beauty of your house"): "The house of the Lord is according to allegory the church, according to anagogy, heaven, or according to tropology, the soul of man" (p. 224). He says that house of God must be understood spiritually, not materially. Sometimes Theodulf adverts to metaphor. When the Greeks cite Psalm 44.13 ("All the rich among the people have sought your face") Theodulf says this has nothing to do with images and in fact the "face" refers to the spiritual teaching of the church and the "rich" are those who have given up everything to follow the Lord. Likewise, when the Greeks bring forward Psalm 29.12 ("You have turned my tears into joy"), Theodulf interprets this passage metaphorically such that tears mean the painfulness of this life and joy means heaven. Occasionally Theodulf uses his responses to Greek psalm interpretation to provide lessons on grammar and disquisitions on tropes and figures of speech. These passages often strike the reader as pompous and sarcastic, but they also serve the author's purpose of explaining why the Greeks simply cannot be trusted to read the Scriptures correctly.

Although 1.30 begins with a psalm citation, this chapter and the immediately following preface to book two served Theodulf as a kind of rhetorical pause in the middle of his analysis of the Byzantine psalm citations in the *acta*. In 1.30 Theodulf takes up Psalm 47.9 ("As we have heard so we have seen"). He first observes that this has nothing to do with "manufactured images" and asks where they have ever heard patriarchs, prophets, or apostles say any such thing. "What we have heard as mortals," he says, "we will see as immortals" (p. 232). We have "heard" about the coming of Christ in the Law and we have "seen" this in the Gospels. For the first time, then, Theodulf opens a theme that will recur constantly later in the *Opus*: the superiority of the Scriptures to images. But, again, Theodulf repeats that the Scriptures, any scripture, must be understood "*typice*." The *Preface* to book two says simply that, having brought forth and combatted some passages that they cite to prop up their vanity, now we must continue, add more such passages, and then turn to some opinions of the holy fathers.

After devoting 2.1 to 2.8 to additional psalm citations, Theodulf turns to three more Old Testament passages which, he insists, possess deep spiritual meanings and have nothing at all to do with images. In commenting on 3 Kings 7.29, where Solomon is reported to have put images of oxen and lions in the Temple, he says they were made by the king "as type figures, and we reject their most insolent, and more than that most superstitious adoration, which we cannot discover ever to have been instituted by patriarchs, prophets, apostles, or apostolic men" (p. 254). The images bear the type of Christ and signify that He would call the apostles who, in their pastoral ministry, would display calm, as the gentleness of oxen, and strictness, as the fierceness of lions. When the Greeks quoted Canticles 2.14 ("Show me your face") Theodulf says this face is spiritual not corporeal and that Canticles as a whole refers to the church as the spouse of Christ. When he came to Isaiah 19.19 ("There will be an altar in the land of Egypt") he argues that this is a prophecy about the calling of the gentiles, that the prophecy was fulfilled in Christ, and that the passage must be interpreted "*spiritualiter*," not "*historialiter*." This long series of biblical passages then ends with Matthew 5.15 ("Neither do men light a candle and put it under a bushel") where Theodulf repeats that this has nothing at all to do with images but that it does refer to Christ and to the apostles whom He sent into the world to radiate His light.

In summary, Theodulf accuses the Greeks of failing to understand the grammatical and rhetorical artifices of the Old Testament. He constantly accuses them of having a poor, even childish, understanding of the Old Testament because they always want to take literally passages that must be understood spiritually, allegorically, typologically. Again and again Theodulf cites either New Testament or patristic passages, or both, that reveal the true sense of any given Old Testament verse. Occasionally he affects bewilderment, often he is starkly sarcastic, sometimes he is like an impatient schoolmaster with a slow pupil, but his basic arsenal of techniques of argumentation is always the same.

With 2.13 Theodulf turns, as he promised in the *Preface*, to patristic texts cited at Nicaea. His first example permitted him to make a number of related points. He cites the story that Pope Sylvester brought images of Peter and Paul to Constantine so that he could recognize them as the very figures he had seen in a dream. This particular passage is one of those that actually derived from Hadrian's letter and which lacks any reference to its origin. He leads with a basic point: "We are often compelled to say in this our special work on images, that it is not forbidden to us to have them, but to adore them, nor must we shrink from seeing them as decorations for churches, since it is adoration which is most insolent, or rather supremely superstitious" (p. 259). Then he goes on to say that Sylvester brought those pictures for Constantine to look at not to adore. He merely wished for the emperor to recognize the persons whom he had seen in his dreams. The pope did so to elevate the emperor's mind from things known to things unknown, from things visible to things invisible, for Constantine was still stuck at the level of visible things. The process was rather like taking Constantine from milk to solid food. Certainly Sylvester had no intention of dragging the emperor from invisible things to visible ones. Finally, Theodulf says, it is dangerous to draw testimony from this story because it is not to be found among the approved books "in the book of blessed Gelasius" (p. 261). After his long preoccupation with biblical texts, this story gave Theodulf an opportunity to signal several themes that would be with him throughout the rest of the *Opus*.

Chapters fourteen to twenty of book two contain Theodulf's rejection of patristic texts cited from Athanasius, Ambrose, Augustine, Gregory of Nyssa, John Chrysostom, and Cyril of Alexandria, with a chapter on the Sixth Ecumenical Council (2.18) in their midst. He accuses the Greeks of failing to understand the texts and of citing them inaccurately. His central point, as always, is that these texts bring no support to the adoration of images. The Augustine passage, incidentally, is the only citation of this father at Nicaea and its text cannot now be traced in any known work of the saint. Having some knowledge of John Chrysostom, Theodulf voices a doubt that the opinion (2.19) cited by the Greeks could have come from this church father. With respect to Cyril (2.20), Theodulf says that he does not know the book in question. Chapter seventeen is a particularly revealing one. The Greeks had cited a passage from Gregory of Nyssa and Theodulf says that his life and teaching are unknown to us. Then he says, with Paul, that everything must be tested to see if it comes from God. He continues by saying that he is not sure if such a passage should or should not have been brought forward but that, for now, he plans to leave it on one side with other teachings about which "we" are ignorant. Moreover, he expresses contentment with the Latin doctors whose lives and teachings are known to us and with the Greek doctors whose writings have been translated into our language. His specific reason for rejecting this passage may have been that he could not trace it in the *Decretum Gelasianum*.[115] The fathers of the Sixth Council mentioned images depicting John the Baptist pointing to the Lamb. Theodulf dismisses this as yet another item in their "accumulation of trifles" and he also complains about the appalling Latin of the text he has before him.

With 2.21 Theodulf turns away from his direct critique of Nicaea's patristic citations to what might be called systematic problems. In 2.21 he rejects the proposition that it is against the Christian faith to refuse to worship images. He says that it would take him too long to enumerate all the instruments that build up the faith, that strengthen the love of God and of neighbor, but that no matter how long he went on, he would never get to the worship of images. No ancient text supports their position and the Scriptures always say that God alone must be worshiped. When they bring in the worship of images they do irreparable damage to the worship of God. Every form of cult, he says, is strictly denied to images. He concludes that he has no intention of saying whether or not you ought to have images for decoration and commemoration, but that if you have them it cannot be for adoration. In 2.22 Theodulf addresses directly the very topic of memory that he has so often raised. He says that he does not want anyone to quote his remarks on memory back to him. Worship, he maintains, can only be in spirit and in truth; it can never be carnal. Thus images are a matter of indifference. But "It is one thing to have them for fear of oblivion and another to have them for love of ornament; one thing for will, another for need; one thing to look to keep from forgetting God and his saints and another thing to look so as to remember things done" (p. 276). He argues that it is utterly demented to say that you have to have pictures to keep from forgetting about God.

Theodulf uses chapters twenty-three to twenty-five to lay down the apostolic tradition. He begins with his only citation of Gregory the Great's letter to Serenus of Marseille, a document that was not cited at Nicaea but that did appear in the *Capitulare* and *Responsum*. Theodulf uses this letter to build an argument that, on impeccable authority, Gregory forbade both the destruction and the adoration of images. Chapters twenty-four and twenty-five then draw heavily on Paul to show that God alone is to be worshiped and that the greatest of Christianity's teachers said nothing at all about images. Theodulf also uses this opportunity to say that the kinds of greetings, or tokens of respect, that are paid to living people are not to be equated honors paid to manufactured images and also to say that if the apostles refused to be worshiped it is inconceivable that they would have approved the worship of their images.

Chapters twenty-six to thirty develop specific topics in ways that are revealing of both Theodulf's deepest concerns and rhetorical skills. These chapters, in brief, unequivocally deny the possibility of drawing comparisons between images and the Ark of the Covenent (26), the eucharist (27), the cross (28), sacred vessels (29), and the Scriptures (30). It is odd that the subject of relics did not come up in this sequence of chapters. Relics figure prominently in Theodulf's discussions in books three and four, and this would have been the natural place to introduce the topic. Theodulf did add a thirty-first chapter to book two, but it argues that the Byzantines are uncharitable toward their parents and ancestors when they call them heretics. In any case, the central subject matter of chapters twenty-six to thirty is the absolute incommensurability between images and other objects that were put into evidence at Nicaea. On many occasions already in the *Opus* Theodulf had put his logical powers on display by slicing through Nicene arguments with razorlike syllogisms.[116] He used two more in this section (2.26, 2.27) but the skill which he really puts on display in these pages is his knack for drawing comparisons that are sarcastic, ironic, angry, verbally adroit, and devastatingly effective. In speaking of the Ark, for example, he says it was commanded by the voice of God, not invented by the artifice of some artist, that it was built by a holy man, not made by somebody or other, that it derived from the lawgiver not from a painter, that it had mysteries, not colors. In discussing the eucharist, Theodulf really warms to his task. First he asserts the difference between the eucharist and images. Then he says that bread and wine are transformed by the consecration of the priest whereas images receive no consecration. Then he starts his combat of comparisons: the Lord commanded to eat His flesh and drink His blood, not to adore images; the eucharist possesses the spirit of God, an image only the skill of the painter. He then concludes this chapter with a barbed question: If those who do not worship images will all perish, what is to be said about small children who were baptized in the Lord but who have not yet had a chance to worship an image? In speaking of the cross, Theodulf notes that the devil was conquered by the cross, not by an image; that humans were redeemed by the cross, not by an image. In the chapter on sacred vessels, in addition to taking another verbal swipe at Tarasius, Theodulf says that all through the scriptures one finds explicit testimony about the necessity of having vessels dedicated to the divine cult but that, on the contrary, one never finds a requirement that an image be used in services. Everything can be done without images, he says, but nothing without vessels. The Lord Himself, at his Last Supper, took up a cup, not an image. The prophet (Isaiah 52.11) did not say "Be you clean you who carry the images of the Lord" but "Be you clean, you who carry the vessels of the Lord" (p. 302). Chapter thirty is the longest in the *Opus*, extending some twenty pages. Just as Theodulf ended book one with a statement about the superiority of hearing—which by implication means reading—to seeing, so too here, despite the tacked-on chapter thirty-one, Theodulf brings up the volume of his music so that no one in his audience will ever forget that images and the Scriptures are absolutely incomparable. He uses a crescendo of quick, punchy comparisons, as before. Paul did not say (Romans 15.4) "Whatever is painted" but "Whatever is written"; and he did not say (2 Timothy 3.16) "every picture" but "every scripture." Moses did not receive a picture but the Law. And so on, at great length. Near the end of the chapter, there is a comparison that is drawn at much greater length and that serves as the great summation of books one and two. First Theodulf repeats that images are without mystery, life, sense, reason, and legitimacy and then he goes on to say that the Bible possesses everything that one needs to know: history, poetic meters, the rules of grammar, eloquence, right reasoning, arithmetic, music, geometry, astronomy. These things, all the liberal arts we may note, are not always present literally or obviously, but they are there just the same and can be discerned by the reader with the right spiritual disposition.

The *Preface* to book three announces Theodulf's intention to demonstrate how the Nicene fathers abandoned the fathers of the church. He does this in book three but, in reality, this book is less cogently organized than books one and two. That is, Theodulf deals with some large theological problems, with the specific topic of painters and images, and with another set of faulty comparisons. But he also includes criticisms of patristic passages that might have fit better in book two, some observations on synods, some complaints about the Byzantine use of language like those found at the beginning of book one, further comments on the unreliability of Byzantine sources, and also some rather random topics that are both hard to characterize and difficult to fit together so as to identify a scheme in book three.

The first chapter of book three, almost five pages long, is a profession of faith. Two things are remarkable about it. First, Theodulf's original draft, probably a series of professions drawn from various fathers, and very much in keeping with his stated intention of adhering to patristic teaching, was erased and replace with a text 131 lines long that is a profession then believed to have been Jerome's but now known to have been Pelagius's. Second, the change seems to have been occasioned by a desire to quote a text that could be read as an explicit refutation of adoptionism. The point of the inclusion of a profession at all seems to have been to establish the Carolingian bona fides. In other words, everything that precedes the profession, and then everything that follows it, puts Carolingian orthodoxy unassailably on the record. By implication, the persons whom the Carolingians are combatting are unorthodox.

Tarasius had come in for direct and personal criticism already in 1.20 and 2.29 but in 3.2 Theodulf flayed him. He accuses Tarasius of having invented the whole idea of worshiping images to draw attention away from his own irregular elevation from the lay state to the patriarchate (a point which he had already made in 1.20). Then Theodulf quotes Paul on what kind of person should be chosen as a bishop, never a neophyte, never a proud man, and on the need for due deliberation (1 Timothy 3.6, 5.22). Theodulf concludes with a quotation from Gregory the Great's *Pastoral Rule* on the necessity for any pastor or teacher—that is, any bishop—to have passed through all the ecclesiastical grades in due order. In 3.3 Theodulf raises the issue of the *filioque* and says that, perhaps, it is not surprising that a person like Tarasius would so misunderstand basic Christian teaching, the very kind of teaching, by the way, that was spelled out in the opening profession of faith, that he would, in offering his profession at Nicaea, say that the Holy Spirit proceeds from the Father *through* the Son. In a way, Tarasius is a foil because chapters three to eight all deal with theology and all except one of them (3.6) deal explicitly with Trinitarian issues. For exam-

ple, in 3.4 Theodore of Jerusalem is attacked for not understanding the coeternity of the Father and the Son. In 3.5 Tarasius comes under fire again for
saying that the Holy Spirit is a *contribulum* (kin, relative) of the Father and Son.
Basil of Ancyra draws an attack in 3.6 for having made an acceptable confession
but, after that, adding that he has faith in images and relics without talking
about sanctification, the remission of sins, or the resurrection of the dead. In 3.7
Theodulf blasts Theodosius of Amorion for being silent altogether about his
faith in the Trinity while asserting "I confess, and I promise, and I receive, and
I kiss images" (p. 367). Chapter eight then returns explicitly to the *filioque*
problem. In a sense, then, 3.1 to 3.8 consist of a profession and an anti-profes-
sion. The latter is made up mainly of the bad trinitarian theology put on display
by the Greeks. But, as so often already in the *Opus*, Theodulf asks repeatedly
how anyone can compare faith in God with faith in images and where anyone
has ever read that images are to be worshiped.

Chapters 3.9 and 3.10 constitute a small set whose purpose is to make two
related points. First, there may be many more errors lurking in the Nicene
documents but there is no time to find them all. This might be an explicit
comment on how Theodulf worked or a veiled reference to his non-continuous
access to the sources. Second, as one more example of Byzantine unreliability,
Bishop Theodore (see not identified) connects two psalm verses in such a way
as to suggest that they are continuous when in fact they come from two entirely
different psalms. However pedantic this may seem, it served Theodulf well as a
rhetorical departure from the theological denunciations contained in the first
eight chapters of book three.

Chapters eleven to fourteen constitute an attack on the synod of Nicaea
itself. Chapter eleven represents one key element in Theodulf's original synodal
theory before the inclusion of 4.28 offered its bold new interpretation. Here
Theoldulf says that it was rash for Nicaea to anathematize people for not worshiping images when no effort had been made to determine the views of "each
and every part of the church" (p. 375). He then gives some pastoral advice:
When a brother errs one goes to him secretly, and then sends others, or maybe
writings. So, legations should have been sent to neighboring churches to sound
out their thinking. The Nicene fathers should have adhered to the teachings of
the fathers, like the rest of the church, rather than try to impose their novel and
unwarranted views on everyone else. If they had adhered to good teaching they
would not have resorted to "useless and irresponsible" councils. Chapter twelve
continues in a similar vein. This time the Greeks are chastised for casting aside
kindness and patience, for not holding their tongues, and for speaking in a
disordered way. He repeats that there are right ways to call councils and correct

issues for them to address. But of their council he says, "Just as light from darkness, life from death, sight from blindness, probity from improbity, purity from impurity health from sickness, so their teaching differs from the teachings of the holy fathers" (p. 380). It is amusing to watch Theodulf administer a tongue-lashing in the midst of a discourse on kindness and patience. Chapter thirteen returns to Empress Irene for the first time since the beginning of the *Opus*. Theodulf expostulates on the report that the Greeks have permitted a woman to teach in their midst. He must have deduced this from the imperial *sacra* because there is no evidence that he would have known that Irene presided at the final session of the council in the Magnaura Palace.[117] Then he helpfully provides a disquisition on the "proper" roles for females. Chapter fourteen pro-voked Theodulf as *"divos,"* *"divalia,"* and *"coregnant"* already had done. That is, he objects to their saying that they "cooperate" with God and that God called them into council in order to establish His will. Predictably, Theodulf calls this arrogance. He then gives a short lesson on the rhetoric of persuasion so that he can conclude that God, who is omnipotent, cannot be persuaded. Besides that, God always said that He and He alone should be worshiped and now they are introducing the novel idea that images are to be worshiped, so it is perfectly obvious that they do not cooperate with God. Surely their foolish synod will not make God change His mind.

Theodulf uses chapters fifteen to twenty-one to establish particular instances of bad Byzantine teaching on images. Not all of the chapters in this section seem equally relevant to this main theme. Moreover, woven through this section is another powerful argument: Rome is the heir of Babylon.

In 3.20 Theodulf criticizes a citation from John Chrysostom on the meaning of the story (4 Kings 19.35) that the angel of the Lord killed 185,000 Assyrians. Chapter twenty-one challenges the authenticity of a story that an image of St. Polemon prevented someone from committing adultery. As with his earlier treatment of a, to him, dubious story from Gregory of Nyssa, so too here Theo-dulf says this story cannot be found in any authentic book. Chapter sixteen takes up one of the oldest chestnuts in the iconophile repertoire, namely the argument that worship conducted before an image is referred to the person whose image it is. Theodulf's rhetorical sabre was especially sharp this time: "Do the saints, who on their merits were able to rise to the heavenly kingdom, and whose images they then plan to adore by irresponsible devotion, solicit these superstitious or irrelevant honors? Do they permit themselves to be adored?" (pp. 407–8). Had the saints been keen for honors while they were alive, they would not be in heaven now. They enjoy the Lord's honor, of what other kind have they need? Many saints spurned honors while alive so how can anyone believe that they would be delighted by having their images adored? Since images are made by the whims of artists and, therefore, some are beautiful and some are ugly, how do they know which ones are more like the saints they supposedly represent? Are more valuable images more worthy of honor than less valuable ones? How fervent can devotion be that is attracted by the skill of the artist or the value of the materials in a picture? If an image is poorly made, or is made of poor materials, does it deserve less devotion? Chapter seventeen drew our attention earlier in connection with Frankfurt. It is the one in which Constantine of Constantia allegedly said that the same worship was to be paid to images as to the Trinity. Chapter eighteen treats Euthimius of Sardis, whose error, Theodulf says, is only slightly less than Constantine's, for he seems to place his whole hope in images. Chapter nineteen, finally, is a studied bit of irony in which Theodulf attacks the Greeks for referring to "our holy scriptures" and asks them just where they got these scriptures and why they cannot be content with the ones everyone else uses.

It is chapter fifteen, however, which stands at the head of the group just discussed, that opens a new theme. For the first, but not the last, time Theodulf here encounters the issue of imperial images. He writes "against those who say" without naming a source. What they say is that when imperial images are brought into a town, people greet them, often with candles and incense, to show respect to the emperor. Thus it is perfectly legitimate that there be in churches pictures of Jesus, Mary, and the saints. Bear in mind that Theodulf will skewer the "referential" argument in the next chapter. For now his target is different and, as always, he punctures it with shafts of irony and sarcasm. He says the Greeks must be drunk, or sick. If, he says, they are going to take arguments from the court or the forum to support image worship, then why don't they take them from the theater or gladiatorial shows? Nowhere in the Scriptures are we instructed to worship images of the emperors so how do we get from imperial images to religious ones? They claim that they worship the emperor in his image because he cannot be everywhere, but how can they worship God in an image, since He is everywhere and cannot be circumscribed in a particular place? God's power and glory are to be sought in pure hearts and pious minds not in pictures. The only people we have ever read about who acted this way are the Babylonians and the Romans, and perhaps the people conquered by them. These kingdoms, Theodulf carries on, are known to have been especially prone to the worship of idols. Then, paraphrasing Orosius, Theodulf strikes to the heart of the matter: "For as the histories say, the Roman Empire received the whole inheritance of Babylon, and between these two kingdoms, as between an old father who was already losing his strength and his young son, who had not yet acquired the power of domination, much was transmitted by two other kingdoms as tutors, that is Macedon and Persia" (p. 404). The coming of Christ should have eradicated all such practices. As the heirs of apostolic teaching, there is no reason for us to adore the images of dead kings. Certain things are implied about Charlemagne's attitude toward Byzantium in book one's opening salvo aimed at Irene and Constantine. In this chapter the full force of this *Staatsschrift* begins to emerge. When the passage drawn from Orosius about Rome's being the heir to Babylon was read out in Charlemagne's presence, a scribe recorded his reaction: "Wonderful!"

Chapters twenty-two to thirty-one treat images under several different headings. Without entering into endless quibbles about Theodulf's intentions in this section, it can be safely said that he addresses painters on the one hand and the authenticity of evidence about images on the other. As at the end of book two, Theodulf spins another set of vicious and effective comparisons at the end of book three. He also offers some of his most detailed, considered views on art and aesthetics.

Chapters twenty-two and twenty-three address art issues directly. In the former, Theodulf got a bit confused in reading his sources and lambasted the Greeks for saying that the Father had called painters pious when actually it had been a church father, Bishop Asterius of Amaseia, who had said this. Nevertheless, Theodulf asks what is unique about the art of the painter. Why is the art of the painter more pious than that of the carpenter, sculptor, bronze founder, engraver, stonemason, woodworker, farmer, or maker of anything else? None of these arts is in and of itself pious or impious, although their practitioners may be either. In 3.23 Theodulf tackles the proposition that "pictures do not contradict the scriptures." As the philosophers have said, according to Theodulf, painters can lead the viewer from truth to falsehood, or from falsehood to truth. They can paint what was, or what never was, what will be, or never will be. Painters can paint many things that are not in the Scriptures. What do they make, he asks, of pictures of the earth and the sea, or of the sun and the moon, as humans? Or winds and months? Or seasons and flowers? Because Scripture contains none of this, surely there is a contradiction here. Many things found in the writings of the gentiles are painted but are not found anywhere in the Bible. Here Theodulf recites a long list of mythical scenes, paintings which he might have seen, or heard about, or read about.[118] His basic argument may be summed up in his own words: "In the scriptures there is nothing vicious, nothing inappropriate, nothing impure, nothing false, except perhaps when the holy scriptures record what wicked people said or did; in paintings, however, there are many things that are false, or inappropriate" (p. 446). He concludes by asking how can they say that "the painters show whatever the scriptures say"? How do you depict, he wants to know, Deuteronomy 6.4, "Hear O Israel, the Lord your God is one"? (p. 446). Conveying what the Lord has said is the work of *writers*, not of *painters*: "Painters can in some way bring the stories of past events back to memory but things that are only perceived by the senses and brought forth by words are comprehended not by painters but by writers" (pp. 446–47).

Chapter twenty-four seems out of place here. It argues that images are not like relics. One might have expected to find this subject covered in the "images are not like . . ." chapters that conclude book two. Here Theodulf argues that some things are made holy by God Himself and some by the consecration of a priest; this repeats what he says earlier about vessels. Images fit into neither category. Relics are holy because they are the bodies, or parts of the bodies, of the saints or else items, like clothing, that saints touched or used. He then goes through a fairly lengthy list of biblical passages, beginning with Abraham's burial of Sarah, to show that the Hebrews tended carefully to the mortal remains of the dead. He concludes by saying that such remains will be resurrected but that images will not be.

Chapters twenty-five and twenty-six rebut arguments to the effect that miracles (or signs) or dreams associated with images are unreliable guides to the truth. As for signs, Theodulf says, he can find no such accounts in the Bible and he doubts that any such stories should be believed. He quotes Gregory and Augustine on the dangers of signs. But he also says that any sign, in so far as it is not diabolical, manifests the power of God. So even if a sign were to have been produced by an image, this is no proof of the power of the image itself and no reason to adore that image or any other one. He then has a little sport at the Greeks' expense. Because God spoke to Moses from a burning bush, should bushes be adored? The Lord was circumcised with a sharp stone so should stones be worshiped? Moses sweetened bitter waters with wood, so should wood be adored? Gideon collected moisture in a fleece, so should fleeces be adored? He gives nearly a dozen examples like these. As for dreams, Theodulf says they cannot be wholly approved or disapproved, for God did sometimes communicate through them. His standard for evaluating dreams is that the information which they convey must accord perfectly with what the Scriptures and the church teach. So if a person had a dream instructing him to worship an image— that is what is at issue in the Nicene passage that he has in his sights—then one ought immediately to regard that as a dubious, perhaps even demonic, dream. In the course of this discussion Theodulf pulls a joker from the deck. After having thrashed the Byzantines in earlier chapters for adhering to pagan standards, and after having shown that depictions of scenes from gentile literature do not agree with the Bible, he cites on the unreliability of dreams a passage from the *(Pseudo-) Disticha Catonis*. Right away, however, he says that if anyone should want to criticize him for doing so, he is in fact "following in the footsteps" of Jerome and Augustine who often cited gentile authors to make their points. His basic point is that neither signs nor dreams can be trusted.

Chapters twenty-seven and twenty-nine are similar to each other and also to some threads in the dense weave of 3.15. The first of these takes up the Nicene statement that images are to be adored "like the place of God." Probably the Greeks meant the holy sites in Palestine but Theodulf professed to be puzzled about just what they meant. Anyway, he argues, God is everywhere, He has no "place." If, he says, they mean churches, then they are wrong because ceremonies and prayers are offered in churches, not in images. If they mean the human soul, then they are terribly wrong because the Redeemer came to save souls, not images. The second of these chapters returns to imperial images, not to trace Rome's Babylonian genealogy but to reject the notion that there is an analogy between worshiping the image of an absent emperor and an image of Christ who can no longer be seen in the flesh. He repeats that God is everywhere and adds that He cannot be worshiped in senseless, lifeless, manufactured images.

Chapter twenty-eight is hard to align with the ones around it. Here Theodulf objects to an assertion that the fear of the Lord is like the adoration of images. He says he has never heard any such thing and then cites numerous biblical passages on the fear of the Lord to demonstrate that there is no connection between fearing God and adoring images.

Chapters thirty and thirty-one have some common elements, and they share a critical perspective with 3.25 and 3.26. In thirty, Theodulf queries apocryphal stories. He returns here to the Polemon story that he already discussed in 3.21. In a section that was erased, he also rejected the story of Abgar of Edessa, to which he would return in 4.10. In 3.31 Theodulf stands incredulous before the story of a, to him, crazy abbot who had suffered a demonic seizure and later said that he would rather enter every brothel in town than refuse to adore images. Here Theodulf is less interested in this colorful character than he is, yet again, in the dubious nature of the stories that the Byzantines brought forward in defense of images.

Book four is full of traps and puzzles. Its *Preface* brings limited succor to an effort to understand it. Theodulf basically says that having challenged their testimonies and attacked their novelties, he now needs to turn to any remaining bits of nonsense that he can identify in their writings. Fair enough: but much of what is in book four is like, in substance, themes, and modes of argumentation, that which had already appeared in books one to three. Freeman has shown that 4.13 was originally intended to be the work's grand finale, with its synodal theory that is in harmony with the ideas expressed in 3.11. Then 4.28 with its bold, new synodal theory wound up at the end of the *Opus*. This already points to some disturbance of the material. The individual chapters in book four can sometimes be arbitrarily grouped into idea clusters, but the order of their appearance in the book is incoherent in the extreme. Perhaps the arrival of the *Responsum* led Theodulf to unload his remaining material in no special order. Quite possibly we have here an unpolished draft.

Book four opens with a series of reflections on the nature of God and of the worship that is due to Him, and to Him alone. These are, of course, topics that Theodulf raises repeatedly, and he does not say much that is new here. Moreover, a much later chapter, 4.23, picks up the same basic theme. In 4.1 Theodulf objects to a person's saying that he can adore an image, call it Christ, and avoid sin. If anyone says that a picture of Christ is the son of God, he lies; if he lies, he does badly; if he does badly, he sins. It was not a picture that was flogged, crucified, rose from the dead, or ascended into heaven. "Since no image can be compared to Christ in nature, none can possibly be compared to him in name" (p. 490). Theodulf the schoolmaster then expatiates on the meanings of names. Chapter two attacks the idea that through a colored image the presence of Christ who was upon the earth comes back to mind. Theodulf counters that the "creative power" of God (His *fortitudo*) is ineffable and cannot be praised with colors. He then names all sorts of biblical characters who adored the power of God without the aid of images. God must be looked for in the heart, not with the carnal eyes but with the eyes of the mind. It is sad to think that a person cannot imagine Christ's presence without an image. Chapter three carries on the discussion by denying the argument that people give no scandal when they bring candles and incense to images. Scandal in fact occurs when things that ought to be offered to God are offered to senseless things. If they object that we offer lights and incense in churches, then we respond that churches are very different, dedicated, as they are, to the divine cult. Chapter twenty-three fits into the context of this discussion too because here Theodulf criticizes the assertion that kissing (or embracing) and adoring are essentially the same and that this is affirmed by their old teachers. Using another classroom lesson on differences and his mordant wit, Theodulf says "God is adored, but he is not kissed. The saints, who left this world with the victory of their merit, are venerated, but they ought not to be adored with the divine cult, and they cannot be kissed. On the other hand, wives, children, and slaves are kissed, but they are not adored" (p. 544). After a careful differentiation between *adoro* and *diligo*,

Theodulf concludes with an explicit statement about how the dialectical art has aided his argument.

One group of chapters extends some earlier criticisms of Byzantium's rulers. In 4.7, 4.8, and 4.22 Theodulf severely censures the current regime for declaring heretical the previous one. He says that the Bible teaches us to honor our parents, not to vilify them and call them heretics. We noted earlier that there appear to be instances where Theodulf did not realize that some statements made at Nicaea were actually Hiereian theses quoted for refutation. Here, however, it is clear that Theodulf did understand that Nicaea was addressing itself explicitly to Hiereia. The implication of these criticisms is that the Franks pay due respect to their parents and ancestors. Chapter five tells the story of an alleged letter of Symeon the Stylite to Justinian urging him to exercise extreme severity with some persons who have destroyed images. Theodulf's special parry is here aimed at the idea that anyone would advise an emperor to be cruel, merciless, relentless, to "return evil for evil." Theodulf insists that, on the contrary, rulers should be mild and gentle, should recall sinners from their offenses, should lead the wayward onto the path of righteousness. Finally, in 4.20 Theodulf treats as ludicrous the idea that the emperor and his mother are like the apostles. The first three chapters, on due reverence for parents, are echoes of many others (*Preface*, 1.2, 1.27, 1.28, 2.23, 2.31). The remaining two chapters are reminiscent of earlier ones too (1.1–4, 3.13, and 3.15). Apart from working in a few new wisecracks, Theodulf really did not advance his argument much here.

At least four chapters address dubious sources. Chapter five was just mentioned for its account of bad advice given to the emperor, but Theodulf also queries Symeon's letter itself. Chapter ten rejects the whole story of Abgar of Edessa. Chapter eleven professes ignorance of a certain book of *Deeds of the Fathers*. And chapter nineteen raises doubts about some stories pertaining to Epiphanius of Salamis and his pupils. These chapters are much like 3.21 and 3.30, not to mention a good many others, where Theodulf objects to sources that are unknown, suspect, or both. Very similar are two chapters that again reject stories about miraculous images. In one case (4.12) Theodulf tosses out of court a story by Dionysius of Ascalon that a certain monk put a light before an image of Mary and it continued burning for six months. In another (4.15) Theodulf refuses to accept a story that grass grew miraculously around a statue of Jesus healing the woman with a flow of blood. His rejections are like those we met in 3.25.

A group of six chapters, in many ways the most interesting and original in book four, treat painters, works of art, and aesthetics. Theodulf begins chapter sixteen with yet another refutation of the referential argument on behalf of images (cf. 3.16) and then turns to the nature of the images themselves. Suppose, he says, you have two pictures of beautiful women. One is thought to be Mary and the other Venus. Now you put a *titulus* on one to identify it as Mary. Where, he asks, was this image's holiness, its power to refer prayers to the Mother of God, before it got a *titulus*? The same theme and some others come up in chapter twenty-one. Here the main point is to refute that idea that because there had been a prophecy that a virgin would conceive and bear a child, no one could resist worshiping an image of Mary holding the baby Jesus. First, Theodulf says that the truths of such prophecies are to be found in the secrets of the heart not in manufactured images. But, he goes on to say, suppose we stipulate adoration. How do we know whose picture it is? What place do we accord to the skill of the artist and the quality of the materials which he used? Perhaps there is no *titulus*. Now, maybe this is a picture of Sarah holding Isaac, or of Rebecca and Jacob, or of Bathsheba and Solomon, or of Elizabeth and John, or maybe just some woman or other and a baby. How would one know? Likewise maybe it is Venus holding Aeneas, or Alcmena holding Hercules, or Andromache holding Astyanax. Wouldn't it be crazy to adore one thing while thinking it was another? The story of the flight into Egypt has been painted many times he says. And it appears on church walls, but also on drinking vessels, silken garments, or even carpets. Are these things to be adored? And if any image of a woman holding her child is to be adored, how about the animals in the picture? This leads to the discussion in chapter twenty-seven where Theodulf says that people can be led astray by badly painted pictures. That is, there are vastly different degrees of skill and understanding among artists. Thus, some will make pretty pictures and others uglier, even perhaps thoroughly ugly, ones. Since people will adore more eagerly the pretty picture, is it the case that holiness is a function of beauty? If that is the case, what happens if someone is tempted to adore an ugly picture? And what is to be said of the poor who, if they can afford images at all, will only be able to buy ugly ones. Do their pictures lack holiness? Theodulf approaches this issue from another angle in chapter twenty-six. Here he asks, if images are truly holy, why do the Greeks put them in the foul, polluted streets? Don't holy objects deserve better treatment? Some of these same issues, but also new ones, appear in chapter nine. Here Theodulf is dealing with a Nicene remark that iconoclasts had cut some pages with images from a book and that a deacon, Demetrius, claimed to have seen silver plaques with images on the cover of the book. Predictably, Theodulf did not miss a chance to say that once the Greeks were heretics for destroying images and now they are heretics for worshiping them. Then he turns directly to the images. Such images he says might appear almost anywhere, say on vessels, for the simple purpose of beautifying them. But what then of silks, clothing, or cloths made for human use and adorned with images? Are these to be adored too? The last chapter in this group to be discussed, eighteen, is mainly concerned to prove that the great figures of the Old Testament did not import gentile practices and engage in the worship of idols. Both the Nicene fathers and Theodulf were here grappling with the differences between images and idols. But whereas at Nicaea the Greeks felt they had reached an understanding that left images safely in a separate category, Theodulf drew upon Isidore to give a history of the emergence of idols in the first place. This chapter is rather like 3.15, the one comparing Rome and Babylon and redounds to the grave disadvantage of the Byzantines. Theodulf's major premise is that all manufactured images are essentially idols and that with the coming of Christ all such gentile practices should have been laid aside.

The remaining chapters are very difficult to group. For instance twenty-four attacks a statement to the effect that the Greeks had come together and made Christ the head of their council. Of course, Theodulf says, the Greeks could do no such thing because Christ, as God, is already the head, the center, the leader of all that His people do. One suspects that Theodulf had simply forgotten to take up this point when he was damning the Greeks for claiming to "reign with God" (1.1), be "chosen by God" (1.2), be *divos* and issue *divalia* (1.3), or have "divine ears" (4.5). Chapter fourteen is full of grammar lessons because Theodulf cannot understand the text in front of him, and chapter seventeen is marked by a comic error. Theodulf may have misunderstood that someone at Nicaea was referring to someone else at Hiereia who had "spoken out of his own belly." The point was obviously that someone was being accused of making things up, or having his own opinions. Theodulf, however, patiently explains the functions of the various parts of the body and assures his readers that the belly cannot talk. One more time he could not resist an opportunity to make the Byzantines look foolish.

We have already discussed the synodal chapters, thirteen and twenty-eight, so we may conclude here this lengthy summation of Theodulf's remarkable, learned, witty, and pungent treatise. In taking leave of the treatise itself, I wish to make two points. In the first three chapters of this book I spent a lot of time discussing the arguments that had been advanced for and against religious art from the fourth century to the eighth. My first point is to emphasize how thoroughly Theodulf had mastered that intellectual heritage. It is not easy to find a single argument with which he was unfamiliar. My second point is that Theodulf dealt so comprehensively with the *acta* of II Nicaea that there should no longer be any question whether or not he had access to the texts—perhaps continuous, perhaps intermittent—and whether or not he could understand the plain words and profound implications that he found on the pages before him. I noted the handful of instances where either a corrupt text or his own misunderstanding led him astray. These lapses do not detract from his achievement.

Conclusion

The problems occasioned by religious images had come up only intermittently during the eighth century. After 769 there was some work in Rome on a florilegium of image-related texts and in 780 images may have figured in discussions about the succession to the patriarchal office in Byzantium. During the 770s the Franks and Byzantines had no serious dealings with one another, perhaps as a consequence of the diplomatic rupture around the time of the synod and assembly of Gentilly. Charlemagne, meanwhile, campaigned in Italy and opened close, productive relations with Pope Hadrian I. In the 780s the overall situation changed in a number of important ways. The Franks and Byzantines reinstated relations and then broke them off again. Byzantium changed secular and ecclesiastical leaders and held a new council to undo the work of Hiereia. Charlemagne and Hadrian continued to interact on a variety of subjects and the pope welcomed the new Byzantine religious orientation.

Against this background, Charlemagne and his key advisers learned of II Nicaea, obtained its *acta*, and embarked upon a massive refutation of the council's decisions. Carolingian views on Byzantium and images took firm shape between about 790 and 794. Clearly the Frankish view of images in the 790s was different from the view to which they had subscribed in 769. It is impossible to say just when the change emerged or became evident. Productive and generally cordial relations between the Carolingians and Byzantium in the 760s and 780s were exchanged for hostility and bitter acrimony. Earlier and uniformly cordial relations between Francia and papal Rome were endangered but never abandoned in the 790s.

A fairly wide array of sources permit insights into all these momentous changes. Those sources help to understand the *Opus Caroli regis contra synodum*, and that treatise puts those sources into context. The *Opus*, however, a product of councils, courts, and the prodigious intellect of Theodulf of Orléans, is the prime evidence for elite thought on images and much else at a decisive time in Charlemagne's long reign. In this chapter, I have described both how that remarkable treatise came into being and what it says. In the next chapter, I shall look more closely at its thematic arguments and then at how those arguments relate to leading ideas in a creative, dynamic segment of Carolingian history. I shall also investigate Carolingian art talk.

CHAPTER FIVE

Tradition, Order, and Worship in the Age of Charlemagne

For we do not know those teachers, nor have their writings come down to us.
—Alcuin, *Against Felix*

No READER OF the *Opus* can possibly miss two fundamental points that recur
constantly. First, the Byzantines were wrong to destroy images and wrong again
to command their worship. Second, images are permitted only for decoration
and commemoration.[1] Yet the polemical tone of the whole work, and the wide
range of seemingly disparate arguments that inform it, authorize a quest for
additional key themes. In my view there are three. The attentive reader will have
noticed Theodulf's concerns about tradition, order, and worship several times
in the preceding summary of the *Opus*. Their identification helps to display the
coherence of the work as a whole and, in the final section of this chapter, will
permit us to situate Theodulf's central concerns within the broader context of
Charlemagne's reign. This section will isolate and discuss these themes for clarity
and emphasis. Of course, there is much in the *Opus* about art. What Theodulf
says under this head will be treated separately in a subsequent section of this
chapter. Theodulf's *Staatschrift*, however, is not at its core about art. Finally,
this chapter will place Theodulf's ideas about tradition, order, and worship into
context by looking at what contemporary writers had to say on these heads.
Alcuin's words quoted above indicate how the Carolingians sought to orient
themselves within a tradition and how confidently they believed that they could
do so independently.

Tradition, Order, and Worship in the *Opus Caroli Regis*

Tradition

Tradition, understood in several different ways, was constantly on Theodulf's mind as he wrote. What he says under the head of tradition may be divided into historical and practical issues. By historical, I mean the way Theodulf himself understood history and how he fitted his own time into the grand sweep. By practical, I mean how Theodulf viewed such issues as interpreting the Scriptures and fathers.

Theodulf's historical sense comes through most clearly in 2.27, a chapter in which he was developing one of his sets of faulty comparisons, this time insisting that images could not be compared to the eucharist. He argues that the eucharist always produces effects that reach far into the future while any effect that an image may have is ephemeral. For instance, he says that the eucharist is food and nourishment for the soul, while an image is food for the eyes alone (p. 295). In the midst of this discussion he says "this confirms *the new antiquity and the ancient novelty*, while a rotten old age will destroy that completely" (p. 295, my emphasis). For Theodulf all of history before the coming of Christ was *antiquus* and everything since the incarnation, *novus*. Before the Christian era there existed an ancient people of Israel and the kingdoms of the world extending from Babylon to Rome. Now there is a new people of Israel and a new kind of kingdom. Everything in the old that foreshadowed the new was *antiqua novitas* while all in the new that hearkens back to the old is *nova antiquitas*. In short, history is a long continuum with a decisive break at its midpoint.[2]

Several of the "practical" manifestations of Theodulf's traditionalist thinking illustrate how his historical sense was always at the center of his thinking. Again and again he says, in refuting one point or another, that we have never heard of patriarchs, prophets, evangelists, apostles, apostolic men, or church fathers saying any such thing.[3] In part, this was a methodological argument. It touched the vital question of how to read the Scriptures and it frames, especially in books one and two, the long series of chapters devoted precisely to exegetical matters. It adds weight to Theodulf's frequent remarks about unknown or dubious books. But it also raises a more theoretical question. Since by implication Theodulf is saying that the Franks do adhere to the ancient and universal teachings whereas the Byzantines do not, then only the Franks can be the heirs of God's promise to Abraham. This point of view, in turn, interprets Theodulf's remark in 3.15 that "the Roman Empire received the whole inheritance of Babylon" (p. 404). The Byzantines themselves claimed to be their heirs of Rome. In one way, that is unfortunate. In another way, it explains a lot. Theodulf's periodic excursions into Byzantine political symbolism and representation permit him to "prove" that, whereas in the Christian era all rulers should bear the type of Christ, Byzantium's rulers are arrogant and violent, Babylonians in short. The contrary argument is then raised explicitly. The Byzantines are like the tribes of Reuben, Gad, and Manasseh, who separated themselves from Israel and built altars of their own (Jos. 22.9),[4] whereas Charlemagne is like David,[5] and the Franks are a new chosen people.[6] Alongside this biblical argument we can place the one Theodulf develops pertaining to church councils. Whereas there have been six councils, and six alone, and only the Franks adhere to them, the Byzantines have created a new and heretical series: Rimini, Hiereia, and II Nicaea—the latter of which shares with I Nicaea only a name.[7]

For Theodulf, then, tradition permitted the elaboration of two kinds of arguments. According to one, there were certain techniques and guidelines for understanding the heritage of the church. The New Testament unlocked the secrets of the Old and the Old provided clues about what would be found in the New. The church fathers, the popes, and the six councils set forth both authoritative teachings and trustworthy techniques for extracting meaning from the texts of Scripture. Each generation was to teach the next only what it had itself learned. Novelty per se was a grave offense.[8] According to the other argument, the more deeply polemical and political of the two, human history consisted of an unfolding relationship between God and His people. God and Abraham concluded a covenant. God inspired prophets to call His people back to the law. God Himself became incarnate to teach His people the way and to call still more people. Evangelists were entrusted with the task of carrying a message to the ends of the earth. A church was built to conserve and disseminate the message. Presently, only the Franks—"the spiritual not the carnal Israel" (2.19)—were faithful to the Abrahamic tradition. Charlemagne was a new David—*nova antiquitas*—and Abraham became an old Frank—*antiqua novitas*. The Byzantines were written out of history, at least out of the history of God's people. Theodulf stands securely in the providential tradition of Augustine's *City of God* but he found a way to use history, which means the past, present, and future, not only as a path to final salvation but also as a discriminating guide to the people who would or would not be saved. *Staatschrift*, indeed.

Order

That a writer who had so ordered a sense of history would reflect on order in other respects is hardly surprising. *Ordo* is a word with a wide range of meanings.

It can mean methodical arrangement, or proceeding in the right order, or behaving and/or thinking in the right way, or arranging something properly, or maintaining rank, station, and hierarchy, or, finally, taking command. In various ways Theodulf touched on all of these possible meanings of the word "order." One of the items in Freeman's appendix of "Characteristic Expressions" is "ordo exposcit": This phrase appears eleven times in the *Opus*.[9] Every time it appears Theodulf is assuring his reader that the Byzantines have failed to do what "order demands."

The *Opus* was ostensibly addressed to the *acta* of a synod: II Nicaea. Accordingly, Theodulf repeatedly turned to the question of councils and synods.[10] We have already seen that he insisted on there having been six, and only six, ecumenical councils. So he objected mightily to Byzantium's having the temerity to label Nicaea as seventh, ecumenical, or universal. This was a contravention of "order," of the order handed down unalterably from the past.

In the same vein, Theodulf criticized Byzantium's secular and ecclesiastical leaders. In calling themselves *"divos"* and their acts *"divalia"* the emperor and his mother offended violently against good order. They displayed "Roman ostentation" (1.1, 1.3). In permitting a woman to teach the Byzantines contradicted established order (3.13). If in claiming too much for themselves they showed arrogance, then in refusing to show mercy and compassion (4.13) they one again failed to imitate Christ, to bear His type. It was extremely pompous of them to compare themselves to the apostles (4.20). Theodulf heaped abuse on Tarasius for violating order in all sorts of ways. He says that "[i]t is no small matter that Tarasius (as they say) was promoted from the lay state to the sacerdotal summit, from military garb to religious, from the circus to the altar, from the tumult of the courtroom to preaching, from the clash of arms to the performance of sacred mysteries" and in consequence "he compelled the people subject to his authority to lapse from the spiritual to the carnal, from the invisible to the visible, from the truth to an image, from the body to a shadow, from the living spirit to a dead letter, from the spirit of adoption to the spirit of fear." All this happened because those things that were permitted and appropriate to him as a layman were unhelpful to him after his illicit promotion to the clergy.[11] Perhaps, Theodulf suggests, Tarasius invented the worship of images to distract people from his own irregular position. Because Tarasius's current situation violates the "norm of ecclesiastical rule," because he has come to his office wrongly, he cannot lead correctly.[12] For this reason, as we have already seen, Tarasius not only misunderstood the central doctrines of the Trinity but also promoted the worship of images and led astray those in his care.[13] On at least one occasion Theodulf plays a bit of dialectical sport with the Greeks. He says that if the current generation wishes to anathematize the previous one, then none of their ordinations and consecrations are valid and they cannot rightly take the actions they are taking.[14] Although Theodulf cites Gregory's *Pastoral Rule* only twice, and not in the connections we have just been discussing, the spirit of that work suffuses the *Opus.* Humility, duty, self-discipline,[15] and sacrifice are the hallmarks of true leaders. Charlemagne possesses all these qualities in abundance and Byzantium's leaders lack them.

In a related vein, Theodulf hectors the Greeks at least nine times for condemning their own parents.[16] The Bible teaches, he says, that parents and ancestors are to be honored. Yet the Greeks chastise and anathematize their parents. Theodulf says, in mock seriousness, that there is a problem because the Greeks of the previous generation were disgusting heretics. But this generation should keep quiet about that and pray for them. In any case, it violates good order for one generation of a family to condemn another.

One key aspect of order is right reasoning. Theodulf approaches this issue obliquely on many occasions when he accuses the Byzantines of poor or muddled reasoning, or when he lambastes them with his scathing rhetoric about being unreasonable, illogical, imprudent, incautious, and so forth. But there is another revealing way in which he makes the same point. He does it by example, so to speak. No fewer than thirty-seven times Theodulf buttresses his own argumentation with acute syllogistic reasoning.[17] His first syllogism appears in 1.1 where he is attempting to disprove the Greek rulers' claim that they "co-reign" with God. He says:

> For if we are still in this world, we are still alive;
> If we are still alive, we do not yet reign with God;
> Since therefore we are still in this world, we do not co-reign with God.[18]

He carries the argument through several more iterations of his major and minor premises to prove that it is logically impossible to argue that we "co-reign" with God. This is a formidable tactic in his "ordered" campaign against Byzantine thought.

For Theodulf order is inextricably bound up with language. Even after acknowledging that he was working with a poor Latin translation, we cannot avoid being struck by the numerous times—I count twenty-one[19]—when Theodulf gave the Greeks a grammar lesson. Sometimes he complained that they did not understand the meanings of words. Sometimes their syntax collapsed. Sometimes they failed to understand the proper use of figures of speech.[20] On several occasions, but never more effectively than in 4.26, Theodulf explains how the "rules of eloquence" can destroy Greek arguments; one may envision him smirking. He was speaking of their statement that images are holy but are nevertheless put into the streets and other profane places. He says that the rules teach one never to juxtapose truth with falsehood, playfulness with seriousness, immodesty with modesty, unchastity with chastity, silly with sad, or profane with religious. Thus the Greeks should not join pure and impure. Theodulf is equally smug in 3.14 when he explains the rules of deliberative rhetoric and the art of persuasion so as to prove that the Greeks cannot persuade God. Theodulf can come off as a pompous boor or as a pedant, but his point is always serious. The Greeks just do not understand the Bible or the traditions of the church. Their learning is so defective, so out of order, that they have no hope of redemption.

Worship

Worship is one key prerequisite to redemption, so we come to Theodulf's third major theme. Amid Theodulf's expressions of anger, irony, and sarcasm I detect an element of bafflement. This was not occasioned by Theodulf's inability to comprehend the subtleties of Greek thought but by sheer, wide-eyed astonishment at what he found on the pages before him. The Greeks actually worshiped images and anathematized those who refused to do so. Under one optic, Theodulf's confusion may be attributed to the chasm that had opened between East and West on the subject of religious art.[21] Under another optic, the one relevant here, Theodulf's absolute commitment to purely spiritual worship led him to condemn without reservation the materiality he perceived in Byzantine worship. The "theological signature" of the work is that mediation between God and humans is through Christ alone. By mistaking anthropology for theology, the Greeks "had put the works of human minds and hands at the center of faith."[22]

Celia Chazelle characterizes Theodulf's view effectively: "although the material world is good, it exists entirely separate from the spiritual realm, so that the mortal who wants to approach God must finally turn away from material things in order to direct his or her attention completely towards the spiritual."[23] Indeed, Theodulf says early and often that God alone is to be worshiped and that He is to be worshiped in "spirit and in truth" (John 4.24, esp. *Opus* 2.22).[24] The Greeks ascribed to images the qualities—life, sense, reason, feeling—that only living beings can possess. In fact, images are totally material and, thus, totally lifeless. Again and again he railed against the worship of "insensate" matter.[25] Then too, no living being can be worshiped with the single exception of God. By failing to realize the complete materiality of images, the Greeks paid to them a worship that was as futile as it was blasphemous.[26]

Theodulf did not build up his argument about the materiality of images from metaphysical reasoning. Instead he grounded himself in positive terms on biblical exegesis and in negative terms on the application of the literary disciplines among the liberal arts to the words of the Byzantines. The centrality of the Bible to Theodulf's thought makes clear why he insisted repeatedly on the superiority of Scriptures to images. The Bible was uniquely God's revelation to His people, God's own words. On the one hand, the Bible provided sure guidance to salvation. On the other hand, the Bible commanded the worship of God alone and never authorized the worship of images; for that matter never authorized the worship of anyone or anything except God. Theodulf says he does not care if people have images or not for the critical question is whether they contribute to salvation. He concludes that they do not.[27] Because Theodulf's understanding of the ontology of images denied them any living reality and assigned them value only insofar as they were made by skilled artists or comprised of valuable materials, he did not need to develop a "Bildmetaphysik" of his own.[28] Thus, he contented himself with deconstructing Byzantine teaching on grammatical, rhetorical, and dialectical grounds. There is also a positive side to Theodulf's arguments. At one point he says that it would take him too long to enumerate all the things that build up faith and also love of God and neighbor but that no matter how long his list might be, he would never get to images.[29] Often, then, Theodulf describes precisely those forms of cult and service which lead the believer to God. Theodulf seems to have perceived that *cultus divinum* and *cultus imaginum* were concepts of the same order but he regarded them as mutually exclusive.[30] For the Byzantines the latter enhanced the former. For Theodulf the former excluded the latter. This is yet another instance where Theodulf understood the Byzantine argument perfectly well but turned it upside down in rejecting it.

Theodulf was not ignorant of the philosophical aspects and implications of some of his arguments. We have seen, for example, that he could discuss with subtlety the differences among image, likeness, and equality. In the *Preface* to book one he criticized the Greeks for failing to understand the difference between *genus*—that is, images—and *species*—that is, idols: every idol is an image but not every image is an idol. Later he borrowed, with full comprehension, Augustine's powerful analogy between the Trinity and the human mind which has knowledge, will, and memory.[31] But he wrote as a theologian, not as a philosopher. Thus his comment that God was everywhere, and could not be circumscribed anywhere, was not a remark about the metaphysical characteristics of the being "God," but a remark grounded in faith and expressed in the language of faith.[32] When Theodulf says that the only way in which humans can image God is in their souls or in their virtuous lives, he is saying something about the utter transcendance of the deity and about the impossibility of any "true" image of a purely spiritual being.[33] Similarly, a picture of a saint cannot reveal the power of God's grace working through the person depicted. Likewise, an image that is alleged to have miraculous qualities is, if it is not diabolical, merely a manifestation of the power of God. Images themselves are superfluous. God suffices.

Theodulf's originality and rigor of thought ought to be acknowledged. Not since late antiquity had any Christian thinker tackled so serious a problem in so independent a way.[34] Theodulf owed a lot to Augustine, but finally his formulations on the subject of worship extend far beyond anything the church father had said.[35] When I look closely at the force and precision of Theodulf's treatment of spiritual and material worship, I cannot help agreeing with Auzépy and Thümmel about the relative superiority of Frankish to Byzantine thought on this topic at least.

Theodulf was also sensitive to the fact that some material things did have a place in Christian worship: sacred vessels, relics, the Scriptures, the cross, the eucharist (more particularly, the elements which became the eucharist), the Ark of the Covenant, and churches.[36] We have seen that Theodulf devoted several lengthy discussions to each of these topics. He organized his comments the same way every time. These things are holy, or can be, precisely because God commanded them to be made and used or else because they are sanctified by the consecration of a priest. Relics are holy because they are the physical remains of, or objects possessed by, persons who are now with God. Moreover, in so far as corporal relics are physical remains, they will be resurrected. Images are not now with God and will not share in the resurrection. Vessels are consecrated to holy purposes. Images are not consecrated. The services of the church cannot be accomplished without vessels, but images are unnecessary and irrelevant. Mass and prayers are offered in basilicas but nothing of value is offered in an image. God Himself commanded Moses to build the Ark and it stood thereafter as a prefiguration of Christ and the church. And so on. Matter is not intrinsically evil, and some types of matter, in particular circumstances, have become holy. Images are not among those types.

Let us sum up. God made a promise to Abraham. For centuries that promise was conserved among a chosen people. God continually revealed Himself to those people, taught them His ways, and called them back when they strayed. Finally, God sent His son into the world as a man to model the life and faith that would secure redemption, return to God. Evangelists told the story of that Son and apostolic men built his church to gather, baptize, and teach the people of God. Rome led the church and pointed the way to authentic teaching. Finally, only the Franks were true to the ancient traditions. The traditions could be known, understood, and disseminated. But doing any of these things depended on following the rules. These rules were dictated by ancient understandings, by good practice, and by careful application of the intellectual tools that may newly be called the liberal arts although they were anciently spelled out in the Scriptures. The God who is the beginning and end of this story is the only being in the universe to whom cult and service may be rendered. Theodulf rose in defense of the unique worship, accomplished in the correct way, of the God who had once spoken to that old "Frank" Abraham and who now guided the steps of the new "Jew," the new David, Charlemagne.

Art and Art Talk in the Age of the *Opus Caroli*

In the preceding section of this chapter I sketched what I take to be the central arguments of the *Opus Caroli*. In the preceding chapters of this book, I included sections on what I have been calling "art talk," meaning the words and concepts which writers employed to talk about art. From the fourth century through the eighth, I have shown, quarrels over art, over images, over icons, were often less about art proper than about theological, ecclesiastical, political, and even ideological issues. Nevertheless, it was the rise and profusion of figural art within the Christian church that prompted the individual reflections or actual controversies. Consequently, it is important to form some sense of how the Carolingians, Theodulf and his contemporaries, talked about art.

Theodulf: Decoration and Commemoration

Theodulf's positive assessment of Christian art appears many times in the *Opus* but never more clearly or succinctly than in these words: "We do not speak against images for the memory of past deeds and the beauty of churches, since we know that they were made thus by Moses and Solomon, although as type figures, but we reject their most insolent or rather most superstitious adoration which we cannot discover to have been instituted by the patriarchs, prophets, apostles, or apostolic men." To this passage Charlemagne responded, "Perfect!"[37] Here we see Theodulf expressing himself at once on tradition, order, and worship. But we also note that he has no objection to figural art per se. In this he differs from the rigorists of the iconophobe period in Byzantium and in late antiquity. But it is also important to note that Theodulf adopts a posture of studied indifference to religious art. He nowhere says that there *ought* to be art in churches, books, or anywhere else. He says simply that, in two kinds of circumstances, art is permissible as long as illicit practices do not come to be associated with it. As Freeman puts it, Theodulf was a "minimalist."

Pope Hadrian I on Art

Theodulf and the Franks had only one interlocutor in the period when the *Opus* was being produced: Pope Hadrian I. The best source for his views is the *Responsum* but we should bear in mind that, in the Nicene *acta*, the Franks had Hadrian's letters to Constantine and Irene, and to Tarasius. Hadrian too took a rather narrow perspective on images, but his views were certainly wider than Theodulf's.[38] Nevertheless, Theodulf and the Franks do not seem to have taken Hadrian's views into account in their continuing work on the *Opus*. It is worth pointing out that the *Capitulare, Responsum,* and *Opus* often appear to represent segments of a dialogue of the deaf. It will be recalled that the Franks severely chastised the Greeks for reading the Bible, especially the Old Testament, literally when they ought to have read it typologically. In writing to Hadrian the Franks often seem to have censured specific Nicene readings as being incorrect on literal grounds (it must be remembered that the *Capitulare* was a list of more or less detailed chapter titles, not a full text). Hadrian routinely answered by citing Augustine, or perhaps another church father, to the effect that Nicaea's exegesis was perfectly acceptable on typological grounds. To take but two examples: The Franks complained about Nicaea's interpretation of Joseph's staff and of the brazen serpent, saying that neither of these pertained to or legitimated images. Hadrian answered that these passages can be read in some ways as bearing on the worship of Christ, whose type the staff and serpent bore.[39] Had Hadrian seen the full Frankish treatment of these passages in the *Opus* (1.13, 1.18) one wonders how he would have reacted to the fact that he and the Franks both read these passages typologically while deriving somewhat different meanings from them. On other occasions, the Franks objected to Byzantine readings of various psalm passages, claiming that the passages in question could not be related to those who refused to worship images. In particular, the Franks cited two verses from Psalm 73 in this connection: verse 2, "how much evil is there in the enemy of your saints," and verse 9, "there is now no prophet and he will recognize us no more." Hadrian, again citing Augustine, says that these verses have always been read as referring to heretics and that because Leo and Constantine were certainly heretics, Nicaea was correct in citing these verses.[40] The Franks also complained that certain things could not be found in the Bible. Hadrian often responded to this charge by asserting the long-standing continuity of papal teaching, but on two occasions he pointed out that not everything that is to be believed is contained in the Bible; in one case he pointed to the existence of the angel Oriel and in another he explicitly cited John 20.30 ("Jesus performed many other signs in the sight of the disciples that are not recorded in this book").[41] In taking Hadrian's testimony on images, therefore, one must be careful to bear in mind that he is responding to charges leveled against II Nicaea, not presenting a systematic treatise. Moreover, his constant refrain is that he is merely upholding the ancient traditions of the church. In fact, he says at one point that he and his predecessors had always rejected "novelties."[42]

Hadrian once defended the idea that acts of worship performed before an image are referred to the prototype. He even cited the appropriate passage from Basil.[43] The pope discretely cited Gregory's letter to Serenus to the effect that images could teach what is otherwise to be read in the Scriptures.[44] Hadrian never discusses the capacity of beautiful things to elevate people's minds and he says nothing about the ability of images to induce joy, sorrow, compunction, or any other emotion. On the matter of whether images had any intrinsic power, Hadrian was cautious. In responding to Frankish objections concerning miracle stories pertaining to the images of Polemon and of the woman with the flow of blood, and to the Abgar image, the pope only says that these stories seem to come from reliable sources.[45] When the Franks insisted that Theodore of Myra was wrong to cite an archdeacon's dream as confirmation for the cult of images, Hadrian replied, a bit weakly, that the Scriptures were full of revelations that came through dreams.[46] If this were all that Hadrian had said explicitly on the subject of images in his fifty-six-page letter defending Nicaea, one would be left with the impression that issues of tradition and authority were fundamental while the specific issue of images was almost incidental or adventitious.

But there is a long chapter (2.19) in the *Responsum* that provides some other intriguing details which themselves shed light on other passages in the document.[47] This chapter consists of Hadrian's response to the Frankish demand that he tell them where in the Holy Scriptures or in the six holy councils it can be read that the worship of images was demanded. Hadrian dodged the Scripture issue. He just did not take it up. His tactic in treating the councils is interesting, however. He begins by citing the story of Sylvester's having shown images to Constantine and points out that this took place close in time to the first council, that is to I Nicaea in 325. Hadrian then goes through each of the councils and mentions images that popes erected around the times of the councils. Only in connection with the sixth council's statement that Christ could be depicted in his human form, does Hadrian actually connect papal images with conciliar remarks. In each case, however, he says that the images erected still exist and have been venerated by us to this day. His remarks read like a litany. He also mentions separately, every single time, *diversae historiae* and *sacrae imagines*. Sometimes Hadrian's words—he routinely uses verbal forms of *venerare*—seem to mean no more than that the images erected by particular popes were understood to be ancient and were much admired, held in great respect. But the veneration to which Hadrian constantly refers might have had other meanings too, meanings that would have been deeply objectionable to the Franks. In replying to the Frankish objection that Tarasius improperly equated images and sacred vessels, Hadrian said that the Franks had not understood the patriarch correctly. Tarasius was, Hadrian said, responding to the heretics of 754 who said that images were not holy because no prayer was said to consecrate them and that accordingly they were no more or less than whatever the artist had made. Hadrian continued, "we say and judge faithfully and truthfully that the custom of our holy Catholic and apostolic church was and is that when holy images or histories are painted they are first anointed with holy chrism and then venerated by the faithful."[48] To my knowledge there is no other statement like this in the whole corpus of early medieval papal documents. If by means of such consecration, images were somehow made holy, then one may ask why Hadrian responded so cautiously to Frankish objections to stories about wonder-working images. Perhaps he was being tactful and taking Frankish sensitivities into account. Perhaps, too, at least at Rome, the sanctification that came from consecration was not understood in miraculous terms. After all, at Rome, relics and the tombs of saints were not as a rule sites of miraculous activity. In this respect, Rome was fundamentally different from Gaul with its profusion of miraculous objects and places.[49] In other words, Hadrian may have deemed images holy and worthy of veneration without thereby concluding that they were naturally miraculous. He was not prepared to deny the possibility of miraculous activity connected with images but neither was he prepared to defend it.

But that same chapter of the *Responsum* contains a curious passage that may qualify what has just been said here. Hadrian seems to have wanted to fit Gregory I into the letter even though he could not attach him to a council. Nevertheless, he mentions that Gregory built an oratory in his house monastery and adorned it with the customary histories and images. He then says that on account of his stomach ailments Gregory entered the oratory with Eleutherius, who was said to have raised a dead man. Both prostrated themselves before the images and then implored "divine mercy." Because of *their* "perfect faith" their prayers were heard. Hadrian completed this Gregorian anecdote by relating that after a miracle occurred in a formerly Arian chuch (Sta. Agata dei Goti) which he had purified, he put images in the place. Hadrian does not connect those images with the miracle, however.

Some insights into these stories can be gained from a close reading of the texts themselves and by juxtaposing this passage with another from the *Responsum*. Note first that Hadrian does not associate a miracle directly with an image. Second, Gregory and Eleutherius called on divine mercy, not on the intercession of a saint. Indeed, Hadrian does not bother to say whose images or what histories Gregory had put in his oratory. Third, Gregory was healed not by the images before which he and Eleutherius prostrated themselves but by the power of Eleutherius's prayer and by the perfect faith of the two men. Fourth, Hadrian again and again insists that Nicaea carefully distinguished between the cult that was due to images and the fundamentally different cult that was owed to God.[50] That may well be why, in telling this story, Hadrian is careful to refer prayers to God alone. Other key insights into this story derive from its ultimate source which Hadrian directly identifies: Gregory's *Dialogues*. Eleutherius appears in this work as a well-known abbot of St. Mark the Evangelist in Spoleto whom Gregory coaxed into joining his house monastery in Rome. Gregory was persistently ill and his stomach was so weak that he had to eat constantly and could not fast. He asked Eleutherius, whose prayer was known to be efficacious, to enter the oratory and pray with him. No sooner did they begin to pray than Gregory was healed sufficiently that he could fast. There is not a word here about images in the oratory or about Gregory and Eleutherius prostrating themselves before them.[51] Gregory also told the rather amusing tale of the miraculous purification of the Arian church that was reconsecrated by him. But once again there is no mention of images.[52] One is left wondering if Hadrian's embellishments on Gregory's simpler narratives arose from local traditions or were of his own devising. In either case, they do not add too much to our view of Hadrian's art talk. He had some sense, some greater sense than the Franks had, that images were venerable. He insisted repeatedly that his predecessors had the same sense; indeed, as we have seen, Roman synods going back to 731 had called for the veneration of images. But he, and perhaps his Roman scene more generally, took a more cautious line than did the Byzantines and a more expansive one than did the Franks.

Theodulf on Art

Theodulf did not produce at any one point in the *Opus* a systematic exposition of his views on the range of possible arguments for and against religious art.[53] The fact that he was responding, more or less *seriatim*, to the Nicene *acta*, which did not themselves contain a single, coherent treatment on the subject, may be one reason why Theodulf did not prepare a treatise-like discussion of his own somewhere in the midst of his massive polemic. His basic indifference to religious art—you can have it; you should not destroy it; you should not worship it—may have dissuaded him from speaking at length and in order on the topic. Nevertheless, at one point or another in the *Opus* Theodulf managed to identify and to counter virtually all of the arguments advanced in defense of religious art between the fourth century and II Nicaea. His art talk is very much up to date, even though it is sometimes difficult to tell just where he extracted his ideas. That he was prompted to speak by the Nicene documents is clear. But, as we have seen, his refutations and rejections sometimes take the form of grammatical, rhetorical, or dialectical counterblasts; sometimes stand on alternative modes of biblical exegesis; sometimes depend on an argument that a particular book or author is unknown; and, finally, sometimes rest on the citation of an alternative patristic passage. What is impressive in the end is the degree to which Theodulf understood the basic issues and responded effectively to them. No less impressive is the extent to which Theodulf profited from the opportunity which the *Opus* provided him to comment in original ways on the aesthetics of religious art.

By now we have become familiar with several basic arguments on behalf of Christian art. Let us see what Theodulf makes of them. One old argument maintained that images of Christ were licit because He appeared on earth as a man and that he could therefore be depicted like any other man. This argument was not prominent at Nicaea so Theodulf had rather little to work with. He mentions the incarnation in one way or another twenty-three times but not once does he do so with specific reference to images of Christ.[54] When he talks about the incarnation he does so either to show that various Old Testament passages were in fact prophecies of Christ's incarnation[55] or else to support authentic Trinitarian theology against the shortcomings he perceived in Byzantine theology owing to its omission of the *filioque*.[56] The closest Theodulf comes to acknowledging the argument from incarnation appears at the start of book four. In 4.1 he says that if anyone shows a picture of Christ and says that it is the Son of God, he lies. For, he says, no picture assumed humanity on our behalf, was flogged, crucified, died, or rose from the dead. A picture cannot reveal the unique Son of God who was with the Father from before all time and was sent by the Father to become man. In 4.2 he carries on the discussion with specific reference to the question of whether or not it is permitted to have pictures to remember Christ "concerning his presence in the world." In responding, Theodulf takes two tacks. First, he says that the "creative power" of God cannot be seen in an image. Then he says, "His power is to be adored not through a picture but through His works, through the very fact that He took on the form of a slave (Philemon 4.7), was born of a virgin, gave hearing to the deaf, speech to the mute, steps to the lame, health to lepers or to others suffering grave afflictions, life to the dead, sight to the blind; he harrowed Hell, conquered death, rose from the grave, and ascended into heaven." So, he goes on, "It is obvious that God is to be sought in the heart, not in visible things, and not in manufactured things."[57] Theodulf effectively sidesteps the argument from incarnation, if he actually spotted it, by saying that nothing revealed by an image of Christ is important in any way. This is consistent with his oft-repeated argument that God cannot be circumscribed in any one place and that it would be a shame if anyone needed pictures to keep from forgetting about God. If images of Christ are simply unnecessary, then they certainly do not prove any central dogmas of the church.

Another old argument held that acts of worship performed before an image were referred to the person whose image it was. This, Theodulf says, is "flatly absurd." In 4.16 Theodulf argues that the very uncertainty surrounding any image, our inability confidently to say whose image it is, renders dubious the possibility that worship performed before such an image will somehow reach its intended recipient. In 3.16 Theodulf argues a bit differently. Here he asks whether saints, who eschewed all outward marks of honor while they were alive and who now enjoy the ultimate honor of life in God's presence, solicit these prayers before their images. Charlemagne said, "To the point!" Theodulf goes on to challenge the Greeks to say where they have ever read any such thing. This suggests that the familiar passage from Basil had not come to his attention (although it did appear in the *Responsum*). He continues once again with his insistence that since images depend on the whim of the artist, absurdities will always attend their worship. For instance, beautiful images will be worshiped more intently than ugly ones. He concludes by saying that even if the learned could avoid traps when praying before images, there is serious danger that the unlearned will be led astray.

Several late antique writers articulated the principle that beauty could inspire, could lift minds from this world to the next. Theodulf was keenly sensitive to beauty, as we have seen and will see in more detail below. Yet beauty was not in itself for him a defense of art. In 2.13, the chapter in which Theodulf discusses the story of Pope Sylvester and the images he presented to Constantine, there is a hint that Theodulf approved the pope's strategy for elevating the still carnally minded emperor's thoughts from the visible to the invisible. But in 1.18 Theodulf reveals once and for all his thinking on the subject of art's capacity to inspire, to liberate the mind from this world. The apostle (Paul) teaches that hope is to be placed in things unseen, not in things seen (Romans 8.24ff.). We must look at the Lord *"internis oculis"* in order to be saved. Theodulf talks some thirty times about our mind's eye, our interior vision. As we have seen, Theodulf says many times that it is permitted to have images to beautify churches. This argument implies that beauty has some positive benefit of its own. Yet Theodulf never connects beauty or the sight of physical objects with the soul's quest for God. For Theodulf spiritual progress comes only when it is possible to see in the depths of the soul things that are invisible to the naked eye. Again one meets Theodulf's principled indifference to art.

What did Theodulf think about the ancient argument that images could teach? The one place where he might have expressed himself in detail on this topic is 2.23 where he cited the first letter of Gregory I to Serenus of Marseille. Yet here, as always, Theodulf held to the Carolingian via media: He cites Gregory only to show that it is wrong to destroy or to worship images. The point Gregory makes in his second letter, namely that images may teach the unlettered what the lettered can read in books, Theodulf does not cite at all.[58] Does he incorporate this point by implication? This is possible[59] and Freeman draws attention to a passage in 2.30[60] where Theodulf suggests that images of past deeds delight the eyes and are committed to the heart and, she goes on, "this is one of the clearest and at the same time most positive expressions in the *Opus Caroli Regis* concerning images above all because here, as otherwise rarely in the work, images are assigned a teaching function."[61] I think that on the balance of his testimony we must conclude that he was unwilling to assign to images a teaching function. The very chapter which Freeman cites as containing, perhaps, an assignment to images of a teaching function, works out at great length the argument that images cannot be equated to the Scriptures. Always, Theodulf upholds the absolute superiority of the written word to the image.[62] He often says that fundamental truths can only be conveyed by words, not by pictures: "Painters can therefore in some way bring the stories of past events back to the memory but things that are only perceived by the senses and brought forth by words are comprehended not by painters but by writers."[63] Theodulf is aware that people will believe what they see and he distrusts painters to depict only what is true.[64] Cavallo has made the astute point that in late antiquity art began to gain autonomy from writing and to develop an independent visual discourse, to develop *loci communes*. For a learned man like Gregory, thinking about his learned contemporaries, it will have been easy to suppose that art was immediately and unambiguously accessible. Indeed, he uses words like *cernere* (to perceive) and *videre* (to see) without qualification. By Bede's time, however, words like *intuere* (to contemplate) and *contuitus* (attentive gazing) have entered the discussion.[65] This was Theodulf's world. Pictures were not transparent. They were potentially dangerous. Fundamental truths, the things that really needed to be learned, were available in words, not pictures. Michael Camille draws attention to the Egino Codex produced in Verona around the time when Theodulf was composing the *Opus*. This book contains pictures of the great Latin church fathers preaching.[66] Theodulf was not in the end hostile so much as cautious about the idea that images could teach. He feared abuses.[67]

Another category of discussions inherited by the eighth century from late antiquity concerns images that were somehow miraculous, that somehow *did* something. This might pertain to images that were miraculous in their origins, to images that themselves performed miracles, or, in milder cases, to images that confirmed dreams or portents. Theodulf had absolutely no sympathy for any such arguments about images. Perhaps this reserved attitude may be attributed to the relative absence of miracle-working images in the West. More likely, however, Theodulf simply did not believe that images themselves could possibly assume any of the powers or actions that he attributed exclusively to God.

Theodulf only dealt with one alleged achieropoieton, the Abgar image. On two occasions he simply rejects the stories told about this image.[68] He likewise had no interest in hearing about images that performed miracles.[69] He dismissed such accounts as either diabolical or else as manifestations of God's power. As far as signs and dreams were concerned, he was simply skeptical.[70] God could do such things, of course. But if He did, then the images themselves were irrelevant to the story.

That Theodulf differed from numerous late antique writers and also from his Byzantine contemporaries on the ontology of images derives from a fundamental point in his theology. Images were purely material and God was purely spiritual. Between images and God no comparisons, no analogies were possible. If I am not mistaken, Theodulf's insistence on the sheer materiality of images, on their "manufactured" quality, is his most commonly repeated point.[71] On one occasion he offers a variant of this story according to which if an image wears out it can be discarded.[72] Images simply were not holy, did not participate in holiness. Any act of worship accorded to an image was blasphemous, idolatrous, superstitious, and a distraction from the proper object of worship, God Himself. Images were wholly unnecessary.

Theodulf's general views on the ontology of images may serve as a bridge to a discussion of his ideas about aesthetics for the two are related in several ways. Theodulf frequently couples denunciations of images as mere "manufactured things" with comments to the effect that images spring from the whims of artists.[73] Again and again he says that artists may depict almost anything, and may do so skilfully or artlessly. The value of an image, he says, depends entirely on the skill of the artist who makes it and on the intrinsic value of the materials of which it is comprised.[74] Some works of art are therefore more beautiful than others and, in consequence, more valuable. But their value does not arise from any intrinsic quality of the image. That is, it does not really matter what the image represents, who made it, or for what purpose it was made. Theodulf does not see why painters should be held in higher esteem than any other kinds of artisans or craftsmen. All have varying degrees of skill and all can make wonderful objects. Images can be painted but they can also appear on cloth, clothing, carpets, or, presumably, almost anywhere. Images can be beautiful or ugly. Images can represent almost any secular or religious subject. One feels in Theodulf's words an exquisite taste and discernment. His appreciation for the differing abilities of artists does not, however, constitute a romantic or modern sense of originality. Although he can detect the difference between a pleasing and a repelling image, he basically distrusts artists and considers their whims to be dangerous. Still, I am unaware of any other early medieval author who spoke at such length and with such feeling about the subject of art for art's sake. If he was an iconophobe, he was no philistine, no primitive. His sensibilities were elegant to a high degree. He had a "conoisseur's interest" in figurative subjects.[75] Perhaps, however, Theodulf's aesthetic sense was more utilitarian than philosophical. That is, no matter how often he praised beauty, "nothing suggests that he conceived of beauty as a universal archetype drawing individuals into cognitive relationship with each other by their likeness to it."[76]

Alcuin on Vision

I have shown that on a number of occasions Theodulf spoke of the "mind's eye." When he did so, he was not speaking of art, or beauty, or sense perception. He was making the point that certain things can only be grasped by a kind of spiritual vision that was not rooted in matter or corporeality. In Chapter 1 I quoted Augustine's words on spiritual sight. Theodulf was clearly influenced by Augustine's way of thinking. And he was not alone in his time.

In a letter that must have been written between 796 and 804, Alcuin replied to a query put to him by Fridugis (d. 834), one of his pupils. We do not know what the query itself was, but here is Alcuin's answer:

> There are three ways of seeing things: One is corporal, another symbolic, and the third is mental. Corporal vision means to see with the eyes of the body. Symbolic vision means that, the body's eyes having nothing to do with it, we perceive in spirit alone through some act of imagination, as when we happen to spot something unfamiliar to our sight and immediately an image of that object is formed in the spirit but the symbolic imagination does not emerge before the corporal perception has been encountered. Mental sight means that we consider with the liveliness of the mind alone, as when we read in the Scriptures "Love your neighbor as yourself." The letters are read by means of bodily sight and the neighbor is called back to the spiritual imagination, and love is seen by the mind's understanding alone.
>
> The first kind of vision is the best known of all. The second is equally familiar to all. The third is unknown to most because they do not know how to differentiate what is symbolic and what is mental. The apostle distinguishes these two with one statement, at that a superbly brief one, when he says "I will pray with my spirit and I will pray with my mind; I will sing with my spirit and I will sing with my mind." He named "Spirit" the hidden meanings that are in the Holy Scriptures and he called "mind" their plain meanings. For he wanted to pray with an understanding of those things which we were talking about. Whence in another place he says "If I have prayed with my tongue, my spirit has prayed but my mind is without fruit." The tongue means here the dark and mystical meanings which are customarily perceived by the spirit and if we have no understanding of them our minds remain fruitless.[77]

Alcuin made these same points at least three other times in his writings.[78] Contemporaries of Theodulf and Alcuin, namely Paulinus of Aquileia and Smaragdus of St.-Mihiel, spoke in almost the same words.[79] What I have been calling Theodulf's "principled indifference" to art was widely shared. There is no reason to think of any of these writers as hostile to art so long as visual representations were kept within their proper sphere. That sphere was carnal and afforded no access to the spiritual sphere. This sharp delineation of boundaries helps to explain why Carolingian writers not only rejected any idea that images were somehow holy but also declined to speak of art's capacity to elevate the mind of the viewer from the material to the spiritual realm. One more point may be relevant. Art was an elite extravagance and, as such, could hardly be required of ordinary believers.[80] Theodulf, as we noted above, said as much.

The Arts in the Age of Charlemagne

For many scholars the *Opus* presents a serious problem. If it can be taken as an authoritative statement of Charlemagne's views, then how, it is asked, can the years between about 780 and 800 have witnessed the exuberant production of figural art in profusion? Was Theodulf's a lonely, rigorist voice, out of step with its times? Did he dominate the 790s and then, after leaving court to take up his duties as bishop of Orléans in 798, did others, perhaps Einhard, who were more sympathetic to art, take his place at Charlemagne's side?[81]

In my view, these old conundra arise from two separate misunderstandings. First, Theodulf was not hostile to art. He was no iconoclast, obviously, but he was not much of an iconophobe either. He repeated ad infinitum his assertion that art was permissible for decoration and commemoration. He mentioned a wide array of artistic representations while saying of them only that they were not holy, that they did not merit adoration. On one occasion he chides the Byzantines for letting churches fall into disrepair while saying that "we" adorn churches with every beautiful thing.[82] It is true that his Bibles are aniconic and that in decorating his chapel at Germigny he confined himself to an image of the Ark and the cherubim.[83] This restraint tells us something about Theodulf himself and his own preferences, but tells us little about his programmatic views as a chief adviser to Charlemagne. Moreover, MS Vaticanus Latinus 7207, the original working manuscript of the *Opus* was intended to have a complete, and stunning, set of beautiful ornamented and colored initials. In her edition, Freeman reproduces, albeit in black and white, nearly one hundred of these initials. Likewise, Theodulf's Bibles were richly decorated. The early books produced at Alcuin's Tours were aniconic, perhaps because the young scriptorium lacked the means to incorporate programs of miniatures. But no one accuses Alcuin of iconoclasm. It is at least a possibility that Theodulf's workshop was incapable of figural production at its inception.[84] Still, the *Opus* defends art and appreciates beauty. That is the "official" position of Theodulf and presumably of Charlemagne in whose name he was writing. The official view does not contradict the artistic production of the age. In his poems he shows the same refined taste we have already noticed. He sent Gisela, Charlemagne's sister, a psalter "sparkling with silver and gold."[85] The verses that accompany one of his Bibles say that it shines, on the outside, with jewels, gold, and purple.[86] I have spoken of Theodulf's principled indifference to religious art. To him such art was potentially distracting and served no essential purpose. But his attitude was by no means hostile or, as we just saw, isolated. Given that his great book was discussed and approved in open court, there is no reason to assume that he was out of step with other key figures in his time.

Second, it is important not to get too carried away in any discussion of the art of Charlemagne's reign or to look for glaring discrepancies between that art and Theodulf's *Opus*. Between 781 and 783 an otherwise unknown scribe named Godescalc produced the evangelistiary that still bears his name.[87] According to the long regnant chronology of the "court" books the years just around 790 saw the production of the Arsenal Gospels,[88] and the first portion of the Trier "Ada" Gospels.[89] In about 795 the aniconic Dagulf Psalter[90] was completed and then, within a few years, the Abbeville[91] and Harley Gospels[92] were finished. Around 800 the high point of the early court's work was attained with the Soissons Gospels.[93] In the next decade the second portion of the Trier "Ada" Gospels[94] and the Lorsch Gospels[95] appeared.[96] An earlier chronology, deriving mainly from the work of Koehler, interlaced with the last of these "court books" the set of books related to the Vienna Coronation Gospels.[97] Today Koehler's overall chronology is not as widely accepted as it once was and in particular there are serious problems with the dating of the Vienna Coronation group; some scholars would place these manuscripts and also the Soissons Gospels well into the ninth century, indeed into the reign of Louis the Pious.[98] Although each of these books is a stupendous achievement in its own right, the fact remains that the total number of illuminated luxury manuscripts that can be regarded as more or less contemporary with the *Opus* and sponsored by the court is not large. This means that we ought to avoid arguing for a sharp dichotomy between polemical aniconism and productional iconism.[99]

This is not the place for an art-historical survey of Charlemagne's reign (and I am not the person to undertake such a survey in any case). But a few basic points may be made about these books as they relate to the arguments of the *Opus*. First, the sequence begins with a book of pericopes and includes a psalter but, apart from a fragment in the Getty Museum and another in Karlsruhe, also books of pericopes, all were full Gospel books. The court did not produce complete Bibles and did not produce, apart from the books of pericopes, luxury liturgical books.[100] In critical respects, this artistic production is fully

consonant with Theodulf's focus on the New Testament not only as *the* bearer
of truth but also as the fulfilment of the Old Testament's prophecies.[101] Second,
the artistic program in all of these books focused on the portraits of the evangelists. Moreover, the evangelists are not presented in iconic repose and isolation
but in the act of writing their Gospels.[102] What is more, in many of the portraits
the evangelists, sometimes a bit awkwardly, present their books to the viewer for
inspection. In short, in every case, it is the word that takes precedence over the
image.[103] This, again, is exactly Theodulf's argument. Third, the evangelists in
the Harley and Soissons books not only hold their texts open but in fact reveal
significant texts that point to themes of orthodoxy and salvation. "These carefully chosen texts," says David Ganz, "put remarkable and unparalleled emphasis on the particular message of each gospel." What is more, Theodulf cited
several of these texts directly in the *Opus*. It is hard to imagine better evidence
for consistence rather than divergence of viewpoint.[104] Fourth, most of these
books display decorative ornamentation that is intricate and beautiful but that
never distracts the viewer's eye from the *text*. In this respect the Carolingian
manuscripts differ significantly from some of the more visually disconcerting
achievements of insular art. Fifth, when in the past art historians tended especially to study style and models, there was a natural tendency to see the Carolingian court books as a kind of fortunate meeting between late antique
perceptions of style and composition and insular decorative traditions. Today it
is more common to see the Carolingian books as comprised of older elements,
to be sure, but as original creations that must be located in a specific time and
place.[105] This means that the key aspect of these books that demands attention
is their affirmation of the proposition that truth comes directly from the text of
the Gospels. Sixth, two of these manuscripts have "Fountain of Life" images
(Godescalc, fol. 3v; Soissons, fol. 6v) and three have images of Christ in majesty
(Godescalc, fol. 3r; Soissons, fol. 124r, where Christ's mandorla is formed by the
Q of the Lucan opening *Quoniam quidem*; Lorsch, part 1, p. 27, a small image
at the top of the page containing the Matthean *argumentum*). The former relate
to baptism, most obviously, but also to the four rivers of paradise, to the origins
of the divine promises, and to the four Gospels.[106] The latter relate to the person
whose story is told in the Gospels, to the "King of Kings," and to the Word
whose words are enclosed in the books. Text and image work together in all
cases. Theodulf did not put such images in his own Bibles but there is absolutely
nothing in the court books that contradicts what Theodulf said in his *Opus*.
And that is as it should be, for the *Opus* was itself a product of the court.
Seventh, only the Soissons Gospels have scenes from the life of Christ, and at
that they appear only in the spandrels of the arches on evangelist pages and on

initium pages. Theodulf was not necessarily opposed to *historiae*, but he did not use them himself and his contemporaries seem to have shared his reluctance.[107] Eighth, and finally, not one of these books contains an image of Charlemagne. Indeed, apart from coins, that is if the imperial bust-portrait coins may be taken as authentic representations, there are no contemporary images of Charlemagne; and the bust-portrait coins date late in the reign, between 804 and 812.[108] This, once more, accords well with Theodulf's abhorrence for the Roman and Byzantine imperial images.

Mayr-Harting has expressed puzzlement that the court books were so sparing in their depictions of Christ while the ivories that were produced at the court do not seem to show the same reserve. He offers four possible explanations: serious divisions of opinion at the court; ivories were different iconographic terrain than parchment pages; ivory was itself precious; ivories were intended for private prayer and meditation. One must be a bit careful with arguments like these because the total number of ivories from Charlemagne's court is not large; about a dozen objects can with some confidence be placed in the period 795–810 and only about half of these can be connected with the court books. Not all books had ivory covers. Some had covers with precious metals and jewels, and some probably had no fine covers at all. It seems likely that, in these earliest years of Carolingian art, harmonious programs encompassing both books and covers had not yet been worked out. Still, it must be remembered at once, Theodulf opposed only the worship of images.

As for the ivories themselves, the plaques that covered two of the court books survive. The covers for the Dagulf Psalter, prepared for a book that was itself written around 795, show David playing a lyre, evidently singing his psalms.[109] Other images show David selecting scribes to copy his psalms, Jerome getting a mandate from Pope Damasus to translate the Bible (but here, of course, the psalms), and Jerome dictating. As its dedication verses make clear, this book was intended as a gift for Hadrian but was probably never sent because the pope died in 795.[110] The psalter itself begins with a remarkable collection of creeds and prefaces that occupy twenty-three folios. The Dagulf Psalter can actually be related both directly and indirectly to the *Opus*. One of the creeds which stands near its beginning is precisely the pseudo-Hieronymian (Pelagian) creed that opens book three of the *Opus*. This is the creed that replaced Theodulf's credal anthology precisely because it could be read as striking a blow against adoptionism. That seems to be a pretty direct connection. That creed was attributed to Jerome. Jerome appears in one of the book's ivories receiving from Pope Damasus his commission to translate the Bible, but perhaps here, in view of the other ivory images, the psalms in particular were meant. Charlemagne was, of course, the new David. Taken together these facts point to at least an indirect connection between the psalter and the *Opus*. After the *Capitulare, Responsum*, and Frankfurt, and all the communications touching on adoptionism and images, it is likely that this book was meant to stress to the pope that the Franks were still loyal, respectful, and orthodox.[111] The covers of the Lorsch Gospels, now divided between the Victoria and Albert Museum and the Vatican, show, as their central scenes, a madonna (V&A) and a Christ triumphing over beasts (Vatican).[112] The latter has a clear parallel in the Douce cover now in the Bodleian and probably originally affixed to a Gospel lectionary prepared for Gisela while she was abbess of Chelles. This cover also features Isaiah holding a scroll on which one can read "Behold, a virgin shall conceive."[113] Once again, these are all Theodulfian themes, all are images that reflect issues discussed at length in the *Opus*.

"Surely," says Udo Reinhold Jeck, "there have been only a few periods in European history when art has been placed in a comparable way at the center of self-consciousness."[114] This lapidary remark will serve to conclude the present section and to lead on to the next one. Theodulf talked at great length about art, and about much else too. His great themes of tradition, order, and worship were central to his thinking. But he was also concerned to legitimize and simultaneously to control art. Beauty both delighted and troubled him. No work of art, no matter how beautiful it might be, and no matter how skilfully it was made, could communicate anything of the essence of the ineffable divinity. Only words could do this. Images were essentially irrelevant to the divine cult and, quite likely, were distracting. Some material things could be holy but only when they had been designated by God Himself or consecrated by a priest. And then, they had to be associated with the rites of the church. The art produced during, as well as just before and after, Theodulf's time at court did not contradict the basic arguments of the *Opus*. That art was relatively restrained in its use of images and concentrated on the word and the Word.

Tradition, Order, and Worship at the Court of Charlemagne

The legalization and then the imposition of Christianity in the fourth century obliged Christians to locate themselves in history.[115] The conversion of ever-larger numbers of people from all walks of life implied the continuous discovery of a new history that began with Adam and Eve and continued to the present. As the writings of Eusebius and Orosius, on the one hand, and those of Augustine, on the other, show very well, Christian and Roman universalism were compatible in some ways and adversarial in others.[116] Nevertheless, as the former western provinces of the Roman Empire were reassembled as kingdoms under the leaders of *gentes*, of peoples, who had no place in previous schemes of either biblical or classical historical consciousness, elites, at least, learned new ways of thinking in universal terms while dissociating themselves from the older frames of reference.[117] By Charlemagne's time something new had emerged in the West, a realm whose leaders had the power and resources, and the will to use them, to create a political entity that could reasonably bear comparison with that world's other two great powers: Byzantium and the Islamic caliphate.[118] Byzantium's view of history was paradoxical, implying at once a dramatic change, represented by the adoption of Christianity, and a total absence of change, implicit in Roman continuity.[119] In the early 790s, the *Opus* "proclaimed, on biblical-typological grounds, a Christian universalism which directly opposed the constitutionally fixed Byzantine claims in world rulership."[120]

Tradition

In important respects the *Opus* was a history book, and history is at least partly about managing tradition and fashioning memory. Let us inquire into the nature of Frankish reflections on tradition in the years around the *Opus*'s composition. There are several indications that the Carolingians were thinking about history, tradition, and time.[121] Around 790 someone with close connections to the court began compiling the *Annals of the Kingdom of the Franks*.[122] This text may have been intended in the narrowest sense to justify Carolingian measures against the refractory Tassilo of Bavaria, but the work reached back to 741, the year when Charles Martel divided his responsibilities between his sons Carloman and Pippin, the latter Charlemagne's father. At around the same time Charlemagne asked Paul the Deacon, famous as the historian of the Lombards, to compile a history of the bishops of Metz.[123] Paul stressed, more than anyone before him had done, the connection between Metz and the Carolingians—Bishop Arnulf was seen as one ancestor of the Carolingian family—and between Metz and St. Peter, the see allegedly having been founded by a disciple of the apostle.[124] Einhard says that histories and the deeds of the ancients were read aloud in Charlemagne's presence.[125] In the early 790s Charlemagne ordered a collection to be made of his family's correspondence with the pope and the with the empire.[126] We know this collection of ninety-nine letters as the *Codex Carolinus*. To our great disappointment, all that survives are papal letters to

Francia. The Frankish letters to Rome and to Constantinople, as well as the imperial letters, have vanished without a trace. In perhaps 794 Charlemagne asked for a collection of the letters of Pope Gregory I.[127] The Sacramentary of Gellone, written in the last decade of the eighth century, contains a litany for the dead that begins with Noah and goes down to Peter and Paul. The point of these prayers was to create a sense of community "not only among the attendants at the death, but between them and those who had preceded them in sacred history."[128] Carolingian libraries were, in a sense, organized historically: first came Bibles, then the school works that permitted an understanding of the plain text, and then the patristic commentaries.[129] Carolingian collections of canon law were generally organized historically; that is, their material was arrayed in more or less chronological order rather than systematically by topic.[130] An episcopal statute from the very early ninth century mentions four great epochs of law giving: natural law before the fall; the Mosaic law of the Old Testament; Christ's law and the New Testament; the legislation of the Frankish church.[131]

In addition to these indications of a widespread awareness of and interest in history and tradition, both contemporary and remote, there are some further hints about interests in time in the circles around Charlemagne. Einhard says that Alcuin taught Charlemagne *computus* and *cursus siderum* to help him arrange time correctly in his world.[132] Surely this meant more than determining the date of Easter. One wonders about Charlemagne's desire to change the names of the months and days. In about 789, at Lorsch, a monastery with close connections to the court, a new calendar was prepared.[133] Unlike those devised earlier by Willibrord (ca. 705) and the one in the Godescalc Evangelistiary, the Lorsch calendar was not primarily designed to serve the liturgy. This calendar, whose origins are obscure, was probably written in clearly readable Caroline minuscule. It was designed for clarity and versatility. It had a solar year beginning with January 1 and it sharply marked off monthly divisions and equipped them with verses. It is laid out in three columns: the left has *computus*; the center, feasts; and the right, astronomical data. The contents were not derived from any single model or tradition. The area devoted to feasts included the great saints acknowledged by all of Christendom and not merely those honored in one place or even by the Franks alone. The main groups of saints seem to come from the Gregorian Sacramentary sent to Charles by Hadrian, although some come from Frankish Gelasian books, and some from Anglo-Saxon sources. But regardless of source, and of Rome's prominence as a source, no previous calendar had focused this way on generally recognized celebrations. The calendar contains biblical commemorations that are not in the liturgy and that served to highlight the Carolingian interest in the Old Testament. There was an orientation to, but not an overarching emphasis on, Roman and papal feasts. The area with the antique astral calendars was meaningless for the reckoning of Easter but useful for spotting particular days in the year. The calendar was in some ways a synthesis of all kinds of ways of imagining, reckoning, and using time. Although it cannot be directly tied to Charles himself, it almost certainly bears connections with people who were close to him and it breathes his spirit of order, precision, and regulation. It also has a way of situating the Franks within their own time and within all of time.

From the quotidian and contemporary we may move to the glimpses of all of time, including the future in quite explicit ways, that a few other sources provide.[134] The Carolingian period has not been prominent in histories of apocalyptic thought. Still, there are indications that some people at least thought that December 25, 800, would mark a new year, a new century, and a new millennium. Such thoughts were prompted by the dissemination of Eusebius's opinion that Christ was born in 5,200. Some, like Beatus of Liebaña, the third redaction of whose Apocalypse Commentary was written in 786, thought the world was about to end. Others, like Ambrosius Autpertus who wrote an influential Apocalypse commentary (between 758 and 767) refused to speculate on the end of time but instead thought in grandly universal terms. Alcuin sometimes spoke of the adoptionists as the "new" heretics whose existence signaled the end of time. Alcuin also talked often of the "*tempora periculosa*," the "dangerous times" (cf. 2 Timothy 3.1). Around 798 at St. Amand someone prepared a substantial set of compustical texts and a few years later at Cologne that set was copied and expanded. It is tempting to connect this activity with the turn of the year 800. And it just might be the case that Charlemagne's profound concern for the Christian people who had been entrusted to his care derived, at least in part, from a sense that time was running out. If there was any widespread sense that time was running out, then Theodulf's concerns about salvation take on a kind of urgency that is more than abstractly theological or momentarily polemical.

Look where we may, we find indications of temporal and historical consciousness. Some of the most important of these involve the Bible and the saints. This is reminiscent of Theodulf's interests. After all, in composing the *Opus* he cited the Old Testament almost eight hundred times and the New more than seven hundred. Carolingian interest in the Bible in Charles's time was intense, as we have seen. And part of that interest was based on an attempt to assimilate the Franks and the Jews.

In the most important capitulary of his royal years, the *Admonitio Generalis* of 789, Charlemagne compared himself to King Josiah (cf. 4 Kings 22, 23) in the "visitation, correction, and admonition" of his realm.[135] Where the Bible tells about Josiah we read that "before him there was no king like him." By implication, there had been no king like Charlemagne.[136] If Charlemagne compared himself to Josiah on this occasion, he was much more often compared to, indeed addressed as, David by his contemporaries. In this connection it is worth bearing in mind that no name except Christ's appears more often than David's in the *Opus*.[137] For the present, however, it is the testimony of others that I wish to invoke. As early as 775 Charlemagne had been called both Solomon and David by Cathwulf.[138] Paul the Deacon called him David in 787.[139] By 794, however, it had become normal to call Charlemagne David, for instance in the dedicatory verses to the Dagulf Psalter,[140] in a poem by Angilbert,[141] and in a letter of Alcuin's.[142] To be sure, many figures at Charlemagne's court received either biblical or classical nicknames.[143] It is hard to know if the Franks knew that at Constantinople the emperor was often called a "second David" and were therefore responding in kind.[144] But the close association between Charlemagne and David was meant to attribute to the great Frank some of David's prophetic wisdom and strength in defense of the faith.

Ubiquitous references to Charlemagne as David nestle in a larger context. Pope Paul I had called the Franks a "new Israel."[145] At about the same time, in the mid-760s, the Franks referred to themselves in the same terms in the second prologue to the Salic Law.[146] It will be recalled that in the *Opus* Theodulf called the Franks the "spiritual Israel." Beginning in the late 780s sources of all kinds refer to the Franks simply as the *populus Christianus*.[147] In writing his *Life of Willibrord*, Alcuin called the Franks, as if they were already so called in the early eighth century, the "chosen people of God."[148] In capitularies of 789 and 792 Charlemagne took oaths of loyalty from all of his subjects and he treated them as a single collectivity, not as a collection of *gentes*.[149] This single "Christian people" was none other that the new "Frankish Israel" led by the new Carolingian David.[150] It would be hard to imagine a clearer evocation of Old Testament traditions in the realms of practical politics or a closer approach to Theodulf's sense of the biblical tradition that culminated in the Franks. On this reckoning, the Franks were the direct heirs of Israel just as, Theodulf had said, the Byzantines were the heirs of Babylon.

The evocations of Israel are not confined to textual evidence. Charlemagne's throne in the palatine chapel at Aachen was intended to evoke the throne of Solomon (3 Kings 10.18–20).[151] To Alcuin, Charlemagne was like Solomon both because of his wisdom and because he erected a chapel like the Temple which Solomon had built in Jerusalem.[152] It is just possible that the Frankish quarrel with Byzantium engendered a new interest in Jerusalem, and thus in ancient Jewish traditions and in Davidic kingship.[153] Alcuin wrote to Patriarch George of Jerusalem on one occasion and said "Jerusalem is our mother and the homeland of the Christian people."[154] Angilbert said that relics had arrived in Aachen from Rome, Constantinople, and Jerusalem.[155] This reference may serve as a final reminder of the omnipresence of Jerusalem in the Carolingian mind while shifting our attention to Rome.

Remember that *Opus 1.6* was a powerful statement of Rome-centeredness that Theodulf was encouraged—forced?—to incorporate as he was revising his book. Remember too that only books approved by the popes or included in the Gelasian canon were acceptable to the Franks. Theodulf repeatedly censured the Byzantines for abandoning Roman standards. Quite apart from willingly shouldering the responsibility of protecting the Roman Church, Charlemagne turned to Rome on many occasions. He sought in 774 a copy of the then-valid Roman canon law and received the so-called *Dionysio-Hadriana*.[156] He turned to Rome for an authoritative service book and received a version of the Gregorian sacramentary.[157] He asked for an authentic copy of the *Rule of St. Benedict*.[158] When books were obtained from Rome and then copied in the Frankish world, they were marked "*ex authentico libro*." To be "authentic" a book had to be Roman.[159]

Roman meant papal or Petrine. Several churches were built in the Frankish world in Charlemagne's time "*more romano*," "in the Roman fashion."[160] Some of these churches—St.-Denis, St.-Maurice d'Agaune, Fulda, Cologne, St.-Riquier—reveal their Roman influences in having T-shaped transepts, ring crypts, or occidentation.[161] To a greater or lesser degree, they are copies of St. Peter's and St. Paul's, the primary churches dedicated to Rome's Christian founders, the religious replacements for Romulus and Remus. The chapel complex at Aachen was sometimes called "the Lateran" (albeit provably only after 800) and its main worship space evokes the octagonal baptistery at the Lateran in Rome.[162] In a justly influential study Richard Krautheimer argued that Charlemagne inaugurated a "renaissance" of Christian Rome.[163] He was thinking in particular of Constantine but I would argue that it was papal Rome that was prominent in Charles's thinking. Perhaps the twenty-four elders of the apocalypse in the cupola of the palatine chapel were meant to evoke the facade of Old St. Peter's.[164] Possibly, too, the stational liturgies implemented in Metz by Chrodegang and then at St.-Riquier by Angilbert are further evocations of Roman usages.[165] There can be no doubt that the great monuments of Christian Rome provided both inspiration and models for the Carolingians. But when the chief Carolingian churches, and especially the chapel at Aachen, are studied in detail, one must be struck by their freshness, their originality. They were something special, something reflective of these people who self-consciously saw themselves as the culmination of all Christian history.[166]

Indeed, while the Roman image in the Carolingian mind is a subject still in need of a full study, it is important to note provisionally how ambiguous secular Rome was as both symbol and reality for the early Carolingians.[167] Theodulf said that Rome was the heir of Babylon and Charlemagne expressed his approval. On one occasion—one only—Hadrian addressed Charles as Constantine.[168] Generally, however, the Constantinian image was only domesticated by the Carolingians after Charlemagne's imperial coronation.[169] Such obvious examples of *imitatio imperii* as coins took on clearly Roman characteristics only after 800.[170] In creating his palace complex at Aachen, Charlemagne may have been asserting his parity with the Baghdad of the Caliphs and the Constantinople of the Byzantines more than laying claim to any specific Roman model of building or behavior.[171] In the famous poem of about 810 which Modoin hoped would secure him the court's patronage, the author spoke again and again of a "New Rome," but this always refers to Aachen. Indeed, the poet speaks of "the palace of David" as "the capital of the world."[172]

Put a little differently, requesting books from Rome, or building *more romano*, was not meant to reanimate a dead past, but to join a living tradition. The Carolingians were acutely aware of history and of tradition, especially Jewish and Roman. Their aim was to join that history. Theodulf reflects these interests faithfully in the *Opus* by his constant evocations of tradition: biblical, patristic, and Roman. And he reflects them in another way. One of the most powerful aspects of his stinging polemic is its ruthless attempt to write the Byzantines out of history.

Order

If tradition and history pointed the way, order told Charles how to get there. Charlemagne's desire to create a well-ordered realm is evident from his first capitulary to his last and from the writings of his contemporaries. That desire manifested itself in concerns about intellectual life and institutions, about secular and ecclesiastical structures, and in the very language used to talk about order.

There has long been a *guerre des savants* over whether the cultural life of the Carolingian period should be understood as a "renaissance" or as a "reform."[173] In fact, it was both. But scholars who energetically defend one view or the other sometimes miss the essential point expressed well a half-century ago by Josef Fleckenstein: Reform was "in its essence the historical realization of a suprahistorical, that is divine, command."[174] Turning to Christian antiquity for inspiration was not merely a matter of taste, and putting the Carolingian house in order was not merely a matter of public utility. Everything, the Franks said, was done to fulfill God's commands and to make it possible for the *populus Christianus* to live by God's law, to achieve salvation. Theodulf spelled this out at the very beginning of the *Opus*: "Since we [i.e., Charlemagne] have taken the rudder in the bay of His realm, with the Lord granting, it is necessary that we struggle with all out might with Christ's help in His defence and for His exaltation that we might thereby be able to be called good and faithful servants."[175] In the *Admonitio Generalis* Charles is called "king and rector of the kingdom of the Franks and humble helper of the holy church," and the document goes on to say that his rule depends on the abundant mercy of Christ and then calls the clergy to aid Charles in "leading the people of God to the pastures of eternal life."[176] Paulinus once called Charles "king and priest and most wise ruler of Christians"[177] while Alcuin called him "a king in power and a bishop in preaching."[178] They both were writing in connection with Charlemagne's efforts to combat adoptionism around the time of Frankfurt. A little earlier Hadrian wrote to Charles to urge him on in his conquest of Saxony so that the Saxons could be offered eternal salvation.[179] Charlemagne's piety may be viewed as simple and militant,[180] but there can be no doubt that he saw himself in the guise of those Old Testament kings who were regularly held up to him for his emulation.

From this discussion of Charles as the divinely instituted *rector* of the *populus Christianus*, we can move to other abstract but nevertheless revealing aspects of the language of order in the world of Charlemagne. We discussed earlier Theodulf's insistence that things be done as "order demands." In the late 740s Pope Zachary wrote to Boniface and urged him to adhere to the "*norma rectitudinis*."[181] The phrase then turned up in Frankish documents. The Synod of Ver in 755 called for a return to the "*rectissima norma*."[182] Chrodegang of Metz often used such phrases as "*norma rectitudinis*" and "*linea rectitudinis*."[183] In the key legislation of the 780s and 790s one encounters over and over words such as "*recte*" and "*ordine*." Tironian notes tell us that Charles four times exclaimed "*Recte*" as the *Opus* was being read in his presence. On one occasion Charles called for baptism to be carried out "*ordinabiliter*."[184] Look where one may, the impression is the same. There were God-given norms, rules, and conventions and the chief responsibility of the king and his clergy was to find them, study them, and implement them. The goal of all of this activity was not to restore or to recover some pristine condition but to make the current situation "right."

Moving from the abstract to the concrete, we may look first at the kind of ruler that Charles imagined himself to be, or supposed that he ought to be. First, let us recall that, in Theodulf's telling—which means in Charles's view too—the Byzantines were arrogant, reckless, imprudent, and violators of unity. Charlemagne was just the opposite. He defended his people from the attacks of pagans and heretics. He promoted justice to such a degree that one scholar has seen the *Admonitio Generalis* as an implementation of the Decalogue.[185] One could easily go through Charles's legislation and find in it a conscious attempt to implement the beatitudes. No issue was too insignificant to escape his attention: the price of food, honest weights and measures, the plight of widows and orphans, the needs of the poor. The Byzantines, as the inheritors of Roman and Hellenistic conceptions of rulership, saw the emperor as "God's image" (μιμητὴς θεοῦ).[186] At Charlemagne's court the ideal of a good bishop and pastor, as sketched by Gregory I in his *Pastoral Rule,* was reformulated to serve as a set of guidelines for a proper ruler. Accordingly, Charlemagne was a *"minister Dei,"* a person assigned an awesome responsibility held in trust for others.[187] Charles was meant to be humble, peaceful, gentle, in short, all those things the Byzantines were not. By extending the argument we can see that Charlemagne was the right kind of ruler, one who measured up to the divine ideal, whereas the Byzantine emperors failed in every critical respect and fomented strife and division. When one reads what Charles himself and his associates said about rulership, it becomes clear why Theodulf was at such great pains to delegitimize Byzantine rulership at every turn.

A rightly ordered ruler can represent himself in many ways. We know all too little about Frankish royal ceremonial, but what we do know suggests that it was designed to promote the ideal of unity and community on the one hand and what one historian has engagingly called "cheerfulness" on the other hand.[188] A focus on the majesty, remoteness, and inaccessibility of the ruler that was a prime Byzantine inheritance from antiquity was largely absent in Francia. Instead the king's oneness with his people and his benevolent care for them were emphasized. The greatest single ceremonial space in Charlemagne's world proclaims the right order of things. In the great chapel at Aachen, the throne was in the west, the altars were in the east, and in the cupola of the dome there was an image of Christ in majesty.[189] This arrangement immediately suggests its own interpretation: in a well-ordered world the humble royal minister surrenders the privileged eastern zone to God's ordained ministers while the only true ruler, Christ, the "King of Kings," reigns from high above. The Frankish royal lauds, often sung in this very place begin and frequently repeat the refrain: *"Christus vincit, Christus regnat, Christus imperat."*[190] But this arrangement of the chapel may also be read as a polemical statement. The imperial Chrysotriklinos at Constantinople placed the imperial throne in the east with an image of Christ regnant behind it and the altar in the west.[191] We cannot be absolutely certain that the Franks knew about the layout of the Chrysotriklinos, but in view of the intense diplomacy that commenced in the mid-750s it seems likely that they would at least have had some reports. The chapel at Aachen was a proper church with a throne in its westwork. The imperial chamber, on the other hand, was primarily a throne room and ceremonial hall. The rulers who officiated there are exactly the ones Theodulf berated for calling themselves "*divos*" and their acts "*divalia*" and for saying that they "co-reign" with Christ. Could anyone who looked at the emperor on his throne with the image of Christ behind him have escaped that impression? And would not a viewer in Aachen have understood the hierarchic significance of a Charles enthroned, like Solomon, beneath a majestically enthroned Christ who reigned supreme from the heavenlike space of the chapel's cupola? Finally, Einhard reminds us that Charlemagne preferred good, old-fashioned Frankish clothing to Roman finery.[192]

Attention to how to talk about rulers and to how rulers ought to behave is mirrored by concerns about the right kinds of clergy. Carolingian interests in this subject parallel Theodulf's blistering attacks on Tarasius's irregular situation. Charlemagne legislated constantly on the clergy. He expressed concerns about their moral fitness and personal excellence. He demanded that they live by "the holy Rule," and that they keep the canons. He continued the efforts begun by his father and the clergy of the 740s to subordinate bishops to metropolitans and local clergy to bishops. He called for regular synods. On this point it is instructive to recall Theodulf's chastisements of the Byzantines for holding synods too often, poorly, and for trivial reasons. On the contrary, Charlemagne spent at least six months preparing for the Synod of Frankfurt and then, in that synod, undertook only necessary actions and did so "*prudenter.*"[193] Again and again, Charles said that the ancient canons or the teachings of the fathers were to be scrutinized and then followed. The Frankish realm seemed to merit God's favor precisely because it had been carefully ordered according to God's own words and commands. And whereas the Byzantine rulers inappropriately intruded themselves into doctrinal matters, Charlemagne always left the matter of dogma to his clergy and then enforced whatever decision they might make.[194]

Theodulf took extreme delight in wordplay. His grammar lessons, explanations of rhetorical conventions, and syllogistic reasoning are evidence enough of that. In virtually every case where Theodulf took the Byzantines to school, he did so on a point of biblical exegesis. If the Bible laid out both the key doctrines of the faith and the rules for right living, then it was crucial to understand it. Manifestly, the Byzantine understanding of Scripture was defective. If the Carolingian was superior, then this was the result not of chance but of design. It would be no exaggeration to say that the very heart of the Carolingian intellectual revival was a broad effort to understand the Bible. McNally puts it this way: "The Carolingian Renaissance can be characterized as a rebirth of the Christian aspiration for biblical spirituality and biblical studies. It was a return to Augustine's idea, expressed in *De doctrina christiana,* that the cultivation of letters should be a propaedeutic to biblical studies."[195] This involved the preparation of acceptable biblical codices, the mastery of the intellectual tools requisite to biblical study, and the acquisition, study, and dissemination of the great commentaries of the patristic era. Surely it is no coincidence that Charlemagne's great school legislation dates from around 789, the year when the *Admonitio Generalis* was issued, and just about the time when the Nicene *acta* arrived at court. The *Admonitio Generalis* itself contains several references to good teaching and learning but its seventy-second *capitulum* is especially important. It was addressed to the bishops first of all, and then to canons and monks. All cathedrals and monasteries were required to establish schools to teach boys psalms, musical notation, singing, computus, and grammar. The clergy were urged "to correct catholic books properly" because uncorrected books can lead astray those who wish to pray correctly. Only mature men were to be permitted to copy books. At, surely, just about the same time Charles sent to the archbishops a circular letter "On the cultivation of letters" that was to be distributed to suffragan bishops and abbots.[196] This letter again urges the creation of schools "for although it is better to do what is good than to know it, nevertheless knowing comes before doing." The letter echoes many of the concerns expressed in the *Admonitio Generalis* and adds that because the Bible is full of "figures of speech, tropes, and similar things" it is important that people gain a "mastery of letters" to make possible and then to enhance their "spiritual understanding." People should be chosen for this work who have both the will and the maturity to carry it out. Knowing and doing are closely related. The Byzantines, perhaps like the Spanish adoptionists, know the wrong things and thus do the wrong things too. The Franks are humble enough to admit that they do not now know everything necessary to their "spiritual understanding" but they are trying hard to remedy their deficiencies. They are seeking to build a better-ordered world.

Worship

Although Theodulf addressed the topic of worship, particularly worship in spirit and truth, this was not a subject that came up often in explicit ways in the legislation of Charlemagne or in the writings of his contemporaries. We may assume in a general way that Theodulf's remarks on worship met with the court's favor in the open discussions held one or more times in Regensburg in 792 and 793. But such a general assumption does not identify or clarify specific examples. In the discussion just above of educational reform we noticed that Charlemagne was concerned about liturgical singing, about *computus*—the arcane science that permitted the correct observation of the feasts of the liturgical year and about prayers offered in the right form. Issues such as these cross between the themes of order and worship. In the *Admonitio Generalis* Charlemagne reminded his contemporaries that his father had begun the process of Romanizing the liturgy, beginning with chant. He himself continued that effort. His words reflect his thinking on this subject and on many others too: "they are to learn the Roman chant . . . in the correct form, in conformity with what our father of blessed memory, King Pippin, strove to bring to pass when he abolished the Gallican chant for the sake of unanimity with the apostolic see and the peaceful harmony of God's holy church."[197] When Charlemagne received from Rome a copy of the Gregorian sacramentary he assigned one of his advisers, Benedict of Aniane, the task of adapting it to Frankish usage.[198] The book was a service book for the pope and for the church of the city of Rome. Some of its material was irrelevant to the operation of the Frankish church, and many feasts that were important in Francia were perforce absent from this Roman book. Once Benedict completed his labors, Charles attempted to impose the book on his whole realm. His effort was unsuccessful but did spawn a greater liturgical uniformity than had ever before existed in the vast Frankish world. In 786 Charles issued a circular letter to accompany a new lectionary that he had asked Paul the Deacon to prepare for him.[199] Again he referred to the work of his father and indicated that he would now extend it: "fired by the example of our father Pippin . . . by whose zeal all the churches of the Gauls became graced by singing in the Roman tradition, we, with wise judgment, are no less concerned to embellish them with a series of readings of great excellence." He went on to say that he had learned that some service books were sloppily compiled and full of errors. Paul, he says, collected from the "catholic fathers" the best possible commentaries for all the feasts of the year. For Charles worship was not only a matter of doing things correctly, but also of doing them in the right times and places. A good example of his attitude is the three days of litanies and solemn masses that he called for in 791 as his army was setting out for a campaign against the Avars.[200] Another indicator of Charles's concerns about correct worship can be extracted from his prohibitions of pagan practices and superstitions. He legislated against soothsayers, magicians, traffickers with spirits, weather prophets, makers of magical ligatures, people who worshiped at sacred springs or trees.[201] In the 780s and 790s Charlemagne was still fully embroiled with the Saxons whose conversion to Christianity was still new and partial. It is worth asking whether some of the *Opus*'s worries about idolatry and superstition might have been born of very real and recent encounters with pagan practices. Charles was also concerned about forms of prophecy of dubious authenticity. Apparently a letter was alleged to have fallen from heaven somewhere and the king said simply that such trash is to be burned and only "canonical books and catholic treatises and the works of holy authors" were to be read.[202] Right practices had to be carried out in the right way, and evil practices extirpated. Charlemagne did not reveal, outside of what the *Opus* attributes to him, Theodulf's zeal for the deep theological implications of worship, but he was second to none in his insistence that things be done correctly. Some of Charlemagne's coins bore the inscription "CHRISTIANA RELIGIO."[203] It is possible to interpret this as a direct affront to what Theodulf called *"Romana Ambitio."*[204] For Einhard, Charlemagne's courtier and eventually biographer, building the "Christian Religion" was a matter of promoting the Christian cult.[205] Without correct forms of worship the Carolingians could not expect to receive the divine favor on which they depended.

A word or two may be said about what I do not find in the age of Charlemagne.[206] Not one panel painting survives from the Carolingian period as a whole. Palladia and prophylacteries were apparently unknown. No icon was carried into battle. Frankish sources are silent on miraculous images. I know of no account of an image's being kissed, embraced, or venerated in any way whatsoever. On just one occasion Theodulf reacted to the possibility that an image might be approached with candles and incense (4.3) but he did not do so in a way that suggests he was familiar with such practices. Instead, he was complaining about what he found in the Nicene *acta*. We have seen that cult practices associated with icons may have arisen later than used to be thought and may not have been as deeply embedded in the tradition as the Nicene fathers insisted. We have seen, too, that a small amount of ambiguous evidence hints at cult practices associated with works of art in Merovingian Gaul and Lombard Italy. In the world of Theodulf and Charlemagne, such practices were either unknown or unrecorded. Images, let alone icons, played no role in worship.

Conclusion

Modern writers interpret the *Opus* in a number of different ways. Schmandt, as noted, called it a *"Staatsschrift"* (political treatise) while Gero prefers *"Streit-*

schrift" (polemic).[207] For Staubach what was at stake was nothing less than the "*Weltstellung*" (place, or rank, in the world) of the Carolingians.[208] Chazelle insists that it is more than merely a polemic because of its profound theological foundations.[209] Folz sees the *Opus* as "a doctrinal manifesto on the part of the Frankish church,"[210] and Jeck appears to agree, saying that however political the work may appear, all of its arguments are carefully grounded in theology.[211] So Berndt sees the *Opus* as a "basic Carolingian course in theology,"[212] while Freeman, who knows the work better than anyone else, calls it a "summa" of Carolingian thought.[213] Mitalaité sees the work as a sophisticated meditation on Trinitarian theology.[214] So we have an oddity: a bare-knuckled political polemic cast as a course in theology.

I contend that each of these scholars has grasped an important part of the truth about the *Opus*. It was political and polemical. One need read only a page or two to see that. But the polemic was not generalized ranting but instead minutely focused dismantling. What was dismantled? Byzantium's claims to biblical and Christian tradition, to authentic rulership, to appropriate ecclesiastical organization. This process of deconstruction was done with small, sharp instruments, not with messy explosives. Thus, indeed, every mincing argument was accompanied by biblical proof-texts, by patristic authorities, and by methodological disquisitions. Moreover, it was not enough to show that the Greeks were always wrong, it was also important to build strong, new things where the old ones had been pulled down. So the Franks understood the Bible, the great commentators on the Bible, and the intellectual tools necessary to careful and correct study. The Franks alone held a place within the lines of biblical and Christian traditions. The Franks had the right kinds of rulers, the right kind of church and churchmen, and the right spiritual attitudes with respect to relationships between the here and the hereafter. There was indeed something "basic," something "summa"-like about the *Opus*.

In closing it is worth reiterating how important and creative were the years between, roughly, 785 and 795. These years witnessed major military and diplomatic successes, the issuance of the most important legislation of Charlemagne's royal period, the real beginnings of Carolingian art and architecture, and the explosion of Carolingian courtly literature. The *Opus* was discussed in open court more than once in these years. It is, therefore, hardly surprising that the work talks of more than just II Nicaea and images. The combination of a thorny issue, a creative moment, and a brilliant author produced a book that opens broad vistas on a decisive time in European history.

CHAPTER SIX

The Age of Second Iconoclasm

For what the present synod [i.e., II Nicaea] teaches about the adoration of
venerable images, your apostolic see has held from ancient times, as many
texts demonstrate; for the universal church has venerated them and venerates
them right up to this day, with the exception of certain bishops of the Gauls
to whom their great usefulness has not yet been revealed. For they say that
nothing whatsoever made by the hands of men is to be adored.
　—Anastasius the Librarian to Pope John VIII,
　　Preface to His Translation of the Acta of II Nicaea

THE HEATED DEBATES over images that attracted so much energy and intelli-
gence in the eighth century cooled noticeably in the years after II Nicaea and
Frankfurt. In the West popes and Franks continued to work together productively and amicably despite their disagreements over images and the *filioque*. In
the East, conditions were less serene. In 797 Irene decided to have her frivolous
son Constantine VI blinded—he died from his wounds—and to assume rule
herself. Irene did rule for five years as *Basilissa*, but she lacked the confidence of
many key constituents in the Byzantine state. Accordingly she was deposed in
802 by Nicephorus, who faced both foreign and domestic problems of huge
magnitude. The Bulgarians were pressing hard on his Balkan frontier and the
redoubtable Harun al-Raschid and his Arab forces were attacking Anatolia. Inside the realm, Nicephorus confronted remedying the state's poor financial position and pacifying bitter quarrels in the church. Nicephorus fell in a battle with
Khan Krum of the Bulgarians in 811, to be replaced for only two years by an
ineffective non-entity, Michael I Rhangabe, who was, in turn, deposed in 813 by

the tough-minded Leo V the Armenian. Leo reinstated iconoclasm in 815 and it is here that this chapter picks up the story in earnest.

Nine years after Leo V reestablished iconoclasm as the official imperial policy, his successor—Leo was himself murdered in 820—Michael II wrote to Louis the Pious, Charlemagne's son and successor. He informed him about the general course of events in Byzantium, told him a little about renewed iconoclasm, and attempted to enlist his intercession with the pope concerning a troublesome iconodule refugee community in Rome.

Louis decided to assemble key theologians for a colloquy—not a council, as we shall see—to meet at Paris in 825 to take up the image question once again. This chapter begins by presenting the background to the Paris Colloquy. That background consists of a few scattered hints about continuing image discussions in the East, the recurrence of Byzantine iconoclasm and its theological dimensions, the tangled skein of Franko-Byzantine relations between Nicaea and the mid-820s, and developments in Rome. The core of the chapter offers a summation and analysis of the extensive records produced by the Paris Colloquy.

The Tangled Legacy of II Nicaea

The roads to Paris in 825 from Frankfurt and Nicaea go through Constantinople and Rome but take some detours along the way. Here we need to follow only a few lengths of the journey: The fate of iconoclasm after 787; East-West relations, both secular and ecclesiastical, in the generation after Nicaea; and the convoluted politics of the Byzantine church. Eighth-century iconoclasm began in the East and so did "Second Iconoclasm," as its heir is usually called. To understand what happened in the West, and why, we must once again begin in the East and ask not only what happened there but also what the West knew about it, and how the West learned about it.

The Official Restoration of Iconoclasm

The astonishingly rapid collapse of iconoclasm between 785, when troops broke up Irene's first attempt to hold a council, and 787, when Nicaea actually met, is one of the most remarkable and puzzling aspects of the whole history of the controversy. As we have seen, Tarasius deserves high marks for his skillful management of II Nicaea with its diplomatic treatment of both the Isaurian legacy and the iconoclasts. Given that iconoclasm was the official policy of the empire for decades, one might suppose that the tendency of the official sources, often late or doctored, to portray iconoclasm as having vanished like a wisp of smoke is a bit deceptive. Yet try as one might to find hints of persistent controversy, the evidence for iconoclast sentiment in the years after II Nicaea is unimpressive.

In 797 Constantine VI threatened Tarasius with a restoration of iconoclasm if he would not agree to the emperor's divorce.[1] It is impossible to gauge whether this threat was taken seriously. In any case, Constantine met his untimely end shortly after this démarche and the issue did not come up again. There is no reason to think that anyone in the West knew about Constantine's threat. The chronicler Theophanes intensely disliked Emperor Nicephorus and implies that he favored a certain "pseudo-hermit" named Nicholas who had an iconoclastic following at Hexakionion. Theophanes further implies that Nicephorus's support for Nicholas may have been prompted by his own quarrels with Patriarch Nicephorus.[2] Under Michael I, Nicholas was forced to make a public recantation of his views and one of his followers who had damaged an image of the Theotokos had his tongue cut out. Theophanes also reports that, on the eve of the Battle of Versinicia, itself a catastrophic defeat for the Byzantines at the hands of the Bulgarians, a band of iconoclasts circulated rumors that Constantine V was going to appear on horseback to lead the Greek forces. The troublemakers were apparently rounded up without much difficulty. The iconoclasts in question appear to have been soldiers, quite possibly veterans cashiered by Michael I.[3] Whether this incident justifies Alexander's remark that "[e]vidently, the 'soldiery' in the capital was still iconoclastic" is open to question.[4] Some scholars have detected in some of Nicephorus's writings an anxiety over iconoclast sentiment among some bishops, without being able to name names.[5] The available evidence for iconoclasm within the empire is minute and ambiguous.

From just outside the empire there is one small piece of contemporary evidence that is more intriguing than revealing. Between 795 and 812 Theodore Abū Qurrah (ca. 740/50–ca. 820/25; one-time monk of St. Saba, briefly bishop of Harrān, and a prolific author) wrote in Arabic a tract in defense of images and their veneration.[6] He was deeply indebted to John Damascene, whose works he may well have encountered when he studied at Mar Saba. Although it seems clear that Theodore was addressing Muslim, and possibly Jewish, opponents of images, it is conceivable that he had some knowledge of the current state of the image controversy in Byzantium and of II Nicaea.[7] Mar Saba had important and continuous connections with Rome and in 808 the monks of this Greek monastery accused Frankish monks on the Mount of Olives of heresy.[8] These Frankish monks wrote to Pope Leo III who forwarded their complaints to Charlemagne. Charlemagne, for his part, had occasional dealings with Patriarch

Thomas of Jerusalem, who may have known Theodore and who may have had relations with the Melkite patriarch of Antioch who deposed Theodore from his bishopric at Harrān in about 812. I would not care to press too hard any element of this story, but I do think that it points to the possibility that people in Rome and in Francia just might have had some intimation that there was a discussion of images going on in the region of Palestine.

Michael I's disastrous defeat at Versinicia in 813 was caused in no small part by the defection of troops who were loyal to Leo the Armenian. Within a few weeks Michael had abdicated and it became clear that Leo was going to succeed to him.[9] Even before he entered the city, Leo sent a letter to Patriarch Nicephorus asserting his orthodoxy and promising not to innovate in religion.[10] When Leo did enter Constantinople, Nicephorus sent a delegation of bishops to him with a statement of orthodoxy for the new emperor to sign. Leo assured the bishops that he agreed with everything in their document and that he would sign it. But he did not do so before his coronation and afterward he declined.[11] Presumably he was keeping open the option of innovating.

Later reports that all emanate from iconophile sources say that almost immediately on becoming emperor Leo began to trumpet the achievements of Leo III and Constantine V. He even renamed his son Symbatios, Constantine. He seems to have made the point that pagans were triumphing over Christians because of icons and he remarked that all iconoclast emperors were successful while all iconodules were failures.[12] It seems that, once again, iconoclasm was "born in the purple." Leo V, like Leo III before him, seems genuinely to have believed that a faith purified of images would once again bring divine favor on the Byzantines.

He moved cautiously. Until his sudden death in 814 Khan Krum was threatening the capital and commanding most of Leo's attention. Moreover, by this time iconophilia had been official policy for decades. The patriarch was a known iconophile as were the influential Studite monks arrayed behind their leader, Abbot Theodore. A later report in the *Life of Nicetas of Medikion* (written before 844/45) says that people began to talk among themselves against the holy icons.[13] Another source says that "in his second year" Leo appointed a study commission that eventually grew to six members under the leadership of the erudite John Hylilas, later called "the Grammarian."[14] The study commission undertook to search the history of the church for evidence that images were a recent innovation and offensive to authentic traditions. The commission also intended to resurrect the teachings of the Council of Hiereia.[15]

In the summer of 814 the commission, then consisting of only three members, John and two imperial bureaucrats, presented Nicephorus with a few hastily assembled passages.[16] The patriarch responded that the passages in question merely condemned pagan idols, not Christian images. Leo's response to this setback was to expand the commission by adding to it two monks and a bishop, men who were more accomplished theologians than John. Initially this commission seems to have been working with the *horos* of 754, which would have been readily available in the *acta* of II Nicaea where it was cited and refuted in detail; an original copy might have been available in the patriarchal library. The *horos* of Hiereia had embedded in it some patristic citations but by no means the full documentation collected in 754. Somehow, then, the commission appears to have gotten its hands on additional material, perhaps the full *acta* of 754, perhaps the patristic florilegium prepared in connection with Hiereia, perhaps the florilegium prepared by Constantine V. Equipped with this much fuller patristic arsenal the commission submitted a substantial report to Leo in December. Leo summoned the patriarch and asked him if he would agree to the removal of images from low and accessible places. Nicephorus refused. Leo then asked him to say where in the Scriptures one might find a requirement to venerate images. Nicephorus responded that many of the church's traditions, long held and deeply believed, were unwritten but no less authentic for that. Leo then said that he in fact had at his disposal a major collection of patristic material that clearly opposed images. This was obviously the dossier the commission had recently given to him. He demanded a serious debate on the issues. Nicephorus declined to debate but did send a deputation of iconophile clerics to present their views to the emperor. At about the same time some troops in the city threw mud and stones at an image of Christ over the Chalké gate of the imperial palace and Leo removed the image, claiming that he did so only to protect it from the mob. As Christmas approached, Nicephorus and the iconophile clergy held a vigil of prayer at Hagia Sophia. Nicephorus then had Leo's dossier read out to the group and asked if they were solidly opposed to it. They were. On Christmas morning Leo summoned the iconophile group to the palace. In a private meeting with the patriarch, Leo venerated a small image that he wore around his neck and assured the patriarch that he had no intention of deposing him. During the celebration of the day's liturgy, Leo publicly venerated an image on an altar cloth. On Epiphany, however, Leo did not venerate the same altar cloth and he began intimidating the members of the patriarch's iconophile group. The emperor won over a good many of them and began to pressure the patriarch. At the beginning of Lent in 815 Leo declared that Nicephorus had abdicated because he could not advance persuasive arguments in favor of images. The patriarch had indeed abdicated under pressure[17] and he was replaced at

Easter by Theodotus Melissenus, a nephew of Constantine V. Shortly thereafter, Leo convened a new council to consider the matter of images.

The council met at Hagia Sophia under the leadership of Patriarch Theodotus and the emperor's son, now called Constantine. The number of participants is not known. Surely the iconophobes who had materialized during 813 and 814 were present, and probably also those former iconophiles won over by the emperor in early 815. The council met in three sessions. During the first, the dossier prepared by Leo's commission in 814 was read out and affirmed. The next day some iconophile bishops were summoned and when they refused to budge on their faith in images they were beaten, spat upon, and expelled. In a third session, this time under imperial presidency, a *horos* was prepared and approved.[18] The *acta* of the Council of Hagia Sophia do not survive as a single, coherent document. However, the decree of the council as well as its accompanying patristic florilegium have been partially reconstructed by Paul Alexander from citations and refutations in works written in exile by Patriarch Nicephorus.[19] By fitting these textual fragments together it is possible to form a reasonably clear picture of what the council actually taught.

The council praised the Isaurians by name, affirmed the teachings of Hiereia, and expressed sadness that "womanly simplicity" had led people astray in the time of Tarasius. Hiereia, as we saw, had three main teachings: 1) images are essentially idols; 2) icons of Christ either circumscribe his uncircumscribable divinity or split his divine and human natures; 3) images cannot convey the resurrected glory of the saints. It will be recalled, too, that in 754 the bishops left aside the theological speculations of Constantine V to the effect that an image and its prototype had to be consubstantial and that, accordingly, only the eucharist was a true and proper image. In 815, the bishops omitted the argument that images were idols. This had been refuted recently by Nicephorus and was always a weak argument. Likewise, and despite its explicit praise for Constantine V, the council followed Hiereia in ignoring the identification of the eucharist with the true image. But the council did affirm Hiereia's other basic teachings although what was said in 815 about Christology is vague. The patristic florilegium of 815 deals at great length with the so-called "ethical theory" of images.

The bishops in 815, then, said little about the old Christological debates and reserved most of their energy for a discussion of the nature of the true image. This nature they equated with the virtue and example of the saints. This argument may be framed both negatively and positively. That is, on the negative side, no image can capture the resurrected glory of the saints or convey any impression of the virtue that had earned the saint a resting place in heaven. On the positive side, only in words—preached or read—could one find true images of saints. These were their deeds and thus a true image is a Christian copying in his or her life the actions of the saints.[20]

Leo and his clerical associates had proceeded very cautiously.[21] They had tried very hard throughout 814 and early 815 to get the patriarch to cooperate in at least some formal criticism of images. They had made an honest effort to survey the sources. They had, apparently, taken to heart the criticism expressed at Nicaea to the effect that the bishops at Hiereia had worked from mere *"pittakia"*—extracts, probably in a florilegium—rather than from full texts. Thus they used the documentation of 754 to carry out thorough research in patristic manuscripts, told Nicephorus of their findings, and then, presumably, verified their extracts in 815 from complete texts. This strategy also permitted the iconophobes to treat II Nicaea with some respect. To be sure, they wanted it set aside. And in 815 they did reject its *horos*. But their tactic involved meeting Nicaea's objections to Hiereia's scholarship with impeccable scholarship of their own on the very matter of patristic tradition. It is as if they were saying that the fathers gathered at Nicaea erred, understandably, because they had never seen the iconophobe case made fully and on its own terms. It is interesting too that whereas Hiereia had labeled iconophiles as either Monophysites or Nestorians, Hagia Sophia avoided these tags, all the while maintaining the same theological position. Invective and name-calling were eschewed. The old argument about idolatry, the one ubiquitous position in iconophobe writing from the fourth century, and surely the primary objection of emperors Leo III and Leo V, was omitted. The council made no explicit statement about the need to destroy images and did not address Leo's suggestion of the previous year that low-hanging images be elevated. The council's positions were few and carefully articulated.

The Iconophile Reaction

This same cautious attitude attended the emperor's actions in the time just after the council.[22] Nicephorus had initially been banished to a monastery he had founded but he was then moved farther away from the capital. Only the most recalcitrant foes of the emperor's policy were exiled, among them the obstreperous Theodore of Studion, who was sent to Metopa in the Opsikion theme. Basically Leo asked bishops and abbots to accept communion with Theodotus, who for his part made statements implying that he was really partial to images; statements in which he was, surprisingly, joined by John the Grammarian. No one was asked to make a public show of desecrating an image. Although imperial efforts focused on Constantinople, there is evidence that pressure was brought to bear everyplace the emperor had any serious authority. After his military successes against the Bulgarians and Muslims in 816, Leo began to move more vigorously against those who opposed him. Theodore, for example, whose correspondence reveals that he was running an extensive opposition network, was moved farther from the capital, to Boneta in the Anatolic theme. Nicephorus, who was also writing extensively, was placed under closer arrest. Some bishops lost their sees. Probably from about this time dates a letter of Theodore's which says that images were being destroyed everywhere.[23] After making allowances for Theodore's usual hysterics and the almost total absence of corroborating evidence, it is probably safest to assume that there was comparatively little actual iconoclasm and that most of those who suffered exile or who were expelled from their offices were punished for flaunting their political opposition to the emperor. The fact is that large numbers of people went along with the emperor. This had also happened in the eighth century.[24] Religious art had once again become a vernacular of Byzantine politics. It was costly to be less than fluent at any given moment.

Where the eighth-century phase of the image controversy is concerned, we noticed a certain paradox. The iconophobes, who were represented by their foes as innovators even though they had solid claims to tradition, were in fact more sophisticated and resourceful in their opposition to images than their iconophile foes, who represented themselves as the keepers of tradition, despite the relative novelty of some of what they believed, were in defending images. In the ninth-century phase this paradox is retained but its polarity is reversed. Each side claimed exclusive possession of the tradition of the church and denied possession to their opponents. That is not new. What is new is that the iconophobes were very modest in advancing their views while the iconophiles soared on flights of philosophical and theological speculation that exceeded even those of John of Damascus who was, in any case, marginalized by the fathers of Nicaea. This point deserves a bit of emphasis for the retrospective light it sheds on the discussion in Chapter 2 of the often ahistorical tendency among some Orthodox theologians and historians to grant a uniquely privileged status to the iconophile view within the history of Christianity and also to assume that all aspects of that view arose simultaneously and early. Another problem with that unhistorical view, as we saw in Chapter 4, is that it erects obstacles to understanding what the eighth-century Franks knew, understood, and responded to. It was actually in their reactions to Second Iconoclasm that Nicephorus and Theodore of Studion set down the terms of what has become the standard Orthodox teaching about icons.

To varying degrees Nicephorus and Theodore responded to both 754 and

815. But their voluminous writings are by no means purely reactionary. They also formulated positive doctrines. Together they achieved, in Alexander's words, "the philosophical climax of the entire controversy."[25] We need here to offer no more than a brief summation of the principal themes and interests in the ninth-century writings of these two Greek writers. Not a line from one of their texts circulated in the West. No florilegium from which they drew evidence was seen or assessed by anyone in the West. The following summary serves mainly as a background reminder of paths not taken by Western thinkers. But the tremendous development of Eastern thought about images is also an interesting counterpart to the relatively more static Western view.

While they were in exile Nicephorus and Theodore produced a vast corpus of literature on the subject of images. Primarily they addressed themselves to what had been said in 754 but they also spoke about the council of 815. Nevertheless, their writings were not merely refutations of what had been said by iconophobes. They also formulated new doctrines and developed new approaches to the whole subject. Together they represent the high point of Byzantine theological reflection on the question of sacred images.[26]

They agreed on many things. For instance, both started from the fundamental Christian mystery of the incarnation. Like so many before them, they believed that the incarnation of God as a man justified images. But they went further than anyone else had gone in saying that the incarnation actually made images *necessary*. That is, because Christ appeared as a man, he had to be depicted. Otherwise, the truth of the incarnation was called into question. A purely spiritual image of Christ is not enough. For Nicephorus, moreover, "It is not Christ but the entire universe that disappears if there is no longer either circumscription or an icon."[27] Both said that if there were no images, then the incarnation might as well have never taken place. It was a bold move to go from saying that the incarnation authorized images to saying that it required them.

They agreed, too, that sight was, compared to sound (which means hearing, in the sense of hearing a text read out), the nobler sense. Likewise they agreed that because of the incarnation Christians had no warrant to devalue or suspect matter. God having become flesh, matter had been elevated in status. Not all matter in all circumstances, obviously, but never again would it be enough to dismiss vile matter or to condemn icons because they consist of dead matter, because they are "soulless." Finally, they shared the view that images somehow conveyed the contemporary reality of the person whom they depicted. They were not merely historical. That is, they show things as they are, not as they were. Icons were, on this view, sharply differentiated from *historiai*.

Although they shared ideas, Theodore and Nicephorus also made individual contributions to the newly emerging theory of images. Theodore used Aristotelian philosophy to work out the relationship between image and prototype, to define the nature of the true image. For Theodore, the image and its archetype differ in material, in nature. But they share a name. In other words, Theodore uses the Aristotelian category of relation to show how image and prototype are connected. He makes relation in a sense the axis that joins the two. He used the analogy of a body and its shadow. No shadow can exist without its body and no body exists that does not cast a shadow. If one sees a shadow, this points inevitably to a body. So, then, an image of Christ points to Christ. Furthermore, since an image has reality only in its prototype, there can be only one kind of veneration accorded to an image, the same veneration that is accorded to the prototype. Finally, whereas the iconoclasts had developed the idea that Christ assumed humanity generally, Theodore responded that Christ had in fact assumed a unique and individual humanity. Furthermore, that humanity was one nature that was joined to a divine nature in a single hypostasis. Thus any image did in fact reveal the hypostasis that exists as Jesus Christ. There could, in other words, be no question of separating or confusing the natures of Christ because these did not exist apart from their presence together in a single hypostasis. From this it follows that an image does not reveal the historical human body of Jesus but the living reality of the hypostasis, Jesus Christ. The image was not Christ, and was not suffused with his *energeia* (John of Damascus had come dangerously close to suggesting this), but shared with him a name and a categorical relationship. Theodore played a high philosophical trump to take an old trick from his foes.

Among Nicephorus's contributions, perhaps the most distinctive is his attempt to settle the matter of circumscriptability. The iconoclasts had always asserted that God could not be circumscribed and that an image either circumscribed God, which was impossible, or circumscribed his humanity, which was tantamount to dividing his natures. As noted, Theodore also spoke to this problem by connecting the doctrine of the hypostatic union to the problem of image and prototype by means of the category of relation. Nicephorus took a somewhat different approach. Also by using Aristotelian philosophy, he argued in the first place that there is a difference between being depicted and being circumscribed. Circumscription, he said, exists in place, time, and apprehension. God chose to circumscribe himself in each of these ways. No painter, that is, did or can circumscribe him. A painter can depict him because he appeared as a true, individual man. But the painter cannot fix God in place, time, or apprehension. Indeed, no painter can ever circumscribe anyone in this way: the subject of a painting is not present *in* the painting and need not have been present *when* the painting was made. Nicephorus used a series of examples of things that could be circumscribed but not depicted: the year, the Law of Moses, idolatry, human life, diseases, breezes, speech. On the contrary, then, many things can be depicted but not circumscribed. This line of reasoning simply destroyed the iconoclast contention that any painted image could possibly circumscribe anything. Iconoclasts had of course argued that an image could only properly circumscribe Christ if Christ and his image were identical. But they were not identical. Thus Nicephorus guarded his flank against an attack of that sort.

In sum, images are necessary, and they are superior to words, to which iconophobes had always accorded precedence. They stand in a particular kind of relationship to what they depict and they do not circumscribe their subjects. These lines of argument advanced by long leaps beyond anything that iconophiles had said in the eighth century and kicked the intellectual props out from under the teachings of the iconophobes. They became Orthodox. But they did not come to the West. And so we leave them.

A Papal Interlude

What did come to the West, then, and when and how did it come? The Carolingian and Byzantine courts undertook a long series of diplomatic encounters beginning shortly after Charlemagne was crowned emperor in 800 and running right down to Michael II's letter to Louis the Pious in 824.[28] This string of negotiations had two primary purposes.[29] One the one hand, there were both discussions and military clashes pertaining to the northern Adriatic region: Istria, Dalmatia, and especially Venice. On this front, the Carolingians finally acknowledged Byzantine rights in Venice, while Istria and Dalmatia remained contested territories well into the ninth century. On the other hand, the Carolingians obtained Byzantine recognition of their imperial office. Emperor Nicephorus appears to have been on his way to conceding that recognition when he died and it was his successor Michael I with whom the pact was concluded. But whereas Michael began his negotiations with Charlemagne, a final agreement was concluded between Leo V and Louis the Pious after Michael was deposed in 813 and Charlemagne died in early 814. In 817 Louis received envoys from Michael at Aachen who wished to talk about Dalmatia. In 821 a Byzantine legation brought news that Leo V had been murdered and that Michael II had succeeded him. There is reason to believe that the two courts were reasonably familiar with each other but, be that as it may, there is not a single hint of the renewed outbreak of iconoclasm in the Frankish annals that report on all this diplomacy. Only under 824 do the *Royal Frankish Annals* remark that "among other things, finally, pertaining to their mission, they brought forth something concerning the veneration of images, on account of which they said they were going to go to Rome to consult the bishop of the apostolic see." Louis heard out the emissaries and dismissed them to go to Rome. Surely this is the legation that brought the letter of Michael II to Louis to which we shall turn shortly. The key point is that the Frankish court either knew little about the new image quarrel at Byzantium or, regardless of what it knew, chose to conduct business as usual with the Greeks. This situation is reminiscent of the 750s and 760s when Constantine V and Pippin III negotiated productively, all the while making Pope Paul I very nervous.

Whether the popes knew more than the Franks did about second iconoclasm, or simply responded more vigorously is hard to say. The nature and timing of the papal responses must, however, be placed firmly into context. Hadrian I had gotten no more than a grudging acknowledgment of his doctrinal authority at the time of II Nicaea and that council declined to address his complaints about his lost church provinces, patrimonies, and revenues. When Leo III crowned Charlemagne the Byzantines regarded him as a schismatic. When Patriarch Tarasius died in 806 and was replaced by Nicephorus, Emperor Nicephorus prohibited the new patriarch from sending his systatic letter to Rome. It was not sent until 811, after the more conciliatory Michael I came to the throne.[30] When Nicephorus did finally write, he explained why he had not written sooner but was not particularly apologetic. Moreover, he addressed Leo as his "brother," talked of their collegial responsibility for the church, stressed that they both served the church under the primacy of Jesus, and repeatedly stressed the work and teaching of St. Paul. In each case, Nicephorus used finely calculated affronts to papal authority and its Petrine bases.

But Leo III had been hearing other things too from the Byzantine East. After Nicaea the stiff-necked Studite monks refused to reconcile themselves to the regime of Tarasius, and then to that of Nicephorus. They were angry about laymen being elevated to the episcopal, indeed to the patriarchal, dignity. They were upset with the lenient way Tarasius treated the former iconoclasts at Nicaea and also at the patriarch's moderate attitude toward various members of the clergy who had been accused of simony. But their real rage was reserved for Tarasius's conduct in the so-called "Moechian" (adultery) affair. Constantine VI had repudiated his wife and wished to divorce her and marry a court attendant. He found a priest, Joseph of Kithara, to bless his new marriage and the patriarch went along with this. Under Emperor Nicephorus, Joseph was exiled but then he performed valuable service to the emperor and was rehabilitated.[31]

This prompted Theodore of Studion to write to Leo III.[32] He did so in terms that were astonishingly deferential to the authority of the Roman see. Theodore may have been sincere to a degree in his lofty attitudes about the papal office, but it should not be forgotten that he and his fellow Studite monks had been for some twenty years bitterly opposed to the reigning patriarchs and that they were, at that very moment, especially incensed because Nicephorus had agreed to Joseph's reinstatement. Theodore really had no where to turn but Rome. Still, he praised the petrine origins of the papal office, spoke of the popes as the leaders of the universal church, called the pope the unique guardian of the faith, and asked for the pope to call a council to hear the Moechian case. Neither Leo nor Hadrian before him had in recent years heard such welcome words from any quarter.[33]

By the time Paschal I ascended the papal throne in January of 817, the Council of Hagia Sophia had already met and both Theodore and Nicephorus had been exiled. Their common opposition to iconoclasm had united the two old foes.[34] Still, Nicephorus does not appear to have dispatched a single word to the West concerning Second Iconoclasm. Theodore did write to the pope, however.[35] Theodore's surviving letters make clear the gravity of the situation, and they repeat and even enhance his earlier comments on the authority of the papacy. He seems to have been well pleased and to have learned that Paschal had taken some steps to deal with the new outbreak of iconoclasm.[36] Unfortunately, his letters do not speak in detail about the theology of Second Iconoclasm so the letters are not themselves good sources for whatever it was that Paschal learned about the case.

The *Life* of the future patriarch, Methodius, provides a few valuable details. Methodius was a Sicilian and, the *Life* says, when iconoclasm broke out and Nicephorus was exiled, he went to Rome.[37] It seems reasonable to suppose that Methodius was a key informant for Paschal. Moreover, he himself entered a Greek monastery in Rome and those monasteries had important contacts with the Greek East. Theodore himself corresponded with Basil, the higoumen of St.-Saba in Rome.[38] As we will see in a moment, there survives one letter of Paschal to Leo V. It is possible that Methodius—and his circle?—inspired that letter. It may be that the dispatch of Paschal's letter to Leo is what pleased Theodore about Paschal. The *Life of Methodius* goes on to say that after Michael II came to the throne, Paschal entrusted Methodius with "books of doctrine" or perhaps "doctrinal teachings" (τόμους δογματικοὺς) to be taken to the emperor in Constantinople.[39] No trace of these "tomes" survives. Against the Byzantine evidence, the one surviving letter of Paschal, and the reference to Paschal's tomes, there is, oddly, not another scrap of written papal evidence for Second Iconoclasm. Unlike his eighth-century counterparts, the author of Paschal's life in the *Liber Pontificalis* is silent about the image controversy even while detailing Paschal's rich endowment of Roman churches with works of art and this pope's close relations with Greek monastic communities in Rome. Similarly, there is not a single papal letter to Francia that so much as mentions the image problem. Perhaps that is not surprising given the cool reception that Hadrian's efforts had received a generation before. But the silence of the *Liber Pontificalis* is puzzling.

Paschal's letter to Leo V survives in a fragmentary state. Cardinal Pitra edited it from a poor and no longer extant Roman manuscript[40] and then Cardinal Mercati produced a new edition from a better Ambrosiana manuscript.[41] The letter seems little known to students of Second Iconoclasm, especially to Western historians.[42] The letter can only be dated between January 25, 817, when Paschal became pope, and December 25, 820, when Leo was murdered. Paschal's letter lacks formal opening and closing matter and one or two rather abrupt shifts in its body suggest that substantive material has fallen out. In short, while it is easy enough to summarize what Paschal said, it is difficult to feel confident that we have all that he said, or that we have what he said in precisely its original order and context.

Paschal's letter not only reveals something about the pope's own thinking on the subject of images but also provides hints about aspects of current thinking in iconophobe circles beyond what can be deduced from the *acta* of the Council of Hagia Sophia. With respect to the latter, Paschal denied that images are idols.[43] As we have seen, this argument, although prominent in 754 and raised in 814, was dropped at Hagia Sophia. Still the fact that both Paschal and Nicephorus felt compelled to rebut it suggests that it had some currency. The letter also counters an apparent citation of the Exodus prohibition against the making of images.[44] This was of course a prominent feature of the earliest stages of the image controversy in the eighth century but had been little heard since then, albeit Leo V and Nicephorus had debated this very issue.[45] Paschal replied in two ways. First, he says, this prohibition was given to those who lived under the law and is no longer applicable to those who live under the new covenant of grace in Jesus Christ. Why, he wonders, would anyone want to place himself under the law. Indeed, anyone who does so cannot call himself a Christian. Christ himself, Paschal argues by means a series of New Testament passages, said that the law had been superceded.[46] Second, Paschal adverts to the cherubim of the Ark of the Covenant. God himself had commanded images to be made.[47]

Most of Paschal's letter as we know it contains arguments of his own that appear to be prompted by his understanding of the central issues as they then stood. He develops the argument from incarnation. The opening line of the letter as it survives says, "They say that no one has ever seen God." This is an old move in the iconophobe game plan. Paschal responds by saying that perhaps there is no image of the invisible God and then he imagines someone's saying that there can be no image of the risen Christ. But, he replies, we make images of the incarnate Christ and depict him, for instance, eating with his disciples.[48] Right away this prompts two observations. First, Paschal seems to have been sensitive to the idea that one cannot admit the possibility that Christ had assumed some sort of generic humanity in his incarnation. This may well have been an issue brought to his attention by his informants. Second, in saying that Christ is depicted in real-life situations Paschal gives one reason to wonder if he has in mind the frontal, static, often isolated images that were common in Byzantine Christ-icons (but would he have known of such icons?) or else the more concrete, historical images such as the very ones that he put into, say, Santa Prassede in Rome. Theodore had argued the same way, of course, so one must be careful not to press too hard any ideas about what kinds of images these writers may have had in mind.

But Paschal went on with the incarnational argument. He says that there can be no possibility of confusing the two natures in Christ unless one does not paint the human Christ who suffered. Whether painted or unpainted, Christ's natures are inseparable and indivisible. And each shares the name "Christ," just as Christ and his image share that name.[49] This is as close as Paschal gets to Theodore's Aristotelian relational argument. One wonders if he got as much of it as he had from letters of Theodore that are no longer extant, or from Greek milieux in Rome, or from Methodius.

Paschal also raised an interesting argument from typology.[50] He spoke at some length of the way the prophets interpreted the glory of the Lord for the benefit of others. Then, he says, the prophets foretold, by means of type figures, the coming of Christ. Why, therefore, will enemies of images not permit an image of the one whom the prophets foretold and who is himself the image of his father? At this point, Paschal, makes an interesting shift. He asks how the enemies of images imagine us to live in this world: in an image or in truth?[51] Here he takes the old iconophobe argument about worship's being in spirit and in truth, divides it, and invests it with a new interpretation. He says, if we live in an image, then we must see that images lead us to truth, for we are images of God. We subsist as images. We may not understand this fully now, as Paul said (quoting "For now we see as through a glass darkly . . ."), but eventually we will. But perhaps you live in "truth." In that case you have no hope of resurrection and if our hope is in this world alone then, as the apostle says, we are the most wretched of men. "Don't you believe that we will rise again, incorrupt?" "Don't you see that when we are said to be filled with virtue, then we are the image of the creator?" "Is not the soul the most distinguished part of the mind, as the eye of the body?"[52] What Paschal has done is argue that the human soul is the aspect of our being that is most fully alive and that it is the image of God. So he concludes that iconophobes draw no distinction between humans and beasts of burden.

Finally Paschal defends images by equating them with sacramental signs.[53] What need would there be of baptism, he asks, if the Father and the Holy Spirit came without signs? If baptism were for you without any work, purely a matter of will, there would be no need of water. To whom would it be of benefit to portray the cross if the faith did not permit signs? The cross is for you just a word, not a sign.

To sum up, Paschal seems to have understood quite clearly what was said at Constantinople in 815. He spoke eloquently and at some length about the incarnational defense of images and in speaking about the virtuous soul as the image of God he indicates some familiarity with the "ethical theory." He also seems to have understood some of the historical background to the whole image controversy. Thus he rejected the equation of images and idols and explained how the Exodus prohibition did not, in fact, prohibit Christian art. In his handling of the old issue of worship in spirit and in truth Paschal made a modest but interesting contribution of his own to the whole debate.

Paschal's letter can be placed into wider contexts. In one or two places, Paschal verges toward the Aristotelianism of Theodore but he never goes far enough to suggest that he was either fully informed about or even sympathetic to the Studite's approach. Compared to Hadrian's extant writings on images, it would appear that Paschal's are more profound. But whereas Hadrian was current with all eighth-century arguments, Paschal knew more than Hadrian did but had fallen behind the most recent thinking in the East. There is no evidence that Paschal's views made any impression on Leo V. Paschal had intense relations with the Carolingians but he did not write to them about images—at any rate no such letter survives.

One further context for Paschal's letter requires somewhat more discussion. Paschal was one of the great patrons of art in early medieval Rome. In erecting a new church at Santa Prassede, Paschal created the first Constantinian-style basilica built in Rome since antiquity and he filled it with Roman relics brought into the city from surrounding regions.[54] The Carolingians, as we have seen, copied Roman forms, built *more Romano*, at St.-Denis and Fulda. And the Carolingians had shown a marked interest in things Christian-Roman, including in Paschal's own time, relics. From one point of view, Paschal may be seen combatting the Carolingians by reclaiming for the papacy the Roman-Christian heritage which the Carolingians had been appropriating. From another point of view, Paschal seems to have behaved like Gregory II and Gregory III in installing sumptuous, public images just as the Byzantines were again campaigning against them. In Chapter 3 we spoke about the papal adoption of the Maria Regina image. It is hardly coincidental, therefore, that Pashcal put a spectacular Maria Regina image in the apse of Santa Maria in Domnica. In this mosaic, Paschal kneels at Mary's feet and looks toward the viewer. His pose is exactly like that of John VII in the Madonna della Clemenza image from Santa Maria in Trastevere.[55] The viewers, that is the Roman community, see the pope as their intercessor with Mary. No emperor, Eastern or Western, intrudes on the scene. Paschal could write letters but he could send comparable messages in other media at roughly the same time.

The Letter of Michael II to Louis the Pious

Soon, however, Paschal would receive a communication from the Frankish court requesting permission to hold a new investigation of the image controversy. That communication was occasioned by Michael II's letter to Louis the Pious.[56] That full and ostensibly frank letter provides the only secure evidence for what the Franks knew about second iconoclasm. It is tempting to suppose that, amid so much diplomacy, the Franks would have garnered a good deal of information in the years just after 815. But there is simply no evidence that authorizes us to act on those temptations.

In a letter that fills 184 lines in the standard (quarto) edition, the topic of images only begins on line 127. Michael begins by telling Louis about the tribulations suffered by the empire since the death of Leo V. In particular, the people had been badly divided because of the dangerous rebellion of Thomas the Slavonian. Michael says that he thinks he should share all of this information with his "peaceful friend and spiritual brother" and he desires a renewal of the peace between them. In the recent past, the peace treaty between Byzantium and the Carolingians had been reaffirmed on each change of throne in both realms. The *Royal Frankish Annals* do say that Louis was somehow informed about the change of rulers in 820 but it seems that Michael's letter constituted the first official contact between the two emperors.[57] The structure of Michael's letter is intriguing. Perhaps he did not regard images as the key item on his agenda. Perhaps he knew that his court and the Frankish court were somewhat closer to agreeing with each other on this topic than either court was to agreement with the pope and the Byzantine clergy. Perhaps he simply wanted to give the impression that the image controversy was a minor detail. Whatever the case may be, did not put images front and center.

But he did come to them eventually.[58] He says he wants Louis to know that some people, both laymen and clerics, have departed from apostolic traditions and have become inventors of evil. He says they cast out crosses from churches and set up images in their place. They place lamps near these images and burn incense before them, giving to those images the same reverence that is customarily paid to the cross. They also sing psalms before these images and ask them for help. Some people wrap these images in linen cloths and make them sponsors of their children in baptism. When young boys receive their first haircuts, or when monks are tonsured, they let their hair fall on these images. Some members of the clergy scrape paint off images and mix the scrapings with the wine of the eucharist and distribute it to the people. Some priests place the consecrated eucharistic bread on an image and invite people to take it from the image. Some use painted panels for altars and celebrate mass not in consecrated churches but in private homes.

Because of these "illicit" practices that are "contrary to our religion," the "orthodox emperors and most learned priests" decided to hold a "local council" to prohibit such things from being done. They caused images to be removed from low places but allowed those placed higher up to remain in place "so that they might serve as scripture but not be worshiped by the unlettered and weak." They also forbade the use of lamps and incense. Michael assured Louis that this was his view and that he had expelled from the church only those who indulged in such wicked practices.

Before I move on to the rest of Michael's letter, one or two points already mentioned call for some comment. Michael did not refer to the Council of Hagia Sophia and instead cited a "local council" which almost certainly took place in 821.[59] One suspects that he was deliberately trying to avoid antagonizing the Franks. Surely the Byzantine court knew how angry the Franks had been when first Hiereia and then Nicaea had been called ecumenical and universal. Michael does not offer Louis a single word of theology on images. He focused exclusively on practices, and indeed on practices that he and his predecessors might well have known to be completely absent in the Frankish world. Finally, Michael said not a word about any kind of iconoclasm. He merely said that low-placed images were raised. He even said that images placed higher were permitted to remain so that they might be instructive. Perhaps the Byzantines knew the Frankish position that, on the one hand, images are permissible for decoration and commemoration and that, on the other hand, it was a grievous offense to worship or to destroy images. As we have seen, Theodulf did not explicitly endorse the idea that images can teach but he did cite the letters where Gregory I had said this. Perhaps, therefore, Michael felt himself to be on safe ground in making the point that elevated images could be permitted for teaching purposes but not for worship. It would be a mistake to suppose that Michael cynically calculated his words to avoid offending the Franks. But it would be wise to suppose that Michael had sufficient knowledge of Frankish views to make his case in the most attractive terms possible.

Michael then went on to say that some people who reject "local councils" have fled from his empire and that many have settled in "Old Rome" where they bear injury and calumny against the church.[60] Michael stresses the wicked words and blasphemies to which the empire and the true church have been subjected because "we" sincerely hold to the symbol of the six holy and universal synods that are accepted by all orthodox Christians. He then appends a brief profession of faith and goes on by saying that he supports belief in the saints and that he venerates their relics. Indeed, he says, he keeps to everything that is taught in the fathers and six councils. Michael concludes by saying that he has written to the pope and that his embassy plans to go on to Rome and hopes to have Louis's intercession with the pope there. What Michael particularly wants is for the pope to expel seducers, pseudo-Christians, and calumniators from Rome. To gain the pope's good will and St. Peter's intercession, Michael has sent beautiful and costly gifts, a Gospel book with gold and gems, and a golden and gemmed paten and chalice.

Once again Michael's words prompt a few reflections. Byzantium had been trying, in the face of foreign threats and domestic rebellions, to attain peace and security for more than a decade. The renewal of iconoclasm was not seen by its promoters as a divisive measure but instead as one that would actually bring together various groups in the empire. Its doctrine was spelled out sparingly and its victims were few and mainly political. All Leo V had asked for was that opponents of his view accept the communion of the new patriarch Theodotus and, basically, keep quiet. Those who refused were exiled but Michael II, on his accession, recalled most of the exiles, including the Studites but not the former patriarch Nicephorus. The problem that he asked Louis for help with was a noisy and treasonous exile community in Rome, a community already revealed to us by the *Life* of Methodius and by Theodore's correspondence. It will be noted that Michael did not ask Louis to endorse his image policy. He simply put the matter before Louis so as to gain favor on the grounds that he was not a maniacal iconoclast. Did Michael suppose that Louis could impose on the pope the way he could impose on a patriarch? It is hard to say. The Byzantine court will surely have known of the close relations between the papacy and the Carolingians so asking for Louis's help was Michael's only available strategy. Michael did not dissemble in the profession of faith in his letter: It does not contain the word *filioque*. Franks and Byzantines had publicly disagreed on that point since the 790s and possibly since 767. In saying that he held to the *six* councils, Michael may well have been making a point that would have found favor at Aachen. The Carolingians had rejected the ecumenicity, the universality, of Hiereia and II Nicaea. But it is striking that Michael did not say a word about Hiereia, a council that had been expressly affirmed by the council of 815. Perhaps discretion was the rule here. My point is that Michael's letter leaves almost as much unsaid as it says. It is diplomatic in all senses of that word. And it did not evoke a howl of protest from the Franks.

To see what impact the letter did have, we must turn to the meeting that Louis the Pious summoned to deal with images. In returning to the Frankish world, we conclude our detour and rejoin the main road. Along the detour we observed how the issue of religious art returned to public discussion in Byzantium, what were the chief characteristics of the renewed Byzantine discussion, and how the issue came once again to the attention of the Franks.

The Paris Colloquy of 825

The collection of documents occupying some seventy-six quarto pages in Werminghoff's edition in the council series of the MGH survives in two different manuscripts which contain the same materials in the same order.[61] The edition presents five items: The letter of Michael II and his son Theophilus to Louis the Pious which was dated in April of 824 and reached Louis in November of that year (pp. 475–80); the *Libellus Synodalis* (hereafter referred to as the *Libellus*), which contains the heart of the Frankish scholarship and reflection on images (pp. 480–532); a letter of Louis to his envoys to Rome on how to comport themselves in the pope's presence (pp. 532–33); a letter of Louis and his son Lothar to Pope Eugenius II (pp. 533–35); an *Epitome* of the *Libellus* which was to be presented to and perhaps read out in the presence of the pope (pp. 535–51).[62] On closer inspection, however, a careful reader detects two additional items embedded in the latter sections of the *Libellus*. One of these is a detailed sketch of a letter which the Paris bishops proposed to Louis for transmission to the pope (pp. 520–23). The other is another very detailed version of a letter which the Paris bishops hoped the pope would send to Constantinople (pp.

523–32). Within this letter, moreover, is a brief section that the pope was to present to the Byzantines as though it had come to the pope from the Franks (pp. 525–26). Taken as a group, these documents bear similarities with the materials relevant to each of the three doctrinal controversies that we have already encountered: images, adoptionism, and *filioque*. The fortunate survival of this apparently complete dossier not only facilitates an understanding of what happened in 825 but also sheds retrospective light on what happened in the 790s and in 809–10.

The Colloquy and Its Work

Early in the *Libellus*, the writers reminded Louis that Bishop Freculf of Lisieux and an otherwise obscure Adegar, merely identified as Freculf's "associate," went to Rome to discuss with the pope the issues raised in Michael's letter. A bit later they reminded Louis that he had sought the pope's permission to explore the problem of images with his own people since "you [Louis] had the will to seek advice but lacked the authority to conduct an investigation."[63] In his letter to his envoys to Rome Louis urged them to present this investigation as done in obedience to the pope's own commission to the Franks.[64] In his own letter to Eugenius Louis says that the pope had given him permission to have his experts look into the image question and that they had done so not to challenge the pope's authority but to be helpful.[65] Finally, in the *Epitome*, Louis stresses how much he wishes to be obedient and helpful.[66]

Sometime, therefore, between November of 824 and the autumn of 825 Louis sent two legates to Rome to ask permission to hold an inquiry into the image question—to explore the evidence, as the dossier repeatedly stresses. Lacking papal sources and without any corroborating narrative records from Francia, we cannot pin down the chronology. Louis's conduct was deplored by an earlier generation of historians who regarded him as weaker, less decisive, than his father. As great an historian as Albert Hauck spoke of Louis "trembling" before the pope.[67] In fact, Louis's conduct is almost identical to that of his father. To be sure, Charles and the papacy disagreed on two doctrinal issues (images and *filioque*) but Charles always desired to cooperate with the pope and, in the end, agreed to disagree without attempting in any way to impose his will on Rome. Moreover, as we saw, the unique Petrine chapter in the *Opus* was added at court to Theodulf's original composition as a gesture of filial obedience. In 825 Louis knew perfectly well that Francia and Rome had different traditions on images.

Louis formulated several different strategies to try to move the pope to the Frankish position. But he no more trembled than his father dictated.

It is not clear why Louis asked his theological advisers to assemble in Paris instead of, say, in Aachen, and it is not clear just what kind of a meeting they attended. Under Charles, Theodulf had worked "at court," probably at Regensburg and later, possibly, at Frankfurt. Those who wrote against adoptionism worked in a variety of places. The theologians whom Charles asked to address the *filioque* controversy wrote in several places but then sent their materials to Aachen where a colloquy was held. So there was some precedent for having important theological matters aired in an official way in various locations. When it is noticed that the sources are lean and ambiguous when they name the meeting that took place in Paris, we may be on the way to understanding one important aspect of this meeting. That is, and despite the title used in the MGH edition and in virtually all the modern scholarship, the texts never once say "council." We read of a *conventum*,[68] and we read that the theologians "came together as one."[69] We also read, in words in the *Libellus* theoretically addressed to the pope, that "we did not ask you in any way for permission to call together a synod but merely sought permission to act," and we have worked "not by calling a synod."[70] In other words, one has here a meeting of the sort that took place regularly in Charles's presence from 792 to 794 and again in 809 and 810. Holding a proper synod or council would have been provocative, would have awakened issues of hierarchy and precedence, and might have called down a papal rebuke.[71] But merely holding a meeting, and indeed one for which the pope had granted his permission, was a way to sail smoothly over troubled waters.

It is not easy to determine who attended the Paris Colloquy. The various documents that we have been discussing provide several names but generally do so in the context of saying who carried which documents to whom. The *Libellus* says that Freculf and Adegar went to Rome to consult with the pope and then adds that Freculf informed those assembled in Paris "*vive voce*" about his experiences there.[72] Form this we may conclude that Freculf was present, but was he summoned to provide details on his meeting with Eugenius or to contribute to the discussions? The *Libellus* also says that Bishop Modoin of Autun was to have been present but was prevented by sickness from actually attending. Bishops Halitgar of Cambrai and Amalar of Metz were deputed by the colloquy to carry its findings to Louis. Presumably they took an active role.[73] Louis wrote to Bishops Jeremias of Sens and Jonas of Orléans to give them advice on how to present the Frankish case to the pope.[74] This constitutes strong presumptive evidence for their presence in Paris. The list of likely participants, then, is a short one: Amalar, Freculf, Halitgar, Jeremias, Jonas. And, for whatever it is worth, we can add that Modoin was meant to have been involved. Apparently Bishop Claudius of Turin, to whom I shall turn below, was summoned to answer for his iconoclastic campaign in northern Italy. That is, I think it unlikely that Claudius had been invited to present his views. Be that as it may, Claudius refused to attend the "gathering of asses."[75] The small number of known participants is a further argument against the Paris meeting's having been a true council. This modest number is, however, reminiscent of the earlier image controversy when only Theodulf and Alcuin can confidently be named as key players, with Angilbert as a possible third participant. Similar too is the set of five who contributed opinions in the dispute over the procession of the Holy Spirit: Adalwin, Arn, Heito, Smaragdus, and Theodulf. Once again, one detects a notable consistency in the way theological problems were handled by the Franks.

We do not know when Louis summoned his theological experts. They began their meeting in Paris on November 1 and sent the *Libellus* to Louis on December 6.[76] The author of the *Libellus* says that "some of us" had to travel a long way.[77] Perhaps Paris was chosen as a meeting point because it was central to those who were coming from Lisieux, Cambrai, Metz, Sens, (Autun), Orléans. But none of these bishops had to make a long or, in late October, particularly arduous journey. Were others involved whose names we do not know, for example bishops from east of the Rhine? The writer also adds that they had been given too little time to make thorough investigations. He goes on to say that some did not even know until they got to Paris why they had been summoned.[78] This suggests to me that the dearth of time applies to the interval between the summons to and the convening of the colloquy and not to the five weeks or so during which they bishops actually worked in Paris. But why were things so rushed? And would Louis really have failed to disclose why he had summoned them in the first place? It is conceivable that he wanted to get his envoys to Italy before the depths of winter made an Alpine crossing all but impossible. The *Royal Annals* say simply that Louis spent the fall hunting and then went to Aachen for the winter.[79] In other words, they do not provide a single clue.

In any case, when the *Libellus* reached Louis he wrote—the letters bear no dates—to Jeremias and Jonas and entrusted to them a letter for Pope Eugenius. In his letter to Jeremias and Jonas, Louis says that Halitgar and Amalar brought him the "excerpts from the books of the holy fathers" that had been collected in Paris and that he had had them read out in his presence. The *Libellus* is a long treatise. Its reading must have taken some time. Then, Louis says, "in all haste" he is informing Jeremias and Jonas of his pleasure with their work and he suggests that they tell the pope only a portion of what has been collected and that they stick to what is most apt and persuasive. Louis encourages them to be "patient and courteous" in their coming "disputation" with the pope.[80]

Louis's words call for two comments. First, it is not surprising that he would speak of a "disputation" with the pope for that is exactly what happened in 810 when Adalhard was sent to Rome to "argue" with Leo III over the procession of the Holy Spirit. The actual text of that argument is extant.[81] Moreover, since his rehabilitation in 821, Adalhard had become one of Louis's principal advisers.[82] It seems possible to hypothesize that we are watching him at work in these proceedings. Second, the "some part of all this" to which Louis refers may well be the *Epitome*. This is a substantial text, but at sixteen pages it is much more manageable than the lengthy *Libellus*—less than one-fourth as long—and it is just twice as long as the *Ratio* that was read out "*per ordinem*" in the presence of Pope Leo III in 810. I think the *Epitome* was intended for oral presentation in Rome.

Louis concludes his letter to Jeremias and Jonas by insisting that Frankish members be included in any papal legation to Byzantium. Louis himself wrote to Eugenius in a spirit of amity and cooperation. He let the pope know that he had acted only out of a desire to be helpful and that he hopes the materials he is sending with Jeremias and Jonas will shed clear light on the old, thorny problem of images. In this letter, Louis does not deal at all with substantive issues pertaining to images.[83] Louis was punctilious. Perhaps he mistrusted the pope or perhaps he knew that Rome and Aachen disagreed in ways that could not easily be overcome.

At this point, the trail of evidence goes cold. Not a word is heard from Eugenius or the Frankish court. Under the year 827 the *Royal Annals* say that envoys from Michael and Theophilus appeared at the court at Compiègne in September "as if to confirm the treaty." They were "received warmly, heard, and dismissed."[84] It is hard to believe that this legation had anything to do with the one of 824 with which we began the present discussion. It is more likely that it was part of routine Franko-Byzantine diplomacy and not unlikely that it had something to do with the constant provocations caused for both Francia and Byzantium by petty potentates in the northern Adriatic region.[85] Likewise, the legation which Louis sent to Constantinople in 828 is nowhere said to have had anything to do with images.[86] Halitgar was a member of this embassy and he had been foreseen as a member of the embassy contemplated in late 825. Louis had informed both Jeremias and Jonas as well as the pope that he was keeping Halitgar and Amalar with him so that they could be included in any papal legation to the East.[87] But Halitgar's companion in 828 was Ansfrid of Nonan-tola, not Amalar, and, in any case, Halitgar was certainly not kept waiting around the court for two or three years. It seems safest to say that, as in the 790s, all parties agreed to disagree and carried on with business as usual.

A *Summary of the* Libellus

Near the beginning of their *Libellus* Louis's "oratores," "spokesmen"—an odd choice of words—provide a good deal of information on how they proceeded with their work. They began by having the *Hadrianum*—Hadrian's letter of 785 to Constantine VI and Irene—read out in their presence. They discussed it carefully. At this point the precise meaning of the text becomes a little murky. I quote in extenso:

> Furthermore when your father of holy memory had that same synod [i.e., Nicaea] read out in the presence of himself and his men, and had criticized it in many places, as was fitting, and when he had particularly noted some passages that were especially open to severe censure, he sent them to Pope Hadrian, through abbot Angilbert, so that they could be corrected by his judgment and authority. The pope himself, on the contrary, by favoring those who had at his instigation inserted both superstitious and ill-suited testimonies into the above mentioned work, tried, in a not quite appropriate way, to offer individual chapters that he wished to stand in their defence.[88]

On one level, this is no more than a narration of what the Paris bishops believed had happened in the early 790s. On another level, however, it is a statement about what those very bishops were themselves reading. It seems clear that they had in their possession and read carefully Hadrian's *Responsum*. It is not so clear whether they also possessed and studied the *Capitulare adversus synodum*, the document sent to Hadrian with Angilbert and to which the *Responsum* was, so to speak, an objectionable objection. A text which the Paris Colloquy never cites or mentions is the *Opus*. This is odd. The *Opus* was clearly very important as a statement of the Carolingian court's view of the image question in the 790s. Moreover, the work must have been available in the palace archives because Hincmar, when has was an *adulescentus*, had a copy made which in fact survives as Paris, Arsenal 663.[89] The passage above seems to leave open just slightly the possibility that the Paris bishops also reviewed the Nicene *acta*, and a close look at the patristic florilegium in the *Libellus* makes it a virtual certainty.[90] The matter of sources is of some importance because, as we will see, much of the *Libellus* consists of lengthy strings of patristic quotations and one wonders where the Paris bishops got either the actual texts they cited or prompts on where to look for them. A bit further on the bishops say that they also read the letter of Michael II to Louis from 824.[91] This is the last concrete statement that the bishops make about their working methods. Otherwise, they content themselves with saying that they used the little time they had to collect relevant testimonies from the Bible and the fathers.

Once they settled into their task, the bishops proceeded in an impressively orderly fashion. Theodulf, as will be remembered, generally followed the structure of the Nicene *acta*, and the various writers who responded to adoptionism tended to follow the arguments of Elipandus and Felix, although Alcuin certainly showed some originality and initiative in composing his own works. The best analogue for 825 is found in the writings of the five theologians who spoke to the *filioque* issue in 809. These writers had no set text to follow as a template and so they grappled with the issues according to their own perception of those issues' importance. In quite traditional fashion, they built up their discussions from biblical passages and extracts from the church fathers, but no one of their contributions is just like any other. What is more, the five authors basically advance their arguments indirectly by heaping up proof-texts. As with Theodulf, although he entered the fray more often and more directly than the 810 authors do, one follows the logic of the argument by noting carefully what was said in, that is, asserted by, the citations. This method permits authors to attack common problems in different ways. The discrepancies between these texts serve as a salutary reminder of how original and independent-minded Carolingian thinkers could be even when they were reflecting on a common problem.

After reviewing the historical record, the bishops at Paris created, in effect, a monograph that develops four major themes on the subject of images (the *Libellus* was not actually provided with any subdivisions at all). The first begins with a brief demonstration that images are permissible but emphasizes why it is wrong to destroy them. The second, which is rather long and somewhat meandering in its reasoning, explores correct and incorrect forms of worship. The third argues the case that images cannot be equated with the cross. The fourth one makes the full case that images are permissible. The bishops may have had to work fast, but they covered a huge range of subjects, evaluated a prodigious corpus of material, and produced a treatise that is both lengthy and cogent. Their achievement is truly impressive.

The *Libellus* contains a lengthy and well-organized florilegium containing

188 separate extracts relating to the four themes just enumerated.[92] The treatise begins and ends, however, with explanatory and interpretive material that provides the reader with not only the Frankish view of what they were doing and why, but also a series of statements that permit historians to form their own judgments about the *Libellus* and its place in Carolingian culture. The bishops rarely intervene personally in their florilegium. They content themselves with saying, "Now we will cite the fathers against those who think *this* . . ." and "That is enough about those who think *that*. . . ." On only a few occasions, which we will note as we move along, do the bishops pause to reflect a little on the topic at hand. Their mandate was to provide raw material.

The compilers say that because a certain reverence should be shown to those who occupy the chair of Peter, they will commence with a discussion of how it is that images are permissible and why it is wrong to destroy them.[93] In documents intended for the pope's eyes, this was a relatively safe way to start because the papacy had defended images and resolutely opposed iconoclasm ever since the early eighth century. "We judge it fitting and necessary to begin," they say, "by collecting the opinions of the holy fathers against those who presume indiscriminately to remove images not only from buildings but even from sacred vessels."[94] A first group defends images. Fourteen patristic passage follow, all of them familiar to us by now in one context or another.[95] The opening citation is the passage in Eusebius's *Ecclesiastical History* about the statue at Paneas of woman with the flow of blood who was healed by touching the hem of Christ's garment. The next passage is the one from the *Acts of Sylvester* concerning the images of Peter and Paul that were shown to Constantine. Then come John Chrysostom on all the things that painters can depict, Paulinus of Nola on the value of looking at scenes from the Old Testament, Gregory of Nyssa on how an image makes him shed tears, the same author on how images can make one think deeply about what is depicted, and then Augustine on how pictures are not real but can bring real things to mind and incite people to compunction. Up to this point, the authors built a very traditional case for the permissibility of images.

The bishops then concentrate on why it is wrong to destroy images. They quote Augustine to the effect that a person would bear injury to God by damaging his image. Then they cite Cassiodorus who himself told of St. Paul destroying altars of the pagan gods. Next they cite Cassiodorus again on how Julian destroyed the image at Paneas and replaced it with his own only to see it destroyed by fire from heaven. The point is made subtly but effectively: Christian images are of *something* and deserve respect but pagan altars, and by extension images, are of *nothing* and can be destroyed with impunity. Then, as if to clinch the case, and perhaps to impress the pope, there follow four separate citations of Gregory I: to Serenus telling him not to destroy images; to Serenus saying that God alone is to be worshiped and not images; to Januarius about the legitimate removal of Christian images from a synagogue where they had been forcibly introduced; and to Secundinus on how images can call things to mind and make one burn with longing for them. Obviously the Frankish writers had to hand very few texts where the fathers actually condemned the destruction of images. So they adopted the stratagem of citing old, familiar texts that authorized images, of demonstrating that pagan images could be destroyed without consequences, and of asserting that damaging Christian images would bring heavenly rebuke. This gave them an opportunity to affirm papal teaching—and five of their fourteen extracts are papal. There may be a subtle point embedded in the list of citations. Of the eight authors cited only one is a pope and the other seven precede that pope—Gregory I—in time. In other words, the compilers are making the point that the popes and the Franks share a tradition. The Byzantines shared that tradition too, so the *Libellus* would not necessarily antagonize the Byzantines. This delicate balancing of Frankish, papal, and Byzantine views is a hallmark of the *Libellus*.

Coming to their second theme, the Paris bishops now say that they are going to speak "against those who serve them [images] and adore them with a cult that is not their due, and call them holy, and who claim that they themselves have gained holiness through them."[96] At this point the bishops embark on a long discussion of worship. The specific subject of images is always front and center, and the basic thesis which the compilers argue is that the worship of images is wrong. But the overall approach is novel in the whole period of image controversies. Never before had there appeared such a sustained presentation of licit and illicit forms of worship, of the nature of worship itself, and of the language available to talk about it.

The bishops start by saying that they need to explore just how the worship of images arose in the first place. There follow six passages, all from various works of Augustine.[97] Image worship is attributed to Simon Magus; to the Carpocratians, a Gnostic sect which allegedly worshiped images of Jesus, Paul, Homer, and Pythagoras; to Epicurus and Democritus whose images were, with their connivance, worshiped by their disciples; and to Hermes Trismegistus. Augustine also is quoted as having said that the Roman Republic began to decline when its citizens turned to images. This section concludes with a declaration from *The City of God* that God is the creator of all and is alone to be loved, not the created things of his world. The tactic here is interesting. Image worship is attributed to pagans, universally recognized heretics, and oddballs. No contemporaries are cited. The problem is placed in the remote, and safe, past.

Having discussed, very briefly and discretely, how image worship arose, the bishops now turn to what "our teachers" say about this superstition.[98] The remark near the end of the discussion of the origins of image worship about the need to worship God alone serves both to identify succinctly the fault of the image worshipers and also to effect a transition to a lengthy elaboration of the argument that worship must be reserved for the creator and not for creation. Thirteen extracts follow, drawn from a wide array of fathers: Fulgentius once, Origen, Jerome, Isidore, and Lactantius twice each, and Augustine four times. This section begins with some reflections by Origen on the twentieth chapter of Exodus. Moving along, the section forbids the worship of images of rulers. Isidore is quoted to show that a picture is nothing in itself but merely a pointer to something else. God alone is to be worshiped and the soul, which cannot be depicted, is the image of God. The whole section stresses the spiritual dimension of worship and warns against the worship of anything created, or made. There is a danger of loving creation more than the creator. These arguments are old, familiar ones. Theodulf would have been happy with this section, although it lacks his persistent and explicit rejection of "manufactured things."

The argument that the creator alone and not his creation is to be worshiped is then carried a bit further in a way that anticipates and meets a potential criticism.[99] The bishops ask about people who seem to think that the mediation of images is necessary because the image of a human body is worth as much as the body itself. Seventeen passages follow with Augustine most frequently represented by far: thirteen extracts as against two from Jerome and one each from Origen and Ambrose. The compilers arrange the extracts in such a way as to make an argument. First, God alone is to be worshiped. Second, it is a great offense to attribute life, an active mode of being, to senseless objects or to demons. Third, angels and saints do not love it if we love them but are only pleased when we love whom they love. Saints indeed may exhibit wonderful qualities, but they are nevertheless not be worshiped. Fourth, Christians do not worship ethereal and celestial beings, such as angels, but only God who created and blessed such beings. Fifth, Christians do not devote the cult to martyrs or to relics that they devote to God. To anchor this point the authors twice cite, once via Augustine and once via Jerome, the passage in Acts 14.10 where the Lycaonians tried to worship Paul and Barnabas. In parallel, the authors cite Acts 10.26 where Peter refused to let Cornelius worship him. Pride might make some men wish to be worshiped like God, but Christians must avoid this temptation. The Paris bishops were being careful to close the door to any argument that, even if the worship of gods and heroes arose among the pagans, and even if Christians show reverence for certain people, that does not mean that Christians also worship created beings—angels, saints, martyrs, even rulers—and, by extension, their images.

This set of reflections carries on with a brief section that once again insists that only the creator and not his creation is to be adored.[100] Custom must always yield to truth. God is not worshiped because He is old, so to speak, but because He is eternal. No mere custom is eternal. The bishops seem to be acknowledging that the worship of images has been around for a long time but saying that they are not thereby impressed by the practice itself or persuaded by the assertion that long usage confers validity.

Now the bishops turn to specific practices which they consider objectionable. They say that since truly holy men and angels did not wish to be adored but to be paid a service of love, and since temples (that is, churches) and sacrifices are not instituted for the martyrs but only for God, then one wonders how it is that the Greeks speak in their letter to Louis of the adoration, lights, incense, and so on, which are offered to images.[101] The Holy, Catholic Church has laid aside every form of superstition and therefore must exercise due discretion with respect to images "just as that outstanding teacher, the blessed Pope Gregory, taught." Here the bishops also announce explicitly a persistent sub-theme: one must avoid giving scandal to "our weaker brothers." The passages cited evince a profound pastoral solicitude. From *The City of God* they cite the story of Moses and the brazen serpent and then the later story of Hezekiah's destruction of the serpent/lance when, after it had been kept for memory, some began to worship it as an idol. The bishops also cite the story of Epiphanius at Anablatha. The bishop had entered a town and found a church veil bearing an image of Christ or of some saint—it was not clear which. Epiphanius removed the veil, gave the cloth to poor people, and gave the church a new veil. In addition, the bishops cite (Pseudo-)Ambrose on the consumption of meat that had been offered in pagan sacrifices. Ambrose says that those who are "wise" can eat such meat but that "weaker brothers" might be confused by the practice. As the section draws to its close, it presents, from Paul (1 Cor. 6.12) via Augustine, the injunction that not everything which is lawful is expedient. The bishops say that when persons have quite properly erected images for memory and love they should be careful that, in satisfying their own devotion, they do not give scandal to weaker people and draw them into an "opportunity for superstition."

At this point the bishops address two familiar Old Testament passages which some "think bring them some support for the adoration of images."[102] The bishops offer Augustine's and Jerome's commentaries on Genesis 47.29–31, where Jacob is said to have "adored" his son Joseph, or the tip of his staff, and then they cite Gregory's *Moralia* on 3 Kings 1.23 where David is reported to have "adored" the prophet Nathan. The interpretations which the bishops offer by means of their patristic citations are completely traditional: this kind of adoration is not religious but is a mark of honor and devotion that people customarily pay to persons worthy of their deepest respect. These two scriptural passages were cited at Nicaea and often figured in iconophile propaganda. But Nicaea cited many more passages than these and the Paris bishops ignore the others. When Theodulf interpreted these texts he did so typologically. The Paris writers seem to cite them as further examples of the kinds of practices that must be approached with discretion.

The discussion of practices concludes with two more brief sections, each buttressed by one citation from Augustine. The first counters the argument that support for the worship of images comes from the fact that they are called holy and are equated with sacred vessels.[103] Augustine says, on the contrary, that vessels are fashioned from gold and silver which God himself made and that they are called holy because they are used to serve God in the sacraments. The vessels are merely the work of human hands and as such deserve no worship in themselves. The second addresses the old matter of the cherubim on the Ark of the Covenant.[104] This time the bishops use a long citation from *On Christian Doctrine* to make the point that it is a grave offense to mistake the sign for what it signifies. Signs are meant to elevate our minds from the corporeal world to the spiritual. The passage does not advert to the old argument that these particular images are licit because God commanded them to be made. These two brief sections should, like the ones dealing with Jacob and Nathan, be taken as additional elements of the preceding discussion about the danger of blurring the line between creator and creation, and of misunderstanding how creation can, properly understood, lead the mind to a contemplation of the creator. Certain traditional practices can enhance the worship of the one, true God but, if due caution is not observed, they can lead anyone, and especially the weaker, the less well educated, to the worship of God's creation.

The next passage extends this argument that worship is to be reserved for God alone. It does so not by talking about practices but instead by exploring the meanings of the words that themselves are usually used in connection with images. It begins thus: "Concerning the due service (*cultu debito*), which the Greeks call *latreia*, or that worship (*religio*) and service (*cultu*) which the Greeks call by one word, *threskian*, or whether or not any manufactured thing is to be cherished (*colendum*) or adored (*adorandum*)."[105] We have seen in earlier chapters that, normally, the Greeks were understood to have observed a distinction between *latreia* and *proskynesis*. The former was reserved for God alone and the latter might be accorded to images. Presumably these words corresponded with the Latin *adorare* and *venerare*. The fullest treatment of this topic in the age of iconoclasm appears in the writings of John of Damascus, but his words were neglected at Nicaea and unknown in the West. Many have argued that Theodulf did not understand the distinction or that the translation from which he worked had missed it by rendering everything as *"adorare."* We have seen, however, that very few authors were careful in maintaining the distinctions between each word in these two pairs, and that the distinctions may be just as much modern scholarly constructs as medieval theological definitions.

Therefore, this section in the *Libellus* seems to be a promising beginning on a fundamental clarification of terms. Yet the bishops turn for "proof" to a brief section from the beginning of Book 10 of *The City of God*.[106] Augustine here inaugurates his ruminations on the various words for worship. He says that there is no single Latin word so, when he needs one very precise word, he will use the Greek *latreia*. He goes on to say that *cultus* is unacceptable as the single word for the worship of God because it has too wide a range of legitimate meanings, although it certainly can apply to the worship of God in the strict sense. The bishops break off their quotation right after Augustine has made this point. Only in the next (uncited) lines does Augustine actually deal with *religio*, which he equates with the Greek *threskeian*. *Religio*, Augustine says, could mean the worship of God alone but, like *cultus*, it has too wide an array of current acceptations. He continues by talking about *pietas*, which the Greeks call *eusebeia*, and says that this word too might refer to the worship of God but can also mean the obligations dutifully performed toward one's parents. Because *eusebeia* could have a range of meanings, Augustine says, the biblical writers sometimes substituted *theosebeia* which had the advantage of referring to God alone. But this word cannot be expressed in Latin with a single word.

Thus far, the Paris bishops neither cited fully nor got full value out of Augustine's comments on the terminology of worship. Then they turn to the well-worn story of Jacob's pillow-stone. On this they cite Augustine's commentary on Genesis to show that when the stone was constituted as a "title" and anointed, Jacob did not become an idolater. Jacob never visited the stone to make sacrifices on it or to adore it. It was a prophetic sign pertaining to the unction that was to come in the one named "Christ." Moreover, Augustine continues, "It must be noted very carefully how he set up those titles as testimony to something, not that they would be served as if gods but that they might signify something." In this brief passage Augustine never uses the words cult, religion, *latreia*, *threskeian*, and so on. He uses *"colerent"* and *"adorando"* once each but the latter does not appear in the quoted selection from *City of God*, although both words appear in the *Libellus* section. The bishops seem to have incorporated this section to advance their contention that God alone is to be worshiped.

To complete our discussion of the second theme of the *Libellus* we have to jump ahead about eighteen pages in the text to a point where the bishops returned to the subject of worship.[107] This time they cite the letter of the Council of Nicaea to Constantine VI and Irene. The relevant passage begins, "For adoration (*adoratio*) is understood in many ways." They carry on by citing several different kinds of adoration: Adoration "according to honor and love and fear, just as princes and their power are adored"; "adoration according to fear proper, as when Jacob adored Esau"; "adoration according to gratitude, as when Abraham adored the sons of Heth from whom he received a plot of land to bury his wife Sarah"; "adoration for someone in a superior position from whom one has gained protection, as when Jacob adored pharaoh." But, they conclude, "there is that true and most certain adoration which is owed to almighty God and the divine majesty alone. It is illicit to transfer this adoration to any creature or to shift it to any manufactured thing." Immediately the bishops return to Augustine, this time citing his *On the Trinity*. Here Augustine reaffirms the difficulties of language and he draws a distinction between *duluein* and *latreuein*. The former may be paid to many persons in many ways but the latter paid to God alone. It appears that the Paris bishops were sensitive to the ambiguities of ordinary language and that they realized clearly that, no matter what words one used oneself, or found in one's texts, there was a kind of "adoration" owed to God alone and another "adoration" that was much broader in application.

The *Libellus* then turns to its third major theme, the problem of those who think that they can adore images because they are just like the cross.[108] This lengthy discussion of the cross is unprecedented in all earlier image disputes. The material treated in this section provoked the longest direct intervention by the bishops in the flow of the florilegium. The bishops start off by addressing those who "in that synod of the Greeks publicly state that they adore images just as they adore the life-giving cross." They reject this contention by means of twelve citations that make three basic points.[109] The first is that miracles are associated with the cross: Constantine saw a cross emblazoned on the sky and he used the cross as a victory-bringing war standard; dead people have been brought back to life by the cross and pagans have been brought to new life in faith through the cross; a woman was cured of cancer by the cross; a relic of the true cross drove away flames. The second point is that the cross brings innumerable benefits to Christians: it brings hope, virtue, consolation, rest, and protection. The third point builds upon the second. The cross is for Christians a universal sign: a sign of punishment has become a sign of glory; the cross gives all who see it hope of the resurrection it signifies. The inescapable inference is that images neither do nor mean any of these things.

Now we encounter the bishops' longest single personal intervention in the florilegium.[110] "Worshipers of images are accustomed to advance in support of their point of view the veneration, adoration, and exaltation of the holy cross. So why [they say] is it not permissible for images to be adored just like the cross?" Their first answer is one that we have encountered before in iconophobe circles:

> When he wished to redeem the human race, Christ chose to be hung upon a cross, not upon an image. And so holy mother church, through-out the whole world, has decreed that the mysteries of the cross, among countless others enumerated far and wide again and again by the holy fathers, are licit for all Catholics on this count alone, the love of the passion. And so wherever they see them they may if they wish venerate them by bowing, and what is more, on the holy day of the Lord's passion that is specially celebrated throughout the world, adore it by prostration as is done with all devotion by the entire order of the clergy and all the people.[111]

The passage then says that nothing like this can be said about images. Moreover, the church uses the cross in consecrating fonts, in baptizing, in making the sign of the cross upon the baptized, and in other blessings too. Ordinary people make the sign of the cross on their foreheads and breasts. The sign of the cross is a powerful weapon against the attacks of Satan. Who can say any of this about images? Furthermore, when the body and blood of the Lord are about to be consecrated in the holy mass, they are signed with the cross. There is no one, be he wise or stupid, who supposes that this consecration may be effected by any other sign.

At this juncture the intervention shifts in mid-course and moves on to the fourth theme, the issue of when and why images are permitted: "Up to here for you, if you are an indiscriminate worshiper (*cultus*) of images and from now on, on the other hand, if you are an intemperate destroyer. Take care that in hearing what follows you do not think some permission has been conceded to your rashness, so that wherever you see images painted or erected not for illicit cult but for a discrete and, therefore, for a licit disposition of mind, you should wish either to pull them down or accord them the mockery of ridicule."[112] The concession to which this refers pertains to the possibility that someone might read the following defense of images, penned in the first place against those who are bent on destroying them, as an authorization to worship them. This passage and the ones surrounding it are mostly in direct address in the second-person singular. This might be taken as a deliberately rude way of speaking to "rash" persons. But the passage was not meant to be seen by anyone except Louis. And it is only in this lengthy intervention that one meets anything like the acrimony of Theodulf. Elsewhere, the calm, moderate tone of the *Libellus* is one of its most striking characteristics.

Because the next chapter will treat art talk in both the *Libellus* and its roughly contemporary treatises, no more will be provided here than a brief summary of the last portion of the florilegium, for it is here that the Paris bishops engage in their art talk.[113] This is the longest section of the *Libellus* and by means of seventy-five extracts, from nineteen different fathers, virtually all of them familiar to us by now, the authors build up a justification for images based on all of the arguments that we have met so far. Images are authorized by God himself who commanded some—as the cherubim—to be made. The incarnation legitimates images. Images can teach, can elevate minds from this world to the next, and can refer worship performed before them to the person whom they represent. Although desecration of an image bears injury to the person represented, the image does not somehow create a duplicate of its subject. Images of Christ do not separate his natures.

Allied Documents from Paris

With the last citation in the florilegium, this section of the *Libellus* comes to an abrupt end. What follows is a draft of a letter that the bishops proposed to Louis for submission to the pope. The letter must be interpreted wholly on its own terms because it lacks any introductory material that might have placed it into context. As we will see shortly, Louis's actual letter to Pope Eugenius differs substantially from the draft letter. In a way, this is fortunate because the discrepancies provide clues as to what the bishops were thinking as well as to what constituted more authoritative, or politic, thinking at the court.

The draft letter begins by arguing that every human effort must be directed to achieving unity, peace, and concord. No one who fails to struggle with all his might in this great effort can have any hope of attaining heaven. The letter then says that some explanation should be offered for why all of the preceding material (i.e., the florilegium) has been transmitted (as these words were being written, it seems, the *Epitome* had not yet been envisaged). The rhetorical strategy is particularly interesting. The letter starts with a reflection on the virtues. Faith, hope, and charity are preeminent, but they can only be preserved and applied when prudence, justice, temperance, and fortitude are present. In turn, these latter virtues cannot be operational if reason, discretion, respectability, and expediency are not in evidence. Now, the letter says, many of these virtues exceed human reason and some of them, indeed, can be attained only by faith. The Bible and the fathers have discussed all this fully. But in its place, reason is a powerful tool. Here reason appears to mean a certain kind of logic, a way of presenting an argument. The implication is that the florilegium constitutes biblical and patristic material that falls into the realm of "divine authority." Divine authority, of course, has its own reason. But so does plain logic, or human ratiocination, and so what follows will in fact take this path.

The letter continues by saying that all are brothers in Christ because all alike are redeemed by the sacrifice in His blood. Therefore, it is painful to know that "our brothers of the whole empire of the eastern Romans" for whom we have unbreakable love have been "irrationally" split into two because some of them, together with "our dearest brothers" Michael and Theophilus, do not wish to have images while others of that same "holy people" wish not only to have images but even to adore them. An altercation ensues because neither party will seek an understanding with the other and both think that reason, the Scriptures, and the fathers are on their side. God has deigned to give the world an arbiter of such disputes, His vicar, the pope. He alone has the name "*universalis papa*," which possesses the authority to intervene. In these "last days" Satan is splitting the bonds of love and unity and the pope alone can lead the struggle against this evil. Indeed, no one has a greater obligation to lead this struggle than the lord apostolic, but if he fails to take up the battle he could not truly be called universal. All this, the letter emphasizes, has been said to show our devotion, to show how we wish to add our help to your (i.e., the pope's) struggle.

The draft letter is about twice as long as the one that Louis eventually sent and is considerably more florid. It is polite albeit a little condescending. Its overall approach is subtle and clever. The problem is a split in Byzantium itself and the pope's pastoral authority is invoked to help heal the division. This line of approach avoids the ticklish matter of the division between the pope and Francia. Moreover, even though the Franks sent their *Libellus*, or at least its *Epitome*, to Rome, this letter did not urge the pope to reflect on those materials, or to use them in any attempt to convince the Byzantines. Instead, the "Franks" counseled an appeal to reason couched in a call for peace, unity, fraternity, and mutual love. This too was a way to evade the obvious difficulty represented by differing papal, Frankish, and Byzantine views of the same biblical and patristic texts.

The next section of the *Libellus* forms a draft of a letter that the bishops proposed to Louis for the pope to send to the Byzantines. This letter opens, courteously, by saying that as we are all sinners and brothers in Christ, then the pope, on the authority of Peter, Paul, and the Lord, wants to call all to peace, love, and unity. The "pope" says he must write to "Michael and Theophilus, the highest sons of the church of God . . . the emperors of the Romans" because the Lord committed the keys to Peter. He asks the Byzantines to heed and obey what he will present to them in three chapters. One will argue with reason in so far as it is rational, discrete, honorable, and advantageous. The second will argue with authority as it is understood by the truth and righteousness of the Catholic faith. The third will lay down a plan, or perhaps give advice, that is pleasing to God.

The first section of the three-part argument is entitled "*Ratio*." In these lines the "pope"—that is, the Franks writing for the pope—says that under the authority of Peter and Paul the whole West has always been free of all taint of heresy and has called back to the right path anyone who has fallen away. This truth is known all over the world and all turn to Rome to find the truth. So it is critical to address the long, harsh controversy that has separated Rome and the Greeks. We must find a way to make peace. Let us start by asking, "What harm would there ever have been to faith, hope, and charity if there had never been an image?" Certainly, if these had never appeared, there would not be this controversy now. When all the clergy and the dignitaries in "the empire of the Franks" heard about this dissension with their brothers they sought authority to look into the matter. They cried out to high heaven that the judgment of God would fall upon us if we did not use all our authority to work for unity. At this point the draft contains a short passage that purports to be a papal quotation of the Frankish point of view. The "quotation" says that it will not seem tedious if "they" add a little on what reason and the ancient fathers say about this case, on what "the reason of truth and the truth of reason" teach, and on "the line of truth that stretches without a break from the ancient fathers right down to us." The "Franks" then tell how Dionysius brought the faith to Gaul from Rome and how it has been kept alive by many others, such as Hilary and Martin, "who may not be known to you because of the size of the earth." But we have never heard that such a question was raised or debated. We find no evidence that anyone ever prohibited images from being painted or erected. No one, in fact, either commands or forbids them. If there were no painted images in all the world, no harm would come to faith, hope, and charity. The knowledgeable sometimes put them up in churches or in the palaces of princes for pious memory or for decoration, while for the unlettered, they are there to teach piety.

They are not there for any cult or religion so they cannot bear any harm to true virtue. People should be able to have them or not, just as they please. Our ancestors have handed down this custom to us, and so we neither require not prohibit images. Those who wish to have them should avoid any illicit cult and those who do not wish to have them should not show any contempt to them or damage them. "Such is then the key point of this whole explanation (*totius huius rationis*), that those who wish may have painted or fashioned images for memory or for sound teaching in suitable places and without any illicit cult, those however who do not wish to have images should not spurn them with any illicit contempt." Here the "pope" concludes by saying that he could have said a lot more but this ought to suffice.

The next section of the draft letter is entitled "*Auctoritas.*" It begins by making the point that the time has come to see if the writings of the holy fathers are in accord with the preceding rationale. The "letter" cites four letters of Gregory I, the very ones that appear in the *Libellus* and in the *Epitome.* The letters to Serenus establish that Gregory opposed the destruction of images and also forbade their adoration. The letter to Januarius tells about a gang led by a converted Jew which entered a synagogue and placed there images of Mary and Jesus, a cross, and a baptismal robe. The Jews appealed to Gregory and he ordered Bishop Januarius to remove the offensive images and let the Jews worship in peace. The letter to Secundinus, still traveling in its heavily interpolated condition, says that Gregory sent this recluse some images because looking at images made his heart burn with desire for the persons represented there. Gregory approves this attitude and remarks that Secundinus does not worship the images as if they were God. The first two letters, then, establish the basic thesis: no adoration, no destruction. The third shows that in some cases images can be removed while the fourth shows the proper attitude and disposition with respect to images. The "pope" says that Gregory's words must be read very carefully so that they do not appear to give aid to those who wish either to destroy or to worship images, or to lead astray the "many persons of lesser understanding" who might misunderstand them.

The last portion of the proposed letter is entitled "*Consilium.*" The "plan" or "advice" returns to but expands on issues raised first in the opening of the letter and in the "*Ratio.*" The "pope" stresses the need to seek peace and concord and to remove the dissension that is dividing "brothers." Then the letter gives a brief history of the controversy. It began when the emperor saw that some of his people were inflamed with a completely inappropriate zeal for images and worshiped them beyond anything that was ever before done in the church. So the emperor sought to remove this superstition and concluded that the vice could not be eradicated unless the offending images were destroyed. But it was not really necessary to remove the images because they were not offensive in themselves. Indeed, they were useful, to the knowledgeable for memory and to the ignorant for teaching. So one offense was exchanged for another and this ought to be easy to fix. After the devil inspired the destruction of images he then led Irene and her son to demand that all people subject to them worship images. We simply need to come back to the right path.

The next item in the dossier is Louis's letter to Jeremias and Jonas as they were preparing to head for Rome. The idealism, perhaps naiveté, evident in the draft letters here gives way to hardheaded realism. Louis first says that the materials which Halitgar and Amalar have brought to him are excellent and well suited to the purpose for which they were collected. But, he continues, you need to select certain items that are most apt for the pope to read and then remind him that these things were only collected with his approval. Be sure, Louis urges, to try to convince the pope about what "reason" teaches concerning images so that neither he nor his people will be able to reject what you say. Be patient and modest in your disputation so that you do not compel him to "irrevocable stubbornness." Lead him by careful, measured arguments. But if "Roman obstinacy" prevents the discussion between you from coming to the desired result, then say that we wish to include our envoys in any legation which he might dispatch to Constantinople.

The focus on reason and on careful argumentation is interesting. Louis does not want his envoys to engage in a battle of florilegia or to argue detailed points of theology. He wants them to stress the kinds of "reason" spelled out at great length in the draft letters. Peace is crucial. It will take some compromise to get peace. Images should not be permitted to cause such deep divisions. The only problem with this "reasonable" position is that it had no chance of being accepted by any convinced iconophile or iconophobe partisan, or perhaps by an obstinate pope.

The following document is Louis's letter to Eugenius. Louis reminds the pope that when the Greeks informed him that they were going to raise certain issues with Rome, he asked the pope for permission to investigate the matter himself, the better to be helpful. Louis says that whatever his bishops collected in so short a time he has read over and now sends on to Rome with his trusted couriers who are themselves learned and skilled in argument. Louis says that he knows the pope himself is aware of the sharp divisions among the Greeks and he hopes that the holy father will work with all his strength to restore peace and unity. If it would be helpful, Louis says, he would be glad to include his own envoys in any papal embassy to the East.

Compared with the long draft letters, this imperial missive to Rome seems pretty unimpressive. Yet it should probably be taken as indicating two things. First, Louis had limited expectations. Second, Louis saw no reason to antagonize the pope with his letter and, anyway, he left a great deal of responsibility, and perhaps initiative, to his legates. Louis was extremely anxious that he be allowed to participate in any papal mission to Constantinople. This suggests to me that the Carolingian court had come to regard relations with Byzantium as being on a par with relations with Rome.

The last document in the 825 dossier is the *Epitome*. This, as Louis's letter to Jeremias and Jonas implies, was intended for presentation to the pope. Perhaps, as in 810, it was to be read *"per ordinem."* The relationship between the *Libellus* and the *Epitome* is a little mysterious. Whereas the *Libellus* contains a florilegium with 188 extracts, the *Epitome*'s florilegium has only 73. In general the organization of the *Epitome* follows that of the *Libellus* but there are some differences and changes that are worthy of note. The most glaring difference is that the *Epitome* omits the longest section of the *Libellus*, namely the one dealing with the patristic justifications for images. Without this section and its 75 extracts, the *Libellus* consists of 113 extracts, a number which resembles more closely the *Epitome*'s 73. On at least three occasions the compiler of the *Epitome* abbreviated specific citations instead of omitting them.[114] But on at least four occasions, the epitomist added references that are not in the *Libellus*. More accurately, in one case the epitomist added a wholly new reference,[115] and in three other cases he included sections of letters of Gregory I that were omitted from the citations of those letters in the *Libellus*.[116] These pertain to the authenticity of Gregory's first letter to Serenus and to the trustworthiness of the bearer of Gregory's second letter. There is also a plea not to detain or abuse the messenger. In a few instances, too, the epitomist(s) mistook extracts contained in the *Libellus* for comments by the compilers of that work or mistook actual comments in the *Libellus* for continuations of an extract.[117] Taken together these differences suggest that the *Epitome* was prepared by different people than the ones responsible for the *Libellus*. One would normally look to the court for the epitomist(s). Louis's letter to Jeremias and Jonas states quite clearly that he thought that they should choose apt material from the *Libellus* for presentation to the pope. Perhaps therefore they were responsible for the *Epitome*. But they had been in Paris; the differences between the *Libellus* and the *Epitome* are impossible to explain.

Some other textual differences between the *Epitome* and the *Libellus* merit a comment or two. Three times the epitomist altered the introductory remark which he found in the *Libellus*. In the first instance, right at the beginning, the epitomist says that he will refute those who reject (*abdicare*) images with indiscriminate zeal, as we read in the letter of Michael, and tell how the fathers permit us to have them. But in the *Libellus* the corresponding remark says that passages will be collected to refute those who efface (*abolere*) images from buildings or even sacred vessels.[118] In the second case, the epitomist says, "Thus far against those who destroy images. Now against those who cherish (*colunt*) them with an unwarranted cult, who place incense before them, or who do other similar superstitious things. . . ." The corresponding passage in the *Libellus* reads, "Now against those who serve and adore them with an unwarranted cult, and call them holy, and insist that they gain some holiness from them, as we find in that synod of the Greeks."[119] The third case shows less alteration. The epitomist asks by what right or authority they bring incense or lights to images as we read in the letter of the Greeks. The *Libellus* is the same except that it does not mention lights.[120] In general, the changes are modest. Yet each one has the effect of softening possible criticisms of the papal position on images.

This softening of implicit criticisms is also apparent in another set of comments that appear in the *Epitome* but not in the *Libellus*. After citing the extract from Eusebius on the Paneas image, the epitomist adds that this passage has been included because it shows that images are to be possessed for love and honor but never for adoration. After the passage on Sylvester, Constantine, and the images of Peter and Paul, the epitomist continues by saying that this "chapter" commends the cult of the one true God and also proves that images are useful for the memory. A citation of John Chrysostom is followed by "If according to the writings of such a great teacher the pictorial art displays a marvellous story to those who view it, why is he contradicted by his disciples?" After a citation of Paulinus we find "Behold how much benefit is conferred by pictures of history." The epitomist talks of Paul destroying pagan altars and says "Destroyers of images should follow this example." After mentioning Marcellina as a heretic, the author adds, "It must be noted that Marcellina is numbered among the heretics because she served images and placed incense before them."[121] There are a few more examples like these, but they are all much the same. In every case, the epitomist's comment serves to impress upon the pope the Frankish interpretation of the relevant passage. These comments are short and carefully stated. They seem to me to correspond with two aspects of the dossier. They reflect the emphasis on "*ratio*," on logical demonstration, and they very much heed Louis's advice to select only apt passages and to argue carefully by means of them.

The *Epitome*, therefore, provides us with privileged access to how the Franks thought it might be possible to mount and win an argument—a disputation—

with the pope. But Louis expected "stubbornness" and "obstinacy" and, as far as we know, his expectations were met. No more is heard of the subject of images from the papal or Frankish courts. As far as we know, there was neither a joint embassy nor an individual papal or Frankish embassy. As in the 790s, the image controversy of 824–25 tells us some interesting things about Frankish views on images but also permits us to listen in on other concerns that were just then important to the Franks. The Paris colloquy evoked both protests and defences. To these we turn in the next chapter in order to create a full context for interpretation.

Conclusion

As in the eighth century so too in the ninth controversy over images emerged in the Byzantine East. We are better informed about the inception of the ninth-century struggle than we are about its eighth-century predecessor, but in both cases we are poorly informed about just why the problem actually arose. It took a long time for the eighth-century controversy in the East to reach a high level of theological sophistication on the iconophobe side whereas, in the writings of John of Damascus, the iconophiles reached a high standard very quickly. The Second Council of Nicaea was theologically moderate. In 815 the Byzantine iconophobes were likewise moderate, returning to some aspects of the theology of Hiereia but mainly contenting themselves with reining in some practices deemed superstitious or irreverent by their opponents. The iconophiles, especially Patriarch Nicephorus and Theodore of Studion, however, far outstripped earlier iconophiles and their contemporary iconophobes in the philosophical rigor and profundity of their argumentation. Much of what Nicerphorus and Theodore said became orthodoxy on the subject of images. But little or nothing of what they said reached the West.

The earliest Western reaction to renewed iconoclasm was papal. Paschal I wrote to Leo V in terms that—as far as can be judged from his fragmentarily preserved letter—hewed closely to traditional papal teaching on the subject of images. The Franks had continuous and intensive relations with Paschal but nothing in the surviving sources permits an assessment of whether the image question played any role at all in Franko-papal relations. The Franks became embroiled in Second Iconoclasm when Michael II sent Louis a letter in November of 824. Louis respectfully requested papal permission to investigate the matter. Perhaps he was mindful of the difficulties occasioned by his father's earlier independent initiative after Nicaea. Louis selected a small group of Frankish bishops and instructed them to meet in Paris and look into the image question. In taking this action he was following traditional Frankish practice in dealing with doctrinal issues. Louis's bishops reviewed a wide array of documents and produced a large corpus of materials destined in the first instance for Louis's eyes and in the second instance for Rome and Constantinople. It is impossible to know the outcome of the whole process. Nevertheless, the Paris documents constitute impressive evidence of the comprehensiveness and sophistication of Frankish reasoning on the matter of images. Essentially, the Franks argued that images were permitted but not essential to faith or worship. It would be good to know if anyone in the West had caught wind of Nicephorus's and Theodore's arguments that images were necessary. The Franks argued again that images were neither to be destroyed nor worshiped. They declined to engage in terminological wrangling. On the whole they commanded the patristic dossier on images and were alert to all the arguments that had been raised on every side of the issue.

CHAPTER SEVEN

Art and Argument in the Age of Louis the Pious

Ask the priests the law.
—Haggai 2.12

CONCURRENT WITH THE Paris Colloquy the Franks discovered a home-grown image quarrel. Bishop Claudius of Turin, perhaps shortly after he became bishop between 816 and 818, began removing and destroying images and preaching against them. Claudius's actions were brought to the attention of Louis's court and the emperor deputed two of his theologian-bishops to investigate the matter. Jonas of Orléans, who had been heavily involved with the Paris proceedings, penned one lengthy treatise and Dungal, the master of the school in Pavia, authored another. In this chapter we shall explore what Claudius did and said. Then we shall turn to the treatises of Jonas and Dungal. In addition, we shall analyze a treatise by Agobard of Lyon that may have been as much a cautious refutation of Paris as a rejection of Claudius. Two other significant Frankish writers, Walahfrid Strabo and Einhard, also weighed in on the image question. On the basis of these writings, we shall turn to art and art talk in the mid-ninth century and then gather in what the treatises, along with the Paris documents, can tell us about the three themes of tradition, order, and worship. Finally, we shall look for signs of these themes in other contemporary writings and issues so as to contextualize the image question as a whole.

Logomachy Carolingian Style

Amid the letters of Bishop Claudius of Turin is a document bearing the title *Apology and Response of Bishop Claudius of Turin against Abbot Theutmir.*[1] Not a letter at all, the *Apology* is a set of brief excerpts from a treatise, later said by Jonas of Orléans to have been equal in length to the psalms of David plus fifty psalms.[2] Claudius took note of Theutmir's concern that a "rumor about me has gone forth from Italy and spread through virtually all of Gaul, right up to the borders of Spain." Jonas later said that he had learned from Theutmir that Claudius had "vomited out a book of such great prolixity to the church of all of Gaul."

This set of clues opens our investigation of the Frankish world's home-grown image quarrel. This quarrel occurred at the same time as the renewed Frankish dispute with Byzantium and Rome. The materials produced in Paris in 825 never explicitly mention Claudius.[3] Louis the Pious commissioned two theologians, Jonas of Orléans and Dungal of Pavia, to respond directly to Claudius. I shall look in turn at what Claudius did, who exactly he was, and what reactions his activities elicited. Then I shall turn to his critics, Jonas and Dungal. Because these texts are not well known, I will summarize each one.[4]

The Teaching of Claudius of Turin

In his *Apology* Claudius says that as soon as he got to Italy to take over the diocese of Turin (816/18) he found "all the basilicas filled against the order of truth with foul images, worthy of anathema, and because everyone paid cult to them (*colebant*) I began to destroy them all by myself." Some evidence suggests that, perhaps after destroying what he found, Claudius had new sculptures prepared for the liturgical spaces in his cathedral and that these items had extremely intricate geometric designs in which cross-symbols are visible. The point seems to be that Claudius was willing to substitute the abstract for the mimetic and representational.[5] Claudius's iconoclasm earned him the severe displeasure of his people and, he says, if God had not helped him they would have taken his life. Claudius and Theutmir carried on a regular correspondence in the 820s. Presumably, Theutmir informed Claudius that reports about his activity had spread widely, and perhaps he chastised him as well. It seems that Claudius responded with the lengthy treatise of which only fragments survive. If Theutmir answered Claudius on the topic of images, his words are not extant. But Theutmir did forward the *Apology* to the palace. This marked at least the second time that Theutmir had brought Claudius to the attention of the emperor and his associates. It is time to learn a little more about Claudius in order to put this affair into perspective.

Claudius's origins and early life are obscure.[6] He was Goth, but it is not clear whether he was Septimanian or Iberian. He seems to have entered the Frankish scene around 800 and to have spent some years with Archbishop Leidrad at Lyon. Felix of Urgel was in sort of honorable incarceration at Lyon for many years and some have assumed that he influenced his countryman, and perhaps that he had been his teacher before they wound up in Lyon. Claudius had little formal education and was unfamiliar with secular letters. In matters theological and exegetical, he may have been an autodidact, or he may have learned from Felix and/or Leidrad. He knew some patristic writings very well and he had a special devotion to St. Augustine. By 811 he had won the favor of Louis the Pious and settled in at the Aquitainian king's palace at Chasseneuil. There he began writing a long series of biblical commentaries (virtually all unedited and unpublished) and teaching some members of the regional clergy. Louis appointed him bishop of Turin sometime between 816 and 818. A good many details about his activities derive from letters he exchanged with his former pupil Theutmir, the abbot of Psalmody near Nimes.[7] In about 820 Claudius published a commentary on First Corinthians and Theurmir sent it to the palace to be inspected by the emperor, bishops, and optimates. By about 823 or 824 Claudius could write to Theutmir, in connection with an ongoing commentary on the Pentateuch, to say that he was continuing with the exegetical work and to upbraid his old student for trying to get him into trouble. Claudius took some pleasure in that fact that friends in high places shielded him.[8] Claudius speaks in some of these letters about the deplorable state of his diocese, about his crushing workload, and about the constant opposition he faced. It is hard to believe that his exegetical work got Claudius into trouble with the locals. He may have encountered opposition from those who were loyal to Bernard of Italy who had rebelled against Louis in 818.[9] Such people might have resented Claudius's close ties with Louis.

It seems more likely that Claudius's efforts to alter customary religious practices in his diocese had people up in arms. But there are puzzles. Claudius says that he found problems as soon as he arrived in Turin (between 816 and 818) and that he immediately set about putting things right. Yet his *Apology* was written after February of 824 because it mentions the death of Pope Paschal I.[10] Moreover, Dungal (see below) says that Claudius declined to appear at a synod whose members he referred to as a "collection of asses."[11] It is possible that this was Paris, November 825. Was Claudius's exchange with Theutmir known to the Paris bishops or did the Colloquy prompt the *Apology*? It is difficult to say. Some of the abrupt and rude passages in the Paris documents referring to "you" seem more understandable if addressed to a renegade like Claudius than to the pope. Dungal also says that the "uncertainty" that had kept him from saying anything "for such a long time" was removed when he received Claudius's *Apology*.[12] This clue would have great value if we knew just when Dungal went to Pavia. His presence there is attested in May of 825 but not before.[13] My hunch is that when Theutmir failed to tarnish Claudius's name on account of his Corinthians commentary, he then denounced him to the court on account of his pastoral excesses. On this reckoning, Theutmir reacted badly to Claudius's vaunting of his support at court in 823 or 824. Claudius had been destroying images and preaching against them, and also criticizing relics and pilgrimage, for six or eight years before anyone really raised a voice against him. But when the charge of iconoclasm hit the court, Louis sprang into action. He and his court elite studied the *Apology* and prepared an extract from it that they sent to Jonas of Orléans and Dungal for refutation. I consider it unlikely that Claudius's iconoclasm had actually gone unremarked for several years. What I do consider likely is that Louis's letter from Michael II along with the Paris Colloquy made it embarrassing for Claudius's activities to be left without response after 825. What is more, Lothar, Louis's eldest son, was sent to Italy in 823 and in 825 he began issuing capitularies intended to put the secular and religious affairs of the kingdom in order.[14] This probably explains why Dungal, master of the school of Pavia, the capital of the kingdom, was deputed to make one of the official responses to Claudius. Jonas says that he stopped writing his book *On the Cult of Images* in 827 when he heard of Claudius's death.[15] This means that Claudius was not deposed for heresy. Nor was he summoned to court or hauled before any synod. He had no colleagues or heirs. His iconoclasm did not evoke the official response that Byzantine iconoclasm did, and he did not receive the punishment meted out to the adoptionist Felix of Urgel.[16]

What did Claudius actually teach? Answering that question is not easy because, as noted, we have mere excerpts from a work that was as long as two hundred psalms.[17] The excerpts were prepared at court on the basis of the book sent to Theutmir and forwarded by him to Aachen. Dungal says that two years before he wrote his *Responses* the ideas of Claudius were the subject of a "very diligent investigation" in the palace,[18] Jonas says that Claudius's book was examined by Louis and "the wisest men of the palace,"[19] and Ermoldus Nigellus addresses Louis about "a senseless person," presumably Claudius, who would dare to deny that the bodies of the saints merited worship.[20] This seems to be further evidence that Claudius's case was aired at court. And let us remember that Theutmir had sent Claudius's commentary on Corinthians to court so that the bishops and magnates could scrutinize it. These examples provide still more testimony about the characteristic Carolingian way of dealing with doctrinal disputes. But my focus is now on the excerpts. Sets of excerpts—presumably identical—were sent to Jonas of Orléans and Dungal and each man responded with a treatise much longer than the surviving (excerpted) version of the *Apology*, and probably longer than Claudius's original treatise.[21] Careful analysis of both treatises fails to disclose additional Claudian material available to them but not to us.[22] We are forced to rely on the substantive and conceptual accuracy of the excerpts prepared at court and sent out for refutation. In the MGH edition, the *Apology* occupies a little less than four pages.

Toward the end of the extant form of the *Apology,* Claudius says to Theutmir, "Your fifth objection to me is . . ." (p. 613). Unfortunately the material that precedes this statement is not organized as four responses to four objections. We may have here a clue as to the original shape of Claudius's hefty *Apology* but we cannot from the mutilated remnant perceive the structure of the original. In my reading of the *Apology* I can see three, and just possibly four, basic themes. Claudius rejects images, using many traditional iconophobe arguments. Claudius rejects the cult of the cross. And Claudius rejects pilgrimage to Rome. Perhaps Claudius also dismissed the cult of the saints or at any rate of their relics.

After a little rhetorical sound and fury, Claudius opens (p. 610) a discussion of worship with the oldest of the arguments with which we have now become familiar, the Exodus prohibition with a few historical accretions: "Since it is clearly commanded that no likeness is to be made of all the things which are in heaven or on the earth, the command is to be understood as pertaining not only to likenesses of foreign gods but also to [those of] heavenly creatures which human wit thinks it can make in honor of the creator." What is old here is obvious. What is "new" calls for just a comment or two. Claudius seems to have understood the normal iconophile countermove which defended images of "our" heavenly creatures while rejecting "their" likenesses. He also picks up on creatures honoring the creator with their own creations, whatever their intentions might be.

At this point some lines have fallen out because Claudius is made to appear to lurch into a discussion of terminology: "To adore is to praise, venerate, ask, beseech, entreat, invoke, pour forth prayer." Possibly these words formed part of a gloss on his treatment of Exodus 20.4, or possibly they are one fragment from a longer discussion. Claudius was a keen student of Augustine and he surely knew Augustine's reflections on these very words. It is not impossible that Claudius knew Theodulf's words on the subject. For present purposes, Claudius's statement may be read as signifying that he was aware of terminological wrangling and that he was having none of it: all of these words attached to beliefs and behaviors which he deemed objectionable. But it may also be that we should read Claudius as providing yet another proof that early medieval people did not draw hard and fast distinctions between the words "adore" and "venerate." In the sections of the *Apology* that deal specifically with the worship of God, and omitting the sentence just quoted, I count thirty-five examples of words that could be translated as "worship": *adorare* 22 times, *colere* 9 times, *venerare* 4 times. Claudius uses them interchangeably. His meaning is perfectly clear and he avoids all sophistries connected with the different shades of meaning borne by one word or another. God alone is to be adored.

Claudius continues by having an imaginary iconophile say, "We do not think that there is anything divine in the image we adore, but instead we adore it with such veneration in honor of him whose image it is" (pp. 610–11). This is another chestnut in the image discussions going back to antiquity. That Claudius chooses to put it into the mouth of an iconophile interlocutor suggests that he really did have lively discussions in his diocese and that his opponents were reasonably well informed (or had he debated the subject with Theutmir?). He then makes basically the same point about images of the saints (p. 611), saying that it is a shame that people who once worshiped demons now worship images of the saints without realizing that they have not deserted their idols at all. The next point in connection with adoration is also cast as if it emerged from a conversation or debate. "If," he says, "you should draw (*scribas*) or paint on a wall images of Peter and Paul, of Jupiter and Saturn or Mercury, the latter are not gods and the former are not apostles, and neither these nor those are men, although the name has been changed for that purpose" (p. 611). This again is a familiar position: images are not actually anything. "If men were to be adored, then it is living rather than dead ones that ought to be adored, that is, those who have the likeness of God not of cattle or what is yet more true, of stones and wood that utterly lack sense, life, and reason." He adds that not only are saints not be honored as God is honored, but that saints "never arrogated divine honors to themselves." Predictably he concludes that if God's creations are not to be adored, how much less then should adoration be paid to the work of men's hands. He asks, "Why do you bow down and humble yourself before false images? Why do you bend your body like a captive before useless representations and earthly inventions? . . . Why do you prostrate yourself in deathly error before that senseless image which you cherish?"

This too is familiar, conventional. Claudius's vision of the worship of God is pure and uncompromising. Material things do not mediate that worship and must not be worshiped themselves. Living humans bear the likeness of God and so in some sense God may be worshiped in His likeness in those humans. (I am almost certain that Claudius's meaning has been distorted here.) Matter is lifeless and irrational. Idols are idols, pure and simple; you cannot give them different names and change their essence. The very points that Claudius rebuts provide us with some hints about the kinds of defenses of images that he was encountering: Images recall to mind; honor paid to an image is referred to the person represented; creation may in some fashion suggest the presence of the creator. Claudius's words provide a further valuable hint: He talks of prostrating, bending, and bowing. Here we have a staunch opponent's version of what image worshipers do. In northern Italy, they did a lot less than in Byzantium.

Claudius also attacks the cult of the cross. His opponents devoted copious attention to this issue and, as Celia Chazelle has recently demonstrated, the cult of the cross and the theology of the crucifixion were topics of intense interest in the first half of the ninth century.[23] I have the impression that the *Apology* as we have it severely abbreviates and quite possibly misrepresents what Claudius said. Nevertheless, it is possible to discern at least the kernel of an argument.

"Those practitioners of false religion and superstition say 'We cherish, venerate, and adore a painted cross for the memory of our Savior and an image fashioned in his honor.'" A bit later on Claudius says, "If they wish to adore every wood made in the shape of a cross. . . ." This leads me to believe that in the first sentence just quoted Claudius is referring to both wall paintings and crucifixes. Be that as it may, Claudius objects because images of the crucifixion depict only the suffering and dead Lord and not the risen one. Such images are idolatrous, in so far as they depict only a man, and cruel, in so far as they crucify Christ again and again. Indeed, if the wood of the cross is to be adored, then all manner of things associated with Christ's earthly existence ought to be adored too: virgins, because Christ was nine months in the womb and only three hours on the cross; mangers and old rags, because Christ was placed in a manger and wrapped in rags (p. 612); boats, because Christ often traveled by boat, taught from a boat, commanded the winds to be calm from a boat, and cast nets from a boat for the miraculous draft of fishes; asses, because Christ rode into Jerusalem on an ass; lambs, because He is called the Lamb of God; lions, because He is called the Lion of Judah; stones, because He was laid in a stone tomb; thorns, because a crown of thorns was placed on His head; reeds, because the soldiers struck Him with reeds; lances, because His side was pierced by a lance. However Augustinian he may have been, Claudius had little sympathy with the father's teachings on signs and symbols. "All those things are ridiculous and to be lamented rather than written," says Claudius, as if his ridicule were not plain enough already. In the midst of this diatribe Claudius cites 2 Corinthians 5.16: "Even though we knew Christ according to the flesh, we now know him that way no longer."

Claudius develops two points with these comments. First, and by no means uniquely in his age, as I shall show in greater detail later in this chapter, Claudius stresses the divinity of the risen Christ almost to the exclusion of the human crucified Jesus. Second, Claudius rejects any worship that is associated with material things, that is not purely spiritual.

Finally, Claudius attacks penitential pilgrimages to Rome and he has a bit of rhetorical sport in doing so. "If you [he means Theutmir here] should say that I prevent men from going to Rome for penance, you would speak falsely. For I neither approve nor disapprove that journey because I know that it neither harms, nor benefits, nor profits, nor damages anyone." He then asks Theutmir, with dripping irony, why he prevents his 140 monks from going to Rome to seek penance. What could cause greater scandal than preventing people from traveling the one sure path to salvation?[24] Sarcasm aside, Claudius has a serious point to make. When Christ said to Peter, "For you are Peter and upon this rock I shall build my church," He was committing His authority to Peter and the apostles and they, in turn, have bequeathed it to each succeeding generation of bishops. Peter is now physically dead but spiritually alive in heaven. Thus his intercession can be sought anywhere and not exclusively in Rome (pp. 612–13).

Here Claudius addresses Theutmir and says, "Your fifth objection against me, indeed you say it displeases you too, is that the lord apostolic is angry with me" (p. 613). Presumably Claudius's views on pilgrimage to Rome had reached Paschal's ears and Theutmir had learned about it. "He is called apostolic," Claudius says, "who guards the [office? teaching?] of the apostle or who fulfills the office of the apostle."[25] Fulfilling the apostolic function, in Claudius's reckoning, is understanding the Lord's teaching correctly. In these circumstances, this precluded the promotion of Rome as the special locus of Peter's holiness.

These three broad themes therefore seem clear, despite Theutmir's five objections. There may just be a fourth theme visible in the *Apology*: Claudius may have had reservations about the cult of the saints. He said that saints cannot be worshiped in their images and that any respect paid to them had to be paid while they were alive. Between his comments on Peter and his jibe at the pope, Claudius says, "What is it to say 'If only Noah, David, and Job were in our midst.' Here's the point: Even if they were, so much sanctity, so much justice and merit, as great as they were, they would not acquit a son or a daughter" (p. 613). No one, he says, is to rely on the intercession of the saints because salvation comes only through possessing the same faith, righteousness, and truth that they possessed. From his surviving statements it is difficult to say if Claudius was hostile or indifferent to the cult of the saints. Clearly, he did not share his contemporaries' zeal.

Jonas of Orléans: On the Cult of Images

Jonas of Orléans was an Aquitainian, born about 780.[26] In his *On the Cult of Images* he says that he remembered having encountered disciples of Elipandus in Asturias and Galicia, probably in around 799.[27] His activities down to 818 when Louis named him to replace Theodulf as bishop of Orléans are unknown. He served in Orléans until 843 and was always a loyal subject of Louis the Pious, and then of his son Charles the Bald. We have already seen that Jonas took a leading role in the Paris deliberations of 825. In 829 he presided, in Paris, at a major reforming synod. He wrote treatises on the lay life and on kingship. He was one of the most influential ecclesiastical figures in the Frankish world. Louis asked him to refute Claudius's teachings and to help him do so sent him the excerpted *Apology* that we have been discussing. Jonas says that when he got news of Claudius's death he laid down his pen, believing that Claudius's teachings died with him. Later, in about 840, partly because he was asked by Charles the Bald and partly because news began to circulate of the activities of some alleged disciples of Claudius, Jonas picked up where he had left off—he says he had made a good start—and carried *On the Cult of Images* to its conclusion in three books.

I observed that three broad themes can be discerned in the *Apology*. Jonas takes them up in order in *On the Cult of Images*, devoting a book to each. In his "Preface," written for Charles the Bald, Jonas provides a brief history of the whole affair. This resumé contains only one surprise (307A–B, 308A–B): Jonas's assertion that he had a credible report that not only had the old heresy (iconoclasm) revived among Claudius's followers but that the Arian heresy was also spreading among them from "some textual recollections" (*quaedam monumenta librorum*). What a shame that we know nothing of that report or who made it. At the end, Jonas says that he is sending this preface, his *opusculum*, and the *excerptum* (the truncated *Apology*) for approval or disapproval. Once again, we have conformation of the Carolingian modus operandi in the case of a theological controversy. The overall structure of *On the Cult of Images* provides no clues as to where Jonas stopped and started again. The work has a general preface (305B–308C) and then Books Two and Three have their own much briefer prefaces (341B–344A, 363D–366B). Book One, at some thirty-five columns, is considerably longer than Book Two, at twenty-one columns, and Book Three, at twenty-five. The lengths of the books and the subjects treated in each may supply a clue as to Jonas's priorities and concerns.

Book One treats worship as its central theme. Jonas opens with some comments about how, in the past, great teachers and defenders of the faith have come from Spain but more recently, only heretics. This leads him to Claudius, a pupil of Felix of Urgel he says.[28] Claudius had some reputation for learning, especially biblical interpretation, and Louis sent him to Italy to tame the locals who "for the most part lacked a sense of the meaning of the holy Gospels." Claudius was a gifted preacher but the devil made him betray his gift and stir up the people with all sorts of foolish notions. Jonas acknowledges that Claudius claimed to be doing the work Louis sent him to do. If, Jonas says, he actually found people worshiping images then, of course, Claudius had a responsibility to teach them better ways. But instead of being a good teacher and pastor, Claudius violated "moderation and discretion" and began to destroy images depicting the "deeds of the saints" and also "material crosses" (crucifixes, I believe)[29] and to call those who worshiped them idolaters. Claudius generated a scandal. Some even say that Claudius taught against relics, but his writings do not prove it. When Theutmir tried to correct him, Claudius ruptured the bonds of ecclesiastical charity and vomited out a huge book which departed from the Bible and the fathers, left behind ecclesiastical traditions, verged on heresy, and established sects (307C–313B).

Jonas then commences his refutation of Claudius's teachings. First, he rejects Claudius's temerity in calling people in Gaul and Germany "members of the devil" for, allegedly, worshiping images. Jonas says indignantly that no one in Gaul or Germany does so, and that everyone in those realms adheres faithfully to the traditions and teachings of the church (313B–314A). Then Jonas rejects Claudius's assertion that he fights, not founds, sects. Jonas blasts Claudius's poor grammar and then says that, again, the whole church is against the bishop of Turin (314A–315A). Jonas continues by warning Claudius that his claim that he had found all the churches and basilicas filled with images worthy of anathema is actually a condemnation of all his predecessors and of the people committed to his care. It is possible that some ignorance has crept in, but it needs careful ministration not scandalous bolts of anathema. To be sure, if there are people who say that images are to be adored with the same cult that is paid to God, then, of course, the whole church stands with you in condemning that idea. But in launching anathemas, you have behaved "rashly and culpably," have departed from the path of "discretion, reason, and patience," and have brought dishonor on your predecessors. What is more, your writing is homely, barbarous, and full of errors. With burning sarcasm Jonas asks Claudius if he alone has defended the catholic faith and if, therefore, all his predecessors in the church—not just in Turin—have been false. Jonas answers Claudius's citation of the Exodus prohibition in three distinct ways: First, this is exactly what everyone believes; second, no right-believing person thinks that any likeness is owed the worship that is owed only to God; third, Moses put cherubim on the tabernacle and Solomon put likenesses in the Temple. Surely these were likenesses of things on the earth, above the earth, and so on. But, Jonas says—in fact he says it twice—these images were made, and we now make images, for decoration and commemoration (315A–319B). Jonas goes on at some length giving Claudius grammar lessons and then turns to a lesson that is at once grammatical and theological. He accuses Claudius of sloppy usage and flawed understanding in his deployment of terms for worship. He draws attention to Book 10 of the *City of God* (as Paris had done), to the Bible, Origen, other works of Augustine, and Fulgentius. He offers points that we have encountered many times: temples are not dedicated to the martyrs but to the God for whom the martyrs died; priests who officiate at the altars of the martyrs serve in the name of God and not of the martyr. He quotes Augustine: "It does not seem to us that a man ought to adore what he makes for it is rightly held that the maker is to be adored by what he has made, and not what has been made by its maker." Angels, finally, do not love it if we adore them, but love it when we adore whom they adore. In other words, this sections lays out the rules and terminology of proper worship (319B–324D).

Jonas now changes the subject and proceeds by a slightly crooked path to a discussion of the saints. He says that Claudius's "highest and most pre-eminent self-flattery" is his claim that he received the church for defending against those who adore images. After criticizing Claudius's grammar Jonas says that Augustine truly received his church for defending against the pagans but Claudius has attacked and disturbed the church. He has stirred up the church because of his defective understanding of key issues. For instance, Claudius says that those against whom he is allegedly defending the church say that they do not suppose that there is anything divine in the images they adore. Jonas says, basically, so what? If they say this, they are correct. If they are like "Orientals" who actually do think that something of the divine essence inheres in images, then the whole church is against them. Jonas goes on to refute Claudius's assertion that people who worship the images of the saints have not left behind the worship of demons but have only changed the name of the demons. Here, Jonas says, people have not substituted images of the saints for idols, for they have truly left their idols behind. If some people seem to show potentially superstitious cult to an image, that person should be taught gently and reasonably. When Claudius says that living rather than dead men ought to be adored because they have the image of God, he speaks rightly. Then Jonas excoriates Claudius for both poor grammar and a serious theological flaw. In this case, I suspect strongly, Claudius's abridger failed him badly. Here is the offending passage in the *Apology*: "Surely, if men may be adored, then it is living rather than dead ones who ought to be adored, that is, where the likeness of God is present, not where there is a likeness of cattle, or what is more to the point, of stones or of wood, lacking in life, feeling, and reason."[30] Jonas tinkers with the grammar of this passage and seems to recognize that something has gone seriously wrong. He says that Claudius should have put "*carentium*" where he put "*carentem.*" That is, Jonas realized that Claudius was talking about images "of things that lack. . . ." Surely Claudius was doing no more than making the old point that living people bear the likeness of God and possess life, feeling, and reason, whereas manufactured things do not. But Jonas took off on a different line. He argues that Claudius has, against the whole tradition of the church, blasphemed against the saints; it is as if Claudius has somehow compared *them* to cattle, stone, and wood. Jonas's defense of the saints brings him around to a discussion of their relics. He accuses Claudius of adhering to the teaching of Eustathius and Vigilantius[31] and of refusing to accept the whole tradition of the church that the remains of the saints are precious. We noted that the material in the *Apology* on saints is too thin to permit a nuanced appreciation of Claudius's view, but it is clear that Jonas understood Claudius to have raised a serious challenge to prevailing ideas about the saints. For his part, Jonas is strictly traditional: the saints were holy; they can now intercede; their tombs and relics are frequent sites of miracles. Although he admits that abuses of the cult can occur, he does not see this possibility as a reason to abandon the cult of the saints. Neither saints, nor their images, nor their relics are worshiped as God alone is worshiped (325A–330B).

Jonas next turns to the cross but in doing so he begins by taking up Claudius's comments about bowing before a cross. He notes right away that Claudius has put forth as his own words about the cross what Cyprian actually said about the pagan gods. Jonas also criticizes Claudius's faulty Latin once again. Then he stretches out over several columns a ringing defense of the cross: It is the universal symbol of salvation; it is the symbol of Christ's triumph over death; it has been defended by Augustine, Gregory, Bede, and others. The cross is "adored, venerated, and cherished" in memory of Christ's passion and in recollection of the redemption that was won on the cross. In some of the most heated language in the whole treatise, Jonas expresses his utter contempt for the idea that depicting Christ on the cross means that people will only see Him tortured and dead, will bring His passion into ridicule, will view Him the way the impious, Jews, and pagans do. Having blasted that contention of Claudius's Jonas turns to the bishop of Turin's faulty understanding of 2 Corinthians 5.16. Of course, Jonas says, we may worship Christ carnally for He Himself chose to become man and dwell among us. Now He is risen and reigns with the Father. The cross reminds us of both states of Christ's existence. This is the teaching of the whole church.

And, of course, the cross is not worshiped with the cult that is paid to God alone, and certainly not in Gaul and Germany, no matter what Claudius might think (330B–336A).

Jonas next quotes Claudius's long, sarcastic rant about the need, if the cross is to be worshiped, to worship other things connected with Christ's life on earth: virgins, rags, mangers, and so on. Jonas gives the by now expected criticism of Claudius's writing skills and also says that he fails to understand how to read the Bible. He refutes explicitly only the comments about virgins and asses. The latter indeed seems to have stung Jonas sharply. In fact, it seems that Jonas took Claudius quite literally, even when he quotes Claudius's own remark that such ludicrous things are better lamented than written about. The central point, however, is that Claudius just does not understand the church's teaching on worship (336B–339A).

Jonas concludes Book One with a refutation of Claudius's idea that depictions of Christ on the cross crucify Him again and again. He begins this section, as usual, with a condemnation of Claudius's writing and censures his departure from the traditions of the church. Jonas catches Claudius using Paul's words as his own. Claudius talked of people who depict Christ on the cross crucifying Him again and making a mockery of him. But Jonas says that this verse relates to Paul speaking about those who have fallen away (Hebrews 6.6). But this is not so for us, for we depict Christ crucified in gold or silver or on plaques of various colors only to commemorate His passion. Claudius is wrong to claim that persons who adore Christ on the cross, or who honor the bodies of the saints, or who salute the banner of the cross associate themselves with demons and banish themselves to eternal damnation. All these practices are the ancient and universal tradition of the church.

Book Two is almost wholly devoted to the cross. Its "Preface" takes up Claudius's barb that if the cross is to be worshiped, then asses ought to be worshiped as well. It again appears that Jonas took Claudius literally on this point. Jonas also stresses that the cross is not worshiped in respect of what it is made of, but because Christ died on it. The cross is never worshiped as God alone is worshiped. Finally, as to bowing and kissing, Jonas asks Claudius if, when celebrating the liturgy, does he not bow his head and kiss the book? If so, does he do this, Jonas asks, in respect of the ink and leather, or because the book contains God's words? So, Jonas says, we bow before and kiss the cross of Christ to commemorate His death. Toward the end, Jonas takes up the other things— virgins, rags, mangers, etc.—which Claudius had urged cross worshipers to adore. All of these points had been touched on in Book One but now Book Two accords each a more expansive treatment.

Book Two itself plunges right in with a series of patristic references to the praises of the cross: a brief citation of Origen; a lengthy set of references to homilies of John Chrysostom; a passage from Eusebius about Constantine and the cross; a story from Augustine's *City of God* about a man miraculously cured of cancer by the sign of the cross; a discussion of Jerome on Ephesians about how the blood of Christ joined heaven and earth; Cassiodorus on Psalm 1 and the way the tree planted near running water foreshadows Christ; again Cassiodorus on Psalm 4; Sedulius's *Paschal Song*; Paulinus's *Deeds of St. Felix*; the *Historia Tripartita*; and finally Gregory's *Dialogues* (3.7). Jonas concludes this section by saying that "these things have been set forth briefly concerning the praise and power of the cross." The force of the argument is carried by the long tradition of the church and by miracles associated with the cross (343B–350C).

Jonas begins section two of Book Two by quoting Claudius back to himself: "For God commanded one thing and they did something else." Jonas, as usual, takes a few swipes at Claudius's grammar and then makes an interesting move. He says that it is natural to the human condition to do otherwise than God commanded, that is, to sin. He asks Claudius "Since that's the way the human condition is, I ask you, if you acknowledge that you are a man, even more, do you think you share in human fragility?" (350C–351B). Jonas goes on this way for a few lines and then says that it would be easy to cite countless examples of human failings but that to avoid prolixity—an avoidance that here and elsewhere he fails to heed—he will choose only some. He begins with Claudius's assertion that "God ordered them to bear the cross, not to adore it; these wish to adore what they do not wish to bear bodily or spiritually." Jonas mixes a blend of biblical exegesis and grammatical instruction to remedy Claudius's poor understanding of Christ's words to His followers, "Take up your cross and follow Me" (Matthew 16.24; Luke 9.23). Jonas concludes this line of argument with a clever reference to St. Augustine: "Listen to blessed Augustine in his book on the sermon on the mount: 'He does not follow Christ, who is not called Christian according to true faith and catholic discipline.' Although you do not seem openly to attack the true catholic faith, you show yourself to be disdainful of following Christ in so far as you work up a sweat slashing away at ecclesiastical decrees, against the teaching of Christians." In sum, Jonas fails to understand the Bible but, what is more serious, departs from authentic tradition (351B–353B). To conclude his treatment of the cross in the *Apology*, Jonas was actually forced to jump ahead in Claudius's text. That is, the *Apology* treats the cross proper, then all the other things that Claudius sarcastically said should be worshiped, and then concludes with the "Take up your cross" reference. Claudius follows this biblical citation with "Unless someone takes utter leave of himself, he does not approach the one who is above him and will not know how to die to what he is." Jonas spots this as a passage from Gregory's *Homilies on the Gospels* and says that Claudius is right on this point because he has, albeit dishonestly, taken his bearings from a distinguished author (353C).

Having exhausted what Claudius says about the cross, Jonas backtracks slightly to treat at length Claudius's sarcastic list of things that cross worshipers ought also to worship: virgins (353C–355A); mangers (355A–B); swaddling clothes (355C–356C); ships (356C–357B); lambs (357C–358B); lions (358C–359A); stones (359A–C); thorns (359C–361A); reeds (361B–D); lances (361D–363A). As he proceeds through these issues, Jonas repeatedly makes six basic points although he expresses them a little differently each time. First, he speaks of why such things are adored, worshiped, or venerated at all. His comment on the Virgin Mary, and by extension on virgins, may stand as an example: "We do not just adore the virgin who bore Christ, but we venerate the holy mother of God with a fitting honor, and we humbly implore her intercession with the divine majesty" (355D). Here Jonas neatly distinguishes between *adorare* and *venerare* but elsewhere he uses them synonymously, and mixes them with *colere*. His meaning is always perfectly clear even as he reveals to us how slippery the terminology was. Second, he hammers Claudius for failing to read the Bible correctly. Third, he serves up yet more grammar lessons. Fourth, he associates Claudius in various ways with a number of ancient heresies and heretics: Montanists, Priscillianists, Manicheaeans, Novatians. Fifth, he asks who Claudius knows who actually does these things since there is no one in Gaul or Germany who does so. As one example, he asks Claudius, "who are these keepers of perverse doctrines who wish to gobble up the living lambs and adore the ones painted on walls? Surely they are not Gauls or Germans who not only avoid bearing adoration to any picture whatsoever but who sound forth with a free voice and shout down the adorers with as much censure as they can muster (358A). Sixth, Jonas tells Claudius that he has violated the terms of the Council of Chalcedon by daring to add something to the faith and that he has risked the auto-abandonment of his priestly office in doing so (360B–C, 364C). All the way through this section, as in the earlier ones dealing with asses, Jonas either took, or affected to take, Claudius *au pied de la lettre*. He says again and again that "you just cannot take the adoration/veneration/devotion/honor of *this* as equal to *that*." Jonas's ability to perceive sarcasm seems inferior to his capacity for dishing it out. But he ends on a nice rhetorical flourish. Having dilated at length on Claudius's errors in equating incommensurables, Jonas says that Claudius cannot be equated with any doctors or doctrines of the church but perhaps can be assimilated to the drunken Silenus, and to drive home his point he quotes some lines from Ovid's *Fasti* and Virgil's *Sixth Eclogue*.

The "Preface" to Book Three (363D–366B) is not particularly helpful in summarizing the contents of the book. Jonas here says only that Claudius has wantonly violated the norms of fraternal charity in heaping abuse on Theutmir who only wanted to help. Jonas does repeat one of his central themes, namely that Claudius has offended the traditions, teachings, and institutions of the church. It was to save him from the consequences of those offenses, Jonas says, that Theutmir and other experienced men had attempted to save him. He says that he needs to add a few additional remarks in case Claudius's writings should in the future come into the hands of a simple brother. Book Three does indeed open with some reflections on Theutmir, but then it moves on to the last sections of the *Apology*, the words addressed to penitential pilgrimages to Rome, to relics of the saints, and to Pope Paschal. Book Three has relatively little to say about the image controversy, but it does serve to remind us that for Claudius and his interlocutors, there were several issues in dispute.

Jonas's tactic in opening Book Three with Claudius's attack on Theutmir is effective for Jonas insists that it was in his attack on Theutmir that Claudius revealed himself most clearly as the "enemy and adversary of our holy mother, the catholic church." Jonas has been arguing this point all along. Generally speaking, however, in Books One and Two Jonas rejects Claudius's teachings because they misconstrue the Bible and deviate from age-old traditions. In Book Three, Jonas speaks more particularly about what people were actually doing in his day and how Claudius affronted them.

Jonas begins with a plea on behalf of Theutmir and then cites Claudius: "If you were to say that I prohibit men from going to Rome for the sake of penance, you would speak falsely" (363D). Jonas then goes on to argue that a look at the rest of what Claudius says proves beyond a doubt that Claudius does object to journeys to Rome and that his words to Theutmir were intentionally deceptive. For had not Claudius also said, "For I do not approve that journey"? Had he not gone on to say, "Because I know that it does not injure, profit, harm, or benefit anyone"? "I can hardly imagine," says Jonas, "that I could ever find stupider words than those." Right away we must note that Jonas has here misquoted Claudius, for the bishop of Turin actually said, "I neither approve nor disapprove of that journey." Be that as it may, Jonas's strategy of argumentation on this point is elegant. First he asks Claudius, rhetorically, if there is any point to many of the practices which we employ in this life to tame our temptations. He discusses fasting, chastity, and almsgiving and acknowledges that these can be done with good or bad intent, and that the benefit of such actions comes not from their nature but from their quality. So, he continues, we know of men who have gone humbly to the threshold of the apostles to pray and to beg their intercession. Having thus circled back on his point, Jonas opens another loop. This one passes by the hill on which Abraham prepared to sacrifice Isaac, the Tabernacle where the Hebrews were especially to pray, the Temple built by Solomon, the sites associated with Jesus' life that induced wonder in St. Jerome, the constant desire of the apostles to pray in Jerusalem, and the hope of St. Paul to spend Pentecost there. Having criticized Claudius's "unreasonable reason" Jonas shows by reasonable reason, so to speak, how certain practices are holy and certain places, too (366C–369B).

Jonas then takes up Claudius's taunt to Theutmir about retaining in his monastery, perhaps to their perdition, so many monks whom he does not permit to go to Rome to seek their redemption. Well, says Jonas, everyone who thinks properly knows that there are in the church many orders that differ not by faith but by manner of life: married, celibate, clerics, pilgrims, monks, canons, and so on. Speaking with the voice of Theutmir, Jonas goes on to say that monks have come to "me" properly seeking the life defined by the *Rule* of St. Benedict and that the canons of Chalcedon permit communities of monks to form and subject them to bishops. Certainly, some can come for the wrong reasons, but this does not militate against the legitimacy of monasticism. Monks live a life of penance and renunciation so they need not seek these things outside the monastery. And, in any case, they are not supposed to leave their communities. Claudius is wrong to say that monks have come to "me" for the sake of penance. They have come to serve the Lord and to seek His mercy. They have renounced the world to seek salvation (369C–371D).

The text of *On the Cult of Images* as we have it now seems to have a flaw. Jonas is wrapping up his point about monks serving God and not Theutmir when he shifts abruptly, in mid-sentence, to St. Jerome on relics (specifically from one of Jerome's letters to Vigilantius). The argument as it moves along makes perfect sense, but some transitional words are clearly lacking. After defending the precious relics of the martyrs, Jonas asks if we are sacrilegious when we enter basilicas. Was Constantine sacrilegious when he transferred so many relics to Constantinople? Was Augustus Arcadius sacrilegious in transferring the bones of Samuel to Thrace? Are all bishops sacrilegious for transporting sacred ashes in silk and in golden vessels? Are the people of every church foolish when they go to visit the relics of the saints and perceive with such great joy that the saints are alive and present there? "Listen, I beg you, to the custom and ancient practice of the holy church, and do not cross the boundaries your fathers have set for you . . . because in the veneration of the relics of the saints by the holy church, Christ is adored, who sanctified them and gave them life" (371D–372C). Then he quotes John Chrysostom: "And so most blessed brothers, let us gather today at the places of the saints, let us hasten to the dwellings of the saints, so that our assembly may be rendered more brilliant by their presence." After a slightly ill-fitting passage on the aid borne by angels to the martyrs and to people now, Jonas cites the *Dialogues* of Gregory I on the benefits brought by the bodily remains of the saints. "May all these gags shut your mouth so that it will no longer gnaw on the dignity of the martyrs" (372C–373D). Relics and the places where they reside, in other words, have been honored for ages. Claudius must abandon his opposition. He objects to Claudius's remark that teaching people to go to Rome will give scandal and that the Lord Himself warned against "one who scandalizes one of the least." The objection is built by a grammatical argument as well as by another citation of John Chrysostom, this time to the effect that all Christians will help people who wish to visit the relics of the saints even those who are unable to do so, perhaps because of physical infirmity. Jonas concludes by saying that preventing people from taking the path of salvation is the greatest scandal (373D–375B). The vehemence of this denunciation is a rather odd reaction to Claudius's oblique reference to relics in the *Apology* and perhaps related to Jonas's earlier remark that he had heard that Claudius taught against the relics of the saints.

The next few columns provide some sense of how Jonas's argument was actually built up—assuming, again, that there is a flaw in the text. Jonas refers to Claudius's argument that those who take Matthew 16.16–18 as a command to go to Rome are failing to read the Gospel spiritually. Jonas's response is at first oblique. He says that from the beginning of the church there have been people not distinguished for their learning who were content in their simplicity. Enemies of the church have always derided their simplicity and now you, Claudius, also an enemy of the relics of the apostles, try to divert the souls of these simple ones and extinguish the fire of their love for the apostles. It is perfectly true, Jonas says, that the intercession of Peter, or of any other saint, is not confined to a particular place, but we know, and the fathers have always taught, that places associated with the saints are especially holy. Then Jonas answers Claudius's charge that the "power of the keys" given to Peter has no relevance to a specific place, that is, does not require visits to Rome. Next Jonas goes back to the kind of argument he had earlier made about the bodies of the saints and says that Peter's happens to be in Rome (375B–377B). The logic of the overall argument is clear: tradition holds that the relics of saints are holy; that the places where those relics are to be found are holy; that saintly intercession is possible anywhere but especially to be found and invoked where the saint's relics are located. Finally, this teaching has always been a special comfort to the "simple."

Then Jonas understands Claudius to say that the power of binding and loosing was handed to Peter and to all the apostles and that, because he does not see Peter sitting on the apostolic throne, then it must be believed that the power is held jointly by all bishops now alive; or in other words, the dead can no longer intercede. This charge sends Jonas off on a somewhat meandering disquisition, buttressed by patristic and biblical citations, designed to prove that the church has always embraced the remains of the holy dead and that the just among the priestly dead not only can and do intercede for the living but also retain something of the authority which they possessed while alive. Jonas agrees with Claudius that one can only please God by having the same "faith, justice, and truth" which the saints possessed, but he cannot see how this supports a denial of intercession (377B–385A). Jonas is obviously defending Rome and St. Peter, but he clearly has in view the larger project of defending relics, saints, intercession, and ecclesiastical traditions. These passages from Book Three reveal further areas of agreement and disagreement between Claudius and Jonas. Both agree that, ontologically speaking, images are nothing at all and worthy of no tokens of respect in connection with their material being. Jonas will, but Claudius will not, accord images a certain utility; they commemorate and decorate. Moreover, Jonas implies several times that this utility may pertain especially to the simple, people whom Claudius seems to dismiss as rustic if not downright heretical. But Jonas accords great significance to the physical remains of the saints and he thinks that Claudius denies this which the bishop of Turin, with his starkly spiritualized faith, may well have done.

The very last section of Book Three, which addresses Claudius's reservations about the authority of the Roman See, must be incomplete in several respects. Jonas begins with Claudius's remark to Theutmir that Pope Paschal is angry with him. Jonas then takes up Claudius' assertion that "One is called apostolic as if the guardian of the apostle" (*Apostolicus autem dicitur quasi apostoli custos*).[32] Jonas rightly says that this phrase makes no sense, but one can hardly believe that this is exactly what Claudius wrote. A bit further on Claudius has said that "[s]urely he is not to be called apostolic who sits on the chair of the apostle, but the one who fulfills the apostolic office." Jonas agrees that this is true but says, basing himself on Gregory, that Claudius ought to observe due prudence and humility in attacking his superiors (385A–386D). It seems that what Claudius was trying to argue is that the pope had departed from apostolic traditions in censuring him and, accordingly, his strictures had no force. Paschal translated a huge number of relics from cemeteries outside Rome to churches in the city.[33]

Perhaps Claudius objected to this action on Paschal's part and prompted some criticism from the pope which escalated into a challenge of papal authority. Jonas was unwilling to agree with Claudius, but he declined to offer a ringing endorsement of either Paschal I or of the papal office itself. Claudius and Jonas both had reservations about papal authority.

Let me sum up provisionally. Jonas's positions are traditional. No material thing is worshiped as God is worshiped. Images are useful for decoration and commemoration. The cross is holy because of its concrete association with Christ's death upon it. Still, the cross is owed a form of cult below that paid to God. It is crucial to read the Bible correctly. Specifically, the Bible must be read in light of the church fathers. Ecclesiastical traditions must be embraced and handed on. It is interesting that a book entitled *On the Cult of Images* devotes so little space to the topic of images.

Dungal of Pavia: Responses against Claudius

Dungal is a mysterious figure.[34] It is always assumed that he was a native Irishman who wound up on the continent in the time of Charlemagne. He was a monk at St.-Denis and may have known Alcuin.[35] He has long been confused with other Irishmen who were his contemporaries and he can be securely identified only with the person whom Charlemagne consulted in the last years of his reign on eclipses and on Fridugisus's treatise *On Nothing and Darkness.*[36] He once wrote to Charlemagne's daughter Theodrada.[37] In addition to a handful of letters, a small amount of his poetry survives. It is not very good. His learning was broad but not exceptional. It is not clear why he was selected to head the school at Pavia although once that choice had been made, he was an obvious person to respond to Claudius.

Dungal's *Responses* are about 20 percent shorter than Jonas's *On the Cult of Images.* Dungal's book has a general "Prologue" and then launches into a single block of text—no divisions into books or chapters (although Paolo Zanna has introduced chapter divisions in his new edition). A distinctive feature of Dungal's book is its lengthy quotations from the Christian poets Paulinus of Nola and (Venantius) Fortunatus; these quotations comprise more than a quarter of the whole book. Like Jonas, Dungal focuses on worship, the cross, and Roman issues, and he also devotes considerable attention to saints and relics. Again very much like Jonas, Dungal builds up his argument on the basis of biblical and patristic references. He has many of the same references that Jonas does, but also a few of his own.[38] As far as style is concerned, Dungal is firm but he ranges between serenity and exasperation. Dungal is more explicit than Jonas on the didactic function of images and he is more positive than Jonas about the capacity of material things to communicate spiritual realities and truths. In general, his line of argument is very much like Jonas's. Nevertheless, Claudio Leonardi argues that alone among the ninth-century commentators on images, Dungal achieved a work of "authentic spirituality" and that he was "certainly the most elevated spokesman for a western iconophilia."[39]

In his "Prologue" Dungal sketches the situation as he sees it in northern Italy.[40] He says that Claudius and his ilk have attacked the cross and holy pictures, the intercession of the saints, and the holiness of relics. All of this is familiar from both Claudius's *Apology* and Jonas's *On the Cult of Images*. One absence is striking: Dungal does not signal that he will speak of Claudius's criticisms of pilgrimages to Rome or of his troubles with Pope Paschal. He does come to these topics later in the *Responses*, however. Slightly different from Jonas's approach is Dungal's immediate assertion that he has written "under the name and in honor of the most Christian rectors of the holy church, the Lord Louis, great and peaceful emperor, and his most noble son, the Augustus Lothar." A bit later Dungal says, "We ask most beseechingly that our most Christian and religious lords, stirred by zeal for God, deign it fitting to run to the aid of their holy mother the church now trembling and shuddering." Perhaps writing for a local Italian audience led Dungal to stress the power and authority, and also religious righteousness, of the rulers. Another remark provides further context for his discussion and differentiates it from Jonas's. He says, "In this area the people are separated and divided into two parts on the matter of ecclesiastical practices, that is on the image of the Lord's passion and the holy picture. Grumbling and arguing the Catholics say that a picture is good and useful, worth almost as much for instruction as sacred letters. The heretic, on the other hand, and the party seduced by him, say 'No, it is all the seduction of evil and idolatry.' "[41] Dungal makes the divisions sound sharp and the discourse acrimonious. This assertion adds weight to Theutmir's charge that Claudius had stirred up sects. Dungal, as the chief teacher in Pavia and a key adviser to Lothar, had to deal with that sectarian strife in a way that Jonas did not.

Dungal opens the *Responses* with a rapid summation of the *Apology* and then settles down to an orderly refutation. His initial gambit is interesting. He says that the whole issue of images was intensely debated at the palace two years earlier where the Scriptures and fathers were so fully and carefully studied that there is no room for further doubts on the subject of painted images. Divine honors are paid to God alone and no one is to destroy images put up for the honor of God. Citing Gregory, Dungal says that images may be useful to the "ignorant" and "those who do not know letters." For 820 years, Dungal says, the basic teachings have been in place so how does one man presume to reject such tradition and blaspheme its founders? Does Claudius think that he alone is wiser than everyone else? Some of the ancient fathers, Dungal insists, wanted pictures not only of the dead saints who live with Christ but even of living holy men. He mentions Severus who put pictures of St. Martin and of Paulinus of Nola in his church. Dungal then cites several selections from the verse of Paulinus to show how pictures can reveal all that is in the Books of Moses and can especially teach the ignorant. As he has cited Paulinus to argue that pictures can inculcate good behavior by imitation, so he continues by referring to Gregory of Nyssa and the emotions evoked by an image. Dungal writes that the Exodus prohibition was written because the Jews were a stiff-necked people who easily lapsed into idolatry. That problem no longer exists so the full force of the prohibition has been relaxed. In fact, God Himself commanded Moses to put cherubim on the Tabernacle and Solomon to put images in the Temple. It is clear, he says, that people who have pictures only for recollecting history to the praise and honor of God are not to be reprehended. In short, before he deals in detail with any one of Claudius's specific arguments, Dungal rejects Claudius's whole case by appealing to authority and tradition. Moreover, Dungal identifies tradition particularly with the use of images for the benefit of the ignorant.[42]

Dungal's distinctive emphases come out again in his next section. He picks up on Claudius's reflections on the various possible meanings of *adorare* and *colere* saying that the bishop of Turin's linguistic skill is defective. He does not understand *adorare* and *colere* to have "precise, distinct meanings" and so he uselessly canvasses all sorts of possible interpretations. Dungal says it would take him too long to discuss all that needs discussing in the heretical book. Then he continues with Claudius's insistence that people who worship images are demon worshipers who have merely changed the names of the objects of their devotions. Dungal claims that this charge is tantamount to reviving the hateful doctrines of Vigilantius and Eunomius[43] and their followers who blasphemed the Catholics, calling them idolaters, worshipers of dead men, and just like the pagans because they venerated the relics of the dead martyrs who had suffered for Christ. Claudius had not mentioned relics but Dungal joins images, saints, and relics into one issue. Then he says, "We on the other hand respond that we do not adore the painted images (*imagines*) of the saints on the walls, nor their bodies laid in tombs, as if they were God, nor do we make sacrifices to them, which would be abominable, as is written . . . but we only venerate in God those whose likenesses (*effigies*) or bodies they are, asking through their intercession that divine help be made present to us."[44] Dungal associates images more closely with relics than Jonas, or anyone else, does and his words hint that the same kinds of veneration that may be paid to relics may also be paid to images. So important are relics to Dungal that he goes on for pages defending the holiness of relics, citing church fathers who defended them, describing miracles associated with them, and insisting that rulers, churchmen, and the people of God have not for centuries behaved stupidly and sacrilegiously in honoring relics.[45] Clearly, Dungal does not say that the adoration due to God alone may be paid to images or relics. But whereas Carolingian authors had normally restricted veneration—no matter what word they used, their meaning is always clear—to the cross, relics, and *res sacratae*, for instance liturgical vessels, Dungal stepped over a line and permitted veneration to pictures albeit only in respect of the God whom the persons depicted had served. Later he makes this point more explicitly.

After a fairly abrupt transition Dungal turns to Claudius's argument that venerators of the cross practice superstition and false religion and, what is worse, bring Christ's passion into disdain and his death into ridicule. Claudius tried to support his contention by citing 2 Corinthians 5.16 but Dungal, quoting Augustine, says that Claudius simply does not know how to read the Scriptures. It is perfectly true that Christ was and is worshiped carnally, because He lived as a Man among men and He appeared with flesh and bones [*sic*] after His resurrection. Claudius, in other words, does not understand the incarnation. Moreover, he fails to acknowledge that the Lord Himself did not tell His followers to conceal information about His death. In increasingly agitated tones Dungal cites biblical and patristic passages to show that the worship of the cross is both traditional and laudable and, almost predictably, he comes back to the words *adoro* and *colo* to argue that Claudius mindlessly thinks that they can be applied to God alone, or believes that if someone applies them to anyone or anything else, then he is superstitious and an idolater.[46] He goes on: "we believe with all our heart, and stretched out humbly in body and soul we confess that God alone must be adored and cherished as the Lord and creator of everything ought to be adored and cherished by His creation. . . . We also adore and cherish God's good and holy creation, that is we humbly honor, love, and embrace a holy angel, or a holy man, or the holy cross, according to their varying degrees of worthiness, and we do so on account of God, and in God, and not at all as we adore and cherish Him."[47] Dungal carries on at some length citing biblical passages in which one person reverences, bows before, "worships," or "adores" another (cc. 86–92). He then cites Jerome on the twofold sense of *adorare* in Scripture: worship, as for God, and honor, as for other worthies (c. 93). The next eight chapters cite biblical and patristic passages illustrating this double meaning. The grammarian Priscian is cited (c. 102) on the meanings of *colo*—to worship, to inhabit, to till—and then Dungal adds his own gloss (c. 104). Nine chapters (105–13), all drawn from poets, illustrate the meanings of these words.

Having warmed to the task of criticizing Claudius's faulty verbal skills, Dungal permitted himself a parting shot: "Just as he went wrong with those words, whence, it seems to me, the very rise of his perversity, so too his imperfect knowledge was already deceived, albeit to lesser danger, by this word: *apostolicus*." Claudius thinks that this word derives from *apostoli custos* which in light of the whole grammatical tradition is nonsense. *Apostolicus* comes from *apostolus* (c. 114).

With some pretty images of sailing and traveling (c. 115), Dungal leaves these grammar lessons behind and reiterates his main point: "No one is able to cross the sea of this life unless he is borne by the cross of Christ." This brings Dungal back to his ongoing consideration of the cross (cc. 116–69). He enumerates the Old Testament passages where the cross is foreshadowed. He discusses the cross in the New Testament, especially in Paul. He selects patristic passages on the cross. He mentions the sign of the cross. Dungal talks of actual crosses, of relics of the true cross, and of mental images of the cross. At one point he says that the cross should be "venerated and cherished" along with the relics of the saints, making again the association that we have already noted.

"With the support and intervention of the blessed prince of the apostles, whose case we have decided to take up right now, we come to the third question. Of the three principal issues which the impudent calumniator argued in his letter, the first concerns breaking and throwing out images; the second pertains to honoring the cross no more than an ass or a thorn; the last, that is the third, prohibits traveling to the memorials of the saints and especially to the church of St. Peter for the sake of praying, saying that this work is empty and useless, without any benefit, and calling those who are seized with a desire to do this blind, foolish, and stupid. He affirms that the bones of any holy man whatsoever are like the bones of cattle, or actually like wood or stones or any other earthly thing you can imagine that is worthy of no more reverence" (c. 170). These lines make a fine provisional summation of Dungal's whole book while also introducing his third major section.

Already in chapter 169 Dungal announced his intention to defend St. Peter against Claudius's attack. In fact, his defense is a meandering one. Dungal first addresses relics (c. 171), shrines (cc. 173), and pilgrimages (cc. 177–78) because, he says, Claudius rejects each. A series of chapters, culminating in a list of miracles (cc. 188–89), clinch his case that the saints are very much alive and well in their remains and in their shrines, and that they continue to intercede for the living. This line of argument finally brings him back to Peter and permits him to rebut Claudius's argument that Peter is no longer involved in the church and that there is no reason to visit his remains in Rome. Several chapters then sum up Dungal's thinking on Peter, the Petrine office, episcopal power generally, and the structure of the church. Dungal then cites poems of Paulinus (cc. 204–17), Prudentius (cc. 220–29), and Venantius Fortunatus on saints, martyrs, relics, shrines, and intercession. It appears that Dungal was particularly stung by what he took to be Claudius's rejection of the familiar features of the cult of the saints. Given that Dungal is more systematic and detailed on saints, relics, cults, and shrines than either Jonas or the fragmentary *Apology*, I wonder if, as a teacher in Pavia, he had more detailed knowledge of Claudius's actual teaching than anyone else.

Yet Dungal was not merely defending traditional practices because they were old and established. He was advancing, against Claudius as he believed, a particular vision of the church: "This church knows that it has two lives divinely spelled out and commended to it; of these, one is in faith and the other in visible shape; one is in the time of pilgrimage, the other is in the eternal mansion; one is in work, the other is in rest, one is on the way, the other is home; one is the fruit of effort, the other is the reward of contemplation" (c. 195). The church is both of this world and not of this world. It is the Body of Christ. Christ gave the power of binding and loosing to Peter and the apostles on behalf of the church. That power persists and as Peter possessed primacy, Peter's successors are to be accorded respect and submission. Claudius is a marvelous new philosopher, wiser than all the teachers of the church in all past time. For he has lacerated the body of Christ by cutting away belief in the intercession of the saints, visits to the *loca* of the saints, hymns and prayers to the martyrs, and the veneration and devotion customarily shown to the saints. Dungal understands Claudius to believe in a heavenly church that is distinct from the one presently visible on the earth. Claudius's heavenly church has no interest in or power over the earthly one. For Dungal, on the contrary, the church is one mystical Body of Christ that exists through time and that joins heaven and earth. Just as Peter was assigned the power of acting and John rested on the breast of the Lord, so too now there are various tasks and responsibilities. But, to sum up, Dungal takes this circuitous route through ecclesiology to defend saintly intercession in general and Peter's intercession in particular.

Near the end of the treatise, Dungal makes explicit his views on the veneration of images: "from everything that has been pulled together above it is most certain and evident that the holy (*sanctam*) picture, the (*sanctam*) holy cross of the Lord, and the sacred (*sacras*) relics of God's elect ought to be venerated (*venerari*) with worthy and fitting honors (*congruis honoribus*) by Catholic and right-believing people in God and on account of God" (c. 240). He adds the necessary caution that honor and cult paid to God alone may not be paid to these other things. To the best of my knowledge, no one in the time of Charlemagne had ever said any such thing.

In his last substantive remarks Dungal asks how Claudius can perform his ecclesiastical duties if he refuses to make the sign of the cross or if he does not believe in the intercession of the saints. Must he not make the sign of the cross in baptism, in conferring chrism, in blessing, in consecrating, in celebrating the mass? Can he omit litanies, or refuse to commemorate the anniversaries of the saints? At the very end, then, Dungal makes a point similar to Jonas's: Claudius has in effect betrayed his priestly office (cc. 242–45).

Let me briefly review what we can learn from Dungal. First, he was in Italy and he said that he had been hearing about Claudius's mischief for some time before he felt empowered to do anything about it. This may mean that Dungal's *Responses* answer not only the *Apology* but also the situation on the ground. He says that Claudius denied and destroyed images but devotes almost no attention to this subject in his *Responses*, or, to put this a little differently, he implies that the image to which Claudius particularly objected was the cross, probably a crucifix but perhaps also painted images on walls. Dungal defends images primarily on grounds of tradition but he also offers the old didactic defense. Dungal again and again defends the intercession of the saints and the holiness of their relics. Just to read the *Responses* is to imagine that Claudius's major preoccupations were saints and relics, not images. Dungal, like Jonas, objected mightily to Claudius's belief that an image of the passion mocked Christ's death and downplayed His resurrection. Like so many authors we have encountered, Dungal appreciates the difficulty of finding unambiguous language to talk about worship. He understands perfectly well, and acknowledges that, generally speaking, Claudius understands too the crucial difference between the worship that is due to God and all other forms of worship. But more than other writers in the Carolingian world, Dungal assigns a kind of worship, or veneration, to material things such as the cross, relics, and images. His words are not as clear as one might wish. Images and the cross are undoubtedly venerable but several times he includes images in a phrase or sentence enumerating those things that may be venerated. In doing so he not only assigns a form of worship to images, but he also equates that form of worship with the cult that is owed to relics and, thereby, invests pictures with a kind of ontological holiness. When those images are of the cross, or are of that particular form, the crucifix, then Dungal's words seem clear, even though he does not elaborate his point. When the image is of the "deeds of the saints" it is much harder to say exactly what Dungal had in mind.

Rippling Discussions: Agobard, Einhard, and Walahfrid

Like a pebble dropped into the Carolingian pond, the image issue kept on rippling from the 820s into the 830s. We have already seen that *l'affaire Claudius* had little demonstrable connection with the letter of Emperor Michael II and the Paris Colloquy. Jonas, we have noted, took up his pen twice, once in about 827 and then again in, probably, 840. Shortly—it seems—after the Paris deliberations Archbishop Agobard of Lyon weighed in on his own with a short treatise *On Pictures and Images*. In the 830s Einhard rose in defence of the holy cross, ostensibly in response to a query by Lupus of Ferrières but quite likely because that controverted subject had often been ventilated in recent years. Likewise in the 830s, the impressively well-connected Walahfrid Strabo included a brief history of the Carolingian image quarrel in his *On the Origins and Developments of Some Aspects of the Liturgy*. Celia Chazelle's work suggests that the cult of the cross continued to prompt some visual duels for another few decades.[48] In Rome, the popes brought up the image question a few times in correspondence with the Byzantine court but they did so in ways suggesting that the issue was spent.

Agobard of Lyons

Abobard (769–840) was yet another of the Goths who have attracted our attention.[49] He seems to have entered the Frankish world in 782 and to have arrived in Lyon by 792. He fell under the influence of Archbishop Leidrad (797/8–816). Ordained a priest in 804, he became chorbishop in 813 and succeeded Leidrad as archbishop in 816. Prolific and querulous, Agobard insinuated himself into most of the great issues of the early ninth century. He opposed Louis the Pious in the insurrections of the 830s and was deposed in 835 only to be reinstated two years later.

The little treatise *On Pictures and Images* is somewhat difficult to interpret.[50] Since there is no evidence that Agobard was among those invited to participate in the Parisian deliberations of 825, it is not easy to say why or when he wrote it. The text has no preface and simply begins "The first precept of the Decalogue is, with God himself speaking, 'I am the Lord your God who led you out of the land of Egypt, etc.'" The text is about thirty pages long (in octavo), considerably shorter than those of Jonas and Dungal, and, presumably, than Claudius's original work. About thee-quarters of *On Pictures and Images* consists of patristic references; indeed, the work looks like a lightly commented florilegium of image texts. Agobard has many of the same texts that the Paris bishops used, and that appeared in the writings of his contemporaries. These overlaps may be attributed to a common intellectual patrimony, but the fact that he cites Hadrian's letter to Irene and Constantine and his *Responsum* suggests that he may well have been in possession of some or all of the Paris dossier. It is possible that he was there and that he wrote his little book as a sort of minority report. It is also possible that he learned of the decisions taken at Paris and spoke on his own, believing that the Paris fathers had indulged in ambiguity and compromise. There are two places in *On Pictures and Images* where Agobard almost certainly quotes Claudius[51] so he may have had either the whole Claudian treatise—when Theutmir sent it to the court it would very likely have gone up the Rhone and right through Lyon—or else the excerpt. It is also possible that Agobard and Claudius knew each other in Lyon before about 816.

For whom did Agobard write? I cannot say. Perhaps the best way to search for a context is to connect *On Pictures and Images* with the Paris Colloquy and the affair of Claudius, on the one hand, and with some of Agobard's other writings, on the other. Agobard wrote scathingly about the Jewish community in Lyon.[52] We have seen that anti-Jewish sentiment often accompanied real or constructed image controversies. There is nothing in Agobard's *Against the Jews* which specifically addresses image-related issues—for instance, charges of idolatry or Claudius's complaint that crucifixes bring the crucifixion into ridicule—so one can only appeal to a generalized context. Agobard also wrote a tough little book against practitioners of weather magic in his own diocese.[53] He knew the dangers of superstition firsthand. What is most significant for our purposes about Agobard's *On Pictures and Images* is that it shows one more variation on the basic Carolingian themes and thereby reveals the subtlety and variety of Carolingian thought.

Agobard, as noted, begins with the Exodus prohibition; he quotes Exodus 20.2–5. He then cites Augustine—although Van Acker, Agobard's most recent editor, cannot find the passage—to explain exactly how the words of Exodus are to be understood: "The first precept prohibits any image of God in human contrivances, not because God has no image, but because no image of him ought to be cherished" (c. 1). The next few chapters develop this theme in several ways. Agobard say that Moses did not see an image of God on Horeb. He also says that if the works of God are not to be adored, then certainly the works of men may not be. At this point, Agobard discusses the lengthy sections of *The City of God* (10.1, 3) dealing with the various words for worship. Like Augustine, Agobard insists that even if language is imprecise the fundamental point is clear: only God is to be worshiped. Agobard then argues that sacrifices are offered only to God, not to holy men or angels. God wishes no creature at all to be worshiped. Agobard seems almost to anticipate a query here for he cites one of Jerome's letters to Vigilantius so that he can use the father's words to say that we do not "worship and venerate" (*colimus et veneramur*) the relics of the martyrs, nor the sun and the moon, nor angels and archangels, nor seraphim and cherubim. "We honor (*honoramus*) the relics of the martyrs so that we might adore (*adoremus*) Him whose martyrs they are; we honor (*honoramus*) the servants so that the honors (*honores*) of the servants might redound to the Lord who said 'Whoever receives you, receives Me.'" He quotes Augustine to argue that we do not despise the bodies of the just dead for the Holy Spirit uses them to effect good works. But we do not build temples to them, dedicate priesthoods to them, nor offer sacrifices to them "since not they, but their God, is our God." He then cites various biblical passages to show how memorials—say, Jacob's pillow-stone—were not idolatrous. Concluding his first section, Agobard says, "Therefore it is God alone, as we have shown abundantly above, in whom we ought to place the hope of our blessedness" (cc. 1–12).

Virtually all of this is familiar to us. Agobard's argumentation is at heart affirmative: Worship God alone. He devotes little time to saying what ought not to be worshiped. In one sense, however, Agobard is rather sharper than his contemporaries. Like them, he acknowledges the problems occasioned by the vocabulary of worship. Like them, too, he insists that God alone is to be worshiped. But whereas others deal with relics, the cross, perhaps even images, by means of the same language which they apply to God, Agobard uses *honor* and *honorare* for the saints and their relics and reserves *adorare*, *colere*, and *venerare* for God. Claudius would have liked the way Agobard opened *On Pictures and Images* but would have parted company as soon as Agobard got to relics. Jonas and Dungal would have seen nothing to concern them in the first twelve chapters of *On Pictures and Images* but I do wonder how they would have reacted to Agobard's meticulous attention to language.

He opens chapter 13 with a quotation from *The City of God* (12.1) where Augustine is saying that only a rational creature can be made happy and that happiness is confined to those who cleave to God. God must be understood to be eternal, unchangeable, and invisible. These divine qualities pose acute problems for human understanding because the human mind grasps things in terms of lines, shapes, colors, sizes, distances, distinctions, intervals, and suchlike properties (c. 14). So, Agobard/Augustine urges, "let us understand God, if we can, as far as we can, as great, but without quantity, as Creator, but without need of anything, as present, but without location, as containing everything, but without a body, as present everywhere, but having no specific location, as eternal, but without time, making changes, but without any change to Himself, and feeling nothing." The next chapter (15) shows us where Agobard is going with this argument. "Just as visible things are harmful to the comprehension of invisible things, so too the love of corporal things, even good ones, is damaging to the contemplation of spiritual things." This sentence is immediately followed by a quotation of John 16.7, "I tell you the plain truth. It is better for you that I go. If I fail to go, the paraclete will not come to you. If however I depart, I will send him to you." Then we find the words of Augustine explaining that had Jesus remained behind, His disciples would only have known Him *carnaliter* whereas it was important for them to begin to know Him *spiritualiter*. Speaking in his own voice, Agobard says a person knows that for a faithful man to benefit himself he must be drawn from the exterior to the interior and not, to his detriment, be driven from the interior to the exterior. "He ought to pass over from the flesh to the spirit, from the body to the soul, from the visible to the invisible, from the world to God." It is even worse than this when foolish people make images and call them holy and pay to the work of their own hand the cult that is due to God, and suppose that sanctification might come from such images. Agobard does not, like Claudius, cite 2 Corinthians 5.16 but he is making the same basic point: Worship is to be in spirit and in truth. Material things cannot be worshiped and, as he repeats several times, no intercession can come through or as a result of material things.

Just as no divine honors are to be offered to likenesses, so too "it is reprehensible to honor the tombs of the saints ostentatiously for the purpose of winning popular acclaim" (17). This remark opens a discussion of the saints which is going to lead to a rejection of their images. Agobard quotes Matthew (23.29–30), "Woe to you, Scribes and Pharisees, you frauds! You erect tombs for the prophets and decorate the monuments of the saints." He then cites Jerome's commentary on this passage and begins the next chapter (18) by saying that one man's testimony should not be spurned for the whole church agrees on this point. To clinch his case he cites, from Eusebius/Rufinus, the case of the martyrdom of Polycarp. Agobard says that this is how the church speaks to Catholics concerning the passion of blessed Polycarp and the veneration (*veneratione*) of the saints. The story is that Polycarp's disciples wanted to take his body away. The officials persuaded the governor to refuse to release Polycarp's body for fear that the Christians would abandon Christ and start to worship (*colere*) Polycarp instead. His disciples, in Eusebius's telling, insisted that they could never abandon Christ, nor worship (*colere*) anyone else. The martyrs, they said, "we love (*diligamus*) and venerate (*veneremur*) as disciples of the Lord." Finally the centurion permitted them to take the body away and they buried it fittingly and later gathered there to reflect upon the example of the martyr. Agobard uses this anecdote to strengthen his contention that, even where the holiest and most famous of martyrs are concerned, they are not paid the cult that is due to God alone. Martyrs may well be due a form of "veneration," a word he earlier restricted to God alone. But here, *colere* is the word that is reserved for the deity. This chapter begins with Agobard saying that the tombs of saints ought not to be ostentatious. The previous chapters had been making points about spiritual worship. Chapter 18, after detouring through Eusebius to validate special affection for the martyrs, concludes by quoting Wisdom 15.4–6: "For neither did the evil creation of men's fancy deceive us, nor the fruitless labor of painters, a form smeared with various colors, the sight of which arouses yearning in the senseless man, till he longs for the inanimate form of a dead image."

On Pictures and Images finally comes directly to the subject of images, first by introducing the cross (19). Agobard almost certainly quotes Claudius when he says "Perhaps someone might say that he does not attribute anything divine to the image which he adores (*adorat*), bur endows it with such veneration (*veneratione*) in honor of him whose likeness it is." Agobard says that this is easy to answer: "If the image which he adores (*adorat*) is not God, then it ought not to be venerated at all (*veneranda*) as if in honor of the saints who never claimed divine honors for themselves." This again is an old argument. It is important to emphasize, however, that Agobard introduces this argument by quoting Claudius but immediately distances himself from the bishop of Turin. Agobard continues by citing Eusebius/Rufinus again, this time the story of the zealous new Christians of Alexandria who demolished idols and then painted crosses on their doorposts, entryways, windows, walls, and columns. "O, What untainted religion! Let the banner of the cross be painted everywhere, not the likeness of some human countenance. God brought this about miraculously, even if perhaps they didn't know it." Following this remark, we read another paraphrase of Claudius to the effect that if they—the newly converted Alexandrites—had put up images of the saints they, who had just abandoned the cult of demons, would think that they had not so much left behind their idols as changed their names. Obviously Agobard and Claudius disagree on the cross, but otherwise it appears that they concur in rejecting images of the saints.

Not so. Agobard now says that images of the apostles and of the Lord Himself were put up by the ancients "on account of love and even more for recollection, but not for any honor of religion or any veneration after the fashion of the gentiles" (20). Eusebius again provides a tale to carry the point: the statue at Paneas of the woman with the issue of blood. Eusebius adds that he himself had seen the statue and that it was one with others made by the gentiles to show their appreciation. So too, therefore, there were images of Jesus, as well as of Peter and Paul. Agobard now turns to Bede (21) and quotes the passages from *On the Temple* which says that if people wish to argue that God forbade images, then how are we to explain the work of Solomon in the Temple, or the brazen serpent, or images in the Scriptures? He carries on with this long passage to the point where Bede says that it is not forbidden to make images but only to worship them, and that the strict biblical prohibitions were uttered because of the grave danger of gentile-style idolatry. Agobard restricts Bede's meaning to the world of the Old Testament: That was then, this is now. Next Agobard tells the story of Sylvester, Constantine, and the images of Peter and Paul (22). This story was told many times in antiquity to validate images. It was repeated at II Nicaea and in Paris. Agobard quotes it just to make this point: Poor Constantine had just come over from paganism and he did not know any better than to recognize the apostles and to adore (*adorare, adorasse*) their images. Remember: Through the last several chapters Agobard has been warning his readers of what is done by the gentiles or in the gentile fashion. Agobard then cites several other well-known stories concerning church fathers who took a dim view of images. Augustine testifies that Christ and his apostles are to be sought in books not in pictures where there is no danger of error, as there is for example in looking at a picture of Jesus, Peter, and Paul, when the three were not contemporary (23). Another passage from *The City of God* is quoted to prove that even the pagans had serious doubts about images and believed it possible to worship without them (24). Some lines from Augustine's *On True Religion* demonstrate the dangers of worship that focuses on the visible and material, the arbitrary and false (25). Augustine, Jerome, and Pope Leo I are quoted to provide evidence for the dangers of bringing into Christianity rites and practices like those of the pagans (26, 27). This leads to a conclusion: If the works of God are not to be adored and worshiped (*adoranda et colenda*) then how much less are the works of man to be worshiped? God made man in His own image and likeness but man cannot make any likeness in which there is an image of the human mind and reason. Quoting or paraphrasing Claudius again, Agobard says that if men had to be adored (*adorandi fuissent*), then surely it would be living and not painted ones. But the point is that only God is to be worshiped (28). The last note sounded here draws attention to the miracles of the martyrs and says that they did nothing on their own; that God worked through them.

I can now sum up *On Pictures and Images* and simultaneously fold in some points from the book's last few chapters. God once forbade images but that was long ago and because of the tendency of the fickle Jews to fall into gentile-style idolatry. God also commanded certain images to be made. What He forbade, absolutely, was that any created thing be worshiped. This has been the universal tradition of the church. It is true that some people have worshiped images, but this has happened when people have recently come over from paganism and/or when they just cannot worship without the support of the visible and the material. Authentic worship must be directed to the invisible and the immaterial. Agobard acknowledges that in olden times images were made for history, for recollection (cc. 20, 22, 32). He does not say that this is still true. And, unlike many of his contemporaries, he never adds a word meaning "decoration." Beauty is simply not an issue for Agobard. Art is not transporting. It does not evoke tears of sorrow or of joy. It is really a matter of indifference, provided of course that it is not idolatrously worshiped.

Should art be destroyed? Agobard is no iconoclast, at least not explicitly. On only one occasion does he give us a hint of his feelings about existing art. He cites Gregory's first letter to Serenus, although he calls him the bishop of Friuli, and says that Gregory told him not to destroy the pictures in his basilica and in fact to leave them for the memory of posterity (22). Was this his view in general? It is hard to say. On one occasion he speaks of images as functioning "in the place of words" to show Catholics victorious in their faith and heretics vanquished after the manner of ancient depictions of civil and foreign wars (32). Does this mean that he endorsed the "didactic" argument? I am not sure. If he did so, he did it once, indirectly, and not in connection with Gregory I. Near the end of *On Pictures and Images* Agobard cites the Elviran canon. He is the only author to do so. If this is to be taken as an indication of his definitive views, then one can only conclude that Agobard, unwilling as he was to endorse the destruction of art, would have preferred that it not exist. Since it did exist, it was not to be worshiped, in any way whatsoever. He said, one senses with an air of resignation, "Let pictures be treated as pictures." He meant that, ontologically speaking, pictures lacked life, reason, feeling. They were not, could not be, holy. Agobard took a spiritual view of worship that was less rigorous than Claudius's but stricter than Theodulf's or Jonas's and, especially, Dungal's. Near the very end of *On Pictures and Images* Agobard says, "For God cried out 'I shall not give my glory to another nor my praise to idols' (Isaiah 42. 8) and the apostle [Paul] said of our Lord and the mediator between God and men 'Because of this God exalted Him above and bestowed on Him the name above every other name' and what this name actually is he went on to say 'That in the name of

Jesus every knee must bend in the heavens, on the earth, and under the earth, and every tongue must confess, to the glory of God the father, that Jesus Christ is Lord.' No holy angel, no holy man, may usurp for himself this name, which is above every other name, or this power, praise, and dominion" (35). Agobard offers no defense of the cult of saints. He says little about relics. He thinks that putting up crosses is a good thing but does not pursue the point. Nothing material is holy, participates in holiness, communicates holiness. Christians must at all costs avoid gentile customs. There is a certain affection that is due to the martyrs and perhaps to saints generally but no worship at all, of any kind. God alone is owed worship. Agobard is a rigorist, an absolutist, an idealist. He also, like almost everyone else who participated in the image discussions of the early Middle Ages, claimed that he was a traditionalist. He believed and taught only what the whole church had always taught.

Einhard

Einhard is different in that he seems so very well known.[54] He was born around 770, the eldest child and perhaps only son of a noble, landed family with holdings east of the Rhine near the Main. After a period of schooling at Fulda he entered Charlemagne's court in 791 or 792. He became one of the king's closest friends and confidants and, of course, wrote his biography. He also enjoyed the confidence of Louis the Pious who gave him estates near Michelstadt and Mulinheim (later called Seligenstadt). Einhard founded a monastery at the latter site and spent the last years of his life in genteel retirement as its lay abbot. Highly educated and a prolific author, Einhard is unusual as the only layman who contributed to the image question; indeed, he is one of the few lay intellectuals in the Carolingian period.

He did not write about images in general but instead about the holy cross in particular, and he did so in response to a query by Lupus of Ferrières. Einhard and Lupus had a touching exchange of correspondence in March and April of 836 occasioned by the death of Einhard's beloved wife.[55] Einhard's letter *On the Adoration of the Holy Cross*[56] says, near its beginning, "When I was attempting . . . to satisfy your curiosity, my dearest Lupus, and to solve the problem you put to me about the adoration of the cross, a question far greater and more encompassing arose from that inquiry . . . I refer to the adoration of God and about how one should call upon and beseech him."[57] Lupus's fourth letter, from April of 836, informs us that he had just received Einhard's letter on the cross. Einhard provides us with precious insights into what *one* educated, well-

connected Carolingian layman thought about some of the issues that have engaged us repeatedly. We do not have the letter in which Lupus asked about the
adoration of the cross, and he did not come back to this subject elsewhere in his
extant correspondence. We simply cannot say specifically why Lupus was interested in this question in the mid-830s. And there is no reason to suppose that
Einhard would have addressed the topic on his own initiative. But Chazelle's
recent work does give us the opportunity to say that the topic of the cross and
the theology of Christ's death on the cross were matters of continuing interest
right through this whole period.[58] We noted above that around 840 Jonas of
Orléans believed that Claudius had followers. Given that Jonas and Dungal
directed some of their sharpest criticisms against Claudius's allegedly wayward
understanding of the cross, it is conceivable that Lupus and Einhard had some
familiarity with the controversy on the topic.

Einhard begins with prayer. He reviews scriptural and conciliar sources to
say that, as far as he can see, prayer is to be addressed to the Father alone.
Moreover, prayers must be in the correct form and must ask for approved things,
the things spelled out in the petitions of the *Pater Noster*. Addressing the wrong
person in the wrong way for the wrong reasons will result in a prayer's not being
answered. Einhard goes on to muse over "the apostles, martyrs, and other spirits
who are with God." He says "I recall hearing it said that there are some people
. . . who think that benefit may come from praying to the saints and that the
saints themselves may even be the beneficiaries of prayers." We know that Einhard was an eager collector of relics, so we ought not to take his musings here
as tokens of skepticism about the saints and the power of their intercession.
Einhard is no Claudius. But he may just be telling us something about the
apprehensions, the uncertainties of an ordinary person in the Carolingian world.
How are we supposed to pray and how do the saints figure in this activity?

In returning to Lupus's "little question" (*rogationculę tuae*) Einhard says,
"It seems to me that the cross ought to be adored . . . and I think I can explain
this more easily if I am able to explain the difference and distinction, as I see it,
between praying and adoring" (147–48/173). "To pray, in my opinion, is to
beseech in mind or voice, or at the same time in mind and voice, without a
gesture of the body." "To adore" (*adorare*), on the other hand, "is to show
veneration (*venerationem exhibere*) to a visible thing placed before one and [actu-
ally] present either by bowing one's head or by bending or prostrating one's
whole body or by extending one's arms or by spreading one's hands or in any
way whatsoever that constitutes a gesture of the body. For we venerate (*veneramur*) many things to which we cannot and ought not to pray. In Sacred Scripture this veneration (*veneratio*) is normally called adoration (*adoratio*)" (148/173).

Einhard continues with a few concrete examples, for instance "when it says I will adore at your temple [Ps. 137.2] it is as if [Scripture] says 'I bow my head or I kneel before your temple.' This adoration signifies only veneration." Furthermore, when Nathan and Bathsheba adored David they did not beseech him as God but venerated him as a man worthy of honor. Likewise when the sons of the prophets fell to the ground to adore Elijah, they did this for the sake of veneration. Einhard says that there are too many examples like this to cite them all and that the key point is that adoration has regularly been put down for veneration. In any case, veneration is "frequently and appropriately shown" to living and sentient beings but also to things "lacking all life" such as churches, tombs, or relics. Einhard expresses puzzlement over the passage in John (4.20–24) where there was a discussion between God and the Samaritan woman about adoration. Einhard does not understand why they did not speak of prayer, "which belongs to God, but concerning adoration, which is shown to a variety of things for the sake of veneration." True adorers, he says, will make their adoration in spirit and in truth, that is without any gesture of the body that belongs to veneration. Again he wonders if here, as elsewhere, adoration has been put down when prayer was meant. But he thinks that John really did understand the difference between prayer, owed only to God, and veneration, owed to many things. He acknowledges, however, that a person might prostrate himself on the ground to pray "at the same time praying in your mind to God and adoring with an action of your body him who is everywhere, as if he were in front of you and present. So it happens that even God may be adored, as if for the sake of veneration, just as other things which we said belong to adoration."

Einhard concludes his reflections on prayer and adoration with a remark that echoes the passage from Book 10 of *The City of God* that we have seen other authors cite and discuss. He says that the Greeks draw a distinction between prayer (*proseuchis*) and adoration (*proschineusis*) wherefore "the former refers to the function of the mind and the latter to the body." As an example he adduces Matthew 6.5–7 where Jesus taught the disciples how to pray: the Bible uses the word *proseuchis* but when the evangelist (2.8) speaks of the Magi "adoring" Jesus, the word is *proschineusis,* "which refers solely to adoration and to bodily function."

Having drawn out at some length his views on prayer and adoration, Einhard judges that "it is now evident that the adoration of the holy cross ought not to be spurned" for Jerome tells of Paula prostrated before the cross and adoring as if she saw the Lord still suspended on it. We too ought to do this, he says, to prostrate ourselves before the cross with our mind's eye open "to adore him, who is suspended on the cross." Thus the cross, "which is without doubt holy, will obtain the honor (*honorem*) appropriate to it." In this way God, who made all things holy that are holy, will be "venerably adored" (*venerabiliter adoratur*).

Einhard was learned and widely read. He says that to solve the problem put to him by Lupus he did a lot of research. But he was not an exegete or theologian. He clearly knew something about the issues that were in the air in his time, but he did not have the confidence of the experienced expert. He is puzzled by the ambiguities of language. We have seen that modern scholars have sometimes too quickly differentiated between adoration and veneration as if this distinction were iron-clad and highly revealing of positions in the image quarrels of the early Middle Ages. In fact, as we have also noted repeatedly, early medieval writers understood that there was a distinction but never created a precise, systematic language to express it. There was always a clear sense that one kind of cult was paid to God and another to anyone or anything else to whom or which cult was paid. Einhard understands that distinction clearly, and he is a little distressed that the biblical writers did not understand it as well as he did! As for adoration and veneration, they are related this way: adoration is the disposition of mind and veneration is what one does as a result of that disposition. His contemporaries would for the most part have said that each is a disposition of mind and that a properly disposed mind understands that some things are done with respect to God alone and other things are done with respect to, say, saints or relics, or, in different circumstances, the cross or images. In the best, the tidiest case, the former is adoration and the latter, veneration. But, to repeat, the case was almost never tidy. Einhard says the cross is holy. He does not elaborate. He says that God alone can make things holy but he does not go on to mention holy things. Does he have a view of *res sacratae*, say, of chalices? We do not know. He says Paula prostrated herself before the cross as if she could see Jesus. Is Einhard here referring obliquely to the didactic defence of images? Is he embracing the long tradition that believes that images can evoke emotional responses? We just do not know. But we can certainly detect the pulse of all these issues beating between the lines of Einhard's little text. And we may suppose that barely audible thump, thump, thump occasioned Lupus's query. Einhard puts one more sheet in our dossier labeled "practices." Claudius mentions bowing and prostration, Dungal, kissing, and Einhard adds various hand gestures. Two points before taking our leave of Einhard: he shows us the wise and practical layman trying to grasp deep issues and cutting right to the heart of the matter; he reminds us again that Carolingian thought is at once impressive and frustrating in its diversity.

Walahfrid Strabo

Walahfrid Strabo was born in about 808, received his early education at Reichenau, and then went on, as so many of his contemporaries did, for a period of study (827–29) with Hrabanus Maurus at Fulda.[59] In 829 Louis the Pious summoned Walahfrid to court to serve as tutor to Charles, his youngest son. In 838, as a reward for services rendered, this son of a poor Swabian father was made abbot of the great monastery of Reichenau. His abbacy was not easy. The Reichenau monks resented the rapid promotion of this thirty-year-old *frater* and when Louis died in 840 his son Louis the German advanced into Swabia and drove out his father's appointee. Only in 842 did Walahfrid make his peace with his brother monks and Louis the German. He drowned in the Loire while on a diplomatic mission in 849. His brief life comes to our attention because, during his period of exile, he wrote what Alice Harting-Correa calls "the first handbook of liturgical history." Chapter 8 of that book, *On Pictures and Images*, is a brief history of and commentary upon the image quarrels of the immediate past.[60] Walahfrid was highly intelligent, superbly educated, and well connected. His views are valuable in their own right, coming as they do from a liturgical expert, and also helpful as an indication of how one more member of the elite, this one a monk, thought about and reacted to the image quarrels.

Walahfrid begins thus: "Some things should now be said about the images and pictures which increase the splendour of churches. They should not be worshiped (*colenda est*) in their various forms with a kind of excessive fervour, as some foolish people do, but on the other hand their splendour should not be scorned with a kind of contempt, as some defenders of nothingness think." The *Libellus* is a long, detailed, and carefully structured work. We may confidently assume that what is true of the whole is also true of the parts. Chapter 8 reveals Walahfrid's priorities. Hence, images are beautiful. They make churches more beautiful. Jonas has some of this too, but for the most part the decoration element of the "decoration and commemoration" formula vanished in the ninth century. Walahfrid not only brings it back but puts it in the privileged position. In another fundamental way he adheres to the Carolingian *via media*: Do not worship images and do not suppress them. He continues by citing the Exodus prohibition followed by an unambiguous statement that neither Moses nor Solomon flouted God's word. Moreover, he says that Moses decorated veils and vestments with pictures and that Solomon "adorned nearly the entire fabric of the temple with pictures and carvings." With these words, Walahfrid lends explicit approval to putting images anywhere. He says that Moses and Solomon understood perfectly well, as we still do, that the "cult and honor" (*cultibus et honoribus*) paid to God ought not to be paid (*colenda est*) to things made by human hands—theirs or ours. This is true no matter why an image is made. And why might one make an image? To signify some mystery, to commemorate great deeds, or to evoke in the minds of viewers a love of the persons portrayed "as in the images of the Lord and His saints." So God Himself commanded images to be made and decreed certain uses for them. They cannot, therefore, be wrong in absolute terms. How might an image be wrong? If one worships it. To prevent this, God gave a further commandment: "You shall not bow down before them or worship them" (Exodus 20.5). Walahfrid seems to take the biblical *Non adorabis neque colis ea* exactly as Einhard did. What must be avoided, finally, is superstition which itself is the transfer of spiritual worship to material things.

Walahfrid anticipates another kind of objection, quite possibly one that sounded frequently in his world. Might not someone protest that the sheer beauty of an image would entice the "foolish" (*insipientes*) to worship it? Well, then, would not such a protester be obliged to object to the works of God: Why did He create the splendid heavenly bodies, or beautiful and fragrant plants, if they would lead away the simple to "adore and reverence them with divine honors"?[61] Demons may lead people to venerate (*venerantur*) these images more than is fitting but this is hardly worse than those who scorn all images as idolatrous and "scandalize the simple of heart." Walahfrid here shows an appreciation for the old idea that one must carefully separate creator and creation but that creation is not intrinsically bad. We see, by refutation and not by explication, that iconophobes hew to the Exodus prohibition and accusations of idolatry. There is nothing philosophical or doctrinal in their misgivings. Lastly, the simple return here. And they seem to me to be here in two guises. By the one, they are scandalized, led astray, by the very clergy who ought to know and behave better. We saw that both Jonas and Dungal taxed Claudius with this charge. In the other guise, the simple are those who may be drawn in, helpfully, pastorally, by images. Jonas, it will be recalled, implies that the wise do not need such things as images but that the simple might find them helpful, not to say indispensable.

Now Walahfrid turns to a history of controversies over images. He goes back to the times of Popes Gregory II and III and he makes a few mistakes that need not detain us. We may remark, however, that he mentions how the Roman Synod of 731 rejected heresy and restored images of the saints to their accustomed place. One wishes he had elaborated on that place. Vaulting over a century, he says that the "controversy of the Greeks" came to Francia in the time of Louis the Pious. No Hiereia, no Nicaea, no Theodulf, no Frankfurt, no

Constantinople (815). Louis duly confuted the Greek view "with synodal documents" (*scriptis synodalibus* the only time Paris is called a synod). Meanwhile a certain Claudius tried to renew the controversy but "he was pierced through by the shafts of diverse opponents." He then says, rather unexpectedly, that anyone who dishonors the emperor's image, even on a coin, has committed a grave offense. I think that this must be an oblique reference to Claudius's iconoclasm and an insistence that Claudius's acts directly offended God or the saints. Walahfrid nowhere raises the familiar defense of Christian images based on their similarity to imperial images. The only reason for him to make this cryptic reference to the seriousness of damaging an imperial image would be to warn off those who might deface a Christian image. It is curious that Walahfrid says so little about Claudius and does not seem to have known his *Apology* given that he was at court from 829. Perhaps we have here an indication that Walahfrid was concerned with a general unease about, or controversy over, images that was simmering away. Agobard wrote, unbidden, at a not quite determinable date. Lupus asked Einhard about the cross in 836. Jonas returned to his *On the Cult of Images* in 840 and Walahfrid composed his *Libellus* between 840 and 842. If I may be forgiven a cliché, I think we are viewing the tip of an iceberg.

Walahfrid carries on with a few thoughts that are, to put it charitably, a little disjointed. He remarks that Jeroboam offended God by making calves and that Hezekiah rightly set up the brazen serpent but that the Hebrews, prone to idolatry as they were, worshiped it and it had to be destroyed. One perceives here fragments of several image conversations. God's prohibition of images was not absolute but specific because the stiff-necked Jews were liable to idolatry. Images could be put up for good or bad ends. Destroying a "graven image" was not iconoclasm. It was perfectly acceptable, even laudable. To be sure, Walahfrid does not draw out these points but he cites the very biblical passages that usually nested in those discursive frameworks. He goes on to say that the Christian people have been so willingly drawn into the "interior chambers of spiritual wisdom" that they do not believe that pictures, images, or even holy men, no matter whether living or dead, should be "reverenced with honors or adored."[62] Here we are in the presence of the principled Carolingian indifference to images. He goes on to say that we do not ask of the saints that they provide salvation but only that we ask them to intercede for us with God, who alone can save. So, there is to be no adoration of the images of saints and no inappropriate address to the saints themselves. Saintly intercession is available and valuable. Walahfrid's prose is taut but the context allows us to relax it a bit. He finishes this point by saying that since Christians have a perfect understanding of this point—that we do not worship the saints but rather ask them to carry our petitions to God—it is wrong to refuse "decent and moderate honors" to their images. Yet again, without elaboration, Walahfrid assumes the validity of the old referential argument: acts of reverence performed before an image go to the person represented.

Walahfrid's final substantive point goes to the issue of the utility of images. He says that since we have it quite straight that icons (he says here, once, *iconas*) are not to be "adored or worshiped" (*adorandas nec colendas*), are we led to conclude that pictures (*picturas*) should be despised and destroyed as unnecessary or even harmful? Should we destroy temples because God cannot be confined within walls and roofs made by human hands? If we did so, he says, we would certainly take away everything by means of which the mind of the simple could err, but we would have virtually no way to practice our devotions or to attract the simple and unlettered to the love of unseen things. More than this, pictures are useful in all sorts of ways. A picture is a kind of literature for the illiterate. Constantine recognized the apostles whom he had seen in a dream after he was shown their images. Simple people who cannot be moved by mere words can often be deeply stirred by a painting of the passion of other wonderful events. So images should be "possessed and loved" (*habendae sunt et amandae*) so that their usefulness is not negated by destroying them or by according them superstitious honors. And damaging images bears harm to the person whom the image represents. Here we encounter the didactic argument was well as the confirmatory and evocative ones. His reference to the simple might be a gentle dose of Carolingian elite condescension, or it might have an evangelizing force such as that noticed by Kessler in the Merovingian world. Dishonor to an image carries over to the person represented just as a prayer does. Walahfrid is a bit more explicit about this than his contemporaries usually were. Still, he never crosses the line and suggests that the image itself is holy. Ontologically the image is nothing more than the materials from which it is made. Walahfrid's use of language is as slippery as that of everyone else we have met. He uses, almost interchangeably, *adorare, colere,* and *venerare.* He adds *amare* and makes repeated use of *honorare.* As always, he understands perfectly well what these words mean when applied to God and what they mean, or must not be permitted to mean, when applied to anyone or anything else. Unlike Einhard, he does not seem to see acts of veneration or honor or reverence as adding up to adoration. But his use of adoration just might imply physical acts in Einhard's sense. Even if this is the case, he does not list or describe those acts.

In his brief chapter *On Images and Pictures* Walahfrid Strabo says much and implies even more. In what he says he shows a familiarity with virtually all of the major Western arguments made on behalf of images. In what he implies, he suggests a deeper understanding of a wider array of image arguments. Although in his time the cross seems to have been the contested issue, Walahfrid speaks of pictures. Walahfrid lays out one traditional argument after another, but he does not, and in this he differs sharply from his contemporaries, with the exception of Einhard, set the church fathers to duelling with each other or with the enemies of images. He writes, finally, with a rather authoritative tone. The matter is settled, he seems to say. Here is the official view.

Tradition, Order, and Worship in the Image Texts

In reviewing the *Opus* it was possible to discern three major themes running through Theodulf's great book. It was also possible to detect those same themes in the interests and work of many of the key people around Charlemagne. In the ninth century, the same three themes are in evidence but with differing emphases. The shifts in focus and interests to which I now turn have two explanations. One is broadly contextual and I shall come to that context in the last section of this chapter. The other is a product of the specific problems that arose in the 820s and of the ways in which a variety of writers responded to them. A group of bishops produced a substantial body of material in Paris in late 825. Two writers replied to the perceived errors of Claudius of Turin. Several other writers weighed in on their own on the topic of images. The texts which we have been summarizing and will now interpret were written over about two decades in widely differing circumstances.

Tradition

Theodulf's polemic, or *Staatsschrift*, was in many respects a theology of history. His aim was to make the new Frankish "Israel" the only legitimate heir to biblical, apostolic, papal, and Roman (understood in a distinctive way) traditions. Theodulf's work evinces agitation among the Frankish elite about their own place in the grand sweep of time and tradition. The Carolingians were usurpers, after all, and recent ones at that. They were only recently embarked on ambitious and unprecedented programs of institutional, intellectual, and ecclesiastical reform. They had conquered many of the old seats of empire and had rolled many *gentes* into a single *populus Christianus*. There was an acute need to define their own identity and to situate that identity in space and time.

In the ninth century these anxieties are all but invisible. The *Libellus* contains an implicit argument that the truth will emerge from key sources, "from the testimonies of Holy Scripture and the opinions of the holy fathers."[63] Jonas refers often to "the tradition of the holy fathers" and "ecclesiasical tradition."[64] Dungal insists that in his world tradition has been properly understood because Scripture and the fathers have been thoroughly studied.[65] Jonas three times says that "Gaul and Germany" are without taint of heresy.[66] Agobard, too, claimed that he adhered strictly to tradition.[67] The *Libellus* states that the "line of truth" extends from Dionysius, whom Peter's successor Clement sent to Gaul, right down to the present.[68] Dungal says that the tradition has been in place for 820 years.[69] These remarks are rather anodyne.

And that is the point. There is a serenity, a sense of self-assurance, that pervades the ninth-century texts but that was noticeably absent in the late eighth century. The Paris fathers, like Jonas and Dungal, worked confidently with a huge store of patristic material. Theodulf routinely cited the Bible to build his case and he addressed the fathers only to the extent that he found them cited in the Nicene *acta*. In the ninth century, only Claudius relied primarily on the Bible. His mutilated *Apology* has twenty-five biblical citations as against a mere two patristic passages. It is as if Claudius were conceding that the church's tradition was against him, but saying it was nevertheless wrong. Dungal asked him how he dared to set himself, a lone man, against the whole tradition. Agobard cited the Bible thirty times and patristic texts forty-seven. Although he begins by relativizing the Exodus prohibition, saying that it applied to the stiff-necked Jews and that the Ark and the cherubim prove that God did not always forbid images, Agobard's main biblical strategy is to insist on purely spiritual worship.[70] The Paris bishops inclined sharply to the patristic side. The fathers *were* tradition for them and they display a real confidence in managing their patrimony. Scholars have noticed that in the ninth century Carolingian exegesis moved from direct commentary on the Scriptures to "exegesis of exegesis," that is to commentary on the commentators.[71] If the eighth-century Carolingian writers struggled to lay claim to a tradition, and to find a place for themselves within it, the ninth-century Carolingans reveal themselves as having assimilated that tradition, having made it their own, and being willing to adjudicate among the exponents of that tradition. This knowledge and confidence, taken together, say something important about intellectual life in the time of Louis the Pious. Or, to put it a little differently, as the "Carolingian Renaissance" moved into its second and third generations, the foundational work of the age of Charlemagne was paying big dividends.

It is interesting, too, to see that while Theodulf was trying hard to deny that Byzantium and the Franks belonged to the same tradition, the Paris *Libellus* calmly asserted that Rome, Byzantium, and the Franks shared a tradition. The current difficulties arose from the fact that the tradition had not alway been properly understood in Rome and Constantinople. Walahfrid reveals a similar concern in his brief history of the quarrel over images. He goes back to the early eighth century to show that recent novelties and misunderstandings have provoked an unfortunate dispute. A correct understanding of the recent past will help to put things right.

Order

If there is a certain serenity in what the ninth-century writers said about tradition, then there is palpable agitation in all that they said about order. They speak a little on government and rulership but have a lot to say about the church and its leadership. They were concerned with grammar, language, and reason. Educational standards attracted their attention. Charity, or a lack of it, prompted some anxious words. Scandal worried them a good deal. Their tone and focus is once again different from Theodulf's.

The world will be rightly ordered when there is "unity, peace, and concord."[72] Michael II insisted that he had brought all the peoples of his empire to peace and concord.[73] For these qualities to be present, Rome and Byzantium must yield to the truth. Theodulf said no such thing. He had rather little to say about the Rome of his own day and contented himself with general remarks about papal traditions. The "papalist" clause in the *Opus* (1.6) was probably not Theodulf's own work. As for the Byzantines, Theodulf was too busy heaping abuse on them to entertain the possibility that concord could be achieved with them. In Louis's time the tone was different. Louis's bishops spoke of his deep concern for his "brothers of the empire of the eastern Romans," and of his solicitude for his "dearest bothers" Michael and Theophilus and their "holy people." Louis was worried about the "God-loving church of the Romans."[74] In his letter to Louis, Michael addressed "our cherished and honorable brother, Louis" and called him "our peaceful friend and spiritual brother."[75] The *Libellus* is not ambiguous about Byzantium's blame for the recent dispute. But Louis must "reprehend the ills of both parties." Dungal agrees that as a Christian ruler Louis must rise up in defense of the truth. Nevertheless, in addition to its talk about fraternal solicitude, the *Libellus* makes some concessions to Byzantine sensibilities. The faults of Irene and Constantine VI that resulted in the unfortunate decrees of II Nicaea are attributed to Satan, not to the personal failings of the rulers.[76] Whereas in the eighth century papal and Frankish writings about the image question stressed Peter's authority, the *Libellus* routinely refers to Peter and Paul, which was normal in Byzantine correspondence and other documents.[77] If there is more than a tinge of condescension in the *Libellus*, there is also a complete lack of invective.

At any rate, Byantium's rulers do not come in for scathing criticism. The same cannot be said for the papacy. The *Libellus* stresses that respect is owed to the Petrine office and to the pope.[78] "Louis"—actually the Paris bishops—emphasizes that he only wishes to be helpful, not to usurp the office of teacher.[79] God has instituted an arbiter of all disputes, the pope. But a controversy is raging and the pope cannot be called "universal" if he fails to take up the battle for the faith.[80] Charlemagne had discovered serious problems and he dutifully submitted them to Hadrian for his "judgment and authority." But Hadrian defended the Greeks, acted improperly, and ordered images to be adored "superstitiously."[81] Hadrian put into his letter "certain testimonies of the holy fathers which, as far as we can understand them, are starkly irrelevant to the issue and scarcely pertinent to it." Hadrian laid aside pontifical authority and many of his objections crashed against truth and authority. He brought forth testimonies that were sometimes irrelevant, sometimes inapplicable, and sometimes even worthy of reprehension."[82] Freculf and Adegar tell how they discussed these issues with Paschal I—that must have been a lively conversation!—and "learned how partly through ignorance of the truth and partly by adherence to wicked custom the plague of that superstition had grown up in those parts." Therefore, the *Libellus* says, "When you [Louis] saw two parties deviating from the royal road, one having fallen into the left ditch by relapsing into image breaking, and one having fallen into the right ditch by superstitiously adoring images, you, on piety's prompting, wished to offer a middle way and to confer life-giving medicine to the deadly ill of each party."[83]

I cannot think of another instance in the early Middle Ages where a ruler and prominent members of his clergy implicitly charged the papacy with heresy. For that is the unmistakable force of the words used in Paris in 825. Not surprisingly, the "allied documents" produced at Paris called for choosing words and arguments very carefully and for using persuasion and flattery. Still, Louis expected his envoys to encounter "Roman obstinacy." There is an interesting ecclesiology, an interesting way of thinking about order, in these documents. The pope holds the Petrine office, is God's duly appointed arbiter, and alone has universal authority. Jonas and Dungal criticized Claudius for, as they understood him, rejecting papal authority. But Jonas had been at Paris and may have been a principal compiler of the *Libellus*. So he also believed that if the pope lapsed from the Catholic faith, his universality ceased. The Franks insist on their obligation to be helpful but never claim an independent right to pronounce on matters of faith and tradition. As far as I can see, it never occurred to anyone in Francia to attempt to coerce the pope. Nevertheless, the Franks were not prepared to submit meekly.

The *Libellus* several times laments the possibility of scandal's arising from the current disordered situation.[84] Walahfrid expresses concern that the image quarrel may give rise to scandal, and Jonas makes the same point twice, speaking about Claudius.[85] "Measured speech and priestly gravity" are necessary, Jonas says, and the *Libellus* calls for discretion, reason, and patience.[86] Jonas charges that Claudius's scandalous behavior has caused "the crown of the priesthood to fall from his head."[87] The Frankish texts reveal a particular concern that the "simple," the "weaker brothers," will be scandalized.[88] If the Franks were worried that ordinary people would be scandalized by the conduct of Turin's bishop, how much more must they have worried about the scandal generated by the pope?

I showed in Chapter 5 that order also pertains to reason, to scrutiny. Theodulf carefully scrutinized the Nicene *acta* so as to decide if they were or were not in accord with the traditions of the church. He faulted the Greeks for their linguistic mistakes, for their poor understanding of the Bible, and for their inappropriate citation of various patristic passages. Dozens of times he displayed his use of "reason" by means of trenchant syllogisms. The ninth-century writers proceeded rather differently. I have not spotted a single syllogism. They cite biblical and, especially, patristic texts in profusion. The *Libellus* says, in effect, that logic is a well-ordered argument.[89] I argued in Chapter 5 that one can discern in Theodulf's overall argumentation a theory of ecumenicity according to which the Franks could argue for their complete, principled adherence to the traditions of the church. I am inclined to think that the *Ratio, Auctoritas,* and *Consilium* of the Paris *Libellus* is in fact a much more "ordered" statement of the same theory. One states the case, assembles the authorities, and lays out the irrefutable argument. Reason involves not finding but yielding to the truth. In a felicitous formulation the bishops speak of the "reason of truth and the truth of reason." The matter is settled. Nothing new is to be added to the faith. Indeed, Jonas reminded Claudius that Chalcedon had forbidden adding anything new.[90] Truth and reason are implicit and explicit in the tradition. The pope himself must "stand aside and let the truth emerge."[91]

The Franks seem sure that their positions are true and reasonable because Gaul and Germany are pure in the faith.[92] Terrible ideas come from Spain.[93] Claudius was sent to Italy to teach the faith but he betrayed his office and led his people astray.[94] One is reminded here of the kinds of issues treated in

Charlemagne's famous letter *On the Cultivation of Letters*. The Franks know better, have been taught better, and must teach better.

Jonas criticizes Claudius for entering into arguments in which he was not competent to participate. Claudius rejects the authority of "experienced men," his title rings absurdly and ridiculously in the ears of "experienced men," and Claudius behaved "inexpertly" in altering the wording of a certain patristic passage. Claudius wields a pen that is "inexpert," writes words that are "inexpert." Claudius's words have come into the hands of men who are, in fact, "expert."[95] Jonas's comments align with Dungal's in reminding Claudius that the issue of images had already been handled diligently by experts at the palace. In other words, the Carolingian writers view order as implicit in the tradition and merely awaiting extraction and presentation. But they also see order as a matter of being expert, or letting the experts pronounce on key issues. In light of this line of argumentation, one can see why the Franks were so distressed about the popes. The pope was the most *peritus* of all, but he was behaving *imperite*. Things were badly out of order.

Theodulf gave the Greeks repeated lessons in grammar and vocabulary. These lessons were central to both his polemical purposes and his method of scrutiny. There is virtually none of this in the *Libellus*. Nevertheless, Jonas and Dungal constantly chided Claudius for his linguistic failings. To some extent, their argument maintains that had Claudius been better educated he would not have made the mistakes he did. Educational standards were once again at the center of an ordered discourse.

Worship

Worship involves specific acts of love or reverence and the persons or objects to which those acts are addressed. The ninth-century authors I have been discussing treat worship and worshipers, often in ways that differ somewhat from Theodulf's treatment of the same topics. Images per se occupy a fairly small place in the writings of the ninth-century authors while relics, the intercession of the saints, and the holy cross emerge as major themes. Just as Theodulf's reflections were prompted by the Nicene *acta*, so too the words of Jonas and Dungal were prompted by their understanding of what Claudius had said. The Paris fathers responded to Michael II, and Agobard, it seems, responded to Paris. Einhard answered questions put to him in a letter. It is not clear that Walahfrid had any specific interlocutors in mind as he wrote. Nevertheless, it is important to keep in mind that, with the possible exception of Walahfrid, no ninth-century writer undertook an independent, systematic, and comprehensive survey of worship as it relates to figural art; not even Jonas who entitled his work *On the Cult of Images*. The Paris bishops asserted that Louis had assembled them "on the matter of images" but their deliberations ranged widely. What we find is a culture of contention where one set of arguments evoked one set of replies. Finally, all of our authors were acutely aware of the challenges of language.

First, then, practices. There is no evidence that the kinds of practices spelled out in Michael's letter existed in Francia. Possibly Louis's legates to Rome in early 825 saw such practices there—the "bad customs" to which the *Libellus* refers. The *Libellus* explicitly rejects the use of lights or incense in connection with images but other texts do not mention them.[96]

Absolutely all the texts agree that God alone is to be worshiped. Interestingly, Einhard alone specifies the form that the worship of God should assume: prayer. Where images, relics, and the cross are concerned, the texts provide numerous clues. The *Libellus* condemns bestowing upon images the adoration that is owed to God as well as "inappropriate," "unnecessary," or "excessive" forms of reverence. Regrettably, the text does not spell out what such unacceptable honors might be like but the text certainly seems to imply that some forms of reverence would pass the test. Dungal is a bit more explicit: "It is perfectly clear and obvious that holy (*sanctas*) pictures, the Lord's holy (*sanctam*) cross, and the sacred (*sacras*) relics of God's elect ought to be venerated with fitting honors by Catholic and right-believing people."[97] Walahfrid agrees. First, he says, pictures and images should not be worshiped with "some immoderate cult" or venerated "more than is fitting." Then he says that "sincere and moderate honors (*honores*) of images should not be altogether rejected." He concludes that images and pictures should be possessed (*habendae*) and loved (*amandae*), not destroyed or paid excessive reverence.[98] Einhard says, "It seems to me that the cross should be adored (*adoranda*)[99] and Hrabanus Maurus (as we shall see below) agreed wholeheartedly.

Theodulf never said anything like this. If his thought accurately reflects currents of opinion in his day, then there was some development in Carolingian thinking. But it should be remembered that Claudius and Agobard continued to reject any forms of reverence shown to any material, created object. It is possible to catch a glimpse of what the authors who were in some fashion favorably disposed toward images may have been talking about. Claudius complained about humbling, bowing, and inclining the body.[100] Jonas criticized Claudius for calling "false worshipers" those who "love, venerate, and adore" painted images *of the cross* and says that kissing the cross itself is an act of reverence.[101]

He does not say this explicitly with respect to painted images of the cross or other images. Einhard says that adoring means bowing one's head, inclining one's body, prostrating oneself, or extending the arms. But to him these are gestures that accompany prayer, that show sincere reverence to God, and that may be performed before the cross.[102] Walahfrid, however, says that the "foolish" "bend" or "bow" (*inclinant*) which leaves one wondering what he considered to be the "sincere and moderate honors" that could be paid to images.[103]

I can cite one document and four pictures that shed some light on how people might have behaved in the presence of images. Between 850 and 853 Prudentius, the bishop of Troyes, composed a sermon on a local holy woman, Maura, who died in 850. Prudentius was a formidable theologian and a close confidant of Louis the Pious, his wife Judith, and their son Charles. He was also a Goth, like Theodulf, Claudius, and Agobard. That is, he is unlikely to have been predisposed in favor of images. In the midst of pressing a case for recognition of Maura's sanctity, he says that, from her youth, Maura entered the Church of the Holy Apostles every day and prayed without cease while lying prostrate before three images. One of these depicted Mary holding Jesus in her lap, another the crucifixion, and the third Christ in majesty.[104] Maura came from a prominent local family and made frequent donations to the church. She hardly qualifies as "simple." Nevertheless, Prudentius's sermon permits us to conclude both that bodily gestures before images occurred and that, in at least one case, did so without provoking criticism. In the Sacramentary of Gellone, probably prepared between 790 and 800, there is an image of the crucifixion in conjunction with an episcopal blessing for the Easter vigil that shows signs of serious wear. It is conceivable that the damage happened through the repeated touching or kissing (the damage may be due to moisture) of this image during the Paschal liturgies.[105] Jonas said that kissing the cross was an act of reverence but, once again, Gellone's image was not reverenced by the "weaker brethren." The last image in Hrabanus Maurus's *In Honor of the Holy Cross* depicts Hrabanus himself kneeling before the cross.[106] Hrabanus prepared copies of his works for many clerical recipients, for Louis the Pious, and for a layman, Duke Eberhard of Friuli. In the dedicatory letter for Eberhard, Hrabanus expresses the hope that the duke would have the book read out frequently in his presence.[107] Perhaps frequent viewing of the pictures made some impression too. Two prayer books made for kings, Charles the Bald and Louis the German, depict these rulers kneeling humbly before the cross.[108] Ordinary people might have seen Maura. The private devotions of monks, dukes, and kings, however, would not have been accessible to the "simple." The pictures are suggestive, therefore, no more.

God alone is the proper and legitimate object of human worship. Nevertheless, some reverence could be paid to manufactured objects, images and crosses, and also to relics. Such reverence took the form of various bodily gestures. In all that they say about worship, however, the ninth-century authors place much more stress on the cross and relics than they do on images.[109] Where relics are concerned, the various writings seem to be responding directly to Claudius's attack on relics and, more generally, on the cult of the saints. Carolingian writers were staunch in their defense of the cult of the saints and of the continuing intercession of the heaven dwellers. The writers make it clear that they do not advocate the worship of the saints themselves but rather that they see the saints, and among them especially the martyrs, as models of the holy life and as signs of faith in God. Images can recall to memory the deeds (*gesta*) of the saints and can teach the unlettered. There is an elite condescension evident in what the authors say about the capacity of images to teach the unlettered and about how the "simple," the "weaker brethren" might be slip into inappropriate belief in or conduct toward images.

The cross is different. To be sure, Jonas and Dungal were appalled at Claudius's insistence that images of the crucifixion brought ridicule on the risen Lord and held Jesus up to mockery.[110] Jonas says that Claudius's followers were tainted by Arianism which may mean that Jonas had adoptionism in mind and, if so, this may explain his effort to associate Claudius with his countryman Felix of Urgel.[111] But both of these authors, and others too, went far beyond Trinitarian and Christological arguments in their defence of the cross. The cross itself, the church's triumphal standard, is truly holy. It deserves an "adoration" that could be paid with various signs of reverence. The cult of the cross was growing in significance right across the Carolingian period. By the ninth century, there were three major liturgical celebrations dedicated to the cross: the *Inventio Crucis* (May 3), the *Exaltatio Crucis* (September 14), and the *Adoratio Crucis* (Good Friday).[112] Depictions of the crucifixion were growing in frequency and the iconography of the finding of the True Cross took shape in the years around 800.[113] Church dedications to the Savior or the cross proliferated as did shrines possessing relics of the True Cross.[114] On Good Friday a plain wooden cross was presented to the faithful for acts of reverence, usually touching or kissing.[115] In his *Liber Officialis*, Amalarius of Metz says, "Let no one be in any doubt that the form of the cross is to be worshiped," and a bit later he says, "We should prostrate ourselves before the cross."[116] Amalar also relates a story which he took from Bede in which King Oswald erected a cross before a battle and then knelt before it with all his men.[117] Amalar also says that "all the world adores this holy cross through which it was redeemed."[118] Some confirmation for this statement comes from the noblewoman Dhuoda, who composed an advice manual for her son William between 841 and 843. After prescribing for him a semi-monastic routine of prayers to be said before bedtime, she says, "When you have done all this, make on your forehead and over your bed the sign of the cross of him by whom you were redeemed . . . and say at the same time: 'I adore your cross, my Lord, and I believe in your holy resurrection. May your holy cross be with me. Your cross is the sign that I have always loved since I came to know it, and that I always adore.' "[119]

In short, defending the cross affirmed central theological teachings and liturgical practices. Dungal and Jonas both ask Claudius how he can celebrate the liturgy if he abhors the cross. Does he make the sign of the cross over the elements at the consecration in the mass? Does he make the sign of the cross in baptism, confirmation, and blessings?[120] If I have read the texts correctly, they tell me that the Carolingian authors saw much more at stake in defending the cult of the cross than in regulating practices connected with images.

Finally, the authors I have been considering struggled mightily with language. At the conceptual level, they understood that true adoration was owed to God alone while other forms of adoration might be paid to physical, manufactured objects—and to relics as well, but they were not *manufacta*. Theodulf was himself concerned with language but his discussion did not lead him to establish relative forms of worship with the possible exception of *res sacratae*—chalices, for example. The ninth-century authors simply do not address consecrated objects (although Jonas does ask Claudius, rhetorically, if he kisses the Gospel book).[121]

In the ninth century one author after another engaged in lexicographical exercises focused on the various words for worship. Claudius, for example, says, "To adore (*adorare)* is to praise, venerate, ask, beseech, implore, invoke, to offer prayer; To worship (*colere*) is to proceed along the right path (*gubernare*), to be attentive, to perform an office, to do repeatedly, to reverence, to love, to cherish."[122] It might appear that Claudius is trying to draw a useful distinction between these two words. Given the fragmentary state of his treatise it is a little difficult to determine just what he had in mind. It should be remembered that he reserved all forms of adoration for God alone. Moreover, right before he offers these definitions he criticizes the practices he discovered in Turin and uses *colebant*. With the exception of Walahfrid's *Libellus*, all the texts I have been considering draw upon the opening of the tenth book of Augustine's *City of God* to make the point that Latin does not have a single word for adoration.[123] Some authors point out that *colo* can mean "to worship," but also "to inhabit" or "to till."[124] Adoration can be the cult paid to God or it can be a form of service (*servitus*) or greeting (*salutatio*). Various biblical passages, sometimes accompanied by patristic interpretations, are cited to show that, for example, in "adoring" David, Nathan greeted him humbly and respectfully.[125] The reader of these materials is drawn to one inescapable conclusion: Words have multiple meanings, can be used almost interchangeably, but should never lead to confusion about the fundamental point at issue. That point is that God is owed one form of adoration and all other persons and things are owed different kinds of adoration, veneration, respect, and honor. Theodulf was certain that relics could be "adored," albeit not like God, but he was ambiguous about the cross. In the ninth century, writers—apart from Claudius and Agobard—were certain that relics, the cross, and images too, could be "adored." This was new in the Carolingian world.

The Arts and Art Talk in the Early Ninth Century

What kinds of art did elite writers see every day? What kinds of art did the "simple" see? After establishing the visual context I shall turn to what the ninth-century writers say about art, to what I have been calling "art talk."

The Visual Environment

Anyone who has even a casual acquaintance with Carolingian art will be able to call to mind gorgeous manuscript illuminations. For many people, Carolingian painting means the images that were painted into books. The delightful introduction *Carolingian Painting* by Florentine Mütherich and Joachim Gaehde presents forty-eight illuminations from fewer than half as many manuscripts. Three points, at least, are lost in this approach to Carolingian art. People in Carolingian Europe were skilled metalworkers, ivory crafters, and occasionally stone sculptors. Not all art was painting. Where painting is concerned, there was a lot more of it on church walls than there ever was in books.[126] Book art was perforce private, even intimate. It is pretty hard to connect the discussions we have been having in this book with the images that were painted into Carolingian manuscripts. Wall paintings, on the contrary, were public, visible to all. Therefore, most of the art talk which we have encountered makes the most sense when connected with wall paintings or with mosaics.

Unfortunately, not much wall painting survives. Or, to put this a little differently, the wall painting that does survive is but a poor hint of the almost unimaginable visual richness that confronted those who entered Carolingian churches and palaces. As great a scholar as Wolfgang Braunfels once said that the Carolingians would have regarded as unfinished any church whose interior was not painted, indeed just about wholly painted.[127] A great Carolingian scholar, Hrabanus Maurus, took painted walls in churches for granted.[128] In the 880s Notker the Stammerer, in his *Deeds of Charles the Great*, took decorated churches for granted too: "If there were any churches belonging to the royal demesne that had to be decorated with paneled ceilings or wall paintings local bishops and abbots looked after this."[129] Much of the surviving painting exists in what were once monastic churches. This accident does not mean that only monks or nuns saw those paintings. Many monastic basilicas accommodated the worship of good-sized surrounding populations. But the almost inexpressibly beautiful frescoes in Santa Maria foris Portas in Castelseprio are eloquent reminders of the kinds of pictures that once graced the walls of one church after another.[130] And the three tall registers of paintings that run right down both sides of the nave in St. John of Müstair reveal the extent to which the eighth- or ninth-century visitor to a Carolingian church was surrounded by pictures.[131] The remains of Carolingian wall painting are well distributed geographically: St.-Germain d'Auxerre is France's chief representative; Germany offers St.-Maximin in Trier, Corvey, Lorsch, Paderborn, Aachen, Steinbach, St.-Emmeram in Regensburg; the Tyrol preserves San Benedetto Po at Malles and St. John of Müstair; without even mentioning Rome or more southerly areas, Italy offers Castel Seprio and nearby Torba, San Protasio and San Satiro in Milan, San Salvatore and Santa Giulia in Brescia, San Procolo in Naturno, and Santa Maria in Valle ("Tempietto Langobardo") Cividale. In all these places what remains tempts us to imagine what was once there. Not many Carolingian buildings are still standing, the impresarios of Romanesque and Gothic having knocked them down or built right over them. Sometimes, we have literary sources that sadden us with their revelations of what we will never see. One thinks of Ermoldus Nigellus's portrayal of the scenes in the church and palace at Ingelheim[132] or of the numerous extant *tituli* that once accompanied pictures that have vanished.[133] And it is worth remembering that some late antique churches with stunning art works, especially mosaics, were visible to people in Carolingian Europe. One thinks of Sant'Ambrogio in Milan, which delights us still, or of the church of La Daurade in Toulouse, whose fifth/sixth-century mosaics are now known only from arduous exploration of a less than satisfactory seventeenth-century description.[134]

The Carolingian elite, lay and clerical alike, had access to pictures all the time, in all sorts of media, in many locations. The famous "Tassilo Chalice," probably donated by the ambitious duke of Bavaria to Kremsmünster, tells us something about the look of those *res sacratae* which Theodulf and others discussed. The beautiful ivory carvings on book covers could have been contemplated at leisure by those who owned the books themselves. Would not the spectacular golden covers of the Lindau Gospels, say, or of the Codex Aureus, have captured more than one rapt gaze? Ordinary people would have caught glimpses of such ivory or golden covers only when books were paraded past them in liturgical processions. The play of candle light on Wolvinius's masterful altar in Milan will have touched off a million sparkles, but could people outside the sanctuary have made out the images on, let us say, the twenty-one panels on the front, never mind those on the sides and back? What everyone, the learned and the simple, could see, often and easily, were the wall paintings. These paintings, as far as we can tell, correlate well with the ways that treatises talk about art. That is, there are scenes from the lives of saints, say from the martyrdom of St. Stephen in Auxerre or Pope Gregory writing his homilies from San Benedetto Po. There were Old Testament scenes, for example depictions of David in Müstair or, again, San Benedetto Po. The New Testament was represented by an amusing picture of Paul being lowered from the wall of Damascus in San Procolo or a hauntingly beautiful series on the nativity in Castel Seprio. Müstair also presents us with a powerful Christ in majesty. In other words, we can see the *kinds* of pictures that they talked about. Thus we know that their discussions were not abstract or academic. Likewise, people in Carolingian Europe saw crosses and crucifixes, to judge from the relative prominence of these objects in the treasury lists published by Bernhard Bischoff.[135] It is well to keep this in mind in light of the prominence of the cross in the image texts discussed above.

Art Talk

Virtually every familiar argument about art that has been presented in earlier chapters recurs in the ninth-century treatises. But some interesting shifts of emphasis and understanding attend the repetition of old arguments. All the way back to the fourth century, writers sometimes argued their own cases and sometimes let biblical and patristic citations argue the point. These rhetorical strategies did not change at all in the ninth century. And the Carolingians seem to have been familiar with all the old arguments. Hence their subtle differences of emphasis and interpretation may be taken as pointing not to ignorance or misunderstanding but instead to originality, advance, and controversy. Shifts in art talk are analogous to those shifts in theology acknowledging that some honor or veneration might be paid to *manufacta* and that some material things, especially crosses, might be holy.

The Carolingian via media is evident where one would expect to find it. That is, Claudius and Agobard are not prepared to say that it is alright to have visual art but wrong to destroy it or to worship it. The Paris *Libellus*,[136] Jonas,[137] Dungal,[138] and Walahfrid[139] explicitly, and in some cases repeatedly, affirm this position.

In Theodulf's time, the via media was accompanied by the argument that art was permissible for commemoration and decoration. In the ninth century, this basic position persists but undergoes some subtle changes. For example, commemoration or recollection do appear as justifications for images, but just as often "love" and "honor" appear as well.[140] I am inclined to think that the explanation for this change is to be found in the heavy attention that the ninth-century texts accord to the cult of the saints and to saintly intercession. Agobard acknowledges that images were erected for commemoration in olden times and "after the fashion of the gentiles" but leaves the impression that he no longer thinks they are necessary now.[141] Only Jonas and Walahfrid mention decoration and neither does so explicitly. That is, Jonas says that images enhance the "loveliness" (*pulchritudinem*) of churches while Walahfrid say that images increase the "splendor" (*decus*) of churches and that "beauty" (*speciositas*) should by no means be scorned.[142] I wonder if there had been so much construction and "decoration" since the 780s and 790s that later writers simply took for granted what Theodulf wished cautiously to authorize?

In Chapter 5 I associated Theodulf's position on figural art with Augustine's and characterized it as "principled indifference." Only in the Paris materials, and then not in the *Libellus* proper presented to Louis but instead in the proposed draft of a letter that Louis might send to the pope, did the old indifference come to articulation. Twice the Paris bishops ask what harm there would be to faith, hope, and charity if images had never existed. They are arguing that the church needs the Christian virtues but can exist nicely without images.[143] Perhaps Agobard was thinking along the same lines when he said that it ought to be possible to worship God without physical images.[144] Bearing in mind that the ninth-century image treatises say surprisingly little about images, I wonder if the desire of the authors of those treatises to defend the intercession of the saints, whose deeds were frequently painted, and the cult of the cross, that was everywhere growing in prominence, induced a certain reluctance to dismiss images as utterly unnecessary?

For ages writers had defended images because God had commanded some images to be made. Although Claudius could dispense with that argument, Agobard said that anyone who reflected on the work of Solomon would never say that images are strictly prohibited. But he does say that in former times people made images in honor of foreign Gods, implying that they do not have to be made any more.[145] The Paris *Libellus* does not cite the biblical texts directly but instead defends the conduct of Moses and Solomon by means of a lengthy quotation from Gregory II's letter to Germanus.[146] Dungal is a bit like Theodulf in arguing that the Jews were a stiff-necked people so prone to idolatry that God had to appease them with images of his own design or approval.[147] Walahfrid argues that neither Moses nor Solomon flouted God's will—that is, the Exodus prohibition—and also suggests that God may have commanded certain images to be made on account of the superstitions connected with other images.[148] Jonas mentions the images commanded by God but stresses that they were erected as type-figures.[149] All the ninth-century writers who defend images do so on the grounds of old ecclesiastical traditions. I wonder if their tendency to appeal to tradition, and their desire to get Byzantines, popes, and Claudius to toe the line, explains why they chose to defend images within the framework of Christian history more than on the basis of divine commands to Moses and Solomon?

One of the oldest arguments on behalf of religious art was that it was valuable for teaching the unlettered, that in certain circumstances art was equivalent to writing. The *Libellus*,[150] Jonas,[151] Dungal,[152] and Walahfrid[153] accepted this argument. Although the argument was older than Gregory I, he was cited as the authoritative interpreter by everyone except Walahfrid who simply did not cite any sources.[154] Even Agobard acknowledged the argument but, once again, suggested that it had more validity in the past.[155] Theodulf, as we saw, would not accept the idea that art could teach. By the middle of the ninth century, it had become normal to argue that it could do so. As I have shown, there was a concern that art truly instruct and not mislead or scandalize the "simple" or the "weaker brothers."

Late antiquity bequeathed other arguments to the early Middle Ages. One of the oldest was the "referential" argument: acts of reverenced before an image were referred to the person represented. The Paris *Libellus* accepts this argument, cites the famous passages from Basil along with others, and draws into the discussion Gregory II's letter to Germanus.[156] Dungal seems to accept this argument though he cites a slightly ambiguous passage from Jerome and also says that intercession comes through images.[157] This is not exactly what Basil had in mind. Agobard may have been implicitly rejecting this argument when he said that "no other mediator is needed between God and man except the One who is God and man."[158] It seems to me that ninth-century authors come much closer to the "referential" argument when they talk about the cross, or about relics. There was also the argument about emotions. The Paris *Libellus* and Dungal cite the famous passage from Gregory of Nyssa, and in his appendix of additional texts Dungal adds a passage in which Augustine says that images may induce compunction.[159] By means of the neoplatonic tradition or else directly through Pseudo-Dionysius, writers had argued that images could elevate the mind, could use the visible to achieve some access to the invisible. The Paris *Libellus* cites (Pseudo-) Dionysius on this point, but no other ninth-century image text does so.[160] Agobard insisted sharply that visible things are harmful to the perception of invisible things.[161] By the time of John of Damascus, another thread in the ancient argumentation had gained strength: the argument from incarnation. The *Libellus* adopts this argument by citing Gregory II to Germanus and Germanus to John of Synada.[162] Theodulf expended some effort qualifying or refuting each of these arguments. His ninth-century successors were in at least some cases familiar with these arguments but simply left them on one side. In so far as they were rooted in the tradition, these arguments ought to have been attractive. But they were not. There continued to be a basic conservatism in how Carolingian writers were prepared to talk about images.

Finally, I come to one of the issues that had been contentious since at least the rise of the icon, namely the ontology of images. All of the authors and texts we have been considering agree that images are material, are *manufacta*, are "senseless things." All agree that senseless things cannot be worshiped as God is worshiped. All agree that nothing divine inheres in any image. In general there is agreement that images have value only in respect of what or whom they represent. Beyond this point, consensus becomes shaky. Einhard says "without doubt the cross is holy" but Agobard rejects the notion that any material thing either is holy or can provide access to the holy. Writers sometimes speak of "holy images" or "holy pictures" but always do so in such a way as to make clear that they are referring to the figures in the pictures and not to the pictures themselves. Ninth-century Carolingian writers uphold the traditional Frankish insistence that the way-of-being of images is never intrinsically holy as some Byzantine writers occasionally insisted. But the language of these writers is broader than Theodulf's and imprecise enough to earn rebukes from Agobard.

Did any image in the Frankish world *do* anything? I know of only two cases. I already introduced Maura who daily prostrated herself before three images in the church of the Holy Apostles in Troyes. Prudentius asked her again and again about her experiences and she was reluctant to reply. Finally, she said that she had heard the baby Jesus cry, the crucified Jesus groan, and the majestic Jesus roar. Moreover, the Christ in Majesty handed her a golden scepter.[163] It is hard to know if these occurrences were singular or repeated. No one else seems to have seen or heard what Maura did. It is not clear from the text whether she was actually relating a vision and not an actual experience. It seems clear, finally, that Prudentius tells the story to buttress his case that Maura deserved to be considered a saint. The second case pertains to an old and worn apse image in the church of Gravedona near Como that glowed for two days in 823. The image was of Mary and Jesus—a madonna, perhaps a regina—with the Magi offering gifts. The Magi did not glow. The story is related in the *Royal Frankish Annals* amid a list of portents.[164] The reader is not told the source for the story. No explanation is offered. Maura's case, as well as the one from Gravedona, are reminiscent of the ones encountered earlier from Ravenna and Frankish Gaul. They are obscure, one-time events with no antecedents and no consequences. No miracles are associated with either image story but Jonas and Dungal go on at length with accounts of miracles wrought at the shrines of saints and martyrs and by the cross. Clearly, whatever one makes of Troyes and Gravedona, images are different than relics and crosses.

Tituli

Tituli, the inscriptions, almost always in verse, that accompanied many images, constitute a particularly intriguing form of art talk. Equipping pictures with inscriptions to identify, explain, or interpret their contents and meaning had a history reaching far back into antiquity.[165] Paulinus of Nola, as we saw in Chapter 1, discussed the *tituli* over the pictures at Nola and said that they would "excite the rustics." Paulinus assumed that the country folk would "read over to each other the subjects painted."[166] Gregory of Tours tells of a man who was inspired to learn to read by *tituli* associated with pictures in Clermont.[167] In the twelfth century Abbot Suger of St.-Denis stated that without *tituli* the complexity of pictures would be difficult for ordinary people to understand.[168] There was a consistent view of the rationale for *tituli* and a long-standing sense that pictures regularly had them. *Tituli* might appear in connection with frescoes and mosaics, or with images in books, or on altars, vessels, ivories, and even cloths. I shall confine myself here to comments on Carolingian *tituli* that pertained to frescoes and mosaics because these were the most visible, public arts of the Carolingian world.

From the Carolingian period, *tituli* survive from Cologne, Fulda, St. Gall, St.-Riquier, and Weissenburg.[169] Sometimes we know the names of the poets who composed them. The vast majority of surviving *tituli* are extant only because someone wrote them down. It is safe to say that only a tiny fraction of Carolingian *tituli* survive. It is sad to say that the surviving *tituli* remind us again and again of works of art that are lost forever. It is only slight compensation that a few *tituli* are sufficiently detailed to permit imaginative reconstructions of the vanished iconographies.[170]

A few *tituli* by Paul the Deacon, Alcuin, and Angilbert survive from the reign of Charlemagne. They were prepared to accompany, respectively, a Last Judgment, a Genesis cycle, and individual scenes of the Annunciation, the Nativity, the Passion, and the Ascension.[171] From the ninth century there are more. Hrabanus Maurus left behind at least four *tituli* pertaining to a portrayal of saints, to an Ascension and perhaps Pentecost, and to two images of Christ.[172] The first of these was placed in the apse of the church of St. Peter in Fulda. The others are more difficult to associate with particular places. Walahfrid Strabo composed a *titulus* at St. Gall for a charming scene of the saint feeding bread to a bear who then served him.[173] Florus of Lyon composed two *tituli* for apse mosiacs.[174] The second of these, in ten hexameters, describes in detail a complex mosaic featuring an enthroned Christ, evangelist symbols, the apostles, the rivers of paradise, Jerusalem, and possibly John the Baptist. Sedulius Scottus created for a gallery or antechamber of some kind *tituli* amounting to twenty hexameters for eighteen New Testament scenes beginning with the angel's appearance to Zachary.[175] He also prepared for Archbishop Gunthar of Cologne (850–69) five *tituli* consisting of fourteen hexameters, arrayed 2-2-3-3-2-2. Apparently the *tituli* described one very complex scene including cherubs, an enthroned Christ, evangelist symbols, the rivers of paradise, and the apostles.[176] At. St.-Riquier a series of poets, possibly Mico, Fredigard, and Odulf, composed numerous *tituli*. Some accompanied crucifixion scenes or images of Christ in majesty. One set, however, portrayed events in the Garden of Eden: Adam eating the forbidden fruit; Adam and Eve covering their genitals with leaves; Adam and Eve being expelled from the garden; Eve being tempted by the serpent. Then there is a scene of Daniel in the lion's den.[177] The monastery of Sts. Peter and Paul in Weissenburg had ten *tituli* in various verse forms which appear to be corrupt in the surviving version. These began with scenes from the Passion of Christ and moved on to moments in the post-Resurrection career of Peter.[178] St.-Gall, finally, presents an especially interesting set of *tituli*. First of all, there is a cycle of eighty-eight hexameters that pertained to forty-four New Testament scenes. They began with "Verses for the Painting of the Gospel." Twenty hexameters attached to ten scenes from the childhood of Christ. These concluded with "Here Ends the Infancy of Christ." Before the next forty, a *titulus* read "These Verses on the Right Wall of the Choir; Those Verses on the Right Wall of the Nave." The scenes of Christ's infancy are "These" while "Those" pertained to forty verses connected to twenty images. The latter set concludes with "Up to Here on the Miracles of Christ on the Right Wall." On the western wall (presumably inside and not outside) there were two *tituli*, or four verses, pertaining to a Last Judgment, with, once again, directions: "These in the Western Front in the Space Which is Above the Throne." The verses here read:

Behold! The horns sound which rescind the rights of death,
The cross shines in the heavens, and fire precedes the clouds.

Another direction follows: "These Beneath the Throne Between Heaven and Hell." The verses here read:

Here live the greatest saints with Christ the Judge,
To justify the pious and damn the wicked to the abyss.

One final direction read, "The Passion of the Lord on the Left Wall of the Nave." It is followed by ten two-line *tituli*.[179]

These verses afford several insights into Carolingian art talk. One gets a sense of how the "simple brethren" might have been instructed, moved, inspired by the combination of pictures and words. I am less confident than Paulinus apparently was that rustics could read the *tituli* to one another, but I am quite prepared to believe that the elite could have, and probably did, explain the pictures and words to the "simple." The verses bristle with words meaning "to stand out," "to shine," "to sparkle," and "to gleam." Here, I think, are *decor* and *splendor*. In other words, the verses articulate the Carolingian sense of "decoration." I have shown that ninth-century writers added "love" to the traditional couplet of "commemoration and decoration." These verses confirm this addition. Sedulius puts into Gunthar's mouth these words: "The venerable bishop Gunthar ordered these verses to be made for the love of Christ."[180] At St.-Riquier, a *titulus* read, "I ordered these images of Christ to be fashioned on account of the love of Christ."[181] One of Angilbert's *tituli* says, "Death's death, therefore, the cross of Christ, is rightly to be worshiped." This accords perfectly with what the treatises say. And how might such worship have been effected? Hrabanus helps. In a *titulus* he wrote for an image of Christ he says, "Bend your knee, you who enter, lie down and adore Christ / whose painted image sparkles above with color." Kneeling, genuflecting, prostrating: These are the kinds of bodily gestures mentioned in the treatises and depicted in images.

Such gestures constituted "fitting" honors. Perhaps Maura only did what *tituli* advised her to do.

Word and Image in Hrabanus Maurus

One of Hrabanus's *tituli* invited an observer to bend his knee before an image of Christ. Hrabanus's most famous work, *In Honor of the Holy Cross*, constitutes one of the most intriguing examples of art talk from the entire Middle Ages. Originally written between 810 and 814, *In Honor of the Holy Cross* consists of prefatory material and twenty-eight figured poems (*carmina figurata*). The work as a whole is divided into two books. Book One contains the poems on left-hand pages and prose explanations of the poems (*declarationes figurarum*) on the right-hand pages. At the foot of the right-hand pages the reader finds the *versus intexti*. These are the verses that Hrabanus ingeniously fitted into the figures that intrude into the space of the full-page poems on the left-hand pages. Because the poems were difficult, and their meanings less than transparent, Hrabanus prepared Book Two, which is a prose explanation of each of the twenty-eight items in Book One. In addition to his original copy, Hrabanus prepared at least eight more down to the mid-840s for a number of notable contemporaries. The work was highly esteemed not only in the Carolingian period but right through the Middle Ages. More than eighty manuscripts are extant and the book was printed for the first time in 1503. When Ernst Dümmler was conducting the initial research that led to the publication by the Monumenta of the volumes of Carolingian poetry, he was disparaging in his assessment of Hrabanus's work. Dümmler's view held sway until fairly recently when Hrabanus and his *In Honor of the Holy Cross* began to receive the careful attention they always deserved.[182] Hrabanus's most famous work received a critical edition only in 1997.[183]

Ironies and oddities attend Hrabanus's work at every turn. One might note, first, that Hrabanus produced a work with twenty-eight complex figures—or twenty-nine if one adds the opening image and poem dedicated to Louis the Pious in the copy Hrabanus prepared for him in the early 830s.[184] Yet in a poem addressed to "Bonosus," that is to his schoolmate Hatto, Hrabanus chided his friend for being too attached to images: "Since a picture seems more pleasing to you than any other art, I ask you not to spurn the work of writing as unpleasant." He goes on to say:

> The sign of writing is worth more than the empty form of an image
> and offers more beauty to the soul than the false picture with colors,

which does not show things correctly. For scripture is the perfect and blessed norm of salvation and is important in all things and is of more use to everyone. It is tasted more quickly, is more perfect in its meaning, and is more easily grasped by the human senses. It serves ears, lips, and eyes, while painting only offers some consolation to the eyes. It shows the truth by its form, its utterance, its meaning, and it is pleasing for a long time. Painting delights the gaze when it is new, but when it is old it is a burden, it vanishes fast and is not a faithful transmitter of the truth.[185]

Hrabanus's words and actions are not in contradiction, as I shall argue presently. For Hrabanus used the old medium of the figured poem to subordinate images to words, indeed to make words into images. But Hrabanus clearly stands in a long tradition in preferring writing to images.

A second irony, or at any rate puzzle, concerns Hrabanus's position within his own intellectual landscape. That is, he was at court shortly after the Franks responded to II Nicaea and Theodulf wrote the *Opus Caroli*. He prepared several copies of *In Honor of the Holy Cross* around the time of the Paris Colloquy, the battle over Claudius, and the Carolingian logomachy over images. Yet *In Honor of the Holy Cross* offers not a single hint of polemical intent or of connection to contemporary issues, except in so far as it testifies to the growing intensity of the cult of the cross.[186] What the work provides is the considered views of an exceptionally learned and well-connected man who was Alcuin's greatest pupil and the teacher of several major ninth-century figures including Walahfrid Strabo, Otfried of Weissenburg, Hartmut of St. Gall, Lupus of Ferrières, and Rudolf of Fulda. Hrabanus was master of Fulda's school, abbot of the monastery (822–41), archbishop of Mainz (847–56), confidant of Louis the Pious and his wife Judith, and later of Louis's son Louis the German. Even if he did not react explicitly to the controversies swirling around him, he certainly spoke with force and authority.[187]

So, what did he say? And why did he say it in the way that he did? He sang—for that is what *carmina* do—the praises (*honores, laudes*) of the holy cross. Right away this is quite different from the intentions of his far-off model, Optatianus Porfyrius, who composed a set of figured poems to celebrate Constantine's *vicennalia*. Between the fourth century and the ninth, several other authors composed figured poems in honor of the cross, but none achieved the sophistication or complexity of Hrabanus's work. Hrabanus created four figured images depicting Christ (no. 1), angels (no. 4), a lamb and the evangelist symbols (no. 15), and a cross with Hrabanus himself kneeling, or bowing profoundly, before it (no. 28). In each case the figure is inserted into a field of poetry and contains within itself further poems, the *versus intexti*. Three times (nos. 3, 26, 27) Hrabanus inserted an equal-armed cross into the field running from border to border. These crosses contain verses. Thirteen times (nos. 5–11, 13, 17, 18, 21, 23, 24) Hrabanus used simple but elegant geometric shapes, circles and triangles for example, to pick out the *versus intexti*. Seven times (nos. 3, 12, 14, 19, 20, 22, 25) Hrabanus ingeniously inserted letters into his field and then inserted *versus intexti* into the letters. These letters can be "read" too: "Crux," "Adam," and "Alleluia," for example. One (no. 19) is a set of chi's (the first letter of Christ in Greek) arrayed in cross-form and another is a set of lambda's (signifying *laus*, praise). No. 22 is particularly clever: a chi-rho, the symbol of Christ, with the *versus intexti* making the names of Christ, and the time of Christ's preaching, the time of judgment, and the reign of Antichrist.[188]

Words and images together praise the cross and Christ. This is what Hrabanus said, over and over again. The cross proclaims the passion, the mystery of the incarnation, and the gift of salvation. Christ is portrayed as the perfect image of the father, as the one who is to come, as the one who came in fulfilment of the prophecies, and as the one whose death and resurrection gave humankind the hope of salvation. The opening image of Christ is particularly revealing. Christ is portrayed frontally and naked apart from a loincloth. Hrabanus's image is precocious in that, except for the slightly earlier crucifixion scene in the Sacramentary of Gellone (see above p. 335), there had been no such depictions in earlier Carolingian art.[189] Novelty is perhaps the least interesting aspect of the image, however. Christ stands erect with his hands extended, as if on the cross, but there is no cross. Moreover, Christ bears no wounds on his hands, feet, side, or head. We see a risen Christ, in other words, portrayed in such a way as to remind the viewer of the results of the passion, namely resurrection and salvation. Christ's nipples and navel reveal the letters D E O. Christ is depicted as God and man. He makes the incarnation visible and reveals the Father whose son became incarnate. In the field, Christ is called "Creator," which further identifies the God-man with God the Father. *In Honor of the Holy Cross* therefore addresses the central truths of the Christian faith. And it places the cross at the center of the faith. Reverence paid to the cross is synonymous with the worship of Christ. Hence, a book in praise of the cross begins with an image of Christ. Hrabanus writes:

> Behold, the image of the savior by the position of its members reminds
> us of the most salvific, sweet, and beloved form of the holy cross that
> we who believe in his name and obey his commandments might though

his passion have hope of eternal life; that, each time we gaze upon the cross, we might be mindful of him who suffered on it for us so that he could seize us from the power of darkness—"swallowing down death that we might be made heirs of eternal life" (1 Peter 3.22). He went to heaven where the angels, powers, and virtues are subject to him, that we might think again and again that we are not redeemed by perishable silver and gold . . . but by his precious blood.[190]

What Hrabanus says does not tell us why he said it in verse, or why his words surround and enclose images. Hrabanus was an accomplished poet. That he wrote in verse is not in itself surprising. Once he chose to create figured poems, obviously, verse had to be his medium. Behind his verses stand a rich assemblage of biblical and patristic sources. But this is true as well of his other, voluminous writings. What Hrabanus seems to have been doing, among other things, was recuperating the late antique heritage of religious poetry on biblical and patristic themes. Behind him stood Paulinus, Prudentius, Sedulius, and Juvencus, to mention only a few prominent figures.[191] His contemporaries, and he himself, labored mightily to recuperate the patristic heritage in biblical exegesis and fundamental theology. Hrabanus anticipated by some years the Paris fathers in adding poetry to the dossier of authoritative texts. He is intriguingly like Dungal in focusing on the Christian poets.

Still, this again tells us *what* he did, not *why*. It is true that Hrabanus subjugated images to words.[192] But this is not the whole truth and Hrabanus need not have created figured poems to do this. *In Honor of the Holy Cross* blends words and images more than subordinating one to the other. *In Honor of the Holy Cross* is fundamentally a linguistic phenomenon because of the strict connection between text and image. All the verse is there without the images, but the images reveal to the reader/viewer another layer of verse. Hrabanus urges his brothers to frequent reading and attentive viewing. In the course of his work, Hrabanus effectively uses *videre*, *ruminare*, and *legere* as synonyms. Hrabanus is alert to the old debate touching on the relative value of sight among the five senses. But he resolves the debate by controlling sight with words and by drawing an equivalence between sign and image, between image and text. Hrabanus' integration of figures and texts is intended to promote a deeper understanding of each and of both together. Hrabanus is also alert to the difference between sign and image. Image as *imago*, or as *pictura*, as he once said to Hatto, raises problems; it does not reveal things correctly; it does not teach holy things. But image as sign points to realities beyond itself, relates to words—to the "perfect norm"—and teaches what is true.[193]

Like his contemporaries, but unlike the generation of his masters, Hrabanus affirmed the value and legitimacy of images for more than decoration and commemoration. They really can teach, but cannot do so if cut off from words. Hrabanus is clearer on this than his contemporaries. Hrabanus refers to memory and recollection and commemoration many times but never, I believe, in union with its old mate "decoration." Unlike Theodulf, Hrabanus believed one particular kind of *manufacta* was holy: the cross. This is a view he shared with other members of his generation. The cross effected the mystery and miracle of human salvation, but crosses work no wonders in this world. No one else was as ingenious as Hrabanus in showing how words and images might work together, or how one might escape the old struggle to place one before the other. Yet like everyone else, Hrabanus did not propose a single, systematic vocabulary. For him acts of viewing, reading, and meditating are also acts of venerating, adoring, and worshiping. Like Einhard, he uses *adorare* and *orare* as synonyms. For Hrabanus, meditating on the mystery of the cross is moving, emotional. Finally, deep and repeated meditation on the words and images in *In Honor of the Holy Cross* can liberate the mind from the world of the senses. In other words, Hrabanus talked about art in new ways but also joined a discourse that was by his time five centuries old.

Tradition, Order, and Worship in the Ninth Century

In the reign of Charlemagne tradition was a matter of grave importance, order figured prominently, and worship was relatively unimportant as a central preoccupation. Tradition occasioned anxiety and polemic as the Carolingians tried hard to discover and articulate their place in the stream of history. Arguments about tradition were ideologically loaded and polemically articulated. Order tended to mean the right ordering of the polity and of the church, not that these entities are always easy to disentangle. Order might also mean right reasoning and legitimate interpreting. Worship played a modest role in contemporary discussions because those discussions were prompted in the first place by a consideration of images and the Carolingians were simply unprepared to accord any form of worship to images. In the age of Louis the Pious tradition was important but in ways that differed significantly from what had been uppermost in the minds of his father's generation. There was a mania for order in Louis's age. Worship figured prominently in the image debates, of course, but also significantly outside outside that framework.

Tradition

The *Twelve Books of Histories*,[194] which Freculf of Lisieux completed in 829 and dedicated to Empress Judith as a gift for her son Charles, provide an excellent listening post to hear contemporary Carolingian concerns about tradition. Freculf's origins are unknown.[195] He was a pupil of Louis's chancellor Helisachar, who apparently brought him to the attention of the court. He served as bishop of Lisieux from 823 or 825 until his death on October 8 in either 850 or 852. In the Prologue to his *Histories* Frechulf speaks of having been "wrapped up in secular and ecclesiastical affairs."[196] He was a *missus* in 822, Louis's envoy to Rome in 824, where he secured permission for the Franks to look into the image question, and a participant in the Paris deliberations of 825 and in the Paris council of 829. He is a particularly interesting case of a busy, well-connected man who was involved in the image case directly and also in a wide array of other current developments.

Freculf's *Histories* constitute an important work that is only just beginning to get its due as a major intellectual achievement.[197] In the Prologue to Part One (containing Books 1 to 7) Freculf reminds Helisachar that he has been working away on the requested history of ancient rulers and realms along with the history of Israel. Part One runs from the creation of the world to the nativity of Christ. It is impossible to say exactly when Frechulf finished Part One. Apparently Freculf continued working on his *Histories* despite the press of other business and he seems to have planned the work as a whole in two parts, the second running from the incarnation to ca. 600.

In order to understand Freculf's purposes it is necessary to begin at the end of his massive work. The *explicit* says, "Here end the books from the incarnation of our Lord Jesus Christ down to the kingdoms of the Franks in Gaul and of the Lombards in Italy."[198] The immediately preceding chapters treat the pontificate of Gregory I as defender of the faith, attentive administrator, evangelizer of Britain, and prolific author (2. 5. 24); the conversion of the Visigoths to Catholicism (2. 5. 25); the deeds of Pope Boniface (actually he conflates Boniface III, 607, and IV, 608–15) who received a decree from Emperor Phocas stipulating that the Roman see was "the head of all churches" and who turned the Pantheon, the temple to all Rome's pagan gods, into the church of St. Mary and All the Martyrs (2. 5. 26); and, finally, a list of the *six* ecumenical councils running from Nicaea (325) to Constantinople III (680–81) (2. 5. 27). These facts are by no means random.

Freculf was the first (or perhaps the first after Isidore) medieval writer to see the post-Roman world as something new. What kind of a new thing was it?

He provides several clues. It was post-Roman imperial; the Romans had been expelled from Italy and the last great monument to Rome's state cults had been transformed. It was Roman, however, but Roman ecclesiastical. Gregory I marked the way and even the Greeks acknowledged that Rome was the head of all churches. It was Catholic. The future of the West was safely in the hands of Catholic Franks and Lombards (he anticipates a little here), the Visigoths had rejected heresy, and the English were on the way to conversion. What is more, the faith itself had been definitively defined.

Freculf's concluding frame of reference takes on a bit more clarity when it is viewed in light of the work as a whole, and of the structure of Part Two. Freculf has had a bad reputation among scholars who dismiss him as a scissors-and-paste compiler and not even a very good one because he abandoned the customary ages-of-the-world or chronological/computistical models for organizing his material.[199] In fact, he had his own sense of the march of history. He traces the rise and fall of rulers, realms, and cults through pagan, pre-Roman antiquity and then through Israel. By juxtaposing Adam and Christ at the beginnings of Parts One and Two he created a perfect typology for two ages centering on the shift from law to grace. By implication the history of Israel was at an end because continued temple service after the incarnation was a perversion. The Rome of Augustus was important only because it created the peace and order through which Christ's church could grow. Rome itself had also passed away, however, leaving behind only the church and the *gentes* which had succeeded Rome and embraced the church. In discussing Ninus, the legendary, eponymous founder of Nineveh, he says, "he lived about twelve hundred years before the founding of Rome, another Babylon in the West."[200]

Freculf's was the most important reception of Augustine's conception of history before Otto of Freising's in the twelfth century. Beginning with Cain and Abel, Freculf traces the rise and course of the "two cities." Freculf's approach blends specific historical accounts with soaring allegorical allusion. Like Augustine, but unlike some other writers, Freculf did not identify the Christianized Roman Empire with the City of God. The identification of regime and cult had been characteristic of all earlier history, including Israel's. In "Christian Times" no such identification was possible.[201] The incarnation changed everything. Once Israel, Rome, and Rome's cults were gone, only the universal church was left as a manifestation of the City of God. The City of Man henceforth included only Jews, pagans, and heretics.[202]

It has puzzled many of his readers that Freculf did not bring his account down to his own times. Sometimes, it is thought, he did not wish explicitly to place the Frankish empire in the City of Man. But the problem has been falsely put. Christian Times were achieved slowly between the incarnation and the early seventh century. The ninth-century Carolingians lived in those Christian Times. In the early fifth century Augustine could not have known how things would turn out. By 829 Freculf had four centuries of hindsight to guide his vision. Freculf told Judith that he had prepared his work as a mirror for Charles so that he could see what to do and what to avoid.[203] Obviously, the work provided all kinds of concrete examples of excellence and depravity. But much more than this, it provided a clear orientation to the march of all time, of all history. Theodulf had done much the same thing but he wrote angrily, polemically, anxiously. Freculf was a better Augustinian and he wrote with a kind of confidence and certainty that had been impossible to achieve some forty years earlier. I noted a kind of serenity in the argumentation of the image texts. Freculf, himself a participant in those controversies, exhibited a similar serenity in locating his contemporaries in time.

Ermoldus Nigellus provides two further examples of an interest in tradition at Louis's court. Ermoldus wrote his *Song in Honor of Louis the Most Christian Caesar* between late 826 and early 828. I noted earlier that Ermoldus made passing reference to Claudius of Turin. He must have been aware of the recent disagreement with Byzantium on the matter of images. Yet instead of heaping abuse on Byzantium Ermoldus says, "And even an organ, which Francia had never built, whence the Greek kingdom boasted so much, and which was the only reason, caesar, Constantinople thought itself superior to you, is now found in the palace at Aachen. Perhaps it will be a sign that they are bending their necks to the Franks that their particular glory has been taken away. Rejoice, Francia! It is only right. Give pious thanks to Louis by whose virtue you receive such gifts. May almighty God, creator of heaven and earth, grant that His name will resound throughout the world for ages."[204] There is something to the story. The *Royal Frankish Annals*, under the year 826, state that a man named George arrived from Venice asserting that he knew how to build organs. Louis sent him to Aachen and instructed that he be given all the materials and help he needed.[205] I would draw attention to the confidence and serenity with which Ermoldus claims that Byzantium has been passed in the march of history.

Another passage in Ermoldus, his famous description of the wall paintings at Ingelheim, also reveals contemporary conversations about history and tradition.[206] There has been some controversy over whether the paintings were installed under Charlemagne or Louis.[207] For present purposes that issue is beside the point because Ermoldus described them in about 827 and it is his words that interest me here. Was he describing real paintings? Probably. And Lawrence Nees says carefully that Ermoldus provides "a fair guide to the fundamental thrust of the iconographic program."[208] Ermoldus starts with a description of the biblical scenes in the palace church. The left wall presented Old Testament scenes extending from Paradise to David, Solomon, and the Temple. The right wall offered New Testament scenes from the Annunciation to the Ascension. While Ermoldus's description is interesting enough, this arrangement of pictures is typical of Roman basilicas and neither the paintings not Ermoldus's words about them are distinctive. The opposite is true of the paintings in the palace hall. The paintings contrast a series of pagan rulers and figures with a series of Christians.[209] One series has Cyrus, Ninus, Phalaris, Romulus and Remus, and Alexander. The other series has Constantine, Theodosius, Charles Martel, Pippin III, and Charlemagne.

Ermoldus's account of the paintings of the pagan and Christian rulers is instructive.[210] On one level the words and pictures functioned as a mirror for Louis. They provided examples of behaviors to be avoided and emulated. On a deeper level the words and pictures present another series of reflections on history and tradition. One can see the passing of peoples and regimes. Cyrus and Ninus, presented in reverse chronological order, account for the end and the beginning of Babylon which had arisen in cruelty and ended in fury. But invoking Ninus and Babylon would, for the learned and alert, have evoked the intertext: Orosius's *Seven Books of History Against the Pagans*, especially the passage where Orosius spoke at length about the connections between Rome and Babylon. This association comes from Augustine. Theodulf cited it, as did Freculf. Now we see it again. Orosius looked more favorably on Christian Rome than Augustine (or Theodulf, or Frechulf) did. Hence, he could take satisfaction in the eclipse of Romulus and Remus's Rome by that of Constantine and Theodosius. Ermoldus, therefore, could situate the Carolingians in a continuous line of divinely ordained historical development. Ermoldus's use of the past is both similar to and different from the almost exactly contemporary Freculf's.

Nevertheless, I see one intriguing parallel. Charles Martel and Charlemagne are praised for defeating pagans, and that is just about all that is said about them. This is not wholly unlike Freculf's idea that *we* live in "Christian Times," in the City of God, and that the City of Man consists of Jews, pagans, and heretics. The very passage from Orosius that may have served as the basis for the Ingelheim iconography and Ermoldus's account uses the words "*Christiana tempora.*" In the late 820s two Carolingian writers who did not agree on all points articulated an acute awareness of time, tradition, and history. Surely Peter Brown is correct, however, in saying that "[t]he frescoes in the main hall of the palace of Ingelheim conjured up the huge confidence of the Franks that their empire represented nothing less than the culmination of Christian history."[211]

If it was important to understand where one fit in the grand scheme of history, it was also critical to understand history's concrete lessons. Ermoldus and Freculf are full of such lessons. But there is another way to view the matter. In the late eighth century Theodulf and Alcuin could complain about books and authors with which they were unfamiliar. Theodulf in particular could also rant about the incorrect ways that Byzantines read known books. He was fighting hard for his right to read, say, patristic texts of biblical passages, in his way. The image texts of the age of Louis the Pious are different in tone and approach. They are almost entirely free of ridicule and insult (at least with respect to Byzantium; Jonas and Dungal pound away at Claudius). They lay out cases with real assurance. They know more and better texts than had been available thirty years before. Again and again they content themselves with saying "The Bible says . . ." or "the holy fathers say. . . ."[212] The authors of these texts knew the tradition and presented it with equanimity. What had to be fought for in 790 had been assimilated by 830.

Several analogies come to mind. First, Carolingian biblical exegesis. For a long time, Carolingian exegetes were disparaged for being unoriginal and sometimes uncomprehending compilers. Gradually it has come to be seen that the Carolingians read the Scriptures themselves with discernment and discretion and that they selected carefully and intelligently among the patristic commentaries that served as their guides. What is more, ninth-century Carolingian commentaries, some 150 in number, often turned into commentaries on commentaries. Carolingian writers set one church father off against another.[213] In Silvia Cantelli's memorable phrase, they did "exegesis of exegesis."[214] That approach reveals a powerful sense of a tradition mastered and deployed. Second, Walahfrid's *Little Book on the Origins and Development of Some Aspects of the Liturgy*[215] as well as Hrabanus Maurus's *On the Instruction of the Clergy*[216] are full of specific, detailed, practical information. But both works offer historically rooted commentaries on ecclesiastical rites and customs. Once again, tradition is a sure guide to the present and a beacon pointing the way to the future. Walahfrid and Hrabanus both contributed to ninth-century discussions of images and both were well-experienced, well-connected men. Both had a profound sense of how tradition could and should guide their own times. Third, there is the proliferation of martyrologies in the ninth century. Monastic legislation required that they be read in chapter. This requirement assured a wide and knowledgeable audience of the ancient, heroic past of the church while, in view of church dedications and liturgical commemorations, putting ninth-century people in constant touch with their ancient Christian forebears.[217] They key point is a widespread familiarity with the stories of the early Christian martyrs—

with history and tradition simultaneously. Fourth, and finally, there are the more than ten thousand canons of Pseudo-Isidore.[218] Amid controversies which are not our concern here, spectacularly gifted forgers created a vast body of material reproducing, allegedly, ancient canonical and papal legislation. Regardless of the authenticity or accuracy of any of this material, it makes no sense, then or now, if it is not seen in the context of the power of the past, of tradition, to confer legitimacy.

Order

The reign of Louis the Pious provides abundant evidence for a quest for order. For a start, let us look at the records of the Council of Paris held in 829. The background may be sketched simply. The empire was suffering attacks on several frontiers. Political struggles were rampant. Louis desired to create a patrimony for his youngest son, Charles.[219] In these circumstances, he gave careful instructions to his archbishops and bishops to meet just after Pentecost in four great councils to be held at Mainz, Paris, Lyon, and Toulouse.[220] Louis had sent his own *missi* throughout the empire to look into everything in need of emendation and he asked the bishops to conduct similar investigations and to report fully to him.[221] Only the records from the Paris council survive. They form a lengthy and revealing dossier.[222] In turning now to those materials we should bear in mind that Jonas of Orléans was their principal redactor and that Freculf was present at Paris.

The Paris materials are set forth in unusual fashion. There is a general introduction, three introductory canons and then, in two books, a mirror for bishops and a mirror for kings. Finally, there is a letter of the bishops to Louis along with a synopsis of the canons. Conciliar canons typically consist of relatively short, detailed, and precise regulations. The Paris canons are generally lengthy, lofty, and occasionally abstract. The canons are studded with biblical references and, just occasionally, with patristic citations. Viewed as a whole, the documents are more like a single treatise than a set of canons.

In the general introduction (pp. 606–9) the bishops say that a review of history—it is biblical history that is under review—shows that God has many times forgiven even grave sinners who have repented and amended their ways. The bishops express their joy that Louis and Lothar have undertaken to ascertain what issues, presumably what sins, might now be in need of amendment. The Lord has entrusted His church to Louis and Lothar to rule and watch over (*regendam tuendamque*). To meet their responsibilities, the rulers have humbly consulted the bishops. The rulers understand that to achieve God's purposes they must "ask the priests the law," citing Haggai (2.12). Pious princes who follow the teaching of the vicars of the apostles merit forgiveness. The bishops, in telling the law, have not boldly transgressed the regulations set down by the fathers but instead have studied them.

The first of the three prefatory canons (pp. 609–10) states that the faith consists in basic doctrine (a creedlike statement is presented) and good works—faith, hope, love, humility, chastity, continence, sobriety, unanimity, concord, justice, piety, mercy, innocence, and simplicity. The second prefatory canon (p. 610) says, "The universal holy church of God is one body whose head is Christ." The third canon (pp. 610–11) says, "The body of this very church is principally divided between two distinguished persons . . . the sacerdotal and the royal." This canon contains the first medieval quotation of the famous dictum of Pope Gelasius I (492–96) from his letter to Emperor Anastasius.[223]

The bishops' words recall Freculf's "Christian Times." After the events of the early seventh century the City of God subsists in the universal church. The foremost duty of the church is to know and teach the faith and to effect proper Christian behavior. Rulers have a duty to use their authority and power to promote the church and its faith, but they have no independent warrant for action. They must consult the priests and implement what they learn. It would be difficult to imagine a clearer or more urgent statement about how the world ought to be ordered.

The bishops then say that because people are to be led to salvation by the vicars of the apostles, it is fitting that, first of all, the bishops look into any of their own actions that stand in need of correction. Accordingly, Book One (canons 4–54), constitutes a lengthy series of statements and admonitions to the episcopal order. Book Two (canons 55–67) asks "What a king is, what he ought to do and to avoid?" Right away one meets the famous tag from Isidore, "A king is called king by ruling rightly." How does a king rule rightly? "The royal ministry consist particularly in governing and ruling the people of God with equity and justice, and in being zealous to promote unity and concord." The king must defend the churches of God and their servitors, protect widows, orphans, and the poor and needy. Cases submitted to the royal ministry are not man's but God's.

Walter Ullmann once spoke of "the king's stunted sovereignty."[224] That is to miss the point. As the bishops saw things, there was only one legitimate entity in the world: the universal church.[225] Authority in the church was entrusted to the vicars of the apostles. As Gelasius had said, the authority of priests is more excellent that the power of kings because priests rule souls and kings, bodies.

What Louis thought about being assigned an auxiliary role in the church is hard to say. In 822, in his *Admonition to All Orders of the Realm,* Louis said, "But although the summit of this ministry is seen to rest in our person, nevertheless by divine authority and human ordination it is understood to be divided into parts so that each of you in your place and rank (*ordine*) is known to have a share in our ministry. Whence it is clear that I ought to be the admonisher of all of you and you ought to be our helpers."[226] In 829 the bishops effectively reversed Louis's sense of the way things ought to be. Still, it is striking that the emperor and the bishops shared a fundamentally similar view of how the world is organized. They seem to have disagreed somewhat on where initiative resided. In either case, they were keen to establish correct order in "Christian Times."

The image texts discussed above give evidence of anxieties about papal authority. Claudius apparently questioned the Petrine office. The Franks were worried about unusual practices tolerated by the papacy. Hadrian was accused of heresy. Louis and his Parisian interlocutors expected papal obstinacy. What is more, in 824 Louis faced the grim prospect of investigating murderous mayhem in Rome. Shortly after the Paris Council of 829 Louis the Pious faced two rebellions, one in 830 and a second in 833. Pope Gregory IV intervened in the second rebellion and Frankish reactions to his participation reveal further concerns about order in the highest levels of the church.

The details of the two rebellions need not detain us (although one could explore the issues on both sides for further evidence of concerns about order).[227] In early 833 Lothar marched north from Italy, to which his father had confined him in 831, bringing Pope Gregory IV with him. The sources relating to the rebellion are partisan in the extreme but they permit a few solid observations. Lothar, his brothers, and their allies among the clergy brought Gregory from Rome to strengthen the legitimacy of their case. Some of Louis's supporters said that Lothar and the others had brought the pope only to excommunicate Louis.[228] They viewed the pope as a tool in Lothar's hands. Some of the more radical clergy among Louis's opponents were prepared to accept papal intervention only if the pope were going to insist on the restoration of the *Ordinatio Imperii* of 817, the succession instrument whereby Louis had made Lothar his sole imperial successor and his younger sons sub-kings. In trying in the late 820s and again in 831 to find a place for Charles, born in 823, Louis adjusted the *Ordinatio* in ways that alarmed the sons of his first marriage. The spokesman for Louis's opponents was Agobard, who wrote to Louis that "if Gregory has showed up just now unreasonably and looking for a fight, then he will leave defeated and repulsed."[229] An impressive number of bishops, including some we have met here such as Jonas and Hrabanus, remained loyal to Louis. They wrote an angry letter to Gregory that does not survive but some of whose contents and tenor can easily be reconstructed from Gregory's response, which repeatedly says, "And then you say. . . ."[230] The loyalists said that the pope should work only for peace and unity and that he should show humble obedience to Louis. They said, further, that if the pope dared to excommunicate Louis he would himself go home excommunicated. Gregory responded powerfully. He chastised the bishops for calling him "brother." He said that the overturning of the *Ordinatio* and the new *Divisio* of 831 were sinful. The loyalist clergy saw Louis "tumbling into mortal danger" yet did nothing to save him. Hence he, Gregory, as the chief priest of the Christian world, had to intervene to restore peace and harmony. The pope also answered the charge that he should show humble obedience to Louis by insisting that he was the *summus pontifex*. As such, it was his responsibility to intervene on account of sin. In the end, Louis's sons deposed their father, and Gregory went home "sadly," unheard and unheeded. His grand claims notwithstanding, he lacked the effective power to intervene.

If the Paris bishops had divided the world in Gelasian terms and assigned primacy to themselves, then Gregory made an identical division but assigned primacy to himself. "For you ought to be aware," he said, "that the rule of souls, which is pontifical, is greater than the imperial which is temporal." For bishops like Agobard, the pope might have an auxiliary, complementary role alongside the Frankish clergy but no independent authority. For the loyalist bishops, the pope had badly exceeded the limits of his authority. The kinds of order so elegantly articulated at Paris in 829 proved hard to apply in contentious circumstances. Yet the desire to discover and implement order is palpable. Order meant the correction and emendation of all that was sinful and scandalous. Peace, unity, justice: these were the signs of order. The intractable problem was how to get there and who was to take the lead.

"Ask the priests the law." The Paris bishops in both 825 and 829 praised Louis for consulting them, first on a thorny dogmatic problem and second on the condition of the "holy universal church." Asked or not, the priests of Louis's age offered advice on a wide variety of issues. Smaragdus of St.-Mihiel, Ermoldus Nigellus, and Jonas of Orléans wrote "mirrors for princes," advice manuals on how to be a good and worthy king.[231] Jonas also wrote a book *On the Lay Estate* for Count Matfrid of Orléans.[232] I have already mentioned Walahfrid's liturgical manual, a how-to book of unusual breadth. Amalar of Metz produced a similar book entitled *On Ecclesiastical Offices*.[233] Hrabanus Maurus, as noted above, wrote a substantial work *Three Books on the Clerical Order* a sort of everything-you-need-to-know-to-be-a-priest manual. Louis's reign commenced with a series of ecclesiastical councils aimed at defining, correcting, and regularizing the monastic and canonical life. From 817 down to the 840s there were no fewer than four commentaries on the *Rule of St. Benedict,* the fundamental text of monastic life and observance.[234] One could go on and on in this vein. Proposed solutions to the problem of how to be good and do well were ubiquitous in the age of Louis the Pious. Order was much on people's minds.

Worship

Practices of and reflections on worship formed prominent issues throughout the reign of Louis the Pious. The Carolingian elite shared a profound conviction that the *cultus divinus* had to be properly observed in order for the peace, stability, and unity of the realm to be maintained.[235] The image texts show that individual, private acts needed scrutiny and regulation. But worship at the grand, public level was no less significant, even if it does not appear to have been a site for controversy. More research is needed on Carolingian court rituals[236] but the religious dimension, the worshipful dimension, of those rituals in Louis's era is so prominent that it provides a first context for thinking about worship generally in the early ninth century.

After the successful conclusion of his siege of Barcelona in 801, Louis processed into the city preceded by his clergy, everyone singing hymns and giving thanks to God.[237] In McCormick's words, Louis managed "to transform the Frankish triumphal entry into a liturgical procession of litanic quality."[238] The religious and ritual dimensions of Louis's coronation by his father at Aachen in 813 and by Pope Stephen IV at Reims in 816 are described in unusual detail by a wide array of sources.[239] We know who was present, where people stood and what they did, and, to some degree at least, what they said. Granted, we can only "see" those rituals in their textualized embodiments.[240] Nevertheless, the sources are unanimous in stressing that the hand of God can be seen in the great moments of Carolingian history and that in great spiritual/ritual moments the Carolingian elite came together as one. Ermoldus Nigellus's minutely detailed account of the preparations for and celebration of the mass in which Harald Klak of Denmark was received into the church was less an improvisation than a revelation of the extent to which court rituals had expanded and elaborated.[241] These rituals were designed to proclaim and to promote consensus and unity. Relations among people here and now, as well as relations between the here and the hereafter, were put right when things were done rightly—one almost said "ritely."

Less auspicious, but no less worshipful, are some other examples of religious rites in Louis's age. In 818 Louis declined to sit in judgment over or to execute sentence upon Bernard of Italy and other rebels during Lent.[242] When Louis was deposed in 833 the bishops charged him with a variety of offenses including: "That against the Christian religion and against his vow, without any public advantage or obvious necessity, having been misled by the advice of wicked men he ordered a general campaign in Lent and he decreed that he was going to hold a general assembly right on the outermost frontier of his realm on Good Friday when the paschal sacraments are supposed to be celebrated by all Christians."[243] Holy seasons were to be observed. And holy moments could be inserted into the regular course of the year. On several occasions Louis called for days of fasting, prayer, and penance before major undertakings such as the issuance of the *Ordinatio Imperii* in 817[244] and the assembling of the four councils in 829.[245]

Who was to worship, and how, when, and where occupied the attention of Hrabanus Maurus. The organization of his how-to book for priests is revealing. Book One discusses the orders of the clergy (cc. 3–12), vestments (cc. 14–23), sacraments (cc. 24–30), and the mass (cc. 30–34). Book Two treats first hours and offices (cc. 1–10), prayer in general terms (cc. 11–16), fasting (cc. 16–27), almsgiving (c. 28), penance (cc. 28–29), the celebration of major feasts (cc. 31– 41), Sundays (c. 42), saints' days (c. 43), masses for the dead (c. 44), commemorations of church dedications (c. 45), weekdays (c. 46), canticles, psalms, hymns, antiphons, responses, and readings (cc. 47–54), and, finally, blessings (c. 55). Book Three treats moral and theological lessons, things clerics "should hold and know." The book is clear, concise, and intensely practical. It is meant to show priests how to celebrate. Celebrating the mass properly was evidently a matter of widespread concern if the nearly two dozen commentaries on the mass from the period are any indication.[246] Walahfrid Strabo's handbook is less cogently organized that Hrabanus but testifies to a similar range of concerns: temples and altars (c. 1), what should and should not be done in churches (cc. 10, 11), bells, vessels, and vestments (cc. 5, 25), regulations for the reception of communion (cc. 20–22), canonical hours, posture in prayer, hymns, and chants (c. 26), and so on. General issues pertaining to worship were under discussion and specific kinds of liturgical books were being refined. Helisachar, Louis's chancellor, apparently re-wrote the night office sung at Aachen and a new hymnary was, it seems, under preparation at the court. The major liturgical scholar Amalar prepared a new antiphonary. Only the prologue survives but in it Amalar says he set to work because "I have been distressed for a long time because of the disagreements (*discordantes*) among the antiphonaries in our province."[247]

Beyond thinking about worship as a way of configuring the polity or as a way of celebrating sacraments properly, Carolingians also worried about avatars of "gentile" practice. In the Danes Louis and his contemporaries saw a very real embodiment of living, yet dead, practices. Ermoldus Nigellus is the best informant and even when some allowance is made for poetic license his account rings true, on the one hand, and lays bare Frankish concerns, on the other. Louis resolved to send a mission to Denmark, identified Ebbo of Reims as his missionary, and secured permission from Paschal I to launch the evangelization project. Ermoldus, as is his wont, puts speeches into the mouths of all the key players in this drama. Some of what he says can be taken seriously. In Ermoldus's telling, Ebbo told the Danes that metal statues made by their own hands cannot possibly benefit them; that they were worshiping empty things and praying to deaf and dumb beings. A bit later, according to Ermoldus, Harald Klak tells Ebbo that he wishes to see Louis's temples and God. If Louis's God is more powerful than his own, he will cast his metal statues into the fiery furnace. Finally, Harald acknowledges that Ebbo had told him that things made by human hands are empty idols so he elects to believe in God and reject statues made by hand.[248] Paganism was still a genuine problem along the frontiers of the Carolingian world. In border zones the battle for correct worship must have been fierce. What is more, it is striking how Ermoldus, surely not Harald, has internalized some of the discourse characteristic of Carolingian image texts: vain or empty idols but especially "things made by human hands." It is important to remember that Ermoldus's poem was written just after the Paris Colloquy and right when Jonas and Dungal were combatting Claudius against whom, as we saw earlier, Ermoldus took a potshot.

In addition to real, live pagans, there were also imperfectly Christianized folks whose modes of belief and worship demanded attention. As early as 815/16 Agobard wrote a treatise "On Hail and Thunder" in which he described various practitioners of and believers in different forms of weather magic: "In these regions almost everyone—nobles and common people, city folk and country folk, the old and the young—believe that hail and thunder can be caused by the will of humans." "Storm-makers" could raise storms when they wished. Ships from Magonia (Magic Land?) sail about in the sky full of crops knocked down by hail. Some people in Agobard's district were about to put to death some people who had allegedly fallen out of such a ship. It was also bruited about in the Lyonnais that Duke Grimoald of Benevento had sent people with a certain magic dust that, once spread in the fields, mountains, and wells, would kill cattle.[249] Agobard does not believe any of this but he accepts the fact that people in his diocese do believe it.[250] Such bizarre beliefs—and practices?—were not localized in time or place. The bishops who gathered at Paris in 829 sent Louis a resumé of their deliberations focusing on some of their most important discoveries and urgent concerns. They mention the existence of practitioners of various evils such as homosexuality and bestiality and then continue, "There are other most pernicious evils which have no doubt survived from the rites of the pagans: magicians, soothsayers, fortune-tellers, sorcerers, false prophets, casters of spells, interpreters of dreams, seers." The bishops also expressed alarm that some people were being led astray by love potions, amulets, and weather magic.[251] At almost the same time the *Penitential of Halitgar* tariffed penances for deaths caused by magic, love magic, the conjuring of storms, auguries, soothsaying, casting lots, practicing wizardry, and bearing amulets.[252] By the end of the ninth century conditions had not improved much judging from Regino of Prüm.[253] The worries expressed in the image texts about the "simple" and the concerns about correct and incorrect worship were by no means academic.

Conclusion

In the early decades of the ninth century Carolingian writers expressed themselves more fully, carefully, and thoughtfully than their predecessors had done a generation earlier. The image controversies of the 820s permit a keen perspective on the forward march of the "Carolingian Renaissance": More schools, scholars, libraries. Those same writers are more numerous than their predecessors. This affords the person who studies them an opportunity to discern areas of agreement and disagreement, to see varying shades of emphasis.

Ninth-century Carolingian authors exhibit full familiarity with all the classic arguments for and against images. Theodulf would not admit that any *manufactum* could be holy and utterly rejected any acts of veneration performed in connection with man-made stuff. Some ninth-century writers accepted that some objects might be holy and that some "moderate" practices might be tolerable. There was more sympathy for the idea that art could teach in the 820s than there had been in the 790s. From the age of Louis the Pious we have some evidence for practices connected with holy objects. While it seems clear that Theodulf would have barked his displeasure at practices that the generation after him tolerated, it is not so clear if more abundant evidence for the 820s and 830s simply reveals practices already present earlier but simply unrecorded.

The ninth century confronts its students with paradoxes. Amid much prudent, conservative verbiage concerning art, there was a profusion of spectacular works of art. Two instances may stand for many. Tours, in the decades after Alcuin's death, produced perhaps two grand, illuminated Bibles per year.[254] Sometime between ca. 816 and ca. 855, somewhere in northern France, an atelier produced the magnificent Utrecht Psalter which equips every psalm with a hauntingly beautiful drawing.[255] Earlier in this chapter I suggested that book art is difficult to draw into the kinds of discussions that I have been conducting. Ordinary people, "the simple," never saw such books, and most prominent laymen probably did not either. But at this stage I can bring this glorious book art back into the discussion by way of saying that the elites who talked about art were clerics—with the sole exception of Einhard—and they did see this art. Did it affect them, teach them, uplift them, inspire them? We do not know. They did not tell us.

Conclusion

Art is notoriously hard to talk about.
  —Clifford Geertz, "Art as a Cultural System"

TWICE BYZANTIUM EMBROILED the Franks in controversies over images. It might have happened a third time. In 842 Emperor Theophilus died. His widow Theodora assumed the regency for their three-year-old son and in 843, abetted by the old iconodule Methodius who had been named patriarch, she effected a "return to Orthodoxy"; that is, she restored icons. The next two decades in the East were filled with familial, political, military, and ecclesiastical strife. When Methodius died in 847 Ignatios replaced him. For eleven years Ignatios navigated dynastic squabbles and tried to balance warring ecclesiastical factions. Iconoclasts were mostly removed from the episcopate but not persecuted. The iconodule zealots, led by the Studite monks, wanted blood. Amid these difficulties Ignatios was deposed in 858 and replaced by the learned layman Photios. Photios announced his election to Nicholas I and thus began another controversy over images.[1]

For more than a decade the popes, emperors, and Byzantine church were ensnared in the "Photian Schism."[2] Most of what happened during that period need not concern us. Several of Nicholas's letters, however, touch upon the image question.[3] After Photios announced his election, Nicholas sent two legates to Constantinople to investigate the circumstances of Ignatios's deposition and replacement by Photios as well as the cause of holy, venerable images. Nicholas repeatedly said that his legates had come to see that images were properly restored to their customary place. He complained that heretical persecutors of images had not been sufficiently punished and that both churchmen and rulers had acted on political not religious imperatives. Nicholas also seems to have believed that Ignatios was a champion of images and that Photios was not. By the mid-860s Photios held a council which excommunicated Nicholas and accused him, as well as the Western church generally, of heresy on issues such as Saturday fasting, the use of unleavened bread in the eucharist, priestly celibacy, and the *filioque*. He did not mention images. Nicholas unleashed an epistolary barrage in the East[4] and also wrote to the east and west Frankish bishops, to Charles the Bald, and to Louis the German enlisting their support against Photios's charges. This marked the first time a pope had ever explicitly requested Frankish assistance in a doctrinal quarrel.[5] In 867 Basil I ascended the throne in Constantinople, deposed Photios, and recalled Ignatios. In 869–70 Ignatios presided over a council in Constantinople whose sixth canon simply embraced papal teaching (*sedis apostolicae praesules*) on the topic of images.[6]

When Nicholas wrote to Michael III in 860 he said that little needed to be said on the specific topic of images because his predecessor Hadrian I had already said everything that needed saying. Then he succumbed to the temptation to add a few comments of his own. He offered a few rather unsystematic defenses of images. He said that images of Christ, his mother, the blessed apostles, and all the saints should be "venerated and worshiped" (*venerari et colere*). He defended images because they increase love and incite emulation. Images painted on the walls of churches and on boards are not adored as if God. Images bring biblical stories and the truths of the faith vividly to mind. Finally, God had appeared to men as a Man. All of this, Nicholas says, is the unbroken tradition of the church.[7]

Exactly what the problem was in the East with respect to images cannot be determined. Nicholas had a loftier sense of papal power and prerogatives than any of his predecessors, and much of his struggle with the East was actually about papal primacy. It may be, therefore, that Nicholas simply wanted to put a papal stamp on Byzantium's return to Orthodoxy on the matter of images. When Nicholas turned to the West for support, he did not put the image question on the table. Several Western replies to Nicholas's request for concurrence survive and not one of them says a word about images.[8] The Franks had said all that they were ever going to say on the subject. They let pass the opportunity that Nicholas presented them to do verbal combat with Byzantium or Rome.

Pope Nicholas's comments in defense of images are briefer than those of Hadrian I or Paschal I. They do tell us, however, that the papacy had not yielded any ground to the Carolingians in argumentation for or against images. The Carolingians themselves exhibited for some fifty or sixty years an essential familiarity with all the basic elements in discussions about sacred art that had been in circulation since at least the fourth century with the sole exception of the philosophical positions adopted by Nicephorus and Theodore in the early ninth century. This is a first important discovery of the present work. It should no longer be possible to say that the Carolingians lacked the books, intellectual traditions, or theological sophistication to grapple with the more complex problems posed by sacred art. This study of art talk may provide food for thought for other investigations of how the Carolingians processed their intellectual inheritance. A second important point demonstrated in the preceding pages is that Carolingians did not agree with each other all the time. In art talk, as in so many other areas of intellectual life, John Contreni's "Inharmonious Harmony" serves as a superb characterization of the richness and complexity, not of the confusion and incomprehension, of Carolingian intellectual life. It is certainly true that the Carolingians sought norms, rules, standards; that they sought "order." But one must neither exaggerate nor misunderstand that quest.

The central Carolingian positions were these: Figural art is acceptable, particularly for commemoration or decoration; art objects should be neither worshiped nor destroyed. Both of these positions were qualified in some ways. Above all, there was what I have called "principled indifference." No Carolingian writer, to my knowledge, said that art was necessary. All Carolingian writers agreed that art could not be worshiped as God is worshiped. All Carolingian writers agreed on that point but they struggled to find the right words to express it. Some Carolingian writers were unprepared to permit any kind of reverence for *manufacta*, for the works of human hands, but other writers were willing to permit certain forms of veneration in certain circumstances. No Carolingian writer except Claudius of Turin believed that art works with Christian subject matter could be destroyed.

Carolingians agreed that art could exist, and of course they produced art in exuberant profusion. Art was permissible, first, because the Old Testament, in certain proof-passages that were cited over and over, said that God Himself had commanded certain images to be made. Moreover, they believed, the church had always countenanced art. Carolingian writers spoke rarely and hesitantly about images not made by human hands. For late antique and Byzantine iconophiles, the *achieropoieton* was a significant proof of the legitimacy of religious images. Some but not all Carolingian writers accepted the idea that art could teach the illiterate what the literate could read in books. Most Carolingian writers agreed that art could help people to recollect the history and mysteries of the faith. Many agreed that art could incite piety and compunction. Only occasionally did art's educative and commemorative functions spawn reflections on the relative excellence of hearing (or reading) versus seeing. The word was superior to the image, Carolingian writers agreed, but the image was useful for the "simple."

Once in a while Carolingian did writers come close to spinning aesthetic arguments to the effect that beauty itself could inspire. A proper Christian aesthetic had to await the massive scholastic compendia of the thirteenth century. Accordingly, the Carolingians had little to say on the (neo-) Platonic, Pseudo-Dionysian proposition that art could transport the laden soul from the material world to higher realms. They often evinced familiarity with the argument but rarely engaged it. Put a little differently, the Carolingians appear to have thought much harder about "commemoration" than they did about "decoration."

Two of late antiquity's most common defenses of art, the argument from incarnation and the referential argument, were widely known and discussed. Yet neither one occupied a central place in Carolingian discussions about art. It is my impression that both arguments were pretty much taken for granted. Further research in Carolingian Christology might help to clarify their attitude to the argument from incarnation. Carolingian writers all agreed that one did not worship an image but only some writers were explicit about praying to, or before, an image. Again, all the writers defended intercessory prayer. It is my impression that, on this point, Carolingian principled indifference led them to think that images were acceptable, perhaps even valuable and helpful, but never strictly necessary. Hence it was not felt imperative to go on at length about the ultimate target of a prayer directed in the first place at an image.

Not one Carolingian writer defended as a general proposition the ontological holiness of images. On the contrary, most of them insisted that images were mere matter, the work of human hands. Images' way-of-being was not different from, separate from, the wood or paint from which they were made. By the mid-ninth century, however, some writers had come to believe that the cross (and the crucifix?) formed an exception.

In the eighth century and then again in the ninth, Carolingian writers seemed baffled by the image practices of the Byzantines. Images in the West—Rome may have been different—did not receive hair or beard clippings, did not stand sponsor at baptism, did not serve as portable altars; their scrapings were not blended with the Eucharist; they were not greeted with lights and incense; they were not carried into battle (but relics were). Byzantine texts often speak of kissing as a common form of reverence bestowed upon images. Carolingian texts in the ninth century allude to kissing, bowing, kneeling, prostrating, and extending of the arms albeit explicitly only in connection with the cross or, depending on how one reads Claudius, with painted images of the cross/crucifix. If the Carolingians generally did not do to or with images what their Byzantine, and possibly Roman, contemporaries did, then neither did Carolingian images themselves do anything. They were not miraculous, did not heal the sick, ward off demons, or identify characters in dreams.

The Carolingian image texts that have been at the center of this study, more than a thousand pages of material, have never before been studied together. I hope the present study makes a contribution in this regard at least. With only a few exceptions[9] the Carolingian texts studied here have never been translated into a modern language, let alone English. I hope that readers will view my lengthy paraphrases and selective translations as another contribution. Finally, even though they wrote a great deal about images, the subject of images itself was rarely at the top of the Carolingian agenda and never alone on that agenda. A third contribution that I have tried to make here consists in paying close attention to the image texts in their contemporary contexts. I always try first to read the image texts on their own terms. Then I look at their actual words and peer between their lines to see if they reveal evidence of attention to, or sensitivity about, other burning issues. I have identified three of these: tradition, order, and worship. I would argue that each of these topics was of intense and durable interest to the Carolingains and that the image texts themselves and a wide range of other sources are mutually illuminating.

After the Carolingians fell silent, image controversies did not cease. Three-dimensional sculptures with embedded relics created a blurring of lines with which the Carolingians did not have to contend. Heretical sects, beginning in the eleventh century, occasioned new attention to the legitimacy of images. Christian-Jewish contention in the twelfth century and later once again generated both real and imagined arguments about religious images. Cisterician "puritanism" militated against the use of images and provoked defenses.[10] The great scholastics Bonaventure and Thomas Aquinas both spoke at some length, albeit in scattered places, about images.[11] It is interesting to see how "Carolingian" their argumentation was even though neither of them cited the texts with which this study has been concerned. They agreed that only God could be worshiped with the highest forms of worship but that images could be paid a lesser form of reverence. They embraced the incarnational and referential arguments. They agreed that images could teach the unlettered. The doctors believed that images could incite a heightened piety. They agreed that the Exodus prohibition applied to stiff-necked Jews and idolatrous pagans. Just as they understood idols and idolatry, so too they knew that images and idols were different. What changed in the thirteenth century was that, as in ninth-century Byzantium, a profound philosophical foundation was laid under the kinds of historical, ecclesiastical, and theological arguments of the Carolingian period. Nevertheless, to understand how the West talked about sacred art, it is necessary, and almost sufficient, to study how the Carolingians received and reflected on their late antique inheritance.

NOTES

ABBREVIATIONS

AASS	*Acta Sanctorum*
AnBol	*Analecta Bollandiana*
AB	*Art Bulletin*
AHC	*Annuarium Historiae Conciliorum*
AHP	*Archivum Historiae Pontificiae*
AK	*Aachener Kunstblätter*
BEC	*Bibliothèque de l'école des chartes*
BMGS	*Byzantine and Modern Greek Studies*
BZ	*Byzantinische Zeitschrift*
CCCM	*Corpus Christianorum, Continuatio Medievalis*
CCSL	*Corpus Christianorum, Series Latina*
CHR	*Catholic Historical Review*
DA	*Deutsches Archiv*
DBI	*Dizionario biografico degli italiani*
DOP	*Dumbarton Oaks Papers*
EHR	*English Historical Review*
EME	*Early Medieval Europe*
FMSt	*Frühmittelalterliche Studien*
JOB	*Jahrbuch der Österreichischen Byzantinistik*
JTS	*Journal of Theological Studies*
LMA	*Lexikon des Mittelalters*
LP	*Liber Pontificalis*
Mansi, Concilia	J. D. Mansi ed., *Sacrorum Conciliorum Nova et Amnplissima Collectio*
MGH	*Monumenta Germaniae Historica*
	Series in MGH
	Cap. *Capitularia Regum Francorum*

Conc.	*Concilia*
Epp.	*Epistolae*
EKA	*Epistolae Karolini Aevi*
PLAC	*Poetae Latini Aevi Carolini*
SSrG	Scriptores rerum germanicarum in usum scholarum
SSRL	*Scriptores rerum Langobardicorum*
SSrM	*Scriptores rerum Merovingicarum*
SCH	*Studies in Church History*
ODCC	*Oxford Dictionary of the Christian Church*
PG	*Patrologia Graeca*
PL	*Patrologia Latina*
PBSR	*Publications of the British School at Rome*
RB	*Revue Bénédictine*
REB	*Revue des études byzantins*
JE	*Jaffé and Ewald., Regesta Pontificum*
SCH	*Studies in Church History*
SSCI	*Settimane di Studio dell'Centro Italiano per il Medioevo*
T&M	*Travaux et mémoires*
W&I	*Word & Image*
ZKG	*Zeitschrift für Kirchengeschichte*

INTRODUCTION

1. Now brilliantly interpreted by Finney, *The Invisible God*. For a wider view, see the recent and engaging Jensen, *Understanding Early Christian Art*.

2. Ladner, "Origin and Significance of the Byzantine Iconoclastic Controversy," p. 127.

3. Florovsky, "Origen, Eusebius and the Iconoclastic Controversy," p. 77.

4. Cameron, "Images of Authority," p. 3.

5. "A Dark-Age Crisis: Aspects of the Iconoclastic Controversy," p. 3.

6. The closest to comprehensive treatments are various chapters in Martin, *History* and Haendler, *Epochen karolingischer Theologie*.

7. A recent, stimulating, and wide-ranging treatment is Besançon, *L'image interdit*.

8. Stock, *The Implications of Literacy*, esp. pp. 88–240.

CHAPTER ONE

1. *The Sayings of the Desert Fathers*, trans. Ward, p. 225.

2. Barasch, *Icon*, pp. 49–60; Metzler, "Bilderstürme und Bilderfeindlichkeit," pp. 14–29; Baynes, "Idolatry and the Early Church," pp. 116–43, esp. 117–19; Bevan, "Idolatry," pp. 253–72; and now, generally, Besançon, *L'image interdit*, pp. 9–10, 27–62.

3. Freedberg, *The Power of Images*, pp. 61–65; Besançon, *L'image interdit*, pp. 66–68.

4. Hossfeld, "'Du sollst dir kein Bild machen!,'" pp. 15–24; idem, "Das Werden des altestamentlichen Bilderverbots," pp. 11–22; Frevel, "Du sollst dir kein Bildnis machen," pp. 23–48; Hartenstein, "Die unvergleichliche 'Gestalt' JHWHs," pp. 49–77; Barasch, *Icon*, pp. 13–22; Nichols, *The Art of God Incarnate*, pp. 3–35.

5. Classic statements of this view are von Campenhausen, "The Theological Problem of Images in the Early Church," pp. 171–200; Koch, *Die altchristliche Bilderfrage*; Elliger, *Die Stellung der alten Christen zu den Bildern*.

6. Jensen, *Understanding Early Christian Art*; Finney, *The Invisible God*; Murray, "Art and the Early Church."

7. The continuing impact of Jewish book art has recently been traced by Kessler, "Through the Temple Veil," pp. 53–77. See also Frey, "La question des images chez les Juifs à la lumière des récentes découvertes," pp. 265–300; Diringer, *The Illuminated Book*, pp. 62–64; Gough, *The Origins of Christian Art*, pp. 28–29. See also the articles cited in n. 4.

8. MacMullen, *Paganism in the Roman Empire*, esp. pp. 1–48.

9. Justin Martyr, *Apologia prima*, c. 9, PG 6: 340A-B; Baynes, "Idolatry," pp. 117–18.

10. Finney, *The Invisible God*, pp. 15–39. See also Thümmel, *Frühgeschichte*, pp. 27–42.

11. Mansi, Concilia, 2: 11, c. 36. For a discussion see Grigg, "Aniconic Worship and the Apologetic Tradition," pp. 428–33.

12. *The History of the Church*, 7.18, trans. Williamson, pp. 301–2.

13. James, *The Apocryphal New Testament*, pp. 228–33. For varying interpretations of such apocryphal images, see Grabar, *Christian Iconography*, pp. 84–86; Breckenridge, "Apocrypha," 101–9; Thümmel, *Frühgeschichte*, pp. 43–44.

14. Mango, *The Art of the Byzantine Empire*, pp. 16–18. The text is in PG 20: 1545–49. See also Gero, "The True Image of Christ," pp. 460–70.

15. *Vita Constantini*, 3.49, PG 20: 1109A-B.

16. *History of the Church*, 7.18, trans. Williamson, p. 301.

17. Ibid., p. 302.

18. *The Divine Institutes*, 2.2, trans. MacDonald, pp. 97–101.

19. *The Case Against the Pagans*, 6.9, 10, 12–13, 14, 16, trans. McCracken, pp. 460–61, 463–65, 466–67, 468–70.

20. *Power of Images*, pp. 59–60, 65. See also Finney, *Invisible God*, pp. 3–14.

21. Finney, *The Invisible God*, pp. 146ff.

22. Jensen, *Understanding Early Christian Art*; Janes, *God and Gold*; Gough, *Christian Art*, pp. 52–136; Christe, "Christian Art from Its Origins to the Beginning of the Eleventh Century," pp. 11–18; Mathews, *The Clash of Gods*, passim; Grabar, *Christian Iconography*, pp. 8–92.

23. Representative are von Campenhausen (above n. 5) and Savramis, "Die abergläubische Mißbrauch," pp. 175–76, 180.

24. Ladner, "The Concept of the Image," p. 20; Kitzinger, "The Cult of Images in the Age Before Iconoclasm," pp. 115–29; Grabar, *Christian Iconography*, pp. 21–36. This thesis has recently been criticized, in ways that are not entirely satisfactory, by Mathews, *Clash of Gods*; See Brown's review in AB, 77 (1995): 499–502; Belting, *Likeness and Presence*, pp. 102–14.

25. Kessler, "'Pictures Fertile with Truth,'" pp. 53–65, quotation p. 54.

26. Kitzinger, "Cult of Icons," pp. 90–91.

27. Dagron, "L'image de culte et le portrait," pp. 125–31; Grabar, "Le portrait en iconographie paléochrétienne," pp. 87–109; Belting, *Image and Presence*, pp. 78–101. Most recently, Sande, "The Icon and Its Origin in Graeco-Roman Portraiture," pp. 75–84 who nevertheless puts the veneration of icons very far back in Christian history by adducing the concept of syncretism and drawing unpersuasive analogies between known pagan practices and alleged Christian ones.

28. Holl, "Die Anteil der Styliten am Aufkommen der Bilderverehrung," pp. 388–98 remains the classic statement of this view. See also Gendle, "The Role of the Byzantine Saint in the Development of the Icon Cult," pp. 181–86.

29. Mathews, *Clash of Gods*, pp. 25–118.

30. Baynes, "Idolatry and the early Church," p. 126.

31. Brenk, "Visibility and (Partial) Invisibility," pp. 140–50.

32. Cameron, *Christianity and the Rhetoric of Empire*; Elsner, *Imperial Rome and Christian Triumph*, pp. 11–15; idem, *Art and the Roman Viewer,* passim; Nees, *Early Medieval Art*, chs. 1–4.

33. Recent discussions are Cormack, *Painting the Soul*, pp. 64–88 and, somewhat more generally, Lowden, *Early Christian and Byzantine Art*, pp. 9–61.

34. Mango, *The Art of the Byzantine Empire*, p. 47 (PG 32: 149). Thümmel, *Frühgeschichte*, pp. 53–55 thinks Basil expressed himself in similes and did not really discuss art per se.

35. PG 26: 332B.

36. Mango, *The Art of the Byzantine Empire*, p. 34 (*De deitate Filii et Spiritus Sancti*, PG 46: 572C).

37. *Homilia in quadraginta martyres*, PG 31: 508C–D.

38. *Homilia encomiastica in patrem nostrum Meletium*, PG 50: 516: καὶ πανταχοῦ τὴν εἰκόνα τὴν ἁγίαν ἐκείνην διαχάραξαν πολλοί.

39. Freedberg, *The Power of Images*, pp. 162–64; Maguire, *Art and Eloquence.*

40. Mango, *The Art of the Byzantine Empire*, p. 37 (*Oratio laudatoria sancti magni martyris Theodori*, PG 46: 737D–740B). The first portion of the translation is Mango's, the second, my own.

41. Maguire, *Art and Eloquence in Byzantium*, pp. 9–12.

42. A subject brilliantly treated by Cameron, *Christianity and the Rhetoric of Empire*. See also n. 32 above.

43. On Epiphanius see: Thümmel, *Frühgeschichte*, pp. 65–73; Maraval, "Épiphane," pp. 51–62; Kitzinger, "Icons," pp. 92–95; Baynes, "Idolatry and the early Church," pp. 126–28; Maas, "Die ikonoklastische Episode in dem Brief Epiphanios und Johannes," pp. 279–86; Holl, "Die Schriften des Epiphanius gegen die Bilderverehrung," pp. 351–64. Recently Speck has, on the grounds of alleged textual anachronisms, argued that what we read is an eighth-century confection, perhaps by another Hypatius: "ΓΡΑΦΑΙΣ Η ΓΛΥΦΑΙΣ: Zu dem Fragment des Hypatios," pp. 211–72, esp. 221–41. I follow the traditional ascription of these fragments to Epiphanius: Thümmel, *Frühgeschichte*, pp. 103–12; Sansterre, "La parole, le texte

et l'image selon les auteurs byzantins," pp. 204–5. Brubaker and Haldon, *Byzantium in the Iconoclastic Era*, p. 253 say that the matter "remains a subject for further discussion."

44. Ostrogorsky, *Studien zur Geschichte des byzantinischen Bilderstreites*, pp. 67–75.

45. Oratio I.25, II.18.

46. Mango, *The Art of the Byzantine Empire*, p. 41.

47. Ibid., pp. 41–42.

48. Ibid., pp. 42–43.

49. Mansi, Concilia, 13: 32C–33C, 36A–D. Mango, *The Art of the Byzantine Empire*, pp. 32–33, has translations of the interpolated versions.

50. Thümmel, "Neilos von Ankyra über die Bilder," pp. 10–21 and *Frühgeschichte*, pp. 78–79. Sansterre accepts Thümmel's interpretation: "Parole," p. 204.

51. Mango, *The Art of the Byzantine Empire*, pp. 43–44.

52. Dumeige, *Nicée II*, p. 41.

53. Clark, *The Origenist Controversy*, pp. 43–104; Schönborn, *L'icone de Christ* pp. 21–85, esp. 7–85; Mathews, *Clash of Gods*, pp. 27–53.

54. Mango, *The Art of the Byzantine Empire*, p. 114.

55. Ibid., p. 115.

56. Hypatius of Ephesus, *Summikta Zetemata*, trans. Alexander, "Hypatius of Ephesus," pp. 178–81. The remainder of this article (181–84) constitutes a brief but careful assessment of the thought of Hypatius. See also Thümmel, *Frühgeschichte*, pp. 103–6; Kitzinger, "Icons," pp. 94, 138; Baynes, "Icons Before Iconoclasm," pp. 93–95; Lange, *Bild und Wort*, pp. 44–60; Gero, "Hypatius of Ephesus," pp. 208–16.

57. PG 93: 1597B–1609A. There is a new edition (pp. 66–72) with a French translation (pp. 72–78) in the second of Déroche's articles cited below. I treat this text at some length because it has not been translated into English. On Leontius, see Thümmel, *Frühgeschichte*, pp. 127–36, 233–36; Lange, *Bild und Wort*, pp. 61–76; Baynes, "Icons Before Iconoclasm," pp. 97–98. Speck calls into question the authenticity of this text: "Graphais ē Glyphais," pp. 242–48; "Anthologia Palatina I.1 and des Apsismosaik der Hagia Sophia," pp. 315–22; "Schweinfleisch und Bilderkult," pp. 367ff. Once again I follow Speck's critics: Déroche, "L'authenticité de l'Apologie contre les Juifs de Léontios de Néapolis," pp. 655–69; idem, "*L'Apologie contre les Juifs*," pp. 45–104; Sansterre, "Parole," p. 205; Mango, "A Byzantine Hagiographer at Work: Leontios of Neapolis," pp. 24–41. Mango dates Leontios's work to 610–50. Thümmel stresses Leontius's later influence. Most recently, see Weitmann, *Sukzession und Gegenwart*, pp. 128–32; Barber, "The Truth in Painting," esp. pp. 1025–33; Brubaker and Haldon, *Byzantium in the Iconoclast Era*, pp. 252–53.

58. Thümmel, *Frühgeschichte*, pp. 118–48.

59. Stephen apparently wrote late in the seventh century. In Rome in about 731 his writing, or some portion of it, was translated into Latin. In, perhaps, the 760s the work was translated back into Greek, possibly in connection with a council of three Oriental patriarchs in Jerusalem. The fragments themselves survive in Paris BNF MS Gr. 1115, an iconophile florilegium that was probably prepared in Rome in the early to late 770s. See Alexakis, "Some Remarks on the Colophon of the Codex *Parisinus Graecus* 1115," pp. 131–43 and "Stephen of Bostra, *Fragmenta Contra Judaeos*: A New Edition," pp. 45–60, with the edition pp. 51–55.

Further details and literature in Brubaker and Haldon, *Byzantium in the Iconoclast Era*, pp. 268–69. For the context see Déroche, "Polémique anti-judaïque," pp. 141–61.

60. De Lange, "Jews and Christians in the Byzantine Empire" pp. 15–32; Haldon, *Byzantium in the Seventh Century*, pp. 345–348; Cameron, "Byzantines and Jews," pp. 249–74.

61. In addition to the works of Déroche and Alexakis cited in nn. 57 and 59 see the studies of Dagron and Déroche that fill almost the whole of vol. II of T&M and, more recently, Hopkins, *World Full of Gods*.

62. *Roman Defeat*, p. 3; for his general discussion of the anti-Jewish material, see pp. 116–79. Cameron, "Byzantines and Jews," passim, finds Olster's views plausible but insufficient as an explanation of the anti-Jewish attitudes of the time. Barber, "The Truth in Painting" adds the nuance that the discussions of images may in fact have reflected attempts by both Jews and Christians to construct identities around the topic of the materiality of images specifically and the created order generally.

63. Ettinghausen, Grabar, and Jenkins-Madina, *Islamic Art and Architecture*, pp. 6, 59–65.

64. Der Nersessian, "Une apologie des images," pp. 379–403. The work of Vrt'anes is translated into French pp. 379–88. I have rendered only a few passages from French into English because I cannot read the Armenian original. Der Nersessian's remains the fundamental study of this issue. See also Baynes, "Icons Before Iconoclasm," pp. 105–6; Alexander, "An Ascetic Sect of Iconoclasts," pp. 151–60; Mahé, "L'Église arménienne de 611 à 1066," pp. 485–86. It is well to remark here, and the point is relevant elsewhere, that the evidence for three-dimensional Christian sculpture is extremely limited: Kilerich, "Sculpture in the Round," pp. 85–97, esp. pp. 89–91.

65. Alexander, "An Ascetic Sect of Iconoclasts," pp. 151–60; text translated by Alexander from the Armenian history of the Caucasian Albanians by Moses of Kaghankatujk, p. 154. See also Thümmel, *Frühgeschichte*, pp. 115, 230, and 328–29 (the latter a reprint of Alexander's English text).

66. Pseudo-Denys, *Celestial Hierarchy* 1.2 ed. and trans. Rorem. On the relationship between Pseudo-Denys and images see Kitzinger, "Icons," p. 137; Kollwitz, "Zur Frühgeschichte der Bilderverehrung," pp. 60–61; Freedberg, *The Power of Images*, pp. 164–65; Barasch, *Icon*, pp. 158–79; Louth, "Truly Visible Things," pp. 15–23.

67. *I Am You*, p. 281. For some interesting reflections on how the writings of Dionysius might have been mediated through those of Maximus the Confessor, who was prominent and controversial in the seventh century, see Zhivov, "The Mystagogia of Maximus the Confessor," pp. 349–76.

68. Mansi, Concilia, 13: 164D–165C. Most of the relevant passage is in Mango, *The Art of the Byzantine Empire*, pp. 140–41 but I have considered a few lines which he omitted. See Thümmel, *Frühgeschichte*, pp. 112–14.

69. Mansi, Concilia, 13: 185B–188A. See Thümmel, *Frühgeschichte*, pp. 109–12.

70. I cite this translation of a passage from Anastasius's *Hodegos* from Barber, "The Body Within the Frame," p. 148.

71. Thümmel, *Frühgeschichte*, pp. 138–40, 236–37, 253–68; Barber, "The Body Within the Frame," pp. 147–48; Kartsonis, "The Emancipation of the Crucifixion," pp. 164–66

and, more generally on Anastasius, *Anastasis*, pp. 41–67; Brubaker, "Perception," 28–31 and "Byzantine Art in the Ninth Century," pp. 70–75. Kartsonis believes that Anastasius may have illustrated his text.

72. Mansi, *Concilia*, 11: 976C–D, c. 73; ed. Nedungatt and Featherstone, p. 155.

73. Mango, *The Art of the Byzantine Empire*, p. 36.

74. Mansi, *Concilia*, 11: 986D, c. 100; ed. Nedungatt and Featherstone, pp. 180–81.

75. Mansi, *Concilia*, 11: 977E–980B; ed. Nedungatt and Featherstone, pp. 162–64, whose translation I cite. On this passage, see Kitzinger, "Icons," p. 121—but Kitzinger says that Lambs were to be "replaced" which is not stated explicitly. Excellent discussion in Barber, *Figure and Likeness*, pp. 40–47.

76. Dagron, "Le christianisme byzantin," p. 65; Robin Cormack, *Writing in Gold*, pp. 98–101; Vogt, "Der Streit um das Lamm," pp. 135–45, adds the idea that the combination of the Lamb and the Forerunner was prophetic and, as such, Jewish and equivalent to the people when they were under the Law. Accordingly, images of Christ in His human form would indicate the present dispensation of "grace and truth." He does not pursue the question of whether or not his thesis contributes to an understanding of anti-Jewish polemics in the seventh century.

77. I would emphasize here that proclaiming the incarnation was not the same as developing a Christological defense of images, or of deriving Christological perspectives from the existence of images. This was done for the first time in the eighth century by John of Damascus, as we will see in the next chapter.

78. "Icons," p. 85.

79. Ibid., pp. 134–35.

80. Mango, *The Art of the Byzantine Empire*, p. 23 and n. 5; Minazzoli, "'Imago'/'Icona,'" pp. 313–16; Belting, *Likeness and Presence*, pp. 17–29.

81. Cameron, "The Language of Images," pp. 7–9; Kitzinger, "Byzantine Art in the Period Between Justinian and Iconoclasm," pp. 48–49; idem, "On Some Icons of the Seventh Century," p. 145. But Brubaker suggests that it may be hazardous to differentiate too sharply between icons and narratives: "Sacred Image," p. 3.

82. *Likeness and Presence*, p. 26. But see also Cormack, *Painting the Soul*, pp. 64–88 for some cogent remarks on the limitations of stylistic assessments of icons.

83. Diebold, *Word and Image*, p. 98.

84. "Sacred Image, Sacred Power," pp. 1–2; "Ruminations on Edible Icons," pp. 47–59.

85. Although Weitzmann, *Monastery of St. Catherine*, vol. 1, pp. 23–26 thinks that the icon of St. Peter was carried in liturgical processions.

86. Brubaker, "Sacred Image," p. 2.

87. "L'iconodulie," in Boespflug and Lossky, *Nicée II*, p. 159.

88. *Bilderlehre und Bilderstreit*, pp. 14–15.

89. *De moribus ecclesiae catholicae* 1.34.75, PL 32: 1342: "Novi multos esse sepulchrorum et picturarum adoratores."

90. *Likeness and Presence*, pp. 30–46, 78–101.

91. Mango, *The Art of the Byzantine Empire*, p. 41.

92. Vikan, "Icon and Icon Piety in Early Byzantium," pp. 569–76; "Byzantine Pilgrims' Art," pp. 229–66.

93. All of this is brilliantly evoked and explained in Maguire, Maguire, and Duncan-Flowers, *Art and Holy Powers*, pp. 1–33. See also for the magical implications of such images Engemann, "Zur Verbreitung magischer Übelwehr," pp. 22–48. The theme is pursued across late antiquity and Byzantium in Maguire and Maguire, *Other Icons*.

94. *Adversus Judaeos et gentiles Demonstratio*, PG 48: 826.

95. Mango, *The Art of the Byzantine Empire*, p. 139. In general see Cormack, *Writing in Gold*, pp. 43–95.

96. Cameron, "Images of Authority," pp. 3–35; McCormick, *Eternal Victory*, pp. 100–110.

97. Cameron, "The Theotokos in Sixth-Century Constantinople," pp. 79–82, quotation p. 81.

98. Frolow, "La dédicace de Constantinople."

99. Mango, *The Art of the Byzantine Empire*, p. 40.

100. Van Esbroeck, "La culte de la Vierge," pp. 181–90.

101. Baynes, "Supernatural Defenders," pp. 165–77; Cameron, "Images and Authority," pp. 20–22; Dagron, "Le christianisme byzantin," pp. 18–20.

102. Grabar, *L'iconoclasme byzantin*, pp. 36–45; Breckenridge, *Numismatic Iconography*.

103. Cameron, "The Language of Images," p. 33.

104. Cameron, "History of the Image of Edessa," pp. 80–94 tells the fascinating story of how the original legend of the epistolary exchange between Jesus and the Edessene king Abgar turned into a story about an image of Jesus sent by the Lord Himself to Abgar through an intermediary.

105. This story is related by the late sixth-century Piacenza Pilgrim's *Travels from Piacenza*, c. 44, ed. and trans. Wilkinson, p. 86.

106. *The Holy Places*, 1.10, ed. and trans. Wilkinson, p. 98.

107. Von Dobschütz, *Christusbilder*, pp. 40–294; Belting, *Likeness and Presence*, pp. 47–65; Cormack, *Painting the Soul*, pp. 93–96. Cormack supposes that the image seen by Arculf may be the one now in Cleveland.

108. For discussions of image practices, see Kitzinger, "Icons," pp. 96–112; Kollwitz, "Frühgeschichte," p. 63; Judith Herrin, *The Formation of Christendom*, pp. 307–15; Dagron, "Le christianisme byzantin," pp. 84–90.

109. Babi, "Les images byzantins," pp. 189–222.

110. "Icons Before Iconoclasm?," pp. 1215–54, esp. 1230–50.

111. *The Spiritual Meadow*, trans. Wortley, nos. 45 (the one that may derive from the seventh century), 81, 180, 230.

112. Brubaker, "Images Before Iconoclasm?," p. 1230 n. 50 citing Geyer's Latin edition. For the English translation, see above n. 105.

113. See below pp. 42–44 for the letters of Pope Gregory I to bishop Serenus of Marseilles discussing *adoratores* of images around 600.

114. See Stephen's *Fragmenta*, ed. Alexakis (as in n. 59 above), pp. 51–55.

115. This is, generally speaking, Thümmel's thesis in *Frühgeschichte*, although I attach somewhat more prominence than he does to the amount of image discussion on both sides of the issue before 700.

116. Paulinus, *Carmen* 27, *Carmina*, ed. De Hartel, pp. 285–88. See also Duggan, "Was Art Really the 'Book of the Illiterate,'" p. 229; Cantino-Wataghin, *"Biblia Pauperum."*

117. John Cassian, *Conférence* X.5, ed. Pichery, pp. 78–79.

118. *De consensu evangelistarum*, 1.10, PL 34: 1049. See Berliner, "The Freedom of Medieval Art," pp. 273–74; Besançon, *L'image interdit*, pp. 141–50; Harrison, *Beauty and Revelation in the Thought of Saint Augustine.*

119. *De Doctrina Christiana Libri IV*, 2.1–5, 25, ed. Martin, pp. 32–35, 61.

120. Dagron, "Holy Images and Likeness," p. 24.

121. *De Trinitate*, 15, 8. 4. 7, ed. Mountain, pp. 275–76.

122. Sermo 264, PL 38: 1214.

123. *De genesi ad litteram*, 12. 6, ed. Zycha, pp. 386–87.

124. Miller, "Relics, Rhetoric, and Mental Spectacles," pp. 28–36.

125. *De fide rerum invisibilium* 20, ed. van den Hout, pp. 1–2.

126. *Regula*, c. 42, PL 67: 1116B.

127. *Etymologiae*, 8.11.4–5, ed. Lindsay, vol. 1, p. 328.

128. *Etymologiae*, 1.73.32, ed. Lindsay, vol. 1, p. 74; 19.16.1 (cf. 16.3.4), vol. 2, np.

129. *Sententiarum Libri Tres*, 2. 11. 9, PL 83: 612B–C.

130. *Decem libri historiarum* 2.17, ed. Krusch and Levison, MGH, SSrM, 1.64–65.

131. *Decem libri historiarum*, 10.31, p. 535. Venantius Fortunatus, Carmen 10, *Opera Poetica*, ed. Leo, pp. 234–38. See Kessler, "Pictorial Narrative and Church Mission," pp. 75–91.

132. Woodruff, "The Iconography and Date of the Mosaics of La Daurade," pp. 80–104.

133. Vieillard-Troiekouroff, *Les monuments religieux de la Gaule*; Knögel, *Schriftquellen zur Kunstgeschichte der Merowingerzeit.*

134. *De gloria martyrum*, 21. MGH, SSrM, 1.2: 51.

135. See his study cited in n. 131.

136. "The Cult of Icons in Sixth-Century Gaul," pp. 151–57; essentially in agreement is Angenendt, Anti-Ikonklasmus," pp. 215–16, noting, however, that images are marginal compared with relics.

137. *De gloria martyrum* 21, MGH, SSrM, 1.2: 51.

138. *De gloria martyrum* 22, MGH, SSrM, 1.2: 51.

139. *De virt. s. Martini*, 1.15, MGH, SSrM, 1.2, p. 597. It was in fact Gregory's friend Venantius Fortunatus who was cured, as he himself relates in his own *Vita Martini*, 4, MGH, AA, 4.1, pp. 369–70.

140. LeBlant, *Inscriptions*, vol. 1, p. 237.

141. Heidrich, "Syriches Kirchengemeinden im Frankenreich im 6. Jahrhunderts," pp. 21–32.

142. Raymond Van Dam, *Saints and Their Miracles in Late Antique Gaul*, pp. 41–42, n. 26.

143. *Glory of the Martyrs*, 6, trans. Van Dam, p. 27.

144. *Virt. Jul.*, 24, MGH, SSrM, 1.2: 124–25; *Gloria martyrum* 5, MGH, SSrM, 1.2: 39–42.

145. *Dreams in Late Antiquity*, p. 104.

146. "The Poet as Visionary." She extends this argument in "Images as 'Mysteries.'"

147. "Images in Texts," quotation at p. 101.

148. Gregory I, *Registrum Epistolarum*, 9.208, ed. Ewald and Hartmann, MGH, Epp., 1, p. 195. See also Duggan, "Book of the Illiterate," with the older literature. The best study of these letters, with even more of the literature, is Chazelle, "Pictures, Books, and the Illiterates," pp. 138–53. On the important matter of the rhetorical style of these letters, see Banniard, "Langages et styles de Gregoire le Grand," pp. 29–46, esp. 37–38.

149. *Registrum Epistolarum*, 11.10, ed. Ewald and Hartmann, pp. 269–72.

150. *Decem libri hist.*, 2.10, MGH, SSrM, 1.2: 58–60.

CHAPTER TWO

1. Ludovico Antonio Muratori, *On the True Devotion to Christ*, quoted by Belting, *Likeness and Presence*, p. 77 (with n. 83, p. 563).

2. Two outstanding books lay out current thinking effectively: Haldon, *Byzantium in the Seventh Century*; Whittow, *The Making of Orthodox Byzantium*.

3. Fowden, *Empire to Commonwealth*.

4. Dagron, "Le christianisme byzantin," p. 93.

5. Cormack, *Writing in Gold*, pp. 47–49; Belting, *Likeness and Presence*, pp. 225–26.

6. Dagron, "Le christianisme byzantin," p. 109.

7. Mansi, Concilia, 13: 208B–C.

8. Ševčenko, "Icons in the Liturgy," pp. 45–57; Beck, "Von der Fragwürdigkeit der Ikone," pp. 33–35; Schreiner, "Der byzantinische Bilderstreit," p. 333. Cf. Sahas, *Icon and Logos*, p. 14: "The icon and the word are in no tension with each other. The icon serves as a reminder of and as a commentary upon the Scriptures and has *always* been an integral part of the liturgical, didactic, and missionary ministry of the Church" (my emphasis).

9. Mango, "Historical Introduction," p. 4; Lowden, *Early Christian and Byzantine Art*, pp. 101–45 passim.

10. Schreiner, "Bilderstreit," pp. 380–81.

11. "Perichoresis: The Christology of the Icon," pp. 67–85.

12. Methodios, Archbishop of Thyateria and Great Britain, "Icons in Patristic Theology and Spirituality Eastern and Western," pp. 17–22.

13. *Icon and Logos*, p. 5. A similarly ahistorical view is taken by Konstantinides, "Die Theologie der Ikone," pp. 42–52, who says that an icon makes a holy person "present" and that the icon is in one sense independent of historical context and in another sense serves alone to interpret context. Again and again he speaks of "the Orthodox tradition" without any reference to historical circumstances.

14. *The Theology of the Icon*, p. 8.

15. *Painting the Soul*, pp. 20, 46.

16. Hetherington, trans. *Painter's Manual*, pp. I–IV; Belting, *Likeness and Presence*, pp. 17–19. See also Cormack, *Painting the Soul*, pp. 29–30.

17. Mansi, Concilia, 13: 252B–C.

18. Most prominently: Grabar, *L'iconoclasme byzantin*, p. 300; Cormack, "Painting after

Iconoclasm," in Breyer and Herrin, *Iconoclasm*, pp. 147–55; de' Maffei, *Icona, pittore e arte al concilio Niceno II,* pp. 69–75, 82–86.

19. Convincingly demonstrated by Yiannias, "A Reexamination of the 'Art Statute' in the *Acts* of Nicaea II," pp. 348–59.

20. Belting, *Likeness and Presence*, pp. 19–21; Thümmel, *Bilderlehre und Bilderstreit*, pp. 35–37.

21. Besançon, *L'image interdite*, p. 158.

22. Nicephorus, *Short History*, cc. 59–60, ed. and trans. Mango, pp. 129–31. Pp. 8–12 of this work discuss the problems involved in dating the text. See also Brubaker and Haldon, *Byzantium in the Iconoclast Era*, pp. 171–72.

23. Theophanes, *Chronographia*, ed. de Boor, pp. 401–13. I cite the translation of Mango and Scott, *The Chronicle of Theophanes Confessor*, pp. 555, 558, 559–61, 563–65. For the basic details on the Beser, Yezid, etc., see Vasiliev, "The Iconoclastic Edict of Yazid II." On Theophanes, Brubaker and Haldon, *Byzantium in the Iconoclast Era*, pp. 168–71.

24. *Life of Stephen the Younger*, c. 10, ed. Auzépy, pp. 100–101, French trans. pp. 193–94. See Brubaker and Haldon, *Byzantium in the Iconoclast Era*, pp. 226–27 with rich bibliography.

25. Cited by Kazhdan and Talbot, "Women and Iconoclasm," p. 392.

26. *Synodicon Vetus*, cc. 147, 148, ed. Duffy and Parker, pp. 122–24.

27. *Vita Gregorii II*, cc. 13–16, LP, ed. Duchesne, 1: 403–4; for general details see Noble, *The Republic of St. Peter*, pp. 28–40.

28. LP, ed. Duchesne, 1: 404; Davis, trans., *The Lives of the Eighth-Century Popes (Liber Pontificalis)*, no. 91, c. 17, p. 11 (my translation differs from Davis's in one or two important ways).

29. Davis, *Lives*, no. 91, cc. 18–24, pp. 13–16.

30. Davis, *Lives*, no. 92, cc. 2–4, pp. 19–21.

31. Mansi, Concilia, 12: 959–82. Cf. Jaffé, RP, nos. 2180, 2182. Caspar asserted the basic authenticity of the texts and supplied an edition that improved on that of Mansi: "Papst Gregor II. und der Bilderstreit," pp. 29–89 (edition, pp. 68–89). Gouillard provides the best edition of the texts, along with a French translation and a superb commentary which makes clear the problems with the texts: "Aux origines de l'iconoclasme: le témoinage de Grégoire II?" pp. 243–307 (edition, pp. 276–307). The primary defender of the authenticity of the letters is Grotz, "Beobachtungen zu den zwei Briefen Papst Gregors II. an Kaiser Leo III.," pp. 9–40; "Weitere Beobachtungen zu den zwei Briefen Papst Gregors II. an Kaiser Leo III.," pp. 365–75; "Die früheste römische Stellungnahme," 150–61. For a review of the issues and comprehensive bibliography see Conte, *Regesto delle lettere*, pp. 46–79. For the most recent arguments against the authenticity of the letters see Michels, "Zur Echtheit der Briefe Papst Gregors II. an Kaiser Leo III.," 376–91 and Vogt, "Der Streit um das Lamm," 145–49; Weitmann, *Sukzession und Gegenwart*, pp. 275–77. Alexakis, *Codex Parisinus Graecus*, pp. 108–10, 119–23, does not finally commit himself on the authenticity of the letters but he does show that they must have been prepared before 754 and that some materials extant before 731 in iconophile florilegia appear in the letters. There still seem to me to be so many problems with the texts of these letters that I decline to draw testimony from them. Only a critical edition of the *acta* of II Nicaea will, perhaps, resolve the matter one way or the other.

32. Mansi, *Concilia*, 13: 92C–100A; Jaffé, RP, no. 2181. See Michels, "Echtheit," p. 384 n. 70. For these three letters see Brubaker and Haldon, *Byzantium in the Iconoclast Era*, p. 277.

33. Mansi, *Concilia*, 13: 100B–105A (John), 105B–108A (Constantine), 108A–118A (Thomas). There is a good discussion of these letters in Thümmel, *Frühgeschichte*, pp. 159–71 but he dates them 720–26. Most recently on Germanus and these letters: Stein, "Germanos," pp. 12–15. Speck, "Die Affäre um Konstantin," pp. 148–54, argues that Germanus and Constantine were essentially in agreement and that the sections of Germanus's letter that appear to support the veneration of images are later interpolations. I am sympathetic to this point but not convinced by this argument.

34. I am inclined to accept the arguments of Stein for dating Germanus' letter to Thomas in about 729: *Der Beginn des byzantinischen Bilderstreites*, pp. 4–88. Speck argues that the letter dates from the 740s and is riddled with later interpolations: *Artabasdos*, pp. 267–81 and again in his *Ich bin's nicht, Kaiser Konstantin ist es gewesen*, pp. 163–67. Stein, "Germanos," pp. 13–15 agrees than the letter to Thomas is a bit later than the ones to Constantine and John, and that it may have been tampered with at some later time. Still, he believes that the letter is official in character and essentially authentic.

35. *De haeresibus et synodis*, cc. 40–41, PL 98:77A–80A.

36. *De haeresibus et synodis*, c. 42, PL 98: 80A–C. On this text see Gouillard, "L'hérésie dans l'empire byzantin des origins au XIIᵉ siècle," pp. 306–7; Dagron, "Le christianisme byzantin," p. 117; Stein, *Der Beginn*, pp. 262–68.

37. *Contra imaginum calumniatores orationes tres*, ed. Kotter. Eng. trans. Louth. For a general account of John's role in the iconoclastic controversy see Louth, *St. John Damascene* and my "John Damascene and the History of the Iconoclastic Controversy," pp. 95–116.

38. Kotter, *Schriften*, pp. 6–7 lays out the traditional chronology. Louth, in the Introduction to his translation of the *Three Treatises*, p. 10 dates no. 1 to 726–30, no. 2 to 730 or shortly after, and no. 3 to the early 740s. Speck argues that all three *Orations* were written between 741 and 750 but holds out the possibility of a date after 752: *Artabasdos*, pp. 179–243. This view has not met with acceptance. Schreiner, "Bilderstreit," p. 325 pronounces the matter unsettled. Alexakis, *Codex Parisinus Graecus*, p. 125 does not commit himself except to say "the end of the second (if not the beginning of the third) quarter of the eighth century." Most recently Brubaker and Haldon, *Byzantium in the Iconoclast Era*, pp. 248–40 opt for a date in the 740s for all three. I certainly agree on the third *Oration* but I believe that the other two are earlier.

39. *Oratio I*, c. 1, ed. Kotter, p. 65 (trans. Louth, p. 19).

40. *Oratio I*, c. 1, ed. Kotter, p. 66 (trans. Louth, pp. 19–20) Where Louth renders the Greek words quoted above as "the word of a king" I have attempted to catch both the literal and ideological force of θεσπίσματα, a common word in imperial diplomas where its use is meant to suggest the divine inspiration of imperial pronouncements. See Dölger, "Die Kaiserurkunde der Byzantiner als Ausdruck ihrer politischen Anschauungen," p. 23.

41. *Oratio II*, c. 12, ed. Kotter, p. 102 (trans. Louth, p. 68).

42. *Oratio II*, c. 16, ed. Kotter, p. 113 (trans. Louth, p. 73).

43. *Oratio II*, c. 12, ed. Kotter, p. 103 (trans. Louth, p. 69).

44. *Oratio I*, c. 3, ed. Kotter, p. 67.

45. *Oratio II*, c. 4, ed. Kotter, p. 71 (trans. Louth, p. 61).

46. *Oratio I*, c. 19, ed. Kotter, p. 94 (trans. Louth, p. 32).

47. The point has been so comprehensively argued that it would be otiose to cite all the contributions. The strongest case for a formal decree in 726 is Anastos, "Leo III's Edict Against Images." For a variety of reasons scholars have been skeptical: Beck, "The Greek Church in the Epoch of Iconoclasm," p. 28; Gero, *Byzantine Iconoclasm During the Reign of Leo III*, pp. 94–105; Mango, "Historical Introduction," p. 2; Stein, *Der Beginn*, pp. 138–77; Speck, "Weitere Überlegungen und Untersuchungen über die Ursprunge der byzantinischen Renaissance," p. 99.

48. Christophilopulu, "Silention," pp. 79–85, esp. 80–82. For the passage in the *Life of Stephen the Younger* see c. 40, ed. Auzépy, pp. 139–40, French trans. p. 235.

49. Gero, *Byzantine Iconoclasm in the Reign of Leo III*, pp. 85–87 says these letters "reveal the existence of an active iconoclastic movement in certain parts of Asia Minor" (p. 87). I think this is an exaggeration of the degree of iconophobia present there and the sources simply do not prove overt iconoclasm.

50. Barnard, *The Greco-Roman and Oriental Background of the Iconoclastic Controversy* lays out the case for Jewish and Muslim influence on Leo. Speck's *Ich bin's nicht* reveals most of the reasons why that case cannot stand. See also Dagron, "Le christianisme byzantin," pp. 101–3.

51. The great study remains Mango, *The Brazen House*, pp. 108–18, where the existence of the image, and Leo's destruction of it, is basically accepted. Belting, *Likeness and Presence*, p. 159 follows Mango. Speck was among the first to suggest a legend: *Kaiser Konstantin VI*, p. 607. In her commentary on Theophanes, Rochow accepts Speck's views and adds some of her own: *Byzanz im 8. Jahrhundert in der Sicht des Theophanes*, pp. 115–18. The most devastating critic of the traditional view is Auzépy, "La destruction de l'icône du Christ?" pp. 445–92.

52. *Vita Stephani*, c. 10, ed. Auzépy, p. 100 (French trans. p. 193). This is, incidentally, the first source to mention the destruction of the image.

53. The one exception might be *Constantinople in the Early Eighth Century: The Parastaseis Syntomoi Chronikai*, c. 5b, ed. Cameron and Herrin, p. 62: τῆς θεανδρικῆς εἰκόνος τοῦ Ἰησοῦ Χριστοῦ. But Auzépy thinks this is a tenth-century interpolation ("La destruction," p. 446) whereas the editors of the text, while acknowledging that this portion of the *Parastaseis* was filled in later, think the material may be authentic, pp. 6, 17.

54. Germanus to Thomas of Claudiopolis: PG 98: 185A; Mansi, Concilia, 13: 124E–125A.

55. LP 1: 426–35 (trans. Davis, pp. 35–50). For the encounter with Constantine V and the gift of the estates of Nimfa and Norma, ed. cit., c. 20, p. 433 (Davis, p. 46).

56. Rouan (Auzépy), "Une lecture 'iconoclaste' de la vie d'Étienne le Jeune," 419. For all issues pertaining to this important text see now the introduction to Auzépy's edition, pp. 5–60.

57. On the reign of Constantine see now Rochow, *Kaiser Konstantin V (741–775)* and Whittow, *The Making of Orthordox Byzantium*, pp. 134–64 passim. Among older works see Lombard, *Constantin V*; Ostrogorsky, *History*, pp. 165–75; Hussey, *The Orthodox Church in the Byzantine Empire*, pp. 38–44.

58. In chronological order these are: (1) George of Cyprus, *Nouthèsia gerontos peri tôn agiôn eikonôn*, ed. Melioranskij. I have not had access to this edition. Dumeige, *Nicée II*, discusses this text (pp. 88–90) and provides extracts in a French translation (pp. 232–36). For additional discussion see: Gero, *Constantine V*, pp. 25–36; Speck, *Bin's nicht*, pp. 565–67. Traditionally the work is dated to around 754 and held to be a source for no. 2 below. Alexakis, *Codex Parisinus Graecus*, pp. 110–15, shows that these two texts are interdependent and that the *Nouthesia* is a "cut-and-paste" job that drew either on No. 2 or on a common source and that it probably dates from the late 760s. (2) *Adversus Constantinum Caballinum*, PG 95: 309–44. The printed version is wrongly attributed to John Damascene. The text is composite: At its base is perhaps a synodical letter of Patriarch John of Jerusalem (cc. 1, 25) written in 730. This was turned into a short version, perhaps at Rome, shortly before 769 (cc. 2–7, 9, 11, 17, 25). The longer version was prepared just before II Nicaea in 787. This is the reconstruction of Auzépy, "L'Adversus Constantinum Caballinum," pp. 323–38, which I accept except that she thinks the long version was prepared in Tarasius's entourage whereas I think that the text's bitter denunciation of Constantine V fits better in the years before Tarasius became patriarch because, as we will see below, he handled Constantine very tactfully. Speck, *Bin's nicht*, pp. 139–90 attempts to make a case for an early section depending on the same source[s] used by the *Nouthesia* and then expanded redactions in the early ninth century and again after 843. This is all quite ingenious but unconvincing. For further discussion see: Gero, *Constantine V*, p. 27; Dumeige, *Nicée II*, pp. 95–97; Dagron, "Le christianisme byzantin," p. 117; Lange, *Bild und Wort*, pp. 147–57. (3) John of Jerusalem, *Adversus iconoclastas*, PG 96: 1348C–1361D. This work, which may not be by John of Jerusalem, appears to date from about 770. It is mainly a theological pastiche and contains fewer details than the first two. For discussion see Dumeige, p. 95 and Dagron, p. 117.

59. Stephen the Deacon, *Life of Stephen the Younger*, ed. Auzépy, pp. 87–178, with an extensively annotated French translation, pp. 179–277. In addition to Auzépy's "Introduction" and annotations, there are several good discussions of this text: Gill, "The Life of Stephen the Younger by Stephen the Deacon," pp. 114–39; Ševčenko, "Hagiography of the Iconoclast Period," pp. 113–31, esp. 115–16; Huxley, "On the *Vita* of St. Stephen the Younger," pp. 97–108; and the article by Rouan (=Auzépy) in n. 56 above. The *Life* was written in about 809 but could date from 807.

60. The so-called *Peuseis* extracted by Ostrogorsky, *Studien*, from the ninth-century writings of Nicephorus. We shall return to these texts below.

61. The council fathers at II Nicaea devoted their sixth cession to a verbatim recitation and lengthy refutation of the documents of the Council of Hiereia: Mansi, Concilia, 13: 203–354.

62. *Short History*, c. 64, ed. Mango, p. 135.

63. *Chronicle*, anno 6233, trans. Mango, p. 575 (ed. de Boor, p. 415).

64. *History of the Byzantine State*, p. 165.

65. Gero, *Constantine V*, pp. 15–17 (quotation p. 17). The key study is Speck, *Artabasdos*, whose chief accomplishment is a revision of the chronology of the revolt from the traditional 742–43 to 741–42. See also Rochow, "Anastasios," pp. 24–29.

66. *Chronicle*, anno 6238, trans. Mango, p. 585 (ed. de Boor, pp. 422–23).

67. *Short History*, c. 67, ed. Mango, pp. 139–41.

68. *Bin's nicht*, pp. 94–105 on Constantine V and pp. 98–104 where he suggests that Anastasius may have issued some sort of decree against images. Rochow, "Anastasios," p. 27, notes that this is all conjecture. For my part, I observe how striking it is that later iconophile writers did not attribute iconoclasm to Anastasius.

69. *Adversus Const. Cab.*, c. 21, PG 95: 337C–340B.

70. *Nouthesia*, trans. Dumeige, p. 232.

71. *Life of Stephen the Younger*, cc. 24, 26, ed. Auzépy, pp. 120, 121 (tr. Fr. pp. 212, 214–15).

72. *Chronicle*, anno 6244 (751–52), trans. Mango, p. 591.

73. *Antirr.* I. 19, PG 100: 232A–B.

74. *Nouthesia*, trans. Dumeige, pp. 232–33.

75. *Life of Stephen the Younger*, c. 26, ed. Auzépy, pp. 121–22.

76. Tarasius, *Apologeticus ad populum a Tarasio*, Mansi, Concilia, 12: 990A. This text stands in the prefatory material to II Nicaea and, as it is not registered by Grumel, *Régestes*, there is reason to suspect it. I cannot independently verify its authenticity.

77. Mansi, Concilia, 13: 356C–D.

78. Mansi, Concilia, 13: 324D–E; trans. Sahas, *Icon and Logos*, pp. 143–44.

79. Mansi, Concilia, 13: 328C; trans. Sahas, *Icon and Logos*, p. 147.

80. *Brief History*, c. 72, trans. Mango, p. 145.

81. Mansi, Concilia, 13: 329E, 332B, D–E.

82. LP 1: 464.

83. Charanis, "The Monk as an Element of Byzantine Society," pp. 63–84; Ringrose, "Monks and Society in Iconoclastic Byzantium," pp. 130–51. Charanis was drawing on an article of Brehier that identified the forty-five monk-patriarchs as having officiated in the years between 705 and 1204: "Le recruitment des patriarches de Constantinople pendant la période byzantine," pp. 221–27.

84. Mango, "St. Anthusia of Mantineon and the Family of Constantine V," pp. 401–9; Auzépy, *La vie d'Étienne le Jeune*, p. 37.

85. *Brief History*, c. 80, ed. Mango, p. 153.

86. *Chronicle*, anno 6253, trans. Mango, p. 598.

87. *Life of Stephen the Younger*, ed. Auzépy, passim.

88. *Short History*, c. 81, ed. Mango, p. 155.

89. *Chronicle*, anno 6257, trans. Mango, p. 604 (ed. de Boor, pp. 436–37).

90. Theosteriktos, *Life of Nicetas*, c. 30, AASS, April 1, pp. 260E–261A. See Ševčenko, "Hagiography of the Iconoclast Period," p. 118.

91. Nicephorus, *Brief History*, c. 83, ed. Mango, p. 157; Theophanes, *Chronicle*, anno 6257, trans. Mango, p. 605. See Rochow, *Theophanes*, pp. 186–89, 191.

92. Theophanes, *Chronicle*, anno 6263, trans. Mango, p. 615.

93. The most penetrating analysis of these developments is Rouan, "Une lecture 'iconoclaste,'" pp. 420–35. The most recent discussion is Rochow, *Konstantin V*, pp. 59–68. Many discussions of the attacks on monks go back to a famous article by Peter Brown, "A Dark-Age Crisis," pp. 1–34. Amid many pointed observations, Brown offered two basic

interpretations: monks were a centripetal force at a time of imperial centralization and monks were especially devoted to icons and the possessors of many famous ones so that "iconomachy in practice was monachomachy." Brown's argument about center and periphery won some support, for instance from Ahrweiler, "The Geography of the Iconoclastic World," pp. 21–27, but seems less prominent today. Brown's association of iconomachy and monachomachy has not been accepted: Gero, "Byzantine Iconoclasm and Monachomachy," pp. 241–48; idem, *Constantine V*, pp. 121–42; Schreiner, "Bilderstreit," pp. 352–58; Thümmel, "Der byzantinische Bilderstreit," pp. 9–40, esp. 16ff. See also the articles by Charanis and Ringrose in n. 83. Generally there is a consensus that the attack on the monks was political and institutional, and perhaps economic.

94. Nicephorus, *Short History*, c. 81, ed. Mango, p. 155; Theophanes, *Chronicle*, anno 6257, trans. Mango, pp. 604–5, 606 n. 5. On Patriarch Constantine generally see Rochow, "Konstantinos II," pp. 30–44 and on his deposition, pp. 37ff.

95. Whittow, *Orthodox Byzantium*, pp. 144–47.

96. I essentially follow the reconstruction of Auzépy, *La vie d'Étienne le Jeune*, pp. 25–42, although I do not think that she fully resolves all the chronological problems.

97. Theodore of Studion, *Laudatio S. Platonis Higoumeni*, PG 99: 805A–849A.

98. The classic study of religious persecution in the iconoclastic era, which began the process of moderating earlier lurid accounts, is Alexander, "Religious Persecution and Resistance in the Byzantine Empire," pp. 238–64. Already Lombard, *Constantin V*, pp. 151–53 had argued for restraint in interpreting the persecutions. See also Mango, "Historical Introduction," p. 4 and Ševčenko, "Hagiography of the Iconoclast Period," p. 115; Dagron, "Le christianisme byzantin," pp. 112–14; Rochow, *Theophanes*, pp. 128ff., 186–88; Auzépy, "La place des moines à Nicée II," pp. 6–7.

99. Mansi, Concilia, 13: 187A–192D.

100. Rodley, *Byzantine Art and Architecture*, p. 126, with the observation that "Otherwise the damage is described in suspiciously general terms."

101. Mango, "Historical Introduction," p. 4; Schreiner, "Bilderstreit," pp. 385–89, who observes that the story about the replacement of the images of the six councils may be a literary duplication of the removal of the image of the sixth council by Philippicus Bardanes; Speck, *Kaiser Konstantin VI*, pp. 71–72.

102. Belting, *Likeness and Presence*, pp. 134–35; Breckenridge, *The Numismatic Iconography of Justinian II*; idem, "The Iconoclasts' Image of Christ," pp. 3–8; Bertolini, *Figura velut qua Christus designatur*, pp. 5–12, 22–36. Moorhead, "Iconoclasm, the Cross and the Imperial Image" argues that iconclasm sparked a cult of the cross and that its origins lie in the era of Constantine the Great.

103. Theophanes, *Chronicle*, anno 6259, trans. Mango, pp. 611, 612 nn. 14, 15 (ed. de Boor, p. 443).

104. Maffei, *Icona, pittore e arte al Concilio Niceno II*, pp. 93–104. Khludov Psalter, fol. 67r, reproduced many times, most recently in Evans and Wixom, eds., *The Glory of Byzantium*, p. 97.

105. Mango, "Historical Introduction," 4; Rodley, *Byzantine Art*, pp. 126–27.

106. Schreiner, "Bilderstreit," p. 387; Dagron, "Le christianisme byzantin, pp. 108–9.

Beck, "Fragwürdigkeit," pp. 31–36 adds that it tended to be the older, noble, well-educated cathedral clergy who designed and celebrated the liturgy so whereas these clerics may have gone along with Constantine V in 754 up to a point, there were limits as to how far they were prepared to go.

107. Cormack, "The Arts During the Age of Iconoclasm," pp. 35–44.

108. Kazhdan and Maguire, "Hagiographical Texts," 9; Brubaker, "Byzantine Culture," pp. 66–67.

109. For Theophanes' account of Leo's reign see *Chronicle*, trans. Mango, pp. 620–31. For varying assessments of the reign of Leo see Dumeige, *Nicée II,* pp. 99–100; Speck, *Konstantin VI*, pp. 54–103; Rochow, *Theophanes*, p. 219; Dagron, "Le christianisme byzantin," pp. 121–22. On Patriarch Paul see Lilie, "Paulos IV," pp. 50–56.

110. Theophanes, *Chronicle*, trans. Mango, p. 625; Cedrenus, *Historiarum Compendium*, ed. Bekker, 2: 19–20.

111. Speck, *Konstantin VI*, pp. 56–58 and Whittow, *Orhtodox Byzantium*, pp. 149–50 with the older literature. For some of the older views see Runciman, "The Empress Irene the Athenian," pp. 101–18. Herrin's is a valiant attempt to make women the particular defenders of images, "Women and Faith in Icons in Early Christianity," pp. 56–83, but the evidence is just too thin, as the article by Kazhdan and Talbot (above n. 25) shows convincingly.

112. For especially good assessments of Irene's position, see Herrin, *Women in Purple,* pp. 51–129; Whittow, *Orthodox Byzantium*, pp. 149–50; Speck, *Konstantin VI*, pp. 105–27; Treadgold, *The Byzantine Revival*, pp. 1–59.

113. Theophanes, *Chronicle*, trans. Mango, pp. 626–31 (quotation p. 626).

114. Rochow, *Theophanes*, pp. 226, 240–41; Hussey, *Orthodox Church*, p. 45; Thümmel, *Bilderlehre*, p. 65; Treadgold, *Byzantine Revival*, pp. 75–77. Treadgold, p. 399 n. 86, provides additional sources, albeit late ones, in support of the traditional view.

115. *Chronicle*, trans. Mango, p. 631. Cf. the fact that in his report for 780/81 Theophanes merely said that "the pious began to speak freely." Born in 759 or 760, Theophanes was an eyewitness and sometime participant in the great events of the 780s: see Mango's superb introduction, pp. xlix–lii, lv–lvi.

116. Speck, *Konstantin VI*, pp. 106–39, esp. 132–35; Schreiner, "Bilderstreit," pp. 345–46; Treadgold, *Byzantine Revival*, pp. 63–71, 75.

117. *Orthodox Byzantium*, p. 150.

118. *Chronicle*, trans. Mango, p. 631.

119. Mansi, Concilia, 12: 984E–986C. The date of August 29, 784 has always been accepted: Dölger, *Regesten*, no. 341; Dumeige, *Nicée II*, p. 100. Maccarrone, "Il papa Adriano I e il concilio di Nicea del 787," p. 433 n. 3 believes that the letter must date from 785 because, he thinks, the letter is of a piece with Tarasius's synodical letter that must date from 785 and because Hadrian's response was not written until October 26, 785—too long, Maccarrone thinks, after a letter of August 29, 784. These arguments are not convincing. See in general, Uphus, *Der Horos*, pp. 39–40.

120. Mansi, Concilia, 12: 986B: "Constantinum praeterea sanctissimum episcopum Leontinum Christo amabilis Siciliae nostrae insulae, quem etiam noscit paterna vestra beatitudo, adduximus ad nos, et facie ad faciem loquentes direximus cum praesenti nostra venera-

bili jussione ad vos . . . porro sanctimssimum episcopum Neapolitanum omnino tenere habet, ut cum ipso ascenderet huc." Martin, *History*, p. 88 n. 3 takes these references to mean that Paul was forced to abdicate and that Irene was looking far afield for a replacement, the bishops of Constantinople's region having been tainted. This view is plausible but runs far ahead of the evidence.

121. *Byzantine State*, p. 177.

122. Theophanes, *Chronicle*, trans. Mango, pp. 632–33. For a fine discussion of Tarasius see Ludwig, "Tarasios," pp. 57–108.

123. Mansi, Concilia, 990A: τινὲς δὲ ὀλίγοι τῶν ἀνθρωπῶν ἀνεβάλλοντο.

124. Hadrian to Irene and Constantine, Mansi, Concilia, 12: 1055A–1071B, 1073A–1076D; to Tarasius, 1078C–1084D. The initial section of the first letter referenced here exists in both Latin and Greek, whereas the second section exists only in Latin. It is in this Latin section that Hadrian's sharp criticisms are expressed. Traditionally it is argued that this section was suppressed in the public reading of the letter at Nicaea in 787 so as to avoid raising thorny issues between East and West and compromising the position of Tarasius. The letter to Tarasius mentions only the matter of his elevation from the laity but does so in rather mild terms and says that, given Tarasius' evident orthodoxy, Hadrian accepts him. Wallach, "The Greek and Latin Versions of II Nicaea, 787, and the *Synodica* of Hadrian I (*JE* 2448)," pp. 3–26 argues that the whole Latin version (Hadrian's original) was translated into Greek and read in 787 but that the Greek version was truncated in 858 to avoid creating problems for Ignatius, another man elevated from the lay state to the patriarchal dignity. Wallach's arguments are learned but have not won much favor (Treadgold, for instance, *Byzantine Revival*, p. 400 n. 98 cites Wallach without comment and Hussey, *Orthodox Church*, p. 46 assumes suppression; Lamberz, "Studien zur Überlieferung der Akten des VII. Ökumenischen Konzils," pp. 41–42 shows that Wallach's arguments rested on shaky foundations as to textual history, but that he may nevertheless have been correct about a later alteration of the letter). Surely there was as much reason to avoid potential insults and tumults in 787 as in 858 and the references to papal patrimonies and episcopal ordinations cannot have had much meaning in 858 whereas they were still live issues in 787. Still, it is odd that the conciliar records have the authenticating testimony of the papal legates after the pope's letters were read in 787 if those letters had been significantly altered. Mansi, Concilia, 1075D, 1083E–1086A. See now Uphus, *Der Horos*, pp. 41–50, 50–53, essentially upholding traditional interpretations.

125. On this monastery see Sansterre, *Les moines grecs et orientaux à Rome*, 1: 22–29.

126. Sansterre, *Moines grecs*, 1: 128; Dagron, "Le christianisme byzantin," pp. 122–23.

127. Henry, "Initial Eastern Assessments of the Seventh Ecumenical Council," pp. 78–79 notes the calculated ambiguity of Hadrian's response, suggesting that all the pope was willing to do was countenance the repudiation of 754.

128. A point (over-)emphasized by Maccarrone, "Adriano e il concilio di Nicea," pp. 433–39 speaking of "una Canossa bizantina," 496, 511–14, 515, and passim. For a more reserved view see Dagron, "Le christianisme byzantin," pp. 132–33.

129. Treadgold, *Byzantine Revival*, pp. 78–79.

130. There are two accounts which complement each other: Theophanes, *Chronicle*, trans. Mango, p. 635; *Syngraphē Syntomos*, Mansi, Concilia, 12: 990B–991D. See Treadgold, *Byzantine Revival*, pp. 78–82.

131. Theophanes, *Chronicle*, trans. Mango, pp. 635–36. See Treadgold, *Byzantine Revival*, pp. 82–82; Alexander, *The Patriarch Nicephorus of Constantinople*, pp. 18–20.

132. An excellent account is Dumeige, *Nicée II*, pp. 101–43.

133. Treadgold, *Byzantine Revival*, p. 81 is good on this issue.

134. Mansi, Concilia, 12: 1031D.

135. Thümmel, *Bilderlehre*, pp. 37–38, 69–76; Speck, *Konstantin VI*, pp. 136–37; Beck, "The Greek Church in the Epoch of Iconoclasm," pp. 37–41.

136. The treatise *Adversus Constantinum Caballinum* (PG 95: 309–44) is a lonely voice from within the empire. Otherwise all known critiques of iconoclasm arose beyond the empire's grasp: In Jerusalem in 760; in the letter of the eastern patriarchs to Pope Paul I in 767; in the Roman synod of 769; in an Antiochene synod of 781. On these see Sahas, *Icon and Logos*, p. 34.

137. Mansi, Concilia, 12: 999B. See Treadgold, *Byzantine Revival*, p. 83.

138. To avoid needless notes, I shall in the following account put the column number(s) from Mansi, Concilia, vols. 12 and 13 in parentheses in the text.

139. The suggestion of Treadgold, *Byzantine Revival*, pp. 84–85.

140. Curiously one of the bishops named in session one, George of Pisidia, disappears from the list of those seated in session three.

141. E.g., Beck, "Fragwürdigkeit," p. 27; idem, *Kirche*, pp. 302–3; idem, "Greek Church," pp. 40–41; Thümmel, *Bilderlehre*, p. 54; Fazzo, "Il concilio di Nicea nella storia cristiana ed i rapporti fra Roma e Bisanzio," pp. 345–60, esp. 358; Dagron, "Le christianisme byzantin," p. 127.

142. This stress on unity is the central argument of de Vries, "Die Struktur der Kirche gemäss dem II Konzil von Nicaea (787)," pp. 47–71. Maccarrone, "Adriano e il concilio," p. 515 sees papal primacy rather than ecclesiastical unity as the key issue. Maccarrone is correct as far as Hadrian's views are concerned but I think de Vries better understands the conciliar records as a whole.

143. Erickson, "*Oikonomia* in Byzantine Canon Law," pp. 225–36.

144. Speck, *Konstantin VI*, pp. 152–59; Treadgold, *Byzantine Revival*, pp. 82–89.

145. Speck, *Konstatin VI*, pp. 156–58; van den Ven, "La patristique et l'hagiographie au concile de Nicée de 787," pp. 325–62, esp. 331ff; Auzépy, "La place des moines à Nicée II," 5–21; idem, "L'iconodulie," pp. 157–65, esp. 157–58.

146. Mansi, Concilia, 13: 417C-439E. Dumeige, *Nicée II*, pp. 142–50; Ciccimara, "La condotta degli ecclesiastici e le disposizione del II Concilio di Nicea," pp. 107–16 Troianos, "Die kanones des VII. ökumenischen Konzils," pp. 289–306.

147. Speck, *Konstantin VI*, pp. 137, 159–60; de Vries, "Struktur der Kirche," pp. 48–49. Ludwig, "Tarasios," p. 64 notes that Ignatius's *Life of Tarasius*, written a generation later, places the blame squarely on Leo III and Constantine V.

148. *Chronicle*, trans. Mango, p. 555.

149. Speck, *Konstantin VI*, pp. 134–40.

150. Van den Ven, "Patristique," pp. 336–38. Another major theologian who received little attention at Nicaea was Maximus the Confessor who, at the time of the Roman Synod of 649, had also issued sharp denunciations of imperial interference in dogma: *Acta Maximi*,

PG 90: 117B–C. Ostrogorsky, *History*, p. 120. These same criticisms are made in the forged or interpolated versions of the letters of Gregory II, which are printed before the conciliar acts in Mansi, 12: 959A–982B and which cannot be shown to have been read at Nicaea. See above, pp. 00–00. It is not implausible that a pope would have condemned imperial intrusion into dogmatic issues but it is hard to know whether this objection was voiced at Nicaea. In a letter to Charlemagne, Hadrian mentions a letter of Gregory III that also criticized Leo III for implicating himself in dogmatic issues (Hadrian, ep. no. 1, MGH, EKA 3, p. 51) but there is no hint anywhere that this letter was read at Nicaea. Finally, the letter of Gregory II to Germanus that was read in session four (92C–100A) is, for all its verbosity, completely vague on the persons who had been attacking images. See also Parry, *Depicting the Word*, p. 136.

151. I cite the translation of O'Connell, *Ecclesiology of Nicephorus*, p. 5.

152. Ludwig, "Tarasios," pp. 73–97 agrees that Tarasius guides Nicaea skillfully but she thinks that the patriarch's moderation was based on a desire to effect a rapprochement with papal Rome and to detach the popes from the Franks. I see no wider evidence to support this view.

153. *L'ideologie politique de l'empire byzantin*, pp. 129–33, quotation p. 132. For a superb historiographical account of the emergence of the concept of Caesaropapism (in Reformation and post-Reformation polemics about "political Christianity") see Dagron, *Emperor and Priest*, pp. 282–95.

154. Dvornik, "Emperors, Popes, and General Councils," pp. 1–23; Michel, "Die Kaisermacht in der Ostkirche (843–1204)," pp. 1–35; Beck, "Kirche und Klerus im staatlichen Leben von Byzanz," pp. 1–24; idem, *Kirche und theologische Literatur*, pp. 36–37, noting that quarrels were usually "Personenfrage" not "Grundsatzfrage."

155. I cite only some representative scholars. Martin, *History*, pp. 16–36; Mango, "Historical Introduction," pp. 2–3, and Herrin, "Context," pp. 15–17; Ahrweiler, *Ideologie*, pp. 25–36; Speck, "Renaissance," pp. 180–83; Carile, "L'iconoclasmo fra Bisanzio e l'Italia," pp. 13, 35; Bertolini, *La persistenza del simbolo delle croce*, pp. 11–12, 22; Thümmel, *Bilderlehre*, pp. 18–21. Older literature is cited by these writers.

156. On this basic point I agree with several writers but we often part company on details and implications. Gero, *Byzantine Iconoclasm under Leo III*, pp. 50–58; idem, "Notes on Byzantine Iconoclasm in the Eighth Century," pp. 40–42; idem, "Byzantine Iconoclasm and the Failure of a Medieval Reformation," pp. 49–62, esp. 53. Haldon, "Some Remarks on the Background to the Iconoclastic Controversy," pp. 181–82; Stein, *Beginn*, pp. 138–77; Dagron, "Le christianisme byzantin," p. 99.

157. Alexakis, *Codex Parisinus Graecus*, pp. 39–40.

158. *Oratio*, 1.1, ed. Kotter, p. 66 (trans. Louth, pp. 19–20).

159. *Die schriften des Johannes von Damaskos*, vol. 3, p. 24.

160. Elsner, "Image and Iconoclasm in Byzantium," pp. 478–79.

161. To streamline referencing in this section I provide only the book and chapter references to John's *Orations*. Translations quoted are Louth's.

162. Excellent discussion in Parry, *Depicting the Word*, pp. 34–43.

163. Parry astutely observes, *Depicting the Word*, pp. 46–48, that John is really defending anthropomorphism and that his Old Testament exegesis is a bit devious because God no where commanded an anthropomorphic image to be made.

164. Kotter, *Schriften*, vol. 3, pp. 10–22; Nikolau, "Die Ikonenverehrung," pp. 138–65.

165. *Depicting the Word*, p. 166.

166. *Early Christian and Byzantine Art*, pp. 150–51.

167. *La vie d'Étienne le Jeune*, p. 179 n. 2.

168. "The Concept of the Image," pp. 4–5, 8–9.

169. "What Was the Iconoclastic Controversy About?" pp. 16–31.

170. *Kunst als Medium*, pp. 45–70.

171. Jevtič, "L'icône et L'Incarnation," pp. 162–70 is a good example of the reigning confusion on this topic. He shows beyond contravention that John introduced the fundamental Christological themes in a serious way but concludes that these arguments had always been present.

172. "Der Bilderstreit und die Kunst-Lehren der byzantinischen und abendländischen Theologie," pp. 1–23, esp. p. 8 n. 22. John refers to the incarnation many times, e.g. 1.4, 9, 16, 3.6. *Oratio* 3.12 is especially revealing of the cast of John's thought: "Reverently we honor and worship His bodily form, and by contemplating His bodily form, we form a notion, as far as is possible for us, of this glory of His divinity." Cf. 3.24. See also Schönborn, *L'icône de Christ*, pp. 191–200 and Parry, *Depicting the Word*, pp. 70–80.

173. Here I follow my "John Damascene and the History of the Iconoclastic Controversy," pp. 102–4, p. 113 n. 54 with further literature.

174. Crucial on the florilegium and on the manuscripts is Kotter, *Schriften*, vol. 3, pp. 24–33 and 34–39.

175. Nasrallah, *Saint Jean de Damas*, p. 95.

176. "Disputations, Polemical Literature and the Formation of Opinion in the Early Byzantine Period," pp. 91–108 and "Texts as Weapons: Polemic in the Byzantine Dark Ages," pp. 198–215. See also Gray, "The Select Fathers," 21–36. An excellent survey of the emergence of florilegia in church councils is Alexakis, *Codex Parisinus Graecus*, pp. 1–41.

177. *History of Dogma*, vol. 4, p. 261.

178. This argument is at the heart of his *Codex Parisinus Graecus,* but see esp. pp. 215–26. His belief that Hadrian sent the 770 version to Constantinople is based on his reading of LP, 1. 511–12 but I am not sure whether he has asked "per testimonia Scriptuarum seu traditionum probabilium patrum" to carry too much weight.

179. See Hennephof, *Textus Byzantinos*, *Peusis I* = frags. 141–61, pp. 52–54, *Peusis II* = frags. 162–70, pp. 54–55; Brief extracts of the texts are given in French translation in Dumeige, *Nicée II*, pp. 229–32; almost all of the fragments (from Hennephof) along with a good German translation are given in Rochow, *Konstantin V*, pp. 177–88. Hennephof thought that there was a third *Peusis* and he gives additional fragments that he believes derive from it (Nos. 171–87, pp. 55–57). This view has not won acceptance: Gero, "Notes on Byzantine Iconoclasm in the Eighth Century," p. 28 n. 6; idem, *Constantine V*, p. 37 n. 1; Rochow, *Konstantin V*, p. 46. Generally on the *Peuseis* see Gero, *Constantine V*, pp. 37–52; Rochow, *Konstantin V*, pp. 43–48; Chifar, *Das VII. ökumenische Konzil von Nikaia*, pp. 61–64.

180. Theosteriktos, *Life of Nicetas of Medikion*, c. 29, AASS, April 1, p. 261A with note g, p. 261D (see Hennephof, frag. 140, p. 52) τριακαίδεκα λογίδρια. Gero, *Constantine V*, p. 39; Rochow, *Konstantin V*, p. 45.

181. Ostrogorsky (*Studien*, p. 11) assumed that the fragments accurately represent Constantine's thought whereas Gero (*Constantine V*, pp. 38–39) has doubts.

182. The first two of these were discussed above (pp. 62–63). The third (PG 96: 1348C–1361D) dates from around 770 and may or may not be by John of Jerusalem whose name stands at the head of Migne's edition. See Schriener, "Bilderstreit," p. 326; Speck, *Bin's Nicht*, pp. 579–635.

183. Parry's discussion of this abstruse issue is particularly clear: *Depicting the Word*, pp. 99–113.

184. Ostrogorsky, *Studien*, pp. 13–17 thought Constantine poorly educated and rather crude in his theology but this view can be countered, as by Rochow, *Konstantin V*, pp. 47–48 and by Gero, *Constantine V*, p. 40.

185. On Hiereia generally, see Gero, *Constantine V*, pp. 53–110 (with an English translation of the *horos*, pp. 68–94); Rochow, *Konstantin V*, pp. 48–55; Chifar, *Das VII. Konzil*, pp. 67–90, a thoughtful and insightful study marred by its insistence that Constantine V and Hiereia were essentially monophysite. This was Ostrogorsky's thesis but it has not been embraced.

186. Gero, *Constantine V*, pp. 100–101 believes that Hiereia saw this argument as "irrelevant."

187. Iconophile sources confirm that these issues were among the key ones raised: *Nouthesia*, trans. Dumeige, p. 234; *Adv. Cons. Cab.*, c. 4, PG 95: 317C–D; *Adv. Iconoclastas*, c. 2, PG 96: 1349C.

188. Helpful is Gero, "The Eucharistic Doctrine of the Byzantine Iconoclasts and Its Sources," pp. 4–22. See also Breckenridge, "Iconoclasts' Image of Christ," pp. 3–8.

189. Gero, *Constantine V*, pp. 95, 106.

190. The author of the treatise *Adv. Cons. Cab.*, c. 3, PG 95: 313B saw this as a key issue: "So why, wicked heretic, do you call me an idolator?" See also c. 7, col. 324A and cf. *Nouthesia*, trans. Dumeige, p. 232.

191. Barber, *Figure and Likeness*, pp. 77–81.

192. For confirmation: *Adv. Cons. Cab.*, cc. 3, 9, PG 95: 315B–D, 317A–B, 325B–C; *Adv. Iconoclastas*, c. 3, PG 96: 1352B. See also Anastos, "The Ethical Theory of Images," pp. 151–66.

193. Florovsky, "Origen, Eusebius and the Iconoclastic Controversy," pp. 77–96 argues that it was not so much Platonism as Origenism, as mediated by Eusebius, that influenced the iconoclasts. It is not clear that there really is an Origenist streak in iconoclast thought, however. See Gero, *Constantine V*, pp. 104–5.

194. Here I disagree with Gero (*Constantine V*, p. 41) and Schönborn (*L'icône de Christ*, pp. 170–78) who argue that Constantine V made the controversy Christological. I would argue that in light of John's thought those who opposed images had to move onto another track than idolatry.

195. Nicephorus, *Antirrhetikoi*, 2.3, PG 100: 340B–C.

196. C. 16, PG 96: 1361A.

197. C. 15, PG 95: 332A–C. John and Gregory were also cited in Hiereia's florilegium: 297A, 300A–B.

198. *Adv. Cons. Cab.*, c. 2, PG, 95: 312A–313B; *Adv. Iconoclastas*, cc. 4–12, PG 96: 1352C–1360A.

199. *Nouthesia*, trans. Dumeige, pp. 233–34; *Adv. Cons. Cab.*, c. 5, PG 95: 320B.

200. *Nouthesia*, trans. Dumeige, p. 233 (Abgar); *Adv. Cons. Cab.*, c. 6, PG 95: 321C (Luke).

201. *Painting the Soul*, pp. 46–47.

202. *Nouthesia*, trans. Dumeige, p. 235; *Adv. Cons. Cab.*, c. 5, PG 95: 320D–321A.

203. Auzépy, "La tradition comme arme du pouvoir," pp. 79–89; Ševčenko, "Search for the Past," pp. 279–93.

204. *Adv. Cons. Cab.*, c. 3, PG 95: 317A.

205. *Iconoclastas*, c. 3, PG 96: 1352B. *Nouthesia*, trans. Dumeige, p. 232; *Adv. Cons. Cab.*, c 9, PG 95: 325B–C.

206. *Adv. Cons. Cab.*, c. 10, PG 95: 325C.

207. Thümmel's "Bilderstreit" and *Bilderlehre* are particularly good on this subject.

208. C. 7, PG 95: 324C; cf. c. 3, col. 315B–D.

209. *Adv. Cons. Cab.*, cc. 6, 8, 10, PG 95: 324A, 324C–D, 325C; *Adv. Iconoclastas*, cc. 14, 15, PG 96: 360C–D.

210. The most extended discussion of Christology in one of these writers actually comes in the midst of a long profession of faith based itself on the six councils. The statements strike me as quite traditional—Christ was a man and can be depicted; depictions do not separate the two natures of Christ; the divinity of Christ cannot be circumscribed: *Adv. Iconoclastas*, cc. 4–12, PG 96: 1352C–1360A.

211. *Adv. Cons. Cab.*, cc. 16, 17, PG 95: 332C, 333A; *Adv. Iconoclastas*, c. 3, PG 96: 1352A. O'Connell, *Ecclesiology of Nicephorus*, pp. 15–18 notes that Hiereia argued explicitly for its own ecumenicity on the grounds that an emperor called it, it adhered to the six councils, and it represented the collegiality of the bishops. Such an argument, if it had been permitted to go unchallenged, would have done grave damage to conciliar doctrines of ecumenicity.

212. C. 20, PG 95: 337A–B.

213. Mango, "Availability of Books," pp. 30–31. Alexakis, *Codex Parisinus Graecus*, pp. 227–33 shows that, despite its explicit claim that it used only books and not extracts, both whole books and florilegia were used. He also shows that the *acta* were scripted to show spontaneity on the part of the persons who presented *testimonia* but that this is a deliberate deception and that the extracts in the *acta* follow so closely the wording and the order of the extracts in pre-conciliar florilegia that it appears as though Tarasius, once again, orchestrated the process.

214. For a superb account of Nicaea's working methods and assumptions see Fazzo, "Il II Concilio di Nicea," pp. 347–57.

215. There is a broad consensus on this point: Fazzo, "Il II Concilio di Nicea," pp. 356–57; Giakalas, *Images of the Divine*, p. 50; Schönborn, *L'icône de Christ*, pp. 139–41; Uphus, *Der Horos*, pp. 338–64, esp. 351–64.

216. *Depicting the Word*, p. 156. See also Brubaker, "Perception," pp. 31–32.

217. Giakalas, *Images of the Divine*, pp. 54–59 is especially good on this topic. Byzantinists all agree on this aspect of images but current discussions often turn on levels of culture and education at Byzantium. This is not our subject here and it is enough to note that specialists disagree. Beck, "Fragwürdigkeit," p. 26 sees images as evidence of the "Folkloristic"

element in iconophile theory. Thümmel, "Eine wenig bekannte Schrift zur Bilderfrage," p. 156 and Treadgold, *Byzantine Revival*, pp. 51–53 hold low estimates of contemporary Byzantine culture. Browning assumes that levels of culture may have been higher than we suspect, "Literacy in the Byzantine World," pp. 139–54 while Beck, "Bildung und Theologie im früh-mittelalterlichen Byzanz," pp. 69–81 holds that traditional education was maintained and Patlagean, "Discours écrit, discours parlé," pp. 264–78 believes that education was sound at the higher levels. In so far as the arguments in 754 and 787 were carried out by elites, it seems safe to say that the didactic argument about images was not a counsel of despair.

218. This is another relatively conservative approach. That is, Nicaea was content to assert that images and words were essentially equivalent. It did not, in other words, harken back to the argument, present certainly in Germanus and John of Damascus, and in writers before them, that sight was the superior sense and that, therefore, images were perhaps supe-rior to mere words. See Barber, "The Body Within the Frame," pp. 147–48; Brubaker, "Per-ception," pp. 28–31 and "Byzantine Art in the Ninth Century," pp. 70–75. She notes that the "triumph of the visual" did not come until the ninth century.

219. Parry, *Depicting the Word*, pp. 46–48; Elsner, "Image and Iconoclasm," pp. 483–85; Brubaker, "Perception," p. 27. This attitude may also lie behind the unease which Wortley detects in the iconophobes' attitude toward relics: "Iconoclasm and Leipsanoclasm," pp. 253–79. I think that Wortley somewhat exaggerates the case with respect to relics. More sensitive on icons and relics is Barber, *Figure and Likeness*, pp. 16–37.

220. Giakalas, *Images of the Divine*, p. 5.

221. Auzépy, "L'évolution de l'attutude face au miracle à Byzance," p. 38.

222. Van den Ven, "Patristique," pp. 336–38 calls it "remarkable" that John is so con-spicuously absent.

223. *Icone, pittore e arte*, p. 42.

224. I have not attempted to verify Van den Ven's enumeration of the sources: "Patris-tique," p. 338. Mango, "Availability of Books," p. 30, arrives at a slightly different count.

225. Dumeige, "L'image du Christ," pp. 258–67 is an excellent discussion of the Chris-tological reserve of II Nicaea. He points out that it was in the ninth century that these themes received fuller development.

226. Meyendorff, *Byzantine Theology*, p. 46 remarks that Nicaea did not choose to elab-orate on the Christology of Hiereia.

227. *L'icône de Christ*, p. 148. Cf. Fazzo, "Il II Concilio di Nicea," p. 358.

228. "The Horos of Nicaea II," p. 172.

229. Auzépy, "La tradition comme arme du pouvoir," p. 89.

CHAPTER THREE

1. Davis, *Lives of the Eighth-Century Popes*, p. 2. But Davis assumes that the version available to Bede went no further than the opening of the pontificate. As we shall see just below, it may be that Bede had a fuller version of the *vita*.

2. For the chronology see Holder, "New Treasures and Old in Bede's 'De Tabernaculo' and 'De Templo,'" p. 237.

3. Bede, *De templo,* 2. 19. 10, ed. Hurst, p. 212; trans. Connolly, *Bede: On the Temple,* pp. 89–90.

4. LP 1. 404.

5. This is the entirely plausible conjecture of Meyvaert, "Bede and the Church Paintings at Wearmouth Jarrow," p. 68.

6. Henderson, *Bede and the Visual Arts*; Parabiaghi, "Pitture ed apparato di culto nelle opere del venerabile Beda," pp. 203–34.

7. *De templo*, 2. 19. 11, ed. Hurst, p. 213; trans Holder, p. 92.

8. Ibid., 2. 19. 10, p. 212; trans. Holder, p. 91.

9. Ibid., pp. 212–23; trans. Holder, p. 91. He makes the same point in Homily 17, *In natale sancti Benedicti episcopi*, PL 94: 228A–B.

10. *De templo*, p. 213.

11. *Bede's Ecclesiastical History of the English People*, 1. 25, ed. Colgrave and Myers, pp. 72–76 (quotation, p. 75).

12. *Historia Abbatum*, 6, ed. Plummer, pp. 369–70.

13. Ibid., c. 9, p. 373. The outstanding study of Bede's account of these paintings remains Meyvaert, "Bede and the Church Paintings," pp. 63–77. Meyvaert was inclined to imagine a sort of iconostasis but this cannot have been the case at so early a date: see Nees, "The Iconographic Program of Decorated Chancel Barriers in the Pre-Iconoclastic Period."

14. *De locis sanctis*, 3. 4–5, ed. Bieler, pp. 229, 231, 233.

15. *Ecclesiastical History*, 5. 15–17; ed. Colgrave and Mynors, pp. 506–12.

16. Laistner and King, *A Hand-List of Bede Manuscripts.*

17. *Die Briefe des heiligen Bonifatius and Lullus,* ed. Tangl, nos. 76 and 91.

18. Ibid., nos. 126, 127 (and see below, pp. 146–47).

19. Noble, *The Republic of St. Peter*, chs. 2 and 3. The issues are summarized in McCormick, "Byzantium and the West," pp. 359–68. I cannot agree with Graf Finck von Finckenstein, "Rom zwischen Byzanz und die Franken," pp. 23–36 who maintains that neither iconoclasm nor imperial tax and institutional policies played a role.

20. The letters of Gregory III and Zachary in the *Codex Carolinus* (nos. 1–3) say nothing about images or Byzantium. Stephen II asks Pippin, "ita disponere iubeas de parte Grecorum, ut fides sancta catholica et apostolica per te integra et inconcussa permaneat in aeterna," and then he goes on to ask that Pippin work against their "pestifera malitia" and seek the restoration of properties in Italy (no. 11, p. 506). Paul I complains that Desiderius is plotting with imperial envoys (nos. 15, 17, pp. 512, 515) and says that six patricians and thirty ships have departed from Constantinople for Rome for reasons he does not know (no. 20, p. 521). Then Paul complains that the imperial envoy George is engaged in "iniqua operatione contra sanctam Dei ecclesiam fidemque orthodoxam" but goes on to say that diplomacy and papal properties are his chief concern (no. 25, pp. 529–30). Diplomacy is still at issue in Paul's next two letters bearing on Eastern relations (nos. 28, 29, pp. 533, 534–35) and then in letter 30 (p. 536) Paul says "non ob aliud ipsi nefandissimi nos persequuntur Greci nisi propter sanctam et orthodoxam fidem et venerandorum patrum piam traditionem quam cupiunt distruere atque conculare." In letter no. 32 (pp. 538–39) Paul calls Pippin the great defender of the orthodox faith but also pleads for help against the "Grecorum malitia" where the "wicked-

ness" can only mean seizures of property thus explaining retrospectively the use of "malitia" by Stephen II in no. 11. Finally in nos. 36 and 37, pp. 543–50, which will be discussed in detail below (pp. 142–43) Paul finally mentions images explicitly. His subsequent letters again drop the subject. So the pope continually asks for territorial security in Italy, occasionally mentions in vague language that the Greeks are heretics, and on one occasion (letters 36 and 37 are related) mentions images. See also Speck, *Kaiser Leo III*, pp. 603–35.

21. JE, nos. 2174–361. The dubious letters are registered as nos. 2180–82.

22. Noble, "A New Look at the Liber Pontificalis," pp. 347–58.

23. LP 1. 404; I cite the translation of Davis (with a modest change), *Eighth-Century Popes*, p. 11.

24. LP 1. 408–10.

25. MGH, Conc., 2: 87 contains much of what remains of *Actio Quarta* (but see below p. 00) of the Roman Synod. It is in the *Life* of Stephen III (LP 1: 476–77) that we find a much fuller account.

26. *Hadrianum*, 1. 5, 12, 2. 19, pp. 15, 19, 51. The letter is edited by Hampe in MGH, Epp., 5, EKA 3, pp. 5–57. I shall hereafter refer to it as "*Hadrianum*" and cite it by section and page number.

27. We will return to some of these details below. For now see Hartmann, *Die Synoden der Karolingerzeit*, pp. 40–43.

28. LP 1. 415; trans. Davis, p. 19.

29. Ibid., 1. 416; trans. Davis, p. 20.

30. Ibid., 1. 477. In the life of Stephen III, where it treats the Roman Synod of 769, we read: "Haec vero omnia promulgata continuo et diversa sanctorum patrum testimonia de sacris imaginibus . . . in eodem adlata sunt concilio." The *Hadrianum* (1. 5, p. 15) says, "domnus Gregorius papa secundus iunior . . . multorum sanctorum patrum testimonia roborantes."

31. There is a voluminous literature on this subject but nothing is better than Sansterre, *Les moines grecs et orientaux à Rome*. See also Alexakis, *Codex Parisinus Graecus*, pp. 257–60.

32. Lanne, "Rome et les images saintes," pp. 172 and 174 n. 41 suggests that because Gregory III was of Syrian extraction, because St. Saba was one of Rome's most important monasteries and maintained close relations with Mar-Saba which was John of Damascus's monastery, it is possible that John's influence was felt in Rome at an early date. This interpretation is not impossible, but given our fragmentary knowledge of Gregory's patristic dossier I see no way to verify it. Moreover, as I have pointed out elsewhere, John's writings cannot be shown to have been known in Rome until some *extracts* were copied there in around 760: "The Declining Knowledge of Greek," 59.

33. LP 1. 476–77.

34. Werminghoff, who edited the records for the Roman Council of 769 for the MGH, published only one patristic extract from the pseudo-Athanasian *Quaestiones ad Antiochum ducem* on the basis of the manuscript that he viewed (MGH, Conc., 2, no. 14, p. 87) but Böhringer ("Zwei Fragmente," 93–105, frag. ed., pp. 102–3) found a longer fragment of the same extract in a manuscript that escaped Werminghoff (BL Add., 16143, fols. 4r–6v). Werminghoff also worked carefully through Hadrian's letter to Charlemagne of 793—the *Hadria-*

num—and found in it several more extracts that, on the basis of Hadrian's own words, seem certain to have come from the synod of 769's repetition of the synod of 731. These extracts add a biblical passage and four patristic texts. Alexakis then worked through the Hadrianum and added two more biblical passages and three patristic texts (*Codex Parisinus Graecus*, pp. 39–40). To this list I think it is possible to add a reference to Gregory I's letter to Serenus because this also appears in the *Hadrianum* (2. 1, pp. 42–43) and was used around 731 by Bede who drew upon Roman sources. Because one text appears in both the Hadrianum and Hadrian's letter of 785 to Constantine VI and Irene, Alexakis thinks that twelve more extracts in the latter may derive from 731 and 769 (*Codex Parisinus Graecus*, p. 39). In fact, Alexakis missed two extracts that appear in both papal letters: The letter of Gregory to Serenus and the *sacra* of Emperor Constantine IV to Pope Donus in 678 (Mansi, Concilia, 12. 1073B; *Hadrianum*, 1. 7, p. 17). I think Alexakis missed another one that appears in both sources: Gregory of Nyssa, *De deitate Filii et Spiritus Sancti* (Mansi, Concilia, 12. 1066B; *Hadrianum*, 1. 37, p. 33). In the latter source this passage appears this way: "Sanctus Cyrillus Alexandrinus *et Sanctus Gregorius Nisenus* uno tenore in istoria Abrahae pro sacris imaginibus veneratione dixerunt" (emphasis added). Gregory's text deals with images in an important way whereas the *sacra* of 678 does not. Wallach (*Diplomatic Studies*, pp. 29, 39) identifies three additional texts that appear in Hadrian's letter of 785 but not in his letter of 793. Alexakis does not include these in his list even though they would appear to belong there according to his methodology and one of them, from the *Actus Silvestri*, appears in the iconophile florilegium that he so painstakingly reconstructs (*Codex Parisinus Graecus*, "Appendix II," no. 124, p. 333). I think it most prudent to hold the count at twelve and to omit the twelve additional passages adduced by Alexakis, or the additional sixteen if Wallach's four new ones are added by using Alexakis's method, or even seventeen if my passage from Gregory of Nyssa is included.

35. LP 1. 432.

36. LP 1. 463, 464; trans. Davis, pp. 80, 82.

37. *Codex Carolinus*, no. 36, ed. Gundlach, pp. 544–45.

38. Noble, "Paradoxes and Possibilities in the Sources for Roman Society in the Early Middle Ages," pp. 55–83.

39. LP 1. 417; trans. Davis, pp. 22–23.

40. Mordek, "Rom, Byzanz und die Franken im 8. Jahrhundert," pp. 123–56; text 123–46, edition 147–56; date device, p. 147, left column. Hartmann, *Synoden*, p. 42 n. 17 says Mordek should not be so certain because only the MS has any kind of date device and perhaps the copyist left out the emperor's regnal years. It may be significant that the Roman Synod of 745 again dated by imperial years: MGH, Conc., 2, no. 5, p. 37. The Synod of 769 then dated "regnante Domino nostro Jesu Christo": ibid., no. 14, p. 79.

41. Mordek, "Rom, Byzanz and die Franken," p. 127.

42. This was the position I took in *The Republic of St. Peter* even before Mordek published his important article on the synod of 732. The chief representative of the old view that the papacy in this period remained fundamentally loyal to the empire is Llewellyn, "The Popes and the Constitution in the Eighth Century," pp. 42–67 and also in an "Afterword" to a 1994 reprint of his book *Rome in the Dark Ages*.

43. LP 1. 418–19: "picturas."

44. Melograni, "Le pitture," pp. 161–78.

45. Andaloro, "La datazione," p. 168.

46. LP 1. 417–18, 419–20, 421.

47. Osborne, "Court Culture, pp. 227–28; Krauthemer, *Rome*, pp. 120–21; Haldon and Ward-Perkins, "Evidence from Rome," pp. 286–96; Speck, *Leo III*, pp. 604–5, 616–17.

48. Herklotz, "Campus Lateranensis," p. 38; Ficthtenau, "Byzanz und die Pfalz zu Aachen," p. 43.

49. LP 1. 432; see also Davis's notes, *Eighth-Century Popes*, pp. 44–45; Osborne, "Papal Court Culture," pp. 223–29.

50. LP 1. 376. See Palazzo and Johansson, "Jalons liturgiques," pp. 15–34.

51. On this image see Belting, *Image and Likeness*, pp. 64–68; Wolf, *Salus Populi Romani*, pp. 38–44; Grisar, *Sancta Sanctorum*, pp. 14, 39–54.

52. A pilgrim's guide from the period 635–45 (*Itineraria Romana IV: Ecclesiae Quae intus Romae habentur*, p. 321) says, "Basilicae quae appellatur Sancta Maria Transtiberis; ibi est imago sanctae Mariae quae per se facta est." Andoloro and Barber (see below n. 76) take this seriously as documenting an early date for the "Madonna della Clemenza," although Barber allows that the extant image could be a copy whereas Andoloro thinks the image itself must be from the sixth century and that the pilgrim reference merely proves that the image was already in place in the 640s. I am dubious about the probative value of the pilgrim reference because it is so starkly isolated and, as far as I know, unique before 753.

53. LP 1. 464–65.

54. Angenendt, "Anti-Ikonoklasmus," pp. 207–8.

55. Andoloro, "Il 'Liber Pontificalis' e la questione delle immagini," pp. 70–72.

56. *Likeness and Presence*, pp. 47–48.

57. Andoloro, "Il 'Liber Pontificalis' e la questione delle immagini," pp. 73–76; Croquison, "L'iconographie chrétienne à Rome," pp. 535–606.

58. *God and Gold in Late Antiquity*.

59. See above p. 15, and p. 374 n. 31.

60. Lawrence, "Maria Regina"; Cecchelli, *Mater Christi*, vol. 1, pp. 80–83, 309–12; Nilgen, "Maria Regina"; Osborne, "Early Medieval Painting in San Clemente"; Ihm, *Die Programm der christlichen Apsismalerei*, pp. 52–68; Stroll, "Maria Regina."

61. Dated to the mid-eighth century on paleographical grounds: Gray, "Paleography of Latin Inscriptions," p. 55.

62. See s.v. "Mappa," *Oxford Dictionary of Byzantium*, 2: 1294.

63. Osborne, "Images of the Mother of God," p. 140.

64. Wolf, *Salus Populi Romani*, p. 119 with the older literature.

65. Osborne, "Mother of God," p. 136.

66. Wolf, *Salus Populi Romani*, p. 120; Osborne, "Mother of God," p. 140.

67. Brenk, *Santa Maria Maggiore*.

68. Klauser, "Rom und der Kult der Gottesmutter Maria"; Cameron, "The Early Cult of the Virgin," pp. 3–15.

69. LP 1. 317.

70. LP 1. 376.

71. Osborne, "Mother of God," p. 139.

72. *In Laudem Iustini*, 1. 52–53, ed. Cameron, p. 49 (trans. p. 95). Cf. the probably sixth-century "Akathistos Hymn," trans. Geanakoplos, *Byzantium*, pp. 193–95: "To Thee, protectress. . . ."

73. Mango, "Constantinople as Theotokoupolis," pp. 17–25; Frolow, "Dédicace de Constantinople," pp. 69–72, 89–101; Baynes, "Supernatural Defenders of Constantinople"; Cameron, "Images of Authority."

74. Belting, *Likeness and Presence*, p. 63.

75. I conclude this from a survey of the images in Ladner, *Papstbildnisse*. See also Osborne, "The Portrait of Pope Leo IV." The last example before John VII is the image of Honorius I (625–38) in the apse of Sant'Agnese.

76. Bertelli, *Trastevere*, pp. 80–86 remains the authoritative view but Cecchelli, *Mater Christi*, vol. 1, pp. 54–55 had already argued for John VII. Wolf, *Salus Populi Romani*, pp. 120–22 adheres to Bertelli's view. Amato, *Effigie*, pp. 25–32 is more cautious and does not take a firm stand. Andoloro, "La datazione della tavola di S. Maria in Trastevere" pp. 139–215 holds for a sixth-century date. Barber, "Early Representations of the Mother of God," pp. 258–59 does not reject Andoloro's arguments but does say that the extant image could be a copy and that early medieval viewers would not have been puzzled or distressed by a supposed lack of authenticity. For my part, I think that the *comparanda* put the picture in the eighth century and point to John VII as the pope represented. This issue has not yet been settled.

77. Romaelli and Nordhagen, *Santa Maria in Trastevere*, pp. 31–36 for a survey of the history of the paintings in this building.

78. LP 1. 385.

79. Wolf, *Salus Populi Romani*, pp. 120, 121; also, Sansterre, "Jean VII ," pp. 377–88.

80. Ladner, *Papstbildnisse*, p. 90; Romanelli and Nordhagen, *Santa Maria Antiqua*, p. 16.

81. Ladner, *Papstbildnisse*, pp. 90–94; Wolf, *Salus Populi Romani*, p. 122; Belting, "Commissions," p. 15; Lawrence, "Maria Regina," p. 161.

82. "Anti-Ikonoklasmus," pp. 201–9.

83. On the deacronries, Noble, *Republic of St. Peter*, pp. 231–34.

84. Some examples from *Le sacramentaire grégorien*, ed. Deshusses: Purification (February 2): no. 126, p. 124: "intercedente beata semper virgine Mariae." Annunciation (March 25): no. 140, p. 128: "ut qui vere eam genetricem dei credimus eius apud te intercessionibus adiuvemur." Assumption (August 15): no. 660, p. 262: "intercessionis eius auxilio a nostris iniquitatibus resurgamus"; no. 662, p. 262: "genetricis filii tui domini nostri intercessione salvemur"; no. 663, p. 263: "subveniat domine plebei tuae dei genetricis oratio"; no. 664, p. 263: "a malis imminentibus eius intercessione libremur." Nativity of Mary (September 8): no. 680, p. 268: "eius intercessionibus complacatus te de instantibus periculis eruamur."

85. Belting, "Commissions," pp. 14–15.

86. Miles, *Image as Insight*, pp. 31–34, noting that the image might direct thoughts to Mary, to Christ, or to the pope and that where the pope is concerned it is either his subjection to Mary or his intercession with her that might be noticed. She quotes the phrase "detachable conclusion" from Frary, "Logic of Icons," p. 398.

87. "Centers, Kings, and Charisma," pp. 122–24.

88. *Pittura politica*, pp. 5–11.

89. "Les représentations mariales," pp. 173–76, 191–95; Noble, "Making of Papal Rome," pp. 61–72.

90. Romanelli and Nordhagen, *Santa Maria Antiqua*, p. 42. I confirmed the existence of these holes by visual inspection in 1997, but I also noted that there do not appear to have been very many of them. There were other Marian images in niches: San Clemente, possibly Santa Susanna, Catacomb of San Valentino, crypt of Santi Cosma e Damiano, and Sant'Urbino: Osborne, "Mother of God," pp. 141–42.

91. This is one of the guiding theses of his magisterial *Likeness and Presence*. See also Maguire, *The Icons of their Bodies*, esp. pp. 5–47, although he is talking about the period following iconoclasm. Romaneli and Nordhagen, *Santa Maria Antiqua*, p. 36 say "probably" eighth century.

92. See s.v. "Maphorion," *Oxford Dictionary of Byzantium*, 1: 1294.

93. These are surveyed and reproduced in Amato, *La vera effigie*, passim.

94. Russo, "L'affresco di Turtura," I. 35–85, II. 71–150.

95. Barber, "Representations of the Mother of God," pp. 253–56, 256–60.

96. Belting, "Eine Privatkapelle"; Matthiae, "La capella di Teodoto"; Lanne, "Rome et Images," 175; Romaelli and Nordhagen, *Santa Maria Antiqua*, pp. 32–37.

97. Teteriatnikov, "For Whom Is Theodotus Praying?" Also, Belting, "Eine Privatkapelle," pp. 55–69.

98. Belting, "Eine Privatkapelle, " pp. 67–69.

99. Belting, *Likeness and Presence*, pp. 120–21.

100. Teteriatnikov, "For Whom Is Theodotus Praying?" pp. 43–44.

101. *Santa Maria Antiqua*, p. 42.

102. *Historia langobardorum*, 5. 41, MGH, SSRL, p. 161.

103. *Liber Pontificalis Ecclesiae Ravennatis*, ed. Deliyannis; Eng. trans by Deliyannis, *The Book of Pontiffs of the Church of Ravenna*, whose "Introduction" constitutes an excellent introduction to Agnellus; also Martinez-Pizarro, *Writing Ravenna*.

104. Deliyannis, "Agnellus and Iconoclasm," pp. 562–69.

105. *Lib. Pont. Rav.*, cc. 24–5, ed. Deliyannis, pp. 170–72; Eng. trans. (*Book of Pontiffs*), pp. 120–23.

106. *Lib. Pont. Rav.*, c. 30, ed. Deliyannis, pp. 178–84; Eng. trans. (*Book of Pontiffs*), pp. 128–33.

107. Sansterre, "La vénération des images à Ravenne," pp. 8–17. The author tracks down the roots of these stories.

108. *Concilium Romanum*, ed. Wermninghoff, p. 77.

109. "La vénération des images à Ravenne," p. 16.

110. Boniface, Epp. nos. 17, 19, 21, 38; Willibald, *Vita Bonifatii*, cc. 4, 6. Cf. Eigil, *Vita Sturmi*, c. 22; Alcuin, *Vita Willibrordi*, cc. 9–12.

111. Ep. no. 35, trans. Emerton (no. XXVI), pp 42–43.

112. Von Padberg, *Christianisierung*, pp. 118–20.

113. MGH, SS, 15: 80–117; trans. Talbot, in Noble and Head, eds., *Soldiers of Christ*, pp. 143–64. On the journey of Willibald, McCormick, *Origin*, pp. 129–34.

114. *Hodoeporicon*, c. 4, trans. Talbot, p. 159.

115. Walser, ed., *Die einsiedler Inschriftensammlung und der Pilgerführer*.

116. *Das Itinerar*, ed. Walser, p. 162.

117. Netzer, *Cultural Interplay*.

118. Full study with plates by Nees, *Gundohinus Gospels*.

119. Nees, *Gundohinus Gospels*, pp. 183–88; idem, "Carolingian Art and Politics," pp. 193–95; idem, "Images and Text," pp. 1–22.

120. *Annales regni Francorum*, s.a. 767, ed. Kurze, pp. 24, 25. The word I have translated as "dispute" is *quaestio*.

121. On the annals, and Carolingian historical writing generally, with the older literature copiously cited, see McKitterick, *History and Memory*.

122. General details: Noble, *Republic of St. Peter*, pp. 61–98. The key source is the *Life* of Stephen II in the LP 1. 452–53.

123. CC, no. 15 shows that George was in Naples in 758 while no. 11 indicates that John was in Francia in 757.

124. *Annales regni Francorum*, ed. Kurze, pp. 14, 15.

125. "Byzantium and the West," p. 365. See also Herrin, "Constantinople, Rome and the Franks," pp. 91–107.

126. McCormick, "Byzantium and the West," pp. 364–66 and "Textes, images et iconoclasme," pp. 110–31; Auzépy, "Constantin V et les Carolingiens," pp. 49–65.

127. "Constantin V et les Carolingiens," pp. 52–53. See CC, nos. 11, 30, pp. 506, 536, for papal anxiety at Franko-Byzantine diplomacy.

128. Not too much is known about this venture. It is mentioned without many details in CC 45, ed. Gundlach, p. 562. Classen, *Karl der Grosse*, p. 26 n. 73 suggests the dating of 766/7 and McCormick, "Textes, images et iconoclasme," pp. 130–31 accepts the suggestion.

129. "Textes, images et iconoclasme," pp. 116–26.

130. *Chronicon*, PL 123: 125A: "facta est tunc temporis synodus anno Incarnationis Domini septingentesimo sexagesimo septimo, et quaestio ventilata inter Graecos et Romanos de Trinitate, et utrum Spiritus sanctus sicut procedit a Patre, ita procedit a Filio, et de sanctorum imaginibus, utrumque fingendae, an pingendae essent in ecclesis." Note that Ado does not mention the Franks as participants in the debate.

131. "Textes, images et iconoclasme," pp. 114–15.

132. This is McCormick's interpretation: "Textes, images et iconoclasme," p. 144. Classen had already observed that there is no way to prove that the *filioque* was discussed in 767 in his *Karl der Große, das Papsttum und Byzanz*, p. 98 with n. 371. The most recent discussion, Gemeinhardt, *Die Filioque-Kontroverse*, pp. 76–81, is also skeptical.

133. For a detailed but partisan view see LP 1. 468–73.

134. MGH, Conc., 2, no. 14, pp. 74–92. For basic details, see Hartmann, *Synoden*, pp. 84–86.

135. LP 1. 473.

136. Emphasized by McCormick, "Textes, images et iconoclasme," pp. 131–32.

137. LP 1. 476–77.

138. MGH, Conc., 2. 88.

139. The surmise of Böhringer, "Zwei Fragmente," p. 94, with which I concur.

140. *Sancti Lulli et Bonifatii epistolae*, nos. 126, 127, ed. Tangl, pp. 264–65.

141. "Textes, images et iconoclasme," p. 132.

142. *Hadrianum*, 1. 12, p. 20; cf. 2. 4, 11, pp. 43, 46. For the letter, Gregory I, Epp., 9. 148, and appendix X, ed. Norberg, pp. 1104–11.

143. McCormick, "Textes, images et iconoclasme," pp. 131–32.

144. MGH, Conc., 2. 90; *Hadrianum*, 1. 18, p. 23.

145. MGH, Conc., 2. 90; *Hadrianum*, 1. 13, p. 20.

146. MGH, Conc., 2, 89–90; *Hadrianum*, 1. 12, p. 20; Gregory I, *Epistolae*, ed. Norberg, pp. 1110–11.

147. Böhringer, "Zwei Fragmente," pp. 104–5.

148. LP 1. 472.

149. Bertelli, "Pittura in Italia," 50, reports this interpretation as having been offered by Dale Kinney in a still-unpublished 1985 conference paper.

150. *Codex Parisinus Graecus*, pp. 222–25; "The Source of the Greek Patristic Quotations."

151. For Franko-papal relations in this period as they are revealed in the surviving papal correspondence see Thoma, "Papst Hadrian I. und Karl der Grosse." On Hadrian and II Nicaea see, briefly (and without serious treatment of the theological issues) Hartmann, *Hadrian I*, pp. 278–91.

152. Pitz, *Papstreskripten*. For example, over 65 percent of the 866 surviving letters of Gregory I, who left the largest collection from the early medieval period, are rescripts.

153. Hadrian's claims on behalf of the Roman Church are discussed in great detail by Maccarrone, "Adriano I e il concilio di Nicea," but the author goes further than I would in interpreting the impact of the pope's writings.

154. LP 1. 511–12.

155. Mansi, Concilia, 12: 1066A–1072B. The texts are listed by Alexakis, *Codex Parisinus Graecus*, p. 40 and Wallach, *Diplomatic Studies*, pp. 29–39.

156. PL 96: 1237D–1240A.

157. For a more traditional view of this issue see Sefton, "Popes and the Holy Images."

158. Noble, "Possibilities and Paradoxes."

159. LP, passim (these numbers are derived from a tabulation across the whole *vita*).

160. LP 1. 501.

161. LP 1. 503, 504, 508, 510.

CHAPTER FOUR

1. LP, 1, 512: "Quam synodum iamdicti missi in greco sermone secum deferentes una cum imperialibus sacris propriis subscriptis, praedictus egregius antistes in latinam eam translatari iussit, et in sacra bibliotheca pariter recondi, dignam sibi orthodoxe fidei memoriam faciens."

2. This was the surmise of von den Steinen, "Entstehungsgeschichte," pp. 20–23. Freeman, "Einleitung" (to her edition), p. 1 accepts this interpretation.

3. Details in von den Steinen, "Entstehungsgeschichte," p. 12. For Anastasius's letter to John: MGH, Epp. 7, p. 416. In his edition of the *Libri Carolini*, Bastgen turned often to the Greek *acta* to control the poor Latin translation from which the Franks had to work. In her edition of the *Opus Caroli*, Freeman uses Anastasius's translation which itself appears in parallel columns with the Greek text in Mansi's edition (Concilia, 12, 991–1154; 13, 1–418) and in PL 129: 195B–512B. These issues are treated in rudimentary fashion by Neil, "Western Reaction."

4. MGH, SS, 1, p. 155.

5. "Einleitung," pp. 2–3.

6. *Opuscula et epistolae quae spectant ad causam Hincmari Laudunensis*, PL 126: 360A–B.

7. *Annales mosellani*, anno 781, MGH, SS, 16, p. 497.

8. Theophanes, *Chron.*, anno 781, trans. Mango and Scott, p. 628. His name was Elissaios and his task was "to teach Rotrud [Erythro] Greek letters and language and educate her in the customs of the Roman Empire."

9. *Annales qui dicuntur Einhardi*, annis 786, 788, ed. Kurze, pp. 75, 83.

10. Excellent on the diplomatic exchanges of these years is McCormick, "Textes, images et iconoclasme," pp. 134–36.

11. *Annales regni Francorum*, anno 798, ed. Kurze, p. 104.

12. Cubitt, *Anglo-Saxon Church Councils*, pp. 153–90, esp. pp. 154–57.

13. Ibid., pp. 170–90.

14. "Alcuin Before Frankfort," p. 578.

15. *Origins of the European Economy,* esp. "Appendix 4," pp. 852–972.

16. *Opus Caroli*, Praef., p. 100.

17. "Einleitung," p. 4 and n. 19.

18. I assume that Theodulf was the primary author of the *Opus Caroli*. Freeman, "Einleitung," pp. 12–23 provides a thorough history of the "Verfasserfrage" from the sixteenth century to the present. Although there were always a few dissenting voices, Alcuin's authorship was generally accepted until von den Steinen, "Entstehung," made a strong, but undocumented, case for Theodulf. In her first publication on the subject, a revised version of her Harvard dissertation, Freeman made it all but certain that Theodulf was the author: "Theodulf and the *Libri Carolini*." In two subsequent publications she clinched her case for every fair-minded reader: "Further Studies in the *Libri Carolini* I and II" and "Further Studies in the *Libri Carolini* III." For some two decades Freeman had to endure the vituperative and frequently beside the point criticisms of Luitpold Wallach, whose many studies were collected in his *Diplomatic Studies*. Paul Meyvaert provided an assessment of Wallach that was careful, balanced, and devastating: "Authorship of the *Libri Carolini*." Oddly, Wirth, *L'image médiévale*, pp. 152–53 still regards the matter as open.

19. Bullough, "Alcuin and the Kingdom of Heaven," pp. 32–34. The point was first made, I believe, by Levison, *England and the Continent*, p. 112.

20. MGH, SS, 13, 155: "scripsit Albinus epistolam ex auctotitate divinarum scriptuarum mirabiliter affirmatam."

21. Weitmann, *Sukzession und Gegenwart,* pp. 181–82; Gero, "Carolingian Orthodoxy," pp. 11–13.

22. Freeman, "Einleitung," pp. 7–8 and "Carolingian Orthodoxy," pp. 86–87.

23. For basic biographical details see Freeman, "Theodulf of Orléans"; Dahlhaus-Berg, *Nova Antiquitas et Antiqua Novitas*, pp. 1–21.

24. Epp. Hadriani, no. 2, MGH, Epp. 5, 5–57.

25. One can compare the contents of Hadrian's letter with those of the *Capitulare* and with the eventual *Opus* in the table in von den Steinen, "Entstehung," pp. 48–49.

26. This issue is carefully discussed by Freeman, "Carolingian Orthodoxy," pp. 81–85.

27. Fundamental on adoptionism and on what the adoptionists believed, as opposed to what the Carolingians *thought* they believed, are: Cavadini, *Last Christology* and "Elipandus and His Critics"; Hainthaler, "Von Toledo nach Frankfurt"; Gemeinhardt, *Die Filioque-Kontroverse*, pp. 90–107, 123–27.

28. Epp. Hadriani, no. 2, MGH, Epp. 5, 7: "Praeterea directus a vestra clementissima precelsa regalis potentia fidelem familiarem vestrum, videlicet Angilbertum . . . edidit nobis *capitulare adversus synodum*, quae pro sacris imaginibus erectione in Nicea acta est" (emphasis added to signal how this text got its common name).

29. McCormick, "Textes, images et iconoclasme," pp. 136–43.

30. MGH, Conc., 2. 2, 481: "Eandum porro synodum cum sanctae memoriae geintor vester coram se suisque perlegi fecisset et multis in locis, ut dignum erat, reprehendisset et quaedam capitula, quae reprehensione patebant, praenotasset eaque per Angilbertum abbatem eidem Hadriano papae direxisset, ut illius iudicio et auctoritate corrigerentur."

31. Another manuscript, Paris, Arsenal 664, prepared for Hincmar of Reims in the 860s, survives intact and thus permits the reconstruction of the whole text of the *Opus*.

32. Schmandt, *Studien*, p. 6. Freeman's quasi-diplomatic edition shows the corrections in every case where they can be discovered. She does not offer a total count and I have not attempted to verify Schmandt's number.

33. "Einleitung," pp. 3–4, 48–50 and "Appendix IV," p. 583.

34. Bullough, "Alcuin and the Kingdom of Heaven," pp. 34–38 sought, cautiously, to discover the influence of Alcuin's lost letter (book?) and he suggested that Alcuin may have had a hand in the drafting of *Opus* 4.23. Subsequently he retracted the latter suggestion but added that Alcuin may have been responsible for *Opus* 4.28, the concluding chapter: "Alcuin before Frankfort," pp. 581–82. Freeman discusses the (to her, slight) possibility of identifying Alcuin's influence in "Additions and Corrections," pp. 163–65. Mitalaité, *Philosophie et théologie*, pp. 37–40 thinks that the additions and corrections may indeed have been by Alcuin or others.

35. "Carolingian Orthodoxy," p. 86.

36. Freeman, "Additions and Corrections," pp. 166–69 and "Einleitung," p. 44.

37. MGH, Conc., 2, nos. 19A and B, pp. 111–19, 120–21.

38. Blumenshine, "Alcuin and the Frankish Kingdom."

39. Freeman, "Einleitung," pp. 44–45 and "Carolingian Orthodoxy," pp. 88–90.

40. Freeman's chronological reconstruction of the development of the *Opus* has been summarized and accepted by Melloni, "L'Opus Caroli Regis,'" pp. 873–79 and Hartmann, "Frankfurt und Nizäa," pp. 320–22. It must now count as the definitive view. The attempt by Arnaldi to date the *Opus* to 794 is not persuasive: "La questione dei 'Libri Carolini,'" pp.

3–19. Wallach, *Diplomatic Studies*, pp. 47–49 also put the preparation of the *Opus* in the years between 791 and 794 but he dates the *Capitulare* to 789 and does not provide as nuanced an account as Freeman does of the crucial years from 791 to 793. Nagel, *Theologischen Herausforderung*, pp. 168–77 dates the *Capitulare* to 790 and the *Responsum* to 790/91 because its speaks only of Constantine VI and not of his mother, who, as Ostrogorsky argued (*History*, pp. 179–80), was away from Constantinople from the spring of 790 to January 792. This is possible, but I prefer Freeman's chronology. The preceding account depends heavily on Freeman's reconstruction while emphasizing more than she does some of the puzzles and uncertainties faced by the historian of these years.

41. See Fleckenstein, "Das frankfurter Konzil von 794," pp. 27–46; Hartmann, "Nizäa und Frankfurt"; idem, "Das Konzil von Frankfurt"; McKitterick, "Das Konzil im Kontext"; Mordek, "Aachen, Frankfurt, Reims"; Nelson, "The Siting of the Council of Frankfurt," pp. 149–65; Staab, "Die Königin Fastrada," pp. 183–217; and the still valuable Ganshof, "Francfort."

42. *Annales regni Francorum*, anno 793, ed. Kurze, pp. 92, 94: "Rex autumnali tempore de Reganesburg iter navigio faciens usque ad fossatum magnum inter Alcmana et Radantia pervenit, ibique missi apostolici cum magnis muneribus praesentati sunt. . . . Inde per Radantia in Mohin navali iter peragens, natalem Domini celebravit ad sanctum Chilianum in Wirzinburg."

43. *Annales qui dicuntur Einhardi*, anno 793, ed. Kurze, p. 95: "celebravitque natalem Domini apud sanctum Kilianum iuxta Moenum fluvium, pascha vero super eundem fluvium in villa Franconovurd in qua et hiemaverat." *Annales regni Francorum*, anno 794, ed. Kurze, p. 94: "Pascha celebratum est in Franconofurt."

44. *Annales qui dicuntur Einhardi*, anno 794, ed. Kurze, p. 95: "quando et generalem populi sui conventum habuit, concilium episcoporum ex omnibus regni sui provinciis in eadem villa congregavit. Adfuerunt etaim in eadem synodo et legati sanctae Romanae ecclesiae, Theophylactus ac Stephanus episcopi . . ."; *Annales regni Francorum*, anno 794, ed. Kurze, p. 94: "ibi congregata est synodus magna episcoporum Galliarum, Germanorum, Italorum in praesentia iamfati principis et missorum domni apostolici Adriani, quorum nomina haec sunt Theofilactus et Stephanus episcopi." Although these annals call both legates "bishops" the *Annales maximiniani*, MGH, SS, 13, 22 calls Theophylact a deacon. Freeman shows that this is likely to be correct: "Carolingian Orthodoxy," p. 93 n. 112.

45. "Carolingian Orthodoxy," p. 90. The Latin is in n. 42 above.

46. Von den Steinen, "Entstehung," pp. 60–65; Freeman, "Carolingian Orthodoxy," pp. 91–92.

47. *Annales regni Francorum*, anno 794, ed. Kurze, p. 94.

48. *Annales qui dicuntur Einhardi*, anno 794, ed. Kurze, p. 95.

49. MGH, Conc., 2, no. 19g, p. 165: "Allata est in medio quaestio de nova Grecorum synodo, quam de adorandis imaginibus Constantinopolim fecerunt, in qua scriptum habebatur, ut qui imagines sanctorum ita ut deificam trinitatem servitio aut adorationem non impenderent, anathema iudicaverunt: qui supra sanctissimi patres nostri omnimodis adorationem et servitutem rennuentes contempserunt atque conscientes condempnaverunt."

50. Mansi, Concilia, 12, 1148B.

51. *Opus Caroli*, 3.17, ed. Freeman, p. 412.

52. Hadrian ep. no. 2, MGH, Epp. 5, 17.

53. Some of the problems in reading this clause are discussed by Freeman, "Carolingian Orthodoxy," p. 94 and Hartmann, "Frankfurt und Nizäa," pp. 308–9.

54. These sources are well discussed by Freeman, "Carolingian Orthodoxy," pp. 92–95 and Hartmann, "Das Konzil von Frankfurt," pp. 331–36.

55. MGH, SS, 1, pp. 35–36.

56. MGH, SS 13, p. 22.

57. Von Dobschütz, ed., *Das Decretum gelasianum de libris recipiendis et non recipiendis.*

58. Theodulf cited the *Decretum* five times (*Opus*, 1.6, 2.13, 4. 10, 4.11, ed. Freeman, pp. 132, 133, 261, 511, 512) and alluded to it another six times (*Opus*, 1.6, 1.11, 2.17, 2.20, 3.21, ed. Freeman, pp. 134, 135, 159, 267, 272, 429).

59. *Opus* 1.6, ed. Freeman, pp. 132–37 with 132 n. 2. For a somewhat different view of the implications of 1.6 see Mitalaité, *Philosophie et théologie*, pp. 45–51.

60. In addressing Migetius, Elipandus held that Matthew 16.18 applied to all the apostles and not just to Peter: PL 96: 859–67. Already Beatus of Liebaña had maintained the same view: *Adversus Elipandum*, 1.3, PL: 96, 916. Freeman, "Einleitung," p. 41. On the issue generally see Ahern, "Late Visigothic Bishops"; on Rome in the early adoptionist quarrel see Cavadini, *Last Christology*, pp. 47–48; on Roman authority in Spain see Firey, "Carolingian Ecclesiology and Heresy" and Nagel, *Theologischen Herausforderung*, pp. 37–43.

61. Noble, "Gregory of Tours and the Roman Church."

62. The specific subject of the inculcation of Rome-centeredness has not advanced far beyond where Levison left it in *England and the Continent.*

63. Hampe, "Hadrians Vertheidigung," p. 102; Hauck, *Kirchengeschichte Deutschlands*, 2. 327–43, esp. 330; Ostrogorsky, "Rom und Byzanz"; Haller, *das Papsttum*, 2. 15; Arnaldi, "La questione dei 'Libri Carolini,'" pp. 3–19; Grape, "Karolingische Kunst und Ikonoklasmus," p. 50; Trompf, "Concept of the Carolingian Renaissance," p. 11 n. 35.

64. This seems to be Freeman's position, "Carolingian Orthodoxy," p. 91 ("The Carolingians were committed, however, before the fact, to an unquestioning acceptance of whatever the pope proclaimed"), and p. 92 ("Defiance of the pope, particularly in a matter of doctrine, would have been unthinkable to any Carolingian king"). Hartmann, *Hadrian I*, pp. 278–91 goes too far in the opposite direction.

65. See the cautious remarks of Hartmann, "Nizäa und Frankfurt," 371, on "publication" of the *Opus.*

66. *Opus* ed. Freeman, p. 97. This page comes from the Paris manuscript (Arsenal 663, fol. 1r), a page that is lacking in the Vatican manuscript. There is no reason to believe that someone in Hincmar's circle invented this title. The long familiar title for the work, *Libri Carolini*, derives from the arbitrary title selected by Bastgen in his 1924 MGH edition: *Libri Carolini sive Caroli Magni capitulare de imaginibus.* For a reproduction of the title page of the Arsenal MS see *Karl der Grosse: Werk und Wirkung*, p. 193 and plate 33.

67. Schatz, "Königliche Kirchenregierung."

68. Codex Carolinus, no. 95, ed. Gundlach, pp. 636–38. Cavadini, *Last Christology*, pp. 11, 73–77.

69. Hadrian ep. 2, MGH, Epp. 5, 7–11.

70. For a brief introduction to the *filioque* issue see Haugh, *Photius and the Carolingians*, pp. 41–81 and Willjung, "Einleitung" (to his *Das Konzil von Aachen*), pp. 5–20. For more detailed analyses see Gemeinhardt, *Die Filioque-Kontroverse*; Ramos-Lissón, "Die Synodalen Ursprung"; Peri, "Il 'Filioque' nel magisterio di Adriano I e di Leone III" and "Leone III e il 'Filioque': ancora un falso e l'autentico simbolo romano"; Borgolte, "Papst Leo III, Karl der Grosse und der Filioque Streit"; Heath, "The Western Schism of the Franks"; Sterk, "Silver Shields of Leo III." The gradual Frankish adoption of *filioque* is traced by Nagel, *Theologischen Herausforderung*, pp. 205–26. Kelly, *Early Christian Doctrines*, pp. 275–76 shows that Augustine is behind western thinking on the double procession of the Holy Spirit.

71. E.g., *Opus* 1.7, 3.3–5, ed. Freeman, pp. 139, 345–60. *Opus* 3.3 appears to have been the original first chapter from the *Capitulare*.

72. These materials are now expertly edited by Willjung, *Das Konzil von Aachen 809*.

73. MGH, Conc. 2, nos. 19 a–g, pp. 111–71 (documents a to f are the treatises and g is the canons).

74. Hartmann, "Das Konzil von Frankfurt," pp. 331–33, 336–41 and "Nizäa und Frankfurt," pp. 309–11.

75. Willjung, "Einleitung," esp. pp. 20–41.

76. MGH, Conc., 2, no. 19, p. 165.

77. Ibid., pp. 165–66.

78. *Das fränkisch-deutsche Synodlarecht*, pp. 252–53, 265–66. See also Depreux, "L'expression *statutum est a domno rege et sancta synodo*" and Staubach, "Cultus Divinus," p. 550: "Nicht Eigenmächtigkeit in Fragen der Glaubensdefinition, sondern Zusammenwirken mit den Bischöfen und dem römischen Stuhl sowie mildtätige Freigebigkeit, insbesondere gegenüber den Kirchen, zeichnet also nach westlichem Verständnis den Herrscher aus. . . ." The same basic point was made already by Folz, *Imperial Coronation of Charlemagne*, pp. 84–85. Most recently Spillung, "Die Sprach des Konzls," pp. 699–727 noting carefully that canons 1 to 3 (canon 3 condemned Tassilo of Bavaria) were impersonal, as were canons 11 to 72. Canons 4 to 10, therefore, reveal Charles's own voice and decisions.

79. Wallach, *Alcuin and Charlemagne*, p. 147; Hartmann, *Die Synoden*, p. 107.

80. MGH, Conc. 2, no. 19f, pp. 157–64.

81. Hadrian, ep. No. 2, MGH, Epp. 5, 55, 57.

82. Peri, "L'ecumenicità di un concilio."

83. Barion, "Der kirchenrechtliche Charakter," p. 167: "In the eyes of the Frankish church and of its leader (Herrn) the council of Frankfurt was a local council."

84. Bastgen, "Das Kapitulare Karls des Grossen," pp. 664–66; von Schubert, *Geschichte der christlichen Kirche*, p. 384; Hauck, *Kirchengeschichte Deutschlands*, 2. 343.

85. *Opus*, 3.11, ed. Freeman, p. 375.

86. Sieben, *das Konzilsidee*, pp. 307–43. Bullough, "Alcuin and the Kingdom of Heaven," pp. 36–38, accepts Sieben's theory. The key study on pentarchy remains Peri, "La pentarchia," pp. 209–311. Valuable too are Schatz, "Oecumenicité du concile et structure de l'église"; Brandmüller, "*Traditio Scripturae Interpres*."

87. For a range of reflections on the meanings of *ratio* see Carruthers, *Craft of Thought*,

pp. 32–35. She notes that *rationes* are not "reasons" but "schemes" or "ordering devices," and that *ratio* means "computation" or "calculation," not "reason" in our senses of that word. It relates to gathering information and building patterns of meaning.

88. I cite Freeman's translation: "Carolingian Orthodoxy," pp. 88–89 from her edition of the *Opus*, p. 557.

89. Schieffer, "Der Papst als Patriarch von Rom," esp. pp. 444–46.

90. Most obviously in his poems on the court and on judges: nos. 15 and 16, ed. Godman, *Poetry of the Carolingian Renaissance*, pp. 150–66.

91. *Studien*, p. 1.

92. *Opus*, 3.17, 3.22 (?), 3.29, 4.14, 4.15, 4.16, ed. Freeman, pp. 412–16, 435–40, 475–79, 522–29.

93. Gero argued for extracts and deep misunderstanding: "The *Libri Carolini* and the Image Controversy." For traditional views on the failure of the Franks to understand Nicaea, see: Martin, *Iconoclastic Controversy*, pp. 228–51; Haendler, *Karolingischer Theologie*, pp. 40–43; Dumeige, *Nicée II*, p. 155.

94. Auzépy, "Francfort et Nicée II," pp. 279–300; Thümmel, "Die fränkische Reaktion," pp. 965–80; Mitalaité, *Philosophie et théologie*. I regret that I became acquainted with Mitalaité's important book only while I was checking the copy-editing of my own. Our approaches are complementary and I wish I had been able to take fuller account of her excellent discussion of the philosophical and theological depths and consistency of Theodulf's arguments.

95. Auzépy, "Francfort et Nicée II," p. 292; Thümmel, "Die fränkische Reaktion," pp. 968–72. For a similar comments see Elbern, "Die liturgische Kunst," p. 15; Froehlich, "Libri Carolini and Lessons," pp. 206–7. This position had already been taken by Ladner, "Kunstlehren," p. 13 n. 41. On the wide range of possible meanings for *proskynēsis* see Lampe, *Patristic Greek Lexicon*, pp. 1174b–1177a.

96. Thümmel, "Die fränkische Reaktion," p. 975.

97. Ibid., pp. 972–77.

98. Auzépy, "Francfort et Nicée II," pp. 284–89.

99. See, for a sense of the issue, the entry "novitas" in Freeman's index, p. 647.

100. Auzépy, "Francfort et Nicée II," p. 292.

101. Thümmel, "Die fränkische Reaktion," pp. 978–80.

102. Morrison, "Anthropology and the Use of Religious Images," pp. 33, 34.

103. *Opus*, ed. Freeman, pp. 97–102.

104. *Opus* 1.1–4, ed. Freeman, pp. 105–15, 115–20, 120–24, 124–28.

105. Freeman, *Opus*, p. 105 n. 61.

106. Although the force and purpose of Theodulf's argument is clear enough, there is a serious textual problem here. The later translation of Anastasius Bibliothecarius reads "nostrum Salvator, qui vobis coimperat." The Greek must have had a ὑμῖν that was misread as a ἡμῖν, accounting for a change of a vobis into a nobis.

107. This is the first time that Theodulf raises the *filioque* issue.

108. On Theodulf's exegetical views see Dahlhaus-Berg, *Nova Antiquitas et Antiqua Novitas*, pp. 35–91 and Noble, "Biblical Testimonies," pp. 106–9.

109. For good comments on Theodulf's attitude to traditional biblical exegesis see Chazelle, "Images, Scripture, the Church," p. 59; Froehlich, "Libri Carolini and Lessons," pp. 199–202.

110. The first four examples come from chapter two, the fifth from chapter fourteen, and the sixth from chapter twenty-two. Theodulf might have gathered all these passages about one person worshiping another into a single chapter, but he is following his sources.

111. *Opus*, 1.13, ed. Freeman, pp. 163–64, and 163 n. 5, 164 n. 1. Theodulf blamed the Greeks for not adhering to the text properly because all he can find is Jacob worshiping "at the foot of the bed" not at the tip of a staff (*virgae*).

112. These discussions may be found in, respectively, 1.10, 1.12, 1.13, 1.18.

113. In order they are: 26.8, 4.7, 44.3, 29.12, 11.3, 11.4, 9.7, 25.8, 47.9, 73.3, 73.9, 72.20, 84.11, 98.5, 98.9, 124.3, 124.5.

114. The first one to draw attention to possible Mozarabic elements in the *Opus* was Allgeier, "Psalmenzitate."

115. *Opus*, ed. Freeman, p. 267 n. 4. See ibid., n. 3 for some of the problems involved in trying to trace the text that is at issue here.

116. Freeman, "Einleitung," pp. 55–56 enumerates the thirty-five syllogisms. See Wirth, *L'image médiévale*, pp. 132–38 on logic in the *Opus*.

117. *Opus*, ed. Freeman, p. 385 n. 4.

118. Freeman devotes Appendix III to this material in 3.23: *Opus*, pp. 577–82. It should be borne in mind that Theodulf's traceable sources are all textual.

CHAPTER FIVE

1. Schmandt, *Studien*, p. 54 counts eighteen repetitions of this point. I did not count them myself.

2. So, generally, Dahlhaus-Berg, *Nova Antiquitas et Antiqua Novitas*, pp. 35–37.

3. E.g., 1.17, 1.30, 2.15, 1.24, 2.25, 2.31, 3 *Praef.*, 3.11, 4 *Praef.*, etc. These are merely representative examples.

4. *Opus, Praef.*, p. 102.

5. *Opus, Praef.*, p. 101; cf. 4.18, pp. 533–34.

6. *Opus*, 1.17, 19, pp. 184, 193. Dahlhaus-Berg, *Nova Antiquitas et Antiqua Novitas*, pp. 196–201; Staubach, "Cultus Divinus," 553.

7. *Opus*, 4.13, pp. 521–22. The council of Rimini was one of two summoned by Emperor Constantius in 359 in an attempt to settle the Arian problem. In the end, its decisions went too far in the Arian direction and were later repudiated.

8. See the index under "novitas," p. 647.

9. *Opus*, p. 564.

10. E.g., *Opus, Praef.*, 1.2, 1.17, 3.11, 3.13, 4.13, 4.28.

11. *Opus*, 1.20, p. 196.

12. *Opus*, 3.2, p. 344.

13. *Opus*, 3.3, 3.8, 3.22, pp. 345–52, 370–71, 435–40.

14. *Opus*, 2.31, p. 322.

15. In *Opus*, 1.19, 4.8, pp. 192, 508 he adds moderation and patience.

16. *Opus*, *Praef.*, 1.2, 1.27, 1.28, 2.23, 2.31, 4.7, 4.8, 4.22.

17. Freeman, "Einleitung," pp. 55–56. See also Marenbon, "Alcuin, the Council of Frankfort and the Beginnings of Medieval Philosophy," who makes the point that whereas for Theodulf logic was a tool for validating or falsifying arguments, for Alcuin, who may have been inspired by Theodulf, logic was a way of apprehending reality.

18. *Opus*, 1.1, p. 113.

19. *Opus*, 1.1, 1.2, 1.3, 1.8, 1.9, 1.11, 1.12, 1.13, 1.17, 1.23, 1.28, 2.15, 2.17, 2.30, 3.9, 4.1, 4.5, 4.14, 4.16, 4.23, 4.26. In some cases these chapters contain numerous complaints on this same issue so the overall number would be higher.

20. Theodulf seems to have taken particular delight in lecturing the Greeks on this point. He mentions ten figures of speech and with much false patience explains how, if the Greeks understood them, they would not have misunderstood the scriptures or spoken "incautiously," "inordinately," "inappropriately": amphibolia—double meaning, ambiguity (3.20, p. 425); ethop(o)eia—inanimate preaching (*Praef.*, p. 98, 1.25, p. 217, 2.30, p. 314); hypozeuxis—a principle of subordination (2.30, p. 308); metabole—repetition to make a point (*Praef.*, p. 98); metaphora—the use of a word in a figurative sense (2.4, p. 245, 2.30, p. 318); parabola—a comparison or an explanatory illustration (1.26, p. 220, 2.20, p. 272); peusis—a searching inquiry (1.23, p. 212); prole(m)psis—anticipation or anachronism (1.1, p. 112, 1.28, p. 223, 2.1, p. 239); somatopoeia—attribution of corporeal qualities to incorporeal things (2.4, p. 244); syllepsis—using one for many or many for one (2.1, p. 240, 3.16, p. 408).

21. Thümmel, "Die Ikonen im Westen," 355–56.

22. Morrison, "Anthropology and the Use of Religious Images," pp. 38, 43.

23. "Images, Scripture, the Church," p. 54. See also eadem, "Matter, Spirit, and Image," pp. 165, 172 and passim, and Froehlich, "Libri Carolini and Lessons," pp. 203–6.

24. Implicit or explicit in *Opus*, 1.2, p. 116, 2.2, pp. 240–41, 2.7, p. 251, 1.15, p. 263, 1.21, p. 274, 2.22, p. 277, 2.24, pp. 280–81, 3.17, pp. 412–16, 3.25, p. 454, 3.28, pp. 470–75, 4.2, p. 491, 4.3, p. 494, 4.18, p. 532, 4.24, p. 550.

25. *Opus*, 1.2, p. 117, 1.9, p. 149, 1.16, p. 179, 1.17, p. 188, 1.19, p. 193, 1.23, p. 211, 1.24, p. 213, 2.5, p. 247, 2.14, pp. 261–62, 2.16, pp. 263–64, 2.26, pp. 286–87, 2.29, p. 301, 2.10, p. 317, 3.18, p. 418, 4 *Praef.*, p. 485, 4.24, p. 550.

26. Excellent is Jeck, "Gott in die Materiae darstellen?"

27. *Opus*, 2.21, p. 275.

28. Jeck, "Gott in die Materiae darstellen?," pp. 95–99.

29. *Opus*, 2.21, p. 273.

30. Staubach, "Cultus Divinum," 547.

31. In order: *Opus*, 1.8, pp. 145–46 and 2.16, p. 265; p. 99; 1.7, pp. 139–40.

32. E.g., *Opus*, 3.15, p. 403, 3.27, p. 466–70, 3.29, pp. 475–79.

33. *Opus*, 1.7, pp. 138–39, 140, 1.17, pp. 185, 187, 2.10, p. 255, 2.16, pp. 263–66, 2.22, p. 275, 3.15, p. 403, 4.2, p. 493, 4.4, pp. 522–24, 4.21, pp. 539–40.

34. I fully concur with Jeck, "Gott in die Materiae darstellen?," p. 98.

35. More than anyone else Chazelle has studied what Theodulf owed to Augustine and where he passed beyond him: "Images, Scripture, and the Church" and "Matter, Spirit, and

Image." Freeman shows that Augustine is by far Theodulf's most frequently cited author "Stellenregister 2: Autoren und Werke," pp. 599–600. Chazelle makes the important point that Theodulf may have thought that he was always reproducing Augustine's thought even when he was advancing beyond him.

36. Relics: *Opus*, 3.16, pp. 409, 411, 3.24, pp. 448–51; the cross: 1.13, p. 166, 1.19, p. 192, 2.15, p. 263, 2.28, pp. 296–300; 4.13, p. 516, 4.16, p. 528; churches: 3.15, p. 403, 3.16, p. 409, 4.3, p. 494; vessels: 2.29, pp. 300–302, 3.24, p. 448, 4.16, p. 527; Scriptures: 2.30, pp. 303–22 (this is the major but not the only theme of this, the longest chapter, in the *Opus*), 3.23, pp. 446–47; eucharist: 2.27, pp. 289–96, 4.13, p. 516, 4.14, pp. 523–24; Ark: 1.15, pp. 169–75, 1.19, pp. 192–93, 1.20, pp. 196–203, 2.26, pp. 286–89, 4.13, p. 516. These themes are partially discussed in Chazelle, "Matter, Spirit, and Images," pp. 165–70 (she omits churches, does not take up the eucharist in detail, and does not make an exhaustive search for her "five" classes of objects [I have seven]) and Appleby, "Holy Relic and Holy Image," esp. pp. 335–36 with particular reference to relics.

37. *Opus*, 1.9, p. 254.

38. Good summary in Weitmann, *Sukzession und Gegenwart*, pp. 198–202.

39. *Responsum*, 1.24, 1.26, pp. 27, 27–28.

40. *Responsum*, 1.15, 1.19, pp. 21, 24.

41. *Responsum*, 1.18, 1.23, pp. 23, 26.

42. *Responsum*, 2.19, p. 51.

43. *Responsum*, 1.8, p. 17.

44. *Responsum*, 2.15, p. 48.

45. *Responsum*, 1.11, 1.18, pp. 18–19, 23.

46. *Responsum*, 1.13, p. 20.

47. *Responsum*, 2.19, pp. 49–52.

48. *Responsum*, 2.19, p. 51.

49. Thacker, "In Search of Saints," pp. 247–69.

50. *Responsum*, 1.54, p. 40 is one good example among many.

51. *Dialogum Libri IV*, 3.33, PL 77: 296B–297C.

52. *Dialogum Libri IV*, 3.30, PL 77: 288A–289A.

53. There is no comprehensive treatment of Theodulf's views. Weitmann, *Sukzession und Gegenwart*, pp. 186–91 is a good start. Less satisfactory is Nagel, *Theologischen Herausforderung*, pp. 182–94.

54. *Opus*, "Wort- und Sachregister," p. 638. I tracked down each reference. Froehlich, "The *Libri Carolini* and the Lessons," p. 208 says that Theodulf neglected the argument from incarnation. That is true but misses the point that Theodulf was not attempting to defend images.

55. *Opus*, 1.22, pp. 207–8, 1.30, pp. 231–32, 2.30, pp. 306–7, 3.6, pp. 362–63, 3.14, pp. 397–98, 3.25, p. 457.

56. *Opus*, 1.29, p. 228, 2.5, p. 248, 3.21, pp. 432–33.

57. *Opus*, 4.2, pp. 492, 493.

58. On Theodulf's condensation of Gregory's arguments see Chazelle, "Images, Scripture, the Church," p. 56.

59. Appleby, "Holy Relic and Holy Image," p. 334 took this view but later abandoned it: "Instruction and Inspiration," p. 89.

60. *Opus*, 2.30, p. 303: "oculis tantummodo faveant per quos (imagines) quasi per quosdam legatos rerum gestarum cordibus mandent."

61. "Einleitung," p. 31.

62. Some examples: *Opus*, 1.14, p. 187, 2.30, passim, 3.23, pp. 446–47, 4.21, p. 539.

63. *Opus*, 3.23, p. 447. See Kessler, "Carolingian Art as Spiritual Seeing," pp. 536–37.

64. *Opus*, 4.27, p. 555.

65. "Testo e immagine," pp. 34–35, 38, 47–54.

66. "Word, Text, and Image," pp. 65–72. Nees, "Godescalc's Career," pp. 21–43 argues that the Egino Codex was painted by Godescalc, a painter with close ties to Charlemagne's court.

67. Appleby, "Holy Relic and Holy Image," p. 334; Freeman, "Scriptures and Images," pp. 170–75.

68. *Opus*, 3.30, p. 480, 4.10, p. 511.

69. *Opus*, 3.21, pp. 428–35 and 3.30, p. 480 (Polemon story), 4.12, pp. 514–15 (light before image story).

70. *Opus*, 3.25–26, pp. 452–66.

71. *Opus*, 1.7, p. 144, 1.18, p. 189, 1.23, p. 209, 1.24, p. 213, 1.29, pp. 224, 225, 1.30, p. 331, 2.1, p. 239, 2.16, pp. 263–64, 2.24, p. 281, 4.2, p. 493.

72. *Opus*, 2.14, pp. 261–62. He is here quoting with approval a story from Athanasius.

73. Another point which he makes countless times: *Opus*, 1.2, p. 117, 1.14, p. 168, 1.20, p. 196, 2.5, p. 247, 2.16, p. 265, 2.26, p. 286, 2.27, p. 290, 3.16, pp. 409–10, 411, 3.18, p. 418, 3.22, p. 438, 3.23, pp. 441–42, 4.16, pp. 528–29, 4.21, p. 541, 4.27, p. 555. Very often Theodulf makes this point by speaking dismissively of a picture's having been made "by some artist or other."

74. *Opus*, 2.27, p. 294, 3.15, pp. 399–400, 3.16, p. 410, 4.19, p. 535; Freeman, "Scripture and Images," pp. 164–65.

75. Godman, *Poetry of the Carolingian Renaissance*, p. 13; Nees, "Art and Architecture," p. 818.

76. Morrison, "Anthropology and the Use of Religious Images," p. 40. See also Mitalaité, *Philosophie et théologie*, esp. pp. 307–21.

77. Alcuin, ep. No. 135, MGH, EKA 2, p. 204.

78. *Commentarium in apocalypsin Libri Quinque*, PL 100: 1089A–B; *Compendium in Canticum Canticorum*, PL 100: 657D; *Commentaria in S. Iohannis Evangelium*, PL 100: 757C–D. See Noble, "Vocabulary of Vision and Worship," pp. 217–18.

79. Noble, "Vocabulary of Vision and Worship," pp. 229–30.

80. Wirth, *L'image médiévale*, pp. 139–54.

81. For some indications of the range of opinions: Schnitzler, "Das Kuppelmosaik," p. 25 and Grape, "Karolingische Kunst und Ikonoklasmus," p. 49 see Theodulf as an exponent of "Carolingian Iconoclasm" and believe that he in some ways imposed this view on his age. Schnitzler adds the view that the 790s, dominated by Theodulf, showed aniconic preferences while the decade after 800, dominated by Einhard, loosened the earlier restraints. Hubert et

al., *Carolingian Art*, pp. 79–81 also see a new spirit after the late 790s and attribute it, tentatively, to Einhard. Mütherich, "I Libri Carolini e la miniatura carolingia," pp. 281–301, Mayr-Harting, "Charlemagne as a Patron of Art," pp. 43, 44–48, and Nees, "Art and Architecture," p. 818 question whether the *Opus* had much influence. Mayr-Harting, pp. 66–75 does discern some influence, but he sees it as mutual between the *Opus* and the court. Schrade, "Zum Kuppelmosaik," p. 28 thinks that gaps in the evidence account for the apparent reserve in figural decoration while Mütherich, "Die Erneuerung der Buchmalerei," p. 564 thinks that limitations in the capacities of the court "school" may have imposed some reserve in figural representations. Bullough, "Imagines Regum," p. 242 thinks the *Opus* reveals a controversy between Theodulf and some "more moderate critics." He thinks the relative aniconism of the 790s owes more to Theodulf or that Theodulf was less out of step with his contemporaries than is usually thought. I am inclined to argue that the overall body of surviving art is too small to permit confident judgments about how much there may once have been.

82. *Opus*, 4.3, pp. 494–95.

83. Vieillard-Troiekouroff, "Les bibles de Théodulphe et la bible wisigothique de La Cava dei Terreni," pp. 153–66 on the books. On the chapel at Germigny, Freeman, "Einleitung," pp. 29–30 where, among other points, she notes that Theodulf did not strictly follow the biblical text in his apse mosaic. See most recently, Schedeler, "Die Pfalzkapelle in Aachen und St. Salvator zu Germigny-des-Prés" and Freeman and Meyvaert, "The Meaning of Theodulf's Apse Mosaic."

84. Mütherich and Gaehde, *Carolingian Painting*, p. 13 (on Tours) and Nees, "Carolingian Book Painters," where he makes the point that painters capable of making fine figural images were probably not common and should not be taken for granted.

85. Poem no. 43, MGH, PLAC, 1, p. 541.

86. Poem no. 41, MGH, PLAC, 1, pp. 532–40. These words virtually echo the dedication verses of the Godescalc Evangelistiary: MGH, PLAC, 1, p. 94: "Aurea purpureis pinguntur grammata scedis." I do not mean to imply that Theodulf's poem was influenced by the Godescalc poem. I merely mean to point to similar modes of expression from Charlemagne's circle.

87. Paris, BNF Lat. Nouv. Acq. 1203; Koehler, *Miniaturen*, 2. 22–28. See Reudenbach, *Das Godescalc Evangelistiar* and, most recently, Nees, "Godescalc's Career."

88. Paris, Bibliothèque de l'Arsenal, ms. 599; Koehler, *Miniaturen*, 2. 29–33.

89. Trier, Stadtbibliothek, ms. 22; Koehler, *Miniaturen*, 2. 34–41.

90. Vienna, Nationalbibliothek, ms. 1861; Koehler, *Miniaturen*, 2. 42–46.

91. Abbeville, Bibliothèque municipale, ms. 4; Koehler, *Miniaturen*, 2. 49–55.

92. London, BL, MS Harl. 2788; Koehler, *Miniaturen*, 2. 56–69.

93. Paris, BNF Lat. Ms. 8850; Koehler, *Miniaturen*, 2. 70–82.

94. Koehler, *Miniaturen*, 2. 83–87.

95. This manuscript was split at some point. The first part, with the gospels of Matthew and Mark, is Alba Julia Rumania; the second part, with Luke and John, is Vat. Pal. Lat. 50. Koehler, *Miniaturen*, 2. 88–100.

96. I follow Mütherich, "Die Erneuerung der Buchmalerei," pp. 563–64. See also Mayr-Harting, "Charlemagne as a Patron of Art," pp. 76–77. All recent chronologies derive

from, or are modifications of, Koehler, *Miniaturen*, vol. 2, pp. 9–16, with his subsequent comments on each of the manuscripts.

97. *Miniaturen*, vol. 3, pp. 7–21. See Mütherich and Gaehde, *Carolingian Painting*, pp. 10–11, 48–51 for a broad affirmation of Koehler's views.

98. Discussed by Nees, "Art and Architecture," p. 843. So too Bischoff, "The Court Library under Louis the Pious," pp. 79–86. Ganz, "'Roman Books' Reconsidered," p. 312 says simply that "Koehler's palace school gospels should rather be regarded as later than the court group."

99. So Bullough, "Imagines Regum," pp. 242–43 and Wiederanders, "Die Auswirkung der Bilderstreits," pp. 152–53.

100. Mütherich, "Die Erneuerung der Buchmalerei," pp. 563–64.

101. Saurma-Jeltsch, "Das Bild in der Worttheologie Karls des Großen," pp. 647–48, 652–54, 673. Her thesis is that the images in Godescalc, and to a degree in Soissons, are not autonomous but serve instead as exegesis of the Word.

102. Reudenbach, *Godescalc*, pp. 12, 45–50. Mütherich, "Die Erneuerung der Buchmalerei," p. 567. The fullest study of the images from the standpoint of style and models remains Rosenbaum, "Evangelist Portraits."

103. Diebold, *Word and Image*, pp. 99–103; McKitterick, "Text and Image," pp. 301, 318, and passim; Wiederanders, "Die Auswirkung der Bilderstreites," p. 154; Brenk, "Bildlichkeit und Schriftlichkeit."

104. Ganz, "'Roman Books' Reconsidered," pp. 313, 314.

105. For a traditional approach to style analysis (apart from Koehler's) see Hubert et al., *Carolingian Art*, pp. 75–92. For alternative modes of interpretation see Reudenbach, *Godescalc*, pp. 27–36; Nees, "Art and Architecture," pp. 809–10, 843; idem, "Carolingian Art and Politics," pp. 178, 187; Brenk, "Schriftlichkeit und Bildlichkeit." Kessler addresses the whole issue: "On the State of Medieval Art History."

106. Studied most fully by Underwood, "Fountain of Life." See also Saurma-Jeltsch, "Das Bild in der Worttheologie Karls des Grossen," pp. 640–41; Reudenbach, *Godescalc*, pp. 68–78.

107. Mayr-Harting, "Charlemagne as a Patron of Art," pp. 46–48.

108. Garipzanov, "The Image of Authority in Carolingian Coinage," pp. 207–15, esp. 208. A single gold coin from the royal period now in the British Museum, which might itself have had a mate in Berlin until sometime after 1840 when it vanished, *may* form an exception to this rule: Schramm, "Goldmünzen aus der Königzeit Karls des Großen," pp. 288–90. The 1965 Aachen exhibition catalogue (*Karl der Grosse*) nos. 10–12 dates the coins merely "after 804."

109. Goldschmidt, *Elfenbeinen*, nos. 3, 4. See Nees, "Art and Architecture," p. 832; idem, "Carolingian Art and Politics," pp. 189–91; Filitz, "Die Elfenbeinarbeiten," pp. 610–12.

110. MGH, PLAC, 1, p. 91.

111. Bullough, "Alcuin and the Kingdom of Heaven," pp. 13–15; idem, "Imagines Regum," pp. 242–43; Nees, "Dagulf Psalter," passim, esp. pp. 688–89.

112. Goldschmidt, *Elfenbeinen*, nos. 13, 14; Filitz, "Die Elfenbeinenarbeiten," p. 610.

113. Goldschmidt, *Elfenbeinen*, no. 5; Nees, "Carolingian Art and Politics," pp. 195–202; Filitz, "Die Elfenbeinenarbeiten," p. 610.

114. "Gott in die Materiae darstellen?" 98.

115. Markus, *Saeculum*, pp. 3–4.

116. Momigliano, "Pagan and Christian Historiography," p. 110.

117. Löwe, *Von Theoderich des Grossen zum Karls des Grossen*; Hauck, "Von einer spätantiken Randkultur zum karolingischen Europa"; Fritze, "Universalis gentium confessio"; Angenendt, "Karl der Große als *rex et sacerdos*."

118. Fleckenstein, "Karl der Große," pp. 29–32.

119. Ševčenko, "The Search for the Past in Byzantium"; Gurevich, *Categories of Medieval Culture*, p. 140; similarly Henry, "Images of the Church," pp. 247–49.

120. Dahlhaus-Berg, *Nova Antiquitas et Antiqua Novitas*, p. 201.

121. McKitterick, *History and Memory*; eadem, "History, Law and Communication."

122. McKitterick, *History and Memory*, pp. 101–11.

123. *Liber de episcopis Mettensibus*, MGH, SS, 2. 260–70. See McKitterick, *History and Memory*, pp. 60–83.

124. Oexle, "Die Karolinger und die Stadt des heiligen Arnulf," pp. 299–301.

125. *Vita Karoli*, c. 24.

126. Gundlach, *Praef., Codex Carolinus*, MGH, Epp. 3. 476.

127. Alcuin, ep. 137, MGH, Epp. 3, p. 215.

128. Paxton, *Christianizing Death*, pp. 118–19.

129. McKitterick, *Carolingians and the Written Word*, pp. 165–210, esp. 196–98.

130. Mordek, "Kirchenrechtliche Autotitäten," pp. 249–50.

131. McKitterick, *Frankish Church*, p. 66.

132. *Vita Karoli* c. 25.

133. Borst, *Die karolingische Kalendarreform*, pp. 231–311, 418–24, 518. Borst's interpretations came in for criticism from Meyvaert, "Discovering the Calendar," and Bullough, "York, Bede's Calendar, and a Pre-Bedan English Martyrology." Borst has now responded in detail: *Der Streit um den karolingischen Kalendar*. Perhaps the "Lorsch Calendar" is less original than Borst thought, but it cannot be explained away. Moreover, the whole issue of time reckoning was a central preoccupation of these years: Contreni, "Counting, Calendars, and Cosmology," pp. 58–67; McKitterick, *History and Memory*, pp. 86–97.

134. Freed, "Awaiting the End of Time," p. 29; Brandes, "Eschatologisches in Vorfeld der Kaiserkrönung"; Landes, "Lest the Millennium Be Fulfilled"; Winandy, *Ambroise Autpert*, pp. 31–37.

135. MGH, Cap. 1, no. 22, pp. 53–54.

136. Contreni, "Carolingian Biblical Culture," pp. 2–3.

137. *Opus*, "Namenregister," pp. 612–13.

138. *Epistolae variorum Carolo Magno regnante scriptae*, no. 7, MGH, Epp. 4. 503.

139. MGH, PLAC, 1. 52.

140. MGH, PLAC, 1. 90–91.

141. MGH, PLAC, 1. 360–63.

142. Ep. No. 41, MGH, Epp. 4. 84.

143. The most recent study of this interesting phenomenon is Garrison, "The Social World of Alcuin."

144. Fichtenau, "Byzanz und die Pfalz," 30. The Sixth Ecumenical Council of 680 addressed the emperor as a "New David" (Dagron, "Le Christianisme byzantin," p. 46) and the Franks, with their emphasis on the "Six" Councils may have known this.

145. Codex Carolinus, no. 39, MGH, Epp. 3, p. 552.

146. Lex Salica, ed. Eckhardt, pp. 1–9. Garrison, "The Franks as the New Israel?" reads the evidence more skeptically than I do.

147. Examples: MGH, Cap. 1, no. 22, c. 62, p. 58; *Annales regni Francorum*, anno 791, ed. Kurze, p. 88; Paulinus of Aquileia, *Libellus adversus Elipandus*, MGH, Conc., 2.2, p. 142; Alcuin, epp. nos. 41, 121, 174, MGH, Epp. 4. 84, 176, 288. Cathwulf speaks of the "populus Dei": MGH, Epp., 4, no. 7, pp. 501–05.

148. Alcuin, *Vita Willibrordi*, c. 9: "electus a Deo populus."

149. MGH, Cap. 1, nos. 23, 24, pp. 63–66; Noble, "From Brigandage to Justice," pp. 53–55.

150. Folz, *Coronation of Charlemagne*, pp. 82–83, 97–100; Wallace-Hadrill, *Early Germanic Kingship*, pp. 98–100; Munz, "Origins," p. 43; Onians, *Bearers of Meaning*, p. 76.

151. Appuhn, "Thron," esp. pp. 130–34; Fichtenau, "Byzanz und die Pfalz," 25–26. But Schramm ("Die Thron des deutschen Königs," pp. 337–44) notes that the throne is not an exact replica of the one described in the Bible and that, in fact, it also evokes Roman precedents and the ancient Germanic tradition. This makes the throne a synthesis of traditions culminating in Charles, exactly like the *Opus* itself. What is more, the throne situated in the gallery today is probably Ottonian.

152. Alcuin, ep. no. 145, MGH, Epp. 4. 235; Notker, *Gesta Karoli*, 1. 27 speaks of the buildings constructed by Charles "following the example of wise, old Solomon." The Solomonic reference had considerable staying power. See Binding, "Zur Ikonologie der Aachener Pfalzkapelle," pp. 195–98.

153. Grabois, "Charlemagne, Rome, and Jerusalem"; Schmid, "Aachen und Jerusalem"; Vauchez, *Spiritualité*, p. 32.

154. Alcuin, ep. no. 210, MGH, Epp. 4. 350–51.

155. *De ecclesia centulensi*, c. 2, MGH, SS, 15.1, p. 175.

156. Mordek, "Kirchenrechtliche Autoritäten." The first fifty-nine capitula of the Admonitio Generalis come from this collection: MGH, Cap. 1, no. 22, pp. 52–57.

157. Hen, *Royal Patronage of Liturgy*, pp. 74–78 with sources and older literature.

158. *Epistula ad regem Karolum*.

159. Bullough, "Roman Books and Carolingian *Renovatio*"; Schieffer, "Redeamus ad fontes," pp. 48–60.

160. Heitz, "More Romano."

161. McLendon, *Architecture*, pp. 85–127; Conant, *Carolingian and Romanesque*, pp. 43–55; D'Onofrio, *Roma e Aquisgrana*, pp. 57, 104–14; Jacobsen, "Gab es ein karolingishcen Renaissance in der Baukunst?" pp. 322–29.

162. Falkenstein, "Zwischenbilanz"; idem, "Charlemagne et Aix-la-Chapelle."

163. "The Carolingian Revival of Early Christian Architecture."

164. Grimme, "Novus Constantinus," p. 11.

165. Claussen *Reform of the Frankish Church*, pp. 276–86; Klauser, "Eine Stationsliste

der Metzer Kirche" and "Notes sur l'ancienne liturgie de Metz"; Rabe, *Faith, Art, and Politics*, pp. 122–32.

166. Untermann, "Die Aachener 'Residenz,' " pp. 158–60; Jacobsen, "Die Renaissance der Frühchristlichen Architektur," pp. 633–34; Nees, "Art and Architecture," pp. 809–10; Schatz, "Königliche Kirchenregierung," p. 367; Schieffer, "Redeamus ad fontes," p. 64; D'Onofrio, *Roma e Aquisgrana*, pp. 125–46.

167. An important first step is McKitterick, *Perceptions of the Past in the Early Middle Ages*, ch. 2.

168. Codex Carolinus, no. 60, MGH, Epp., 3. 587.

169. Nees, *Tainted Mantle*, pp. 3–17, esp. p. 6, shows that Constantinian imagery is all post-800. See also Grimme, "Novus Constantinus," pp. 9–11; Ewig, "Das Bild Constantins des Großen."

170. Fallon, "Imperial Symbolism," pp. 122–27.

171. Falkenstein, "Charlemagne et Aix-la-Chapelle," pp. 282–89, although he does not mention Baghdad.

172. Modoin, *Eclogue*, ed. Godman, *Poetry of the Carolingian Renaissance,* pp. 192–96.

173. The most recent assessment is Brown, "The Carolingian Renaissance." Without citing all of the older literature, I can offer the following titles as effective summations and original contributions: Contreni, "The Carolingian Renaissance"; idem, "Inharmonious Harmony"; Guerreau-Jalabert, "La 'Renaissance carolingienne' "; Trompf, "Concept of the Carolingian Renaissance"; Morrison, "The Church, Reform, and Renaissance."

174. *Die Bildungsreform Karls des Grossen*, p. 11.

175. *Opus, Praef.*, p. 98.

176. MGH, Cap. 1, no. 22, *Praef.*, pp. 53–54.

177. *Libellus Sacrosyllabus*, MGH, Conc., 2.2. p. 142: "sit rex et sacerdos."

178. *Adversus Elipandum*, 1. 16, PL 101: 251.

179. *Codex Carolinus*, no. 76, MGH, Epp. 3, pp. 607–8; cf. Alcuin ep. 110, MGH, Epp. 4, pp. 157–59.

180. Waas, "Karls des Grossen Frömkigkeit."

181. Zachary to Boniface in Boniface, epp. 58, 61, ed. Tangl, pp. 108 ("norman rectitudinis") 121 (viam rectitudinis); in general, Fleckenstein, *Bildungsreform*, pp. 7–23.

182. MGH, Cap. I, no. 14, p. 33.

183. *Regula canonicorum*, prologue, c. 20, PL 89: 1057C.

184. MGH, Conc., 2.2, p. 294.

185. Wormald, "Lex scripta," p. 132. See also Contreni, "Carolingian Biblical Culture."

186. Treitinger, *Die oströmische Kaiser- und Reichsidee.*

187. A king was first called *minister Dei* in c. 75 of the Fourth Council of Toledo (589): PL 84: 385–86. Markus, "The Latin Fathers," p. 119 captures beautifully the Gregorian position: "One of the threads running through Gregory's *Regula Pastoralis* is the insistence that the exercise of power must be a mission of service to those subject to it, and humility its indispensable condition." There is no controversy on the degree to which Gregory influenced Carolingan ideas of kingship, but at the same time, no one has studied the issue carefully and in detail. See Ewig, "Königsgedanken," pp. 3–4, 39–63; Folz, *Coronation*, p. 77; Russell, *Just*

War, pp. 27–29; Fritze, "Universalis Gentium Confessio," pp. 106–13; Leonardi, "Alcuino," pp. 483–84.

188. Nelson, "The Lord's Anointed," pp. 154–57, 175–80.

189. D'Onofrio, *Roma e Aquisgrana*, pp. 132, 150–55; Folz, *Coronation*, pp. 104–5. The controversial element in Aachen is the mosaic in the cupola. A seventeenth-century image by Ciampini shows a Christ in majesty, rather like the now-visible image that was heavily restored in the nineteenth century. Charlemagne put the first image in the cupola and Frederick Barbarossa, in order to hang a chandelier, cut through the ceiling and then replaced it and the image. Did he restore it faithfully or did he replace an adoration of the Lamb with a maiestas? Schnitzler, "Kuppelmosaik" made the most impressive case for an original lamb. Mayr-Harting, "Charlemagne as a Patron," pp. 45–46 tends to agree. Schrade, "Kuppelmosaik" argued for a maiestas image. This is also the view of Wallace-Hadrill, *Early Germanic Kingship*, pp. 194–95; Bullough, "Imagines Regum," pp. 241–42; and Wehling, *Die Mosaiken*, pp. 12–48, who also studies the paintings.

190. Kantorowicz, *Laudes Regiae*, p. 15.

191. Cameron, "Justin II"; Fichtenau, "Byzanz und die Pfalz," 7–12; Folz, *Coronation*, pp. 104–6.

192. *Vita Karoli*, c. 23.

193. Fleckenstein, "Karl der Große," pp. 41–43 stresses how long Charlemagne spent in preparation for Frankfurt.

194. Two old studies set thinking on this topic on correct foundations: Kampers, "Rex et Sacerdos" and Delaruelle, "Charlemagne et l'église." The key point is that Charlemagne was not addressed as "king and priest" very often and never considered himself a priest. Moreover, he always stayed short of the line separating his protection of the church from outright intrusion. See also Fichtenau, "Karl der Grosse und das Kaisertum," 278–80; Folz, *Coronation*, p. 84; McCormick, "Paderborn 799," pp. 74–78. For a slightly different way of assessing the subject and of evaluating Alcuin's influence: Leonardi, "Alcuino."

195. *Bible*, p. 20. See also Contreni, "Carolingian Biblical Studies" and "Carolingian Biblical Culture"; Hartmann, "Die karolingische reform und die Bibel"; Gorman, "Wigbod and Biblical Studies under Charlemagne."

196. MGH, Cap. 1, no. 29; Martin, "Bemerkungen."

197. MGH, Cap. 1, no. 22, p. 60. See, in general, Hen, *Reform of the Liturgy* and Vogel, "Les échanges liturgiques."

198. Deshusses, *Le sacramentaire grégorien*; idem, "Le supplement au sacramentaire grégorienne."

199. MGH, Cap. 1, no. 30.

200. *Annales regni Francorum*, anno 791, ed. Kurze, p. 88.

201. For some examples: MGH, Cap. 1, no. 19, c. 6, p. 45, no. 22, c. 65, pp. 58–59, no. 26, cc. 6, 7, 9, pp. 68–69, no. 35, cc. 5, 40, 41, pp. 102, 104.

202. MGH, Cap. 1, no. 22, c. 78, p. 60.

203. Grierson and Blackburn, *Coinage*, pp. 201, 209–10, 524–25.

204. Fallon, "Imperial Symbolism," pp. 122–23; Nees, *Tainted Mantle*, p. 131.

205. Staubach, "Cultus Divinus," pp. 561–62, 567–71.

206. Cf. Wirth, *L'image médiévale*, pp. 121–27, 139–40, 163–64.

207. "Libri Carolini," p. 9.

208. "Cultus Divinus," p. 547.

209. "Matter, Spirit, and Image," 184.

210. *Coronation*, p. 95.

211. "Gott in die Materiae darstellen?" pp. 96–98.

212. "Kristallisationspunkt," p. 542.

213. "Theodulf of Orléans and the *Libri Carolini*," p. 665.

214. *Philosophie et théologie*.

CHAPTER SIX

1. Alexander, *Patriarch Nicephorus*, p. 111.

2. Theophanes, *Chronicle*, trans. Mango and Scott, pp. 671–72. See also Alexander, *Patriarch Nicephorus*, p. 111 and Treadgold, *Byzantine Revival*, pp. 169, 182.

3. Theophanes, *Chronicle*, trans. Mango and Scott, pp. 684–85; Alexander, *Patriarch Nicephorus*, pp. 112–13; Treadgold, *Byzantine Revival*, p. 182.

4. *Patriarch Nicephorus*, p. 112.

5. Barber, *Figure and Likeness*, p. 41; O'Connell, *Ecclesiology of Nicephorus*, pp. 126–28.

6. Griffiths, "Theodore Abū Qurrah's Arabic Tract," pp. 53–73. For some more details on Theodore see Sieben, "Theodore abū Qurra über 'unfehlbare' Konzilien," pp. 489–509; Graf, *Geschichte der christlichen arabischen Literatur*, pp. 7–26; Weitmann, *Sukzession und Gegenwart*, pp. 144–45. Further on Theodore's thought: Bratu, *Représenter le Christ*, pp. 209–60. Some of Theodore's writings are available in a new English translation: *Theodore abu Qurrah*, trans. Lamoreaux.

7. Griffiths (see n. 6) thinks that Theodore had no knowledge of current events in Byzantium and that he wrote only for Christian Arabs who were being challenged by their militantly iconophobic neighbors. This may be true and I would not dare to challenge Griffiths on the history of Christian Arabic literature. But Griffiths did not take into account connections between Palestine and Rome or Francia which seem to have been continuous. In turn, both Rome and Francia had constant contacts with Byzantium. Knowledge could have circulated more fully than Griffiths thinks. McCormick, *Origins of the European Economy*, documents hundreds of cases of trans-Mediterranean contact.

8. See above, p. 175.

9. Details in Treadgold, *Byzantine State and Society*, pp. 429–33 and *Byzantine Revival*, pp. 196–200. See also Ostrogorsky, *History*, pp. 175–80.

10. *Scriptor Incertus*, PG 108: 1016C; Theophanes, *Chronicle*, trans. Mango and Scott, p. 685.

11. Ignatios, *Life of Nikephoros*, pp. 72–74.

12. *Scriptor Incertus*, PG 108: 1021A–B, 1024C–D.

13. AASS, Aprilis 1, Appendix, col. xxvii; Brubaker and Haldon, *Byzantium in the Iconoclast Era*, p. 222.

14. Ignatios, *Life of Nikephoros*, p. 75. On John see Lemerle, *Le premier humanisme byzantin*, pp. 135–46.

15. *Scriptor Incertus*, PG 108. 1024C–1025B.

16. For what follows the basic sources are *Scriptor Incertus*, PG 108: 1024C–1036D, who provides most key details but does so in a somewhat chaotic order; Ignatios, *Life of Nikephoros*, pp. 75–107. The basic events are narrated by Treadgold, *Byzantine Revival*, pp. 209–13; Alexander, *Patriarch Nicephorus*, pp. 125–35; Ostrogorsky, *History*, pp. 129–30.

17. *Life of Nicetas of Medikion*, AASS, Aprilis 1, Appendix, p. xxv.

18. Alexander, "Iconoclastic Council," pp. 37–44; idem, "Church Councils and Patristic Authority," pp. 493–505; idem, *Patriarch Nicephorus*, pp. 137–40; Anastos, "Ethical Theory of Images," pp. 153–60, esp. pp. 156–60.

19. "Iconoclastic Council," pp. 58–66.

20. In the 1950s Alexander ("Iconoclastic Council") and Anastos ("Ethical Theory of Images") waged a battle of florilegia worthy of the combatants in the struggle whose history they were writing. First, Alexander claimed that the teaching of 815 on images and saintly virtue was essentially new and a departure from 754. Then Anastos said that the passages adduced by Alexander in connection with 815 were basically all there in 754. In his *Patriarch Nicephorus*, pp. 138–39, Alexander ignored Anastos's criticism of his earlier views and reformulated his own as positive and negative expressions. I have basically adopted this interpretation here as it seems to me to make the best sense of the scanty and ambiguous evidence. Recent scholars have not really returned directly to this problem.

21. I follow the interpretations of Alexander "Iconoclastic Council," pp. 41–42 and "Councils and Patristic Authority," pp. 498–99, 501–2. See also Treadgold, *Byzantine Revival*, pp. 212–13.

22. Alexander, *Patriarch Nicephorus*, pp. 140–47; Treadgold, *Byzantine Revival*, pp. 213–17.

23. *Epistolae* 2.12, PG 99: 1152D. To this letter may be added the extremely general remarks of Ignatios, *Life of Nikephoros*, pp. 125–26.

24. Alexander, "Religious Persecution and Resistance," pp. 238–64.

25. "Iconoclastic Council," p. 37.

26. The paragraphs that follow constitute a synthesis of Bratu, *Représenter le Christ*, pp. 261–460; Barber, *Figure and Likeness*, pp. 98–137; Alexander, *Patriarch Nicephorus*, pp. 189–213; Pratsch, *Theodoros*, pp. 203–91; Gardner, *Theodore*; Meyendorff, "L'image de Christ," pp. 115–17; Thümmel, "Positionen im Bilderstreit," pp. 184–91; Baget-Bozzo, "L'immagine di Christo," pp. 462–72; Schönborn, *L'icone de Christ*, pp. 220ff; Tsigaris, "Philosophisches Instrumentum der Christologie," pp. 268–77; Parry, "Theodore Studites and the Patriarch Nicephorus on Image Making," pp. 164–83; Jeck, "Prototyp—Ikon—Relation," pp. 206–14; Weitmann, *Sukzession und Gegenwart*, pp. 147–61. The key sources are: Theodore, *Antirrhetici I, II, III*, PG, 99. 328–436, with an English translation by Catherine Roth, *St. Theodore the Studite on the Holy Icons*. For Nicephorus, the key accessible source is his *Antirrhetici*, PG 100: 205–533 with a French translation by Mondzain-Baudinet, *Discours contre les iconoclastes*. Alexander identifies and discusses Nicephorus's other writings, as above, pp. 156–88.

27. *Antirr.* 1.20, PG, 100. 244D.

28. The elementary details are presented under the appropriate years in *Annales regni Francorum*, ed. Kurze, annis 803, 806, 807, 809, 810, 811, 812, 813, 814, 817, 821, 824, pp. 118, 122–24, 127, 130, 133, 136, 137, 140–41, 145, 155, 165.

29. See in general Hägermann, *Karl der Grosse*, pp. 561–64, 592–96.

30. PG 100: 169A–200C. On this letter see O'Connell, *Ecclesiology of Nicephorus*, pp. 68–78; Mainka, "Zum Brief des Patriarchen Nicephoros."

31. On these various affairs see: Pratsch, *Theodoros*, pp. 83–178; Treadgold, *Byzantine Revival*, pp. 103–8, 153–57, 178–80; Henry, "The Moechian Controversy."

32. *Epistolae*, 1.33, 1.34, PG 99: 1017B–1021A, 1021B–1028C.

33. With the possible exception of southern Italy. Patlagean, "Les moines grecs d'Italie" makes a good case for considerable sympathy for papal doctrinal primacy in hagiographical writings from southern Italy, but it is hard to know if such ideas were known in Rome.

34. Alexander, *Patriarch Nicephorus*, pp. 147–55.

35. *Epistolae*, 2.12, 2.13, PG 99: 1152B–1153C, 1153C–1156C. On Theodore's correspondence with Rome, see Pratsch, *Theodoros*, pp. 175–78, 253–54; van der Vorst, "Les relations de S. Théodore Studite avec Rome"; Grumel, "Quelques témoinages byzantines sur la primauté romaine"; idem, "Les relations politico-religieuses entre Byzance et Rome sous le regne de Léon V l'Arménien," pp. 19–44; O'Connell, *Ecclesiology of Nicephorus*, pp. 195–226; Gouillard, "L'église d'Orient et le primauté romaine," esp. pp. 46–53; Patlagean, "Les Stoudites, l'empereur et Rome."

36. *Epistolae*, 2.63, PG 99: 1281A–1284C.

37. *Vita Methodii*, c. 4, PG 100: 1248A–B.

38. *Epistolae*, 1.35, PG 99: 1028C–1032A, esp. 1029C.

39. *Vita Methodii*, c. 5, PG 100: 1248B–C.

40. *Iuris ecclesiastici Graecorum Historia et Monumenta*, vol. 2, pp. xi–xvii.

41. "La lettera di Pasquale I a Leone V," pp. 228–35.

42. The letter's basic context is laid out by Grumel, "Les relations politico-réligieuse," pp. 19–44. The most recent discussion is Thunø, *Image and Relic*, pp. 135–40.

43. *Epistola* c. 13, ed Mercati, p. 231. In this one instance I think that Pitra's reading (p. xiii) is superior. Mercati has Ἀλλὰ βλάπτῃ τῇ τῶν εἰκόνων ἀντιπαραθέσει πρὸς τὰς εἰκόνας but Pitra reads εἰδώλων for εἰκόνων which makes more sense.

44. *Epistola*, c. 14, ed. Mercati, p. 231.

45. Ignatios, *Life of Nikephoros*, pp. 83–100.

46. *Epistola*, cc. 15–18, 20, ed. Mercati, pp. 231–33, 233–34.

47. *Epistola*, cc. 21–22, ed. Mercati, pp. 234–35.

48. *Epistola* cc. 1–2, ed. Mercati, p. 228.

49. *Epistola*, c. 3, ed. Mercati, p. 229.

50. *Epistola*, cc. 6, 9, ed. Mercati, pp. 229–30, 230.

51. *Epistola*, cc. 7–8, ed. Mercati, p. 230.

52. *Epistola*, c. 10, ed. Mercati, pp. 230–31.

53. *Epistola*, cc. 5–6, ed. Mercati, pp. 229–30.

54. On Paschal's work generally, Thunø, *Image and Relic*. On the churches and mosaics, McClendon, *Origins of Medieval Architecture*, pp. 143–48; idem, "Louis the Pious, Rome, and

Constantinople"; and Noble, "Making of a Papal Rome," pp. 61–68. On the relics, Smith, "Old Saints, New Cults."

55. McClendon, *Origins of Medieval Architecture*, pp. 146–47 notes the parallel between the Trastevere image and Santa Maria in Domnica's apse (and in the same vein he points out that the apse mosaic in Santa Prassede, another of Paschal's churches, "quotes" the apse of Santi Cosma e Damiano). But McClendon thinks that because the Mary in Santa Maria in Domnica wears only a maphorion she is not a regina type but rather a Greek type and thus a rebuke to Michael II (or perhaps Leo V?). I agree on the rebuke. I have adopted the observation on tradition. But I do not quite follow the logic of the two Marys. If one quotes the other, if the Romans were expected to "get it," if the Santa Maria in Trastevere image is unquestionably a regina type, then I do not see why the absence of a crown in Santa Maria in Domnica makes this Mary, seated as she is on a jeweled throne, less "queenly."

56. MGH, Conc., 2.2, pp. 475–80. The letter is dated April 10, 824.

57. *Annales regni Francorum*, ed. Kurze, anno 821, p. 155: "Adlatum est et de morte Leonis Constantinopolitani imperatoris. . . ."

58. Michael II, *Epistola ad Hludowicum*, pp. 478–79.

59. Mansi, *Concilia*, 14, 399A–402A.

60. Michael II, *Epistola ad Hludowicum*, pp. 479–80.

61. MGH, Conc. 2. 2, pp. 475–551. Generally, Hartmann, *Konzilien*, pp. 168–71.

62. Werminghoff tags the five items A to E but I shall refer to them by name.

63. *Libellus*, p. 482 (lines 10–13 and 30–31).

64. Letter to Jeremias and Jonas, p. 533.

65. Letter to Eugenius, p. 534.

66. *Epitome,* p. 535.

67. *Kirchengeschichte Deutschlands*, 2, pp. 499, 502.

68. Letter to Jeremias and Jonas, p. 533.

69. *Libellus*, pp. 481, 483.

70. *Libellus*, pp. 522, 522–23.

71. Hartmann, *Synoden*, pp. 168–69.

72. *Libellus*, p. 482.

73. *Libellus*, p. 483.

74. Letter to Jeremias and Jonas, p. 533.

75. Dungal, *Responsa*, c. 246, ed. Zanna, p. 250. See also Dungal, ep. no. 9, MGH, Epp. 4, p. 585.

76. *Libellus*, p. 481: "proximis Kalendis Novembris . . . in unum convenimus"; Letter to Jeremias and Jonas, p. 533: "Venerunt ad praesentiam nostram Halitgarius et Amalarius episcopi VIII. Idus Decembris."

77. *Libellus*, p. 483: "Nam quidam nostrorum de longe venientes."

78. *Libellus*, p. 483: "Vere enim fatemur, quia angustia temporis praepediente nec quanta voluimus nec quanta potuimus collegimus"; "quidam vero nec causam, pro qua ad hunc conevntum venire iussi sunt, donec pervenerunt, veraciter nosse potuerunt."

79. *Annales regni Francorum*, ed. Kurze, anno 825, p. 168: "Ipse autem autumnali venatione complete circa hiemis initium Aquisgrani reversus est."

80. Letter to Jeremias and Jonas, p. 533.

81. *Ratio Romana,* ed. Willjung, *Das Konzil von Aachen,* pp. 287–94.

82. Kasten, *Adalhard,* pp. 138–44.

83. Letter to Euhenius, pp. 534–35.

84. *Annales regni Francorum,* ed. Kurze, anno 827, p. 174.

85. McCormick, *Origins of the European Economy,* pp. 911–12 lists ten East-West encounters between 825 and 827 which are primarily diplomatic but which do tend to confirm that there was a steady flow of information in both directions.

86. *Annales regni Francorum,* ed. Kurze, anno 828, p. 174.

87. This is not stated explicitly but is implied strongly in the Letter to Jeremias and Jonas, p. 533, and more weakly in the letter to Eugenius, p. 534.

88. *Libellus,* p. 481.

89. Freeman, "Carolingian Orthodoxy," pp. 96–99.

90. In the last, long section of the *Libellus* there are twenty extracts that do appear in the records of II Nicaea but that do not appear in Hadrian's letters: Two extracts from the Quinisext (p. 513), three extracts from Gregory II's (interpolated or forged) letter to Germanus (pp. 508–10), an extract from Basil to Amphilocion *On the Holy Spirit* (pp. 510–11), five extracts from Leontius of Neapolis (pp. 513–14), two extracts from Athanasius's sermons *Against the Arians* (pp. 516–17), an extract from Anastasius of Theopolis to Symeon of Bostra (p. 517), four extract from Germanus to John of Synada, one extract from II Nicaea to Constantine VI and Irene, and the weird story of Yezid, Tessarakontapechys, and the origins of iconoclasm.

91. *Libellus,* p. 484.

92. The number 188 is based on my own count. Down to no. 76, the enumeration is provided by Werminghoff. But even between nos. 1 and 76, there are actually additional extracts because a given numbered passage will often be followed by one or more, always from the same author but not always from the same work by that author, that are labeled "and again," "likewise," or something similar. After no. 77 one continues to find main extracts followed by subsidiary ones. I do not attempt in what follows to refer to extracts by number because there are no textual references to turn to.

93. *Libellus,* p. 484.

94. *Libellus,* p. 484.

95. *Libellus,* pp. 484–89.

96. *Libellus,* p. 489.

97. *Libellus,* pp. 489–90.

98. *Libellus,* pp. 490–93.

99. *Libellus,* pp. 493–96.

100. *Libellus,* p. 497.

101. *Libellus,* pp. 497–99.

102. *Libellus,* pp. 499–500.

103. *Libellus,* p. 500.

104. *Libellus,* pp. 500–501.

105. *Libellus,* p. 501.

106. *Libellus*, pp. 501–2.

107. *Libellus*, pp. 518–19.

108. *Libellus*, pp. 502–6.

109. *Libellus*, pp. 502–6 (the quotation is on p. 502).

110. *Libellus*, p. 506.

111. *Libellus*, p. 506.

112. *Libellus*, pp. 506–7.

113. *Libellus*, pp. 507–20.

114. A poem of Paulinus is slightly abbreviated: cf. pp. 486 and 538; a passage from Ps.-Ambrose is shortened (cf. pp. 498 and 538); a reference to Paul (1 Cor. 8.13) is shortened by means of an ellipsis (cf. pp. 498 and 548).

115. To John Chrysostom, *Twelfth Homily on the Epistle to the* Hebrews (an inauthentic work, in any case): *Epitome*, p. 541.

116. *Epitome*, pp. 539–40.

117. *Epitome*, pp. 540 (lines 31–36) and 544 (lines 22–24) are clear examples; p. 547 (lines 10–11) is either another example or a place where the text of the *Epitome* is corrupt; p. 549 (lines 8–9) is curious for here the letter of Michael and Theophilus is attributed to Michael and Patriarch Anthony.

118. *Epitome*, p. 536, *Libellus*, p. 484.

119. *Epitome*, p. 540, *Libellus*, p. 489.

120. *Epitome*, p. 544, *Libellus*, p. 494.

121. *Epitome*, pp. 536, 537, 537, 538, 538, 541, respectively.

CHAPTER SEVEN

1. Claudius, ep. No. 12, pp. 610–13. Gorman, "Commentary on Genesis of Claudius of Turin," 282 n. 15 provides evidence for the form Theutmir(us) instead of the more familiar Theodimir.

2. *De cultu imaginum*, PL 106: 312C.

3. Chazelle, *Crucified God*, p. 121 assumes that the Paris fathers were concerned with Claudius.

4. Claudius's *Apology* has been translated into English by McCracken (*Early Medieval Theology*, pp. 241–48) but my readings sometimes differ from his and I offer my own here. Jonas has neither been translated nor given a modern edition. I work with the PL edition. Dungal has been newly edited and translated into English by Palo Zanna. He makes relatively few changes to the PL edition, which I use unless otherwise noted.

5. Casartelli Novelli, "L'immagine della croce," pp. 109–15.

6. For basic details on Claudius see Boulhol, *Claude de Turin*, pp. 37–65, 87–224; Gorman, "Commentary on Genesis of Claudius," pp. 279–83; Ferrari, "Note su Claudio," pp. 291–307; Leonardi, "Claudio," LMA, 2, cols. 2132–33; Sergi, "Claudio," DBI, 26, pp. 158–61; Wattenbach-Levison, *Deutschlands Geschichtsquellen*, 3, pp. 310–11; Manitius, *Geschichte*, 1, pp. 390–96.

7. Claudius, epp. 6, 7, 8, 9, 10, pp. 600–610.

8. Claudius, ep. 10, pp. 609.

9. Louis's treatment of Bernard was indeed controversial well into the 820s: Jarnut, "Kaiser Ludwig der Fromme und König Bernhard von Italien."

10. Claudius, ep. 12, p. 613.

11. Dungal, *Responsa*, PL 105: 529A. Dungal says that Claudius refused to attend a "conventum episcoporum" and that he called their "synodum" a "congregationem asinorum." We have no corroborating evidence that Claudius was summoned to Paris, nor do we know of any other assembly before which he was called. Boshof, *Agobard*, p. 145 thinks Paris was not at issue. Boulhol dates the *Apologeticum* to early autumn 825: *Claude de Turin*, p. 35; Leonardi, "Gli irlandesi," p. 751 dates it to 727; Heil, "Claudius," 398, makes a good case that Claudius was discussed in the palace in the winter of 824–25.

12. *Responsa*, PL 105, 467C.

13. MGH, Cap. 1, no. 163, p. 327.

14. Ferrari, "Note su Claudio," p. 291: "forse per mutate condizioni di convenienza politica."

15. *De cultu imaginum*, PL 106: 307A (that Jonas was speaking of 827 is a widespread scholarly inference for which there is no proof). He was in any case mentioned in May of 827 in a charter for Novalesa: see Gorman, "Commentary on Genssis of Claudius," p. 283 and n. 23.

16. Claudius's lenient treatment has been variously explained. Matter, "Theological Freedom," p. 58, believes that "Carolingian Europe was a relatively open field for theological speculation . . . there was little as yet in the way of monolithic consensus." I think this goes too far. Heil, "Claudius," pp. 400–403, emphasizes that in the early 820s there was a significant change of leadership around Louis. The Goths (he overlooked Prudentius) were all dead (Theodulf, Benedict of Aniane) or under suspicion (Agobard). All of the Goths were hostile to images and it may be that the pupils of Alcuin, for example Hilduin and Hrabanus, wanted to widen the narrow space left to images by the *Opus*. They were also great collectors of relics and cannot have welcomed Claudius's attack on them. Boureau, "Les théologiens carolingiens," pp. 250–53 does not think that Claudius was sufficiently heterodox to merit deposition.

17. It survives in a single manuscript, Vat. Reg. Lat. 200, fols. 1r–6v. Folios 7r to 92r of this manuscript are filled with Dungal's *Responsa*. There is a similar manuscript, Milan, Biblioteca Ambrosiana, B 102 sup, which contains the *Responsa* and whose now missing initial folios almost certainly contained the excerpts. Ferrari, "Dungal," pp. 12–15 assumes that the Vatican and Ambrosiana manuscripts are revised copies of Dungal's original.

18. *Responsa*, PL 105: 468B.

19. *De Cultu imaginum*, PL 106: 306C.

20. *In honorem Hludowici*, lines 2594–99, ed. Faral, p. 196.

21. Both say explicitly that they received only excerpts: Jonas, *De cultu imaginum*, PL 106: 306C; Dungal, *Responsa*, PL 105: 467C.

22. Ferrari, "Dungal," p. 10 says that Dungal might have had the whole text of Claudius' work because he once cites a few lines that are not in the excerpts (*Responsa* 497A). Banning, "Claudius," pp. 747–48 represents (and cites) a tradition that Dungal had all of Claudius. The evidence is too thin for a confident argument on this point.

23. *Crucified God.*

24. Claudius was like Theodulf who says (Carmen 67, MGH, PLAC 1. 557), "It is better to live honestly at home than to go to Rome. One will not get to heaven by feet, but by good morals."

25. Something may be wrong with this sentence in the extant version of the *Apology*: "Apostolicus autem dicitur quasi apostoli custos aut apostoli fungens officium." Apostoli custos could require another word, as suggested in the text.

26. Savigni, *Giona*; Brunhölzl, *Histoire*, vol. 1, pt. 2, pp. 155–59; Anton, "Jonas," LMA, 5, col. 625; Wattenbach, Levison, Löwe, *Deutschlands Geschichtsquellen,* vol. 3, pp. 311–12; Manitius, *Geschichte,* pp. 374–80.

27. *De cultu imaginum,* PL 106: 308D. Defourneaux, "Charlemagne et le monarchie asturienne," p. 181. It is not clear why he was in Spain.

28. This is almost certainly untrue: Heil, "Claudius," p. 391.

29. It used to be thought that monumental crucifixes had not yet appeared in the early ninth century. The words used by Claudius and Jonas seem to me to imply that this old view needs correcting. For a start, see Nees, "On the Image of Christ Crucified."

30. *Apology,* p. 611; *De cultu imaginum,* col. 326C–D.

31. It is a littler hard to see what Eustathius (ODCC, p. 483) is doing here. Vigilantius (fl. 400) did oppose the cult of saints and their relics, as we know from Jerome's arguments with him (ODCC, p. 1440).

32. Surely something has fallen out of this formulation, perhaps an *esse* that would have created a statement in indirect discourse which, in view of *quasi,* would be taken as doubtful.

33. LP, 2, p. 54.

34. Zanna, "Introduction" (to his edition of the *Responsa*), pp. xv–xxii; Brunhölzl, *Histoire,* vol. 1, pt. 2, pp. 63–64; Ferrari, "Dungal," DBI, 42, pp. 11–14; eadem, "In Papia conveniunt ad Dungalum," pp. 1–52; Leonardi, "Dungal," LMA, 3, cols. 1456–57; Manitius, *Geschichte,* 1, pp. 370–74.

35. Alcuin, ep. no. 280, p. 437.

36. *Epistolae variorum,* no. 35, p. 552; Dungal, ep. no. 1, pp. 570–78.

37. Dungal, ep. no. 7, p. 582.

38. Ferrari, "In Papia conveniunt ad Dungalum," pp. 23–28 provides a helpful tabulation of the sources used in Hadrian's *Responsum,* Paris 825, Jonas, and Dungal. This is followed by lists of the sources used only at Paris (pp. 29–30) or only by Dungal (pp. 30–31).

39. "Gli Irlandesi," p. 757.

40. Cc. 1–18, ed. Zanna, pp. 2–10.

41. C. 5, ed. Zanna, p. 4.

42. Cc. 27–41, ed. Zanna, pp. 16–28.

43. Jonas assimilated Claudius's teachings to those of Vigilantius and Eustathius. Eunomius (d. 394) was an Arian who taught about a single and utterly remote divine substance: ODCC, p. 480. Perhaps Claudius could be called Eunomian in the sense that he had such a remote, thoroughly spiritualized view of God and no room for inferior levels of holiness.

44. Cc. 46–47, ed. Zanna, p. 30. Leonardi, "Dungal," LMA, 3, col. 1457; idem, "Gli Irlandesi," pp. 756–57; Ferrari, "Dungal," DBI, 42, p. 13 both argue that Dungal believed in the possibility of spiritual mediation through material things, including pictures.

45. Cc. 45–60, ed. Zanna, pp. 30–46. In general, Dungal is speaking of the relics of martyrs. On relics and their cult in this period see, in general, Geary, *Furta Sacra*, chs. 1 and 2.

46. C. 78, ed. Zanna, p. 58.

47. C. 84, ed. Zanna, p. 62. On the cross in general, cc. 61–73, 79–83, pp. 48–54, 58–62.

48. *Crucified God.*

49. Boshof, *Agobard*; Brunhölzl, *Histoire*, pp. 166–77; Manitius, *Geschichte*, pp. 380–90.

50. *De picturis et imaginibus*, ed. Van Acker, pp. 151–81. Bellet's attempt, "Il 'Liber de imaginibus,'" to attribute the treatise to Claudius of Turin has not met with acceptance: Van Acker in Agobard's *Opera*, pp. xxiv–xxxiii; Brunhölzl, *Histoire*, pp. 168–69; Boshof, *Agobard*, pp. 153–56.

51. *De picturis*, c. 19, p. 168, c. 28, p. 177.

52. Agobard, *De insolentia Iudaeorum*, ed. Van Acker, pp. 189–95; *De iudaicis superstitionibus et erroribus*, ed. Van Acker, pp. 197–221; Boshof, *Agobard*, pp. 102–38.

53. Agobard, *De grandine et tonitruis*, ed. Van Acker, pp. 1–15; Boshof, *Agobard*, pp. 170–85.

54. For an excellent introduction to Einhard, see Dutton, *Charlemagne's Courtier*, pp. xi–li.

55. Lupus to Einhard: Lupus, epp. 2, 4, 5; Einhard to Lupus, apud Lupus ep. 3, ed. Levillain, pp. 10–50.

56. *Einharti Quaestio de adoranda cruce*, ed. Hampe, pp. 146–49; trans. Dutton, *Charlemagne's Courtier*, pp. 171–74.

57. Ed. Hampe, p. 146; trans. Dutton, p. 171.

58. *Crucified God.*

59. There is no comprehensive modern monograph on Walahfrid. Details on his life and assessments of his many writings may be found in Manitius, *Geschichte*, 1, pp. 302–15; Brunhölzl, *Histoire*, pp. 102–15; Harting-Correa, *Walahfrid Strabo's* Libellus, pp. 1–37, esp. 6–12. She also provides an outstanding edition of the text of the *Libellus de exordiis et incrementis* with an excellent English translation.

60. *Libellus*, c. 8, ed. Harting-Correa, pp. 72–80 (Latin), 73–81 (English).

61. 61.*Libellus*, p. 76: "a quibusdam errantibus divinis honoribus adorata sint et culta." Harting-Correa (p. 77) has "adored and worshipped in the liturgy," which, I believe, stretches the meaning that these words habitually possess.

62. *Libellus*, p. 78: "divinis credat colendos honoribus vel adorandos." Again, Harting-Correa takes *divinis honoribus* as a specific reference to "the liturgy."

63. *Libellus*, pp. 482–83.

64. *De cultu imaginum*, 331A–332D.

65. *Responsa*, 468B–C; Jonas, *De cultu imaginum*, 308C–309B. In this, they were hardly exaggerating. Between 500 and 750 about 35 biblical commentaries were composed. From 750 to about 900, more than 150: Contreni, "Carolingian Biblical Culture," p. 7.

66. *De cultu imaginum*, 312A, 334C–D, 358A.

67. *De picturis et imaginibus*, c. 30, pp. 178–79.

68. *Libellus*, p. 525.

69. *Responsa*, 469B–C.

70. So in his *De iudaicis superstitionibus et erroribus*, ed. Van Acker, pp. 199–221 Agobard felt obliged to defend Christians against a Jewish accusation that they worshiped idols. Was this a real dispute or was it, as in seventh-century Byzantium, a literary exercise? Given that he was so dead set against any form of reverence to be paid to any material thing, one wonders just what he was defending.

71. Cantelli, *Angelomo*, p. 61; Contreni, "Carolingian Biblical Culture;" idem, "'By Lions, Bishops are Meant'"; Noble, "Biblical Testimonies."

72. *Libellus*, pp. 521, 523, 530, 531–32.

73. Michael to Louis, as in n. 54, p, 478.

74. *Libellus*, pp. 521, 524.

75. *Letter*, pp. 475, 478.

76. *Libellus*, p. 522.

77. Ibid., pp. 523, 525. This usage appears in the proposed letter for Eugenius II to send to Constantinople. Therefore it was doubly significant in that a papal letter would normally have stressed Peter alone.

78. *Libellus*, p. 484.

79. *Libellus*, pp. 482, 534.

80. *Libellus*, p. 522.

81. *Libellus*, pp. 481, 534.

82. *Libellus*, p. 481.

83. *Libellus*, p. 482 (both quotations).

84. *Libellus*, pp. 497, 499, 525, 528.

85. *Libellus*, p. 483; *De cultu imaginum*, 311A, 373D–375A.

86. *De cultu imaginum*, 313B; *Libellus*, p. 521.

87. *De cultu imaginum*, 364C–D.

88. Jonas, *De cultu imaginum*, 311A, 366A, 373D–375A, for example.

89. *Libellus*, p. 521. See further on logic, reason, and truth, pp. 483, 521, 523, 525.

90. *De cultu imaginum*, 360B–C.

91. *Libellus*, p. 482.

92. Jonas, *De cultu imaginum*, 312A, 334C–D, 358A.

93. Jonas, *De cultu imaginum*, 308C, 309C–310C; Dungal, *Responsa*, cc. 12–14, ed. Zanna, pp. 6–8.

94. Jonas, *De cultu imaginum*, 306B; by implication, Dungal, *Responsa*, cc. 3–6, ed. Zanna, pp. 2–4.

95. *De cultu imaginum*, 312B, C, 330D, 334C, D, 365A, C. In every case, the relevant word is some form of *imperitus*.

96. *Libellus*, p. 497.

97. *Responsa*, c. 240, ed. Zanna, p. 244.

98. *Libellus*, c. 8., ed. Harting-Correa, pp. 72, 76, 78, 80.

99. *Quaestio de adoranda cruce*, ed. Dümmler, p. 147.

100. *Apology*, p. 611.

101. *De cultu imaginum*, 331D–332A, 312C, 342C–D.

102. *Quaestio de adoranda sancta cruce*, p. 148.

103. *Libellus*, c. 89, ed. Harting-Correa, p. 72.

104. *Sermo de vita et morte Maurae*, PL 115: 1371D–1372B. Castes, "La dévotion privée et l'art a l'époque carolingienne," pp. 3–18. Castes argues that the images were a crucifix and two statues. The matter is of small consequence here. See also Ganz, "'*Pando quod ignoro*,'" p. 30.

105. Paris, BNF, cod. lat. 12048, fol. 152v. For the date, Palazzo, *History of Liturgical Books*, p. 97 with further references. For the interpretation adopted here, Chazelle, *Crucified God*, pp. 96–97, with her Figure 10, p. 96.

106. *In honorem sanctae crucis*, B 28, ed. Perrin, p. 216 (see also C 28 and D 28, pp. 219–21, 285–87).

107. Hrabanus, ep. 42, MGH, Epp. 5, p. 481.

108. Prayer Book of Charles the Bald (860s), Munich, Schatzkammer der Residenz, fols. 38v–39r; see Nees, *Early Medieval Art*, p. 171. Prayer Book of Louis the German (ca. 869), Berlin, Staatsbibliothek zu Berlin—Preussischer Kulturbesitz, MS Theol. lat., fol. 58, with the image on fol. 120r; see also Goldberg, *Struggle for Empire*, pp. 285–87. Crivello, "Herrscherbild," 216–19 thinks the picture was added later than Goldberg does and that, in fact, it may represent Arnulf of Carinthia. The identity of the person depicted does not materially affect my argument. On the prayer book of Charles the Bald see Deshman, "Exalted Servant," pp. 387–88 and n. 13.

109. The Paris *Libellus*, pp. 502–6, devotes one of its longest sustained discussions to the cross. Jonas devotes his whole second book to the subject (with scattered comments elsewhere) and Dungal assigns cc. 61–179 to the cross.

110. Jonas, *De cultu imaginum*, 333D–336A; Dungal, *Responsa*, cc. 6, 23. ed. Zanna, pp. 4, 14.

111. *De cultu imaginum*, 307B–309C; cf. Dungal, *Responsa*, c. 12, ed. Zanna, p. 6.

112. Chazelle, *Crucified God*, pp. 30, 118–31, 139–40.

113. Ferrari, *Il "Liber Sanctae Crucis,"* pp. 360–78; Baert, *Heritage of Holy Wood*, pp. 54–80.

114. On the churches, Heitz, *Recherches*, pp. 147–49; on the shrines, Wilhelmy, "Kreuzverehrung im Karolingerreich," pp. 29–32, with the useful map on p. 31.

115. As Jonas affirms, with citation of the prayers: *De cultu imaginum*, 332A.

116. *Liber Officialis*, 1. 14. 4, 5, ed. Hanssens, p. 100.

117. *Liber Officialis*, 1. 14. 11–12, ed. Hanssens, pp. 103–4; cf. Bede, *Historia Ecclesiastica*, 3. 2, ed. Plummer, pp. 128–31.

118. *Liber Officialis*, 1. 14. 20, ed. Hanssens, p. 107.

119. *Liber manualis*, 2. 3, ed. Riché, pp. 128–30; trans. Neel, p. 19.

120. Dungal, *Responsa*, c. 242, ed. Zanna, p. 246; Jonas, *De cultu imaginum*, 332B.

121. Jonas, *De cultu imaginum*, 312D–313A, 342D–343A.

122. *Apologeticum*, p. 610.

123. Paris *Libellus*, pp. 501–2; Jonas, *De cultu imaginum*, 319B–D; Dungal, *Responsa*, c. 103, ed. Zanna, p. 76; Agobard, *De picturis*, cc. 2–3, ed. Van Acker, pp. 152–54. Einhard, *Quaestio de adoranda sancta cruce*, pp. 148–49, does not cite Augustine but instead talks about

the different meanings of the Greek words (*proseuchin, proschinusis*) for adoration in Matthew's Gospel. He may well have had Augustine in mind because Augustine himself discusses these, and other, Greek words.

124. Jonas, *De cultu imaginum*, 319C–D; Dungal, *Responsa*, cc. 78, 102, 104, ed. Zanna, pp. 58, 74, 76.

125. *Libellus*, pp. 499–500; Jonas, *De cultu imaginum*, 320C–D; Dungal, *Responsa*, cc. 86–92, ed. Zanna, pp. 64–66.

126. *Carolingian Painting* has no wall paintings. Braunfels, *Die Welt der Karolinger*, has 312 B&W and 54 color plates. Of these, 9 B&W plates are wall paintings and 3 are mosaics. The index has no entry for, e.g., "Wandmalerei." But Braunfels did devote a few pages to wall paintings ("Die Wandmalerei," pp. 473–75, along with catalogue entries nos. 650–88) in *Karl der Grosse: Werk und Wirkung*, the catalogue of the 1965 Aachen exhibition. Hubert et al., *The Carolingian Renaissance*, pp. 5–11 presents a cursory treatment of wall painting with 4 plates from St.-Germain d'Auxerre and 11 from the North Italian/Tyrolean region. Dodwell, *Painting in Europe*, mentions wall painting *en passant* and devotes 4 of 43 Carolingian plates to the subject. Bergamini, "La pittura e la miniatura," pp. 326–39 is better for Lombard Italy. Preißler, "Fragmente einer verlorenen Kunst," pp. 197–206 handles only Paderborn and its putative *comparanda* while mentioning that more than 13,000 fragments have been found. In his outstanding new survey, *Early Medieval Art*, Nees provides plates for 3 Carolingian-era wall paintings (Sta. Maria in Valle, Santa Maria Antiqua [Theodotus chapel], and San Vincenzo al Volturno) along with Theodulf's mosaic at Germigny. My point is not to criticize any of these great scholars but to illustrate that "painting" has tended to mean book painting.

127. "Wandmalerei," p. 475.

128. *Homilia*, no. 37, PL 110: 73B–74C.

129. *Gesta Karoli Magni Imperatoris*, 1. 30, ed. Haefele, p. 41.

130. Sironi, *Castel Seprio*, with rich bibliography down to 1995 (pp. 47–58). Carver, "Carbon-14 Dating of Wood," and "S. Maria foris Portas at Castel Seprio" brings some precision to the dating by excluding dates before the late eighth century. On balance, mid-ninth century seems most likely.

131. Goll, Exner, and Hirsch, *Müstair*.

132. *In honorem Hludowici*, ll. 2062–163; for interpretation, Lammers, "Ein karolingisches Bildprogramm," pp. 226–89.

133. These may be found strewn through von Schlosser's *Schriftquellen* or vols. 1 and 2 of MGH, PLAC. See also Arnulf, *Versus ad Picturas*, pp. 147–200; Ganz, "'Pando quod ignoro,'" p. 27.

134. Woodruff, "Mosaics of La Daurade."

135. *Mittelalterliche Schatzverzeichnisse*, nos. 12, 15, 27, 28, 56, 66, 74, 97, 110. Of the 151 documents in Bischoff's collection, 22 are Carolingian and 9 of these explicitly mention crosses or crucifixes.

136. *Libellus*, 481, 482, 483, 484, 506, 521–22, 526.

137. *De cultu imaginum*, 311D–312B, 329C–330B.

138. *Responsa*, cc. 5–6, ed. Zanna, p. 4

139. *Libellus*, c. 8, ed. Harting-Correa, p. 80.

140. *Libellus*, 484, 489, 499, 501, 526; Jonas, *De cultu imaginum*, 310D, 332A, 330B, 318B; Dungal, *Responsa*, cc. 22, 42, 240, ed. Zanna, pp. 13, 28, 245.

141. Agobard, *De picturis,* cc. 20, 32, ed. Van Acker, pp. 168–69, 180.

142. *De cultu imaginum*, 318C; *Libellus*, c. 8, ed. Harting-Correa, pp. 72, 74.

143. *Libellus*, pp. 524, 526.

144. Agobard, *De picturis,* c. 24, ed. Van Acker, pp. 172–74.

145. Agobard, *De picturis,* c. 21, ed. Van Acker, pp. 169–70.

146. *Libellus*, 510. A bit further on (p. 513) the *Libellus* make the same point by means of a quotation from Leontius of Neapolis in Cyprus.

147. *Responsa*, cc. 39–41, ed. Zanna, pp. 26–28.

148. *Libellus,* c. 8, ed. Harting-Correa, p. 74.

149. *De cultu imaginum*, 318B.

150. *Libellus*, 487; and in the later sections, pp. 526, 530.

151. *De cultu imaginum*, 310D, 312C.

152. *Responsa*, cc. 5, 28, ed. Zanna, pp. 4, 16.

153. *Libellus*, c. 8, ed. Harting-Correa, pp. 74, 80.

154. *Libellus*, pp. 487–88, 497, 507–8, 527–29; Jonas, *De cultu imaginum*, 310D, 311A; Dungal, *Responsa*, cc. 28–29, ed. Zanna, pp. 16–18.

155. Agobard, *De picturis,* c. 32, ed. Van Acker, pp. 180.

156. *Libellus*, pp. 507, 510–11 (Basil), 507–8 (Gregory II to Germanus on Basil), 511 (Athanasius), 513 (Gregory of Nyssa).

157. *Responsa*, cc. 47, 49, ed. Zanna, pp. 30, 34.

158. Agobard, *De picturis,* c. 3, ed. Van Acker, pp. 154.

159. *Libellus*, pp. 486, 513 (Gregory) and 486 (Augustine); Dungal, *Responsa*, c. 35, ed. Zanna, p. 24, Appendix, no. 10, p. 256.

160. *Libellus*, p. 512. The Byzantine court in 827 sent Louis the Pious a luxury manuscript of (Pseudo-) Dionysius, which Abbot Hilduin of St.-Denis translated into Latin (rather poorly!) and presented to Louis in 832. The Paris fathers got their "Dionysius" from the texts which they reviewed. It is difficult to see, on chronological grounds, how Claudius, Agobard, or Dungal could have seen the new, full text. Jonas, Walahfrid, and Einhard *could* have seen it. In any case, it seems to have made no impression until a generation later when Eriugena studied the work and translated it anew.

161. Agobard, *De picturis,* c. 15, ed. Van Acker, pp. 164–65.

162. *Libellus*, pp. 509, 518.

163. Prudentius, *Sermo*, 1371C.

164. *Annales regni Francorum*, anno 823, ed. Kurze, p. 163.

165. Arnulf, *Versus ad Picturas*, pp. 9–11, 17.

166. Poem no. 27, ed. Hertel, p. 288; trans. Walsh, p. 291. See Arnulf, *Versus ad Picturas*, pp. 47–50.

167. *The Lives of the Fathers,* 12.2, trans. James, p. 93.

168. Arnulf, *Versus ad Picturas*, pp. 13–14.

169. List, references, and brief comments in Ganz, "'Pando quod ignoro,'" pp. 27–29.

170. Arnulf, *Versus ad Picturas*, pp. 147–63 suggests some reconstructions.

171. Discussed by Arnulf, *Versus ad Picturas*, pp. 148–51.

172. MGH, PLAC, 1, nos. 44, 48, 60, 61, pp. 211, 213, 220, 222.

173. MGH, PLAC, 2, no. 53, p. 400.

174. MGH, PLAC, 2, nos. 18, 20, pp. 547, 548.

175. MGH, PLAC, 3, no. 48, p. 210.

176. MGH, PLAC, 3, no. 82, p. 231.

177. MGH, PLAC, 3, nos. 7–10, 14, 130–32, 154, 155, pp. 296, 297, 347, 348, 359.

178. MGH, PLAC, 4, pp. 1047–50.

179. MGH, PLAC, 2, pp. 480–82.

180. MGH, PLAC, 3, p. 231.

181. MGH, PLAC, 2, p. 296.

182. Ferrari, *Il "Liber Sanctae Crucis,"* pp. 1–7 summarizes the older scholarship.

183. Rabanus Maurus, *In honorem sanctae crucis*, ed. Perrin. Perrin has also published a fine facsimile along with helpful introductory material (now largely superceded by the "Introduction" to his edition), transcriptions of the *versus intexti*, and French translations: *Louanges de la sainte croix*. It may be observed that I use Perrin's title *In Honor of the Holy Cross*. In his "Introduction," pp. xxvi–xxix he explains why the preponderance of evidence argues for *honorem* instead of the more familiar *laudem*.

184. The copy for Louis was made between 831 (it alludes to that year's "Persian" embassy to the court) and Louis's death in 840. Sears, "Louis the Pious as *Miles Christi*" makes an impressive case that the book was made for Louis's imperial restoration in 834.

185. Hrabanus, *Carmen* no. 38, ed. Dümmler, MGH, PLAC, 2, p. 196. The first part of the translation is my own. For the second part I rely on Ganz's translation, " 'Pando quod ignoro,' " p. 29 with some slight modifications. It must be acknowledged that we do not know when Hrabanus wrote this poem and we do not know what picture(s) he was referring to: Ferrari, *Il "Liber Sanctae Crucis,"* pp. 18–22, 314–15.

186. Scholars have sketched Hrabanus's intellectual background without being able to connect him to specific features: Chazelle, *Crucified God*, p. 114; Ferrari, *Il "Liber Sanctae Crucis,"* pp. 292–315; Wilhelmy, "Die Entstehung von *De laudibus* im Spannungsfeld," pp. 23–26.

187. On Hrabanus in general, who lacks a modern monograph, see *Rabanus Maurus*, ed. Kotzur, pp. 15–19; Perrin, "Introduction," pp. v–vii; Kottje, "Hrabanus Maurus," LMA, 5. 144–47. Brunhölzl, "Zur geistigen Bedeutung des Hrabanus Maurus," pp. 1–17; Manitius, *Geschichte*, 1, pp. 288–302; Brunhölzl, *Histoire*, vol. 1, part 2, pp. 84–101.

188. These figures are readily available in Perrin's *Louanges*, a facsimile, and in his edition of *In honorem sanctae crucis*.

189. Ferrari, *Il "Liber Sanctae Crucis,"* pp. 325–37, 343.

190. *In honorem sanctae crucis*, C 1, ed. Perrin, p. 29 (lines 1–12). Outstanding on Hrabanus's theology of the cross is Chazelle, *Crucified God*, pp. 99–119.

191. On Hrabanus' debts to his poetic heritage see Ferrari, *Il "Liber Sanctae Crucis,"* pp. 396–410.

192. Diebold, *Word and Image*, pp. 109–11.

193. Chazelle, *Crucified God*, pp. 110–14; Ferrari, *Il "Liber Sanctae Crucis,"* pp. 316–19, 323, 343–57.

194. Ed. Allen, CSEL, vols. 169, 169A (2002).

195. Allen, ed. cit., vol. 169A, pp. 11–81; Schmale, "Frechulf," LMA, 4. 882–83.

196. *Prologus*, ed. Allen, vol. 169, p. 19.

197. Fundamentally owing to the reevaluation by Staubach, "*Christiana Tempora.*"

198. Ed. Allen, vol. 169, p. 724.

199. The older literature is fully discussed by Staubach, "*Christiana Tempora,*" pp. 167–70, 175–76, 189–98.

200. *Historiae*, 1. 2. 1, ed. Allen, p. 91.

201. The phrase "Christian Times" (*Christiana tempora*) is not arbitrary. Although Frec-ulf never uses *Christiana Tempora* he uses forms of the word *tempus* 220 times. He virtually always says "In the time of . . ." or "In the times of. . . ." This was his way of marking time. His intertexts explain his copious use of time words. Augustine uses *Christiana Tempora* 12 times, including once in the *City of God* (12.21, ed. Dombart and Kalb, CC 48, p. 378). Orosius uses the phrase five times (3.8, 4.6, 6.1, 6.22, 7.43, ed. Zagemeister, CSEL 5, pp. 152, 223–24, 354, 429, 563. Each time he uses the phrase he does so to contrast "Christian Times" with pagan times. The last instance is revealing: "I . . . would permit Christian times to be blamed freely, if, from the founding of the world to the present, any equally fortunate period can be pointed out" (trans. Deferrari, p. 363). Freculf was able to look back to that "present" from the vantage point of his own. The numbers specified here were derived from searches of electronic databases and then verified against the texts.

202. Staubach, "*Christiana Tempora.*"

203. *Historiae*, 2, *Prologus*, ed. Allen, p. 436.

204. *Carmen*, ed. Faral, vv. 2520–29.

205. *Annales regni Francorum*, anno 826, ed. Kurze, p. 170.

206. *Carmen*, ed. Faral, vv. 2068–163.

207. Lammers, "Bildprogramm," pp. 243–47 argues for the time of Louis and cites older literature. Nees, *Tainted Mantle*, pp. 276–77 discusses the issues.

208. *Tainted Mantle*, p. 276.

209. Ermoldus implies strongly that the pagan and Christian images opposed each other on the side walls: "Regia namque domus late persculpta nitescit" (v. 2126); "Parte alia tecti . . ." (v. 2148). Persculpta cannot be taken literally. Lammers, "Bildprogramm," pp. 282–86 thinks the Christian images were in the apse with the pagan one on flanking walls. I have no view on the matter.

210. Excellent discussion in Nees, *Tainted Mantle*, pp. 270–77, with older literature.

211. *Rise of Western Christendom*, p. 269.

212. Noble, "Biblical Testimonies."

213. Notably, Contreni, "Carolingian Biblical Culture."

214. *Angelomo e la scuola esegetica di Luxeuil*, p. 61 (cited by Contreni, "Carolingian Biblical Culture," p. 20 n. 42).

215. Ed. Harting-Correa.

216. *De institutione clericorum*, ed. Zimpel.

217. Lifshitz, *The Name of the Saint*, pp. 110–22.

218. The definitive study is Fuhrmann, *Einfluss und Verbreitung*, 3 vols.

219. Boshof, *Ludwig der Fromme*, pp. 173–81.

220. *Constitutio de synodis*, MGH, Conc., 1, pt. 2, no. 50A, pp. 596–97.

221. *Hludowici et Lotharii epistola generalis*, MGH, Conc., 1, pt. 2, no. 50B, pp. 597–601.

222. *Concilium parisiense*, MGH, Conc., 1, pt. 2, no. 50D, pp. 605–80. On the council generally: Hartmann, *Konziliengeschichte*, pp. 179–87.

223. *Duo quippe sunt*, ed. Schwartz; Eng. trans. Tierney, *Crisis of Church and State*, pp. 13–14. Knabe, *Zweigewaltentheorie*.

224. *Carolingian Renaissance*, pp. 111–34.

225. These issues have been discussed endlessly. Fundamental still is Arquillière, *L'augustinisme politique*. See also Mohr, *Reichsidee*; Morrison, *The Two Kingdoms*; Nelson, "Kingship and Empire."

226. MGH, Cap. 1, no. 150, c. 3, p. 303.

227. These issues are now brilliantly discussed in Booker, *Past Convictions*, forthcoming.

228. Astronomer, *Vita Hludowici*, c. 48, ed. Tremp, p. 474.

229. *De privilegio apostolicae sedis*, ed. Van Acker, pp. 304–6, quotations p. 305.

230. Apud Agobardi epistolae, no. 16, MGH, Epp. 5, pp. 228–32.

231. Smaragdus, *Via Regia*, PL 102: 931–70; Ermoldus, *Ad Pippinus Regem I, II*, ed. Faral, pp. 202–32; Jonas, *Ad Pippinum regem Ludovicii Pii augusti filium admonitio et opusculum de munere regio (De institutione regia)*, ed. Dubreucq. The basic study of these texts is Anton, *Fürstenspiegel*, pp. 132–98.

232. *De institutione laicali*, PL 106: 121–278.

233. Amalar, *Opera liturgica omnia*, ed. Hanssens, vol. 1, pp. 361–63.

234. Benedict of Aniane, *Concordia regularum*, ed. Bonnerue; Smaragdus, *Expositio in regulam S. Benedicti*, ed. Szpannagel; Hildemar, *Exposition regulae*, ed. Mittermüller; Grimlaicus, *Regula solitariorum*.

235. Staubach, "Cultus Divinus."

236. Nelson, "The Lord's Anointed and the People's Choice"; McCormick, *Eternal Victory*, pp. 362–84.

237. Astronomer, *Vita Hludowici*, c. 13, ed. Tremp, pp. 318–20.

238. *Eternal Victory*, p. 375. See also Hen, *Royal Patronage of the Liturgy*, pp. 108–9.

239. 813: *Annales regni Francorum*, ed. Kurze, p. 138; Ermoldus, *Carmen*, ed. Faral, vv. 652–735; Thegan, *Gesta Hludowici*, c. 6, ed. Tremp, pp. 180–84; Astronomer, *Vita Hludowici*, c. 20, ed. Tremp, pp. 340–44. 816: *Annales regni Francorum*, ed. Kurze, p. 144; Ermoldus, *Carmen*, ed. Faral, vv. 848–1131; Thegan, *Gesta Hludowici*, cc. 16, 17, ed. Tremp, pp. 196–98; Astronomer, *Vita Hludowici*, c. 26, ed. Tremp, pp. 364–68.

240. A nod, but not a bow, to Buc, *Dangers of Ritual*.

241. *Carmen*, ed. Faral, vv. 2164–351. See Hen, *Royal Patronage of the Liturgy*, pp. 115–16.

242. *Annales regni Francorum*, anno 818, ed. Kurze, p. 148.

243. MGH, Cap, 2, no. 197, c. 6, p. 53.

244. MGH, Cap., 1, no. 136, *Praef.*, p. 271.

245. MGH, Conc., 1, pt. 2, no. 50B, p. 601.

246. Keefe, *Water and the Word*, vol. 2, pp. 126–27, provides a list of the manuscripts containing these *expositiones missae*.

247. Hen, *Royal Patronage of the Liturgy*, pp. 102–5 with the older literature and sources.

248. *Carmen,* ed. Faral, vv. 1950–53, 2034–47, 2222–27.

249. *De grandine et tonitruis,* ed. Van Acker. Essential extracts trans. Dutton, *Carolingian Civilization*, pp. 220–23.

250. Dutton, "Fire and Hail"; Riché, "La magie à l'époque carolingienne." There is much of value in Flint, *Rise of Magic*, especially pp. 110–15 on Agobard, but I disagree with the fundamental premises of the book.

251. MGH, Conc., 1, pt. 2, p. 669.

252. McNeill and Gamer, eds., *Handbooks of Penance*, pp. 305–6.

253. *Libri duo de synodalibus causis,* 2. 354–75, ed. Hartmann, pp. 412–25.

254. Kessler, *Illustrated Bibles from Tours.*

255. Chazelle, "Utrecht Psalter."

CONCLUSION

1. Basic details: Treadgold, *Byzantine State and Society*, pp. 446–57; Ostrogorsky, *History*, pp. 217–35.

2. Dvornik, *Photian Schism* remains fundamental.

3. Epp. nos. 82, 85, 88, 90, 91, 92, 94, 98, ed. Perels, MGH, Epp. 6, EKA 4, pp. 433–39 (esp. 436–38), 443–46, 454–87 (esp. 472–73, 482–83), 491–93, 495, 514, 516, 517, 519, 522, 534, 544, 554–55, 557–58. In almost every case the references are brief and say no more than that Nicholas's legates attempted to look into the matter.

4. On November 13, 866, Nicholas wrote twice to the Eastern archbishops and bishops, to Michael III, to Photios, and to Ignatios: Epp. 90–94, 98.

5. Epp. nos. 100–102, ed. Perels, MGH, Epp. 6, pp. 600–610.

6. Constantinople IV, *Actio* VII, c. 6, Mansi, *Concilia,* 15, cols. 109E–110B.

7. Ep. no. 82, ed. Perels, MGH, Epp. 6, pp. 436–38.

8. Ratramnus, *Contra graecorum opposita*, PL 121: 223–346; Aeneas of Paris, *Liber adversus Graecos*, PL 121: 685–762; *Responsis episcoporum Germaniae de fide sanctae Trinitatis*, PL 119: 1201–12.

9. Claudius, Dungal, Einhard on the Cross, Walahfrid's chapter, and parts of Hrabanus.

10. Nicely surveyed in Schmitt, *Le corps des images.*

11. I make no pretense to thoroughness on this topic. See Besançon, *L'image interdit*, pp. 155–64; Feld, *Der Ikonoklasmus des Westens*, pp. 63–68; Dillenberger, *Theology of Artistic Sensibilities*, pp. 42–44.

BIBLIOGRAPHY

SOURCES

Adamnan. *De locis sanctis.* Ed. Ludwig Bieler. CCCM 175, pp. 183–234. Turnhout, 1965.

Ado of Vienne. *Chronicon.* PL 123: 23A–138D.

Adversus Constantinum Caballinum. PG 95: 309–44.

Agnellus of Ravenna. *Liber Pontificalis Ecclesiae Ravennatis.* Ed. Oswald Holder-Egger. MGH, SSRL, pp. 265–391. English translation by Deborah Deliyannis. *The Book of Pontiffs of the Church of Ravenna.* Washington, D.C., 2004.

Agobard of Lyon. *De picturis et imaginibus.* In L. van Acker, ed., *Agobardi Lugdunensis Opera Omnia,* pp. 151–81. CCCM 52. Turnhout, 1981.

———. *De grandine et tonitruis.* In L. van Acker, ed., *Agobardi Lugdunensis Opera Omnia,* pp. 1–15.

———. *De insolentia Iudaeorum.* In L. van Acker, ed., *Agobardi Lugdunensis Opera Omnia,* pp. 189–95.

———. *De iudaicibus superstitionibus et erroribus.* In L. van Acker, ed., *Agobardi Lugdunensis Opera Omnia,* pp. 197–221.

———. *De privilegio apostolicae sedis (ad Ludovicum).* In L. van Acker, ed., *Agobardi Lugdunensis Opera Omnia,* pp. 303–6.

Alcuin, *Epistolae.* Ed. Ernst Dümmler, MGH, Epp. 4, EKA 2, pp. 1–481. Berlin, 1895.

———. *Adversus Elipandum Libri IV.* PL 101: 231A–300A.

Amalarius of Metz. *Liber Officialis.* Ed. John Michael Hanssens, S.J. Studi e Testi 139, 140. Vatican City, 1948.

Anastasius Bibliothecarius. *Praefatio Anastasi Bibliothecarii in septimam synodum ad Joannem VIII. pont. max.* Mansi, Concilia, 12: 981C–984B.

Annales mosellani. MGH SS 16: 491–99.

Annales regni Francorum. Ed. Friedrich Kurze. MGH, SSrG. Hannover, 1895.

Apocryphal New Testament: A Collection of Apocryphal Christian Literature in an English Translation. Ed. J. K. Elliott. Oxford, 1993.

Arnobius. *The Case Against the Pagans.* Trans. George McCracken. 2 vols. Westminster, Md., 1949.

Augustine. *Libri quattuor de consensu evangelistiarum.* PL 34: 1041A–1230A.

———. *De genesi ad litteram libri duodecim.* Ed. J. Zycha. CSEL 28.1. Vienna, 1894.

————. *De Magistro.* Ed. G. Weigel. CSEL 77. Vienna, 1961.

————. *De doctrina christiana Libri IV.* Ed. Joseph Martin. CCSL 32. Turnhout, 1962.

————. *De Trinitate libri XV.* Ed. W. J. Mountain. CCSL 50. Turnhout, 1968.

————. *De fidem rerum invisibilium.* Ed. M. J. Van den Hout. CCSL 46. Turnhout, 1969.

Basil. *Homilia XIX in sanctos quadraginta martyres.* PG 31: 508B–525A.

Bede. *De templo.* Ed D. Hurst. CCCM 119A. Turnhout, 1969. English translation by Seán Connolly. *Bede On the Temple.* Translated Texts for Historians 21. Liverpool, 1995.

————. *De tabernaculo.* Ed. D. Hurst. CCCM 119A. Turnhout, 1969. English translation by Arthur Holder. *Bede: On the Tabernacle.* Translated Texts for Historians 18. Liverpool, 1994.

————. *Venerabilis Baedae Opera Historica.* Ed. Bertram Colgrave and R. A. B. Mynors. Oxford, 1969.

————. *Historia Abbatum.* Ed. Charles Plummer. Oxford, 1896.

Benedict of Aniane. *Concordia regularum.* Ed. Pierre Bonnerue. CCCM 168, 168A. Turnhout, 1999.

Boniface. *Die Briefe des Heiligen Bonifatius und Lullus.* MGH. Berlin, 1916. English translation by Ephraim Emerton. *The Letters of St. Boniface.* Repr. New York, 2000.

Caesarius of Arles. *Regula ad virgines.* PL 42: 1105C–1120D.

Cedrenus. *Historiarum Compendium.* Ed. I. Bekker. 2 vols. Bonn, 1838–39.

Charlemagne: Translated Sources. Ed. and trans. P. D. King. Lancaster, 1987.

Claudius of Turin. *Epistolae.* Ed. Ernst Dümmler, MGH, Epp. 4, EKA 2, pp. 590–603. Berlin, 1895.

————. *Defense and Reply to Abbot Theodimir.* Trans. George E. McCracken, pp. 241–46. In his *Early Medieval Theology.* London, 1957.

Codex Carolinus. Ed. Wilhelm Gundlach. MGH, Epp. 3, pp. 469–657. Berlin, 1892.

Constantinople in the Early Eighth Century: The Peristasis Syntomoi Chronikai. Ed. Averil Cameron and Judith Herrin. Leiden, 1984.

The Council in Trullo Revisited. Ed. George Nedungatt and Michael Featherstone. Kanonika 6. Rome, 1995.

Dhuoda. *Liber Manualis Dhuodane quem ad filium suum transmisit Wilhelmum.* Ed. Pierre Riché. Sources chrétiennes 225bis. Paris, 1997. Trans. Carol Neel, *Handbook for William.* Lincoln, Nebr., 1991.

Dionysius of Fourna. *The Painter's Manual.* Trans. Paul Hetherington. Torrance, Calif., 1989.

Divalis sacra directa a Constantino et Irene Augustis as sanctissimum et beatissimum Hadrianum papam senioris Romae. Mansi, Concilia, 12: 984E–986C.

Dungal. *Dungali responsa contra perversas Claudii taurinensis episcopi sententias.* PL 105: 465A–530A.

————. *Responsa contra Claudium: A Controversy on Holy Images. A New Edition.* Ed. Paolo Zanna. Per verba 17. Florence, 2002.

————. *Epistolae.* Ed. Ernst Dümmler. MGH, Epp. 4, EKA 2, pp. 570–85. Berlin, 1895.

Einhard. *Quaestio de adoranda cruce.* Ed. Karl Hampe. MGH, Epp. 5, EKA 3, pp. 146–48. Berlin, 1898.

Epistula ad regem Karolum de monasterio sancti Benedicti directa et a Paolo dictata. Ed. Kassius Hallinger, Corpus Consuetudinum Monasticarum, vol. 1, pp. 157–75. Siegburg, 1963.

Ermenrich, *Vita Hariolfi*, MGH, SS, 10, pp. 11–15.

Ermoldus Nigellus, *In Honorem Hludowici Christianissimi Caesaris Augusti Elegiacum Carmen.* Ed. Edmond Faral. *Ermold le Noir: Poème sur Louis le Pieux et Épitres au roi Pépin.* Les classiques de l'histoire de France au moyen age 14. Paris, 1932.

Eusebius. *The History of the Church.* Trans. G. A. Williamson. Harmondsworth, 1965.

———. *De vita beatissimi imperatoris Constantini.* PG 20: 209C–1229B.

Ex vetustis annalibus nordhumbranis. MGH SS 13: 154–56.

Freculf. *Historiarum Libri XII.* Ed. Michael I. Allen. *Frechulfi Lexoviensis Episcopi Opera Omnia.* CCCM, 169. Turnhout, 2002.

Germanus. *Epistolae.* PG 98: 156B–188B; Mansi, Concilia, 13: 100B–118A.

———. *De heresibus et synodis.* PG 98: 40A–88B.

Gregory I. *Registrum Epistolarum.* Ed. Paul Ewald and Ludovicus M. Hartmann. MGH, Epp. 1. Repr. Berlin, 1957.

Gregory IV. *Epistola.* Apud Agobardi epistolae, no. 16. Ed. Ernst Dümmler. MGH, Epp. 5, EKA 3, pp. 228–32.

Gregory of Tours. *Decem Libri Historiarum.* Ed. Bruno Krusch and Wilhelm Levison. MGH, SSrM, 1. Repr. Hannover, 1951.

———. *De gloria martyrum.* Ed. Krusch and Levison. MGH, SSrM, 1.2, pp. 34–111. Hannover, 1885. Trans. Raymond Van Dam, *Gregory of Tours: Glory of the Martyrs.* Translated Texts for Historians 3. Liverpool, 1988.

———. *Liber de passione et virtutibus sancti Iuliani episcopi.* MGH, SSrM, 1.2: 112–34.

———. *De virtutibus sancti Martini episcopi.* MGH, SSrM 1.2: 134–211.

Grimlaicus. *Regula solitariorum.* PL 103: 575–664.

Hildemar. *Expositio regulae.* Ed. Rupert Mittermüller. Regensburg, 1880.

Hincmar of Reims. *Opuscula et epistolae quae spectant ad causam Hincmari Laudenensis.* PL 126: 287A–684C.

Hrabanus Maurus. *Carmina.* Ed. Ernst Dümmler. MGH, PLAC 2, pp. 154–258.

———. *De institutione clericorum libri tres.* Ed. Detlev Zempel. Freiburger Beiträge zur mittelalterlichen Geschichte 7. Frankfurt, 1996.

———. *De laudibus sanctae crucis.* Trans. (into French), ed., and annotated by Michel Perrin. Paris, 1988.

Ignatios. *The Life of Patriarch Nikephoros I of Constantinople.* Trans. Elizabeth A. Fischer. In Alice-Mary Talbot, ed., *Byzantine Defenders of Images,* pp. 41–142. Washington, D.C., 1998.

———. *The Life of the Patriarch Tarasios: Introduction, Text, Translation, and Commentary.* By Stephanos Efthymiadis. Birmingham Byzantine and Ottoman Monographs 4. Aldershot, 1998.

Inscriptions chrétiennes de la gaule antérieure au VIIIe siècle: Réunies et annotées. Ed. Edmond Frederic Le Blant. 2 vols. Paris, 1856–65.

Isidore of Seville. *Etymologiae Libri XX.* Ed. W. M. Lindsay. 2 vols. Oxford, 1911.

———. *Sententiarum Libri Tres.* PL 83: 537D–738B.

Itineraria Romana IV, Ecclesiae quae intus Romae habentur. Itineraria et alia geographica, pp. 321–22. CCSL 175. Turnhout, 1965.

John Cassian. *Conférences VIII–XVII.* Ed. E. Pichery. Sources Chrétiennes 54. Paris, 1958.

John Chrysostom. *Homilia encomiastica in patrem nostrum Meletium.* PG 50: 515–20.

———. *Adversos Judaeos et gentiles demonstratio, Quod Christus sit Deus.* PL 48: 813–48.

John Moschus. *The Spiritual Meadow.* Trans. John Wortley. Kalamazoo, 1992.

John of Damascus. *Contra imaginum calumniatores orationes tres.* Vol. 3 of *Die Schriften des Johannes von Damaskos.* Ed. Bonifatius Kotter OSB. Patristische Texte und Studien 17. Berlin, 1975. English translation by Andrew Louth. John of Damascus. *Three Treatises on the Divine Images.* Crestwood, N.Y., 2003.

John of Jerusalem (?). *Adversus iconoclastas.* PG 96: 1348C–1361D.

Jonas of Orléans. *De cultu imaginum.* PL 106: 305B–388A.

———. *De institutione laicali.* PL 106: 121D–278B.

———. *Le métier de roi (De institutione regia).* Ed. Alain Debreucq. Sources Chrétiennes 407. Paris, 1995.

Justin Martyr. *Apologia prima pro christianis.* PG 6: 327A–440C.

Das Konzil von Aachen 809. Ed. Harald Willjung. MGH, Concilia 2, Supplementum 2. Hannover, 1998.

Lactantius. *The Divine Institutes.* Trans. Sr. Mary Francis MacDonald, O.P. The Fathers of the Church 49. Washington, D.C., 1964.

Leontius of Neapolis. *Sermo contra Judaeos.* PG 93: 1597A–1609A.

Le Liber Pontificalis: Texte, Introduction et Commentaire. Ed. L. M. O. Duchesne. 2nd ed. by Cyrille Vogel. 3 vols. Paris, 1955. English translations: Raymond Davis, *The Lives of the Eighth-Century Popes.* Translated Texts for Historians 13. Liverpool, 1992. Davis, *The Lives of the Ninth-century Popes.* Translated Texts for Historians 20. Liverpool, 1995.

Mansi, J. D., ed. *Sacrorum Conciliorum Nova et Amplissima Collectio.* 31 vols. Florence-Venice, 1759–98.

Medieval Handbooks of Penance. Trans. John T. McNeill and Helena M. Gamer. Repr. New York, 1979.

Nicephorus. *Antirrhetici I–III.* PG, 100: 205D–533A.

———. *Short History.* Ed. and trans., Cyril Mango. Corpus Fontium Historiae Byzantinae 13. Washington, D.C., 1990.

———. *Discours contre les iconoclastes.* Trans. Marie-José Mondzain-Baudinet. Paris, 1989.

Orosius, Paulus. *Historiarum adversus paganos libri VII.* Ed. Carolus Zagenmeister. CSEL 5. Vienna, 1892. English translation Roy J. Deferrari. *The Seven Books of History Against the Pagans.* The Fathers of the Church 50. Washington, D.C., 1964.

Paschal I, *Epistola ad Leonem V.* In "La lettera di Pasquale I a Leone V sul culto delle sacre imagini." In Giovanni Mercati, *Note di letterature biblica e cristiana antica,* pp. 227–35. Studi e Testi 5. Rome, 1901.

———. *Epistola ad Leonem V.* In J. B. Pitra, ed., *Iuris ecclesiastici graecorum historia et monumenta,* vol. 2, pp. xi–xvii. Rome, 1868.

Paschasius Radbertus. *Expositio in evangelium Matthaei.* PL 120: 31B–994C.

Paulinus. *Carmina.* Ed. Guillelmus De Hartel. CSEL 30. Vienna, 1894.

Paul the Deacon. *Liber de mettensibus episcopis.* MGH, SS, 2, pp. 260–68.

Piacenza Pilgrim. In *Jerusalem Pilgrims Before the Crusades,* pp. 79–89. Ed. and trans. John Williams. Warminster, 1977.

Prudentius of Troyes. *Sermo de vita et morte gloriosae virginis Maurae.* PL 115: 1367D–1376A.

Pseudo-Dionysius. *The Complete Works.* Trans. Colm Luibheid with Paul Rorem. Classics of Western Spirituality. New York, 1987.

Regino of Prüm. *Libri duo de synodalibus causis et disciplinis ecclesiasticis.* Ed. and trans. Wilfried Hartmann. Ausgewählte Quellen zur deutschen Geschichte des Mittelalters, Freiherr-vom-Stein Gedächtnisausgabe 42. Darmstadt, 2004.

Le Sacramentaire Grégorien: Ses principales formes d'après les plus ancient manuscrits. Vol. 1, *Le sacramentaire, le supplément d'Aniane.* Ed. Jean Deshusses. Spicilegium Friburgense 16. Fribourg, 1971.

The Sayings of the Desert Fathers: The Alphabetical Collection. Trans. Benedicta Ward. Kalamazoo, 1975.

Schriftquellen zur karolingischer Kunst. Ed. Julius von Schlosser. Quellenschriften für Kunstgeschichte und Kunsttechnik des Mittelalters und der Neuzeit, n.s. 4, Bd. 3. Repr. Hildesheim, 1988.

Scriptor Incertus de Leo Armeno. PG 108: 1009C–1037A.

Smaragdus. *Via regia.* PL 102: 931D–970C.

———. *Expositio in regulam Sancti Benedicti.* Ed. Alfred Spannagel. Corpus Consuetudinum Monasticarum 8. Siegburg, 1974.

Synodikon Vetus. Ed. John Duffy and John Parker. Corpus fontium historiae Byzantinae 18. Washington, D.C., 1979.

Tarasius. *Apologeticus ad populum a Tarasio.* Mansi, Concilia, 12: 986D–990B.

Textus Byzantinos ad iconomacham pertinentes. Ed. Hermann Hennephof. Byzantina Neerlandica, series A Textus 1. Leiden, 1969.

Theodore Abū Qurrah. *Selections.* Trans. John C. Lamoreaux. Provo, Utah, 2005.

Theodore of Studion. *Antirrhetici I–III.* PG 99: 328–436.

———. *Laudatio Sancti Platonis Higumeni.* PG 99: 805A–849A.

———. *On the Holy Icons.* Trans. Catharine P. Roth. Crestwood, N.Y., 1981.

Theodulf of Orléans. *Opus Caroli Regis contra Synodum (Libri Carolini).* Ed. A. Freeman. MGH, Conc.2, Supplementum 1. Hannover, 1998.

Theophanes. *The Chronicle of Theophanes Confessor: Byzantine and Near Eastern History AD 284–813.* Trans. Cyril Mango and Roger Scott. Oxford, 1997.

Theosteriktos. *Life of Nicetas of Medikion.* AASS, April 1: 254B–265F.

Vita Methodii. PG 100: 1244D–1261C.

Walahfrid Strabo. *Walahfrid Strabo's* Libellus de exordiis et incrementis quarundam in observationibus ecclesiasticis rerum: *A Translation and Liturgical Commentary.* By Alice L. Harting-Correa. Mittellateinische Studien und Texte 19. Leiden, 1996.

LITERATURE

Aherne, Sister Consuelo Maria. "Late Visigothic Bishops, their Schools and the Transmission of Culture." *Traditio* 22 (1966): 435–44.

Ahrweiler, Hélène. "The Geography of the Iconoclastic World." In Bryer and Herrin, eds., *Iconoclasm,* pp. 21–27.

————. *L'idéologie politique de l'empire byzantin.* Paris, 1975.

Alexakis, Alexander. *Codex Parisinus Graecus 1115 and Its Archetype.* Dumbarton Oaks Studies 34. Washington, D.C., 1996.

————. "The Source of the Greek Patristic Quotations in the *Hadrianum* (JE 2483) of Pope Hadrian I." AHC 26 (1994): 14–30.

————. "Stephen of Bostra, *Fragmenta Contra Iudaeos*: A New Edition." JOB 43 (1993): 45–60.

————. "Some Remarks on the Colophon of Codex *Parisinus Graecus* 1115." *Revue d'histoire des textes* 22 (1992): 131–43.

Alexander, Paul J. "Religious Persecution and Resistance in the Byzantine Empire of the Eighth and Ninth Centuries: Methods and Justifications." *Speculum* 52 (1977): 238–64.

————. *The Patriarch Nicephorus of Constantinople.* Oxford, 1958.

————. "Church Councils and Patristic Authority: The Iconoclastic Councils of Hiereia (754) and St. Sophia (815)." *Harvard Studies in Classical Philology* 63 (1958): 493–505.

————. "An Ascetic Sect of Iconoclasts in Seventh-Century Armenia." In Kurt Weitzmann, ed., *Late Classical and Medieval Studies in Honor of Albert M. Friend Jr.,* pp. 151–60. Princeton N.J., 1955.

————. "The Iconoclastic Council of St. Sophia (815) and Its Definition (Horos)." DOP 7 (1953): 35–66.

————. "Hypatius of Ephesus: A Note on Image Worship in the Sixth Century." *Harvard Theological Review* 45 (1952): 178–84.

Allgeier, Arthur. "Psalmenzitate und die Frage nach der Herkunft der Libri Carolini." *Historisches Jahrbuch der Görresgesellschaft* 46 (1926): 333–53.

Amato, Pietro. *De Vera Effigie Mariae: Antiche Icone Romane.* Milan, 1988.

Anastos, Milton V. "Leo III's Edict against Images in the Year 726/27 and Italo-Byzantine Relations between 726 and 730." *Byzantinische Forschungen* 3 (1968): 5–41.

————. "The Transfer of Illyricum, Calabria and Sicily to the Jurisdiction of the Patriarch of Constantinople in 732–33." *Studi byzantini e neoellenici* 9 (1957): 14–31.

————. "The Argument for Iconoclasm as Presented by the Iconoclastic Council of 754." In Kurt Weitzmann, ed., *Late Classical and Medieval Studies Presented to Albert Mathias Friend, Jr.,* pp. 177–88. Princeton, 1955.

————. "The Ethical Theory of Images Formulated by the Iconoclasts in 754 and 815." DOP 8 (1954): 153–60.

Anderson, Jeffrey C. "The Byzantine Panel Portrait Before and After Iconoclasm." In Robert Osterhout and Leslie Brubaker, eds., *The Sacred Image in East and West,* pp. 25–44. Illinois Byzantine Studies 4. Urbana, 1995.

Andoloro, Maria. "Il *Liber Pontificalis* et la questione delle immagini da Sergio I a Adriano I." In *Roma e l'età carolingia,* pp. 69–77. Rome, 1976.

————. "La datazione della tavola di S. Maria in Trastevere." *Rivista dell'istituto nazionale d'archeologia e storia dell'arte* 19/20 (1972/73 [1975]): 139–215.

Angenendt, Arnold. "Der römische und gallisch-fränkische Anti-Ikonoklasmus." FMSt 35 (2001): 201–25.

————. "Karl der Große als *rex et sacerdos*." In Berndt, ed., *Das Frankfurter Konzil,* pp. 255–78.

———. "Princeps Imperii—Princeps Apostolorum: Rom zwischen Universalismus und Gentilismus." In Angenendt and Theodor Schieffer, eds., *Roma—Caput et Fons: Zwei Vorträge über das päpstliche Rom zwischen Altertum und Mittelalter*, pp. 7–94. Kleve, 1989.

Anton, Hans Hubert. *Fürstenspiegel und Herrscherethos in der Karolingerzeit*. Bonner historische Forschungen 32. Bonn, 1968.

Appleby, David F. "Instruction and Inspiration Through Images in the Carolingian Period." *Micrologus* 8 (2001): 83–109.

———. "Sight and Church Reform in the Thought of Jonas of Orléans." *Viator* 27 (1996): 11–33.

———. "Holy Relic and Holy Image: Saints' Relics in the Western Controversy over Images in the Eighth and Ninth Centuries." W&I 8 (1992): 333–43.

Appuhn, Horst. "Zum Thron Karls des Großen." AK 24/5 (1962/63): 127–36.

Arnaldi, Girolamo. "Rinascita, fine, reincarnazione e successive meta morfosi del senato romano (secoli V–XII)." *Archivio della Società Romana di Stories Patria* 105 (1982): 5–56.

———. "Il papato e l'ideologia del potere imperiale." SSCI 27 (1981): 341–407.

———. "La questione dei *Libri Carolini*." *La Cultura* 17 (1979): 3–19; also in *Culto cristiano politica imperiale carolingia*, pp. 61–86.

Arnulf, Arwed. *Versus ad Picturas: Studien zur Titulusdichtung als Quellengattung derKunstsgeschichte von der Antike bis zum Hochmittelalter*. Kunstswissenschaftliche Studien 72. Munich, 1997.

Arquillière, Henri-Xavier. *L'Augustinisme politique*. L'Église et l'état au moyen-age 2. 2nd ed. Paris, 1955.

Ashanin, Charles B. "Western Reaction to the Seventh Ecumenical Council." *Patristic and Byzantine Review* 7 (1988): 59–66.

Auzépy, Marie-France. "La tradition comme arme de pouvoir: L'exemple de la querelle iconoclaste." In Jean-Marie Sansterre, ed., *L'autorité du passé dans les sociétés médiévales*, pp. 79–92. Brussels, 2004.

———. "Le Christ, l'empereur et l'image (VIIe–IXe siècle)." In Εὐψυχία: Mélanges offerts à Hélène Ahrweiler, pp. 35–47. Byzantina Sorbonensia 16. Collection de l'école française de Rome 333. Paris, 1998.

———. "Francfort et Nicée II." In Berndt, ed., *Das Frankfurter Konzil von 794*, pp. 279–300.

———. *La Vie d'Étienne le Jeune par Étienne le Diacre: Introduction, Édition et Traduction*. Birmingham Byzantine and Ottoman Monographs 3. Aldershot, 1997.

———. "L'Adversus Constantinum Caballinum et Jean de Jérusalem." *Byzantinoslavica* 56 (1995): 323–38.

———. "L'évolution de l'attitude face au miracle à Byzance (VIIe–IXe siècle)." In *Miracles, prodiges et merveilles au moyen age*, pp. 31–46. Publications de le Sorbonne, Série Histoire Ancienne et Médiévale 34. Paris, 1995.

———. "De la Palestine à Constantinople (VIIIe–IXe siècles): Étienne le Sabaïte et Jean Damascène." T&M 12 (1994): 183–218.

———. "Constantin V, l'empereur isaurien et les Carolingiens." In Odile Redon and Bernard Rosenberger, eds., *Les assises du pouvoir: Temps médiévaux territoires africaines*, pp. 49–65. Paris, 1994.

————. "La destruction d l'icône du Christ de la Chalcé par Léon III: Propagande ou réalité?" *Byzantion* 60 (1990): 445–92.

————. "La place des moines à Nicée II." *Byzantion* 58 (1988): 5–21.

————. "L'iconodulie: défense de l'image ou de la dévotion à l'image?" In Boespflug and Lossky, eds., *Nicée II*, pp. 157–65.

Azkoul, Michael. "Perichoresis: The Christology of the Icon." *Patristic and Byzantine Review* 7 (1988): 67–85.

Babić, Gordana. "Les images byzantines et leurs degrés de signification: L'exemple de l'Hodigitria." In Guillou and Dwand, eds., *Byzance et les images*, pp. 189–222.

Baert, Barbara. *A Heritage of Holy Wood: The Legend of the True Cross in Text and Image.* Cultures, Beliefs, and Traditions 22. Leiden, 2004.

Baget-Bozzo, Gianni. "L'immagine di Cristo e dei santi." *Renovatio* 12 (1977): 462–72.

Baker, Derek, ed. *Renaissance and Renewal in Christian History.* SCH 14. Oxford, 1977.

Banniard, Michel. "*Zelum discretione condire*: Langages et styles de Gregoire le Grand dans sa correspondence." In P. Guichard, M.-T. Lorcin, J.-M. Poisson, and M. Rubelin, eds., *Papauté, Monachisme et Théories politiques, vol. 1: Le pouvoir et l'institution ecclésiale: Etudes d'histoire médiévale offertes à Marcel Pacaut*, pp. 29–46. Collection d'histoire et d'archéologie médiévales 1. Lyon, 1994.

Banning, Joop van. "Claudius von Turin als eine extreme Consequenz des Konzils von Frankfurt." In Berndt, ed., *Das Frankfurter Konzil*, pp. 731–49.

Barasch, Moshe. *Icon: Studies in the History of an Idea.* New York, 1992.

Barber, Charles. *Figure and Likeness: On the Limits of Representation in Byzantine Iconoclasm.* Princeton, 2002.

————. "Early Representations of the Mother of God." In Vassilaki, ed., *Mother of God*, pp. 253–61.

————. "Writing on the Body: Memory, Desire, and the Holy in Iconoclasm." In Liz James, ed., *Desire and Denial in Byzantium*, pp. 111–20. Aldershot, 1999.

————. "The Truth in Painting: Iconoclasm and Identity in Early-Medieval Art." *Speculum* 72 (1997): 1019–36.

————. "The Body Within the Frame: A Use of Word and Image in Iconoclasm." W&I 9 (1993): 140–53.

Barion, Hans. *Das fränkisch—deutsche Synodalrecht des Frühmittelalters.* Kanonistische Studien und Texte 5–6. Bonn-Köln, 1931.

————. "Das kirchenrechtliche Charakter des Konzils von Frankfurt 794." *Zeitschrift der savigny-Stiftung für Rechtsgeschichte, kanonistische Abteilung* 19 (1930): 139–70.

Barnard, L. W. *The Graeco-Roman and Oriental Background of the Iconoclastic Controversy.* Leiden, 1974.

————. "The Emperor Cult and the Origins of the Iconoclastic Controversy." *Byzantion* 43 (1973): 13–29.

Bastgen, Hubert. "Das Kapitulare Karls des Grossen über die Bilder oder die sogennanten *Libri Carolini*." *Neues Archiv* 36 (1911): 629–66; 37 (1912): 13–51, 453–533.

Baynes, Norman H. "Idolatry and the Early Church." In his *Byzantine Studies and Other Essays*, pp. 116–43. London, 1955.

————. "The Icons before Iconoclasm." *Harvard Theological Review* 44 (1951): 93–106.

————. "The Supernatural Defenders of Constantinople." AnBol 67 (1949): 165–77.

Beck, Hans-Georg. "The Early Byzantine Church." In Hubert Jedin and John Dolan, eds., Anselm Biggs, trans., *History of the Church, vol. 2: The Imperial Church from Constantine to the Early Middle Ages*, pp. 421–514. London, 1980.

————. *Kirche und Theologische Literatur im byzantinischen Reich*. 2nd ed. Munich, 1977.

————. "Von der Fragwürdigkeit der Ikone." *Bayerische Akademie der Wissenschaften, philosophisch-historische Klasse, Sitzungsberichte, Jahrgang 1975, Heft 7*. Munich, 1975.

————. "The Greek Church in the Epoch of Iconoclasm." In Friedrich Kempf et al., eds., *The Church in the Age of Feudalism*, pp. 26–53. Vol. 3 of *Handbook of Church History*, ed. Hubert Jedin and John Dolan, trans. Anselm Biggs. New York, 1969.

————. "Kirche und Klerus im staatlichen Leben von Byzanz." *Revue des études byzantines* 24 (1966): 1–24.

————. "Bildung und Theologie im frühmittelalterlichen Byzanz." In *Polychronicon: Festschrift für Franz Dölger*, pp. 69–81. Heidelberg, 1966.

Bellet, Paolino. "El Liber de imaginibus sanctorum bajo el nombre de Agobardo de Lyon obra de Claudio de Turin." *Analecta Sacra Terraconensia* 26 (1953): 151–94.

Belting, Hans. *Likeness and Presence: A History of the Image Before the Era of Art*. Chicago, 1994.

————. *The Image and Its Public in the Middle Ages: Form and Function of Early Paintings of the Passion*. Trans. Mark Bartusis and Raymond Meyer. New Rochelle, N.Y., 1990.

————. "Papal Artistic Commissions as Definitions of the Church in Rome." In Hellmut Hager and Susan Scott Munshower, eds., *Light on the Eternal City: Observations and Discoveries in the Art and Architecture of Rome*, pp. 13–30. Papers in Art History from the Pennsylvania State University, 2. University Park, Pa., 1987.

————. "Eine Privatkapelle im frühmittelalterlichen Rom." DOP 41 (1987): 55–69.

————. "Die beiden Palastaulen Leos. III und die Entstehung einer päpstlichen Programmkunst." FMSt 12 (1978): 55–83.

————. "I mosaici dell'aula Leonina come testimonianza della prima 'renovatio'dell'arte di Roma." In *Roma e l'età carolingia*, pp. 167–82.

Bergamini, Giuseppe. "Le pittura e la miniatura." In Menis, ed., *I Longobardi*, pp. 326–39.

Berliner, Rudolf. "The Freedom of Medieval Art." *Gazette des Beaux-Arts*, 6th ser., 28 (1945): 163–88.

Berndt, Rainer, S.J. *Das Frankfurter Konzil von 794: Kristallisationspunkt karolingischer Kultur*. Quellen und Abhandlungen zur mittelrheinischen Kirchengeschichte 80. 2 vols. Mainz, 1997.

Bertelli, Carlo. *La Madonna di Santa Maria in Trastevere: Storia, Iconografia, Stile di un dipinto dell'ottavo secolo*. Rome, 1961.

————. "Pour an évaluation positive de la crise iconoclaste byzantine." *Revue de l'art* 79 (1988): 9–16.

————. "Pittura in Italia durante l'iconoclasmo." *Arte Cristiana* 76 (1988): 45–54.

Bertolini, Paolo. *Figura velut qua Christus designatur: La persistenza del simbolo delle croce nell'iconografia numismatica durante il periodo iconoclasta: Constantinopoli e Benevento*. Istituto Storico Italiano per il medioevo, Studi Storici 99. Rome, 1978.

Besançon, Alain. *L'image interdit: Une histoire intellectuelle de l'iconoclasme.* Paris, 1994.

Bevan, Ernst. "Idolatry." *Edinburgh Review* 243 (1926): 253–72.

Binding, Günther. "Zur Ikonologie der Aachener Pfalzkapelle nach der Schriftsquellen." In Dieter Bauer et al., eds., *Mönchtum-Kirche-Herrschaft*, pp. 187–211. Sigmaringen, 1998.

———. "*Multis arte fuit utilis*: Einhard als Organisator am Aachener Hof und als Bauherr in Steinbach und Seligenstadt." *Mittellateinisches Jahrbuch* 30 (1995): 29–46.

Bisanzio, Roma e l'Italia. SSCI 34. Spoleto, 1986.

Bischoff, Bernhard. *Manuscripts and Libraries in the Age of Charlemagne.* Trans. Michael Gorman. Cambridge Studies in Paleography and Codicology 1. Cambridge, 1994.

———. "The Court Library of Charlemagne." In his *Manuscripts and Libraries in the Age of Charlemagne*, pp. 56–75.

———. "The Court Library under Louis the Pious." In his *Manuscripts and Libraries in the Age of Charlemagne*, pp. 76–92.

———. "Libraries and Schools in the Carolingian Revival of Learning." In his *Manuscripts and Libraries in the Age of Charlemagne*, pp. 93–114.

———. *Mittelalterliche Schatzverzeichnisse: Erster Teil von der Zeit Karls des Grossen bis zur Mitte des 13. Jahrhunderts.* Veröffentlichungen des Zentralinstituts für Kunstgeschichte in München 4. Munich, 1967.

———, ed. *Das Geistige Leben.* Karl der Grosse: Lebenswerk und Nachleben, vol. 2. Düsseldorf, 1965.

Blaauw, Sible de. *Cultus et Decor: Liturgia e archittetura nella Roma tardoantica e medievale.* 2 vols. Vatican City, 1994.

Blumenshine, Gary B. "Alcuin's *Liber Contra Heresim Felicis* and the Frankish Kingdom." FMSt 17 (1983): 222–33.

Blumenthal, Uta-Renate, ed. *Carolingian Essays.* Washington, D.C., 1983.

Boespflug, François, and Nicolas Lossky, eds. *Nicée II, 787–1987: Douze siècles d'images religieuses.* Paris, 1987.

Böhringer, Letha. "Zwei Fragmente der römischen Synode von 769 im Codex London, British Library, Add. 16143." In Hubert Mordek, ed., *Aus Archiven und Bibliotheken: Festschrift für Raymund Kottje zum 65. Geburtstag*, pp. 93–105. Frankfurt, 1992.

Bonini, Roberto. "Giustiniano e il problema italico." SSCI 34 (1988): 73–92.

Booker, Courtney M. *Past Convictions: The Penance of Louis the Pious and the Decline of the Carolingians.* Philadelphia, 2009.

Borgolte, Michael. *Petrusnachfolge und Kaiserimitation: Die Grablegen der Päpste, ihre Genese und Traditionsbildung.* Veröffentlichungen des Max-Plancks Instituts für Geschichte 95. Göttingen, 1989.

———. "Papst Leo III., Karl der Große, und der Filioque-Streit von Jerusalem." *Byzantina* 10 (1980): 403–27.

Borst, Arno. *Der Streit um den karolingishchen Kalendar.* MGH, Studien und Texte 36. Hannover, 2004.

———. *Die karolingische Kalendarreform.* MGH, Schriften 46. Hannover, 1998.

Boshof, Egon. *Ludwig der Fromme.* Darmstadt, 1996.

———. *Erzbischof Agobard von Lyon: Leben und Werk.* Kölner historische Abhandlungen 17. Cologne, 1969.

Boulhol, Pascal. *Claude de Turin: Un évêque iconoclaste dans l'occident carolingien. Étude suivi de l'édition du* Commentaire sur Josue. Collection des Études augustiniennes, Série Moyen Âge et Temps Modernes 38. Paris, 2002.

Boureau, Alain. "Les théologiens carolingiens devant les images: La conjuncture de 825." In Boespflug and Lossky, eds., *Nicée II*, pp. 247–62.

Brandes, Wolfram. "*Tempora periculosa sunt.* Eschatologisches im Vorfeld der Kaiserkrönung Karls des Großen." In Berndt, ed., *Das Frankfurter Konzil*, pp. 49–80.

Brandmuller, Walter. "*Traditio Scripturae Interpres*: The Teaching of the Councils on the Right Interpretation of Scripture up to the Council of Trent." CHR 73 (1987): 523–40.

Brandon, S. G. F. "Christ in Verbal and Depicted Imagery: A Problem of Early Christian Iconography." In Jacob Neusner, ed., *Christianity, Judaism, and Other Greco-Roman Cults: Studies for Morton Smith at Sixty*, pp. 164–72. Studies in Judaism in Late Antiquity 12.2. Leiden, 1975.

Bratu, Mihaita Gh. *Représenter le Christ: Recherches doctrinales au siècle de l'iconoclasme (723–828)*. Strasbourg, 2001.

Braunfels, Wolfgang. *Die Welt der Karolinger und ihre Kunst.* Munich, 1968.

———. "Die Wandmalerei." In *Karl der Grosse: Werk und Wirkung*, pp. 473–88.

Braunfels, Wolfgang, and Hermann Schnitzler, eds. *Karolingische Kunst.* Karl der Grosse: Lebenswerk und Nachleben, vol. 3. Düsseldorf, 1965.

Breckenridge, James D. "Apocrypha of Early Christian Portraiture." BZ 67 (1974): 101–9.

———. "The Iconoclasts' Image of Christ." *Gesta* 11 (1972): 3–8.

———. "Evidence for the Nature of Relations between Pope John VII and the Byzantine Emperor Justinian II." BZ 65 (1972): 364–74.

———. *The Numismatic Iconography of Justinian II.* New York, 1959.

Bredekamp. Horst. *Kunst als Medium sozialer Konflikt: Bilderkämpfe von der Spätantike bis zur Hussitenrevolution.* Frankfurt, 1975.

Brehier, Louis. "Le recruitment des patriarches de Constantinople pendant la période byzantine." *Actes du VIᵉ congrès international des études byzantines*, vol. 1, pp. 221–27. Paris, 1950.

Brenk, Beat. "Visibility and (Partial) Invisibility of Early Christian Images." In de Nie, Morrison, and Mostert, eds., *Seeing the Invisible in Late Antiquity and the Early Middle Ages*, pp. 139–83.

———. "Schriftlichkeit und Bildlichkeit in der Hofschule Karls des Großen." SSCI 41 (1994): 631–82.

———. *Die frühchristlichen Mosaiken in Santa Maria Maggiore zu Rom.* Wiesbaden, 1975.

Brown, Giles. "Introduction: The Carolingian Renaissance." In Rosamond McKitterick, ed., *Carolingian Culture: Emulation and Innovation*, pp. 1–51. Cambridge, 1994.

Brown, Peter. *The Rise of Western Christendom.* 2nd. ed. Oxford, 2003.

———. "A Dark-Age Crisis: Aspects of the Iconoclastic Controversy." EHR 88 (1973): 1–34.

———. Review of Thomas Mathews *Clash of Gods*. AB 77 (1995): 499–502.

Brown, Thomas S. "The Interplay Between Roman and Byzantine Traditions in the Exarchate of Ravenna." SSCI 34 (1988): 127–60.

Browning, Robert. "Literacy in the Byzantine World." BMGS 4 (1978): 139–54.

Brubaker, Leslie. "Icons before Iconoclasm?" SSCI 45 (1998): 1215–54.

———. "Byzantine Culture in the Ninth Century: An Introduction." In Leslie Brubaker, ed., *Byzantium in the Ninth Century: Dead or Alive?*, pp. 63–71. Aldershot, 1998.

———. "Introduction: The Sacred Image." In Robert Osterhout and Leslie Brubaker, eds., *The Sacred Image in East and West*, pp. 1–24. Illinois Byzantine Studies 4. Urbana, 1995.

———. "Byzantine Art in the Ninth Century: Theory, Practice, and Culture." BMGS 13 (1989): 23–93.

———. "Perception and Conception: Art, Theory and Culture in Ninth-Century Byzantium." W&I 5 (1989): 19–32.

Brubaker, Leslie and John Haldon. *Byzantium in the Iconoclast Era (ca. 680–850): The Sources. An Annotated Survey.* Birmingham Byzantine and Ottoman Monographs 7. Aldershot, 2001.

Brunhölzl, Franz. *Histoire de la litterature latine du moyen age.* Vol. 1, parts 1 and 2. Turnhout, 1990.

Bryer, Anthony and Judith Herrin, eds. *Iconoclasm: Papers Given at the Ninth Spring Symposium of Byzantine Studies, University of Birmingham.* Birmingham, 1977.

Buc, Philippe. *The Dangers of Ritual.* Princeton, 2001.

Bullough, Donald A. "York, Bede's Calendar and a Pre-Bedan English Martyrology." AnBol 21 (2003): 329–55.

———. "Alcuin before Frankfort." In Berndt, ed., *Das Frankfurter Konzil*, pp. 571–86.

———. "*Aula Renovata*": The Carolingian Court Before the Aachen Palace." *Proceedings of the British Academy* 71 (1985): 269–301.

———. "Albinus deliciosus Karoli regis: Alcuin of York and the Shaping of the Early Carolingian Court." In L. Fenske et al., eds., *Insititutionen, Kultur und Gesellschaft im Mittelalter: Festshcrift für Josef Fleckenstein zum 65. Geburtstag*, pp. 72–92. Sigmaringen, 1984.

———. "Alcuin and the Kingdom of Heaven: Liturgy, Theology, and the Carolingian Age." In Uta-Renate Blumenthal, ed., *Carolingian Essays*, pp. 1–69. Washington, D.C., 1983.

———. "Roman Books and Carolingian *Renovatio*." In Derek Baker, ed., *Renaissance and Renewal*, pp. 23–50. SCH 16. Oxford, 1977.

———. "'Imagines Regum' and Their Significance in the Early Medieval West." In Giles Robertson and George Henderson, eds., *Studies in Memory of David Talbot Rice*, pp. 223–76. Edinburgh, 1975.

———. *The Age of Charlemagne.* 2nd ed. London, 1973.

Cameron, Averil. "The Early Cult of the Virgin." In Vasillaki, ed., *Mother of God*, pp. 3–15.

———. "Byzantines and Jews: Some Recent Work on Early Byzantium." BMGS 20 (1996): 249–74.

———. "Texts as Weapons: Polemic in the Byzantine Dark Ages." In Alan K. Bowman and Greg Woolf, eds., *Literacy and Power in the Ancient World*, pp. 198–215. Cambridge, 1994.

———. "The Language of Images: The Rise of Icons and Christian Representation." In Diana Wood, ed., *The Church and the Arts*, pp. 1–42. SCH 28. Oxford, 1992.

———. "Disputations, Polemical Literature and the Formation of Opinion in the early Byzantine Period." In G. J. Reinink, ed., *Disputes, Poems and Dialogues*, pp. 91–108. Orientalia Louvanensia Analecta 42. Louvain, 1991.

———. *Christianity and the Rhetoric of Empire*. Berkeley, 1991.

———. "The History of the Image of Edessa: The Telling of a Story." In *Okeanos: Essays Presented to Ihor Ševčenko*, pp. 80–94. Harvard Ukrainian Studies 7. Cambridge, Mass., 1983.

———. "The Artistic Patronage of Justin II." *Byzantion* 50 (1980): 62–84.

———. "Images of Authority: Elites and Icons in Late Sixth-Century Byzantium." *Past & Present* 84 (1979): 3–35.

Camille, Michael. *The Gothic Idol: Ideology and Image-making in Medieval Art*. Cambridge, 1989.

———. "Word, Text, Image and the Early Church Fathers in the Egino Codex." SSCI 41 (1994): 65–92.

———. "Seeing and Reading: Some Visual Implications of Medieval Literacy and Illiteracy." *Art History* 8 (1985): 26–49.

———. "Die Bilderfrage als theologisches Problem der alten Kirche." In Kollwitz, ed., *Das Gottesbild im Abendland*, pp. 77–108.

Cantelli, Silvia. *Angelomo e la scuola esegetica di Luxeuil*. 2 vols. Biblioteca di Medioevo Latino 1. Spoleto, 1990.

———. "L'esegesi al tempo di Ludovico Pio e Carlo il Calvo." In *Giovanni Scoto nel suo tempo: L'organizzazione del sapere in età carolingia*, pp. 261–336. Atti del XXIV convegno storico internazionale. Spoleto, 1989.

Cantino-Wataghin, Gisella. "*Biblia Pauperum*: A proposito dell'arte dei primi cristiani," *L'antiquité tradive* 9 (2001): 259–74.

Capitani, Ovidio, ed. *Culto Christiano Politica Imperiale Carolingia*. Convegni del Centro de Studi sulla Spiritualità medievale, Università degli Studi de Perugia 13. Todo, 1979.

Carile, Antonio. "L'iconoclasmo fra Bisanzio e l'Italia." In *Culto delle immagine e crisi iconoclasta*, pp. 13–54. Atti del convegno di Studi Catania, 16–17 Maggio 1984. Palermo, 1986.

Carruthers, Mary. *The Craft of Thought: Meditation, Rhetoric, and the Making of Images, 400–1200*. Cambridge Studies in Medieval Literature. Cambridge, 1998.

Carver, M. O. H. "Carbon-14 Dating of Wood from the East Apse of Santa Maria at Castel Seprio." *Gesta* 26 (1987): 17–18.

———. "S. Maria foris Portas at Castel Seprio: A Famous Church in a New Context." *World Archaeology* 18 (1987): 312–29.

Caspar, Erich. "Papst Gregor II. und die Bilderstreit." *Zeitschrift für Kirchengeschichte* 52 (1933): 29–89.

Castes, Albert. "La dévotion privée et l'art à l'époque carolingiene: Le cas de Sainte-Maure de Troyes." *Cahiers de civilisation médiévale* 33 (1990): 3–18.

Cavadini, John. "Elipandus and His Critics at the Council of Frankfort." In Berndt, ed., *Das Frankfurter Konzil*, pp. 787–808.

———. *The Last Christology of the West: Adoptionism in Spain and Gaul, 785–820*. Philadelphia, 1993.

Cavallo, Guglielmo. "Testo e immagine: Una frontiera ambigua." SSCI 41 (1994): 31–62.

———. "Interazione tra scritture greca e scritture latina a Roma tra VIII e IX secolo." In Pierre Cockshaw, Monique-Cécile Garand, and Pierre Jodogne, eds., *Miscellanea Codicologica F. Masai Dicata*, pp. 23–29. Les publications de Scriptorium 8. Ghent, 1979.

Cecchelli, Carlo. *Mater Christi*. 4 vols. in 3. Rome, 1946–54.

Chadwick, Henry. *East and West: The Making of a Rift in the Church*. Oxford, 2003.

Charanis, Peter. "The Monk as an Element of Byzantine Society." DOP 25 (1971): 63–84.

Chazelle, Celia. *The Crucified God in the Carolingian Era*. Cambridge, 2001.

———. "Archbishops Ebbo and Hincmar of Reims and the Utrecht Psalter." *Speculum* 72 (1997): 1055–77.

———. "Not in Painting But in Writing: Augustine and the Supremacy of the Word in the *Libri Carolini*." In Edward English, ed., *The 'De doctrina christiana' of Augustine in the Middle Ages*, pp. 1–22. Notre Dame Conferences in Medieval Studies 6. Notre Dame, 1995.

———. "Images, Scripture, the Church, and the *Libri Carolini*." *Proceedings of the PMR Conference* 16/17 (1992/93): 53–76.

———, ed. *Literacy, Politics, and Artistic Innovation in the Early Medieval West*. Lanham, Md., 1992.

———. "Pictures, Books, and the Illiterate: Pope Gregory I's Letters to Serenus of Marseilles." W&I 6 (1990): 138–53.

———. "Matter, Spirit, and Image in the *Libri Carolini*." *Recherches augustinienne* 21 (1986): 163–84.

Chifar, Nicolae. *Das VII. ökumenische Konzil von Nikaia: Das letzte Konzil der ungeteilte Kirche*. Oikonomia 32. Erlangen, 1993.

Cholij, Roman. *Theodire the Stoudite: The Ordering of Holiness*. Oxford, 2002.

Christe, Yves. "Christian Art from Its Origins to the Beginning of the Eleventh Century." In Yves Christe, Tania Velmans, Hanna Losowska, and Roland Rechd, eds., *Art of the Christian World A.D. 200–1500: A Handbook of Styles and Forms*, pp. 9–120. New York, 1982.

Christophilopulu, Aikatherine. "ΣΙΛΕΝΤΙΟΝ." BZ 44 (1951): 79–85.

Chrysos, Evangelos. "Codex Parisinus Graecus 1115 und die Konziliengeschichte." AHC 26 (1994): 8–13.

———. "Byzantine Diplomacy, A.D. 300–800: Means and Ends." In Shepard and Franklin, eds., *Byzantine Diplomacy*, pp. 25–39.

Ciccimarra, Francesco. "La condotta degli ecclesiastici e le disposizione del II Concilio di Nicea." *Euentes Docete* 41 (1988): 107–16.

Clark, Elizabeth. *The Origenist Controversy: The Cultural Construction of an Early Christian Debate*. Princeton, N.J., 1992.

Claussen, Martin A. *The Reform of the Frankish Church: Chrodegang of Metz and the* Regula Canonicorum *in the Eighth Century*. Cambridge, 2004.

Conant, John Kenneth. *Carolingian and Romanesque Architecture: 800 to 1200*. 2nd ed. Harmondsworth, 1966.

Conte, P. *Regesto delle lettere dei papi del secolo VIII*. Milan, 1984.

Contreni, John J. "'By Lions, Bishops Are Meant; By Wolves, Priests': History, Exegesis, and the Carolingian Church in Haimo of Auxerre's *Commentary on Ezechiel*." *Francia* 29 (2002): 29–56.

———. "Counting, Calendars, and Cosmology: Numeracy in the Early Middle Ages." In

John J. Contreni and Santa Casciani, eds., *Word, Image, Number: Communication in the Middle Ages*, pp. 43–83. Florence, 2002.

———. "Carolingian Biblical Culture." In Gerd Van Riel et al., eds., *Iohannes Scottus Eriugena: The Bible and Hermeneutics,"* pp. 1–23. Ancient and Medieval Philosophy, De Wulf Mansin Centre, Series 1, 20. Leuven, 1996.

———. "The Carolingian Renaissance." In Warren Treadgold, ed., *Renaissances Before the Renaissance*, pp. 59–74. Stanford, 1984.

———. "Carolingian Biblical Studies." In Uta-Renate Blumenthal ed., *Carolingian Essays*, pp. 71–98. Washington, D.C., 1983.

———. "Inharmonious Harmony: Education in the Carolingian World." *Annals of Scholarship* 1 (1980): 81–96.

Cormack, Robin. *Painting the Soul: Icons, Death Masks, and Shrouds*. London, 1997.

———. *Writing in Gold: Byzantine Society and Its Icons*. London 1985.

———. "The Arts During the Age of Iconoclasm." In Bryer and Herrin, eds., *Iconoclasm*, pp. 35–44.

———. "Painting After Iconoclasm." In Breyer and Herrin, eds., *Iconoclasm*, pp. 147–55.

Corrigan, Kathleen. "Wort und Bild in Byzanz zur Zeit des Ikonoklasmus und seines Nachleben." In Janowski and Zchomelidse, eds., *Die Sichtbarkeit des Unsichtbaren*, pp. 131–45.

Cramer, Peter. *Baptism and Change in the Early Middle Ages, c. 200–1150*. Cambridge Studies in Medieval Life and Thought, 4th ser., 20. Cambridge, 1993.

Crivello, Fabrizio. "Eine Name für das Herrscherbild des Ludwigspsalters." *Kunstchronik* 60 (2007): 216–19.

Croquison, J. "L'iconographie chrétienne à Rome d'après le 'Liber Pontificalis.'" *Byzantion* 34 (1964): 534–606.

Cubitt, Catherine. *Anglo-Saxon Church Councils c. 650–c. 850*. London, 1995.

Culto crististiano politica imperiale carolingia. Convegni del centro di studi sulla spiritualità medievale, Università degli studi di Perugia 18. Todi, 1979.

Dagron, Gilbert. *Emperor and Priest: The Imperial Office in Byzantium*. Trans. Jean Birrell. Cambridge, 2003.

———. "L'image de culte et le portrait." In Guillou and Durand, eds., *Byzance et les images*, pp. 121–50.

———. "Le christianisme byzantin du viie au milieu du xie siècle." In Mayeur et al., eds., *Histoire du Christianisme*, pp. 9–371.

———. "Judaïser." T&M 11 (1991): 359–80.

———. "Holy Images and Likeness." DOP 45 (1991): 23–33.

———. "Rome et Italie vues de Byzance (IVe–VIIe siècles)." SSCI 34 (1988): 43–64.

———. "Le culte des images dans le monde byzantin." In Jean Delumeau, ed., *Histoire vécu du peuple Chrétien*, vol. 1, pp. 133–60. Toulouse, 1979.

Dagron, Gilbert, Pierre Riché, and André Vauchez. *Histoire du Chritianisme, tome IV: Évêques, moines et empereurs (610–1054)*. Paris, 1993.

Dagron, Gilbert, and Vincent Déroche. "Juifs et Chrétiens dans l'Orient du VIIe siècle." T&M 11 (1991): 17–273.

Dahlhaus-Berg, Elisabeth. *Nova Antiquitas et Antiqua Novitas: Typologische Exegese und isido-*

rianisches Geschichtebild bei Theodulf von Orléans. Kölner historische Abhandlungen 33. Cologne, 1975.

De Bruyne, Donatien. "La composition des *Libri Carolini.*" RB 44 (1932): 227–34.

Défourneaux, Marcelin. "Charlemagne et la monarchie asturienne." In *Mélanges d'histoire du moyen age dédiés à le mémoire de Louis Halphen,* pp. 177–84. Paris, 1951.

De Lang, Nicholas. "Jews and Christians in the Byzantine Empire: Problems and Prospects." In Diana Wood, ed., *Christianity and Judaism,* pp.15–32. SCH 29. Oxford, 1992.

Delaruelle, Etienne. "Charlemagne et l'église." *Revue d'histoire de l'Église de France* 39 (1953): 165–99.

Deliyannis, Deborah Mauskopf. "Agnellus of Ravenna and Iconolasm: Theology and Politics in the Ninth-Century Historical Text." *Speculum* 71 (1996): 559–76.

de'Maffei, Fernanda. *Icona, pittore e arte al Concilio Niceno II e la questione della scialbatura delle imagini, con particolare referimento agli Angeli della Chiesa della Dormizione de Nicaea.* Rome, 1974.

De Nie, Giselle, Karl F. Morrison, and Morco Mostert, eds. *Seeing the Invisible in Late Antiquity and the Early Middle Ages: Papers from "Verbal and Pictorial Imaging: Representing and Accessing the Invisible, 400–1000" (Utrecht, 11–13 December 2003).* Utrecht Studies in Medieval Literacy 14. Turnhout, 2005.

———. "Images as 'Mysteries': The Shape of the Invisible." *Journal of Medieval Latin* 9 (1999): 78–90.

———. "The Poet as Visionary: Venantius Fortunatus's 'New Mantle' for Saint Martin." *Cassiodorus: Rivista di studi sulla tarda antichità* 3 (1997): 49–83.

Depreux, Philippe. "L'expression *statutum est a domno rege et a sancta synodo* annonçant certains dispositions du capitulaire de Francfort (794)." In Berndt, ed., *Das Frankfurter Konzil,* pp. 81–102.

Deshman, Robert. "The Exalted Servant: The Ruler Theology of the Prayerbook of Charles the Bald." *Viator* 11 (1980): 385–417.

Der Nersessian, Sirarpie. "Une apologie des images du septième siècle." In her *Études byzantines et arméniennes,* vol. 1, pp. 379–403. Louvain, 1973.

Déroche, Vincent. "Polémique anti-judaïque et émergence de l'Islam." REB 57 (1999): 141–61.

———. "*L'Apologie contre les Juifs* de Léontios de Néapolis." T&M 12 (1994): 45–104.

———. "La polémique anti-judaïque au VIe et VIIe siècle: Un memento inédit, Les *Kephalaia.*" T&M 11 (1991): 275–311.

———. "L'Authenticité de l'"Apologie contre les Juifs' de Léontios de Néapolis." *Bulletin de correspondence hellenique* 90 (1986): 655–69.

Deshusses, Jean. *Le sacramentaire grégorien.* 2nd ed. Freiburg, 1979.

———. "Le supplément au sacramentaire grégorien: Alcuin ou Saint Benoît d'Aniane?" *Archiv für Liturgiewissenschaft* 9 (1965): 48–71.

DeVries, Wilhelm. "Die Struktur der Kirche gemäss dem II Konzil von Nicäa (787)." *Orientalia Christiana Periodica* 33 (1967): 47–71.

Diebold, William. *Word and Image: An Introduction to Early Medieval Art.* Boulder, Colo., 2000.

———. "Verbal, Visual, and Cultural Literacy in Medieval Art: Word and Image in The Psalter of Charles the Bald." W&I 8 (1992): 89–99.

Dillenberger, John. *A Theology of Artistic Sensibilities: The Visual Arts and the Church*. New York, 1986.

Diringer, David. *The Illuminated Book: Its History and Production*. New York, 1967.

Dodwell, C. R. *Painting in Europe 800–1200*. Harmondsworth, 1971.

Dölger, Franz. "Die Kaiserurkunde der Byzantiner als Ausdruck ihrer politischen Anschauungen." In his *Byzanz und die europäische Staatenwelt*, pp. 9–33. Darmstadt, 1964.

D'Onofrio, Mario. "La Königshalle di Lorsch presso Worms." In *Roma e l'età carolingia*, pp. 129–38.

———. *Roma e Aquisgrana*. Collana di Studi di Storia dell'arte 4. Rome, 1983.

Duggan, Lawrence G. "Was Art Really the 'Book of the Illiterate'?" W&I 5 (1989): 227–51.

Dumeige, Gervais. "L'Image du Christ, Verbe de Dieu." AHC 20 (1988): 258–67.

———. *Nicée II*. Histoire de conciles oecuméniques 4. Paris, 1978.

Dümmler, Ernst. "Über leben und Lehre Bischofs Claudius von Turin." *Sitzungsberichte der kgl. Preußischen Akademie de Wissenschaften zu Berlin* 23 (1895): 427–43.

Dutton, Paul. "Thunder and Hail over the Carolingian Countryside." In his *Charlemagne's Mustache and Other Cultural Clusters of a Dark Age,* pp. 169–88. New York, 2004.

———. *Carolingian Civilization: A Reader*. 2nd ed. Peterborough, Ontario, 2004.

———. *Charlemagne's Courtier: The Complete Einhard*. Peterborough, Ontario, 1998.

Dvornik, Francis. *The Photian Schism*. Cambridge, 1948, repr. 1970.

———. *Byzantium and the Roman Primacy*. New York, 1966.

———. *Early Christian and Byzantine Political Philosophy, Origins and Background*. Dumbarton Oaks Studies 9. Washington, D.C., 1966.

———. "The Patriarch Photius and Iconoclasm." DOP 7 (1953): 67–97.

———. "Emperors, Popes, and General Councils." DOP 6 (1951): 1–23.

Elbern, Victor. "Die 'Libri Carolini' und die liturgische Kunst um 800." AK 54 (1986/7): 15–32.

Elliger, Walter. *Die Stellung der alten Christen zu den Bildern in den ersten vier Jahrhunderten*. Leipzig, 1930.

Elsner, Jaś. *Imperial Rome and Christian Triumph*. Oxford History of Art. Oxford, 1998.

———. *Art and the Roman Viewer: The Transformation of Art from the Pagan World to Christianity*. Cambridge, 1995.

Elsner, John. "Image and Iconoclasm in Byzantium." *Art History* 11 (1988): 471–91.

Engemann, Josef. "Zur Verbreitung magischer Übelwejhr in der nichtchristlichen und christlichen Spätantike." *Jahrbuch für Antike und Christentum* 18 (1975): 22–48.

Erickson, John H. "*Oikonomia* in Byzantine Canon Law." In Kenneth Pennington and Robert Somerville, eds., *Law, Church and Society: Essays in Honor of Stephan Kuttner*, pp. 225–36. Philadelphia, 1977.

Ettinghausen, Richard, Oleg Grabar, and Marilyn Jenkins-Madina. *Islamic Art and Architecture, 650–1250*. New Haven, 2001.

Ewig, Eugen. "Zum christlichen königsgedanken im Frühmittelalter." In Theodor Mayer, ed., *Das Königtum*, pp. 7–73. Darmstadt, 1963.

Ewig, Eugen. "Das Bild Constantins des Großen in den ersten Jahrhunderten des Abendländischen Mittelalters." *Historisches Jahrbuch* 75 (1956): 1–46.

Falkenstein, Ludwig. "Charlemagne et Aix-la-Chapelle." *Byzantion* 61 (1991): 231–89.

———. "Zwischenbilanz zur Aachener Pfalzenforschung." *Zeitschrift der Aachener Geschichtsvereins* 80 (1970): 7–71.

Fallon, Hugh. "Imperial Symbolism on Two Carolingian Coins." *American Numismatic Society: Museum Notes* 8 (1958): 119–32.

Fazzo, Vittorio. "Il concilio di Nicea nella storia cristiana ed i rapporti fra Roma e Bisanzio." In *Cultura e società medievali: Studi per Paolo Brezzi,* pp. 345–60. Studi Storici, fasc. 184, 187. Rome, 1988.

Feld, Helmut. *Der Ikonoklasmus des Westens.* Studies in the History of Christian Thought 41, ed. Heiko Oberman. Leiden, 1990.

Ferluga, Jadran. "L'Italia bizantina dalla caduta dell'esarcato di Ravenna alla metà del secolo IX." SSCI 34 (1988): 169–193.

Ferrari, Michele Camillo. *Il "Liber sanctae crucis" di Rabano Mauro: Testo—Immagine—Contesto.* Lateinische Sprach und Literatur des Mitttelalters 30. Bern, 1999.

Ferrari, Mirella. "Dungal." DBI 42 (1993): 11–14.

———. "Note su Claudio di Torino 'Episcopus ab ecclesia damnatus.' " *Italia medioevale e umanistica* 16 (1973): 291–308.

———. " 'In Papia conveniant ad Dungalum.' " *Italia medioevale e umanistica* 15 (1972): 1–52.

Fichtenau, Henrich. "Karl der Große und das Kaisertum." MIOG 61 (1953): 257–333.

———. "Byzanz und die Pfalz zu Aachen." MIOG 59 (1951): 1–54.

Fillitz, Hermann. "Die Elfenbeinen des Hofes Karls des Großen." In Stiegemann and Wemhoff, eds., *Kunst und Kultur der Karolingerzeit,* pp. 610–22.

Finney, Paul Corby. *The Invisible God: The Earliest Christians on Art.* New York, 1994.

Firey, Abigail. "Carolingian Ecclesiology and Heresy: A Southern Gallic Juridical Tract Against Adoptionism." *Sacris Erudiri* 39 (2000): 251–316.

Fischer, Bonifatius. "Bibeltext und Bibelreform unter Karl dem Grossen." In Bischoff, ed., *Karl der Grosse,* vol. 2, pp. 156–216.

Fleckenstein, Josef. "Karl der Große, seine Hofgelehrten und das Frankfurter Konzil von 794." In Berndt, ed., *Das Frankfurter Konzil,* pp. 27–48.

———. *Die Bildungsreform Karls des Grossen als Verwirklichung der Norma Rectitudinis.* Bigge, 1953.

Flint, Valerie I. J. *The Rise of Magic in Medieval Europe.* Princeton, 1991.

Florovsky, George. "Origen, Eusebius and the Iconoclastic Controversy." *Church History* 19 (1950): 77–96.

Folz, Robert. *The Coronation of Charlemagne.* Trans. J. E. Anderson. London, 1974.

Fowden, Garth. *Empire to Commonwealth: Consequences of Monotheism in Late Antiquity.* Princeton, 1993.

Freed, Johannes. "Awaiting the End of Time around the Year 1000." In Richard Landes et. al., eds., *The Apocalyptic Year 1000,* pp. 17–65. Oxford, 2003.

Freedberg, David. *The Power of Images: Studies in the History and Theory of Response.* Chicago, 1989.

Freeman, Ann. "Scripture and Images in the Libri Carolini." SSCI 41 (1994): 163–88.

———. "Additions and Corrections to the Libri Carolini: Links with Alcuin and the Adoptionist Controversy." In Sigrid Krämer and Michael Bernhard, eds., *Scire Litteras: Forschungen zur mittelalterlichen Geistesleben*, pp. 159–69. Munich, 1988.

———. "Theodulf of Orléans and the Psalm Citations of the *Libri Carolini*." RB 97 (1987): 195–224.

———. "Carolingian Orthodoxy and the Fate of the *Libri Carolini*." Viator 16 (1985): 65–108.

———. "Further Studies in the *Libri Carolini* III: The Marginal Notes in Vaticanus Latinus 7207." *Speculum* 46 (1971): 597–612.

———. "Further Studies in the *Libri Carolini*." *Speculum* 40 (1965): 203–89.

———. "Theodulf of Orléans and the *Libri Carolini*." *Speculum* 32 (1957): 663–705.

Freeman, Ann, and Paul Meyvaert. "The Meaning of Theodulf's Apse Mosaic at Germigny-des-Prés." *Gesta* 40 (2001): 125–39.

Frevel, C. "Du sollst dir kein Bildnis machen!—Und wenn doch? Überlegungen zur Kultbildlosigkeit der Religion Israels." In Janowski and Zchomelidse, eds., *Die Sichtbarkeit des Unsichtbaren*, pp. 23–48.

Frey, J. B. "La question des images chez les Juifs à la lumière des récentes découvertes." *Biblica* 15 (1934): 265–300.

Fritze, Wolfgang H. "Universalis gentium confessio: Formeln, Träger und Wege universal missionarischen Denkens im 7. Jahrhundert." FMSt 3 (1965): 78–130.

Froehlich, Karlfried. "The *Libri Carolini* and the Lessons of the Iconoclastic Controversy." In H. George Anderson, J. Francis Stafford, and Joseph A. Burgess, eds., *The One Mediator, the Saints, and Mary*, pp. 193–208. Lutherans and Catholics in Dialogue 8. Augsburg, 1992.

Frolow, A. "La dédicace de Constantinople dans la tradition byzantine." *Revue de l'histoire des religions* 127 (1944): 61–127.

Fuhrmann, Horst. "Das Papsttum und das kirchliche Leben im Frankenreich." SSCI 27 (1981): 419–56.

———. *Einfluss und Verbreitung der pseudoisidorischen Fälschungen*. 3 vols. Schriften der MGH 24. Stuttgart, 1972–73.

Ganshof, F. L. "Observations sur le synode de Francfort de 794." In *Miscellanea historica in honorem Alberte de Meyer*, vol. 1, pp. 306–18. Louvain, 1946.

Ganz, David. " 'Roman Books' Reconsidered: The Theology of Carolingian Display Script." In Smith, ed., *Early Medieval Rome and the Christian West*, pp. 297–315.

———. "Theology and the Organisation of Thought." In McKitterick, ed., *New Cambridge Medieval History*, vol. 2, pp. 758–85.

———. " '*Pando quod ignoro*': In Search of Carolingian Artistic Experience." In Lesley Smith and Benedicta Ward, eds., *Intellectual Life in the Middle Ages: Essays Presented to Margaret Gibson*," pp. 25–32. London, 1992.

———. *Corbie in the Carolingian Renaissance*. Beihefte der Francia, 20. Sigmaringen, 1990.

Gardner, Alice. *Theodore of Studium: His Life and Times*. London, 1905.

Garipzanov, Ildar H. "The Image of Authority in Carolingian Coinage: The *Image* of a Ruler and Roman Imperial Tradition." EME 8 (1999): 197–218.

Garrison, Mary. "The Franks as the New Israel? Education for an Identity from Pippin to Charlemagne." In Yitzhak Hen and Matthew Innes, eds., *The Uses of the Past in the Early Middle Ages,* pp. 114–61. Cambridge, 2000.

———. "The Social World of Alcuin: Nicknames at York and at the Carolingian Court." In *Alcuin of York: Scholar at the Carolingian Court,* pp. 59–79 Germania Latina 3. Groningen, 1999.

———. "The Emergence of Carolingian Latin Literature and the Court of Charlemagne (780–814)." In McKitterick, ed., *Carolingian Culture,* pp. 111–40.

Geary, Patrick J. *Furta Sacra: Thefts of Relics in the Central Middle Ages.* Rev. ed. Princeton, 1990.

Geertz, Clifford. "Art as a Cultural System." In his *Local Knowledge: Further Essays in Interpretive Anthropology,* pp. 94–120. New York, 1983.

———. "Centers, Kings, and Charisma: Reflections on the Symbolics of Power." In his *Local Knowledge,* pp. 121–46.

Gemienhardt, Peter. *Die Filioque-Kontroverse zwischen Ost- und Westkirche im Frühmittelalter.* Arbeiten zur Kirchengeschichte 82. Berlin, 2002.

Gendle, Nicholas. "The Role of the Byzantine Saint in the Development of the Icon Cult." In Sergei Hackel, ed., *The Byzantine Saint,* pp. 181–86. University of Birmingham Fourteenth Spring Symposium of Byzantine Studies. London, 1980.

Gero, Stephen. "The True Image of Christ: Eusebius' Letter to Constantis Reconsidered." JTS 32 (1981): 460–70.

———. *Byzantine Iconoclasm During the Reign of Constantine V with Particular Attention to the Oriental Sources.* Corpus Scriptorum Christianorum Orientalium, Subsidia 52. Louvain, 1977.

———. "Byzantine Iconoclasm and the Failure of a Medieval Reformation. In Gutmann, ed., *The Image and the Word,* pp. 49–62.

———. "Byzantine Iconoclasm and Monachomachy." *Journal of Ecclesiastical History* 28 (1977): 241–48.

———. "Hypatius of Ephesus on the Cult of Images." In Jacob Neusner, ed., *Christianity, Judaism and Other Greco-Roman Cults: Studies for Morton Smith at Sixty,* pp. 208–16. Studies in Judaism in Latin Antiquity 12.2. Leiden, 1975.

———. "The Eucharistic Doctrine of the Byzantine Iconoclasts and Its Sources." BZ 68 (1975): 4–22.

———. "Notes on Byzantine Iconoclasm in the Eighth Century." *Byzantion* 44 (1974): 23–42.

———. *Byzantine Iconoclasm During the Reign of Leo III with Particular Attention to the Oriental Sources.* Corpus Scriptorum Christianorum Orientalium, Subsidia, 41. Louvain, 1973.

———. "The *Libri Carolini* and the Image Controversy." *Greek Orthodox Theological Review* 18 (1973): 7–34.

Giakalis, Ambrosios. *Images of the Divine: The Theology of Icons at the Seventh Ecumenical Council.* Studies in the History of Christian Thought 54. Leiden, 1994.

Gill, J. "The Life of Stephen the Younger by Stephen the Deacon: Debts and Loans." *Orientalia Christiana Periodica* 6 (1940): 14–139.

Godman, Peter. *Poets and Emperors: Frankish Politics and Carolingian Poetry.* Oxford, 1987.

―――. *Poetry of the Carolingian Renaissance.* London, 1985.

Goldberg, Eric J. *Struggle for Empire: Kingship and Conflict under Louis the German, 817–876.* Ithaca, 2006.

Goldschmidt, Adolf. *Die Elfenbeinskulpturen aus der Zeit der karolingischen und sächsischen Kaiser.* 4 vols. Berlin, 1914–26.

Goll, Jürg, Matthias Exner, and Susanne Hirsch. *Müstair: Die mittelalterlichen Wandbilder in der Klosterkirche.* Munich, 2007.

Gorman, Michael. "Wigbod and Biblical Studies under Charlemagne." RB 107 (1997): 40–76.

―――. "The Commentary on Genesis of Claudius of Turin and Biblical Studies under Louis the Pious." *Speculum* 72 (1997): 279–329.

―――. "The Commentary on Kings of Claudius of Turin and Its Two Printed Editions." *Filologia mediolatina* 4 (1997): 99–131.

Gough, Michael. *The Origins of Christian Art.* New York, 1973.

Gouillard, Jean. "L'église d'Orient et le primauté romaine au temps de l'iconoclasme." *Istina* 21 (1976): 25–54.

―――. "Aux origines de l'iconoclasme: Le témoinage de Gregoire III?" T&M 3 (1968): 276–305.

―――. "L'hérésie dans l'empire byzantin des origines au XIIe siècle." T&M 1 (1965): 299–324.

Grabar, André. "L'Asymétrie des relations de Byzance et de l'Occident dans le domaine des arts au moyen age." In Irmgard Hutler, ed., *Byzanz und der Westen: Studien zur Kunst des europäischen Mittelalters*, pp. 9–24. Österreichische Akademie der Wissenschaften, phil.-kist. Klasse, Sitzungberichte 432. Vienna, 1984.

―――. *Christian Iconography: A Study of Its Origins.* Bollingen Series 35. Princeton, 1968.

―――. "Le portrait en iconographic paléochrétienne." *Revue des sciences religieuses* 36 (1962): 87–109.

―――. *L'iconoclasme byzantin: dossier archéologique.* Paris, 1957.

Graboïs, Aryeh. "Charlemagne, Rome, and Jerusalem." *Revue belge de philologie et d'histoire* 59 (1981): 792–809.

Graf, Georg. *Geschichte der christlichen arabischen Literatur.* Vol. 1. Vatican City, 1944.

Grape, Wolfgang. "Karolingische Kunst und Ikonoklasmus." AK 45 (1974): 49–58.

Gray, N. "The Paleography of Latin Inscriptions in the Eighth, Ninth, and Tenth Centuries in Italy." PBSR 16 (1948): 38–170.

Gray, Patrick. "The Select Fathers: Canonizing the Patristic Past." *Studia Patristica* 23 (1989): 21–36.

Grierson, Philip and Mark Blackburn. *Medieval European Coinage.* Vol. 1. Cambridge, 1986.

Griffith, Sidney H. "Theodore abū Qurrah's Arabic Tract on the Christian Practice of Venerating Images." *Journal of the American Oriental Society* 105 (1985): 53–73.

Grigg, Robert. "Constantine the Great and the Cult without Images." *Viator* 8 (1977): 1–32.

―――. "Aniconic Worship and the Apostolic Tradition: A Note on Canon 36 of Elvira." *Church History* 45 (1976): 428–33.

Grimme, Ernst Günther. "Novus Constantinus: Die Gestalt Konstantins des Großen in der imperialen Kunst der mittelalterlichen Kaiserzeit." AK 22 (1961): 7–20.

Grisar, Hartmann, S.J. *Die römische Kapelle Sancta Sanctorum und ihr Schatz*. Freiburg im Breisgau, 1908.

Grotz, Hans. "Die früheste römische Stellungnahme gegen die Bildersturm (Eine These, die es zu beweisen gilt)." AHC 20 (1988): 150–61.

———. "Weitere Beobachtungen zu den zwei Briefen Papst Gregors II. an Kaiser Leo III." AHP 24 (1986): 365–75.

———. "Beobachtungen zu den zwei Briefen Papst Gregors II. an Kaiser Leo III." AHP 18 (1980): 9–40.

Grumel, Venance. "Les relations politico-religieuses entre Byzance et Rome sous le regne de Léon V L'Arménien." REB 18 (1960): 19–44.

———. *Les regestes des actes du patriarchat de Constantinople*. Vol. 1, Les actes des patriarches, fasc. 2, Les regestes de 715 à 1043. Paris, 1936.

———. "Quelques témoinages byzantines sur la primauté romaine." *Echos d'Orient* 30 (1931): 422–30.

———. "L'iconologie de St. Théodore Studite." *Echos d'Orient* 20 (1921): 257–68.

Guerreau-Jalabert, Anita. "La 'Renaissance carolingienne': Modèles culturels, usages linguistiques et structures sociales." *Bibliothèque de l'École des Chartes* 139 (1982): 5–35.

Guillou, Abdré. "Le monde des images à Byzance." In Guillou and Durand, eds., *Byzance et les images*, pp. 13–39.

Guillou, André, and Jannic Durand, eds. *Byzance et les images*. Paris, 1994.

Gundlach, Wilhelm. "Über den Codex Carolinus." *Neues Archiv* 17 (1892): 525–66.

Gurevich, A. J. *Categories of Medieval Culture*. London, 1985.

Gutmann, Joseph, ed. *The Image and the Word: Confrontations in Judaism, Christianity and Islam*. Missoula, 1977.

Haendler, Gert. "De byzantinische Bilderstreit und das Abendland 815–825." In Helga Köpstein and Friedhelm Winkelmann, eds., *Studien zum 8. und 9. Jahrhundert in Byzanz*, pp. 159–62. Berliner byzantinistische Arbeiten 51. Berlin, 1981.

———. "Kirchenpolitische Rückwirkungen des byzantinischen Bilderstreites auf das Papsttum bis zur Frankfurter Synode 794." In Johannes Irmscher, ed., *Der byzantinische Bilderstreit: Sozialokonomische Voraussetzungen, ideologische Grundlagen, geschichtliche Wickungen*, pp. 130–48. Leipzig, 1980.

———. *Epochen karolingischer Theologie*. Theologische Arbeiten 10. Leipzig, 1958.

Hägermann, Dieter. *Karl der Grosse: Herrscher des Abendlandes*. Munich, 2000.

Hainthaler, Theresia. "Von Toledo nach Frankfurt: Dogmengeschichtliche Untersuchungen zur adoptianistischen Kontroverse." In Berndt, ed., *Das Frankfurter Konzil*, pp. 809–60.

Haldon, John. *Byzantium in the Seventh Century: The Transformation of a Culture*. Cambridge, 1990.

———. "Some Remarks on the Background to the Iconoclastic Controversy." *Byzantinoslavica* 38 (1977): 161–84.

Haldon, John, and Bryan Ward-Perkins, "Evidence from Rome for the Image of Christ on the Chalke Gate in Constantinople." BMGS 23 (1999): 286–96.

Haller, Johannes. *Das Papsttum*. Vols. 1 and 2. Basel, 1951.

Hampe, Karl. "Hadrians I. Vertheidigung der zweiten nicaenischen Synode gegen die Angriffe Karls des Großen." *Neues Archiv* 21 (1896): 83–113.

Harnack, Adolf. *History of Dogma*. Trans. Neil Buchanan. Vol. 4. New York, 1961.

Harrison, Carol. *Beauty and Revelation in the Thought of Saint Augustine*. Oxford, 1992.

Hartenstein, F. "Die unvergleichliche 'Gestalt' JHWHs: Israels Gesichte mit den Bildern im Licht von Dtn. 4, 1–14." In Janowski and Zchomelidse, eds., *Die Sichtbarkeit des Unsichtbaren*, pp. 49–77.

Hartmann, Florian. *Hadrian I (772–795): Frühmittelalterliches Adelspapsttum und die Lösung Roms vom byzantinischen Kaiser*. Päpste und Papsttum 34. Stuttgart, 2006.

Hartmann, Wilfried "Das Konzil von Frankfurt 794: Nachwirkung und Nachleben." In Berndt, ed., *Das Konzil von Frankfurt*, pp. 331–56

———. *Die Synoden der Karolingerzeit im Frankreich und in Italien*. Paderborn, 1989.

———. "Das Konzil von Frankfurt 794 und Nizäa 787." AHC 20 (1988): 307–24.

———. "Die karolingische Reform und die Bibel." AHC 18 (1986): 58–74.

Hauck, Albert. *Kirchengeschichte Deutschlands*. 5th ed. Pt. 2. Leipzig, 1935.

Hauck, Karl. "Von einer spätantiken Randkultur zum karolingischen Europa." FMSt 1 (1967): 3–93.

Haugh, Richard. *Photius and the Carolingians: The Trinitarian Controversy*. Belmont, Mass., 1975.

Heath, R. G. "The Western Schism of the Franks and the 'Filioque.'" *Journal of Ecclesiastical History* 23 (1972): 97–113.

Hefele, Charles Joseph and Henri Leclercq. *Histoire des conciles*. Vol. 3, pt. 2. Paris, 1910.

Heidrich, Ingrid. "Syrische Kirchengemeinden im Frankenreich des 6. Jahrhunderts." In Hubert Mordek, ed., *Aus Archiven und Bibliotheken: Festschrift für Raymund Kottje zum 65. Geburtstag*, pp. 21–32. Freiburger Berträge zur mittelalterlichen Geschichte 3. Frankfurt, 1992.

Heil, Johannes. "Claudius von Turin—eine Fallstudie zur Geschichte der Karolingerzeit." *Zeitschrift für Geschichtswissenschaft* 45 (1997): 389–412.

Heitz, Carol. *Recherches sur les rapports entre architecture et liturgie à l'époque carolingienne*. Paris, 1963.

———. "L'image du Christ entre 780 et 810: Une éclipse?" In Boespflug and Lossky, eds., *Nicée II*, pp. 229–46.

———. "More romano: Problèmes d'architecture et liturgie carolingiennes." In *Roma e l'età carolingia*, pp. 27–37.

Hen, Yitzhak. *The Royal Patronage of Liturgy in Frankish Gaul*. The Henry Bradshaw Society, Subsidia 3. London, 2001.

Henderson, George. *Bede and the Visual Arts*. Jarrow Lecture. Newcastle, 1980.

———. *Early Medieval*. Medieval Academy Reports for Teaching 29. Toronto, 1993.

Henry, Patrick. "Images of the Church in the Second Nicene Council and in the *Libri Carolini*." In Kenneth Pennington and Robert Somerville, eds., *Law, Church, and Society: Essays in Honor of Stephan Kuttner*, pp. 237–52. Philadelphia, 1977.

———. "What Was the Iconoclastic Controversy About?" *Church History* 45 (1976): 16–31.

———. "Initial Eastern Assessments of the Seventh Oecumenical Council." JTS 25 (1974): 75–92.

———. "The Moechian Controversy and the Constantinopolitan Synod of A.D. 809." JTS 20 (1969): 495–522.

Herklotz, Ingo. "Der Campus Lateranensis im Mittelalter." *Römisches Jahrbuch für Kunstgeschichte* 22 (1985): 1–42.

Herrin, Judith. *Women in Purple: Rulers of Medieval Byzantium.* Princeton, 2001.

———. *The Formation of Christendom.* Princeton, 1987.

———. "Women and Faith in Icons in Early Christianity." In R. Samuel and Gareth Stedman Jones, eds., *Culture, Ideology and Politics,* pp. 56–83. London, 1982.

———. "Constantinople, Rome and the Franks in the Seventh and Eighth Centuries." In Shepard and Franklin, eds., *Byzantine Diplomacy,* pp. 91–107.

Hiltbrunner, Otto. "Die Heiligkeit des Kaisers." FMSt 2 (1968): 1–30.

Holder, Arthur G. "New Treasures and Old in Bede's 'De Tabernaculo' and 'De Templo.'" RB 99 (1989): 237–49.

Holl, Karl. "Die Schriften des Epiphanios gegen die Bilderverehrung." In his *Gesammelte Aufsätze zur Kirchengeschichte,* vol. 2, pp. 351–64. Tübingen, 1928.

———. "Die Anteil der Styliten am Aufkommen der Bilderverehrung," In his *Gesammelte Aufsätze zur Kirchengeschichte,* vol. 2, pp. 388–98. Tübingen, 1928.

Hopkins, Keith. *A World Full of Gods: Pagans, Jews, and Christians in the Roman Empire.* London, 1999.

Hossfeld, F.-L. "Das Werden des alttestamentlichen Bilderverbotes im Kontext von Archäologie, Rechtsentwicklung und Prophetie. Thesen." In Janowski and Zchomelidse, eds., *Die Sichtbarkeit des Unsichtbaren,* pp. 11–22.

———. "'Du sollst dir kein Bild machen!' Funktion des alttestamentlichen Bilderverbots." In Josef Wohlmuth, ed., *Streit um des Bild: Das zweite Konzil Nikäa (787) in ökumenischer Perspektive,* pp. 15–24. Studium Universale 9. Bonn, 1989.

Hubert, Jean, Jean Porcher, and W. F. Volbach. *Carolingian Art.* London, 1970.

Hugot, Leo. "Die Königshalle Karls des Großen in Aachen." AK 30 (1965): 38–48.

Hussey, Joan. *The Orthodox Church in the Byzantine Empire.* Oxford, 1990.

Huxley, George. "On the *Vita* of St. Stephen the Younger." *Greek, Roman and Byzantine Studies* 18 (1977): 97–108.

Ihm, Christina. *Die Programm der christlichen Apsismalerei vom 4. Jahrhundert bis zur Mitte des 8. Jahrhunderts.* 2nd ed. Stuttgart, 1992.

Irmscher, Johannes ed. *Der byzantinische Bilderstreit: Sozialokonomische Voraussetzungen, ideologische Grundlagen, geschichtliche Wirkungen.* Leipzig, 1980.

Iogna-Prat, Dominique, Eric Palazzo, and Daniel Russo, eds. *Marie: Le culte de la vierge dans la société médiévale.* Paris, 1996.

Jacobsen, Werner. "Gab es die karolingische 'Renaissance' in der Baukunst?" *Zeitschrift für Kunstsgeschichte* 51 (1988): 336–57.

Jaffé, Phillip. *Regesta Pontificum Romanorum.* 2nd ed. by S. Loewenfeld, F. Kaltenbrunner, and P. Ewald. Vol. 1. Leipzig, 1885.

James, M. R. *The Apocryphal New Testament.* Oxford, 1960.

Janowski, Bernd, and Nino Zchomelidse, eds. *Die Sichtbarkeit des Unsichtbaren: Zur Korrelation von Text und Bild in Wirkungskreis der Bibel.* Stuttgart, 2003.

Jarnut, Jörg. "Kaiser Ludwig der Fromme und König Berhnard von Italien." *Studi Medievali,* 3rd ser., 30 (1989): 637–48.

Janes, Dominic. *God and Gold in Late Antiquity.* Cambridge, 1998.

Jeck, Udo Reinhold. "Die frühmittelalterliche Rezeption der Zeittheorie Augustins in den *Libri Carolini* und die Temporalität des Kultbildes." In Berndt, ed., *Das Frankfurter Konzil,* pp. 861–84.

———. "Gott in der Materie darstellen? Zum Grundverständnis des Kultbildes in *Libri Carolini.*" *Hermeneia* 9 (1993): 95–108.

———. "Prototyp—Ikone—Relation." *Hermeneia* 9 (1993): 206–14.

Jensen, Robin Margaret. *Understanding Early Christian Art.* London, 2000.

Jevtič, Athanasijè. "L'Icône et L'Incarnation." AHC 20 (1988): 162–70.

Kaczynski, Bernice. *Greek in the Carolingian Age: The St. Gall Manuscripts.* Speculum Anniversary Monographs 13. Cambridge, Mass., 1988.

Kampers, Franz. "Rex et Sacerdos." *Historisches Jahrbuch* 45 (1925): 495–515.

Karl der Grosse: Werk und Wirkung. Aachen, 1965.

Kartsonis, Anna. "The Emancipation of the Crucifixion." In Guillou and Durand, eds., *Byzance et les images,* pp. 151–87.

Kazhdan, Alexander. "The Notion of Byzantine Diplomacy." In Shepard and Franklin, eds., *Byzantine Diplomacy,* pp. 3–21.

Kazhdan, A. P. and A. M. Talbot. "Women and Iconoclasm." BZ 84/5 (1991/92): 391–408.

Kazhdan, Alexander and Henry Maguire. "Byzantine Hagiographical Texts as Sources on Art." DOP 45 (1991): 1–22.

Keefe, Susan A. *Water and the Word: Baptism and the Education of the Clergy in Carolingian Europe.* 2 vols. Notre Dame, 2002.

Kennedy, Kevin. "The Permanence of an Idea: Three Ninth-Century Frankish Ecclesiastics and the Authority of the Roman See." In Hubert Mordek, ed., *Aus Kirche und Reich: Studien zu Theologie, Politik und Recht im Mittelalter: Festschrift für Friedrich Kempf,* pp. 105–16. Sigmaringen, 1983.

Kessler, Herbert L. "Images of Christ and Communication with God." SSCI 52 (2005): 1099–1136.

———. "'Facies Bibliothecae Revelata': Carolingian Art as Spiritual Seeing." SSCI 41 (1994): 533–84.

———. "'Pictures Fertile with Truth:' How Christians Managed to Make Images of God Without Violating the Second Commandment." *Journal of the Walters Art Gallery* 49/50 (1991/92): 53–65.

———. "An Apostle in Armor and the Mission of Carolingian Art." *Arte medievale,* 2nd ser., 4 (1990): 17–39

———. "Through the Temple Veil: The Holy Image in Judaism and Christianity." *Kairos* 32/33 (1990/91): 53–77.

———. "On the State of Medieval Art History." AB 70 (1988): 166–87.

———. "Pictorial Narrative and Church Mission in Sixth-Century Gaul." In Kessler and

Marianne Schreve, eds., *Pictorial Narrative in Antiquity and the Middle Ages*, pp. 75–91. Studies in the History of Art 16. Washington, D.C., 1985.

——. *The Illustrated Bibles from Tours*. Studies in Manuscript Illumination 7. Princeton, 1977.

Kilerich, Bente. "Sculpture in the Round in the early Byzantine Period: Constantinople and the East." In Rydén and Rosenqvist, eds., *Aspects of Late Antiquity*, pp. 85–97.

Kitzinger, Ernst. "Römische Malerei vom Beginn des 7. bis zur Mitte des 8. Jahrhundert." Reprinted in his *Studies in Late Antique Byzantine and Medieval Western Art*, vol. 2, pp. 829–85. London, 2003.

——. "Byzantine Art in the Period Between Justinian and Iconoclasm." *Berichte zum XI. Internationalen Byzantinisten Kongress*, vol. 4, pp. 1–50. Munich, 1958.

——. "On Some Icons of the Seventh Century." In Weitzmann, ed., *Late Classical and Medieval Studies in Honor of Albert Mathias Friend, Jr.*, pp. 132–50.

——. "The Cult of Images in the Age Before Iconoclasm." DOP 8 (1954): 83–150.

Klauser, Theodor. "Rom und der Kult der Gottesmutter Maria." *Jahrbuch für Antike und Christentum* 15 (1972): 120–35.

——. "Eine Stationsliste der Metzer Kirche aus dem 8. Jahrhundert, wahrscheinlich ein Werk Chrodegangs." *Ephemerides Liturgicae* 44 (1930): 162–93.

——. "Notes sur l'ancienne liturgie de Metz." *Annuaire de le Société d'histoire et d'archéologie de la Lorraine* 38 (1929): 497–510.

Knabe, Lotte. *Die gelasianische Zweigewaltentheorie bis zum Ende des Investiturstreits.* Historische Studien 292. Berlin, 1936.

Knögel, Elsmarie. *Schriftquellen zur Kunstgeschichte der Merowingerzeit.* Bonner Jahrbücher des rheinischen Landesmuseums in Bonn und des Altertumsfreunde im Rheinlande 140/41. Darmstadt, 1936.

Koch, Hugo. *Die altchristliche Bilderfrage nach den literarischen Quellen.* Göttingen, 1917.

Koehler, Wilhelm. *Die Karolingischen Miniaturen.* Dritter Band: Erster Teil: Die Gruppe des Wiener Krönungs-Evangeliars Zweiter Teil: Metzer Hanschriften. Berlin, 1960.

——. *Die Karolingischen Miniaturen. Vol. 2: Die Hofschule Karls des Grossen.* Berlin, 1958.

Kollwitz, Johannes. *Das Gottesbild im Abendland.* Glaube und Forschung 13. Witten, 1957.

——. "Zur Frühgeschichte der Bilderverehrung." In his *Das Gottesbild im Abendland*, pp. 52–76. Glaube und Forschung 13. Witten, 1957.

——. "Bild und bildertheologie imMittelalter." In his *Das Gottesbild im Abendland*, pp. 109–38. Glaube und Forschung 13. Witten, 1957.

Konstantinides, Chrysostomos. "Die Theologie der Ikone." AHC 20 (1988): 42–52.

Kottje, Raymund. "Kirchliches Recht und päpsticher Autoritätsanspruch. Zu den Auseinandersetzung über die Ehe Lothars II." In Mordek, ed., *Aus Kirche und Reich*, pp. 97–103.

——. "Einheit und Vielfalt des kirchliche Lebens in der Karolingerzeit." ZKG 76 (1965): 323–42.

Kotzur, Hans-Jürgen, ed. *Rabanus Maurus: Auf den Spuren eines karolingischen Gelehrten.* Mainz, 2006.

Krautheimer, Richard. *Rome: Profile of a City, 312–1308.* Princeton, 1980.

——. "The Carolingian Revival of Early Christian Architecture." *Art Bulletin* 24 (1942).

Repr. in his *Studies in Early Christian, Medieval and Renaissance Art*, pp. 203–56. New York, 1969.

Ladner, Gerhart. "The Concept of the Image in the Greek Fathers and the Byzantine Iconoclastic Controversy." DOP 7 (1953): 1–34.

————. *Die Papstbildnisse des Altertum und des Mittelalters*. Vol. 1. Monumenta di antichità cristiana, 4. Rome, 1941.

————. "Origin and Significance of the Byzantine Iconoclastic Controversy." *Mediaeval Studies* 2 (1940): 127–49.

————. "I moasici e gli affreschi ecclesiastico-politici nell'antico palazzo lateranense." *Rivista di archeologia cristiana* 12 (1935): 265–92.

————. "Der Bilderstreit und die Kunst-Lehren der byzantinischen und abendländischen Theologie." ZKG 50 (1931): 1–23.

Lahne, Emmanuel. "Rome et les images saintes." *Irénikon* 59 (1986): 163–88.

Laistner, M. L. W., and H. H. King. *A Hand-List of Bede Manuscripts*. Ithaca, 1943.

Lamberz, Erich. "Studien zur Überlieferung der Akten des VII. Ökumenischen Konzils: Der Brief Hadrians I. an Konstantin VI und Irene (JE 2448)." DA 53 (1997): 1–43.

Lammers, Walter. "Ein karolingisches Bildprogramm in der Aula Regia von Ingelheim." In *Festschrift für Hermann Heimpel zum 70. Geburtstag am 19. September 1971*, vol. 3, pp. 226–89. Göttingen, 1972.

Lampe, G. W. *A Patristic Greek Lexicon*. Oxford, 1961.

Landes, Richard. "Lest the Millennium Be Fulfilled: Apocalyptic Expectations and the Pattern of Western Chronography 100–800CE." In Werner Verbeke, Daniel Verhelst, and Anders Welkenhuysen, eds., *The Use and Abuse of Eschatology in the Middle Ages*, pp. 137–211. Leuven, 1988.

Lange, Günter. *Bild und Wort: Die katachetische Funktion des Bildes in der griechischen Theologie des sechsten bis neunten Jahrhunderts*. Schriften der Religionspädogogik und Kerygmatik 6. Würzburg, 1969.

Lanne, Emmanuel. "Rome et Nicée II." In Boespflug and Lossky, *Nicée II*, pp. 219–28.

————. "Rome et les images saintes." *Irénikon* 59 (1986): 163–88.

Lawrence, Maria. "Maria Regina." AB 7 (1925): 150–61.

Lemerle, Paul. *Le premier humanisme byzantin: Notes et remarques sur l'enseignement et culture à Byzance des origines au Xe siècle*. Paris, 1971.

Leonardi, Claudio. "Dungal." LMA 3 (1985): 1456–57.

————. "Claudius von Turin." LMA 2 (1983): 2132–33.

————. "Gli Irlandesi in Italia: Dungal e la controversia iconoclastica." In Heinz Löwe, ed., *Die Iren und Europa im früheren Mittelalter*, pp. 746–57. Stuttgart, 1982.

————. "Alcuino e la scuola palatina: le ambizioni di una cultura unitaria." SSCI 27 (1981): 459–96.

Levison, Wilhelm. *England and the Continent in the Eighth Century*. Oxford, 1946.

Levison, Wilhelm, and Heinz Löwe. *Deutschlands Geschichtsquellen im Mittelalter. Vorzeit und Karolinger*. 2 Heft: *Die Karolinger vom Anfang des 8. Jahrhunderts bis zum Tod Karls des Grossen*. Weimar, 1953.

Lewis, Suzanne. "A Byzantine 'Virgo Militans' at Charlemagne's Court." *Viator* 11 (1980): 71–93.

Lifshitz, Felice. *The Name of the Saint: The Martyrology of Jerome and Access to the Sacred in Francia, 627–827.* Notre Dame, 2006.

Lilie, Ralph-Johannes, ed. *Die Patriarchen der ikonolastichsen Zeit.* Berliner byzantinische Studien 5. Frankfurt, 1999.

———. "Paulos IV." In his *Die Patriarchen,* pp. 50–56.

Llewellyn, Peter. "The Popes and the Constitution in the Eighth Century." EHR 101 (1986): 42–65.

Lombard, Alfred. *Constantin V, empereur des Romains (740–775).* Université de Paris, Bibliothèque de la faculté des lettres 16. Paris, 1902.

Loos, Milan. "Einige strittige Fragen der ikonoklastischen Ideologie." In Helga Köpstein and Friedhelm Windelmann, eds., *Studien zum 8. und 9. Jahrhundert in Byzanz,* pp. 131–51. Berliner byzantinistische Arbeiten 51. Berlin, 1983.

Louth, Andrew. *St. John Damascene: Tradition and Originality in Byzantine Theology.* Oxford, 2002.

———. "'Truly Visible Things Are Manifest Images of Invisible Things': Dionysius the Areopagite on Knowing the Invisible." In de Nie et al., eds., *Seeing the Invisible,* pp. 15–24.

Lowden, John. *Early Christian and Byzantine Art.* London, 1997.

Löwe, Heinz. *Deutschlands Geschichtsquellen im Mittelalter. Vorzeit und Karolinger:* Vol. 3, *Die Karolinger vom Tode Karls des Grossenbis zum vertrag von Verdun.* Weimar, 1957.

———. *Von Theoderich dem Grossen zu Karl dem Grossen.* Darmstadt, 1956.

Ludwig, Claudia and Thomas Pratsch. "Tarasios (784–806)." In Lilie, ed., *Die Patriarchen,* pp. 57–108.

Maas, Paul. "Die ikonoklastische Episode in dem Brief Epiphanios und Johannes." BZ 30 (1929/30): 279–86.

Maccarrone, Michele. "Il papa Adriano I e il concilio di Nicea del 787." In his *Romana ecclesia cathedra Petri,* ed. Piero Zerbi et al., pp. 433–540. Italia Sacra 47. Rome, 1991.

MacMullen, Ramsay. *Paganism in the Roman Empire.* New Haven, 1981.

Maguire, Eunice Dauterman, Henry Maguire, and Maggie J. Duncan-Flowers. *Art and Holy Powers in the Early Christian House.* Illinois Byzantine Studies 2. Urbana, 1989.

Maguire, Henry and Eunice Dauterman Maguire. *Other Icons: Art and Power in Byzantine Secular Culture.* Princeton, 2007.

Maguire, Henry. *The Icons of Their Bodies: Saints and Their Images in Byzantium.* Princeton, 1996.

———. *Art and Eloquence in Byzantium.* Princeton, 1981.

Mahé, Jean-Pierre. "L'Église arménienne de 611 à 1066." In Mayeur et al., *Histoire du Christianisme,* pp. 457–547.

Mainka, Rudolf M. "Zum Brief des Patriarchen Nicephoros I. von Konstantinopel an Papst Leo III." *Ostkirchliche Studien* 13 (1964): 273–81.

Mango, Cyril. *The Art of the Byzantine Empire, 312–1453.* Toronto, 1986.

———. "Constantinople as Theotokoupolis." In Vassilaki, ed., *Mother of God,* pp. 17–25.

———. "A Byzantine Hagiographer at Work: Leontios of Neapolis." In Irmgard Hutter, ed., *Byzanz und der Westen: Studien zur kunst des europäischen Mittelalters,* pp. 25–41.

Osterreichische Akademie der Wissenschaften, phil.-hist. klasse, Sitzungsberichte 432. Vienna, 1984.

———. "St. Anthusia of Mantineon and the Family of Constantine V." AnBol 100 (1982): 401–9.

———. "Historical Introduction." In Bryer and Herrin, eds., *Iconoclasm*, pp. 1–6.

———. "The Availability of Books in the Byzantine Empire, A.D. 750–850." In *Byzantine Books and Bookmen*, pp. 29–45. Dumbarton Oaks Colloquium, 1971.

———. *The Brazen House: A Study of the Vestibule of the Imperial Palace of Constantinople*. Copenhagen, 1959. Washington, D.C., 1975.

Manitius, Max. *Geschichte der lateinischen Literatur des Mittelalters, Erster Teil: von Justinian bis zur Mitte des zehnten Jahrhunderts*. Munich, 1911.

Maraval, Pierre. "Épiphane, 'docteur des iconoclastes.'" In Boespflug and Lossky, eds., *Nicée II*, pp. 51–62.

Marenbon, John. *From the Circle of Alcuin to the School of Auxerre: Logic, Theology and Philosophy in the Early Middle Ages*. Cambridge Studies in Medieval Life and Thought, 3rd ser., 15. Cambridge, 1981.

———. "Alcuin, the Council of Frankfort and the Beginnings of Medieval Philosophy." In Berndt, ed., *Das Frankfurter Konzil*, pp. 603–16.

Markus, Robert. *Saeculum: History and Society in the Theology of St. Augustine*. Rev. ed. Cambridge, 1988.

———. "The Latin Fathers." In J. H. Burns, ed., *The Cambridge History of Medieval Political Thought*, pp. 92–122. Cambridge, 1988.

———. "Gregory the Great's Europe." *Transactions of the Royal Historical Society*, 5th ser., 31 (1981): 21–36.

———. "The Cult of Icons in Sixth-Century Gaul." JTS 29 (1978): 1151–57.

———. "Papal Primacy: The Early Middle Ages." *The Month* 229 (1970): 352–61.

———. "Papacy and Hierarchy." In Robert Markus and Eric John, eds., *Papacy and Hierarchy*, pp. 1–50. London, 1969.

Martin, Edward James. *A History of the Iconoclastic Controversy*. London, 1930.

Martin, Thomas. "Bemerkungen zur 'Epistola de litteris colendis.'" *Archiv für Diplomatik* 31 (1985): 227–72.

Mathews, Thomas C. *The Clash of Gods: A Reinterpretation of Early Christian Art*. Princeton, 1993.

Matter, E. Ann. "Theological Freedom in the Carolingian Age: The Case of Claudius of Turin." In *The Concept of Freedom in the Middle Ages: Islam, Byzantium and the West*, pp. 51–60. Penn-Paris-Dumbarton Oaks Colloquia 4. Paris, 1985.

Matthiae, Guglielmo. *Pittura politica del medioevo romano*. Rome, 1964.

———. "La capella di Teodoto." In *Pittura del medioevo secoli IV–X*, vol. 1, pp. 138–47. Rome, 1987.

Mayeur, Jean-Marie, Charles and Luce Pietri, André Vauchez, and Marc Venard, eds. *Histoire du Christianisme*. Vol. 4, *Évêques, moines et empereurs (610–1054)*. Paris, 1993.

Mayr-Harting, Henry. "Charlemagne as a Patron of Art." In Diana Wood, ed., *The Church and the Arts*, pp. 43–77. SCH 28. Oxford, 1992.

McClendon, Charles B. *The Origins of Medieval Architecture.* New Haven, 2005.

———. "Louis the Pious, Rome, and Constantinople." In Cecil L. Striker, ed., *Architectural Studies in Honor of Richard Krautheimer,* pp. 103–6. Mainz, 1997.

McCormick, Michael. *The Origins of the European Economy: Communications and Commerce AD 300–900.* Cambridge, 2001.

———. "Paderborn 799: Königliche Repräsentation—Visualisierung eines Herrschaftskonzepts," pp. 71–81. In Stiegemann and Wemhoff, eds. *Kunst und Kultur der Karolingerzeit.*

———. *Eternal Victory.* Cambridge, 1986.

———. "Byzantium and the West." In McKitterick, ed., *The New Cambridge Medieval History,* vol. 2, pp. 349–80.

———. "Textes, images et iconoclasme dans le cadre des relations entre Byzance et l'occident carolingien." SSCI 41 (1994): 95–158.

McKitterick, Rosamond. *Perceptions of the Past in the Early Middle Ages.* The Conway Lectures in Medieval Studies 2004. Notre Dame, Ind., 2006.

McKitterick, Rosamond. *History and Memory in the Carolingian World.* Cambridge, 2005.

———. "History, Law and Communication with the Past in the Carolingian period." SSCI 52 (2005): 941–79.

———. *History and Its Audiences.* Inaugural Lecture, University of Cambridge, 2000. Cambridge, 2000.

———. "Das Konzil im Kontext der karolingischen Renaissance." In Berndt, ed., *Das Frankfurter Konzil,* pp. 671–34.

———, ed. *The New Cambridge Medieval History.* Vol. 2. Cambridge, 1995.

———, ed. *Carolingian Culture: Emulation and Innovation.* Cambridge, 1994.

———. "Text and Image in the Carolingian World." In her *The Uses of Literacy in Early Mediaeval Europe,* pp. 319–33. Cambridge, 1990.

———. "Carolingian Book Production: Some Problems." *The Library,* 6th ser., 12 (1990): 1–33.

———. *The Carolingians and the Written Word.* Cambridge, 1989.

———. *The Frankish Church and the Carolingian Reforms, 789–895.* London, 1977.

Melloni, Alberto. "L'Opus Caroli Magni contra Synodum' o 'Libri Carolini.'" *Studi Medievali,* 3rd ser., 29 (1988): 871–86.

Melograni, Anna. "Le pitture del VI e VIII secolo nella basilica inferiore di S. Crisogono in Trastevere." *Rivista dell'Istituto nazionale d'archeologia e storia dell'arte,* 3rd ser., 13 (1990): 139–78.

Menis, Gian Carlo ed. *I Longobardi.* Milan, 1990.

Mercati, Angelo. "Per la storia del codice Vaticano dei Libri Carolini." *Bessarione* 37 (1921): 112–19.

Metzler, Dieter. "Bilderstürme und Bilderfeindlichkeit in der Antike." In Marten Warnke, ed., *Bildersturm: Die Zerstörung des Kunstwerks,* pp. 14–29. Munich, 1973.

Meyendorff, John. *Imperial Unity and Christian Divisions: The Church 450–680 A.D.* Crestwood, N.Y., 1989.

———. *Byzantine Theology.* New York, 1974.

———. "L'image du Christ d'après Théodore Studite." In *Synthronon: Art et archéologie de la fin de l'Antiquité et du Moyen Age,* pp. 115–17. Bibliothèque des Cahiers Archéologiques 2. Paris, 1968.

Meyvaert, Paul. "Discovering the Calendar (*Annalis Libellus*) Attached to Bede's Own Copy of the *De temporum ratione.*" AnBol 120 (2002): 5–64.

———. "The Authorship of the *Libri Carolini*: Observations Prompted by a Recent Book." RB 89 (1979): 29–57.

———. "Bede and the Church Paintings at Wearmouth Jarrow." *Anglo-Saxon England* 8 (1979): 63–77.

Michel, Anton. "Die Kaisermacht in der Ostkirche (843–1204)," *Ostkirchliche Studien* 2 (1953): 1–35.

Michels, Helmut. "Zur Echtheit der Briefe Papst Gregors II. an Kaiser Leo III." ZKG 99 (1988): 376–91.

Miles, Margaret R. *Image as Insight: Visual Understanding in Western Christianity and Secular Culture.* Boston, 1985.

Miller, Patricia Cox. *Dreams in Late Antiquity: Studies in the Imagination of Culture.* Princeton, 1994.

———. "Relics, Rhetoric, and Mental Spectacles in Late Christian Antiquity." In de Nie et al., eds., *Seeing the Invisible in Late Antiquity and the Early Middle Ages,* pp. 25–52.

Minazzoli, Agnès. " 'Imago'/'Icona': Esquisse d'une problematique." In Boespflug and Lossky, eds., *Nicée II,* pp. 313–16.

Mitalaité, Kristina. *Philosophie et théologie de l'image dans les* Libri Carolini. Collection des Études Augustiniennes, Série Moyen Âge et Temps Modernes 43. Paris, 2007.

Mohr, Walter. *Die karolingische Reichsidee.* Münster, 1962.

Momigliano, Arnaldo. "Pagan and Christian Historiography in the Fourth Century A.D." In his *Essays in Ancient and Modern Historiography*, pp. 107–26. Middletown, Conn., 1982.

Moorhead, John. "Iconoclasm, the Cross and the Imperial Image." *Byzantion* 55 (1985): 165–79.

Mordek, Hubert, "Aachen, Frankfurt, Reims. Beobachtungen zu Genese und Tradition des *Capitulare Francofurtense.*" In Berndt, ed., *Das Frankfurter Konzil,* pp. 125–48.

———, ed. *Aus Archiven und Bibliotheken: Festschrift für Raymund Kottje zum 65. Geburtstag.* Freiburger Beiträge zur mittelalterlichen Geschichte 3. Frankfurt, 1992.

———. "Rom, Byzanz und die Franken im 8. Jahrhundert: Zur Überlieferung und kirchenpolitischen Bedeutung der Synodus Romana papst Gregors III. vom Jahre 732 (mit Edition)." In Gerd Althoff, ed., *Personen und Gemeinschaft im Mittelalter: Karl Schmid zum fünf und sechsigsten Geburtstag,* pp. 123–56. Sigmaringen, 1988.

———, ed. *Aus Kirche und Reich: Studien zu Theologie, Politik und Recht im Mittelalter: Festschrift für Friedrich Kempf.* Sigmaringen, 1983.

———. "Kirchenrechtliche Autoritäten im Frühmittelalter." In Peter Classen, ed., *Recht und Schrift in Mittelalter,* pp. 237–55. Vorträge und Forschungen 23. Sigmaringen, 1977.

Morrison, Karl F. "Anthropology and the Use of Religious Images in the *Opus Caroli Regis* (*Libri Carolini*)." In Jeffrey Hamburger and Anne-Marie Bouché, eds., *The Mind's Eye: Art and Theological Argument in the Middle Ages,* pp. 32–45. Princeton, 2006.

————. "Know Thyself: Music in the Carolingian Renaissance." SSCI 39 (1992): 369–479.

————. *I Am You: The Hermeneutics of Empathy in Western Culture*. Princeton, 1988.

————. *The Two Kingdoms: Ecclesiology in Carolingian Political Thought*. Princeton, 1964.

————. "The Church, Reform, and Renaissance in the Early Middle Ages." In Robert S. Hoyt, ed., *Life and Thought in the Early Middle Ages*, pp. 143–59. Minneapolis, 1967.

Munitiz, Joseph A. "Le Parisinus Graecus 1115: Description et arrière plan historique." Scriptorium 36 (1982): 51–76.

Munz, Peter. *The Origin of the Carolingian Empire*. Leicester, 1960.

Murry, Sister Charles. "Art and the Early Church." JTS 28 (1977): 303–45.

Mütherich, Florentine. "Die Erneuerung der Buchmalerei am Hof Karls des Großen." In Stiegemann and Wemhoff, eds., *Kunst und Kultur der Karolingerzeit*, pp. 560–609.

————. "I *Libri Carolini* e la miniatura Carolingia." In Capitani, ed., *Culto Christiano Politica Imperiale Carolingia*, pp. 281–301.

Mütherich, Florentine and Joachim Gaehde. *Carolingian Painting*. New York, 1976

Nagel, Helmut. *Karl der Große und die theologischen Heruasforderungen seiner Zeit: Zur Wechselwirkung zwischen Theologie und Politik im Zeitalter des großen Frankenherrschers*. Freiburger Beiträge zur mittelalterlichen Geschichte 12. Frankfurt am Main, 1998.

Nees, Lawrence J. "Godescalc's Career and the Problem of 'Influence.'" In John Lowden and Alixe Bovey, eds., *Under the Influence: The Concept of Influence and the Study of Illuminated Manuscripts*, pp. 21–43. Turnhout, 2007.

————. "On the Image of Christ Crucified in Early Medieval Art." In Michele Camillo Ferrari and Andreas Meyer, eds., *Il Volto Santo in Europe: Culto Immagini del Crocefisso nel Medioevo*, pp. 345–85. Atti del Convegno internazionale di Engelberg (13–16 Settembre, 2000). Lucca, 2005.

————. *Early Medieval Art*. The Oxford History of Art. Oxford, 2002.

————. "On Carolingian Book Painters: The Ottoboni Gospels and Its Transfiguration Master." AB 83 (2001): 209–39.

————. "Carolingian Art and Politics." In Sullivan, ed., *"The Gentle Voices of Teachers,"* pp. 186–226.

————. "Art and Architecture." In McKitterick, ed., *The New Cambridge Medieval History*, vol. 2, pp. 809–44.

————. *The Tainted Mantle: Hercules and the Classical Tradition at the Carolingian Court*. Philadelphia, 1991.

————. "The Originality of Early Medieval Artists." In Chazelle, ed., *Literacy, Politics, and Artistic Innovation*, pp. 77–109.

————. *The Gundohinus Gospels*. Medieval Academy of America Books 95. Cambridge, 1987.

————. "Image and Text: Excerpts from Jerome's *De trinitate* and the *Maiestas Domini* Image from the Gundohinus Gospels." *Viator* 18 (1987): 1–22.

————. Review of Kurt Holter, ed., *Der goldene Psalter "Dagulf Psalter."* AB 67 (1985): 681–90.

————. "The Iconographic Program of Decorated Chancel Barriers in the Pre-Iconoclastic Period." *Zeitschrift für Kunstgeschichte* 46 (1983): 15–26.

Neil, Bronwen. "The Western Reaction to the Council of Nicaea I." JTS 51 (2000): 533–52.

Nelson, Janet L. "The Siting of the Council at Frankfort: Some Reflections on Family and Politics." In Berndt, ed., *Das Frankfurter Konzil.*, pp. 149–65.

———. "Women at the Court of Charlemagne: A Case of Monstrous Regiment?" In John Carmi Parsons, ed., *Medieval Queenship*, pp. 43–61. London, 1994.

———. *Charles the Bald.* London, 1992.

———. "Kingship and Empire in the Carolingian World." In McKitterick, ed., *Carolingian Culture*, pp. 52–87.

———. "The Lord's Anointed and the People's Choice: Carolingian Royal Ritual." In David Cannadine and Simon Price, eds., *Rituals of Royalty: Power and Ceremonial in Traditional Societies*, pp. 137–80. Cambridge, 1987.

———. "Symbols in Context: Rulers' Inauguration Rituals in Byzantium and the West in the Early Middle Ages." In SCH 13, pp. 97–119. Oxford, 1976.

Netzer, Nancy. *Cultural Interplay in the Eighth Century.* Cambridge Studies in Paleography and Codicology 3. Cambridge, 1994.

Nichols, Aidan. "The Horos of Nicaea II: A Theological Re-appropriation." AHC 20 (1988): 171–81.

———. *The Art of God Incarnate: Theology and Image in Christian Tradition.* New York, 1980.

Nikolau, Theodor. "Die Ikonenverehrung als Beispiel ostkirchlicher Theologie und Frömmigkeit nach Johannes von Damaskos." *Ostkirchliche Studien* 25 (1976): 138–65.

Nilgen, Ursula. "Maria Regina—Ein politischer Kultbildtypus?" *Römisches Jahrbuch für Kunstgeschichte* 19 (1981): 3–33.

Noble, Thomas F. X. "The Vocabulary of Vision and Worship in the Early Carolingian Period." In de Nie et al., eds., *Seeing the Invisible in Late Antiquity and the Early Middle Ages*, pp. 213–38.

———. "Gregory of Tours and the Roman Church." In Ian Wood and Kathleen Mitchell, eds., *The World of Gregory of Tours*, pp. 145–62. Cultures, Beliefs, Traditions 8. Leiden, 2002.

———. "Topography, Celebration, and Power: The Making of Papal Rome in the Eighth and Ninth Centuries." In Frans Theuws and Mayke de Jong, eds., *Places of Power in the Early Middle Ages*, pp. 45–91. Leiden, 2001.

———. "The Varying Roles of Biblical Testimonies in the Carolingian Image Controversies." In E. Cohen and M. B. De Jong, eds., *Medieval Transformations: Texts, Powers, & Gifts in Context*, pp. 101–19. Cultures, Beliefs and Traditions 11. Leiden, 2001.

———. "Paradoxes and Possibilities in the Sources for Roman Society in the Early Middle Ages." In Smith, ed., *Early Medieval Rome and the Christian West*, pp. 55–83.

———. "Tradition and Learning in Search of Ideology." In Sullivan, ed., *"The Gentle Voices of Teachers,"* pp. 227–60.

———. "The Papacy in the Eighth and Ninth Centuries." In McKitterick, ed., *The New Cambridge Medieval History*, vol. 2, pp. 563–86.

———. "From Brigandage to Justice: Charlemagne, 785–794." In Chazelle, ed., *Literacy, Politics, and Artistic Innovation*, pp. 49–75.

———. "Literacy and the Papal Government in Late Antiquity and the Early Middle Ages." In McKitterick, ed., *The Uses of Literacy in Early Mediaeval Europe*, pp. 82–108.

————. "John Damascene and the History of the Iconoclastic Controversy." In Thomas F. X. Noble and John J. Contreni, eds., *Religion, Culture and Society in the Early Middle Ages: Studies in Honor of Richard E. Sullivan,* pp. 96–116. Studies in Medieval Culture 23. Kalamazoo, 1987.

————. "A New Look at the Liber Pontificalis." *Archivum Historiae Pontificiae* 23 (1985): 347–58.

————. "The Declining Knowledge of Greek in Eighth- and Ninth-Century Papal Rome." BZ 78 (1985): 56–62.

————. *The Republic of St. Peter: The Birth of the Papal State, 680–825.* Philadelphia, 1984.

Nordhagen, Per Jonas. "Italo-Byzantine Wall Painting of the Early Middle Ages: An 80-year-Old Enigma in Scholarship." SSCI 34 (1980): 593–624.

Novelli, Silvana Casartelli. "L'immagine della croce nella scultura longobarda e nell''entrelacs' carolingio della diocesi di Torino." In Schmid, ed., *Riforma religiosa,* pp. 109–15.

Oakeshott, Walter. *Classical Inspiration in Medieval Art.* London, 1959.

O'Connell, Patrick, S.J. *The Ecclesiology of St. Nicephorus I (758–828) Patriarch of Constantinople: Pentarchy and Primacy.* Orientalia Christiana Analecta 194. Rome, 1972.

Ohnsorge, Werner. "Orthodoxus Imperator: Vom religiösen Motiv für das Kaisertum Karls des Großen." In *his Abendland und Byzanz,* pp. 54–78. Darmstadt, 1958.

O'Loughlin, Thomas. "Adomnán and Arculf: The Case of an Expert Witness." *Journal of Medieval Latin* 7 (1997): 127–46.

Olster, David M. *Roman Defeat, Christian Response, and the Literary Construction of the Jew.* Philadelphia, 1994.

Onians, John. *Bearers of Meaning: The Classical Orders in Antiquity, the Middle Ages, and the Renaissance.* Princeton, 1988.

Osborne, John. "Images of the Mother of God in Early Medieval Rome." In Anthony Eastmond and Liz James, eds., *Icon and Word: The Power of Images in Byzantium. Studies Presented to Robin Cormack,* pp. 135–56. London, 2003.

————. "Papal Court Culture during the Pontificate of Zacharias (AD 741–52)." In Catherine Cubitt, ed., *Court Culture in the Early Middle Ages: The Proceedings of the First Alcuin Conference,* pp. 223–34. Studies in the Early Middle Ages 3. Turnhout, 2003.

————. "Early Medieval Painting in San Clemente, Rome: The Madonna and Child in the Niche." *Gesta* 20 (1981): 299–310.

————. "The Portrait of Pope Leo IV in San Clemente, Rome: A Re-examination of the So-called 'Square' Nimbus in Medieval Art." PBSR 47 (1979): 58–65.

Ostrogorsky, George. *History of the Byzantine State.* Translated from the German by Joan Hussey. Rev. ed. New Brunswick, N.J., 1969.

————. *Studien zur Geschichte der byzantinischen Bilderstreites.* Breslau, 1929; repr. Amsterdam, 1964.

————. "Rom und Byzanz im Kampfe um die Bilderverehrung: Papst Hadrian I. und das VII. Ökumenische Konzil von Nikäa." *Seminarium Kondakovianum* 6 (1933): 73–87.

Ouspensky, Leonid. *The Theology of the Icon.* Trans. Anthony Gythiel. Crestwood, N.Y., 1992.

Oxford Dictionary of the Christian Church. Ed. F. L. Cross and E. A. Livingstone. 3rd ed. Oxford, 2005.

Padberg, Lutz E. von. *Mission und Christianisierung: Formen und Folgen bei Angelsachsen und Franken in 7. und 8. Jahrhundert.* Stuttgart, 1995.

Palazzo, Eric. *A History of Liturgical Books from the Beginning to the Thirteenth Century.* Collegeville, Minn., 1998.

Palazzo, Eric, and Ann-Katrin Johanssen. "Jalons liturgiques pour une histoire du culte de la vierge." In Iogna-Prat et al., eds., *Marie*, pp. 15–43.

Parabiaghi, Mario. "Pitture ed apparato di culto nelle opere del venerabile Beda." *Ecclesia Orans* 4 (1987): 203–34.

Parry, Kenneth. *Depicting the Word: Byzantine Iconophile Thought in the Eighth and Ninth Centuries.* The Medieval Mediterranean 12. Leiden, 1996.

———. "Theodore Studites and the Patriarch Nicephorus in Image Making as a Christian Imperative." *Byzantion* 69 (1989): 164–83.

Patlagean, Evelyne. "Les Stoudites, l'empereur et Rome: Figure byzantine d'un monachisme réformateur." SSCI 34 (1988): 429–60.

———. "Discours écrit, discours parlé: Niveaux de culture à Byzance aux VIIIᵉ–XIᵉ siècles." *Annales ESC* 35 (1979): 264–78.

———. "Les moines grecs d'Italie et l'apologie des thèses pontificales (VIIIᵉᵐᵉ–IXᵉᵐᵉ siècles)." *Studi Medievali*, 3rd ser., 5 (1964): 579–602.

Paxton, Frederick S. *Christianizing Death: The Creation of a Ritual Process in Early Medieval Europe.* Ithaca, 1990.

Pelikan, Jaroslav. *Imago Dei: The Byzantine Apologia for Icons.* Bollingen Series 36. Princeton, 1990.

Peri, Vittorio. "L'ecumenicità di un concilio come processo storico nella vita della chiesa." AHC 20 (1988): 216–44.

———. "La pentarchia: instituzione ecclesiale (IV–VII sec.) e teoria canonico-teologica." SSCI 34 (1988): 209–311.

———. "Il 'Filioque' nel magisterio di Adriano I e di Leone III." *Rivista di storia della chiesa in Italia* 41 (1987): 5–25.

———. "Leone III e il 'Filioque': Ancora un falso e l'autentico simbolo romano." *Rivista di storia e letteratura religiosa* 6 (1970): 268–97.

Picker, Hanns-Christoph. *Pastor Doctus: Klerikerbild und karolingische Reformen bei Hrabanus Maurus.* Veröffenlichungen des Instituts für Europäische Geshichte 186. Mainz, 2001.

Pizarro, Joaquín Martinéz. "Images in Texts: The Shape of the Visible in Gregory of Tours." *Journal of Medieval Latin* 9 (1999): 91–101.

Polara, Giovanna. "Parole e immagine nei carmine figurati di età carolingia." SSCI 41 (1994): 245–73.

Pratsch, Thomas. *Theodoros Studites (759–826) zwischen Dogma and Pragma.* Berliner byzantinistische Studien 4. Frankfurt am Main, 1998.

———. "Nikephoros I (806–815)." In Lilie, ed., *Die Patriarchen*, pp. 109–47.

Preißler, Matthias. "Fragmente einer verlorene Kunst: Die Paderborner Wandmalerei." In Stiegemann and Wemhoff, eds., Kunst und Kultur der Karolingerzeit, pp. 197–206.

Rabe, Susan A. *Faith, Art, and Politics at Saint-Riquier.* Philadelphia, 1995.

Ramos-Lissón, Domingo. "Die synodalen Ursprünge des 'Filioque' im römisch-westgotischen Hispanien." AHC 16 (1984): 286–99.

Reudenbach, Bruno. *Das Godescalc-Evangelistar: Ein Buch für die Reformpolitik Karls des Grossen.* Frankfurt am Main, 1998.

———. "Imago—Figura: Zum Bildverständnis in den Figurengedichten von Hrabanus Maurus." FMSt 20 (1986): 25–35.

Riché, Pierre. "La magie à l'époque carolingienne." In *Comptes-rendus des séances de l'Académie des Inscriptions et Belles-Lettres, Janvier-Mars, 1973*, pp. 127–38. Paris, 1973.

Ringrose, Kathryn M. "Monks and Society in Iconoclastic Byzantium." *Byzantine Studies* 6 (1979): 130–51.

Robertson, Giles, and George Henderson, eds. *Studies in Memory of David Talbot Rice.* Edinburgh, 1975.

Rochow, Ilse. *Kaiser Konstantin V (741–775).* Berliner byzantinistische Studien 1. Frankfurt, 1994.

———. *Byzanz im 8. Jahrhundert inder Sicht des Theophanes: Quellenkritisch historischer Kommentar ze den Jahren 715–813.* Berliner byzantinistische Arbeiten 57. Berlin, 1991.

———. "Anastasios (730–754)." In Lilie, ed., *Die Patriarchen*, pp. 22–29.

———. "Konstantinos II (754–766). In Lilie, ed., *Die Patriarchen*, pp. 30–44.

Rodley, Lyn. *Byzantine Art and Architecture: An Introduction.* Cambridge, 1994.

Roma e l'età carolingia: Atti del giornate del studio 3–8 Maggio 1976. Rome, 1976.

Romanelli, Pietro, and Per Jonas Nordhagen. *Santa Maria Antiqua.* Rome, 1964.

Romanides, John S. *Franks, Romans, Feudalism, and Doctrine: An Interplay Between Theology and Society.* Patriarch Athenagoras Memorial Lectures. Brookline, Mass., 1981.

Rosenbaum, Elizabeth. "The Evangelist Portraits of the Ada School and Their Models." AB 38 (1956): 81–90.

Rouan (Auzépy), Marie-France. "Une lecture 'iconoclaste' de la vie d'Étienne le Jeune." T&M 8 (1981): 415–36.

Runciman Steven. "The Empress Irene the Athenian." In Derek Baker, ed., *Medieval Women*, pp. 101–18. SCH, Subsidia 1. Oxford, 1978.

Russell, Frederick H. *The Just War in the Middle Ages.* Cambridge, 1975.

Russo, Daniel. "Les représentations mariales dans l'art d'Occident: Essai sur la formation d'une tradition iconographique." In Iogna-Prat et al., eds., *Marie*, pp. 173–291.

Russo, Eugenio. "L'affresco di Turtura nel cimiterio di Comodilla, l'icona di S. Maria in Trastevere e le piu antiche feste della madonna a Roma." *Bullettino dell'Istituto storico italiano per il medio evo e archivio muratoriano,* (I) 88 (1979): 37–85; (II) 89 (1980–81): 71–150.

Rydén, Lennart and Jan Olof Rosenqvist, eds. *Aspects of Late Antiquity and Early Byzantium.* Swedish Research Institute in Istanbul, Transactions 4. Uppsala, 1993.

Sabev, Todor. "L'iconoclasme." In Guillou and Durand, eds., *Byzance et les images*, pp. 329–69.

Sahas, Daniel J. *Icon and Logos: Sources in Eighth-Century Iconoclasm.* Toronto Medieval Texts and Translations 4. Toronto, 1986.

Sande, Siri. "The Icon and Its Origin in Graeco-Roman Portraiture." In Rydén and Rosenqvist, eds., *Aspects of Late Antiquity*, pp. 75–84.

Sansterre, Jean-Marie. "Attitudes occidentales à l'égard des miracles d'images dans le haut moyen age." *Annales ESC* 53 (1998): 1219–41.

———. "La vénération des images à Ravenne dans le haut moyen age: Notes sur une forme de dévotion peu connue." *Revue Mabillon*, n.s. 7, 68 (1996): 5–21.

———. "La parole, le texte et l'image selon les auteurs byzantine des époques iconoclaste et posticonoclaste." SSCI 41 (1994): 197–240.

———. "Le monachisme byzantin à Rome." SSCI 34 (1988): 701–46.

———. *Les moines grecs et orientaux à Rome aux époques byzantine et carolingienne (milieu de VIe s.–fin du IXe s.).* Academie Royale de Belgique, Mémoires des classes des lettres, 2nd ser., vol. 66, fasc. 1–2. Brussels, 1983.

———. "Jean VII (705–707): Idéologie pontificale et réalisme politique." In Lydie Hedermann-Misguich and George Raepsaet, eds., *Rayonnement grec: Hommages à Charles Delvoye*, pp. 377–88. Brussels, 1982.

Saurma-Jeltsch, Lieselotte E. "Das Bild in der Worttheologie Karls des Großen: Zur Christologie in karolingishcen Miniaturen." In Berndt, ed., *Das Frankfurter Konzil*, pp. 635–76.

Savigni, Raffaele. *Giona di Orléans: Una ecclesiologia carolingia.* Bologna, 1989.

Savramis, D. "Der abergläubische Missbrauch der Bilder in Byznaz." *Ostkirchliche Studien* 9 (1960): 174–92.

Schade, Herbert. "Die Libri Carolini und ihre Stellung zum Bild." *Zeitschrift für katholische Theologie* 79 (1957): 69–78.

Schatz, Klaus, S.J. "Königliche Kirchenregierung und römische Petrus-Überlieferung im Kreise Karls des Großen." In Berndt, ed., *Das Frankfurter Konzil*, pp. 357–72.

———. "Oecumenicité du concile et structure de l'Église à Nicée II et dans les *Livres Carolins*." In Boespflug and Lossky, eds., *Nicée II*, pp. 263–70.

Schedler, Uta. "Die Pfalzkapelle in Aachen und St. Salvator in Germigny-des-Prés—Vorbild und Widerspruch," pp. 677–98. In Berndt, ed., *Das Frankfurter Konzil.*

Schiebe, Friedrich-Karl. "Alcuin und die *Admonitio Generalis*." DA 14 (1958): 221–29.

Schieffer, Rudolf. "Der Papst als Patriarch von Rom." In Michele Maccarone, ed., *Il primato del vescovo di Roma nel primo millennio: Ricerche e testimonianze,* pp. 433–51. Pontificio Comitato di scienze storiche, Atti e Documenti 4. Vatican City, 1991.

———. " 'Redeamus ad fontem': Rom als Hort authentischer Überlieferung im frühen Mittelalter." In Arnold Angenendt and Theodor Schieffer, eds., *Caput et fons: Rom zwishen Universlismus und Gentilismus*, pp. 45–70. Zwei Vorträge über das papstliche Rom zwischen Altertum und Mittelalter. Kleve, 1989.

Schmandt, Walter. *Studien zu den Libri Carolini.* Mainz, 1966.

Schmid, Alfred, ed. *Riforma religiosa e arti nell'epoca carolingia.* Bologna, 1983.

Schmid, Karl. "Aachen und Jerusalem: Ein Beitrag zur historischen Personenforschung der Karolingerzeit." In his *Gebetsgedenken und adliges Selbstverständnis im Mittelalter: Ausgewälte Beiträge*, pp. 106–26. Sigmaringen, 1983.

Schmitt, Jean-Claude. *Le corps des images.* Paris, 2002.

———. "Rituels de l'image et récits de vision." SSCI 41 (1994): 419–59.

———. "L'Occident, Nicée II et les images du VIIIe au XIIIe siècle." In Boespflug and Lossky, eds., *Nicée II*, pp. 271–301.

Schnith, Karl Rudolf, and Roland Pauler, eds. *Festschrift für Eduard Hlawitschka zum 65. Geburtstag.* Münchener historische Studien, Abteilung mittelalterliche Geschichte 5. Kallmünz, 1993.

Schnitzler, Hermann. "Das Kuppelmosaik der Aachener Pfalzkapelle." AK 29 (1964): 17–44.

Schönborn, Christoph. L'icone de Christ. Paradosis 24. Fribourg, 1976.

Schrade, Hubert. "Zum Kuppelmosaik der Pfalzkapelle und zum Theoderich-Denkmale in Aachen." AK 30 (1965): 25–37.

Schramm, Percy Ernst. "Die Throne des deutschen Königs." In his Herrschaftszeichen und Staatssymbolik, pp. 336–44. Schriften der MGH, 13.1. Stuttgart, 1954.

———. "Goldmunzen aus der Königszeit Karls des Großen." In his Herrschaftszeichen und Staatssymbolik, pp. 288–90.

Schramm, Percy Ernst, and Florentine Mütherich. Denkmale der deutschen Könige und Kaiser: Ein Beitrag zur Herrschergeschichte von Karl dem Großen bis Friedrich II. 768–1250. Veröffentlichungen des Zentralinstitutes für Junstgeschichte in München 2. Munich, 1962.

Schreiner, Peter. "Der byzantinische Bilderstreit: Kritische Analyse der zeitgenössichen Meinungen und das Urteil der Nachwelt bis Heute." SSCI 34 (1988): 319–407.

Schwarzlose, Karl. Der Bilderstreit: Ein Kampf der griechischen Kirche ihre Eigenart und ihre Freiheit. Gotha, 1890.

Sears, Elizabeth. "Louis the Pious as Miles Christi: The Dedicatory Image in Hrabanus Maurus's De laudibus sanctae crucis." In Peter Godman and Roger Collins, eds., Charlemagne's Heir: New Perspectives on the Reign of Louis the Pious, pp. 605–28. Oxford, 1990.

Sergi, G. "Claudio." DBI 26 (1982): 158–60.

Ševčenko, Ihor. "The Search for the Past in Byzantium around the Year 800." DOP 46 (1992): 279–93.

———. "Hagiography of the Iconoclast Period." In Bryer and Herrin, eds., Iconoclasm, pp. 11–32.

Ševčenko, Nancy Patterson. "Icons in the Liturgy." DOP 45 (1991): 45–57.

Shepard, Jonathan, and Simon Franklin. Byzantine Diplomacy: Papers from the Twenty-fourth Spring Symposium of Byzantine Studies, Cambridge, March 1990. Aldershot, 1992.

Sieben, Hermann-Josef. Die konzilsidee der alten Kirche. Konziliengeschichte, ed. Walter Brandmuller. Reihe B: Untersuchungen. Paderborn, 1979.

———. "Theodor abū Qurra über 'unfehlbare' Konzilien." Theologie und Philosophie 49 (1974): 489–509.

Sinding-Larsen, Staale. Iconography and Ritual: A Study of Analytical Perspectives. Oslo, 1984.

Sironi, P. G. Castel Seprio: Storia e Monumenti. 2nd ed. Colombo Tradate, 1997.

Smith, Julia M. H., ed. Early Medieval Rome and the Christian West: Essays in Honour of Donald A. Bullough. Leiden, 2000.

———. "Old Saints, New Cults." In Smith, ed., Early Medieval Rome and the Christian West, pp. 317–39.

Sot, Michel. "Autorité du passé lointain, autorité du passé proche dans l'historographie épiscopale (VIIIe–IXe siècle)." In Jean-Marie Sansterre ed., L'autorité du passé dans les sociétés médiévales, pp. 139–62. Collection de l'École français de Rome 333. Rome, 2004.

Speck, Paul. Kaiser Leo III., Die Geshcichtswerke des Nikephoros und des Theophanes und der Liber Pontificalis. Poikila Byzantina 19, 20. Bonn, 2002, 2003.

———. Die Interpolationen in den Akten des Konzils von 787 und die Libri Carolini. Poikila Byzantina 16. Bonn, 1998.

————. "Die Affäre um Konstantin von Nakoleia." BZ 88 (1995): 148–54.

————. *Ich bin's nicht, Kaiser Konstantin ist es gewesen die Legenden vom Einfluss des Teufels, des Juden und des Moslem auf den Ikonoklasmus.* Poikila Byzantina 10. Bonn, 1990.

————. "Anthologia Palatina I, 1. und das Apsismosaic der Hagia Sophia." In *Poikila Byzantina* 6, pp. 285–329. Bonn, 1987.

————. "Weitere Überlegungen und Untersuchungen über die Ürsrpunge der byzantinischen Renaissance." In *Poikila Byzantina* 6, pp. 253–83. Bonn, 1987.

————. "Ikonklasmus und die Anfänge der makedonischen Renaissance." In *Poikila Byzantina* 4, pp. 175–210. Bonn, 1984.

————. "ΓΡΑΦΑΙΣ Η ΓΛΥΦΑΙΣ: Zu dem Fragment des Hypatios von Ephesos über die Bilder mit einem Anhang Zu den Dialog mit einem Juden des Leontios von Neapolis." In *Poikila Byzantina* 4, pp. 211–72. Bonn, 1984.

————. "Schweinfleisch und Bilderkult: zur Bilderdebatte in den sogennanten Judendialogen." In John Langdon et al., eds., *TO EΛΛHNIKON: Studies in Honor of Speros Vryonis, Jr.*, 2 vols., vol. 1, pp. 367–83. New York, 1983.

————. *Artabasdos: Der rechtgläubige Vorkämpfer der göttlichen Lehren.* Poikila Byzantina 2. Bonn, 1981.

————. *Kaiser Konstantin VI.* Munich, 1978.

Staab, Franz. "Die Königin Fastrada." In Berndt, ed., *Das Konzil von Frankfurt*, pp. 183–217.

Staubach, Nicholas. "*Christiana Tempora*: Augustin und das Ende der alten Geschichte in der Weltchronik Frechulfs von Lisieux." FMSt 29 (1995): 167–206.

————. "'Cultus Divinus' und karolingische Reform." FMSt 18 (1984): 546–81.

Stein, Dietrich. *Der Beginn des byzantinischen Bilderstreites und seine Entwicklung bis in die 40er Jahre des 8. Jahrhunderts.* Miscellanea Byzantina Monacensia 25. Munich, 1980.

————. "Germanos I (715–730)." In Lilie, ed., *Die Patriarchen*, pp. 5–21.

Sterk, Andrea. "The Silver Shields of Pope Leo III: A Reassessment of the Evidence." *Comitatus: A Journal of Medieval and Renaissance Studies* 19 (1988): 62–79.

Stewart, Columba. *Cassian the Monk.* Oxford, 1998.

Stiegemann, Christoph, and Matthias Wemhoff, eds. *799. Kunst und Kultur der Karolingerzeit: Karl der Große und Papst Leo III. in Paderborn.* Beiträge zum Katalog der Ausstellung Paderborn 1999. Mainz, 1999.

Stock, Brian. *The Implications of Literacy: Written Language and Models of Interpretation in the Eleventh and Twelfth Centuries.* Princeton, 1983.

Stoclet, Alain J. "Dies Unctionis: A Note on the Anniversaries of Royal Inaugurations in the Carolingian Period." FMSt 20 (1986): 541–48.

Stroll, Mary. "Maria Regina: Papal Symbol." In A. J. Duggan, ed., *Queens and Queenship in Medieval Europe*, pp. 173–203. London, 1997.

Sullivan, Richard E., ed. *"The Gentle Voices of Teachers": Aspects of Learning in the Carolingian Age.* Columbus, Ohio, 1995.

Teteriatnikov, Natalia. "For Whom Is Theodotus Praying? An Interpretation of the Program of the Private Chapel in S. Maria Antiqua." *Cahiers archéologiques* 41 (1993): 37–46.

Thacker, Alan. "In Search of Saints: The English Church and the Cult of Roman Apostles and Martyrs in the Seventh and Eighth Centuries." In Smith ed., *Early Medieval Rome and the Christian West,*" pp. 247–77.

Thoma, Gertrud. "Papst Hadrian I. und Karl der Große. Beobachtungen zur Kommunikation zwischen Papst und König nach den Briefen des Codex Carolinus." In Schnith and Pauler, eds., *Festschrift für Eduard Hlawitschka*, pp. 37–58.

Thümmel, Hans Georg. *Die Frühgeschichte der ostkirchlichen Bilderlehre: Texte und Untersuchungen zur Zeit vor dem Bilderstreit.* Texte und Untersuchungen zur geschichte der altchristlichen Literatur 139. Berlin, 1992.

———. *Bilderlehre und Bilderstreit: Arbeiten zur Auseinandersetzung über die Ikone und ihre Begründung vornehmlich im 8. und 9. Jahrhundert.* Das östliche Christentum, Neue Folge 40. Würzburg, 1991.

———. "Die fränkische Reaktion auf das 2. Nicaenum in den Libri Carolini." In Berndt, ed., *Das Frankfurter Konzil*, pp. 965–80.

———. "Die Ikonen im Westen." AHC 20 (1988): 354–67.

———. "Eine wenig bekannte Schrift zur Bilderfrage." In Helga Köpstein and Friedhelm Winkelman, eds., *Studien zum 8. und 9. Jahrhundert in Byzanz*, pp. 153–57. Berliner byzantinistische Arbeiten 51. Berlin, 1983.

———. "Der byzantinische Bilderstreit: Stand und Perspektiven der Forschung." In Johannes Irmscher, ed., *Der byzantinische Bilderstreit: Sozialökonomische Voraussetzungen, ideologische Grundlagen, geschichtliche Wirkungen*, pp. 9–40. Leipzig, 1980.

———. "Neilos von Anlcyra über die Bilder." BZ 71 (1978): 10–21.

———. "Positionen im Bilderstreit." In Johannes Irmscher and Peter Nagel, eds., *Studia Byzantina*, 2nd ser., Berliner byzantinistische Arbeiten 44. Berlin, 1973.

Thunø, Erik. *Image and Relic: Mediating the Sacred in Early Medieval Rome.* Analecta Romana Instituti Danici, Supplementum, 32. Rome, 2002.

Toynbee, J. M. C. "Pagan Motifs and Practices in Christain Art and Ritual in Roman Britain." In M. W. Barley and R. P. C. Hason, eds., *Christianity in Britain, 300–700*, pp. 177–92. Leicester, 1968.

Travis, John. *In Defense of the Faith: The Theology of Patriarch Nikephoros of Constantinople.* Brookline, Mass., 1984

Treadgold, Warren. *A History of the Byzantine State and Society.* Stanford, 1997.

———. *The Byzantine Revival, 780–842.* Stanford, 1988.

———. "The Empress Irene's Preparation for the Seventh Ecumenical Council." *Patristic and Byzantine Review* 7 (1988): 49–58.

Treitinger, Otto. *Die oströmische Kaiser- und Reichsidee nach ihrer Gestaltung im höfischen Zeremoniell.* 2nd unchanged edition. Darmstadt, 1956.

Troianos, Spyros. "Die Kanones des VII. ökumenischen Konzils und die Kaisergesetzgebung." AHC 20 (1988): 289–306.

Trompf, G. W. "The Concept of the Carolingian Renaissance." *Journal of the History of Ideas* 34 (1973): 3–26.

Troupeau, Gérard. "Église et Chrétiens dans l'Orient Musulman." In Mayeur et al., eds., *Histoire du Christianisme*, pp. 375–456.

Tsigaris, Georg. "Philosophisches Instrumentarium der Christologie von Theodorus Studites über die Darstellung des menschgewordenen Logos." AHC 20 (1988): 268–77.

Ullmann, Walter. *The Carolingian Renaissance and the Idea of Kingship.* London, 1969.

Underwood, Paul A. "The Fountain of Life in Manuscripts of the Gospels." DOP 5 (1950): 43–138.

Untermann, Matthias. "'*Opera mirabili constructa*': Der Aachener 'Residenz' Karls des Großen." In Stiegemann and Wemhoff, eds., *Kunst und Kultur der Karolingerzeit*, pp. 165–73.

Uphus, Johannes Bernhard. *Der Horos des Zweiten Konzils von Nizäa: Interpretation und Kommentar auf der Grundlage der Konzilsakten mit besonderen Berüchsichtigung der Bilderfrage*. Paderborn, 2004.

Van den Ven, Paul. "La patristique et l'hagiographie du Concile de Nicée de 787." *Byzantion* 25–27 (1955–57): 325–62.

Van der Vorst, Charles. "Les relations de S. Théodore Studite avec Rome." AnBol 32 (1913): 439–47.

Van Esbroeck, Michel. "La culte de al Vierge de Jérusalem à Constantinople aux 6e–7e siècles." REB 46 (1988): 181–90.

Vasiliev, Alexander A. "The Iconoclastic Edict of the Caliph Yazid II. AD 721." DOP 9/10 (1956): 25–47.

Vassilaki, Maria, ed. *Mother of God: Representations of the Virgin in Byzantine Art*. Milan, 2000.

Vauchez, André. *La spiritualité du Moyen Âge occidental: VIIIe–XIIe siècles*. Vendôme, 1975.

Vieillard-Troiekouroff, May. *Les monuments religieux de la Gaule d'après les Oeuvres de Grégoire de Tours*. Lille, 1977.

———. "Les bibles de Théodulphe et la bible wisigothique de La Cava dei Terreni." In *Synthronon: Art et archéologie de la fin de l'Antiquité et du Moyen Age. Recueil d'études par André Grabar et un groupe de ses disciples*, pp. 153–66. Bibliothèque des Cahiers Archéologiques 2. Paris, 1968.

Vikan, Gary. "Byzantine Pilgrims' Art." In Linda Safran, ed., *Heaven on Earth: Art and the Church in Byzantium*, pp. 229–66. University Park, Pa., 1998.

———. "Icons and Icon Piety in Early Byzantium." In C. Moss and K. Kiefer, eds., *Byzantine East, Latin West: Art-Historical Studies in Honor of Kurt Weitzmann*, pp. 569–76. Princeton, 1995.

———. "Ruminations on Edible Icons: Originals and Copies in the Art of Byzantium." *Studies in the History of Art* 20 (1989): 47–59.

———. "Sacred Image, Sacred Power." In Gary Vikan, ed., *Icon: Four Essays*, pp. 6–19. Washington, D.C., 1988.

Voci, Anna Maria. *Nord o Sud: Note per la storia del medioevale Palatium Apostolicum apud Sanctum Petrum e delle sue capelle*. Capellae Apostolicae Sextinaque Collectanea Acta Monumenta 2. Vatican City, 1992.

Vogel, Cyrille. "Les motifs de la romanisation du culte sous Pépin le Bref (751–768) et Charlemagne (774–814)." In Capitani, ed., *Culto Cristiano, Politica imperiale Carolingia*, pp. 13–41.

———. "La reforme liturgique sous Charlemagne." In Bischoff, ed., *Das Geistige Leben*, pp. 217–32.

———. "Les échanges liturgiques entre Rome et les pays francs jusqu'à l'époque de Charlemagne." SSCI 7 (1959): 185–295.

Vogt, Hermann J. "Der Streit um das Lamm." AHC 20 (1988): 135–49.

Von den Steinen, Wolfram. "Der Neubeginn." In Bischoff, ed., *Das Geistige Leben*, pp. 9–27.

———. "Karl der Grosse und die Libri Carolini: Die Tironischen Randnoten zum Codex Authenticus." *Neues Archiv* 49 (1931): 207–80.

———. "Entstehungsgeshcichte der Libri Carolini." *Quellen und Forschungen aus italienischen Archiven und Bibliotheken* 21 (1929–30): 1–93.

Von Campenhausen, Hans Freiherr. "The Theological Problem of Images in the Early Church." In his *Tradition and Life in the Church*, pp. 171–200. Trans. A. V. Littledale. London, 1968.

Von Dobschütz, Ernst. *Christusbilder: Untersuchungen zur christlichen legende.* Leipzig, 1899.

Von Finckenstein, Albert Graf Finck. "Rom zwischen Byzanz und den Franken in der ersten Hälfte des 8. Jahrhunderts." In Schnith and Pauler, eds., *Festschrift für Eduard Hlawitschka*, pp. 23–36.

Waas, Adolf. "Karls des Grossen Frömmigkeit." *Historische Zeitschrift* 203 (1966): 265–79.

Wallace-Hadrill, J. M. *Early Germanic Kingship in England and on the Continent.* Oxford, 1971.

Wallach, Luitpold. *Diplomatic Studies in Latin and Greek Documents from the Carolingian Age.* Ithaca, 1977.

———. "The Greek and Latin Versions of II Nicaea, 787 and the *Synodica* of Hadrian I (*JE* 2448)." In his *Diplomatic Studies*, pp. 3–26.

Walser, Gerold. *Die einsiedler Inschriftensammlung und der Pilgerführer durch Rom (Codex Einsidlensis 326).* Historia Einzelschriften 53. Stuttgart, 1987.

Wattenbach, Wilhelm. *Deutschlands Geschichtsquellen im Mittelalter: Vorzeit und Karolinger.* 2 Heft *Die Karolinger vom Anfang des 8. Jahrhunderts bis zum Tode Karls des Grossen*; 3 Heft, *Die Karolinger vom Tode des Karls des Grossen bis zum Vertrag von Verdun.* Rev. Wilhelm Levison and Heinz Löwe. Weimar, 1952.

Wehling, Ulrike. *Die Mosaiken im Aachener Münster und ihre Vorstufen.* Arbeitsheft der rheinischen Denkmalpflege 46. Bonn, 1995.

Weitmann, Pascal. *Sukzession und Gegenwart: Zu theoretischen Äußerungen über bildende Künste und Musik von Basileios bis Hrabanus Maurus.* Spätantike—Frühes Christentum—Byzanz: Kunst im ersten Jahrtausend ed. Beat Benk, Johannes G. Deckers, Aren Effenberger, Lieselotte Kötzsche. Reihe B: Studien und Perspektiven, 2. Wiesbaden, 1997.

Weitzmann, Kurt, ed. *Late Classical and Medieval Studies in Honor of Albert Mathias Friend, Jr.* Princeton, 1955

———. *The Monastery of St. Catherine at Mount Sinai: The Icons.* Vol. 1. Princeton, 1976.

Whittow, Mark. *The Making of Orthodox Byzantium.* London, 1996.

Wiederanders, Gerlinde. "Die Auswirkung des Bilderstreites auf die Entwicklung der kunst im Karolingerreich." In Johannes Irmscher, ed., *Der byzantinische Bilderstreit: Sozialökonomische Voraussetzungen, ideologische Grundlagen, geschichtliche Wirkungen,"* pp. 149–59. Leipzig, 1980.

Wilhelmy, Winfried. "Rabanus Maurus: Auf den Spuren eines karolingischen Gelehrten," "Die Entstehung von *De laudibus* im Spannungsfeld von Bilderstreit und Glaubenswahrheit," and "Kreuzverehrung im Karolingerreich." In Kotzur, ed., *Rabanus Maurus,* pp. 15–32.

Wilkinson, John. *Jerusalem Pilgrims Before the Crusades.* Jerusalem, 1977.

Winandy, Jacques. *Ambroise Autpert: Moine et théologien.* Paris, 1953.

Winkelmann, Friedhelm. *Der monoenergetisch-monothelitische Streit.* Berliner Byzantinistische Studien 6. Frankfurt am Main, 2001.

Wirth, Jean. *L'image médiévale: Naissance et développements (IVᵉ–XVᵉ siècle).* Paris, 1989.

Wohlmuth, Josef, ed. *Streit um das Bild: Das zweite Konzil von Nicäa (787) im ökumenischer Perspektive.* Studium universale 9. Bonn, 1989.

Wolf, Gerhard. *Salus Populi Romani: Die Geschichte römischer Kultbilder im Mittelalter.* Weinheim, 1990.

Wolfram, Herwig. "Political Theory and Narrative in Charters." *Viator* 26 (1995): 39–51.

Woodruff, Helen. "The Iconography and Date of the Mosaics of La Daurade." *AB* 13 (1931): 80–104.

Wortley, John. "Iconoclasm and Leipsanoclasm: Leo III, Constantine V and the Relics." *Byzantinische Forschungen* 8 (1982): 253–79.

Yiannias, John J. "A Reexamination of the 'Art Statute' in the Acts of Nicaea II." *BZ* 80 (1987): 348–59.

Zhivov, V. M. "The Mystagogia of Maximus the Confessor and the Development of the Byzantine Theory of the Image." *St. Vladimir's Theological Quarterly* 31 (1987): 349–76.

INDEX

ACKNOWLEDGMENTS

The first lines of this book were written thirteen years before the last. Teaching and administrative responsibilities along with a move from Virginia to Notre Dame took tolls on the progress of this work. Beyond these explanations—not excuses—the book itself kept changing shape as I worked on it. Every change pushed me into new sources and scholarship. One happy result of the book's long gestation is that I got a lot of advice and support along the way. I am delighted now to be able to acknowledge at least some of it.

The book was begun and almost finished during two stints (1994, 2006) at the incomparable Institute for Advanced Study in Princeton. Those who have been there will know its superb blend of interaction and isolation. I also had a wonderful year at the Netherlands Institute for Advanced Study (1999–2000). The National Endowment for the Humanities provided a fellowship in 1993–94 that permitted me to launch the study in a serious way. The University of Virginia and the University of Notre Dame supported me morally, materially, and administratively.

Institutions are important, of course, but to me, people matter even more. At an earlier stage in its development, Charlie Barber, Karl Morrison, and Larry Nees read my manuscript. Later on Larry, along with Rosamond McKitterick, read the whole thing. Such labors both display and stretch the ties of friendship. Along the way, I received help, advice, and encouragement from many friends. In listing some I am sure that I will omit others, and I am sorry that I cannot always remember, and have no space to record, what each person's support has meant to me. So permit me to thank David Appleby, Barbara Baert, Franz Alto Bauer, Claudia Bolgia, Beat Brenk, George Brown, Peter Brown, Leslie Brubaker, Celia Chazelle, Martin Claussen, John Contreni, Mayke de Jong, Giselle de Nie, Deborah Deliyannis, Paolo Delogu, the late Robert Deshman, William Diebold, Judson Emerick, Ann Freeman, David Ganz, Eric Goldberg, Caroline Goodson, Jeffrey Hamburger, Johannes Heil, Catherine Karkov, Herbert Kessler, Dale Kinney, Genevra Kornbluth, Federico Marazzi, Robert Markus,

Charles McLendon, Paul Meyvaert, John Mitchell, Jinty Nelson, Éamonn Ó Carragáin, John Osborne, Daniel Sheerin, Julia Smith, Paolo Squatriti, the late Richard E. Sullivan, Erik Thunø, John Van Engen, Robert Louis Wilken, Ian Wood, the late Patrick Wormald, John Yiannias, and Paolo Zanna. I must also thank Jerome Singerman, my editor at the University of Pennsylvania Press, without whose faith and gentle prodding I might never have finished this book.

I also record with gratitude a generous publication subsidy form the Institute for Scholarship in the Liberal Arts of the College of Arts and Letters in the University of Notre Dame.

The dedication says all, but much less than I wish I could say.